ONE WEEK LOAN

OXFORD READINGS IN SOCIO-LEGAL STUDIES

A Reader on Regulation

A READER ON

Regulation

EDITED BY

Robert Baldwin

Colin Scott

Christopher Hood

OXFORD UNIVERSITY PRESS

1998

Oxford University Press, Great Clarendon Street, Oxford OX2 6DP

Oxford New York

Athens Auckland Bangkok Bogota Bombay Buenos Aires
Calcutta Cape Town Dar es Salaam Delhi Florence Hong Kong Istanbul
Karachi Kuala Lumpur Madras Madrid Melbourne Mexico City
Nairobi Paris Singapore Taipei Tokyo Toronto Warsaw

and associated companies in Berlin Ibadan

Oxford is a registered trade mark of Oxford University Press

Published in the United States
by Oxford University Press Inc., New York

© Oxford University Press 1998
The moral rights of the authors have been asserted

First published 1998

British Library Cataloguing in Publication Data
Data available

Library of Congress Cataloging in Publication Data
Data available

ISBN 0–19–876529–0
ISBN 0–19–876530–4 (pbk)

1 3 5 7 9 10 8 6 4 2

Typeset by Pure Tech India Ltd, Pondicherry
Printed in Great Britain
on acid-free paper by
Bookcraft Ltd., Midsomer Norton, Somerset

Preface

We have prepared this book in order to make a good range of readings on regulation available to the growing number of students for whom regulation is now a course of study or a key part of some broader course. We have generally selected readings which would not otherwise be easily available, and which reflect the main currents of ideas, not just within socio-legal studies, but within regulation scholarship more generally. We have written an introductory chapter which we hope will be helpful both to the reader who is new to the study of regulation and to the more experienced reader who may want to engage with the argument which we seek to develop about the direction of both regulatory scholarship and practice.

The immediate context for the preparation of the book was our own teaching on the interdisciplinary Masters Programme in Regulation at the London School of Economics. We are grateful to our colleagues and past and present students for discussion and testing of ideas, to Mandy Tinnams who assisted with the preparation of the text for the press and Charlotte Hadfield who acted as research assistant. We owe particular thanks to those friends and colleagues who commented on the introductory chapter and/or choice of readings, especially to: Julia Black, John Braithwaite, Terence Daintith, Cosmo Graham, and Sol Picciotto. Finally we would like to thank all of those who gave their kind permission to use the works we have selected as readings.

Robert Baldwin
Colin Scott
Christopher Hood

March 1998

Contents

Acknowledgements

Grateful acknowledgement is made to all the authors and publishers of extract material which appears in this book, and in particular to the following for permission to reprint material from the sources indicated:

Blackwell Publishers Ltd: J.-M. Sun and J. Pelkmans, 'Regulatory Competition in the Single Market'. Reprinted by permission of the publisher from *Journal of Common Market Studies*, 33 (1995), 67–89, © 1995 by Blackwell Publishers Ltd.

*Brookings Institution: S. Peltzman, 'The Economic Theory of Regulation after a Decade of Deregulation'. Reproduced by permission of the publisher from *Brookings Papers on Microeconomics* (1989), 1–59.

Cambridge University Press: J. O. Freedman, 'Crisis and Legitimacy in the Administrative Process: A Historical Perspective'. Reprinted by permission of the publisher from J. O. Freedman, *Crisis and Legitimacy* (Cambridge: Cambridge University Press, 1978), © 1978 Cambridge University Press. T. Makkai and J. Braithwaite, 'In and Out of the Revolving Door: Making Sense of Regulatory Capture'. Reprinted by permission of the publisher from *Journal of Public Policy*, 1 (1995), 61–78 © 1995 Cambridge University Press.

Centre for the Study of Regulated Industries: C. Graham, 'Is there a Crisis in Regulatory Accountability'. Reprinted by permission of the publisher from C. Graham, *Is there a Crisis in Regulatory Accountability?* (London: CIFPA, 1997), © 1997 CIFPA.

Frank Cass and Co. Ltd: C. Majone, 'The Rise of the Regulatory State in Europe.' Reprinted by permission of the publisher from *West European Politics* 17 (1994), 77–101.

Harvard University Press: S. Breyer, 'Typical Justifications for Regulation'. Reprinted by permission of the publisher from S. Breyer, *Regulation and its Reform* (Cambridge, Mass.: Harvard University Press, 1982) © 1982 by the President and Fellows of Harvard College.

Oxford University Press: L. Hancher and M. Moran, 'Organizing Regulatory Space'. Reprinted by permission of the publisher from L. Hancher and M. Moran (eds.) *Capitalism, Culture and Economic Regulation* (Oxford:

Oxford University Press, 1989), © Leigh Hancher and Michael Moran 1989. K. Hawkins, 'Law as Last Resort'. Reprinted by permission of the publisher from K. Hawkins, *Environment and Enforcement* (Oxford: Oxford University Press (1994), © Social Science Research Council 1984. A. Ogus 'Rethinking Self-Regulation'. Reprinted by permission of the publisher from *Oxford Journal of Legal Studies* (1995), 97–108, © 1995 Oxford University Press.

Northeastern University Press: N. Reichman, 'Moving Backstage: Uncovering the Role of Compliance Practices in Shaping Regulatory Policy'. Reprinted by permission of the publisher from Shlegel and Weisburd (eds.), *White-collar Crime Reconsidered* (Boston: Northeastern University Press, 1992), 245–67, © 1992 Northeastern University Press.

University of California Press: K. Shrader-Frechette, 'Uncertainty and the Producer Strategy'. Reprinted by permission of the publisher from K. Shrader-Frechette, *Risk and Rationality* (Berkeley and Los Angeles: University of California Press, 1991), ch. 9, © 1991 University of California Press.

University of Chicago Press: S. Shavell, 'The Optimal Structure of Law Enforcement'. Reprinted by permission of the publisher from *Journal of Law and Economics*, 255 (1993), 270–87, © 1993 by The University of Chicago.

Walter de Gruyter and Co.: T. Daintith, 'Legal Measures and their Analysis'. Reprinted by permission of the publisher from *Law as an Instrument of Economic Policy: Comparative and Critical Approaches* (Berlin: Walter de Gruyter, 1988), 25–47, © 1988 Walter de Gruyter and Co. Gunther Teubner,' Juridification: Concepts, Aspects, Limits, Solutions.' Reprinted by permission of the publisher from Gunther Teubner (ed.), *Juridification of Social Spheres* (Berlin: Walter de Gruyter, 1987), 3–48, © 1987 Walter de Gruyter and Co.

* Yale Law Journal Co. Inc.: C. Diver, 'The Optimal Precision of Administrative Rules'. Reprinted by permission of the publisher from *Yale Law Journal*, 93 (1983), 65–109, © 1983 The Yale Law Journal Company and Fred B. Rothman & Company.

Despite every effort to contact the copyright holders and obtain permission prior to publication in some cases this has not been possible. If notified, the publisher undertakes to rectify any errors or omissions at the earliest opportunity.

Introduction

I. Regulation Grows Up: Into its Prime or Mid-Life Crisis?

Were Sam Goldwyn to lunch with Adam Smith today, he might remark that regulation is so pervasive you cannot see the invisible hand of the market. Imagine the case of Ada Smith (a descendant of Adam), an astute British business woman who has identified a gap in the market for the production of pins and decides to establish a company to manufacture this product. Ada finds that every stage of establishing the firm and producing and marketing the product is likely to be regulated. (This is not to suggest that Ada's business is necessarily overregulated, but that we are all enmeshed within an elaborate web of regulatory requirements). Fig. 1.1 shows the business path and some of the likely regulation to which she will be subjected by UK authorities.

Regulation has, moreover, become a central form of state intervention in the economy, and it has grown towards maturity in two senses. One is an intellectual maturation, reflected in the development of distinct analytic approaches and generic understandings of regulatory processes that are capable of being applied across different regulatory sectors. The other is a maturation of practice: administrative processes which were once seen as sector specific, and peculiar to individual domains such as consumer protection, financial services, pollution, or occupational health and safety,

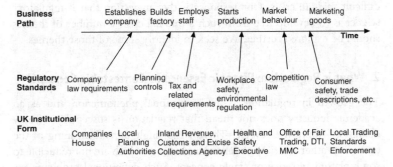

Fig. 1.1. Regulating Ada

are coming to be seen as part of a generic 'set' of instruments and strategies deployed by the state.[1]

The study of regulation has also produced themes that have travelled across the boundaries of different states and legal systems. Much of the early literature and policy interest in regulation developed in the United States, but more recently European approaches to regulation have been developed, reflecting the distinctive cultural and institutional make-up of European states.[2] This development reflects the way that regulation has replaced or is replacing other forms of state intervention in the economy (notably public enterprise), not just in the United Kingdom but in Europe more generally.[3] The memory of state-provided utilities fades as key services are associated with the work of private providers and such agencies as OFTEL, OFWAT, OFFER, and OFGAS. Accompanying this increased emphasis on regulation at national level has come a parallel growth in supra-national regulation—raising questions about how far regional and global markets can be steered by regulatory institutions above the level of the state. As more weight has come to be placed on regulation as a policy instrument, sharper questions have been asked about regulatory regimes, with increasing discussion both of 'accountability deficits' in regulation and of the excessive burdens that are imposed on business by regulatory compliance costs.[4]

In this introductory chapter we have two aims. First we examine regulation as a topic for study; review major developments in regulation; and outline central themes in regulation. To this end, section 2 looks at approaches to the definition of regulation, section 3 describes landmarks in British regulatory theory and practice, and sections 4, 5, and 6 look at major themes. Second, we present an argument. In section 7 we ask whether regulation is entering its prime as a science or approaching a difficult mid-life crisis. Our response is the suggestion that if regulatory science is to develop free from such a mid-life crisis a number of themes should be explored further. We seek to identify some of those themes.

2. What is Regulation: Platonic Essence or Contestable Concept?

The growth in regulation as an institutional phenomenon and as an academic industry does not mean that regulation is susceptible of easy definition—quite the reverse. There is no single agreed meaning of the term, but rather a variety of definitions in usage which are not reducible to some platonic essence or single concept. Such definitional problems are inevitable given the competition by academics and professionals to colonize new or newly important fields of activity, thereby constructing them in their own image.[5] Three main meanings are discussed here, namely regulation as targeted rules, regulation as direct state intervention in the economy more generally, and regulation as encompassing all mechanisms of social control, by whomsoever exercised.

At its simplest, regulation refers to the promulgation of an authoritative set of rules, accompanied by some mechanism, typically a public agency, for monitoring and promoting compliance with these rules. Rule-making and monitoring/enforcement mechanisms need not be located in a single institution. Whereas in the United States the powerful federal independent regulatory commissions typically have exercised these functions together with powers to sanction,[6] in Europe, and certainly in the United Kingdom, rule-making powers have more usually been retained by central government and legislature, with monitoring and enforcement powers devolved to local authorities or to central agencies such as the Health and Safety Executive or the utilities regulators.[7] In many instances enforcement bodies do not seek routinely to apply the ultimate administrative or criminal sanctions which are available, but where such sanctions are sought, application must be made to the courts. The purposes that such regulatory regimes are directed towards may be social or economic in character,[8] but traditional criminal law is generally excluded from the definition on the basis that it seeks to punish anti-social conduct rather than encourage particular forms of purposive activity. This distinction is conventional, but not everyone finds it convincing.

A second, broader, conception of regulation, commonly found in the political economy literature, takes in all the efforts of state agencies to steer the economy.[9] Thus, while rule-making and application through enforcement systems would come within such a definition, a wide range of other government instruments based on government authority such as taxation and disclosure requirements might also be included. Even those government tools which rely on government expenditure or direct organization such as contracting and public ownership might be considered as alternative tools of regulation.[10] Such an approach has the merit that a variety of tools are considered as possible alternatives to traditional 'command and control' type regulation (discussed below), so that where rule-making seems to be inappropriate as a means for achieving policy objectives, other tools may be used. Some commentators have drawn a broad distinction between regulatory mechanisms that are based on the creation of incentives to behave in certain socially desirable ways and mechanisms that are based on commands.[11] Nor should regulation be seen as devoted only to *restriction*: an important aspect of regulation may be *enablement*—the creation not merely of incentives but of those conditions that allow activities to take place (for example, the allocation of airwave frequencies to provide ordered broadcasting rather than chaos). A disadvantage of this second approach is that regulation so conceived potentially takes in all instruments directed towards the achievement of economic and perhaps social policy ends. Consequently it no longer appears to be a distinctive form of governance.

A third definition, broader still, considers all mechanisms of social control—including unintentional and non-state processes—to be forms of regulation.[12] Thus the range of government instruments noted above comes within the definition, but such a definition extends also to mechanisms which are not the products of state activity, nor part of any institutional arrangement, such as the development of social norms and the effects of markets in modifying behaviour. Thus a notion of *intentionality* about the development of norms is dropped, and anything producing effects on behaviour is capable of being considered as regulatory. Furthermore a wide range of activities which may involve legal or quasi-legal norms, but without mechanisms for monitoring and enforcement, might come within the definition.

While lawyers and economists studying regulation have tended to work within the first two definitions, the distinctive contribution of socio-legal studies has been to eschew any distinction between activities based on formal differences between state and non-state activity or between rule-based oversight and other forms of social control. The selection of readings for this book draws on all three definitions. While following the first two definitions the study of regulation has a reasonably clear boundary based on intentional state (and self-regulatory) activity directed towards the modification of behaviour by reference to systems of authoritative rules. Taking into account the third definition we see the importance of the activities of businesses and their professional advisers in shaping regulatory fields, both in terms of policy-making and implementation.

3. Landmarks in UK Regulation

Regulation, like privatization, has become a policy buzzword in the United Kingdom over the past twenty years. But, just as Molière's M. Vautrin (in *Le Bourgeois Gentilhomme*) discovered one day that what he had been speaking all his life was prose, the phenomenon of government regulation is far from new and long predates the current preoccupation with this policy instrument in politics and social science. The state has exercised regulatory functions over the economy for hundreds of years. Many of those functions that have existed since the nineteenth century, and local enforcement functions going back much further, have evaded sustained study. The extensive use of public ownership as a tool of government in the middle years of the twentieth century also contributed towards a lack of memory of the long history of regulation. Thus, to suggest that state activity in the United Kingdom has been transformed by the extensive development of new regulatory institutions is to present only one side of the picture. From another perspective, we can see a pattern of continuity and incremental change in many regulatory areas, and, in the case of the utilities sectors, reversion to a model not dissimilar from that of nineteenth-century public regulation of privately provided services.

Market regulation by local officials is no new phenomenon. It was considered to be a basic function of the state (in ensuring *neteté*, *sûreté*, and *bon marché*) in eighteenth-century 'police science'.[13] Even before that, markets were subject to detailed common law rules in medieval England to ensure produce was only sold on market-day at the appointed place, and that middlemen did not buy and resell in the market for profit.[14] Additionally, statutory schemes were developed to prevent the dilution of staples such as bread and beer with cheaper impurities,[15] and universal standards to be enforced locally were developed for regulating weights and measures.[16] Today analogous functions are exercised through legislative standard setting for consumer protection, for example in the Trades Descriptions Act 1968, the Consumer Credit Act 1974, the Consumer Protection Act 1987, and the Food Safety Act 1990. Enforcement continues to be local, even though the old weights and measures departments of local authorities have been renamed as trading standards departments.[17] Recently the membership of the United Kingdom in the European Union has been an important new source of regulatory norms in relation to domains such as consumer protection, occupational health and safety, equality regulation, and environmental protection.[18]

Though such centralized regulation as developed in the sixteenth and seventeenth centuries was substantially removed in the eighteenth century,[19] local administration and enforcement of a wide range of measures continued.[20] The nineteenth century (conventionally portrayed as an era of *laissez-faire*) saw the introduction of a broader range of legislative standards and schemes of statutory arbitration in a range of social and economic areas, frequently followed up by the development of agencies for monitoring and enforcement.[21] New institutions for social protection included the Factories Inspectorate (1833)[22] and, for economic regulation, the Railways Commissioners (1844).[23] Local authorities also took on more developed enforcement functions in relation to public health, housing,[24] and food safety.[25]

In the twentieth century, discrete regulatory control by local and central agencies was maintained in many areas and expanded to new areas such as minimum wage regulation (1909).[26] Though such social regulation continued to develop, the shifting 'economic borders of the state'[27] resulted in many economic tasks which had once been undertaken by regulatory bodies being subsumed into the ownership and operation of nationalized industries, notably in the utilities sectors. Telegraphs were nationalized by a Conservative government as early as 1869; telephones followed in 1911, being incorporated in the Post Office, the government department already responsible for telegraphs, and the electricity, gas, and rail industries were subsequently nationalized in order to promote rationalization and make the control of natural monopoly elements more straightforward in the light of what was seen at that time by many as the failure of regulation to ensure efficient and accessible public services. Notwithstanding the considerable amounts of continuing regulation, these functions were relatively hidden and public ownership, not regulation, was the policy buzzword of that time. It was an era when government operated its own public houses (in Scotland and the North of England) as a legacy of First World War concerns with drunkenness among munition workers and ran its own Wool Disinfection Plant to deal with the risk of anthrax in imported wool and goat hair: the idea that such problems might be tackled by regulation rather than direct government action only slowly gained favour.

Nevertheless, in the years after the Second World War new models of central regulatory agencies started to develop with the creation of the Independent Television Authority, created in 1954 to oversee the provision of commercial television by private companies. Many new agencies were created in the 1960s and 1970s, both for economic regulation (as in the case of the Civil Aviation Authority established in 1972) and for social regulation (as with the Equal Opportunities Commission of 1976).

In the 1980s and 1990s great emphasis has been placed on the failure of regulation and 'the regulatory crisis'.[28] Paradoxically, in a period when deregulation has been claimed to be the driving force of public policy under the influence of the neo-liberal strand of New Right ideas, more new central regulatory agencies have been created than ever before. Indeed, like quangos, regulation is something that British Conservative governments in the years from 1979 to 1997 could neither quite live with or live without. This result has arisen in part because government has viewed the regulation of private activity as less interventionist than public ownership, and so has created new regulatory agencies to oversee privatized utilities sectors in telecommunications (OFTEL, 1984), gas (OFGAS, 1986), electricity (OFFER, 1989), water (OFWAT, 1990), and rail (Office of the Rail Regulator, 1993). Additionally, the removal of environmental regulation functions, once exercised by the water companies themselves, resulted in the creation of a National Rivers Authority (1990), now subsumed, with other functions, into the Environment Agency (1996), and the creation of the first National Lottery in the United Kingdom since the 1830s was accompanied by the creation of an Office of the National Lottery (1993) to oversee the private company that provides it. For the Labour government elected in May 1997, the attraction of regulation as an instrument of government policy is that it provides mechanisms for indicating government commitments and priorities without heavy costs in public expenditure terms, since most of the costs are compliance costs borne by the regulatees or passed on to consumers.[29]

'Deregulation' itself implied a form of new regulation over government departments, to be led by the Department of Trade and Industry's Enterprise and Deregulation Unit, established in 1985 to oversee the review of all new legislative instruments for the costs of compliance by those affected.[30] That unit, now called the Better Regulation Unit, and housed in the Cabinet Office, subsequently extended its jurisdiction into the review of existing regulatory measures in 1993, resulting in a promise of a 'bonfire of red tape' from the then President of the Board of Trade, Michael Heseltine. Perhaps the pinnacle of this deregulatory initiative was the Deregulation and Contracting Out Act 1994 which, *inter alia*, gave Ministers powers, exercisable by statutory instrument, to eliminate or reduce the burdens of other legislative controls.[31] No evaluation of the impact of this review has yet been undertaken and no examination has been carried out in respect of the costs to *public* bodies of complying with regulatory requirements such as inspection and audit.[32] A similar review (the *fiche d'impact* system) has also been pursued at European Community level since 1985, concerned with balancing regulatory costs and benefits and ensuring that new and existing Community measures comply with principles of subsidiarity (on which see below). These processes have been accompanied by a search for ostensibly less interventionist modes of regulation, such as self-regulation, tax rules, liability rules, disclosure rules, franchising, and mechanisms for enhancing or preserving competition. Self-regulation, which has a long history in the United Kingdom, has been particularly favoured as a means of regulating without so-called 'command and control' systems (a term of rhetoric coined to discredit orthodox forms of regulation, on which we comment below).

4. Two Major Themes in Regulation

The study of regulation in the United Kingdom has by no means been restricted to academic lawyers and sociologists. Economists have taken a particular interest in the regulation of the utilities sectors, developing normative accounts of the best mix of regulatory instruments for protecting consumers and promoting competition.[33] Political scientists have focused more on the origins of regulation, implementation, and regulatory processes,[34] and regulation has been analysed from many other disciplinary perspectives, including anthropology, social administration, social psychology, and geography.[35]

Out of the many analytic questions raised by such approaches, two major themes emerge as recurrent intellectual concerns. The first relates to the natural history of regulation—the evolution, development, and observable life processes of regulation, the behaviour of regulatory actors in the regulatory landscape, and the practices of implementation and enforcement. The second looks to the various species of regulation—the variety of strategies used, scales of control encountered, and modes of evaluation and holding to account.

Here we organize our discussion around these themes. In section 5 we review work on the origins, development, and reform of regulation and consider the issues of standard-setting, rule-choices, and enforcement in regulation. In section 6 we look at different styles of regulation, the international dimension to regulation, the accountability of regulators, and the measurement of their performance.

5. The Natural History of Regulation

Regulatory origins, development, and reform

Just as the origins of life and the universe are fundamental questions in natural science, the genesis and change of regulatory regimes attract a range of explanatory theory. The technical reasons that justify regulation and the rationalizations for regulating are also central issues. Our first reading, taken from Stephen Breyer's well-known book *Regulation and its*

Reform (1982), offers a classic review of common rationales for regulating and outlines, *inter alia*, a series of justifications based on the alleged inability of the market-place to deal with particular problems.

Whether 'market failure' is in fact a technical problem or whether it reflects differences in perception and cultural bias, even among economists, is a contested issue.[36] Some claim that the best way of explaining the political ebbs and flows of regulation calls for reference not to the changing technical properties of markets but to the tides of received ideas concerning regulation. Whether the latter view is sustainable is itself contentious—arguments can be made that such ebbs and flows can better be explained in terms of pressures of interests; or with reference to changes in socio-economic circumstances; or by looking at the inherently self-destructive forces that typically lie within regulatory policies and institutions.[37] It would be difficult, nevertheless, to hold with conviction that currents of thought never have relevance in charting developments in regulation.[38] It is, therefore, for practical as well as intellectual reasons, useful to look to past progressions of thought on the origins and development of regulation.[39]

A first approach to regulation, associated with the growth of regulatory activity in the United States from the late nineteenth-century Progressive era, is the public interest or functionalist analysis.[40] It holds that the state acts in the public interest to tackle market imperfections. Public officials thus translate public preferences into legal regulatory regimes and elected legislatures direct such officials in pursuit of the public good. Those pressing for regulation, on such a view, act as agents for the public interest.[41] Consistent with such an approach is an emphasis on the trustworthiness of expert regulators in whose public spiritedness and efficiency the public can have confidence.[42] Often decried as old fashioned, the public interest approach continues to attract sophisticated defenders arguing for the maintenance and development rather than abandonment of traditional regulation.[43]

Nevertheless, the public interest approach is conventionally argued to suffer from several weaknesses. It has been said to understate the extent to which regulation is the product of clashes between different interest groups[44] and (alternatively) the degree to which regulatory regimes are established by, and run in, the interests of the economically powerful.[45] Observers of regulation in practice have also contested the disinterestedness and efficiency that the public interest approach attributes to regulators. Some observers have pointed to venal tendencies among regulators, their corruption into private profit seekers, and their instinct to protect their own positions and employment as first priorities.[46] This attack on the public interest approach is consistent with that of 'capture theorists' who hold that regulation becomes (or in some versions begins life as) captured by the regulated parties and so serves their interests rather than any wider public interest.

More generally, the public interest perspective has been attacked on the ground that regulation often seems to fail to deliver public interest outcomes. For some this observation indicates that we must learn from failures and design better regulatory institutions.[47] For others, it suggests that regulatory projects are doomed and ought to be replaced by policies of deregulation. Chief among these critics of the public interest approach in the US literature are proponents of a second, and very different, vision of regulation. Interest-group theorists see regulation as the product of relationships between different groups and between such groups and the state. Instead of conceiving regulation as reflecting the public spiritedness of a Hegelian state élite, such theorists range from open-ended pluralism to corporatism.[48] Pluralists see competing groups as struggling for power and elections as won by coalitions of groups who use their power to shape regulatory regimes. Corporatists, on the other hand, see successful groups as being taken into partnership with the state and producing regulatory structures that exclude non-participating interests.[49]

A third broad approach to regulation draws on microeconomic theory, encompassing perspectives variously known as 'capture', 'special interest', 'economic', 'private interest' 'rent-seeking', and 'public choice'. Generally these approaches see regulatory origins and developments to be driven by the pursuit of rational self-interest by policy participants. Such participants pursue their preferences in a manner akin to market activity. The focus thus rests on the individual actor rather than the group or the state. Organizations and bureaucracies are thus to be analysed with reference to the pursuit of the competing preferences of the individuals that make up such collectivities. Stress is placed on the propensity of such individual actors to circumvent official regulatory goals by substituting objectives that are self-serving and to act in pursuit of such ends as job retention or aggrandizement, re-election, or the accumulation of personal wealth.[50] From such a viewpoint, public interest plays a very small role in the establishment and operation of regulatory regimes. Regulation is better seen as another commodity, 'bought' by the economically powerful and used in a manner calculated to gain further wealth for the powerful.[51] Political activities, on such a view, can be seen as no less rationally self-interested than actions taken in private lives or markets.

Policies are put into effect with the purpose of enhancing wealth or utility positions.[52]

As already noted, the attacks on the public interest stance that have come from the public choice stable have been seen as helping to found the deregulation movements in the United States and the United Kingdom in the 1970s and 1980s and the popularity of ideas of 'government by the market'.[53] As theories, however, the public choice perspectives can themselves be attacked on a number of grounds.[54] They cannot explain where the preferences in the 'market' (taken as given in conventional economic analysis) come from, why they are diverse, how far they vary, and why they change. Parties, moreover, may lack determinate preferences on political or regulatory issues. They may behave altruistically in important respects (e.g. identifying with group, bureaucracy, agency, or legislative objectives) and may behave in different ways according to the roles they adopt—for example, as market purchasers, career movers, or designers of policies in their professional lives. Informational deficiencies may prevent regulators or bureaucrats from acting in a rational, self-serving way. The interest group process may affect regulation in a manner uncontrollable by private preference realizers and regulatory bureaucracies may have a life beyond the sum of lives that make up their parts. Moreover, one of the major challenges presented to the economic theory of regulation is precisely that experience of deregulation seems to confound the theory's predictions. In the face of that challenge, Sam Peltzman has been in the lead of attempts to rework the economic theory so that it can accommodate both the extension of self-seeking regulation and deregulation.[55]

Our second reading is Sam Peltzman's 1989 article in the *Brookings Papers on Microeconomics* in which he reviews the economic theory and assesses its power to explain regulatory developments between the mid-1970s and mid-1980s. He concludes that although such theory 'can tell a coherent story about most of the examples of deregulation' it leaves some important questions unanswered—for instance about the design of institutions and their adaptability.

Perceived deficiencies in the public choice approach constitute a gap that has been filled by 'agency theories'—sometimes called 'postrevisionist' accounts.[56] These theories again draw on economists' tools, including information analyses, to explore the mechanisms by which voters' preferences are translated through political processes into policy. Legislators' ideological preferences are, in such accounts, taken on board in looking at voting practices,[57] and the focus is on monitoring and agency relationships.[58] A major theme of such approaches is that conventional democratic systems and processes allow for only limited oversight over actors and agencies: voters have problems in controlling legislatures, legislators have difficulties in controlling agencies, and similar difficulties permeate government at all levels. A central issue is the cost and difficulty to controlling parties of obtaining information of a quality adequate for effective oversight.[59] In the 'institutionalist' strain of agency theory, such questioning focuses on the modes of behaviour of different kinds of governmental body and the ways in which analysis of informational and transactional restraints aids the understanding and prediction of regulatory behaviour.

A variant of the same themes of institutional evolution is found in Oliver MacDonagh's path-breaking study of the Passenger Acts between 1800 and 1860, which was referred to above, and suggests that the pattern of regulatory growth in nineteenth-century Britain largely reflects an independent process by which administrative processes tend to grow into bureaucracies. In his micro-study of the regulation of passenger ships, substantially used for emigration, he shows that once a problem was officially recognized (namely the risks to life experienced by emigrants on what could be a twelve week passage across the Atlantic in crowded sailing vessels), the process of standard-setting led to the growth of bureaucratic procedures for monitoring and enforcing those standards which continued to develop long after the original problem had been largely solved by the development of steamships.[60]

Others have emphasized the role of institutions[61] or of systems[62] in explaining shifts and changes in governmental arrangements. Leigh Hancher and Michael Moran, in our third reading, do not suggest that the interests of various actors should be ignored but they question the value of conventional notions of regulatory capture and portrayals of regulation as contests between public authorities and private interests. Regulation, they argue, involves an unavoidable intermingling of public and private characteristics and accordingly it is more fruitful to attempt to understand the complex and shifting relationships between and within organizations at the heart of regulation—to understand the way in which different institutions come to inhabit a shared 'regulatory space' marked out by a range of regulatory issues subject to public decision.

Theories of capture are subjected to empirical testing in our fourth reading by Toni Makkai and John Braithwaite. They claim capture is a multi-dimensional concept, with a number of distinct forms ranging from an absence of toughness, through sympathy with an industry in difficulties concerning compliance, to actual identification with the industry. They see capture not as the product of regulatory structure, but rather as a more contingent process arising in particular situations.

Similar institutional analyses focus on the way institutions shape the playing of the regulatory game on the international stage. Thus, Giandomenico Majone, in our fifth reading, looks at the rise of the 'regulatory state' in Europe and, blending institutional and self-interest analyses, points to the role of institutional structures in explaining why Member States of the EU become prepared to delegate regulatory powers to a supranational authority such as the European Commission.

Institutional analyses have value in emphasizing that caution should be exercised in drawing institutional comparisons across jurisdictions. They indicate, further, that other influences on regulation should not be neglected—that interests (even public spirited and altruistic) can be seen as shaping regulation alongside institutional factors. Similarly, changes may be driven at least in part by economic or technical considerations or by the force of ideas.

At its simplest, attributing change to the power of ideas might simply reproduce public interest accounts. Alternative approaches emphasize the role that private interest attacks on regulation have had in reshaping perceptions and forming the basis for new policies.[63] The most developed attempt to show how ideas matter is the work of Martha Derthick and Paul Quirk who seek to show that normal interest group politics was displaced by neo-liberal New Right ideas which held that state intervention was undesirable and that diffuse consumer interests would benefit from deregulation at the expense of concentrated consumer interests.[64] Superficially appealing, such theories do not adequately explain the tenacious resistance of some regulatory regimes to this intellectual climate, and in particular the growth in regulation which has accompanied deregulation. Nor is the 'power of ideas' a theme which is ultimately falsifiable, because ideas are in practice impossible to distinguish from interests.

Can such theories of origins and development be subjected to synthesis and a metatheory developed so that the political economy of regulation can be understood 'well enough to generate reliable predictions about the behaviour of regulatory processes'?[65] To put the issue thus is perhaps to ignore the familiar trade-offs that have to be made in choosing among ways to explain social phenomena. The broader the thrust of a theory, the more it provides a frame for understanding, but the more it requires refinement to explain particular circumstances. The narrower the range of an account the sharper its thrust in relation to the focused—upon topic, but the poorer its capacity to serve as a frame for general understanding. In regulation, as in other spheres, it is perhaps wise to develop a nose for the kernels of truth in varying theories, a sense of the limitations of, and assumptions underpinning, such theories and an awareness of the information necessary for applying and testing them.

Standard-setting and rule choices

Some regulatory regimes are intended to be no more than paper schemes, designed to appease international bodies or to operate as a sop to domestic pressures. The history of regulation is full of this type of scheme and in the contemporary world states often accuse one another of applying regulation in a tokenistic way (for example, in disputes over the regulation of fishing to conserve stocks or over agricultural disease-prevention measures). The Biscay 'tuna war' of 1994 was founded on resentments concerning alleged non-enforcement of European regulations by the Spanish authorities.

A regulatory regime of any form has, however, to be applied on the ground if it is to be more than a symbolic or token gesture. Implementation has implications for the way standards and rules are designed, promulgated and enforced. One major issue is, accordingly, the problems, informational, political, and other, that regulators face in devising standards that are appropriate to designated ends and which can be enforced effectively. A related issue concerns the type of rule that is employed in regulation and how rule-type may affect both compliance seeking and the attainment of desired regulatory objectives.

Within the so-called 'command and control' approach to agency regulation, major tasks are perceived to be rule-making, enforcement, and application of sanctions. The design of appropriate regulatory rules has been the subject of a substantial and growing literature.[66] In the United Kingdom more attention has been focused on the making of rules by government, than by agencies. It is in the UK financial services and health and safety sectors that we find the most sustained attempts to understand the selection of appropriate rule-types.[67] Rules have been treated by some analysts as having four dimensions: 'substance (what the rule says); character (whether it is permissive or mandatory: may or shall); status (its legal force and the sanction attaching to it) and structure . . . Rule type is a function of only three of the dimensions: character, status/sanction and structure.'[68] For regulators and regulatees one of the key issues is the ideal degree of precision of a particular rule.

Colin Diver looks at this question in our sixth reading. He defines the concept of rule precision and distinguishes three qualities of regulatory rules—transparency, accessibility, and congruence. He develops criteria to determine the appropriate degree of regulatory precision and applies the resultant analytical framework to a number of policy areas.

Eugene Bardach and Robert Kagan have noted that regulatory agencies tend to shy away from broad discretionary standards as such standards tend to be more difficult to enforce, at least in the United States' legal and cultural setting. Thus, where a broad standard is set, agencies tend to try to fill it in with detailed specifications. 'It is easier to gather evidence and convince a judge that a nursing home has failed to maintain a specified numerical staff–patient ratio, for example, than it is to show that it failed to provide "adequate staffing to maintain a decent standard of care".'[69] Precisely-stated rules may be easier to comply with or to enforce, but may be under- or over-inclusive, and therefore not actually achieve the outcome sought (they may fail to cover behaviour or dangers that should be covered or take in matters that should be left unregulated). Strategies of 'creative compliance' among regulatees (discussed in the following section) may also render the effects of precise rules nugatory.[70] Less precisely-drafted rules may give the regulator more discretion, or may make enforcement more difficult, in either case affecting legitimacy.

Major questions also arise over *which* factors regulatory standards should focus on. Should they relate to matters of physical design (for example, of road gradients or curvatures), to standards of performance without narrowly specifying design parameters (for example, of the impacts that vehicle bumpers should be able to withstand), or to organizational decision procedures (for example, that there should be safety committees with defined responsibilities)? What 'justice models' should they incorporate? For instance, should they follow standard economic optimization rules when faced with the inevitable choices about how to judge the desirability of measures which make some people better off at the expense of others, or opt instead for an egalitarian bias, favouring the worst off? What approach should they incorporate in terms of the avoidance of errors, in the real-world situation where avoidance of all error is impossible?

The latter issue is the subject of our seventh reading, taken from Kristin Shrader-Frechette's *Risk and Rationality* (1991). It concerns the question of where the regulatory bias should lie between what are conventionally called Type I and Type II errors. A Type I error in statistics means rejection of a null hypothesis (= no harmful effect, in this case) that turns out to be true, whereas a Type II error means acceptance of a null hypothesis that turns out to be false. Regulators ineluctably face the choice of what kind of error they would 'prefer' to make, for example in setting standards for nuclear safety plants which might conceivably be operated (as in the Chernobyl disaster in 1986) by engineers who choose to disconnect all the automatic safety systems to conduct an experiment, or over the treatment of meat potentially affected by 'mad cow disease' (aka bovine spongiform encephalopathy) which in turn conceivably exposes humans to a greater risk of contracting Creuzfeld-Jakob disease. To err may be human, but in which of those two directions—Type I or Type II—should regulators aim to err?

Shrader-Frechette's argument is that conventional standards across much of risk regulation lay an exaggerated emphasis on the avoidance of Type I errors at the expense of Type II errors, and that the conventional bias reflects the instinct of natural scientists to come down on the side of 'conservative errors'—as does even the preference normally built into the criminal law to acquit the guilty rather than convict the innocent. If it comes to a choice of errors, Shrader-Frechette argues that a bias in favour of avoiding Type I errors ought not to be echoed in public risk regulation, where the opposite bias—to make Type II errors at the expense of Type I errors, if need be—is more appropriate.

The problem with Shrader-Frechette's proposal is where exactly does the principle stop? As it is, economists often argue that electoral pressures typically lead governments to be much more unwilling to make Type II than Type I errors, even where the costs of such a bias are very substantial—for example, resulting in patients who die because of the non-release of drugs that could save their lives but might conceivably have harmful side-effects. As Geoffrey Brennan claims: 'governments will tend to be led to act too conservatively in Type I contexts and too casually in Type II contexts, and to trade Type I errors for Type II errors, even where the Type II error involves the greater expected loss.'[71] Whether that political bias is really as universal as Brennan claims is debatable—after all, cases such as tobacco regulation might be considered to be examples of the opposite kind of bias at work—but certainly the development of the so-called *Versorgensprinzip*, or 'precautionary principle', adopted by Germany in 1976 for risk regulation and extended more generally into many areas of EU regulatory decision-making (for example, over nitrate levels in water or growth hormones in meat[72]) is a clear development of the doctrine Shrader-Frechette advocates. But whether her preferred egalitarian solution to the balancing of risks and benefits in regulation—in effect, an updated version of Bentham's idea of a 'Public Opinion Tribunal' to guide public policy—could really avoid the besetting sins of 'tunnel vision', 'random agenda selection', and 'inconsistency' that Judge Breyer[73] sees as endemic to the political and legal process of risk regulation, must be open to debate.

Enforcement

Central concerns in the analysis of enforcement are the devices and approaches that can be employed; the values that underpin and are served by enforcement activity; the effectiveness of different enforcement styles; and the relationships between enforcers and those who make the rules.

Enforcement in regulation is a multi-layered term. It may refer simply to the prosecution of those in breach of the rules in response to complaints, a model familiar from our notions of general policing. But regulatory enforcement often consists of a more subtle range of techniques of monitoring, inspecting, advising, and warning, with prosecution constituting only a small part of the agency's activities. Enforcement officers may have powers going beyond simple prosecution, including the seizure and destruction of dangerous goods or shutting down of dangerous activities.[74] The interest of researchers concerned with regulatory enforcement has often been to discover the ways in which the mix of powers is used, whether it is reactive or proactive in seeking out infractions, whether it uses a negotiating or adversarial technique in its approach to compliance.[75] Much of the literature has been concerned with enforcement in regimes where penalties for breaches are criminal, leading to the development of a new branch of criminology concerned with regulatory crime as opposed to traditional crime.[76] This literature has paid less attention to problems of regulatory enforcement in areas where criminal sanctioning has given way to administrative controls as in the UK utilities sectors, and areas dominated by licensing such as consumer credit and estate agencies and administrative oversight of public sector activities.[77]

A key debate about enforcement has been concerned with the appropriate approach to be taken by enforcement authorities. Many regulatory statutes in the United Kingdom prescribe criminal sanctions as the stick with which to beat offenders. Enforcement authorities may not have sufficient resources to prosecute every infraction which they discover or they may take the view that their resources are more efficiently used in taking action falling short of prosecution. It may even be that enforcement authorities do not actually have the resources to shape the behaviour of firms in the way they want. In these circumstances, officers may exploit the absence of lawyers in enforcement situations and use bluffing and illusion to secure compliance.[78] A number of empirical studies of enforcement have shown that enforcement authorities, like football referees, frequently develop a hierarchy of sanctions in which the first stage may be to offer education and advice to the offender, the second is a warning for a subsequent offence, and only when offending appears to be serious and culpable, or the flagrantly routine conduct of the offender, to think of prosecuting.[79]

This pattern is captured in our seventh reading, from Keith Hawkins's well-known study, *Environment and Enforcement*, and in John Braithwaite's well-known model of the enforcement pyramid.[80] In characterizing enforcement approaches, Albert Reiss draws an important distinction between 'compliance' approaches which emphasize the use of measures falling short of prosecution in order to seek compliance, and 'deterrence' approaches, which rely on penalizing violators so as to deter future infractions:

> although both compliance and deterrence law enforcement systems are oriented towards *preventing* the occurrence of violations, compliance systems are *premonitory*, attending to conditions that induce conformity or to foreloading of harm. By contrast, deterrent law enforcement systems are *postmonitory*, reacting to violations that have occurred. Deterrence systems assume that penalties have causal effect, the principle of which is to prevent future violations. Compliance systems, correlatively, either reward or withhold imposing penalties to induce states of compliance.[81]

Having seen that enforcement authorities have choices between compliance and deterrence approaches, we might next ask whether certain factors are likely to lead to the routine use of one rather than the other within any given regulatory regime.[82] For some, the adoption of compliance approaches may be the product of capture (as discussed above), or of regulator and regulatee having sufficient identification with each other, through shared experience, frequent contacts, staff exchanges, or familiarity (components affecting 'relational distance', that is, the degree of social distance between regulator and regulatee[83]), that routine prosecution would be unthinkable. Deterrence approaches may be more common where the relationship between regulator and regulatee is less close, social contact less frequent, or where enforcement officers have an image of those whom they regulate as offenders needing punishment for offences. Such a view seems to be much less common where regulatees are large firms, and prosecutions by agencies chiefly regulating large firms are consequently much less common.[84] A major empirical study by Peter Grabosky and John Braithwaite was only able to substantiate two hypotheses concerning factors relevant in determining the extent to which regulatory agencies resort to prosecution. These were the relational distance hypothesis (prosecution less frequent when regulators and regulatees are close in social background) and the company size hypothesis (prosecution less frequent when regulatees are large firms).[85] Hawkins has, however, stressed the role of moral and social attitudes in the judgements made by prosecutors and has argued that prosecutions are most likely to be pursued when infringements are flagrant, repeated, or extreme in their culpability or consequences.[86]

For some there is an optimal level of enforcement. In the ninth reading in this volume, Steven Shavell examines 'the optimal structure of enforcement' and advances an economic model which links the various dimensions of law enforcement to the various means by which regulatory law may be enforced. More generally, economists, have sought to identify the conditions under which compliance approaches to regulation can be seen as economically rational.[87]

In a classic, but controversial, study[88] Eugene Bardach and Robert Kagan identified several advantages in tough enforcement. They found many instances of improved standards and reduced risks when enforcement was strict. They observed systematic responses in larger firms to develop management systems which reduced the risk of infraction, thus changing the corporate culture.[89] Arguably this general change in corporate culture, under which a form of self-regulation at the level of the firm is taken seriously, is the most positive aspect of the deterrence approach to enforcement. In the United Kingdom self-regulation in this form is encouraged through the construction of strict liability offences with defences that permit firms to show that they exercised all due diligence to avoid committing the offence. Thus, where infractions are discovered, for example over food safely, firms that have installed systems for protecting against the infraction may escape liability.[90] In the case of large organizations, enforcement officers may, in any case, be too heavily dependent upon internal control systems within the firm to be effective to enact the firm's general wish to comply with the requirements of the regulatory regime.[91]

The Bardach and Kagan study found a variety of problems with tough enforcement strategies. First they suggested that many of the features which make the operation of an industry work well are not capable of being reduced to enforceable rules. Amongst these features they include kindness among health care workers, and, more generally, aspirations to do better among workers. Routinization of inspection linked to compliance with rules may reduce the capacity of inspectors to identify new problems. Resentment and hostility in organizations inspected in a legalistic manner may reduce the efficiency of enforcement, particularly where inspectors are dependent on the firm for information, and may lead to organizations pursuing only the minimal compliance required. They note, additionally, that legalistic enforcement is much more costly than pursuit of compliance strategies.[92] Bardach and Kagan set out a scheme of appropriate and flexible enforcement for regulatory regimes which resembles the description of actual practices in UK studies of the enforcement process.[93] Ian Ayres and John Braithwaite have subsequently offered a more formal model, based on developments in game theory (notably Axelrod's well-known iterated Prisoner's Dilemma studies),[94] in which they suggest that enforcement will be most effective in securing compliance where enforcement officers use a tit-for-tat strategy. This idea implies that the enforcement officers will seek co-operation with the regulated unit initially and up to the point when the regulate fails to co-operate. At that stage the enforcement officers no longer co-operate and invoke sanctions, which may be statutory penalties, or some other action which will damage the regulatee such as adverse publicity.[95] This strategy addresses both the regulation of organizations which seek to be co-operative, and those which calculate to co-operate only when it serves their interests. For both motivational sets tit-for-tat is said to encourage co-operation and therefore compliance. Yet, in Bardach and Kagan's terminology, it does not necessitate unreasonable regulation. This approach is also consistent with earlier work by Braithwaite in setting out enforcement pyramids, but questions may be asked concerning the extent to which the move up the sanctions ladder can be assumed to be free from political lobbying, or capture and concerning restrictions that limitations of resources, information, and rule-making capacities place on such a strategy. Whatever conclusions are drawn by the participant in the compliance versus deterrence debate, the flexible enforcement approach casts doubt on portrayals of enforcement in such dichotomous terms.

The idea of compliance may itself pose difficulties and securing compliance may not necessarily produce the results desired by legislators or regulators. Some commentators have thus pointed to the problem of creative compliance.[96] This phenomenon arises when regulatees avoid the intention of a law or rule without technically breaching that rule or law—they may, for instance, restructure a mode of operation so that it escapes a legal definition yet, for all practical purposes, reproduces the kind of behaviour and results that the law at issue seeks to curtail. Thus, confronted with a law stating, say, that shops with floor areas over 10,000 square metres may only open for six hours on Sundays, an enterprise might divide its site into two 6,000 square metre units ('Homes' and 'Groceries') and escape the rule while continuing to trade as formerly. The difficulties of controlling creative compliers have been described in some detail by Doreen McBarnet and Christopher Whelan,[97] who argue that certain types of regulatory rule (notably those formalistic in nature) are liable to produce creative compliance yet are the kinds of formulations that are pressed for (with some success) by certain interests and regulated parties.

In our tenth reading Nancy Reichman seeks to build on earlier work on regulatory enforcement by showing that regulated firms and their professional advisers play a key role not just in securing compliance, but in actually negotiating the meaning of regulatory rules.[98] She develops the concept of cultural authority to explain the circumstances under which such development of roles is likely and possible. This analysis again poses questions concerning the drawing of clear distinctions between enforcement approaches, since we find that regulatees may be shaping the interpretation of rules at early stages in the regulatory process.

A particular concern of some commentators is to explain instances where there is a lack of uniformity in enforcement. Lack of uniformity across what are supposed to be similar, but locally-based regimes, has also often led to criticism. Many enforcement functions are carried out by local authorities in the United Kingdom, for example, in town planning, consumer protection, and environmental health. One hypothesis would suggest that local authorities might compete with each other to create regimes which are favourable to businesses setting up in their area, as Tiebout suggests they might compete on local taxation.[99] Such a hypothesis would lead us to expect a general downward pressure on enforcement standards. Other explanations of lack of uniformity emphasize differing levels of resources across local authorities, or differing cultures within local authority departments. A number of responses to problems of lack of uniformity have been observed, notably in response to concerns within EC institutions that such lack of uniform enforcement is inconsistent with the principles of the Single Market. (We return to the theme of regulatory competition in section 6 below).[100]

6. Species of Regulation

Varieties of regulatory styles and techniques

A wide range of regulatory styles may be found across jurisdictions, even dealing with issues that are apparently quite similar. For example, federal regulation in the United States is dominated by a formalized and legalistic style of regulation, administered by powerful agencies having rule-making, enforcement, and sanctioning powers.[101] Processes are formal, relatively transparent, and often involve lengthy decision cycles. In the United Kingdom regulation has tended to be much less formal and less transparent, with regulators wielding substantial powers with little procedural check. Consideration of the experience of regulation in other jurisdictions makes the British informal style look somewhat normal, and the formalism and legalism of the United States seem pathological. The success of the Japanese economy has been built, in part, on a regulatory structure of informality in which regulatory authorities exercise wide discretion in issuing guidance, but where compliance is largely voluntary.[102] Low relational distance in regulation is a product of an old boy network in which retired government officials commonly transfer to the management of businesses.[103] A series of scandals in relation to financial regulation in the early 1990s may herald efforts to reform this system.[104]

Indeed, in an important study contrasting styles of environmental regulation in the United States and the United Kingdom, David Vogel concluded: 'the American approach to environmental regulation is the most rigid and rule-oriented to be found in any industrial society; the British, the most flexible and informal'.[105] Relations between government and industry in the United Kingdom have, additionally, been closer and more consensual in character.[106] Similar observations may be made about utilities regulation, where British regulatory agencies have been able to deploy relatively limited policy making powers, focused on licence modification, for the management of sectors which in most cases are moving from statutory monopoly to a greater degree of competition.[107] This outcome contrasts with the results achieved by the formally more powerful American agencies whose effectiveness has been constrained by the maze of procedural requirements and opportunities for hearings about, and appeals from, regulatory decisions. Nevertheless, it has been argued that the American Progressive-era independent commission model has been better suited to regulatory reform and deregulation. The Federal Communications Commission, the Civil Aeronautics Board, and the Interstate Commerce Commission have been at the forefront of agency-led deregulation which has occurred in ways that are substantially independent of the executive.[108] In the United Kingdom, deregulatory efforts have necessarily been focused on central government, and notably the Cabinet Office Better Regulation Unit discussed earlier, and have consequently been more political and more difficult. Where the less powerful regulatory agencies have attempted regulatory reform they have found themselves lacking the powers needed for the task.[109]

A frequently claimed feature of the UK style of regulation (and the associated structure of convention and common law surrounding parliamentary government) is that regulation has been regarded as almost a private affair between regulator and regulated, in which third parties are assumed to have little interest or even right to information or consultation.[110] A related observation is that UK governments have been much more willing to use self-regulation as a means towards achieving policy outcomes,[111] with self-regulatory regimes often having operated and developed in the shadow of threatened legislative developments.[112]

How may we account for such divergent regulatory styles both over time and in different states? Can it be assumed that styles of regulation within jurisdictions are homogeneous? A focus on national styles may tend to obscure variations in attitudes and approaches to regulation within states. Cultural theory is one approach which prompts a look for such variations and which aims to provide an analysis of preferences for different forms of organization. Cultural theorists claim that organizations, institutions, and individuals embody a finite number of ways of life or cultural biases which in turn translate into views about social justice, blame, accountability, and organizational design. The argument is that ways of life reflect two fundamental variables in human organizations— group and grid—which when dichotomized into high and low variations combine to produce four polar ways of life. Group refers to the extent to which individuals are integrated into collectives and grid refers to the extent to which transactions among individuals are governed by general rule rather than every transaction needing its own negotiations and *ad hoc* bargaining. Dividing grid and group into strong and weak varieties produces four possible ways of life: hierarchism (strong group, strong grid); fatalism (weak group, strong grid), individualism (weak group, weak grid), and egalitarianism (strong group, weak grid). Hierarchist societies are likely to favour a heavy reliance on generalized rules and organization founded on the presumption that individuals may need to be sacrificed for collective gain. Individualist and egalitarian societies are unlikely to favour such policy styles and the former are more likely to prefer deregulation or, at most, light touch regulation while the latter will put the stress on highly participatory models of regulation. Fatalist societies are likely to involve a substantial state presence, not necessarily in a regulatory form and without social participation.[113]

What difference does it make whether regulation is conducted in one form or another? In the current UK model the comparatively weak powers given to the regulators *vis-à-vis* the firms they regulate has created the potential for a sophisticated form of game-playing and process of negotiation in which all institutional resources may potentially be used.[114] There may ultimately be the threat of new legislation or some form of drawn-out enforcement process, but, in many instances, regulators and firms are likely to seek the best position they can in some sort of regulatory compromise.

In understanding different styles and processes of regulation key concerns are the choices that are made between different techniques of control and how those choices are made. The range of policy instruments available to secure the regulatory ends identified have been reviewed by a number of authors.[115] In that vein, the various typologies of policy instruments are reviewed by Terence Daintith in our eleventh reading and Daintith himself attempts to trace out the steps through which such a typology can be derived a priori. He argues that policy instruments link the objectives of economic policy to the specific legal measures of implementation and it is accordingly necessary, when developing a typology of policy instruments, to avoid the circularity implicit in defining instruments by reference to legal measures and then comparing measures by reference to instruments.

The classical model of regulation has come to be called command and control regulation, and involves the regulator making and enforcing the rules. It is typically associated with US Progressive-era regulation. The term 'command and control' is in fact a later coinage: as John Dryzek puts it: 'In this democratic age, and following the manifest failure of centrally controlled economics, who could possibly favour "command and control" of anything (except perhaps the military)?'[116] Perhaps because of the success of such rhetorical tactics, a number of alternative styles have assumed importance in the modern regulatory debate. Some of these alternatives involve agency regulation with less prescriptive rules, others involve the use of alternatives to sanction-based commands, such as taxes and contracts, and a third type uses non-government resources in the form of self-regulatory institutions and rules.[117]

The regulation of the British utilities sectors following privatization is, or was thought to be, a key example of light rein agency regulation, under which the regulated firms would have certain obligations in their licences which the agencies would enforce (principally RPI − X price controls),[118] but under which there would be few, if any, detailed sectoral rules. A key aspect of such regimes is that although all players in the market are obliged to have licences, only those with a dominant market position are exposed to all the regulatory requirements. Thus there is a form of 'partial industry intervention' which affects not only the firms subject to the regulatory requirements, but also, implicitly, all the other players in the market.[119] The experience of partial industry regulation is most notable in telecommunications where only British Telecom, the largest player, is subject to price control and the broadest social obligations.

In some sectors general antitrust or competition rules may be seen as providing a substitute for detailed sectoral provision.[120] The mode of regulation provided by competition rules tends, however, to be biased towards liberalization. The key issue to be addressed in the utilities sectors is the dominance and potential for abuse of position by vertically integrated monopolies. Competition rules may provide a spur to liberalization but there are doubts whether competition rules and enforcement can substitute for regulation. In both the United States and the EU competition rules have been important in the liberalization of key utility sectors such as telecommunications and energy. In the United States application of the antitrust rules resulted in the structural separation (or break-up) of the dominant telecommunications provider, AT&T, in 1984, which was divided into regional companies providing local services and a long-distance operator. Even though such structural solutions to the competition problems raised by the utilities sectors were technically possible, and arguably more straightforward in the United Kingdom, at the time when the utilities were privatized, such options were in most cases not pursued for political reasons.[121] Only in the case of the privatization of rail under the Railways Act 1993 has infrastructure ownership been separated from service provision,[122] a structural solution which may have reduced some of the competition problems, but which seems likely to increase the co-ordination problems in providing rail services.

The main concern of competition rules is likely to be the prevention of unfair conduct by major players, for example in 'predatory pricing'[123] (i.e. pricing below cost to chase others out of the market) or cross-subsidizing from monopolistic to competitive sectors. Where a dominant incumbent has control over 'essential facilities' such as network infrastructure, as applies to many of the utilities sectors, competition rules may be concerned to ensure that other firms have access to those facilities.[124]

The decision whether to use general competition rules in regulation gives rise to complex questions as to the design of institutions and rule-types.[125] In relation to institutions: should rules be adjudicated/enforced only through the courts (as at present), through a system of mandatory arbitration, through a sectoral regulatory agency, or through a government department? In relation to rules: should there be no rules beyond the general competition rules? Should there be broad statutory rules for the sector? Should there be detailed sectoral rules?[126]

The UK model has been based on detailed sectoral rules and agency enforcement, but with some evidence of a shift towards more general anti-competitive conduct rules, notably in telecommunications. At present this shift falls short of accepting proposals to give affected third parties the right to enforce the competition rules, though such rights do exist in EC competition law. The Labour government elected in 1997 has committed itself, however, to introducing new legislation which will substantially align UK competition rules to those of the EC.

An alternative to command and control regulation, but one which is more prescriptive than the application of competition rules, and in practice often combined with other forms of regulation, is franchising. Firms wanting to carry out the regulated activity bid for the right to do so. The franchise is issued to the most favoured bidder (typically on the most favourable bid—be this lowest price or highest quality—or mixture of price and quality) for a fixed period of years. The franchise agreement will typically include provisions relating to such matters as quality, and pricing of the franchised service. The regulator will then seek to enforce the terms of the franchise. In Britain this form of regulation has been used for commercial broadcasting, the National Lottery, and privatization of the rail network.[127] Its advantages are said to be that even though a monopoly is ultimately granted, the process of bidding has created a form of competition for the field which provides a market mechanism for securing information about the price/quality ratio which the regulator can expect in the sector.[128] The regulatory rules are effectively institutionalized in a contract between the regulator and the firm.

A related technique is referred to as 'regulation by contract'.[129] Here the government uses its wealth (derived from taxes) and its need to obtain goods and services, to seek certain objectives by specifying them in the contract. A classic example is provision that employees of companies providing goods and services to the public sector shall be paid a minimum wage. The key difference between this and franchising is that the contracts issued are not entered into for the primary purpose of regulating, but rather regulatory aspects to the contract are incidental to the main purposes which are likely to be the procurement of goods and services. The effect, however, is to achieve a regulatory standard across all firms contracting with government without ever issuing a mandatory rule. Compulsory competitive tendering (CCT) of local authority-provided services, a form of contracting-out, has been used by government as a means to reduce costs associated with local service provision and brings with it regulation by contract of service providers by local authorities.[130] Related trends include: the pressing of public sector contractors to submit to quality assessment regimes as conditions of securing such contracts; the move towards market testing of services provided by central government; and separation of policy-making and operation of services, with the relationship between service providers and policy-makers being variously governed by quasi-contractual documents (framework agreements in the case of Next Steps Agencies, and (unenforceable) contracts in the case of health provision under the NHS and Community Care Act 1990).[131] It may be added that the dependence of some sectors on public funding has also been used as a lever to encourage both the development of self-regulation and to impose consensual forms of regulation.[132]

Another way of securing objectives without issuing mandatory rules is through the use of taxes and subsidies.[133] Subsidies alter the incentives faced by individuals or organizations, for example, in inducing firms to set up in particular areas (as with regional policy) or to offer particular services (as with railways). Taxes may be used to increase the costs of certain activities, for example, of polluting. (The differential duty levied on leaded and unleaded petrol, introduced in Britain in 1987, is often cited as a tax with regulatory effect.) If they can ensure that the costs of negative externalities are really paid by those creating the externalities then taxes provide incentives to carry out those activities at economically efficient levels. Where government or regulators decide the maximum level of acceptable pollution they may be able to sell the rights to pollute in permits which in total reach the maximum. Such a permit may be tradeable, and therefore a market in the right to pollute is created, with such rights being a scarce resource for which firms will pay.[134] The idea of tradeable permits in pollution has been a fashionable idea among economists for several decades, though the idea has largely remained on the drawing board as politically unacceptable and administratively impractical.[135]

The development of self-regulatory regimes in key areas of the economy has also been an important sub-theme of British regulation over the past 25 years.[136] The term self-regulation has no accepted definition. At its simplest it may refer to the capacity and tendency of all individuals and organizations to regulate their own conduct. Used in the context of regulation, self-regulation more usually refers to a scheme whereby a representative organization, for example a trade association, develops a system of rules which it will then monitor and enforce against, in some cases, its members, or, in rarer cases, a larger community.[137] Such self-regulatory regimes may be set up wholly independently of any encouragement by government. More commonly, the development of such regimes may be carried out to discourage the government from legislating—as with the Press Complaints Authority, the Advertising Standards Authority[138] regime, and the Association of British Insurers' Statements of Insurance Practice.[139] Alternatively, the regime may be mandated under legislation—as is the case with much professional regulation and the extensive network of self-regulatory organizations (SROs) established under the terms of the Financial Services Act 1986.[140] Statutory schemes may, moreover, subject self-regulatory mechanisms to scrutiny and approval by a government agency, as is the case with the trade association codes of practice approved by the Director General of Fair Trading under the terms of the Fair Trading Act 1973.[141]

Self-regulation has become popular not just in terms of the number of appearances self-regulatory regimes make in the contemporary world, but in the enthusiasm for the approach on the part of some influential academics. In particular, John Braithwaite, with various collaborators, has suggested that a system of enforced self-regulation under which firms, or industry associations, make their own rules but have to submit them to public agencies for approval might prove more efficient, more flexible, and less costly to government than traditional command and control methods.[142] In such regimes enforcement is to be carried out through compliance officers within firms who will have responsibilities to report infractions and act upon them.[143]

Ian Ayres and John Braithwaite have, moreover, suggested that different styles of regulation, involving differing degrees of intervention in the market, can be reconciled by thinking in terms of a pyramid of regulatory strategies. In this model self-regulation should be favoured as the initial approach, and, where it proves unsuccessful, 'enforced self-regulation', which involves greater state monitoring, should be introduced. Only where these strategies fail should state regulation with discretionary punishment, and finally with mandatory punishment, be resorted to.[144] It is in this sense that their 1992 book *Responsive Regulation* attempts to transcend the deregulation debate.

In our twelfth reading Anthony Ogus discusses the array of criticisms of self-regulation that has emerged from lawyers and other social scientists and suggests that insufficient attention has been given to the wide range of institutional arrangements that may properly be labelled 'self-regulation'. Ogus goes on to argue that self-regulators' regimes based on consensual bargaining, or involving competition between self-regulatory structures, have the potential to meet traditional criticisms if such regimes incorporate some measure of external constraint. Self-regulatory regimes, containing powers to make and enforce rules, and to sanction transgressors, may, nevertheless, be regarded as constituting 'mini-systems of government' which raise difficult doctrinal questions as to their broader subjection to the principles of administrative law.[145]

As for the general limitations of regulatory law and of juridification, these are analysed by Gunther Teubner in our thirteenth reading. Teubner considers potential solutions to the problems posed by such limitations and considers the possibilities offered *inter alia* by a more sophisticated approach to implementation (and attention to 'enforcement deficits'); by deregulation; by 'controlled self-regulation'; by 'constitutive strategies of law', and by negotiated regulation.

Such a critique is broadly based on the concern that giving legal powers to public authorities to intervene in markets for social or economic ends may render a legal system hitherto based on general principles too specific, or may create expectations of the legal system and of the interventionist state that it cannot possibly meet. The legal system is only likely to respond to instructions from the political system on its own terms, and these may or may not coincide with those of the political system. The regulated sphere will also respond to instructions from the regulated system on its own terms. Such an analysis suggests that the most successful regulation is likely to be that which is most in sympathy with the culture and values of the regulated, and thus makes a strong argument for self-regulation.

Varieties of regulatory scale

Regulation operates at different governmental levels. Thus, few aspects of UK regulation are unaffected by international, and notably EU, inputs. Indeed, the EU has given rise to a new species of regulation characterized by a combination of rule-making at the supranational and rule-application at the national levels. Central concerns are how integration of regulatory regimes can be brought about; how domestic and non-domestic regulatory systems will interact; how choices can be made concerning the appropriate governmental level at which to regulate; and how implementation is to be supervised.

For most UK students of regulation it is membership of the EU that provides the central focus for interest,[146] as well as supranational regulation through the World Trade Organisation (formerly the GATT) and other international organizations. From its creation in 1957, a key objective of what was then the European Economic Community was the creation of a common market. New institutions were established at that time, including the European Commission, the European Court of Justice, the Assembly (since 1986 known officially as the European Parliament), and the Council of Ministers. At the time of its creation it appeared the creation of a common market would require laws which were harmonized to remove barriers to trade. The implication of this requirement was that new regulatory regimes operating at the Community level would replace domestic regimes. However, the processes of harmonization proved to be difficult, partly because the creation of detailed vertical standards was very time consuming, and partly because the institutional structure of the Community, requiring as it did unanimous approval from the Council for measures put forward by the Commission, made the passage of contentious measures virtually impossible. A period of 'Euro-sclerosis' in the 1970s was ended partly by judicial activism and partly by institutional reforms designed to make the completion of what was to be called the Internal Market more straightforward. As noted earlier, regulatory policy making is very attractive for Eurocrats keen to enhance their power, since it costs little for a bureaucracy which has little scope to expand programme expenditure.[147]

The key move made by the Court of Justice was the development of a principle of 'mutual recognition' in a case brought under Article 30 of the (then) EEC Treaty (free movement of goods).[148] An importer of alcoholic drinks alleged that German rules which set a minimum alcohol content for spirits above the level of many French alcoholic products (including a liqueur called *Cassis de Dijon* which it wished to import into Germany) was in breach of Article 30, as a measure 'having equivalent effect' to import restrictions. In upholding the case of the importer, the Court held that, subject to the exceptions contained in Article 36 of the Treaty, 'any product lawfully produced and marketed in one of the Member States' should be permitted to be imported and sold in any other Member State. The principle of 'mutual recognition' that this judgment embodied created fears of negative integration—that there would be a race to the bottom because each Member State would aim to develop standards rather less stringent than its rivals, producing a beggar-my-neighbour effect. Partly in response to such fears, the European Commission has developed the framework approach to legislation under which minimum requirements are set out, but much of the detailed regulation is to be set by Community or national standard-setting organizations without the need for time-consuming consideration of such standards in the Council of Ministers.[149] Additionally, the Treaty was revised by the Single European Act (1986) to permit legislation directed towards the completion of the Internal Market to be passed by a qualified majority in the Council of Ministers. With that new impetus, the Community proceeded to identify and enact the legislation needed to complete the Internal Market by 1992.

Debate over EU regulation today focuses on the appropriate level for regulatory legislation. The EC Treaty was amended by the Treaty on European Union (Maastricht Treaty) in 1993 to incorporate formally the much-discussed principle of subsidiarity, the concept that legislation and regulation should be carried out at the lowest appropriate level for success —a concept familiar in some continental legal system, but foreign to the UK tradition.[150] At the same time, new objectives were formally incorporated into the Treaty structure such as consumer protection and environmental protection. The consequence of the adoption of the subsidiarity principle is that many proposed Community measures have been abandoned and some existing measures are being reviewed.[151] Some argue that the new emphasis on subsidiarity will lead to competition between the legal systems of the Member States to attract businesses to invest and that this regulatory competition will have produced the optimal level of regulation in the Community as a whole as the appropriate level is worked out effectively through the market.[152] Others argue that it merely raises the stakes for races to the bottom, with the risk that important standards of social protection will be abandoned in favour of securing investment.[153] Indeed, the refusal of the last Conservative British government to sign up to the Social Chapter of the Maastricht Treaty (arguing that it would increase costs to industry to an unacceptable degree and thereby cause unemployment), provided a demonstration of how a state may seek to compete by adopting a lower set of standards. In this case, however, there appear to be some corporate counterweights to race-to-the bottom pressures: many corporations operating in the United Kingdom declared that they would voluntarily adopt one of the key aspects of the Chapter, the creation of Works Councils, because they operated in several EC Member States and preferred to have a uniform set of institutional arrangements for all their plants. This particular example has been overtaken by the decision of the Labour government to implement the Social Chapter in the United Kingdom.

The regulatory competition discussion originates in the observation that in the United States there was competition between states which were attempting to secure the incorporation of national firms within their jurisdiction.[154] The state of Delaware pursued this strategy so vigorously that it has given its name to the effect induced by such competition. Ideas of regulatory competition have now become fashionable as a way of explaining the behaviour of national governments which increasingly perceive themselves as acting on a world stage in which they compete for the favours of increasingly global industries, and the logic of this viewpoint is that EU regulatory standards need to be made competitive with those of newly industrialized countries like Korea. Much of the argument in favour of liberalization of key global markets, such as telecommunications, has arisen from the perception that such a strategy will enhance the ability of nations to compete in economic terms.

In the fourteenth reading in this volume, Jeanne-Mey Sun and Jacques Pelkmans provide a rigorous critique of the application of theories of regulatory competition to the European Community. They conclude that the benefits of regulatory competition, in terms of the development of optimal levels of rules, may be outweighed by the costs when considered concretely in the EC environment. They argue for a balanced mixture of harmonization and minimum requirements coupled with regulatory competition for levels of regulation above this minimum.

Having formally achieved the objectives of the Internal Market programme in 1993, EU institutions have turned their attention to other areas of economic activity hitherto neglected by Community policy. Of central interest for regulation has been the development of policies of liberalization affecting public utility services which have in many Member States been provided hitherto by public monopolies.[155] Though the Treaty precludes the Community from requiring privatization of such enterprises, the lack of political or other advantage in public ownership of utilities under conditions of liberalization has triggered a wave of privatizations, accompanied by the development of regulatory bodies which would in any case be required by Community law. We are thus seeing the development of new principles of Community regulation in these sectors, thereby raising, at the EU level, many of the procedural and substantive questions concerning regulation that have become familiar in the United Kingdom.[156]

An important theme in considering market and governance effects on regulation in an international context is the pressure on the transitional economies of Central and Eastern Europe and of developing countries to carry out market and regulatory reforms which mirror changes in the industrialized economies. In many of the transitional European economies the reform agenda is partly driven by the concern to render economies internationally competitive once more, and to introduce regulatory regimes which comply with the requirements for entry to the European Union in the next century.[157] With developing countries, though similar concerns with competitiveness may be present, a more immediate source of pressure is conditions placed on the granting of loans and the restructuring of funds by international agencies, notably the World Bank and the International Monetary Fund. The emphasis of such conditions has been largely on a reduction in the size of the public sector, and hence privatization. The development of regulatory measures to meet local economic and social concerns has received less emphasis, and this aspect has been the subject of trenchant criticism.[158] Dezalay describes:

[an] Entire export-oriented—and imperialistic—service industry of symbolic production, which aims to substitute the market economy for the various more or less interventionist systems of planning erected by communist regimes, as well as the welfare states and the 'developing' states.[159]

Variety in accounting for regulation

Casting a critical eye on regulation demands an investigation of the benchmarks by which regulatory performance may be assessed. Under this heading, therefore, fall questions about the values that should be served by regulation and issues of regulatory legitimacy.

In the fifteenth reading in this volume James Freedman explores some of the consequences of delegating substantial power to administrative agencies in the United States when the 1937 Brownlow Commission famously dubbed the independent regulatory commissions a 'headless fourth branch of government'. Criticism of such wide powers has been concerned with legitimacy, the capacity of such agencies to make good policy, and more general efficiency. Some British commentators[160] have built on North American studies of regulatory legitimacy,[161] and have argued for the application of benchmarks incorporating reference to such factors as the regulator's statutory mandate; the appropriateness of any mechanisms that create regulatory accountability; the fairness of procedures employed, the expertise applied, and the efficiency of regulation. Further questions arise concerning the methods by which such benchmarks can be applied in practice.

Particular regulations have, as noted earlier, been subjected to cost-benefit testing and compliance cost analysis.[162] Since 1981 US executive agencies have been required to submit all major regulations to cost-benefit analysis and to put forward for presidential approval only those with a surplus of benefits. In 1985 the UK government, as indicated above, embarked on a simpler exercise looking at costs but not at benefits in a formal CBA approach.[163] Some commentators have explored how the processes of economic appraisal can be made more democratically legitimate and have been sanguine[164] about the prospects of effecting such a shift, while others have emphasized the problems of access, arbitrariness, and lack of transparency posed by such processes; the preference given to the business voice within the UK system; the dangers that distributional questions are begged; and the difficulties of imposing accountability within such systems.[165]

For some commentators, the conferring of substantial powers on regulators gives particular urgency to questions of accountability.[166] Accountability issues are perhaps most central for those regulators who possess the greatest arrays of powers and greatest independence from elected government.[167] Such issues have been debated for the UK utilities regulators,[168] and the debate has broadened to include issues both of accountability and of appropriate procedures for regulatory bodies.[169] The final reading in this volume, by Cosmo Graham, examines the alleged crisis in UK utilities regulation and suggests how the utilities regulators may best be brought within accountability processes without hindering their ability to perform their regulatory tasks. Graham argues that problems of legitimacy and issues of accountability of regulators are part of a wider problem: namely that mechanisms of public government accountability have not been changed sufficiently to reflect changes in governance generally associated with privatization, contracting out, and deregulation. He sees three key issues which need resolving; namely the relationships of ministers and regulators; the oversight and accountability of the regulators; and the framing of the general duties of the regulators.

7. The State of Regulatory Science: Into Its Prime or Towards Mid-Life Crisis?

At the beginning of this chapter, we suggested that regulation may be maturing, both as a subject of study and as an institutional process. But precisely what sort of maturity is it developing into? Superficially unexceptionable, the idea of regulation maturing turns out to be a double-edged metaphor, or perhaps even a treble-edged one. In one sense it might imply a regulatory paradigm coming into its prime in a process of essentially incremental change in which the institutions and analytic approaches that were developed in the brashness of youth come to be steadily perfected. In another sense, it might imply the regulatory paradigm is starting to be over the hill, and moving into a phase of growing rigidity, declining innovativeness, and intellectual fatigue. Somewhere in between those two possibilities is a third possible type of growing up: outgrowing and rejecting early tastes and ideas and becoming willing to strike out in new directions.

Whatever might be happening to regulatory institutions, academic approaches to regulation do not seem to display the narrowing of vision and reduction of energy[170] that is often associated with stereotypes of middle age. On the contrary, the trend seems to be in the opposite direction, in at least four ways. First, more emphasis is coming to be laid on inter-disciplinary approaches, with research crossing the traditional academic boundaries between law, sociology, political science, and economics,[171] and indeed extending to fields such as anthropology and history. Second, not only are disciplinary barriers being crossed, but bridges are being built between different sectors within disciplines. For example, connections have been made between competition law, corporate law, and regulatory law,[172] and writers in areas such as family law have come to address regulatory issues and even to use the terminology of regulation.[173] Third, regulatory theory is becoming ever-more diffuse as it absorbs a steadily expanding range of analytic sources and areas—from legal theory[174] to political science[175] and anthropology.[176]

Fourth, the issues occupying centre stage in the analytic agenda for regulation have changed as well. In particular, the theme of risk and blame is emerging as a central preoccupation of contemporary regulatory studies.[177] This development both seems to reflect long-term changes in social attitudes (as 'risk' becomes increasingly politicized and construed as 'danger' rather than its original technical meaning of statistical or mathematical probability) and the fact that risk and blame is a unifying theme cutting across all the social sciences.

Indeed, far from following what is said to be the pattern of development in 'normal science',[178] in which scientists come to know more and more about less and less, regulation is, if anything, in danger of following the opposite dynamic and producing excessive theoretical diffusion. It is easy to see why. The field encompasses fundamental issues in law and social science and it is studded with deep policy disagreements among 'experts' as well as between 'expert' and 'lay' responses. It cuts to basic issues of accountability, trust, and institutional dynamics. It prompts discussion of the boundaries of public and private provision and of national and institutional competence. It spans a wide range of organizational types, from highly personalized regimes to the high point of legal and bureaucratic formalism. Such questions recognize no tidy borders, and the subject is no longer owned by any one discipline or analytic approach.

There are dangers as well as opportunities in such developments. The danger is of intellectual over-extension, the loss of disciplinary focus and coherence, and consequent lack of immunity to academic fads and fashions. To make sense as an emerging sub-discipline, regulation either needs to involve a special perspective on a general field of activity or a general perspective on a special field of activity—but not a general perspective on a general field of activity. After all, if regulation is everything, perhaps it is nothing more than another naked emperor?

Such heretical thoughts, however, cannot obscure the undoubted rise of regulation as an institutionalized field of study, with the conventional academic trappings. True, there is as yet no dedicated cross-disciplinary UK academic journal devoted to regulation, no regular conference event for major academic papers, and no professional association. But possible indicators of regulation having arrived as a mature field of study in the United Kingdom include the appearance of indigenous textbooks, such as Anthony Ogus's *Regulation: Legal Form and Economic Theory* of 1994, which have replaced the scattering of journal articles and hand-me-down US material that previously served as 'the literature' for British students of regulation. Along with the textbooks, graduate course programmes have emerged with regulation as their central focus, and there has been a notable growth of research projects and centres in regulation culminating in the designation of the field as a thematic priority for research funding by the ESRC in 1995. On the face of it, such developments might be taken as signs of a subject well on its way to academic self-confidence and institutionalized security—unless, even more heretically, one takes official sponsorship and recognition to be the kiss of death for intellectual vibrancy and coherence in the field, and a sign of incipient decline. Clearly, 'regulatology' has to tread a narrow path to ensure such opportunities do not threaten its future.

Indeed, in so far as academic concerns are driven by political and governmental priorities, it is to be expected that pressure to develop regulatory studies will be sustained. The forces behind the development of the 'regulatory state', as identified by Giandomenico Majone in 1994,[179] seem unlikely to slacken in the short term and the regulatory regimes established in the 1980s seem unlikely in the short or medium term to be replaced by non-regulatory alternatives, whatever else happens to them. Indeed, new areas of regulatory activity are constantly emerging, often in response to technological innovation such as food irradiation, genetic manipulation of plants and animals, and the internet. That does not mean, however, that an incremental future for the study of regulation—filling a gap here, extending an established argument or analytic approach there—is the only possible scenario for the intellectual middle age of this field. Nor is it necessarily the most desirable one. Cumulative development is important in science, but so are lateral shifts. Too much emphasis on smooth incremental progress can be a formula not so much for perfecting established methods and theories as for a tram-lined adherence to analytic and problem-solving approaches that will inevitably become outdated, either because of habitat change or because of observer paradoxes turning into self-defeating or self-fulfilling prophecies. Accordingly, a different vision for the future of regulation might involve not just polishing up existing approaches but also a more basic debate about the ABC of institutional design[180] and analytic approaches in the field.

The possibility that regulation might be heading for a mid-life crisis over fundamental assumptions and perspectives in its intellectual middle age can thus be viewed as uncomfortable but also as exciting. It is the sort of prospect likely to be uncomfortable for those with their roots firmly grounded in one of the approaches surveyed in the first part of this Introduction, but it could be an exciting possibility for those who believe regulation deserves a basic rethink and not just more of the same.

One of the possible reasons for a rethink is that the intellectual tools appropriate for early exploration of a new subject—such as basic mapping skills and practico-descriptive analysis—may be quite different from what is wanted at a later stage of inquiry. Indeed, it could be argued that several themes that might be expected in a mature social science analysis of regulation are still lacking—or at least seriously underdeveloped—in the subject. Three in particular are the analysis of *language*, *culture*, and *consequences*, on which we will briefly comment in conclusion.

The language of regulation

What makes for a winning argument in contemporary regulation? The analysis of what makes ideas persuasive and what closes arguments (in the absence of systematic analysis of cases or irrefragable logical proofs) is the oldest field of study in the humanities, but in recent decades it has undergone a marked revival—for example, as a means of understanding how the master tropes of rhetoric are employed to produce a Nobel Prize winning article in economics.[181] Regulation has often been argued to be a field dominated by the politics of ideas.[182] Murray Edelman's classic analysis of symbolic politics[183] ('words that succeed and policies that fail', as his subtitle puts it) is often cited in writing about regulation; and the same goes for Giandomenico Majone's defence of rhetoric in policy analysis.[184] An analysis focused on how the rhetoric of contemporary UK regulation works would pay close attention to elements like the use of structural metaphor or the selection of which premises to expose and which to suppress in regulatory argument. Structural metaphor (and the associate forms of metonymy and synecdoche) is embedded in the command and control metaphor for traditional regulation on which we commented earlier (implicitly likening it to a form of regulating a command economy), in the analogy between utility regulation and fair trading regulation (from which the institutional form of the UK utilities regulators was derived) or in background ideas about what the world is like (e.g. network industries). The exposure and suppression of a premises is critical for the success of enthymemes, the normal form of rhetorical argument. If ideas matter in regulation, we need to pay more attention to the way they are packaged.

The culture of regulation

What different bundles of attitudes and beliefs about justice, blame, and preferred ways of life are encountered in contemporary regulatory politics? Much contemporary analysis of regulation adopts a taken-for-granted economistic or practico-descriptive account of how the process works. Such an approach itself tells us something about the dominant academic culture of regulatory analysis, but it does not help us to understand the range of different preferences and the (growing?) clash of cultures that make up the process of regulation. For environmental and risk regulation, cultural analysis is deservedly coming to occupy a central place in elucidating who fears what and why, but analogous questions need to be asked about regulation more generally.[185] Schwarz and Thompson's analysis[186] of the clash between the hierarchist logic of a major multinational corporation and the egalitarian logic of dark green campaigners over the design of an environmentally acceptable lavatory rim-block is an example of such an exploration, that is in principle applicable to other areas of regulation which occupy a cultural crossroads. Debates about regulatory accountability for instance, need to be understood in the context of cultural variation, yet too often they are conducted as if accountability was some Platonic essence rather than a marker of cultural bias. A widespread assumption up to now has tended to be that regulatory culture is mainly exposed by comparative whole-nation studies. Yet cultural variety and clashes of different world-views may merit attention at a much more disaggregated level. For instance, do the econocratic regulatory offices presiding over the privatized utilities in the United Kingdom represent islands of individualist attitudes in a sea of popular egalitarianism? What cultures clash inside regulatory bureaucracies? If, as some claim, popular attitudes in the wealthy Western countries are moving from a mixture of hierarchism and fatalism to a polarization of individualist Chicago school and egalitarian dark green attitudes, where does such a shift leave the position of regulatory bureaucracies?

The consequences of regulation

Does regulation always produce the results that were intended? How often are side-effects anticipated, and how often are they surprising? Under what conditions do reverse effects obtain—producing the very opposite of what was originally intended? Contemporary regulatory studies do not tell us much about the answers to those questions, and indeed the questions are frequently left unasked as well as unanswered.[187] But they are fundamental to every form of social intervention. For example, it is conventionally assumed that the promotion of competition through regulation will tend to reduce prices; yet the National Consumer Council report on UK utilities regulation in 1993 argued that for services like telephones and gas the very opposite had tended to apply in key cases.[188] Similarly, it is conventionally assumed that mandatory introduction of safety devices will reduce accidents, yet heretics argue that they often simply redistribute risk through a risk compensation effect (for example, in more dangerous driving to compensate for the effect of safer vehicles)[189] and may even increase the danger of accidents through a Titanic effect of perceived invulnerability (a placation process, encouraging a belief that nothing can possibly go wrong). The study of the unintended consequences of social action dates back at least to the eighteenth-century Scottish enlightenment and has the potential to be a unifying analytic theme across all the social sciences engaged in the study of regulation, including sociology, economics, and political science.[190] Yet that theme has not hitherto been a notable *leitmotiv* of contemporary regulatory analysis. The potential for developing a fatalist approach to the consequences of regulation through the application of chaos theory modelling has not been developed at all, and much of the analysis of regulation still embodies a taken-for-granted approach about the consequences of the regulatory state.

These themes are of course interlinked. Persuasion is linked to culture, and culture is linked to beliefs about the consequences of social action. As regulation grows up as a field of study, such themes may come to haunt its middle age more than they did its youth. And while linear development of the earlier themes will help this emerging subject to come into its prime, a certain amount of mid-life crisis—reaching out to alternative themes not yet fully explored—could be productive in putting regulation at the centre of contemporary social science.

Notes

1. T. Daintith, 'A Regulatory Space Agency' (1989) 9 *Oxford Journal of Legal Studies* 534–46, 534. Daintith suggests that the 'vocabulary and conceptual apparatus of "regulation" ' only spread to the UK from across the US at the end of the 1970s, and explains this by reference to 'apparent parallelism of the approach to government-industry relations pursued by the Carter and Reagan administrations in the United States and the Thatcher government in the United Kingdom' at 535.

2. L. Hancher and M. Moran, 'Introduction', in L. Hancher and M. Moran (eds.), *Capitalism, Culture and Regulation* (Oxford: Oxford University Press, 1989).

3. A comparative account of the use of the public sector as a policy instrument, is provided by L. Hancher, 'The Public Sector as Object and Instrument of Economic Policy', in T. Daintith (ed.), *Law as an Instrument of Economic Policy* (Berlin: Walter de Gruyter, 1988), 165–236. For North America see M. J. Trebilcock and J. R. S. Prichard, 'Crown Corporations: The Calculus of Instrument Choice', in J. Robert S. Prichard (ed.), *Crown Corporations in Canada—The Calculus of Instrument Choice* (Toronto: Butterworth, 1983). An account of the shift away from public ownership towards regulation of the private sector in Europe is provided by G. Majone, 'The Rise of the Regulatory State in Europe', *West European Politics*, 17 (1994), 77–101. See also T. Prosser and M. Moran, 'Conclusion: From National Uniqueness to Supra-National Constitution', in T. Prosser and M. Moran (eds.), *Privatization and Regulatory Change in Europe* (Buckingham: Open University Press, 1994).

4. Department of Trade and Industry, *Lifting the Burden* (London: HMSO, 1985), Cmnd 9571; *Burdens on Business* (London: HMSO, 1985); Deregulation and Contracting Out Act 1994; Deregulation Unit, Cabinet Office, *Regulation in the Balance* (London: Cabinet Office, 1996); *Checking the Cost of Regulation* (London: Cabinet Office, 1996).

5. Y. Dezalay, 'Between the State, Law and the Market: The Social and Professional Stakes in the Construction and Definition of a Regulatory Arena', in

J. McCahery, W. Bratton, S. Picciotto, and C. Scott (eds.), *International Regulatory Competition and Coordination* (Oxford: Oxford University Press, 1996), 59–60.

6. See P. Selznick, 'Focusing Organisational Research on Regulation', in R. Noll (ed.), *Regulatory Policy and the Social Sciences* (Berkeley: University of California Press, 1985), 363, and, on the history of US regulation, R. Rabin, 'Federal Regulation in Historical Perspective', in P. H. Schuck (ed.), *Foundations of Administrative Law* (New York and Oxford: Oxford University Press, 1994).

7. G. Majone, 'The Rise of the Regulatory State in Europe' (1994) 17 *West European Politics* 77–101, 81.

8. A distinction is sometimes drawn between economic (or direct) and social regulation. For the former the object of regulation is conventionally to substitute for competition in order to discipline natural monopolies into the consumer responsiveness and innovation that rivalry would otherwise produce and to correct inevitable market failures or to provide the conditions under which competition can develop. Social regulation tends to operate across all sectors of the economy and commonly involves the exercise of state influence in relation to the unwanted effects of industrial activity on society—such as pollution or risks to the health and safety of employees and consumers. See *Responsible Regulation: An Interim Report of the Economic Council of Canada* (1979), 43–4, extracted in I. Ramsay, *Consumer Protection: Text and Materials* (London: Weidenfeld and Nicholson, 1989), 59–62.

9. Thus the French and German 'regulationist' schools place state activity generally at the centre of their approaches. See B. Jessop, 'Regulation Theories in Retrospect and Prospect' (1990) 19 *Economy and Society* 153–216.

10. C. Hood, *The Tools of Government* (London: Macmillan, 1983); T. Daintith, 'A Regulatory Space Agency' (1989) 9 *Oxford Journal of Legal Studies* 534–46.

11. See e.g. S. Breyer, *Regulation and its Reform* (London: Harvard University Press, 1982). For a general review of how the law influences the state's relationship with the economy see T. Daintith, 'Regulation', in *International Encyclopaedia of Comparative Law*, xvii (1997), ch. 10.

12. Majone, 'The Rise of the Regulatory State in Europe', 78.

13. A. Smith, *Lectures on Jurisprudence*, ed. R. L. Meek, D. D. Raphael, and P. G. Stein (Oxford: Clarendon Press, 1978), 331 ff.

14. P. Atiyah, *The Rise and Fall of Freedom of Contract* (Oxford: Clarendon Press, 1979), 128–30.

15. Assize of Bread and Ale, 1266.

16. J. O'Keefe, *The Law of Weights and Measures* (London: Butterworth, 1966), ch. 1.

17. G. Rhodes, *Inspectorates in British Government* (London: Allen and Unwin for the Royal Institute of Public Administration, 1981), ch. 3.

18. See generally G. Majone, *Regulating Europe* (London: Routledge, 1996).

19. A. I. Ogus, 'Regulatory Law: Some Lessons from the Past' (1992) 12 *Legal Studies* 1.

20. H. W. Arthurs, *'Without the Law' Administrative Justice and Legal Pluralism in Nineteenth Century England* (Toronto: University of Toronto Press, 1985), 91.

21. Ibid., ch. 4. O. McDonagh, *A Pattern of Government Growth, 1800–1860* (London: McGibbon and Kee, 1961), 59, notes that the Passenger Act 1803, which set safety standards for ships carrying emigrant passengers introduced 'a revolutionary principle into English law, a principle of first importance which was to have no true counterpart in other fields for thirty years to come. This innovation was interference with the legislature with freedom of contract…upon the ground that the free, sane and adult citizens concerned required a peculiar statutory protection in these transactions.' What was peculiar was that central government would so legislate at this time. Local and common law intervention in freedom to contract clearly existed at this time, and central government had interfered with freedom of contract at earlier periods.

22. G. Rhodes, *Inspectorates in British Government* (London: Allen and Unwin, 1981), ch. 4.

23. On the forgotten early history of railway regulation see Sir Christopher Foster, *Privatization, Public Ownership and the Regulation of Natural Monopoly* (Oxford: Blackwell, 1992), chs. 1 and 2.

24. R. Cranston, *Legal Foundations of the Welfare State* (London: Weidenfeld and Nicholson, 1985), 109–14.

25. I. Paulus, *The Search for Pure Food* (London: Martin Robertson, 1974).

26. Cranston, *Legal Foundations of the Welfare State*, 118–20. For a history of government inspectorates see G. Rhodes, *Inspectorates in British Government* (London: Allen and Unwin, 1981).

27. D. Helm (ed.), *The Economic Borders of the State* (Oxford: Oxford University Press, 1989).

28. Concerns with the inefficiency, ineffective, and even counter-productive effects of regulation in such fields as rent control and minimum wages have long been a source of criticism. See Cranston, *Legal Foundations of the Welfare State*, 155–60. See generally N. Reich, 'The Regulatory Crisis: Does it Exist and Can it be Solved? Some Comparative Remarks on the Situation of Social Regulation in the USA and in the European Economic Community' (1984) 2 *Environment and Planning C: Government and Policy* 177–97.

29. M. Loughlin and C. Scott, 'The Regulatory State', in P. Dunleavy *et al.*, *Developments in British Politics 5* (London: Macmillan, 1997).

30. See the government White Paper, *Building Business… Not Barriers*, Cmnd 9794 (1986), para. 3.3. See also the two White Papers, *Lifting the Burden*, Cmnd 9751 (1985), *Releasing Enterprise*, Cm 512 (1988), and Department of Trade and Industry, *Burdens on Business: Report of a Scrutiny of Administrative and Legislative Requirements* (1985). On Compliance Cost Assessment see Cabinet Office *Checking the Cost of Regulation* (London: HMSO, 1996), and *Regulation in the Balance* (London: HMSO, 1996); J. Froud *et al.*, 'Toeing the Line: Compliance

Cost Assessment in Britain' (1994) 22 *Policy and Politics* 311; R. Baldwin, *Rules and Government* (Oxford: Oxford University Press, 1995), ch. 7.

31. Deregulation and Contracting Out Act 1994, sect. 1; Department of Trade and Industry, *Deregulation: Cutting Red Tape* (1994).

32. J. Q. Wilson and P. Rachal, 'Can the Government Regulate Itself?' (1977) 46 *Public Interest* 3–14; C. Hood and C. Scott, 'Bureaucratic Regulation and New Public Management in the United Kingdom: Mirror-Image Developments?' (1996) 23 *Journal of Law and Society* 321–45. The new 'Regulatory Appraisals', heralded in the Deregulation Unit's *Regulation in the Balance* document of 1996, do, however, demand that cost assessments for regulatory proposals should look at costs not merely to business (as formerly) but also to consumers and the government.

33. J. Vickers and G. Yarrow, *Privatisation: An Economic Analysis* (Cambridge, Mass. and London: MIT Press, 1988); M. Armstrong, S. Cowan, and J. Vickers, *Regulatory Reform: Regulation of Economic Activity* (Cambridge, Mass.: MIT Press, 1994); M. Bishop, J. Kay, and C. Mayer (eds.), *Privatisation and Economic Performance* (Oxford: Oxford University Press, 1994). A broader range of concerns (going beyond the utilities sectors) and approaches (going beyond economics) may be found in M. Bishop, J. Kay, and C. Mayer (eds.), *The Regulatory Challenge* (Oxford: Oxford University Press, 1995).

34. B. Hogwood, *Trends in British Public Policy: Do Governments Make Any Difference?* (Buckingham: Open University Press, 1992); J. Hills, *Deregulating Telecoms* (London: Frances Pinter, 1986).

35. See R. G. Noll, 'Government Regulatory Behavior: A Multidisciplinary Survey and Synthesis, in R. G. Noll (ed.), *Regulatory Policy and the Social Sciences* (Berkeley: University of California Press, 1995).

36. See J. Malkin and A. Wildavsky, 'Why the Traditional Distinction between Public and Private Goods Should be Abandoned' (1991) 3 *Journal of Theoretical Politics* 335–78; and compare R. D. Adams and K. McCormick, 'The Traditional Distinction between Public and Private Goods Needs to be Expanded, Not Abandoned' (1993) 5 *Journal of Theoretical Politics*.

37. See C. Hood, *Explaining Economic Policy Reversals* (Buckingham: Open University Press, 1994), chs. 1 and 2.

38. Thus the deregulation movement of the 1970s and 1980s has been said to have been partially shaped by the theoretical critiques of regulation developed in the 1950s and 1960s:—see J. G. Francis, *The Politics of Regulation: A Comparative Perspective* (Oxford and Cambridge, Mass.: Blackwell, 1993) 6; M. Derthick and P. Quirk, *The Politics of Deregulation* (Washington DC: Brookings Institution, 1985), ch. 7; S. Skelman, 'Public Choice and Public Spirit' (1987) 87 *Public Interest* 80. On the politics of ideas see J. Q. Wilson, *The Politics of Regulation* (New York: Basic Books, 1980), ch. 10; Hood, *Explaining Economic Policy Reversals*, 28.

39. For an attempt to compare the broadest range of theories of regulation using data relating to the passing of the Railways Act 1844 see I. McLean and

C. Foster, 'The Political Economy of Regulation: Interests, Ideology, Voters and the UK Regulation of Railways Act 1844' (1992) 70 *Public Administration* 313–32.

40. Francis refers to the public interest approach as the 'public interest/legal perspective' (Francis, *The Politics of Regulation*, 7), which may be to credit academic lawyers with rather greater naïvety than is merited.

41. See e.g. J. M. Landis, *The Administrative Process* (New Haven: Yale University Press, 1938); R. E. Cushman, *The Independent Regulatory Commissions* (New York: Octagon Books, 1941); see B. Mitnick, *The Political Economy of Regulation* (New York: Columbia University Press, 1980), 91.

42. See Landis, *Administrative Process*.

43. C. R. Sunstein, *After the Rights Revolution: Reconceiving the Regulatory State* (Cambridge, Mass.: Harvard University Press, 1990).

44. See Francis, *The Politics of Regulation*, 8.

45. See G. Stigler, 'The Economic Theory of Regulation' (1971) 2 *Bell Journal of Economics and Management Science* 1–21; G. Kolko, *Railroads and Regulation 1877–1916* (Princeton: Princeton University Press, 1965); Mitnick, *The Political Economy of Regulation*, 111–20.

46. See R. Cushman, *The Independent Regulatory Commissions* (New York: Octagon Books, 1941), 52.

47. C. R. Sunstein, 'Paradoxes of the Regulatory State' (1990) 57 *University of Chicago Law Review* 407–41.

48. Francis, *The Politics of Regulation*, 8; G. Wilson, *Interest Groups* (Oxford: Blackwell, 1990).

49. See O. Newman, *The Challenge of Corporatism* (London: Macmillan, 1981).

50. Cf. the arguments to the effect that an agency may inflict capture on itself through a process of self-deception as to the task to be achieved: R. A. Litz, 'Self-Inflicted Capture—an Exploration of the Role of Self-Deception in Regulatory Enforcement' (1995) 26 *Administration and Society* 419–33.

51. See G. Stigler, *The Citizen and the State: Essays on Regulation* (Chicago and London: University of Chicago Press, 1975); R. Posner, 'Theories of Economic Regulation' (1974) 5 *Bell Journal of Economics and Management Science* 335; S. Peltzman, 'Towards a More General Theory of Regulation' (1976) 19 *Journal of Law and Economics* 211; W. A Jordan, 'Producer Protection, Prior Market Structure and the Effects of Government Regulation' (1972) 15 *Journal of Law and Economics* 151.

52. See A. Downs, *An Economic Theory of Democracy* (New York: Harper and Rowe, 1957); M. Olson, *The Logic of Collective Action: Public Goods and Theory of Groups* (Boston and Oxford: Harvard University Press and Oxford University Press, 1965).

53. See P. J. O. Self, *Government by the Market?* (Basingstoke: Macmillan, 1993).

54. See Hood, *Explaining Economic Policy Reversals*, 24, and, generally, P. Dunleavy, *Democracy, Bureaucracy and Public Choice* (London: Harvester, 1991).

55. S. Peltzman, 'The Economic Theory of Regulation after a Decade of Deregulation' (1989) *Brookings Papers on Microeconomics* 1–59. Compare the institutional analysis of M. A. Eisner, *Regulatory Politics in Transition* (Baltimore: Johns Hopkins University Press, 1993), ch. 8.

56. See e.g. M. E. Levine and J. L. Forrence 'Regulatory Capture, Public Interest and the Public Agenda: Towards a Synthesis' (1990), 6 *Journal of Law, Economics and Organization* 167; M. D. McCubbins, R. G. Noll, and B. R. Weingast 'Administrative Procedures as Instruments of Political Control' (1987) 3 *Journal of Law, Economics, and Organization* 243; J. R. Macey, 'Organizational Design and Political Control of Administrative Agencies', (1992) 8 *Journal of Law, Economics, and Organization* 93; B. Mitnick, 'The Theory of Agency: The Policy "Paradox" and Regulatory Behaviour' (1975) 24 *Public Choice* 27–47; M. J. Horn and K. A. Shepsle 'Commentary on "Administrative Agreements and the Political Control of Agencies"' (1989) 75 *Virginia Law Review* 499. For a European perspective on agency theories see Michael Bergman and Jan-Erik Lane, 'Public Policy in a Principal-Agent Framework' (1990) 2 *Journal of Theoretical Politics* 339–52.

57. See e.g. M. Fiorina and R. Noll, 'Voters, Bureaucrats and Legislators: A Rational Choice Perspective in the Growth of Bureaucracy' (1978) 9 *Journal of Public Economics* 239; J. Kan and P. Rubin, 'Self-Interest, Ideology and Logrolling in Congressional Voting' (1979), 22 *Journal of Law and Economics* 365; J. Kalt and M. Zupan, 'Captive and Ideology in Economic Theory of Policies', (1984) 74 *American Economic Review* 279.

58. An early attempt to apply a principal–agent approach to regulation is provided by M. J. Trebilcock and J. R. S. Prichard, 'Crown Corporations: The Calculus of Instrument Choice', in J. Robert S. Prichard (ed.), *Crown Corporations in Canada—The Politics of Instrument Choice* (Toronto: Butterworth, 1983).

59. See B. Weingast, 'Regulation, Reregulation and Deregulation: The Foundation of Agency–Clientele Relationships' (1981) 44 *Law and Contemporary Problems* 147–77; for the UK see D. Helm, 'British Utility Regulation: Theory, Practice and Reform' (1994) 10 *Oxford Economic Review* 17–39.

60. MacDonagh, *A Pattern of Government Growth, 1800–1860.* See also Arthurs, *'Without the Law',* 103 ff.

61. Central among the institutional approaches is the development of the concept of 'regulatory space' in L. Hancher and M. Moran, 'Organizing Regulatory Space', in Hancher and Moran (eds.), *Capitalism, Culture, and Regulation.* See also Daintith, 'A Regulatory Space Agency' (1989) 9 *Oxford Journal of Legal Studies* 534–46. The concept is further developed in C. Shearing, 'A Constitutive Conception of Regulation', in P. Grabosky and J. Braithwaite (eds.), *Business Regulation and Australia's Future* (Canberra: Australian Institute of Criminology, 1993), ch. 5. Shearing argues that the sharp distinction between regulation and the market is unhelpful as is the notion of regulation as the only form of

control over businesses. See also M. A. Eisner, *Regulatory Politics in Transition* (Baltimore: Johns Hopkins University Press, 1993).

62. The application of systems theory to regulation is most closely associated with Gunther Teubner: 'Juridification—Concepts, Aspects, Limits, Solutions', in G. Teubner (ed.), *Juridification of Social Spheres* (Berlin: Walter de Gruyter, 1987), 3–48. See also W. H. Clune, 'Implementation as Autopoietic Interaction of Autopoietic Organizations', in G. Teubner and A. Febbrajo (eds.), *State, Law and Economy as Autopoietic Systems—Regulation and Autonomy in New Perspective* (Milan: Guiffre, 1972), 485–513. Applying the theory to self-regulation see J. Black, 'Constitutionalising Self-Regulation' (1996) 59 *Modern Law Review* 24–55.

63. Hood, *Explaining Economic Policy Reversals*, 28.

64. Ibid. 29.

65. See Levine and Forrence, 'Regulatory Capture, Public Interest and the Public Agenda: Towards a Synthesis', 167–71.

66. See e.g. Baldwin, *Rules and Government*; G. Ganz, *Quasi-Legislation* (London: Sweet and Maxwell, 1987); C. Hood, *Administrative Analysis* (Brighton: Wheatsheaf, 1986).

67. J. M. Black, '"Which Arrow": Rule Type and Regulatory Policy' (1995) *Public Law* 94–117; J. M. Black, *Rules and Regulators* (Oxford: Oxford University Press, 1997); Baldwin, *Rules and Government*, chs. 5 and 6 and 'Why Rules Don't Work' (1990) 53 *Modern Law Review* 321.

68. Black, 'Which Arrow?', 96; but see also Baldwin, *Rules and Government*, 7–11, and generally W. Twining and D. Miers, *How to Do Things with Rules* (London: Weidenfeld and Nicholson, 1991), and F. Schauer, *Playing by the Rules* (Oxford: Clarendon Press, 1991).

69. E. Bardach and A. Kagan, *Going by the Book—The Problem of Regulatory Unreasonableness* (Philadelphia: Temple University Press, 1982), 35; Baldwin, *Rules and Government*, ch. 6. See also J. Braithwaite and V. Braithwaite, 'The Politics of Legalism: Rules versus Standards in Nursing-Home Regulation' (1995) 4 *Social and Legal Studies* 307–41.

70. See D. McBarnet and C. Whelan, 'The Elusive Spirit of the Law: Formalism and the Struggle for Legal Control', (1991) 54 *Modern Law Review* 848.

71. G. Brennan, 'Civil Disaster Management: An Economist's View' (1991) 64 *Canberra Bulletin of Public Administration* 30–3, 33.

72. See Royal Society, *Risk, Analysis, Perception, Management* (London: Royal Society, 1992), ch. 6, 'Risk Management', 135–92, 155.

73. S. G. Breyer, *Breaking the Vicious Circle: Toward Effective Risk Regulation* (Cambridge, Mass.: Harvard University Press, 1993).

74. Bardach and Kagan, *Going by the Book*; Baldwin, *Rules and Government*, ch. 5, 31–2.

75. J. Braithwaite, J. Walker, and P. Grabosky, 'An Enforcement Taxonomy of Regulatory Agencies' (1987) 9 *Law and Policy* 323–51.

76. J. Rowan-Robinson, P. Watchman, and C. Barker, *Crime and Regulation—A Study of the Enforcement of Regulatory Codes* (Edinburgh: T. T. Clark Ltd., 1990). See also the acrimonious exchanges between F. Pearce and S. Tombs, 'Ideology, Hegemony and Empiricism' (1990) 30, *British Journal of Criminology* 423, and K. Hawkins, 'Compliance Strategy, Prosecution Policy, and Aunt Sally', (1990) 30 *British Journal of Criminology* 444.

77. But on estate agencies see M. McConville, D. Smith, and M. Clarke, *Slippery Customers: Estate Agents, the Public and Regulation* (London: Blackstone, 1994).

78. K. Hawkins and B. M. Hutter, 'The Response of Business to Social Regulation in England and Wales: An Enforcement Perspective' (1993) 15 *Law and Policy* 199–217, 206–7.

79. See K. Hawkins, *Environment and Enforcement* (Oxford: Clarendon Press, 1984); B. Hutter, *Compliance: Regulation and Environment* (Oxford: Clarendon Press, 1997); R. Cranston, *Regulating Business—Law and Consumer Agencies* (London: Macmillan, 1979). Cranston has recently noted: 'I am afraid that my moral sense revolted at the advice and persuasion philosophy, as did that of some of the consumer protection officers with whom I worked as a participant observer. Not only were some consumer protection offences very close to traditional crime, but . . . I was troubled by how the economically powerful could render the law pliable' (R. Cranston, ' "A Wayward, Vagrant Spirit": Law in Context finds its Rich and Kindly Earth', in Geoffrey P. Wilson (ed.), *Frontiers of Legal Scholarship* (Chichester: Chancery Law Publishing Ltd., Wiley, 1995), 1–20.

80. I. Ayres and J. Braithwaite, *Responsive Regulation—Transcending the Deregulation Debate* (Oxford: Oxford University Press, 1992), 35.

81. See A. J. Reiss, 'Selecting Strategies of Social Control over Organisational Life', in K. Hawkins and J. Thomas (eds.), *Enforcing Regulation* (Boston: Kluwer-Nijhoff, 1984), 23, 24.

82. One major study suggests that there are 127 variables which may be examined to explain regulatory behaviour: P. Grabosky and J. Braithwaite, *Of Manners Gentle: Enforcement Strategies of Australian Business Regulatory Agencies* (Melbourne: Oxford University Press, 1986), ch. 15.

83. D. Black, *The Behaviour of Law* (New York: Academic Press, 1974), 40–8.

84. Grabosky and Braithwaite, *Of Manners Gentle*, 215 ff.

85. Ibid. 217–18.

86. See also B. Hutter, *The Reasonable Arm of the Law?* (Oxford: Clarendon Press, 1988).

87. See P. T. Fenn and C. J. Veljanovski, 'A Positive Economic Theory of Regulatory Enforcement' (1988) 98 *Economic Journal* 1055. See also G. J. Stigler, 'The Optimum Enforcement of Laws' (1970) *Journal of Political Economy* 78; G. S. Becker, 'Crime and Punishment: An Economic Approach' (1968) 76 *Journal of Political Economy* 169.

88. Bardach and Kagan, *Going by the Book* which Hutter and Sorenson cite as an example of research on regulation which is 'heavily ideological in tone and

content' and which they describe as taking a 'strong pro-business stance'
    B. Hutter and P. Sorensen, 'Editors' Introduction' (1993) 15 *Law and Policy*
    169–77, 170.

89. Bardach and Kagan, *Going by the Book*, 93–5.

90. C. Scott, 'Criminalising the Trader to Protect the Consumer: The Frag-
    mentation and Consolidation of Trading Standards Regulation', in Ian
    Loveland (ed.), *Frontiers of Criminality* (London: Sweet and Maxwell, 1995),
    ch. 7.

91. Hawkins and Hutter, 'Response of Business to Social Regulation', 208–9.

92. Bardach and Kagan, *Going by the Book*, 98–119, and see Fenn and Veljanovski,
    'A Positive Economic Theory'.

93. Bardach and Kagan, *Going by the Book*, ch. 6; K. Hawkins, 'Bargain and Bluff:
    Compliances, Strategy and Defence in the Enforcement of Regulation' (1983)
    Law and Policy Quarterly 35.

94. R. Axelrod, *The Evolution of Cooperation* (New York: Basic Books, 1984).

95. Ayres and Braithwaite, *Responsive Regulation*, 21–2.

96. See McBarnet and Whelan, 'The Elusive Spirit of the Law', 848; D. McBarnet,
    'Law, Policy and Legal Avoidance' (1988) *Journal of Law and Society* 113;
    Baldwin, *Rules and Government*, 185–9.

97. McBarnet and Whelan, 'The Elusive Spirit of the Law', 848.

98. See also J. McCahery and S. Picciotto, 'Creative Lawyering and the Dynamics
    of Business Resolution', in Y. Dezalay and D. Sugarman (eds.), *Professional
    Competition and Professional Power* (London: Routledge, 1995).

99. See C. Tiebout, 'A Pure Theory of Local Expenditures' (1956) *Journal of
    Political Economy* 64. Other commentators emphasize distinctions between
    classes of regulatees and the case for adopting different strategies for different
    types of regulatee, see Baldwin, *Rules and Government*, ch. 6.

100. Vogel, *National Styles of Regulation* (Ithaca, NY: Cornell University Press,
    1986), 29, notes that the concerns of the EC derive not just from the fact of
    decentralized enforcement in the UK, but also because of the extensive
    reliance on self-regulation. The British preference for self-regulation has
    been recognized in recent EC legislation, for example in Council Directive
    on Control of Misleading Advertising (EEC 84/450) which permits the
    Member States to require that self-regulatory remedies are exhausted before
    administrative enforcement of the rules may be applied. See the Control of
    Misleading Advertisements Regulations 1988 SI no 915. Proposals for a new
    focus on uniformity in enforcement are set out in European Commission, *The
    Internal Market after 1992—Meeting the Challenge* (Sutherland Report) (Brussels:
    Commission of the European Communities, 1992).

101. An excellent introduction to US regulation, directed at a European audience is
    provided by S. Breyer, 'Regulation and Deregulation in the United States:
    Airlines, Telecommunications and Anti-Trust', in G. Majone (ed.), *Deregula-
    tion or Reregulation?* (London: Pinter, 1990), ch. 1.

102. Harald Baum, 'Introduction: Emulating Japan?', in H. Baum (ed.), *Japan: Economic Success and Legal System* (Berlin: Walter de Gruyter, 1997), 12–13.

103. Ulrike Schaede, 'The "Old Boy" Network and Government-Business Relationships in Japan', in Baum (ed.), *Japan: Economic Success and Legal System*, 343.

104. E. B. Keehn, 'Virtual Reality in Japan's Regulatory Agencies', in Baum (ed.), *Japan: Economic Success and Legal System*.

105. Vogel, *National Styles of Regulation*, 21, and see generally ch. 7.

106. Ibid. 24–5. See also G. K. Wilson, *The Politics of Safety and Health* (Oxford: Clarendon Press, 1985).

107. Armstrong, Cowan, and Vickers, *Regulatory Reform*, 360. For a critique of the UK model from an economist see D. Helm, 'British Utility Regulation: Theory, Practice and Reform' (1994) 10 *Oxford Economic Review* 17–39. A comparison of UK and US styles of utility regulation is provided by M. Stelzer, 'Regulatory Methods: A Case for "Hands Across the Atlantic"', in C. Veljanovski (ed.), *Regulators and the Market* (London: IEA, 1991), ch. 3. For a general economic assessment of the UK privatization programme see M. Bishop, J. Kay, and C. Mayer (eds.), *Privatization and Economic Performance* (Oxford and New York: Oxford University Press, 1994).

108. G. Majone, 'Paradoxes of Privatization and Deregulation' (1994) 1 *Journal of European Public Policy* 53–69, 66–7.

109. See, for example, Oftel's attempts at removing detailed regulation for the UK telecommunications sector: C. Scott, 'The Future of Telecommunications Regulation in the United Kingdom: Tinkering, Regulatory Reform or Deregulation' (1995) 6 *Utilities Law Review* 13–17.

110. D. Larson-Bennett, 'Access Avenues to Environmental Regulatory Information in England' (1996) 22 *IALS Bulletin* 14–20, 14.

111. Vogel, *National Styles of Regulation*, 21.

112. R. Lewis, 'Insurers' Agreements Not To Enforce Strict Legal Rights: Bargaining with the Government and in the Shadow of the Law' (1985) 48 *Modern Law Review* 275; R. Baggott and L. Harrison, 'The Politics of Self-Regulation' (1986) 14 *Policy and Politics* 143.

113. For a comparison of cultural and institutional theories see G. Grendstad and P. Selle, 'Cultural Theory and New Institutionalism' (1995) 7 *Journal of Theoretical Politics* 5–27. The *locus classicus* on fatalism is E. C. Banfield, *The Moral Basis of a Backward Society* (New York: Free Press, 1958). For a sociolegal account of the importance of culture in understanding regulatory regimes see E. Meidinger, 'Regulatory Culture: A Theoretical Outline' (1987) 9 *Law and Policy* 355–86.

114. A. Melville, 'Power, Strategy and Games: Economic Regulation of a Privatized Utility' (1994) 72 *Public Administration* 385–408. For a critique of the conception of regulation as a game see P. K. Manning, 'Commentary: Regulation as a Game?' (1993) 15 *Law and Policy* 235–8.

115. See e.g. R. Mayntz, 'The Conditions of Effective Public Policy: A New Challenge for Policy Analysis' (1983) 11 *Policy and Politics* 123; Hood, *The Tools of Government*.

116. J. Dryzek, 'The Informal Logic of Institutional Design', ch. 4 in R. Goodin (ed.), *The Theory of Institutional Design* (Cambridge: Cambridge University Press, 1996), 107.

117. See R. Baldwin, 'Regulation: Beyond Command and Control', in K. Hawkins (ed.), *The Human Face of Law* (Oxford: Oxford University Press, 1996); Robert Howse, 'Retrenchment, Reform or Revolution? The Shift to Incentives and the Future of the Regulatory State' (1993) 31 *Alberta Law Review* 455–92; Richard H. Pildes and Cass R. Sunstein, 'Reinventing the Regulatory State' (1995) 62 *University of Chicago Law Review* 1–129.

118. D. Helm, 'RPI Minus X and the Newly Privatised Industries: A Deceptively Simple Regulatory Rule' (1987) *Public Money* 47–51; Armstrong, Cowan, and Vickers, *Regulatory Reform*, ch. 6.

119. Ayres and Braithwaite, *Responsive Regulation*, ch. 5.

120. A critical evaluation of this claim is provided by H. Janisch, 'From Monopoly Towards Competition in Telecommunications: What Role for Competition Law?' (1994) 23 *Canadian Business Law Journal* 239–78. For a regulatory approach to competition law in the UK see P. Craig, 'The Monopolies and Mergers Commission: Competition and Administrative Rationality', in C. McCrudden and R. Baldwin (eds.), *Regulation and Public Law* (London: Weidenfeld and Nicholson, 1987).

121. C. Scott, 'Privatisation, Control and Accountability', in McCahery, Picciotto, and Scott, *Corporate Control and Accountability* (Oxford: OUP, 1993); J. Moon, J. Richardson, and P. Smart, 'The Privatisation of British Telecom: A Case Study of the Extended Process of Legislation' (1986) 14 *European Journal of Political Research* 339–55.

122. D. Corry, D. Souter, and M. Waterson, *Regulating Our Utilities* (London: Institute for Public Policy Research, 1994).

123. J. Vickers, 'The Economics of Predatory Prices' (1985) 6 *Fiscal Studies* 24.

124. D. Glasl, 'Essential Facilities in EC Antitrust Law: A Contribution to the Debate' (1994) 15 *European Competition Law Review* 306–14.

125. For a discussion of New Zealand difficulties in applying general competition rules in the telecommunications sector see *Clear Communications* v. *New Zealand Telecommunications Corp* [1994] 6 TCLR 138. For an attempt to outline the common law principles which might govern the New Zealand utilities operators in the absence of statutory regulation see M. Taggart, 'Public Utilities and Public Law', in P. Joseph (ed.), *Essays on the Constitution* (Wellington: Brookers, 1995), 214–64.

126. New Zealand Government, Department of Commerce and Treasury, *Regulation of Access to Vertically-Integrated Monopolies—A Discussion Paper* (1995).

127. On British franchising see R. Baldwin and M. Cave, *Franchising as a Tool of Government* (London: CRI, 1996); S. Domberger, 'Regulation Through Franchise Contracts', in J. Kay, C. Mayer, and D. Thompson (eds.), *Privatisation and Regulation—The UK Experience* (Oxford: Clarendon Press, 1986); National Economic Research Associates, *Franchising Passenger Rail Services* (1993); D. Kennedy, *Bus Tendering in London* (London Department of Transport, 1994); A. W. Dnes, 'Franchising Passenger Rail' (1993) 40 *Scottish Journal of Political Economy* 420; 'Bidding for Commercial Broadcasting' (1993) 40 *Scottish Journal of Political Economy*.

128. W. Baumol, R. Panzer, and R. Willig, *Contestable Markets and the Theory of Industry Structure* (New York: Harcourt Brace, 1982). Principles of competition for the field or contestability may also be applied to the regulation of so-called public 'intermediate institutions', quangos and their ilk. See G. Mulgan, 'Democratic Dismissal, Competition and Contestability Among the Quangos' (1994) 10 *Oxford Review of Economic Policy* 51–60.

129. T. Daintith, 'Regulation by Contract: The New Prerogative' (1979) *Current Legal Problems* 41.

130. P. Vincent-Jones, 'Hybrid Organisation, Contractual, Governance and Compulsory Competitive Tendering in the Provision of Local Authority Services', in S. Deakin and J. Michie (eds.), *Contracts, Co-operating and Competition* (Oxford: Oxford University Press, 1997).

131. S. Richards, 'Devolving Public Management' (1994) 10 *Oxford Review of Economic Policy* 40–50. On the NHS see A. Maynard, 'Reforming the NHS', in M. Bishop, J. Kay, and C. Mayer (eds.), *The Regulatory Challenge* (Oxford: Oxford University Press, 1995), ch. 3. More generally see I. Harden, *The Contracting State* (Buckingham: Open University Press, 1992); Deakin and Michie, *Contracts, Co-operating and Competition*.

132. M. Cave, R. Dodsworth, and D. Thompson, 'Regulatory Reform in Higher Education in the UK: Incentives for Efficiency and Product Quality', In Bishop, Kay, and Mayer (eds.), *The Regulatory Challenge*.

133. Robert Howse, 'Retrenchment, Reform or Revolution? The Shift to Incentives and the Future of the Regulatory State' (1993) 31 *Alberta Law Review* 455–92.

134. B. O. Van Dyke, 'Emissions Trading to Reduce Acid Deposition' (1992) 100 *Yale Law Journal* 2707.

135. J. Dryzek, 'The Informal Logic of Institutional Design', ch. 4 in Goodin (ed.), *The Theory of Institutional Design*.

136. See J. Black, 'Consitutionalising Self-Regulation' (1996) 59 *Modern Law Review* 24, A. Page, 'Self-Regulation: The Constitutional Dimension' (1986) 49 *Modern Law Review* 141; 'Financial Services: The Self-Regulatory Alternative', in Baldwin and McCrudden, *Regulation and Public Law*; R. Baggott and L. Harrison, 'The Politics of Self-Regulation' (1986) 14 *Policy and Politics* 143.

137. A key example of a self-regulatory regime with jurisdiction extending beyond the membership of a trade association is provided by the Advertising Standards Authority. In the absence of contract it is unclear whence the authority for such extensive jurisdiction derives. However, in the case of advertising the authority problem is arguably less important since once the self-regulatory route is exhausted, the Director-General of Fair Trading has powers to seek injunctions against firms which put out misleading advertising likely to adversely affect the economic interests of consumers (Control of Misleading Advertisements Regulations 1988 SI no 915 and see *DGFT* v. *Tobyward* [1989] 2 All ER 288).

138. Baggott and Harrison, 'The Politics of Self-Regulation'.

139. R. Lewis, 'Insurers' Agreements Not To Enforce Strict Legal Rights: Bargaining with the Government and in the Shadow of the Law (1985) 48 *Modern Law Review* 275.

140. A. C. Page and R. B. Ferguson, *Investor Protection* (London: Weidenfeld and Nicholson, 1992); C. Mayer, 'The Regulation of Financial Services: Lessons from the UK for 1992', in Bishop, Kay, and Mayer (eds.), *The Regulatory Challenge*.

141. By Apr. 1994, 26 trade association codes of practice had been approved by the Director General of Fair Trading, including a number of new ones, the most recent being that of the Finance and Leasing Association (1993). For details see W. H. Thomas, *Encyclopedia of Consumer Law* (London: Sweet and Maxwell, 1980 and supplements), para. 4-751. See also I. Ramsay, 'The Office of Fair Trading', in Baldwin and McCrudden (eds.), *Regulation and Public Law*. On defining the relationship of self-regulatory regimes to government generally cf. Black, 'Constitutionalising Self-Regulation'.

142. Ayres and Braithwaite, *Responsive Regulation*; cf. S. Dawson *et al.*, *Safety at Work: The Limits of Self-Regulation* (Cambridge: Cambridge University Press, 1988).

143. Initially worked out in J. Braithwaite, 'Enforced Self-Regulation' (1982) 80 *Michigan Law Review* 1466–1507.

144. Ayres and Braithwaite, *Responsive Regulation*.

145. Black, 'Constitutionalising Self-Regulation'.

146. See generally G. Majone (ed.), *Regulating Europe* (London: Routledge, 1996); F. McGowan and P. Seabright, 'Regulation in the European Community and its Impact on the UK', in Bishop, Kay, and Mayer (eds.), *The Regulatory Challenge; Journal of European Public Policy*, special issue on European Regulation, 1996.

147. G. Majone, 'Cross-National Sources of Regulatory Policy Making in Europe and the United States' (1991) 11 *Journal of Public Policy* 79–106, 96.

148. Case 120/78, *Rewe-Zentrale AG* v. *Bundesmonopolverwaltung für Branntwein* [1979] ECR 649, [1979] 3 CMLR 494. See generally P. Craig and G. de Búrca, *EC Law, Text, Cases and Materials* (Oxford: Clarendon Press, 1995).

149. G. Majone, 'Introduction', in G. Majone (ed.), *Deregulation or Reregulation? Regulatory Reform in Europe and the United States* (London; Pinter, 1990), 1–6 (and see also the chapters by Joerges and Kaufer).

150. McGowan and Seabright, 'Regulation in the European Community'.

151. I. Maher, 'Legislative Review by the EC Commission: Revision Without Radicalism', in J. Shaw and G. More (eds.), *New Legal Dynamics of European Union* (Oxford: Clarendon Press, 1995).

152. H. Siebert and J. Koop, 'Institutional Competition Versus Centralization: Quo Vadis Europe?' (1993) 9 *Oxford Review of Economic Policy* 15–30.

153. The tension between the apparent needs of integration and the protection of regulatory objective is captured in R. Dehousse, 'Integration v. Regulation? On the Dynamics of Regulation in the European Community' (1992) 30 *Journal of Common Market Studies* 383–402. See also A. McGee and S. Weatherill, 'The Evolution of the Single Market—Harmonization or Liberalization' (1990) 53 *Modern Law Review* 578–96; McGowan and Seabright, 'Regulation in the European Community', 232–6.

154. See generally J. McCahery, W. Bratton, S. Picciotto, and C. Scott, 'Introduction: Regulatory Competition and Institutional Evolution', in McCahery, Bratton, Picciotto, and Scott (eds.), *International Regulatory Competition and Coordination*.

155. L. Hancher, 'The Public Sector as Object and Instrument of Economic Policy', in Daintith (ed.), *Law as an Instrument of Economic Policy*, 240–4.

156. L. Hancher, 'European Utilities Policy: The Emerging Legal Framework' (1991) 1 *Utilities Policy* 255–66; C. Scott, 'Changing Patterns of European Community Utilities Law and Policy: An Institutional Hypothesis', in Josephine Shaw and Gillian More (eds.), *New Legal Dynamics of European Union* (New York: Clarendon Press, 1995).

157. T. Prosser and M. Moran, 'Conclusion: From National Uniqueness to Supra-National Constitution', in Prosser and Moran, *Privatization and Regulatory Change in Europe* (Buckingham: Open University Press, 1994); T. Markowski, 'Privatization and Regulatory Change in Hungary', ibid.

158. J. Nellis and S. Kikeri, 'Public Enterprise Reform: Privatization and the World Bank' (1989) 17 *World Development* 659–72.

159. Y. Dezalay, 'Between the State, Law and the Market: The Social and Professional Stakes in the Construction and Definition of a Regulatory Arena', in McCahery, Bratton, Picciotto, and Scott (eds.), *International Regulatory Competition and Coordination*, 59.

160. See Baldwin and McCrudden (eds.), *Regulation and Public Law*, ch. 3; Baldwin, *Rules and Government*, ch. 3; T. Jones, 'Administrative Law, Regulation and Legitimacy' (1989) *Journal of Law and Society* 16.

161. See e.g. G. E. Frug, 'The Ideology of Bureaucracy in American Law' (1984) 97 *Harvard Law Review* 1277; J. Freedman, *Crisis and Legitimacy* (Cambridge: Cambridge University Press, 1978), ch. 5, J. Mashaw, *Bureaucratic Justice*

(New Haven: Yale University Press, 1983); 'Administrative Due Process: The Quest for a Dignitary Theory' (1981) 61 *Boston University Law Review* 885.

162. See generally T. O. McGarity, *Reinventing Rationality* (Cambridge: Cambridge University Press, 1991); Baldwin, *Rules and Government*, ch. 7; G. Bryner, *Bureaucratic Discretion* (New York: Peryaman Press, 1987), chs. 3 and 4.

163. But see the movement from mere compliance cost assessment towards cost-benefit analysis in Deregulation Unit, Cabinet Office, *Regulation in the Balance* (HMSO, 1996).

164. See e.g. K. S. Shrader-Frechette, *Risk and Rationality* (Berkeley: University of California Press, 1991).

165. See e.g. P. Self, *Administrative Theories and Politics* (London: Allen and Unwin, 2nd edn., 1978; McGarity, *Reinventing Rationality*; Bryner, *Bureaucratic Discretion*; Baldwin, *Rules and Government*.

166. See C. Graham and T. Prosser, *Privatizing Public Enterprises* (Oxford: Clarendon Press, 1991); T. Prosser, 'Privatisation, Regulation and Public Services' (1994) 3 *Juridicial Review* 3; C. Graham, *Is There a Crisis in Regulatory Accountability?*, CRI Discussion Paper No. 13 (1995).

167. T. Prosser, 'Regulation, Markets and Legitimacy', in Jowell and J. D. Oliver (eds.), *The Changing Constitution* (Oxford: Clarendon Press, 3rd edn., 1994), 237–60.

168. The early comments came from: J. F. Garner, 'After Privatization: Quis Custodiet Ipsos Custodies' [1990] *Public Law* 329–37; C. Graham, 'The Regulation of Privatised Enterprises' [1991] *Public Law* 15–20. See also Graham, *Is There a Crisis in Regulatory Accountability?*; Centre for the Study of Regulated Industries; *Regulating the Utilities—Accountability and Processes* (London: CRI, 1993).

169. See C. Veljanovski, *The Future of Industry Regulation in the UK* (London: European Policy Forum, 1993); Adam Smith Institute, *Who Will Regulate the Regulators?* (London: Adam Smith Institute, 1992); P. Hain, *Regulating for the Common Good* (London: GMB, 1994); Centre for the Study of Regulated Industries, *Regulating the Utilities—Accountability and Processes* (London: CRI, 1994); National Consumer Council, *Paying the Price* (London: HMSO, 1993); Baldwin, *Regulation in Question*; Sir C. Foster, *Natural Justice and the Process of Natural Monopoly Regulation*, Centre for the Study of Regulated Industries, Discussion Paper 9 (1994).

170. See e.g. D. Helm (ed.), *British Utility Regulation* (Oxford: OXERA Press, 1995).

171. Ibid.

172. See e.g. J. McCahery, S. Picciotto, and C. Scott (eds.), *Corporate Control and Accountability* (Oxford: Clarendon Press, 1993).

173. See e.g. J. Eeklaar, *Regulating Divorce* (Oxford: Oxford University Press, 1991).

174. See e.g. J. Black, 'Constitutionalising Self-Regulation' (1996) 59 *Modern Law Review* 24.

175. See e.g. J. T. Scholz, 'Co-operative Regulatory Enforcement and the Politics of Administrative Effectiveness' (1991) 85 *American Political Science Review*, M. J. Horn, *The Political Economy of Public Administration* (Cambridge: Cambridge University Press, 1995).

176. See e.g. M. Douglas, 'Risk as a Forensic Resource' (1990) 119 *Daedalus* (Journal of the American Academy of Arts and Sciences) 1–16.

177. See Royal Society, *Risk: Analysis, Perception, Management* (London: Royal Society, 1992); M. Power, *The Audit Society* (Oxford: Oxford University Press, 1997).

178. T. S. Kuhn, *The Structure of Scientific Revolutions* (Chicago: University of Chicago Press, 1962).

179. Majone, 'The Rise of the Regulatory State in Europe', 77–101.

180. Goodin (ed.), *The Theory of Institutional Design*.

181. See D. N. McCloskey, *The Rhetoric of Economics* (Madison, Wis.: Wisconsin University Press, 1985), and *If You're So Smart: The Narrative of Economic Expertise* (Chicago: University of Chicago Press, 1990).

182. See M. Derthick and P. Quirk, *The Politics of Deregulation* (Washington, DC: Brookings Institution, 1985) and P. Quirk, 'In Defence of the Politics of Ideas' (1988) *Journal of Politics* 31–41.

183. See M. Edelman, *The Symbolic Uses of Politics* (Urbana, Ill.; Illinois University Press, 1964).

184. See G. Majone, *Evidence, Argument and Persuasion in the Policy Process* (New Haven: Yale University Press, 1989). For a discussion of legitimating arguments in British regulation see Baldwin, *Rules and Government*, ch. 3.

185. See E. Meidinger, 'Regulatory Culture: A Theoretical Outline' (1987) 9 *Law and Policy* 355–86.

186. M. Schwartz and M. Thompson, *Divided We Stand: Redefining Politics, Technology and Social Choice* (Hemel Hempstead: Harvester Wheatsheaf, 1990).

187. But see the taxonomy developed by P. Grabosky, 'Counterproductive Regulation' (1995) 23 *International Journal of the Sociology of Law* 347–69.

188. National Consumer Council, *Paying the Price: A Consumer View of the Gas, Electricity and Telephone Regulation* (London: National Consumer Council, 1993).

189. See J. Adam, *Risk and Freedom: The Record of Road Safety Regulation* (Cardiff: Transport Publishing Projects, 1985).

190. See S. Sieber, *Fatal Remedies: The Ironies of Social Intervention* (New York: Plenum, 1981).

PART I
Regulatory Origins Development and Reform

Typical Justifications for Regulation

S. BREYER

The major objectives of most economic regulatory efforts fall within one of the categories discussed in this chapter.[1] The *justification* for intervention arises out of an alleged inability of the market-place to deal with particular structural problems. Of course, other rationales are mentioned in political debate, and the details of any program often reflect political force, not reasoned argument. Yet thoughtful justification is still needed when programs are evaluated, whether in a political forum or elsewhere. Usually this justification is one (or more) of the following.[2]

The Control of Monopoly Power

The most traditional and persistent rationale for governmental regulation of a firm's prices and profits is the existence of a 'natural monopoly.' Some industries, it is claimed, cannot efficiently support more than one firm. Electricity producers or local telephone companies find it progressively cheaper (up to a point) to supply extra units of electricity or telephone service. These 'economies of scale' are sufficiently great so that unit costs of service would rise significantly if more than one firm supplied service in a particular area. Rather than have three connecting phone companies laying separate cables where one would do, it may be more efficient to grant one firm a monopoly subject to governmental regulation of its prices and profits. To understand why this may be so, we must examine the underlying arguments.

The Traditional Economic Rationale for Regulation
In a perfectly competitive market, firms expand output to the point where price equals incremental cost—the cost of producing an additional unit of their product.[3] A monopolist, if unregulated, curtails production in order to raise prices. Higher prices mean less demand, but the monopolist willingly forgoes sales—to the extent that he can more than compensate for the lost revenue (from fewer sales) by gaining revenue through

increased price on the units that are still sold.[4] The result is waste: Consumers compare the high monopoly price of the monopolized product with the relatively cheaper prices of competitively produced products and buy more of the latter even though (1) they may prefer more of the former and (2) it costs society less in terms of real resources to produce more of the former and less of the latter.[5] Thus, where economies of scale render competition wasteful, the classical economist or regulator will try to set price near incremental cost in order to induce the natural monopolist to expand its output to a socially preferred level—where buyers do not inefficiently substitute consumption of socially more costly goods for consumption of the monopolized good.[6]

Monopolists may also lack sufficient incentive to hold production costs at low levels. They do have some incentive to lower costs, since lower costs will increase their profits. But although there is a 'carrot,' there is no 'stick': they do not feel the pressure of competitors who would threaten to lower their own costs, subsequently lower their prices, and thereby capture sales. For this reason, the monopolist may be lazy about production costs. The extent to which regulation can counteract this tendency is doubtful.[7]

Objections to the Traditional Economic Rationale

There are serious objections to the basic rationale for regulation just described. While none of them suggests outright rejection of the economic model, they do seriously temper the enthusiasm with which we embrace its results.

The 'second best' problem. The theory of the 'second best'[8] casts doubt on the value of forcing prices down toward incremental costs. Under perfect competition, the price of each and every good reflects its incremental cost; buyers cannot be misled into choosing goods that they desire less but that cost society more to produce; resources are allocated so as to maximize social welfare. However, in the real world, differences between price and true economic cost not only exist, but vary greatly across goods and industries. The theory of the second best posits that one cannot readily determine what sort of price changes are needed to correct the resulting inefficiency. The prices of goods *relative* to one another, not their absolute level, direct purchasing decisions. Thus, monopoly may raise prices, but an equal degree of monopoly throughout the economy should lead to relative prices roughly similar to those of perfect competition. And it should give consumers much the same information about relative production costs as would perfect competition. In an economy in which there are varying competitive conditions and in which there is no accurate, practical method for measuring cost/price differences, one cannot be certain whether lowering the price of a single product will provide consumers with *more* or with *less* accurate information about the relative costs of products. Thus, one cannot be certain whether lower prices and increased production generated by regulation are more or less wasteful of society's resources.

The 'second best' argument weakens but does not destroy the classical rationale for regulation. One might confess to uncertainty but still believe that lower regulated prices are more likely to move the economy toward rather than away from allocative efficiency. Large sectors of the American economy are competitive—with prices that are presumably near incremental costs—and unregulated monopoly can raise prices far above costs. In addition, monopoly can significantly distort buying decisions within particular sectors in a way that is entirely independent of its affect on the economy as a whole. Assume, for example, that within the energy sector coal and natural gas are produced competitively but oil is monopolized. Relative prices induce consumers to use some coal that (in relative terms) is more socially costly to produce than equivalent oil. Increased competition in the oil industry improves allocational efficiency within the energy sector regardless of the effect it has on buying decisions elsewhere.[9] In the absence of a strong empirical showing that such proregulation premises are untenable, one may find 'second best' considerations ignored in regulatory debates for an important practical reason: agencies and courts need principles and standards to determine the substantive validity of regulatory decisions governing price and other (particularly anticompetitive) practices. The competitive model—based upon the desirability of incremental cost pricing—provides such standards. Given the difficulty of elaborating acceptable substitute standards, it is unlikely that it will be abandoned.

Price discrimination. Without regulation, natural monopolists will not necessarily restrict output, if they can discriminate in price.[10] 'Price discrimination' means charging, say, different customers two or more different prices for the identical product. For most producers price discrimination is impractical, because the customer who is charged a low price for a unit of the product can turn around and resell it to the customer whom the producer wishes to charge a high price. The very nature of telephone service, electricity, and natural gas, however, makes it difficult for a user to resell the service he receives. Thus, if the telephone company, electric producer, or natural gas distributing company can discern the relative value of the service to each customer (that is, the maximum price each would pay for the service), it can dramatically increase revenues by raising the price to those who will continue to use its service, while keeping prices low to prevent abandonment by others. There would then be none of the service curtailment that the classical economist/regulator fears the monopolist would bring about without regulation.[11]

The force of this argument depends upon the ease with which the monopoly firm can in fact discriminate. To discriminate in price, customer by customer, is administratively impractical for these firms, as is price discrimination over individual units sold to a single customer. A practical discriminatory pricing system would divide customers into classes, and services into categories. Railroads, for example, charge higher rates to transport more valuable commodities; airlines, seeking to charge business travelers more, give discounts to those who can stay away for a week or longer; electric utilities have 'business' and 'residential' rates. The unregulated profit-maximizing monopolist presumably would raise the prices of some services across the board within some classes and categories. Thus, to some extent, without regulation service will be curtailed. The seriousness of the classical 'output curtailment' problem depends upon the practicality of determining appropriate price classifications, which in turn depends upon the firm's knowledge of how demand responds to price changes. The less accurately the monopolist firm can estimate its customers' response to price changes, the more likely that it would, if unregulated, impose price increases that lead to curtailed service.[12]

Not much market power. A related argument assumes that demand for natural monopoly services is fairly elastic—that is to say, a fairly small increase in price leads to a significant cut in demand for the product. If so, the monopolist will not make substantial price increases for fear that buyers will switch to other products. Alternatively, it may be fairly easy for new firms to enter the market to produce this or a related product, and higher prices may induce new (but less efficient) competitors to enter and attract customers. Thus, the natural monopolist—even without regulation—may be unlikely to raise prices very high, and, in the absence of regulation, production will not be curtailed significantly.[13]

But this argument and the 'price discrimination' arguments raise several empirical questions: To what extent is price discrimination possible? How does one go about determining elasticity of demand for different sets of customers over different ranges of price? What is the height of entry barriers? Given the difficulty of answering these questions, it is not surprising that intuitive judgments about them differ when applied to particular industries—just as do estimates of the importance of 'inadequate output' as a rationale for regulating monopoly.

The need to pay for investment. The classical 'inadequate output' argument may be thought of as an argument for nationalization and not regulation. Consider Hotelling's[14] example of a bridge that costs $25 million to build and will last virtually forever. Assume that the resource cost per crossing—the wear and tear on the bridge—is 50 cents. To charge more than 50 cents will reduce bridge use and prompt inefficient expenditures (such as driving an extra ten miles to avoid the toll). Yet if the bridge owner charges only 50 cents, how is he to pay back the investors who put up the $25 million to build the bridge? The answer, the argument goes, is nationalization. If the government invests $25 million, needed bridges are built, and if it charges a toll of only 50 cents once the bridge is built, no one is unnecessarily discouraged from using it.

Nationalization, however, has its own problems. Consider two common ones related to allocation and efficiency: (1) *How is the government to know when and where to build bridges?* Unless bridge users are prepared to pay not only 50 cents for wear and tear, but also enough additional money to pay the investment cost (whether through tolls or taxes), it is wasteful to build the bridge.[15] A private investor will build bridges only where users can, and will, pay enough to cover investment costs. The government can try to reproduce (or improve upon) the private investor's decision by developing a cost/benefit calculus for each project and investing only in those that demonstrate adequate social returns. However, there is serious doubt as to whether such studies produce results as accurate as those flowing from the discipline imposed upon investors by the knowledge that users must in fact pay sufficient tolls if the investment is to be recovered.[16] (2) *Are nationalized industries less efficiently operated than those run by private firms?* Do they run the risk of undue political interference? Ambrose Bierce, for example, defined a lighthouse as 'a tall building on the seashore in which the government maintains a lamp and the friend of a politician.'[17]

If nationalization is rejected, then capital must be raised from private sources, and regulators must set prices that allow fixed investment—investment in rights of way or railway beds, representing unrepeatable expenditure—to be paid for and recovered. This need, in the case of a natural monopoly, may well lead to prices that exceed incremental costs. Thus, even when regulation works perfectly, it cannot, by setting prices equal to incremental costs, totally cure the 'misallocation' that natural monopoly theoretically might cause, but rather it will aim at setting higher prices that allow recovery of investment costs when incremental cost pricing would not do so.

In sum, the traditional 'inadequate output' justification for natural monopoly regulation rests upon the assumption that a natural monopoly, operating without fear of present or future legislation, would set prices not simply higher than incremental cost, but significantly higher. It assumes that the regulated prices (including the recovery of investment) generate product prices (in a sector or in the economy generally) that reflect relative resource costs better than would unregulated prices. Such a proposition is logical, but rests upon a host of empirical assumptions that are unproved or, as a practical matter, unprovable.

Additional Bases for Regulation

In addition to the economically based 'increased output' rationale, three other justifications for regulating the natural monopoly are often advanced.

Income transfer. Even if the monopolist maintains output at roughly the competitive level—by practising price discrimination, for example—he will raise the price of some of his services far above a regulated or competitive level. The effect is to transfer income from the users of the service to investors—an income transfer that is generally believed to be regressive, and hence undesirable.[18] From the investor's perspective, this transfer of wealth takes place only once. If, for example, an electricity company were suddenly deregulated and found it could earn profits equivalent to, say, 50 percent on its equity investment instead of its previous earnings of 10 percent on the stock's market value, the price of the company's shares would rise, so that earnings on the new higher share value would be roughly equivalent to returns earned by other competing investments.[19] Initial investors receive a windfall; future investors, who pay more for the shares, do not. Consumers indefinitely pay the extra charges each year that constitute the increased profits that the firm now enjoys. The more essential the service, the greater the amount that this income transfer is likely to be. Unlike monopoly rents, or patents, or rents accruing to firms that improve their products, there is no natural limitation to the time period over which increased profits are earned, nor is there any obvious social advantage in allowing the firm to earn them. Although the amount of probable income transfer in any specific case is almost always unknown, proponents of regulation may assume it to constitute a strong reason for regulating the prices and profits of the natural monopolist.

Fairness. The competitive market does not provide the firms within it much opportunity for the arbitrary or unjustifiably discriminatory exercise of personal power. If grocery store A hires rude salesmen or provides inadequate service, the customer can switch to store B. If an unregulated telephone company were to treat a customer unfairly, he or she would have no ready recourse. Given the high costs of litigation, courts are not readily accessible. Appeals to higher levels within the firm's bureaucracy may not be very effective when the firm is aware that the customer must continue buying the firm's service regardless of the outcome. The regulatory system, by providing recourse for grievances against the monopolist, offers a remedy that to some extent makes up for the lack of competition's guarantees against unjustified discrimination.[20]

Power. Regulation is also advocated by those who fear concentration of substantial social or political power in the hands of a single firm that controls an essential product. Whether regulation is in fact effective in achieving this end is, of course, debatable. Yet the need to file reports, the fear that improper conduct might prompt hostile governmental action, the feeling of public responsibility that regulation may engender in the minds of the firm's executives—all suggest that regulation may have some effect (for better or worse) on the social or political activities of a large firm. Though the meaning and desirability of 'corporate social responsibility' is controversial, it can be argued that regulated firms such as the telephone company will take actions popularly regarded as socially responsible, though there is no empirical data about whether regulation makes such actions more likely.

This survey of the classic case for economic regulation—regulating the prices and profits of the natural monopoly—although brief, suggests that the case for regulation rests partly on economic grounds, partly on political and social grounds, and upon a host of unproved (and possibly unprovable) assumptions. However, enough of these assumptions are plausible to make regulation an apparently reasonable governmental response to the natural monopoly.

Rent Control or 'Excess Profits'

What Is a Rent?

Since 'economic rent' is often confused with 'monopoly profit,' the problem of rent control is often confused with that of controlling monopoly power. Yet rents and monopoly profits are very different.

A firm will earn an economic rent if it controls a source of supply that is cheaper than the current market price.[21] It is a rent and not a monopoly profit if the cheap source could not supply the entire market. If, for example, coal sells in a competitive market for $20 a ton, and if Smith finds a small but unusually rich seam that can be mined for $1 a ton, Smith will earn a rent of $19 a ton. Smith's profit is best thought of as a rent because his output is limited. He cannot expand production to the point where he could supply the entire coal market—his seam is too small. Thus, if all non-Smith coal costs $20 to produce, and buyers are willing to pay $20, those buyers will bid the price of Smith's coal up to $20.

Unlike a monopoly profit, the existence of a rent does not mean that there is 'inefficiency' or 'allocative waste.' Assume that the coal industry is highly competitive and sells 15 billion tons per year—including 50 million from Smith's mine—at a price of $20 per ton. By definition, Smith can produce no more; by definition, additional coal will cost $20 or more per ton to produce. To sell coal at $20 equates demand with supply and allows each buyer to see the additional resource cost of supplying his (extra) demand. To force the price of coal down below $20 will yield no more coal, for it costs $20 or more per ton to produce more than the existing 15 billion tons. In fact, a price below $20 will bring about a shortage because customers will demand more coal and their demand cannot be satisfied at less than $20. To lower price (below the resource cost of satisfying their demand) causes distortions in the prices of coal and related commodities.

It should be noted that rents are common throughout the economy, in competitive and noncompetitive industries alike. Any firm that finds a more efficient production process, that finds an unusually cheap supply source, that luckily buys a machine at a time when they are cheap, that has unusually effective managers—but that cannot expand to the point of satisfying a significant share of industry demand at prices that reflect its lower costs—earns a rent. To discourage the earning of rents is highly undesirable, for it would impede the search for efficiency. In many instances it seems perfectly fair that rents should accrue to producers who, through talents or skill, produced them.

The Rationale for Regulation

Many of those who demand regulation of rents may not be aware of the precise nature of the problem. They may see large producer profits and believe that they are monopoly profits or they may simply see prices rising, and, without inquiry into the cause, exert political pressure to bring about lower prices through regulation.[22] Mistake, confusion, or political power may cause regulation but cannot justify it. Yet a plausible justification for regulation to control some rents exists. The justification rests upon the desirability of transferring income—from producers to consumers—in a very few instances in which producer rents are large and occur suddenly.

Thus, one finds plausible arguments for rent control made where producers of certain products particularly important to consumers suddenly find that they, through no particular initiative of their own (through luck or change in general economic conditions), have earned very large rents.[23] During World Wars I and II owners of urban housing and property found that increased immigration into cities combined with the curtailment of new building (as construction workers were called to defense work) forced up the price of old housing.[24] Similarly, it has been argued that producers of natural gas that had been found at low cost could earn huge profits—by selling this old cheap gas in a free market, where increased demand and vastly increased exploration costs made natural gas far more expensive.[25] And, of course, between 1973 and 1980 the Arab cartel multiplied the value of existing oil stocks by a factor of ten.

These cases argue for regulation for reasons related not to more efficient use of the world's resources, but to a fairer income distribution. First, it is felt that the extra profit accruing to these producers is somehow undeserved. It does not reflect wise investment decisions—money was not attracted into oil exploration by anticipation of a future Arab boycott. Rather, it reflects plain luck. Second, the income transfer from consumers to producers or to their shareholders that these profits represent is thought to be *regressive*. Of course, the transfer will in part be taxed away—through tax rates on unearned income, for example, that approach 70 percent (compared with a 50 percent rate on earned income). But tax rates may fall, and producers may find ways within the tax laws to shelter the increased income from these high rates of tax. Third, the amounts involved are *large*—so large that the government should intervene to ensure that 'windfall' rents are captured for the benefit of the consumer rather than the producer.

The claim for regulation is strengthened if the price of a product increases not just drastically but also *suddenly*, as did, for example, the price of oil during the Arab oil embargo. The uncontrolled market price of $10–12 per barrel was five to six times the preembargo price; and the increase took place within a period of weeks. Such jumps obviously generated high rents for those controlling oil stocks. The rents were arguably 'undeserved'; the transfer was regressive, and the amounts involved were large. Moreover, the *suddenness* of this rise might have required consumers to cut back other expenditures drastically in order to pay increased oil bills without significantly eroding their savings. The net result might have been to hasten economic recession.

In essence, rent control is aimed at transferring income and is undertaken for reasons of 'economic fairness.' It may also seek to avoid certain adverse social effects—dislocation and hardship—of a significant increase in the price of an essential household item. These hardships may result from the suddenness of the price increase rather than the existence of the rent.

Compensating for Spillovers (Externalities)

What Are Spillovers?

A considerable amount of regulation is justified on the grounds that the unregulated price of a good does not reflect the true cost to society of producing that good. The differences between true social costs and unregulated price are 'spillover' costs (or benefits)—usually referred to by economists as 'externalities.'[26] If a train emits sparks that occasionally burn the crops of nearby farmers, the cost of destroyed crops is a spillover cost imposed upon the farmers by those who ship by train—so long as the shipper need not pay the farmer for the crop lost.[27] Similarly, if honeybees fertilize nearby apple orchards, the beekeepers provide a spillover benefit to the orchard owners—so long as the latter do not pay the former for their service.[28] Spillover benefits have sometimes been thought to justify government subsidy, as when free public education is argued to have societal benefits far exceeding the amount which students would willingly pay for its provision. Yet when one considers regulatory systems, spillover costs—not benefits—are ordinarily encountered.

The Classical Rationale for Regulation

Like the regulation of natural monopoly, the regulation of spillover costs is justified by the desirability of avoiding economic waste. Suppose a factory can produce sugar either through production method A or production method B. Method A costs 9 cents per unit of production but sends black smoke billowing throughout the neighborhood to the annoyance of neighbors for miles around. Method B costs 10 cents per unit of production and produces no smoke at all. The profit maximizing factory owner adopts A although, if those injured by the smoke would willingly pay more than 1 cent (per pound of sugar) to be rid of it, method A is socially more expensive. Then B, not A, should be chosen, because its total social costs—including costs of harm inflicted—are lower. As long as the affected public prefers reduced pollution to its noisome effects, it should bribe the producer to choose method B. Where the public prefers reduced pollution yet finds no practical way to bribe the producer, too many of society's resources are attracted (by lower prices not reflecting the cost of pollution) into polluting processes and products, and too few are attracted into pollution-free products and processes. Government intervention arguably is required to help eliminate this waste.

Objections to the Classical Rationale

It can be argued that spillover costs do not call for government intervention but, rather, for a rearrangement of private property rights.[29]

First, as Ronald Coase[30] has pointed out, if bargaining were costless, spillovers would not exist. Those suffering the pollution in the example above would simply band together and offer to pay the factory to use process B rather than A. The factory owner would switch only where the coalition was willing to pay more than 1 cent per pound. Precisely the same result would occur if the factory were required to compensate residents for pollution damage (both physical and psychological) it created, or if the government intervened and stopped pollution precisely and only in each instance where the public would rather pay abatement costs than suffer the effects of pollution. Thus, one might argue, why not let people bargain privately to abate pollution rather than introduce government regulation?

The answer to this question is that bargaining is not costless. Thus, the residents may suffer the pollution despite a willingness to pay more than 1 cent per pound to avoid it, simply because it is too difficult for them to band together. As the number of affected people increases, communication becomes more expensive, bargaining becomes more complicated, and a clear consensus is harder to obtain.[31] Furthermore, there is the added problem that some participants may systematically underestimate the true value of abatement to them in the hope of minimizing their contribution to the cost of abatement.[32] Thus, transaction costs may permit the continuance of spillover costs even though society would be better off without them.

Second, one may object to the classical rationale for regulation on the grounds that inefficient spillovers could still be eliminated by allocating relevant property rights to those who are most likely to achieve the efficient result through bargaining (were bargaining practical). For example, making the factory liable for the damage it causes will prompt it to switch to process B where doing so is cheaper than compensating sufferers. Freeing the factory of liability places the burden of organizing on the sufferers, so that they can bribe the producer to switch to B—an impractical alternative.

Third, one might argue that rather than introducing governmental regulation, it might be better to create liability rules to allocate the burden of paying for the harm of pollution in a way that leads to 'efficient' solutions. However, court-administrated liability rules, although they may indeed have theoretical and practical merit for dealing with some spillovers, cannot adequately deal with others. For one thing, government officials must determine the precise shape and location of liability rules. This in itself may prove a herculean task. For example, should liability be placed upon the party best able to calculate the relevant costs?[33] Upon the party best able to organize? Upon the party most likely to reach the socially optimal result? It may be as difficult for a 'liability rule maker' to determine the correct response in a particular instance as for a central administrator to choose between process A and process B. Moreover, the court enforcement of liability rules may be nonuniform, expensive, and have as many harmful side effects as central administrative direction. Thus, despite the theoretical existence of a system of private rights to deal with spillovers, direct governmental intervention is often believed desirable.

Another, less serious objection to governmental regulation rests upon the belief that spillovers do not exist. Undesired air pollution, for example, is caused not only by a process that sends smoke up the stack but also by the presence of nearby residents who breathe the smoke. The discomfort is as much a result of living near the factory as of using process A: while the cost is external to the good produced by A, it is internal to those who live near the factory and affects the behavior of those thinking of moving. And moving away eliminates the problem just as would the factory's switch to process B.[34]

This objection, however, misses the point. As a technical matter, externalities (or spillovers) are defined in relation to particular products. That is to say, air pollution is spillover in relation to the production of sugar; it is not claimed to be a spillover in relation to living near a sugar factory. Moreover, the justification for governmental intervention to deal with this spillover rests upon the judgment that society is better off where firms are encouraged to control polluting processes than where persons are encouraged not to live near polluting factories. Insofar as this justification relates to the spillover, it reflects the belief that those affected by air or water pollution would rather pay the cost of reducing the pollution than suffer from the pollution itself. Furthermore, the difficulties of organizing coalitions to bribe producers are just too great under the present allocation of private rights and liabilities. Thus, governmental intervention is likely to approximate better the amount of pollution that affected consumers are willing to pay for.

Of course, intervention itself is not costless. Moreover, intervention—or rearrangement of rights and liabilities—changes the distribution of wealth and income. Those who buy sugar (and the owners of sugar factories) are made poorer and those who suffer pollution are made richer by intervention or liability adjustments leading to reduced pollution. Insofar as intervention is designed to produce the result that would be paid for were bargaining feasible, those suffering pollution will gain more than the others lost. Whether this is a sufficient basis for intervening or altering liabilities may be debated. Traditionally it has been argued that changes should be made when the beneficiaries can compensate the losers out of their gains and have some gain left over; others have claimed that since the compensating is only hypothetical and not actually carried out, there is no clear justification for making the change. Regardless of the merits of these arguments, it is sufficient to note here that this rationale is one of 'economic efficiency.' To satisfy it is to move closer to a world in which all resources are used in a manner that maximizes the welfare of the world's individuals as measured by their preferences revealed in the market-place. And it is the same rationale of allocative efficiency that underlies many governmental economic decisions and actions, including regulation of natural monopolies.

In sum, a spillover rationale must be phrased in terms of a particular product; it must assume that obstacles to bargaining lead to significantly greater use of a product (or production process) than would be the case if costless bargaining were possible; and it must assume that the result of intervention (taking into account the costs of intervention) will better approximate the bargained-for solution. If these assumptions are correct, then intervention will reduce allocative inefficiency.

A Caveat

One can too readily classify as a spillover cost or benefit almost any policy reason for taking actions that lead to results other than those dictated by existing market arrangements. Thus, law enforcement can be seen as securing the 'external benefits' of security, or the laws prohibiting blood feuds can be justified as elimination of the 'external costs' of chaos and disruption. Where it is used to describe those commodities, the value of which is incapable of even rough monetary estimation—commodities such as justice, security, and so on—the 'spillover' notion is virtually useless. The more readily monetary values of the commodities or objectives can be estimated, the more directly useful 'spillover' characterization is likely to prove. In other cases, one is better off speaking directly of noneconomic reasons for and against taking a particular action rather than explicitly invoking the notion of 'spillover.'

Moreover, since there is always some possible beneficial effect in reversing a market-made decision, one can always find some (broadly defined) spillover cost rationale for regulating anything. Thus, the rationale, if it is to be intellectually useful, should be confined to instances where the spillover is large, fairly concrete, and roughly monetizable.

Inadequate Information

For a competitive market to function well, buyers must have sufficient information to evaluate competing products.[35] They must identify the range of buying alternatives and understand the characteristics of the buying choices they confront. At the same time, information is a commodity that society must spend resources to produce. The buyer, looking for alternative suppliers, spends time, effort, and money in his search.[36] The seller spends money on research, labeling, and advertising to make his identity and his product's qualities known. In well-functioning markets, one would expect to find as much information available as consumers are willing to pay for in order to lower the cost or to improve the quality of their choices.

The Classical Rationale for Regulation

Markets for information may on occasion not function well for several reasons. First, the incentives to produce and to disseminate information may be skewed. Like the bridge in Hotelling's example, some information (particularly that requiring detailed research) is expensive to produce initially but very cheap to make available once produced. Since it can be repeated by word of mouth, televised, or printed and reprinted at low cost, it may easily benefit many recipients who never pay its original producer. Thus, those in the best position to produce the information may not do so, or they may hesitate to disseminate it, for fear that the benefits will go not to themselves but only to others.

The importance of this problem varies considerably depending upon the type of information and its use. A firm that manufactures breakfast foods, for example, would have every incentive to produce information showing that its cereal was more nutritious than that of its competitors and to disseminate that information widely. Moreover, the production, use, and dissemination of much information is protected by copyright and patent laws.[37] Further, the inadequate incentive to produce information typically leads to a demand not for regulation but for governmental support of production and dissemination.

Nonetheless, occasionally the problem may lead to a demand for regulation. Drug manufacturers, for example, are required to print the generic (general scientific) name of their product, as well as the brand name, on the label. Thus, the buyer sees that a host of competitors in fact offer to sell the same product. This labeling requirement can be seen as lowering the cost to buyers of searching for competing sellers,[38] by quickly making them aware of the competitors' existence. And it does so by requiring those with the information most readily at hand to make it available.

Second, one of the parties to a transaction may seek deliberately to mislead the other, by conveying false information or by omitting key facts. A seller of securities may lie about the assets of the company; a seller of a used car may turn back the mileage indicator. Of course, false statements or active misrepresentations may be grounds for rescinding a contract or suing for damages. Yet the cost of court action is often high enough to weaken it or give it minimal effect as a deterrent. Nor can one necessarily rely upon fear of declining reputation to act as a deterrent. The importance of reputation in securing sales depends upon the particular product, the particular seller, and a host of other circumstances. The rationale for governmental action to prevent false or misleading information rests upon the assumption that court remedies and competitive pressures are not adequate to provide the consumer with the true information he would willingly pay for. Thus, the Securities and Exchange Commission (SEC) regulates the issuances of securities, while the buyer of used cars is typically left to his basic judicial remedies.

Third, even after locating potentially competing sellers, the buyer may not be able to evaluate the characteristics of the products or services they offer. The layman cannot readily evaluate the competence of a doctor or lawyer. Nor can he, unaided, evaluate the potential effectiveness or dangers of a drug. And he is unlikely at the time of purchase to know if a car is a lemon. Formal or informal understandings among those on the supply side—whether doctors, lawyers, or drug producers—may make difficult or impossible the creation of objectively applied labels that aid evaluation.[39] Governmental intervention may be desired to prescribe the type of information that must be provided, as well as to help buyers evaluate the information that is being supplied.[40]

Fourth, the market may, on the supply side, be insufficiently competitive to provide all the information consumers would willingly pay for. Until the government required disclosure, accurate information was unavailable to most buyers concerning the durability of light bulbs, nicotine content of cigarettes, fuel economy for cars, or care requirements for textiles.[41] In the 1930s automobile manufacturers advertised the comparative safety of their product. Subsequently this advertising disappeared, since auto makers felt that calling attention to safety problems hurt the industry more than it benefited individual firms. For similar reasons one does not find individual airlines advertising safety records. Since the airline industry is highly competitive in many respects, this fact suggests that tacit understandings not to supply certain varieties of information may be easier to reach (the industry need not be highly concentrated) than are tacit agreements not to compete in price or in service quality.

Criticisms of the Rationale

Criticisms of the rationale for regulating the provision of information usually focus on whether the rationale applies to the particular case at issue. Critics may claim, for example, that in a particular case the market is functioning competitively, consumers are sufficiently capable of evaluating a product's qualities, or there is little deliberate deception. They may argue that a particular agency's efforts to provide information are too expensive, that the information is unnecessary, that disclosure itself may mislead consumers, or that it may interfere with the competitive workings of the market-place. For example, the efforts of the Federal Trade Commission (FTC) to require that imported products have a 'country of origin' label have been criticized as at best a waste of time and at worst as an effort to protect American manufacturers from foreign competition by imposing costly labeling requirements on foreigners.

In sum, there is little quarrel with governmental efforts to help consumers obtain necessary information when the information is in fact needed and the intervention lowers the cost of providing it. Critics of intervention tend in particular cases to quarrel with the claim that regulation will lower the costs of its provision.

Excessive Competition: The Empty Box

A commonly advanced rationale for regulation of airlines, trucks, and ships is that competition in those industries would otherwise prove 'excessive.' This rationale has been much criticized as incoherent or at least inapplicable to the transportation regulation it is meant to justify. In fact, the difficulty with the term is that it has been used to describe several different types of rationale—some of which are no longer acceptable justifications for regulation. The notion common to all those rationales is that prices, set at unprofitably low levels, will force firms out of business and result in products that are too costly.

Historical Use

The history of airline and trucking regulation offers some insight into two possible uses of the term 'excessive competition.'

Airlines. The federal government began to regulate prices and profits of the airline industry in the 1930s, when it was still subsidizing the industry to encourage its development. The subsidy consisted of contracts to carry airmail at prices that exceeded the cost of carriage. A major scandal arising out of subsidy awards by the United States Postal Service led Congress, first, to transfer subsidy authority to the Interstate Commerce Commission (ICC), and, second, to consider comprehensive change of the subsidy system. The ICC administered the subsidy by asking the airlines to bid for the right to carry U.S. airmail. It awarded the contract to whichever line was willing to fly for the lowest subsidy. But the airlines believed that once the government awarded a contract to a particular carrier, it would increase the subsidy should the initial payment prove insufficient to cover the airline's costs. As Colonel Gorell, an industry representative, testified before Congress in 1937, 'The law put a premium upon an unreasonably low bid since there is always the possibility that later on, a rate first put unjustifiably low will be raised by the action of the Interstate Commerce Commission . . . [which] is ultimately under the duty of fixing a reasonable rate.'[42]

As a factual matter, it is not clear that competition in the 1930s was 'excessive' in any sense. Colonel Gorell also testified before Congress in 1937 that excessive competition had not actually occurred, but that it had been 'much closer than I would like to talk about.'[43] Moreover, the classical price and profit regulatory provisions of the act may reflect the fact that its framers borrowed many of its provisions from the act governing the ICC.[44] But, at least in theory, a subsidy offer provides one perfectly sensible rationale for 'excessive competition': the airlines' belief that the ICC would increase the subsidy award to a firm under contract provided an incentive to bid for the initial contract at a price well below cost. By doing so, an airline could expand the size of its route system, with the government making up the difference. Indeed, each airline would charge low prices to all customers, for the objective of each would be to expand system size and not to earn profits or to minimize losses. Thus, a government seeking to minimize the amount of subsidy required would have to prevent prices that were 'unreasonably low,' and regulation would be justified in order to minimize government outlay.[45]

This rationale for regulation, while coherent, is not applicable today, when almost all airlines are unsubsidized.

Trucks. Demand for regulation of trucking prices, profits, and entry arose in the 1930s for three reasons. First, the railroads, regulated by the ICC, complained that truckers were undercutting their prices. They did not argue that trucking prices were below costs, but rather that the ICC required the railroads to charge more than incremental costs on routes where they could compete with trucks; thus, the trucks took away business that, on a 'least cost' basis, should have belonged to the railroads. This argument does not offer a strong rationale for regulation of trucking, but rather suggests the need for changing the way railroads are regulated.

Second, the truckers argued that an unregulated market would lead some firms to cut prices and drive others out of business. Regulation would keep more firms in business and provide more employment. In principle, however, competition drives firms out of business because the survivors can do the same job better, more efficiently, or with fewer employees. To keep *unnecessary* firms in business is likely to sound more reasonable at a time of very serious depression (like the 1930s) than today.

Third, in the 1930s the competitive process itself was often blamed for the Depression. The framers of the National Industrial Recovery Act, for example, believed that agreements among firms not to cut prices would increase profits, encourage investment, and maintain employer purchasing power. Thus, ordinary competition in many industries was viewed as 'excessive.' The NIRA cure for recessions, however, has been discredited. In a world in which competition is the desired norm and regulation the exception, the NIRA theory does not provide a coherent rationale for selective regulation.[46]

Current Use

Currently, 'excessive competition' might be used to refer to any of three alleged justifications for regulation.

The 'natural monopoly.' The 'excessive competition' argument would make sense as applied to an industry that is a natural monopoly. One might claim that, without regulation, too many firms would seek to enter, and the resulting fight for market share would lead to the demise of all but one—the one that obtained the lion's share of the market by achieving the lowest unit costs.[47] According to the argument, this competitive process is wasteful of resources; a regulator should make certain that only one firm enters the industry and others do not seek to displace it.

Those opposed to regulation argue the opposite. They claim that any potential waste is justified by (1) the ability of the competitive process to pick the 'best' firm out of the contenders; and (2) the tendency of the competitive battle to demonstrate empirically whether or not the industry is in fact a natural monopoly.

Regardless of the outcome of this argument, it does not apply to airlines, trucks, or ships, because those industries are generally conceded to be structurally competitive—not natural monopolies. Yet it is in the case of airline, trucking, and ocean shipping regulation that one finds the excessive competition argument used.

The cyclical nature of demand. 'Excessive competition' might refer to a claim that, unless a particular industry is regulated, the cyclical nature of demand for its product will produce waste. When demand falls during, say, an economic downswing, competition among firms results in prices that cover only short-run incremental costs and prompts capacity curtailment. When the next upswing occurs, a firm will have to reopen its plant or rebuild its capacity. It might be argued that, rather than have firms go through the expensive process of closing and reopening plants, the government should set minimum prices—or allow firms to agree on minimums. Prices would remain high enough to cover fixed costs and plants would continue to operate during the recession. The extra costs of the agreements to consumers, one might claim, would be less than the cost of closing and reopening during the business cycle.

This argument assumes, however, that firms cannot raise sufficient funds in the capital markets to support excess capacity during periods of soft demand. If capital markets are functioning well, the firm ought to be able to attract funds to keep its plant open during the downswing on the basis of the expected future profits in the upswing. If it cannot do so, perhaps the capacity ought to close permanently, for consumers will not pay enough for the product (in the upswing) to justify maintaining it (in the downswing). Only if markets fail accurately to reflect the firm's future earning ability is it desirable to keep the plants operational.[48]

Moreover, to prevent excessive competition by maintaining higher-than-competitive downswing prices may easily encourage overinvestment. Firms would be prevented from the otherwise unprofitable consequence of overpredicting demand for the industry and product. Any resulting overinvestment is a wasteful byproduct of an effort to prevent 'waste.'

In any event, this excessive competition argument applies to industries with large fixed investments and comparatively small variable costs—industries such as steel or copper.[49] One can understand that a recession might drive copper prices so low that mines must close, that the expense of reopening them may be great, and that capital markets may be unwilling to finance them so that they could remain open. But the argument does not apply to trucking, where fixed costs are low, or to airlines, where fixed costs can be reduced by leasing or storing planes during the downswing in the cycle.

Predatory pricing. Another variation of the excessive competition argument is that a particular industry is subject to 'predatory pricing.' Competition leads some firms to price below costs, driving their competitors out of business. The remaining firm then raises its prices to excessive levels, leaving the public worse off than before.

For a firm to have an incentive to price predatorily, however, two preconditions must be met: (1) the predator must be powerful enough to outlast its competitors once prices are cut below variable costs; and (2) re-entry into the market must be so difficult that the predator can maintain prices well above costs long enough to recoup its prior losses. Unless a firm is reasonably certain that both these conditions will obtain, it is irrational for it to attempt predatory pricing.[50]

For this reason, it seems unlikely that predatory pricing will ever justify regulation. In fact, regulation can make predatory pricing easier, since it often provides the barriers to entry necessary for a potential predatory pricer to succeed. Furthermore, the antitrust laws make predatory pricing unlawful.[51] Those firms suffering its consequences can bring antitrust suits and appeal to enforcement agencies. Of course, the enforcement agencies may not be effective, but that is no argument for regulation since the regulatory agency is as likely to be ineffective.

Moreover, unfortunately, ordinary price competition is easily confused with predatory pricing. The former generally involves low-cost firms charging lower prices that take business from higher-cost firms;[52] the latter involves short-term prices well below costs, set with the object of destroying competition and later recouping losses through prices well above cost. Those advocating regulation on these grounds in the transportation field may well have confused the two.

Other Justifications

The reader should be aware of several other possible justifications for regulatory systems. While important, they have been used less often in the United States than elsewhere to justify governmental regulation of individual firms.

Unequal bargaining power. The assumption that the 'best' or most efficient allocation of resources is achieved by free-market forces rests in part upon an assumption that there is a 'proper' allocation of bargaining power among the parties affected. Where the existing division of such bargaining power is 'unequal,' it may be thought that regulation is justified in order to achieve a better balance. It is sometimes argued, for instance, that the 'unequal bargaining power' of small sellers requires special legislative protection. While in principle one might regulate the 'monopoly buyer' in order to protect these sellers, the more usual congressional response is to grant an exemption from the antitrust laws, thus allowing the sellers to organize in order to deal more effectively with the buyer. This rationale underlies the exemption granted not only to labor, but also to agricultural and fishing cooperatives.[53]

Rationalization. Occasionally governmental intervention is justified on the ground that, without it, firms in an industry would remain too small or would lack sufficient organization to produce their product efficiently.[54] One would ordinarily expect such firms to grow or to cooperate through agreement, and to lower unit costs.[55] But social or political factors may counteract this tendency.[56] In such circumstances, agencies have sought to engage in industry-wide 'planning.' In the 1960s, for example, the Federal Power Commission argued that increased coordination in the planning and operation of electric power generation and transmission facilities would significantly lower unit costs. The commission felt that environmental, political, regulatory, and managerial problems make it difficult for firms to plan jointly. The result was a relatively unsuccessful federal agency effort to encourage industry-wide rationalization.[57]

Moral hazard. The term 'moral hazard' is used to describe a situation in which someone other than a buyer pays for the buyer's purchase.[58] The buyer feels no pocketbook constraint, and will purchase a good oblivious to the resource costs he imposes upon the economy.[59] When ethical or other institutional constraints or direct supervision by the payer fail to control purchases, government regulation may be demanded.

The most obvious current example is escalating medical costs.[60] As medical care is purchased to an ever greater extent by the government or by large private insurers (with virtually no constraint on the amount demanded by the individual users), medical costs have accounted for an ever greater proportion of the national product.[61] The fact that purchases are paid for by others frees the individual from the need to consider that using more medical care means less production of other goods; thus, he may 'unnecessarily' or 'excessively' use medical resources. If one believed that too much of the gross national product is accounted for by medical treatment, and also believed that the problem of moral hazard prevents higher prices from acting as a check on individual demand for those resources (which in turn reduces incentive to hold down prices), one might advocate regulation to keep prices down, improve efficiency, or limit the supply of medical treatment.[62]

Paternalism. Although in some cases full and adequate information is available to decision makers in the market-place, some argue that they nevertheless make irrational decisions and that therefore governmental regulation is needed. This justification is pure paternalism: the government supposedly knows better than individuals what they want or what is good for them. Such distrust of the ability of the purchaser to choose may be based on the alleged inability of the lay person to evaluate the information, as in the case of purchasing professional services, or the belief that, although the information could be accurately evaluated by the lay person, irrational human tendencies prevent this. The latter may be the case where small probabilities are involved, such as small risks of injury, or where matters of life and death are implicated, such as when those suffering from cancer will purchase a drug even though all reasonably reliable information indicates that it is worthless or even harmful. Whether the brand of paternalism based on mistrust of consumer rationality is consistent with the notions of freedom of choice that underlie the free market is questionable. However, it plays an important role in many governmental decisions.

Scarcity. Regulation is sometimes justified in terms of scarcity.[63] Regulation on the basis of this justification reflects a deliberate decision to abandon the market, because shortages or scarcity normally can be alleviated without regulation by allowing prices to rise. Nonetheless, one might decide to abandon price as an allocator in favor of using regulatory allocation to achieve a set of (often unspecified) 'public interest' objectives, such as in the case of licensing television stations. Sometimes regulatory allocation is undertaken because of sudden supply failures: to rely on price might work too serious a hardship on many users who could not afford to pay the resulting dramatic price increases, as in the case of the Arab oil boycott. 'Scarcity' or 'shortage' calling for regulation may also be the result of the workings of an ongoing regulatory program, as when natural gas must be allocated because of rent control or when an agency awards licenses to enter an industry.

The Mixture of Rationales

Many existing regulatory programs rest upon not one but several different rationales. Thus, for example, one might favor regulation of workplace safety for several reasons. One might believe that employers and employees can bargain fairly and equally for improved workplace safety (greater safety expenditures), but argue that accidents impose costs on others who are not represented at the bargaining table; thus, bargaining alone will produce inadequate expenditures for safety devices. This is a *spillover* rationale. Or one might believe that the worker does not know enough about the risks or consequences of accidents, so that he will fail to insist upon adequate safety expenditures. This is to argue that there is an *informational defect* in the market. Or one might feel that the worker is too poor or too weak to bargain for the safety he needs—that he has *unequal bargaining power*. Finally, one might claim that workers (indeed, all people) are simply incapable of understanding their likely future feelings about accidents that hurt them. They inevitably underestimate the risk. If regulation is an effort to give them what they 'really' want (contrary to their expressed views), a *paternalistic* rationale is at work.

The importance of distinguishing rationales lies in the extent to which different rationales may suggest different remedies. Thus, one who believes that the primary problem is informational will tend to favor not classical regulation, but governmental efforts to provide more information. Although one who accepts a paternalistic rationale may disagree with one who believes the problem is informational, the clear statement of their points of difference can form the basis of empirical work that will lead them toward agreement upon the basic rationale and thus help choose the regulatory weapon best suited to the problem at hand.

Similarly, the debate over the need for regulation of medical costs might be clarified if its proponents specified the rationale, or mixture of rationales, for regulation and the relative importance of each. To point to the increased price of medical care does not, by itself, suggest a need for regulation. The increased price might reflect cost increases due, for example, to medical advances. If scientific progress means that few older people die of pneumonia, more will (eventually) die of cancer or strokes, which require more expensive care and treatment. Moreover, labor costs may be increasing, as well as the costs of technology. Demand may increase because people have more money to spend on medical care. If rising prices reflect no more than increased demand for medical care (greater relative desire for medical care compared with other goods, greater ability to pay for it) and increased costs of supply (more technology, higher labor costs), regulation of these prices would not rest upon a 'market failure' rationale. Indeed, rising prices might be a consequence of highly desirable actions taken by governments on grounds of equity—namely, supporting medical care for those who cannot readily afford it.

The proponent of regulation might cite other factors, however. He might argue that there is excess demand because so many patients do not pay their own bills—a problem of *moral hazard*. He might point to the difficulty potential patients have in determining whether they need care or what sort they may need. He might add that doctors themselves may not fully comprehend the economic costs of the treatment choices they make and thus choose treatment that is too expensive. All these are *informational problems*. Finally, he might fear that sudden increases in demand for medical care will lead to higher profits for hospitals, which, being 'non-profit' institutions, invest the 'excess' in new, more expensive technology and plants. This is a problem akin to *rent control*.

Again, a breakdown by rationale does not determine whether hospital prices ought to be regulated. To know that, one would have to obtain empirical confirmation that the rationale is empirically important. Nonetheless, analysis may help clarify and focus the debate and thereby help policy makers reach more sensible conclusions.

This chapter has surveyed the major economic rationales for regulatory programs. Individually or in combination they underlie most major regulatory programs, which are themselves of several different types. This chapter has provided a survey of most major types of regulatory programs and the economic justifications that underlie them.

Notes

1. The list of 'market defects' discussed in this chapter does not treat separately one justification for regulation—namely, 'income redistribution,' which some

have thought an important basis for regulatory action. The decision not to treat income redistribution separately is based upon several considerations. For one thing, it is typically difficult to evaluate the redistributive consequences of regulatory decision making. The effort, for example, to help small towns by cross-subsidizing airline costs may or may not help those who are poor. The users of small-town service may, in general, be richer than those who use transcontinental service. Indeed, those persons who use natural gas to heat their homes and thus are helped by price controls on gas may or may not be richer than those forced to turn to other higher-cost fuels due to a regulation-induced shortage. Regulatory statutes, despite their broad language, rarely call for pure income redistribution. Further, virtually every regulatory program has redistributive effects, and could be claimed to benefit some group of people who arguably are worse off than some other group that the decision harms. Thus, pure redistribution as a justification would impose little or no standard upon regulatory actions. Finally, 'redistributive consequences,' like other justifications not treated in this chapter, is better left as a rebuttal argument by those supporting a program. Often, it will not be made. Thus, for example, when airline regulators sought to force an increase in transatlantic charter rates, their objective was basically redistributive; they feared the bankruptcy of Pan American Airlines and they were trying to help Pan American and its employees. It is unlikely, however, that they would have advanced such a claim as justifying forcing Pan Am's competitors to charge higher charter fares, simply because the action, even if it could be shown to help 'the poor,' would not have been seen as a legitimate justification for regulatory intervention.

2. For a sampling of the literature dealing with the economic justifications for regulation, see A. Kahn, *The Economics of Regulation: Principles and Institutions*, 2 vols. (New York, 1970, 1971); R. Posner, 'Natural Monopoly and Its Regulation,' 21 *Stan. L. Rev.* 548 (1969); G. Stigler, 'The Theory of Economic Regulation' 2 *Bell J. Econ. & Mgmt. Sci.* 3 (1971); H. Demsetz, 'Why Regulate Utilities?' 11 *J. Law & Econ.* 55 (1968).

3. The economist's model of a perfectly competitive market assumes that (1) individual sellers are unable to affect market price by varying output, (2) resources move freely among productive uses, (3) sellers produce identical products, and (4) actors in the market-place possess perfect information about prices, technology, and consumptive choices. Several conclusions that flow from these assumptions are illustrated in Fig. 1.1. When a firm first enters the market, the owner finds that he can sell his product for price P_i. This, in turn, leads him to expand his output to X_i units, where the price it can obtain in the market-place is equal to the cost of producing the last unit of output (i.e., the marginal cost of $X_i = P_i$). At output levels below X_i the owner earns revenue in excess of his costs and it pays to expand; at levels above X_i it costs the seller more to produce additional units than he can recoup in the market-place, and output will be cut back. Where the firm is able to produce at output X_i and price P_i, it earns profits

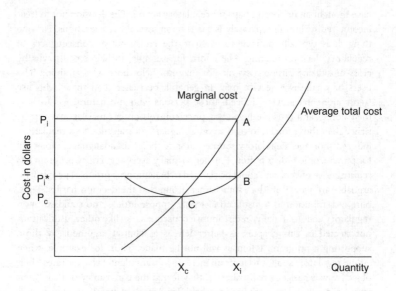

Fig. 1.1 The competitive model

exceeding total costs (Profits = Revenue − Costs = AREA OP_iAX_i − AREA $OP_i^*BX_i$ = AREA $P_iABP_i^*$). The availability of such profits will prompt new firms to enter the industry until price has been pushed down to P_c and no firm earns supranormal profits (the average cost curve reflects the rate of return necessary to keep firms in the industry). At this point price equals marginal and average costs and each firm will produce at the minimum point of its average total cost curve. For an intuitive discussion of these concepts in a public-utilities setting, see A. Lerner, 'Conflicting Principles of Public Utility Rate Regulation', in P. MacAvoy, ed., *The Crisis of the Regulatory Commissions* (New York, 1970), at 18–29. See also A. Kahn, *supra* note 2, vol. 1, at 65–70. The classic exposition of the welfare economic model of production is F. Bator, 'The Simple Analytics of Welfare Maximization,' 47 *Am. Econ. Rev.* 22 (1957).

4. A monopolist differs from a competitive producer in that he can unilaterally affect price by varying his level of output. If he charges the same price to all consumers, he will restrict output to the point where marginal cost equals marginal revenue (the latter term is the difference between the price paid by the marginal consumer and the decrease in revenue from reducing the price charged to every other consumer). In Fig. 1.2, a competitive market would generate output Q_c at price P_c while monopoly results in output Q_m and price P_m. The monopoly price exceeds marginal cost by the length of segment BD and the monopolist benefits by increased profits (vis-à-vis the competitive

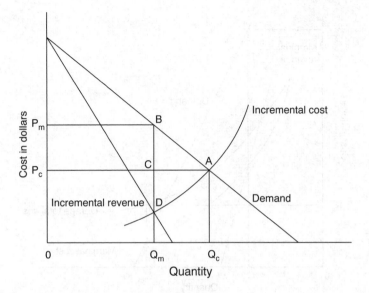

Fig. 1.2. Monopoly

solution) of $P_m BCP_c - ADC$. For a more extensive treatment, see R. Posner, *Economic Analysis of Law*, 2nd edn. (Boston, 1977), at 195–205; or F. Scherer, *Industrial Market Structure and Economic Performance*, 2nd edn. (Chicago, 1980), at 14–17, 229–236. The ambitious reader should consult J. Robinson, *The Economics of Imperfect Competition* (London, 1933), esp. bks. 2 and 4.

5. Consumer surplus is the difference between the price consumers actually pay for a good and the maximum price that they would have been willing to pay to obtain the good. In Fig. 1.2, competitive output Q_c generates consumer surplus $P_c AE$, while monopolistic output Q_m results in consumer surplus $P_m BE$. The difference between these quantities $P_m BAP_c$ consists of an income transfer from consumers to producers of $P_m BCP_c$ (known as the producers' surplus) and a net loss of consumers' surplus of BAC. This latter quantity is the absolute or 'deadweight' loss to society due to monopoly.

   Price in excess of true social costs also creates misperceptions concerning the relative values of producing monopolized and competitive goods. Artificially high prices in one sector of the economy will lead consumers to purchase fewer of those goods than is efficient. As a result, insufficient resources will be allocated to the monopolized sector and society will fail to produce as much as it could. For a lucid illustration of this proposition see F. Scherer, *supra* note 4, at 17–20.

6. A natural monopoly differs from an ordinary monopoly (the type illustrated in notes 4 and 5) in that its average total costs decrease throughout the relevant

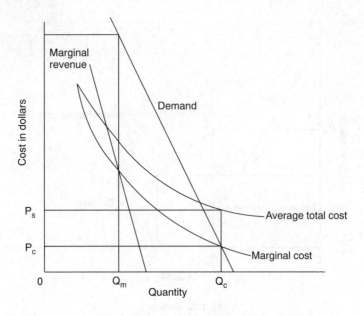

Fig. 1.3. Natural Monopoly

range of output. Average total costs exceed marginal cost at all points and there exists no output at which a monopolist is able to recoup his total investment by setting a single price equal to marginal costs. This is indicated in Fig. 1.3. Government intervention to increase output from Q_m (the monopoly output) to Q_c (the competitive output) would require payment of a subsidy to the monopolist of $(P_s - P_c) \, Q_c$ in order to allow him to cover his total costs.

7. This is called the X-efficiency loss from monopoly. See H. Leibenstein, 'Allocative Efficiency vs. "X-Efficiency,"' 56 *Am. Econ. Rev.* 392 (1966); W. Comanor and H. Leibenstein, 'Allocative Efficiency, X-Efficiency and the Measurement of Welfare Losses,' 36 *Economica* 304 (1969).

8. The seminal article is R. Lipsey and K. Lancaster, 'The General Theory of Second Best,' 24 *Rev. Econ. Stud.* 11 (1956–1957). See also E. Mishan, 'Second Thoughts on Second Best,' 14 *Oxford Econ. Papers* 205–217 (October 1962); O. Davis and A. Whinston, 'Welfare Economics and the Theory of Second Best,' 32 *Rev. Econ. Stud.* 1 (1965); as well as the collection of papers appearing in 34 *Rev. Econ. Stud.* 301–331 (1967).

9. The greater the independence of the sector in question from the rest of the economy, the greater the likelihood that imposition of competitive forces will have a positive effect. See Davis and Whinston, *supra* note 8; E. Mishan, *supra* note 8; and F. Scherer, *supra* note 4, at 28.

10. Strictly defined, price discrimination is the sale of individual units of the same product at different prices, independent of any differences in the cost of production.

11. Generally, three types of price discrimination are distinguished. *First degree* (*or perfect*) discrimination describes the situation where the monopolist charges each consumer the maximum price he or she is willing to pay for the good. As such, the monopolist acquires the entire consumer surplus accruing from production of the good and expands output until price equals marginal cost. Under *second degree* discrimination, the monopolist is only able to set a finite number of prices and charges consumers the highest price they are willing to pay. *Third degree* discrimination obtains where the monopolist is able to divide consumers into two or more groups with distinct demand functions. The monopolist charges each group a distinct price and expands output until the marginal revenues generated by the two (or more) markets is equal. The above distinctions were developed by A. C. Pigou and appear in *The Economics of Welfare*, 4th edn. (London, 1962), at 275–289. For a relevant illustration of third degree discrimination see A. Kahn, *supra* note 2, vol. 1, at 137–140. See also P. Steiner, 'Peak Loads and Efficient Pricing,' 71 *Q.J. Econ.* 585 (1957).

12. The perfectly discriminating monopolist will always expand production to the competitive equilibrium. The second-degree monopolist will usually expand output beyond the nondiscriminating monopoly outcome. The output decision of a third-degree monopolist will depend on the shape of the relevant demand and cost curves. See J. Robinson, *supra* note 4, at 179–202, esp. 188–195. Demand elasticities, however, are notoriously difficult to estimate.

13. See 'Economic Analysis of the Telecommunications Industry,' Charles River Associates, Report 338.01, ch. 4 (Cambridge, Mass., 1979).

14. H. Hotelling, 'The General Welfare in Relation to Problems of Taxation and of Railway and Utility Rates,' 6 *Econometrica* 242 (1938); J. DuPuit, 'On the Measurement of the Utility of Public Works,' *Annales des Ponts & Chaussées*, 2nd Ser., 8 (1844), reprinted in *International Economic Papers* 2 (London, 1952).

15. A single-price monopolist confronted with the cost and demand curves depicted in Figs. 1.4 and 1.5 will not build the bridge, since there is no one price at which his revenues will cover total costs. If the monopolist is permitted to price discriminate perfectly, his revenues increase (Fig. 1.4) to $OADQ_c$. He will build the bridge as long as P_s AB >BCD. Even imperfect discrimination (Fig. 1.5) will permit construction of the bridge as long as P_x FGP_y >HIJK. Here consumers are left with consumers' surplus equal to EFP_x + FBH +HKJ. Alternatively, the government could build (or subsidize a monopolist to build) the bridge (Fig. 1.4) at cost P_c DCP_s. Such an action will be socially justified as long as AP_s B >BCD. Otherwise, social benefits accruing from building the bridge will not cover costs.

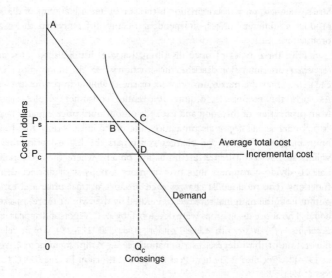

Fig. 1.4. The fixed-cost problem (I)

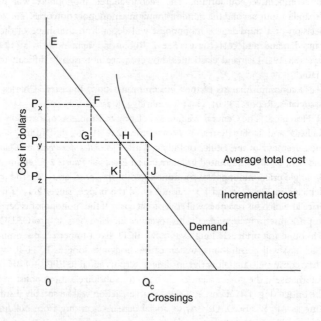

Fig. 1.5. The fixed-cost problem (II)

16. On the difficulties of determining criteria for public investment, see, e.g. E. Mishan, 'Criteria for Public Investment: Some Simplifying Suggestions,' 75 *J. Pol. Econ.* 139 (April 1967), and Mishan's reply to critics in 78 *J. Pol. Econ.* 178 (1970).

17. A. Bierce, *The Devil's Dictionary* (1957 edn.), at 107.

18. But see R. Posner, *supra* note 2, at 564.

19. See generally on matters of fairness in this area A. Okun, *Equality and Efficiency: The Big Tradeoff* (Washington, D.C., 1975).

20. Moreover, the 'natural monopolist' may be the firm that arrived first in the field, rather than a firm that outcompeted its rivals. The 'unfairness' of the fact and the foreclosure of the field to others partly account for the ethical attractiveness of ideas such as those of Demsetz and Williamson to allow firms to bid for monopoly franchises. See Demsetz, *supra* note 2.

21. An economic rent can alternatively be defined as the excess revenue over and above the minimum amount required to keep a factor in its current use.

22. See e.g., P. Douglas, 'The Case for the Consumer of Natural Gas,' 44 *Geo. L.J.* 566 (1956).

23. See A. Kahn, 'Economic Issues in Regulating the Field Price of Natural Gas', 50 *Am. Econ. Rev.* 506, no. 2 (1960).

24. See *Building the American City*, Report of the National Commission on Urban Problems to the Congress and the President of the United States, 91st Cong., 1st Sess., House Doc. No. 91–34 (1968).

25. See S. Breyer and P. MacAvoy, 'The Natural Gas Shortage and the Regulation of Natural Gas Producers,' 86 *Harv. L. Rev.* 941 (1973).

26. The two seminal articles in this area are F. Bator, 'The Anatomy of Market Failure,' 72 *Q.J. Econ.* 351 (1958); and R. Coase, 'The Problem of Social Cost,' 3 *J. Law & Econ.* 1 (1960). For a very readable account of the literature see E. Mishan, 'The Postwar Literature on Externalities: An Interpretative Essay,' 9 *J. Econ. Lit.* 1 (1971).

27. In this case, the cost that should be internalized is the expected value of damage per train trip (since fires caused by sparks do not occur on every trip). However, the courts have generally not seen the problem this way. See *LeRoy Fibre Co. v. Chicago, Milwaukee and St. Paul Railway*, 232 U.S. 340 (1913). See also R. Posner, *supra* note 4, at 38–39.

28. See F. Bator, *supra* note 26, at 358–360.

29. See generally G. Calabresi and A. Melamed, 'Property Rules, Liability Rules and Inalienability: One View of the Cathedral,' 85 *Harv. L. Rev.* 1089 (1972); H. Demsetz, 'Toward a Theory of Property Rights,' 57 *Am. Econ. Rev.* 347 (November 2, 1967); and F. Michelman, 'Pollution as a Tort: A Non-Accidental Perspective on Calabresi's Costs,' 80 *Yale Law J.* 647 (1971).

30. R. Coase, *supra* note 26.

31. See J. Buchanan, 'An Economic Theory of Clubs,' 32 *Economica* 1 (1965); and M. Olson, *The Logic of Collective Action: Public Goods and the Theory of Groups* (Cambridge, Mass., 1965).

32. There are two essential factors at work here. The first is that enjoyment of benefits accruing from successful bribery of producers ofttimes cannot be limited to those who paid for them (nonexcludability of consumption). This, in turn, gives rise to incentives for individuals (the 'free-rider' problem) to strategically misrepresent their preferences so that they might enjoy all the benefits without bearing any costs. Unfortunately, such behavior often causes socially beneficial activities to be forgone. On the first problem see F. Bator, *supra* note 26; and J. Buchanan, *supra* note 31. On the free-rider problem see R. Posner, 'Theories of Economic Regulation,' 5 *Bell J. Econ. & Mgmt. Sci.* 335 (1974); G. Stigler, 'Free Riders and Collective Action: An Appendix to Theories of Economic Regulation,' 5 *Bell J. Econ. & Mgmt. Sci.* 359 (1974).

33. This is Calabresi's suggestion. See Calabresi, *The Costs of Accidents, A Legal and Economic Analysis* (New Haven, 1970).

34. See Coase, *supra* note 26, at 11–12. See also *Spur Industries, Inc.* v. *Del E. Webb Development Co.*, 108 Ariz. 178, 494 P.2d 700 (1972).

35. The classic article on the information problem is F. Hayek, 'The Use of Knowledge in Society,' 35 *Am. Econ. Rev.* 519 (1945).

36. When an individual initially considers buying a product (such as a car, a watch, or a house), he is usually unaware of all the prices that various sellers are currently charging. To obtain the lowest price, he must identify potential sellers and consult them to learn their prices. The search process is not costless, however, and the consumer must weigh the potential gains against the cost of searching. The greater the dispersion of prices among sellers and the greater the dollar amount of the purchase, the greater the potential benefits of searching. In general, the consumer will buy information ('search') until he reaches the point at which the expected incremental gain from additional searching equals the incremental cost of conducting the search. Alternative methods of providing information are justified where their cost is lower than that of private searches. See G. Stigler, 'The Economics of Information,' 69 *J. Pol. Econ.* 213 (1961). For an interesting variation on this discussion, see M. Spence, 'Job Market Signaling,' 87 *Q.J. Econ.* 355 (1973).

37. Even if subsequent users of the information, once generated, can obtain it 'free,' there may be adequate incentive to provide it without patent or copyright protection. Much depends on whether a producer believes its production will give him a substantial advantage over his competitors. These and related issues are fiercely debated in the areas of patents and copyrights. See F. Machlup, *An Economic View of the Patent System* (Washington, D.C., 1958); S. Breyer, 'The Uneasy Case for Copyright: A Study of Copyright in Books, Photocopy, and Computer Programming,' 84 *Harv. L. Rev.* 281 (1970).

38. See *Abbott Laboratories* v. *Gardner*, 387 U.S. 136 (1966).

39. P. Nelson, 'Information and Consumer Behavior,' 78 *J. Pol. Econ.* 311 (1970), distinguishes two general classes of goods. *Search* goods are products whose

quality attributes may be determined by inspection. Items such as clothing, garden tools, and barbells fall into this category. *Experience* goods denote those items whose quality attributes can only be determined through purchase and consumption. For example, one cannot assess the quality of canned lima beans without eating them—nor can one assess ex ante whether a particular automobile is a lemon (even automakers with good reputations make lemons). See G. Akerlof, 'The Market for "Lemons": Quality Uncertainty and the Market Mechanism,' 84 *Q.J. Econ.* 488 (1970); and P. Nelson, 'Advertising as Information,' 82 *J. Pol. Econ.* 729 (1974). The functional difference between these categories is not great where the consumer makes repeated purchases over time. One can easily sample all brands of lima beans and settle on the best price/quality combination with little sacrifice. However, where a one-shot purchase is contemplated, the differences may be substantial—and in some cases irrevocable. With search goods there is little danger of incorrect decisions, since all relevant attributes are known prior to purchase. Such is not the case with experience goods. For example, one cannot protect ex ante against negligent automobile design which might dramatically increase the likelihood of serious injury. Nor can one assess the probability that particular employment might lead to cancer ten or twenty years hence.

40. In addition to problems that arise where consumers have imperfect information concerning product quality, there is also the problem that *even in the presence of perfect information* individuals may still inaccurately evaluate the magnitude of the risks they face. See, e.g., Calabresi, *supra* note 33, at 56; and T. Schelling, 'The Life You Save May Be Your Own,' in S. B. Chase, ed., *Problems in Public Expenditure Analysis* (Washington, D.C., 1968).

41. See R. Pitofsky, 'Beyond Nader: Consumer Protection and the Regulation of Advertising,' 90 *Harv. L. Rev.* 661 (1977); J. Ferguson, 'Consumer Ignorance as a Source of Monopoly Power,' 5 *Antitrust Law & Econ. Rev.* 2 (29) and (3) 55 (1971–72); and R. Posner, 'The Federal Trade Commission,' 37 *U. Chicago L. Rev.* 47 (1969).

42. Hearings on § 2 and § 1760 before a subcommittee of the Senate Committee on Interstate and Foreign Commerce, 75th Cong., 1st Sess. (1937). For a brief account of regulation at this time, see U.S. Senate Comm. on the Judiciary, Subcomm. on Admin. Practice and Procedure, *Civil Aeronautics Board Practices and Procedures*, Subcomm. report, 94th Cong., 1st Sess., 31–35 (1975) [hereinafter referred to as the *Kennedy Report*].

43. Aviation: Hearings on H.R. 5234 and H.R. 4652 before the House Comm. on Interstate and Foreign Commerce, 75th Cong., 1st Sess., 76 (1937).

44. See *Kennedy Report, supra* note 42, at 61–62.

45. See *Kennedy Report, supra* note 42.

46. See National Industrial Recovery Act, 48 Stat. 195, 196, 15 U.S.C. 703 (1933) § 3 (declared unconstitutional in *A.L.A. Schechter Poultry Co.* v. *United States*, 295 U.S. 495 (1934).

47. For a sample of the developing literature on the sustainability of natural monopoly see G. Faulhaber, 'Cross-Subsidization: Pricing in Public Enterprises,' 65 *Am. Econ. Rev.* 966 (1975); J. Panzar and R. Willig, 'Free Entry and the Sustainability of Natural Monopoly,' 8 *Bell J. Econ. & Mgmt. Sci.* 1 (1977); and W. Baumol, E. Bailey, and R. Willig, 'Weak Invisible Hand Theorems of the Sustainability of Multiproduct Natural Monopoly,' 67 *Am. Econ. Rev.* 350 (1977).

48. Of course, government action here might lower costs by lowering risks, but that claim can be made of a host of cartel and other anticompetitive agreements.

49. See F. Scherer, *supra* note 4, at 205–212.

50. For a further discussion and some illustrations see F. Scherer, *supra* note 4, at 335–340.

51. See P. Areeda and D. Turner, *Antitrust Law* ¶ 711 (1978); Areeda and Turner, 'Predatory Pricing and Related Practices under Section 2 of the Sherman Act,' 88 *Harv. L. Rev.* 697 (1975).

52. In such a case, exit of firms from the industry is appropriate, since they are replaced by firms who can satisfy societal needs at lower costs.

53. 15 U.S.C. ¶ 17 (1976), labor organization; Capper-Volstead Act of 1922, 7 U.S.C. §§ 291–292 (1976), farming; Fisherman's Cooperative Marketing Act, 15 U.S.C. §§ 521–522 (1976), fishing.

54. See, e.g., S. Breyer and P. MacAvoy, 'The Federal Power Commission and the Coordination Problem in the Electrical Power Industry,' 46 *S. Cal. L. Rev.* 661, 680–682, 685–687, 688–694 (1973).

55. See Breyer and MacAvoy, *supra* note 25, at 665–669.

56. See generally, F. Scherer, *supra* note 4, at 174–175, 506–509, 563–569.

57. U.S. Federal Power Commission National Power Survey (1964); Breyer and MacAvoy, *supra* note 25.

58. See Calabresi, *supra* note 33.

59. For a descriptive example see K. Arrow, *Essays in the Theory of Risk Bearing* 142–143 (1971).

60. See R. Gibson and M. Mueller, *National Health Expenditures, Fiscal Year 1976*, 40 Soc. Security Bull. 3, no. 4 (April 1977).

61. See M. Feldstein and A. Taylor, *The Rapid Rise of Hospital Costs*, Staff Report of the Council on Wage and Price Stability, Executive Office of the President (1977).

62. See Conference on Health Planning, Certificate of Need, and Market Entry, Regulating Health Facilities Construction (1974).

63. G. Brannan, 'Prices and Incomes: The Dilemma of Energy Policy,' 13 *Harv. J. Legis.* 445, 447 (1976).

The Economic Theory of Regulation after a Decade of Deregulation

S. PELTZMAN

What has come to be called the economic theory of regulation, or ET, began with an article by George Stigler in 1971.[1] The most important element of this theory is its integration of the analysis of political behavior with the larger body of economic analysis. Politicians, like the rest of us, are presumed to be self-interested maximizers. This means that interest groups can influence the outcome of the regulatory process by providing financial or other support to politicians or regulators.

Simultaneously with Stigler, Richard Posner provided an important critique, and several years later he gave the theory its grandiose name. The major theoretical development of the ET has been an article by Peltzman in 1976 and one by Gary Becker in 1983.[2] By conventional measures the theory has been an academic success. In this paper I evaluate that success in light of the changes in regulatory institutions that have occurred since the ET's early development.

The most notable changes have meant a reduction or substantial elimination of regulatory constraints whose scope is unprecedented in modern American history. The challenge posed by these changes for the ET seems obvious. One strand in the theory is that the producers' interest in restricting competition dominates the political system. But deregulation was sweeping aside many long-standing legal barriers to competition even as the ink was drying on the theory. Doesn't deregulation then decisively falsify the theory?

One easy answer would be that the deregulation movement was a special case—a one-shot response to the peculiar macroeconomic and political conditions of the late 1970s. That was a time of increased concern about inflation and of disillusion with the efficacy of government intervention generally. It was also a time when most of the ultimately successful legislative initiatives toward deregulation bore fruit. It is hard to treat the conjunction of the rightward shift in the political mood and deregulation as entirely coincidental. But it is also hard to push this, or any, special-purpose explanation too far.

This particular special-purpose explanation has factual problems. For example, the deregulation movement was selective. Many areas of regulation escaped essentially unscathed; others, such as the regulation of labor contracts and health care, even prospered. Because of this selectivity, the plausible role of deregulation in the fight against inflation is largely symbolic. No serious investigation could attribute to deregulation more than a microscopic effect on the overall inflation rate. Also, the timing of the political change is not quite right. The culmination of the rightward shift in American politics and of the inflationary spiral occurred in the same year (1980) that saw the end rather than the beginning of de jure deregulation.[3]

Ultimately, however, I eschew a special-purpose absolution of the ET on methodological grounds. The theory purports to be a general model of the forces affecting regulation; that is, it suggests the common elements underlying regulatory change. In evaluating the theory, one must weigh the importance of these common elements before considering what might be special about the 1970s.

Seen in this light, if the theory implied that every restriction of competition was permanent, one could easily dispose of the ET as a useful model for the deregulation movement. But that is, I will argue, too simple a characterization of the theory. One complication is that the theory does not speak with one voice on the subject of entry into and exit from regulation. Another is the lack of a satisfactory alternative theory. Not one economist in a hundred practising in the early 1970s predicted the sweeping changes that were soon to happen. Most believed that, however desirable, events like the demise of the Civil Aeronautics Board (CAB) and the shriveling of the Interstate Commerce Commission (ICC) were unlikely to occur soon. This was hardly the first or last forecasting failure in economics, and the methodological pitfalls of evaluating theory by forecasting ability are well known. Nevertheless, the fact that deregulation was such a surprise partly reflects, I will argue, some general problems in the theory of regulatory entry and exit. I will also argue that no version of that theory, including the ET's, is sufficiently well developed to generate sharp predictions about where and when entry or exit will occur.

It is possible, nevertheless, to take advantage of the hindsight afforded by the experience of the past decade in order to evaluate the ET. Though the ET is not a full-blown theory of institutional change, it does suggest circumstances under which such change is more or less likely to occur.

Accordingly, one may ask whether the circumstances surrounding the changes of the last decade are broadly consistent or inconsistent with those emphasized by the ET. This is the procedure I follow. To see the underlying motivation, consider entry and exit theory in the more familiar context of ordinary markets. The theory says distressingly little about the speed or timing of entry or exit. But one would recognize a serious shortcoming of the theory if, for example, it frequently took a long time for entry to respond to profits. And it would be hard to take the theory seriously at all if new firms usually entered in the wake of losses and exit followed profits. Here I will ask, in effect, if the ET's version of 'losses' in the political market had any plausible connection to the deregulation that took place. Perhaps unsurprisingly, my overall answer is positive. But the exit-follows-profits phenomenon is not entirely absent.

In the first section of the paper I summarize the development of the ET and the historical background in which it occurred. I then discuss the shortcomings of the ET as a theory of entry. Finally, I review some of the important changes in regulation that occurred after the theory was developed and evaluate each of them against the relevant elements of the theory.

The Economic Theory in Historical Perspective

The ET made its debut in 1971 after a decade of unusual ferment in the economic analysis of regulation. Until the early 1960s the prevailing theory of regulation was what Joskow and Noll have called the 'normative analysis as a positive theory' (or NPT).[4] This theory, which has been around in one form or another since Adam Smith, regarded market failure as the motivating reason for the entry of regulation. Once established, regulatory bodies were supposed to lessen or eliminate the inefficiencies engendered by the market failure. The ingenuity of economists ensures that the list of potential sources of market failure will never be complete. But in the early 1960s the most popular culprit was natural monopoly followed at a distance by externalities.

The main problem with the NPT was that until the 1960s it was not systematically tested. To be sure, some economists had expressed dissatisfaction with its predictions in such industries as truck and air transportation where the natural-monopoly rationale for entry and rate regulation did not seem readily applicable.[5] But these were exceptions to a general belief that most regulatory activity was compressing the gap between price and marginal cost that would otherwise exist. Perhaps the first formal test of that belief was, appropriately enough, Stigler and Friedland's analysis in 1962 of the effects of regulation of electricity rates.[6] At the time, nothing seemed more settled in the economics of regulation than the presumptive effects of such regulation. Surely restricting entry and imposing maximum rates in this quintessence of a natural monopoly would make rates lower than otherwise. The authors concluded, however, that regulation had not resulted in lower electricity rates.

The importance of the Stigler-Friedland article lies less in this particular result than in its catalytic role. It stimulated an ongoing empirical literature on the effects of regulation. The seeds of the ET were planted by the pattern of results emerging from the first decade of that literature.

That pattern was uncongenial to the NPT. Indeed, it suggested a synthesis that was the exact opposite of the NPT. In 1972 William Jordan provided a good summary of this new synthesis, sometimes called the capture theory of regulation, or CT.[7] After surveying the extant literature on the effects of regulation, he concluded that Stigler and Friedland's finding of ineffective regulation did not hold for all forms of regulation. But the available examples in which regulation did affect prices shared striking similarities. All were found in naturally competitive or nonmonopolistic industries like surface and air transportation, and in all these instances the effects of regulation were to raise prices and reduce the number of competitors. By contrast, regulation did not change prices in natural monopoly industries, where, Jordan argued, the NPT led us to expect that regulation would have suppressed monopoly power. Thus the correct generalization seemed to be the CT—that regulation served the producer interest either by creating cartels where they would otherwise not exist or by failing to suppress monopoly.

Stigler

The capture theory was not new by the early 1970s. Well-known versions had appeared earlier.[8] What was new was its broad appeal to economists based on the accumulating evidence of empirical research within their discipline. However, this new version of the CT shared a conceptual problem with the NPT. Both were empirical generalizations without a theoretical foundation. Neither had a ready answer to the question 'why should regulation be expected to encourage or suppress monopoly?' Stigler's version of the ET sought to fill that theoretical lacuna.[9] The specific conclusions Stigler reached bear the imprint of the then accumulating evidence in favor of some form of the CT. Indeed, his article comes across as an effort to rationalize those results. And Stigler had important predecessors. The notion that ordinary voters are 'rationally ignorant,' which is associated with Anthony Downs, and the free-rider obstacle to collective action, which appears in Olson, are prominent features of Stigler's theory.[10] But as with the Stigler-Friedland article, the lasting significance of Stigler's 1971 article is less in its specific conclusions or elements than in the question it poses—the why of regulatory behavior—and in the structure of its answer.

As mentioned earlier, in Stigler's formulation political actors are presumed to be self-interested maximizers. Just what is in their objective function is not completely spelled out, but surely it includes securing and maintaining political power. For clarity and simplicity, Stigler ignores both the fact that regulators are usually agents of an executive or legislature rather than agents of voters and the many problems of stability and existence of equilibrium in political modeling. He assumes that regulators do the bidding of a representative politician who has the ultimate power to set prices, the number of firms, and so on.[11]

Stigler's next step is to specify the concrete objects of choice in this politician's utility function. These come down to two—votes and money. That is, one consequence of a regulatory decision is that members of groups affected by the decision will be moved to vote for or against the representative politician. Because his ultimate goal is securing and enhancing his power, the politician prefers decisions that directly elicit favorable votes. Regulatory decisions can also elicit campaign contributions, contributions of time to get-out-the-vote, occasional bribes, or well-paid jobs in the political afterlife. Because the more well-financed and well-staffed campaigns tend to be the more successful and because a self-interested politican also values wealth, he will pay attention to these resource (money) consequences of regulatory decision as well as to the direct electoral consequences. Accordingly, groups that may themselves be too small to offer many votes directly in support of a regulatory policy can nevertheless affect that policy by delivering other valuable resources. This notion is another durable feature of the ET literature.

Another durable aspect of Stigler's contribution is his emphasis, already implicit in the preceding, on the distributional aspects of regulatory decisions. Self-interested politicians and constituents exchange objects of utility—a price or entry certificate for votes and money—and what matters to each actor is their wealth or utility, not the aggregate social wealth. Aggregate welfare does matter, in the sense that slices of a pie tend to be larger if the pie is larger. But Stigler's criticism of the NPT is simply that aggregate welfare as such is not what a politician plausibly maximizes.

The results of any analysis of utility-maximizing behavior usually hinge more critically on its specification of the constraint than on the objective function. This is true for Stigler. Though he makes no formal analysis of a constrained maximization problem, one clearly emerges from the discussion. If regulators bestow benefits in exchange for votes and money, the latter must be delivered. (Whether this is done before or after a regulatory decision is one of those suppressed details of the machinery of politics.) Because the benefits typically accrue to groups rather than individuals, the technology for delivery entails group organization. Stigler's results follow more or less directly from his specification of this technology.

Stigler emphasizes two related kinds of costs that constrain a group's ability to deliver votes and money: information and organization costs. Groups must organize to lobby and to deliver campaign contributions, and their members must know enough to vote 'right' on election day. Because knowledge and organization consume resources, low-cost groups tend to be favored at the expense of high-cost groups. And more important, if, as is typical in regulatory issues, the relevant groups are of widely different size, the numerically larger group will tend to be the loser. To see why, consider a decision on how high or low a price should be set or on how many firms should be allowed in. In the relevant range, having more firms and lower prices benefits buyers and harms sellers. Though Stigler alludes to complexities, such as the potentially disparate interests of subgroups, the main issue is whether the buyers or the sellers win a more-or-less fixed prize. Since the number of buyers is usually manyfold greater than the number of sellers, the buyers will probably face prohibitively high costs of organization. The number of collections required and the incentives to free riding will ensure this. Moreover, because each buyer's stake in the outcome is trivial compared with that of the typical seller, it is unlikely that all buyers will know enough to reciprocate any benefits (or punish costs) at the polls unless considerable resources are spent on educating them. The larger per capita stakes yield a saving of information costs to the smaller group (consider the odds that a typical taxpayer knows more about the National Science Foundation's budget than a typical economist), and their smaller numbers make for lower organization cost. Thus the main conclusion of Stigler's analysis is that the producer interest will win the bidding for the services of a regulatory agency. More generally, in any similar political contest between groups of disparate size, the compact organized interest (say, farmers in a developed economy) will usually win at the expense of the diffuse group (taxpayers).

The general framework developed by Stigler, with its emphasis on self-interested political behavior and the importance of organization and information costs, became a hallmark of the subsequent ET literature. But it quickly became apparent that the generalization that regulation served the producer interest had moved too far from the NPT. Indeed, in the same issue of the *Bell Journal* in which Stigler's article appeared, his colleague Richard Posner demonstrated some of the infirmities of the CT as empirical generalization.[12] He did so by emphasizing the phenomenon of 'internal subsidization' (sometimes called cross subsidization), the enforced provision of service to selected consumer groups at especially low, often below-cost, prices. Those consumers are 'subsidized' out of potential producer rents generated elsewhere in the regulated industry. Posner's argument was that cross subsidies are so pervasive and important that no fig-leaf modification of the CT can cover them. Consider just one of many examples offered by Posner: the pre-Amtrak perpetuation of railroad passenger service by the ICC. In CT revisionism, the ICC's raison d'être is to cartelize surface transportation. But how can such devotion to the producer interest be reconciled with the preservation of money-losing passenger service? The simple answer, repeated for many other examples, is that it cannot. The losses were too great and the efforts of the railroads to escape them were too strenuous for any CT explanation to be plausible.

Posner's discussion of cross subsidies illustrates a more general point. Viewed from afar, a particular type of regulation often seems to fit the CT or NPT mold. But a closer look usually uncovers too many exceptions for this dichotomy to be plausible. Consider, for example, areas of regulation like antitrust or health-safety-environmental regulation. If these had been put to the vote in a two-theory election, most economists would have voted for the NPT even after the ascendancy of the CT. But when economists analyze these modes of regulation more closely, they turn up at least as many exceptions to the NPT as confirmations and even a healthy dose of CT-like results.[13]

Peltzman

The notion that no single economic interest captures a regulatory body plays a prominent role in the 1976 article by Peltzman.[14] He derives an equilibrium in which the utility-maximizing politician allocates benefits across groups optimally—that is, in accord with the usual *marginal* conditions. Thus as long as some consumers can offer some votes or money for a small departure from the cartel equilibrium, pure producer protection will not, in general, be the dominant political strategy. Two factors work against such a solution. First, the organization and information costs emphasized by Stigler make it unlikely that the producers will withdraw all their support for the regulatory system for a small reduction in cartel rents. Second, those rents need not be spread to all consumers. Subgroups can organize (or be organized by the regulator) with the appropriate characteristics for efficiently reciprocating a regulatory benefit. Considerations like these led Peltzman to a general characterization of the politician's problem that is distinctly familiar to economists. Economic benefits to any group are reciprocated according to a technology of diminishing returns with the usual continuity properties. As a result, politicians normally hire the services of all groups. A similar general statement applies within groups. Given the usual constraints on discrimination, regulators will allocate benefits across consumer and producer groups so that total political utility is maximized.

This result—that all groups will share in the rents at the regulators' disposal—is as essentially empty as any similar result of constrained maximization analysis. It is the analytical equivalent of results such as 'consumers buy food as well as clothing' or 'firms hire capital as well as labor.' And like these results, Peltzman's gives no guidance on expenditure shares, that is, whether the producers, the consumers, or neither group typically gets the lion's share of the rents. The interesting results in Peltzman come, as is usual in constrained maximization problems, from the comparative static analysis of the constraints on the utility function rather than from any worry over the detail of what is in that function.

In that formulation, the regulator wants to make everyone (with any marginal political weight) as happy as possible, but he is constrained by the demand and cost functions of the regulated industry. Peltzman then investigates the effect of changes in (or different types of) demand and cost conditions on the nature of the resulting equilibrium. Though some of the results are standard CT, or second-best welfare-economics fare (such as less elastic demand or supply functions imply higher prices), two predictions deserve special mention. They are the tendency toward systematic, cost-based cross subsidization and the tendency for regulation to offset the effect of market forces on the division of rents between producers and consumers.

A simple example helps illustrate these results. Suppose a regulated firm, X, sells to two customers, A and B. Suppose further that A and B have equal demands and equal political weight (that is, their utility enters the regulator's utility function in the same way), but that the marginal cost (MC) is higher for serving A than for serving B. Now recall the general result that X will not get maximum profits; for simplicity call this 'tax' on maximum profits, T, and assume it is fixed. Since X cares only about the size of T, not its distribution among A and B, and since A and B are politically equal, the regulator has only one remaining task: to make the price (P) to A and B (P_A and P_B), and thereby A's and B's consumer surplus, as nearly equal as possible, given T. The result will be a lower P_A/MC_A than P_B/MC_B. If T is big enough to permit it, the regulator will completely ignore the fact that $MC_A \neq MC_B$ and set $P_A = P_B$. While there are the inevitable complications and ambiguities, this tendency for the high-cost customer to get the low P/MC is common. It rests on the lack of any general connection between the cost differences and the political importance of the two buyers. And it is a result that does not obtain in CT or NPT regulation or unregulated markets.

The regulator-as-buffer result can be illustrated by a cost or demand change that would leave prices unchanged in the absence of regulation— say a change in fixed cost. This change would, however, alter the distribution of rents between sellers and buyers. Since the regulator is seeking to maintain a politically optimum distribution, he will change prices to offset the distributional effect of the cost or demand change. Thus an increase in fixed cost does not come entirely out of X's hide, as in standard monopoly analysis; it gets translated into higher P_A and P_B to recover some of X's lost rents. Later I give examples of both results—the cost-based cross subsidization and the regulator as buffer—in the discussion of specific cases of regulatory change.

Becker

Results like these come from a view of regulation in which industry wealth (producer and consumer rents) is the prime political currency to be disposed of in ways that best suit the regulator. This view provides a link between the ET, with its emphasis on redistribution, and the NPT, with its emphasis on efficiency. That link has been most extensively developed by Gary Becker, first in his comment on Peltzman's paper and then in his 1983 article.[15] His setup is similar to Peltzman's: groups organize to exert pressure on the political process to grant them benefits or exempt them from paying for others' benefits. And the equilibrium represents a balancing of marginal pressure exerted by winners and losers. Becker's central argument is that in a setup like this deadweight losses are a constraint on inefficient regulatory policies. The reason is simple: as the regulator moves output away from the efficient level, the deadweight loss increases at an increasing rate. (The marginal deadweight loss is the difference between the heights of the demand and the supply function, which gets bigger the further quantity is pushed from the efficient level.) Deadweight loss is nothing more than the winner's gain less the loser's loss from the regulation-induced change in output. These gains and losses are what motivate the competing pressures on the political process. So rising marginal deadweight loss must progressively enfeeble the winners relative to the losers. The pressure the winners can exert for each extra dollar's gain must overcome steadily rising pressure from the losers to escape the escalating losses.

Becker's formulation produces a political equilibrium with some deadweight loss. It does, however, suggest a bias against the unbounded deadweight losses implicit in the CT. Among the concrete manifestations of this bias is what Becker calls the 'tyranny of the status quo.' Most structurally competitive industries, for example, are not subject to price or entry regulation, even though the producers have Stiglerian organization and information cost advantages. But rising marginal deadweight loss can offset the producers' other advantages unless the demand and supply functions are sufficiently inelastic to attenuate it. The other side of this avoidance of inefficiency is a search for greater efficiency. Becker argues that the political process will be drawn toward efficient modes of re-distribution in general and to efficiency-enhancing regulation in particular. The reason is simply that neither winners nor losers would rationally oppose changes that eliminated some deadweight loss. This is an important point for at least two reasons.

First, economists have a well-honed instinct for separating allocational from distributive issues. So there appears to be an obviously more 'efficient' way of accomplishing the redistribution that the ET ascribes to regulation: why not directly pay off the winners without messing up a nice $P = MC$ equilibrium? In a world of competing pressure groups, however, no redistributive mechanism, not even the proverbial lump-sum tax, is without its deadweight cost. Payers and payees will incur costs to generate pressure and to alter their behavior so as to maximize the benefits or minimize the costs meted out by the political process. Given this situation, it is no longer obvious that all the costs associated with tax-transfer redistribution will be smaller than the costs of comparable redistribution through regulation. In fact, if regulatory redistribution survives, the presumption must be that it is the less costly mode. Otherwise both winners and losers would press for a change.

Second, market failure, the standby of the NPT, creates incentives for regulation. If regulation can reduce the resulting inefficiency, there will be more wealth available for distribution. This extra wealth can induce greater pressure for regulation from winners and can attenuate the opposition of losers. In contrast to the NPT, the ET says that the regulation will not maximize the extra wealth, because buyers and sellers are not in general equally well organized politically. But faced with a portfolio of potential areas to regulate, the political process will tend to be attracted to industries where it can increase wealth as well as to those where deadweight losses are small.

Summary of ET Findings

A useful way to summarize the foregoing discussion is to list some of the important characteristics of regulation that emerge from the literature on the economic theory of regulation.

—Compact, well-organized groups will tend to benefit more from regulation than broad, diffuse groups. This probably creates a bias in favor of producer groups, because they are usually well organized relative to all consumers. But the dominant coalition usually also includes subsets of consumers.

—Regulatory policy will seek to preserve a politically optimal distribution of rents across this coalition. Thus, over time, the policy will tend to offset changes in this optimal distribution arising from shifts in demand or cost conditions. At any one time, the price structure will cross-subsidize high-cost consumers from rents generated by prices to other groups.

—Because the political payoff to regulation arises from distributing wealth, the regulatory process is sensitive to deadweight losses. Policies that reduce the total wealth available for distribution will be avoided, because, other things being equal, they reduce the political payoff from regulation.

The Academic Effect of the ET

While some of these features of the ET literature have received more attention than others, the literature as a whole has made its mark on academic analyses of regulation. Table 2.1 summarizes one measure of this impact, the number of citations to the three articles I have just summarized. To put this number in perspective, I have included citation counts for two recognized classics in the same general area—Coase's 1960 article on social cost and Averch and Johnson's 1962 article on rate-of-return regulation. By now all three ET articles have passed Averch-Johnson in the citation derby. The two mature ET articles—Stigler and Peltzman—have run considerably ahead of Averch-Johnson and below Coase in recent

Table 2.1. *Number of Citations to Selected Articles, 1972–86*

| Year | Economic theory of regulation articles[a] | | | Other articles[b] | |
	Stigler	Peltzman	Becker	Coase	Averch and Johnson
1972	16[c]	...	...	61	21
1973	7	...	...	59	22
1974	18	...	...	58	20
1975	17	...	...	81	27
1976	27	...	...	66	30
1977	16	6[c]	...	53	30
1978	29	11	...	56	19
1979	28	19	...	74	32
1980	48	33	...	90	25
1981	42	31	...	84	14
1982	53	46	...	102	28
1983	60	34	...	100	29
1984	67	48	12[c]	86	21
1985	79	62	23	88	13
1986	77	70	31	93	26
Annual average					
1972–86	38.9	36.0	22.0	76.7	23.8
1980–86	60.9	46.3	22.0	91.9	22.3

Source: Social Science Citation Index.

a. George J. Stigler, 'The Theory of Economic Regulation,' *Bell Journal of Economics and Management Science*, vol. 2 (Spring 1971), pp. 3–21; Sam Peltzman, 'Toward a More General Theory of Regulation,' *Journal of Law and Economics*, vol. 19 (August 1976), pp. 211–40; and Gary Becker, 'A Theory of Competition among Pressure Groups for Political Influence,' *Quarterly Journal of Economics*, vol. 98 (August 1983), pp. 371–400.

b. Ronald H. Coase, 'The Problem of Social Cost,' *Journal of Law and Economics*, vol. 3 (October 1960), pp. 1–44; and Harvey Averch and Leland L. Johnson, 'The Behavior of the Firm under Regulatory Constraint,' *American Economic Review*, vol. 52 (December 1962), pp. 1052–69.

c. Includes previous (publication) year.

years. Stigler has been getting about two-thirds and Peltzman about one-half the citations accruing to Coase. Moreover, interest in this literature seems to be growing. Note the jump in the Stigler and Peltzman citations from 1980 on and the rapid growth in the Becker citations since publication. Becker's article is getting about twice the citations of its two predecessors at a comparable post-publication stage. Though citation counts are an obviously crude index, the data suggest that academics have been treating the ET as an important piece of intellectual capital that is not yet fully depreciated.

I leave an assessment of the reasons for this impact to others. Here I evaluate whether this academic success is somehow justified in light of recent real-world developments. Many of these involve deregulation—that is, exit from regulation. Exit is the logical and chronological successor to entry. So, before discussing the ET's success in coping with exit, I evaluate its utility as a theory of entry into regulation. I argue that as entry theories both the ET and its competitor, the NPT, have specific weaknesses that affect their ability to cope with deregulation.

Entry in the Theory of Regulation

Most of the development of the ET concerns the behavior of established regulatory bodies: whom they will favor and how and why their policies will change. But the question of why the body was established in the first place cannot be ignored. The ET's answer to that question is about what one would expect from a maximizing theory of institutional behavior: politicians seek politically rewarding fields to regulate and avoid or exit from the losers. The difficulty with the ET as an entry theory is precisely that it never gets much beyond this level of generality.

Consider Stigler's version. In some absolute sense, the lopsided advantages that producers have over consumers are essentially universal. This fact suggests that regulation which generates rents for producers should also be universal. To the non-Marxist, or anyone concerned with making distinctions, such a formulation obviously says too much. Accordingly, Stigler implicitly imposes a budget constraint on the entry problem. To find the prime candidates for regulation, he looks for industries where the producers' advantage is unusually large. Operationally this means searching for a link between the probability that an industry is regulated and variables like the geographic concentration of sellers which are proxies for organization or information cost advantages of producers. Stigler has only limited success with this strategy, nor has it led to a literature with much stronger results. Given the lack of explicit attention to constraints on entry, one leaves Stigler's model with the nagging question of why minimum rate or entry regulation of structurally competitive industries is comparatively rare.[16]

Peltzman's version is hardly an improvement. Given its emphasis on the optimal allocation of wealth among potentially conflicting interests, almost anything that makes the wealth pool 'large' or its allocation politically nonoptimal should induce regulatory entry. Thus *both* naturally competitive and naturally monopolistic industries ought to attract regulation (they are at a 'corner' and hence farthest from the optimal rent distribution). Growth in demand, technological progress, inelastic supply and demand curves (all of which generate large or growing wealth), and unexpected disturbances in supply and demand (which upset the optimal wealth distribution) are all mentioned as conducive to regulation. This list is still reasonably compact, but it is unclear that the extra variables buy much more explanatory power. That is, Peltzman's model, like Stigler's, seems incapable of explaining why substantial and continual regulation of important structural or behavioral characteristics seems concentrated in a few industries.

In this respect, Becker's article marks an advance. In its full generality—efficiency in producing pressure for regulation generates regulation—Becker's formulation shares the infirmities of its two predecessors. But the specific emphasis on economic efficiency leads Becker to emphasize correction of market failure as an important motive for regulation. If market failure is comparatively rare, Becker's version of the ET gives some insight into the pattern of regulation. Consider a political decision on whether industries $A_i, A_2, \ldots, A_n$ or B should be regulated, where the A_i are all structurally competitive and B is ridden with market failure. The proregulation pressure group in each of the A_i is handicapped by the regulation-induced deadweight losses, and the group in B is helped by the potential efficiency gains. If regulation is not universal, B would, all else the same, end up as the only regulated industry.

Read this way, the ET comes close to merging with the NPT's entry story—entry occurs only to correct market failure. Shouldn't we then just invoke Occam's razor and prefer the NPT? The answer, given our present state of knowledge, is a resounding maybe. If there is an empirical basis for the NPT's continuing attraction for economists, it is probably its apparent success as an entry theory. Consider Hotelling's classic statement in 1938 of the natural monopoly version of the NPT.[17] In this purely theoretical piece, railroads and utilities are presumed, without much evidence, to be the main real-world examples of natural monopoly. They also occupied most of the regulatory (including public ownership) effort when Hotelling wrote. This correspondence between the NPT and the real-world allocation of regulatory effort seems striking. Now consider the postwar expansion of regulation. In terms of the resources involved, the biggest single chunk is probably accounted for by environmental regulation, where the externalities aspect of the NPT scores another success. As for much of the impossible-to-catalogue remainder—health, safety, old-age security, and so on—the NPT becomes frayed at the edges. To be sure, a good economist needs no more than fifteen minutes' notice to produce a market failure to 'explain' any of these interventions. But credulity is strained when the list of market failures grows at roughly the same rate as the number of regulatory agencies. And even in Hotelling's time the regulation of trucks and airlines, agriculture, labor markets, and many professions was already taxing the NPT's explanatory power. In sum, if the ET overpredicts the incidence of regulation, the NPT underpredicts it. If a case exists for favoring the NPT as a general entry model, it would be that underpredicting a comparatively rare phenomenon produces a smaller average error than overpredicting it.

Regulatory Change in Theory and Practice

The topography of American regulation has changed considerably in the last two decades. Some types of regulation have grown or consolidated their position: regulation of the environment, product and workplace safety, the medical industry (such as prices and entry of hospitals), the disclosure of financial information, the operation of financial institutions (such as the de facto nationalization of distressed banks and savings and loan associations), and labor contracts (especially race and sex pay differentials). The avidity with which particular administrations pursue these areas may vary, but the strength of the governing institutions has grown or remained unchallenged. Here I focus on a historically more interesting change: the substantial reduction or elimination of the regulation of entry/exit or rates, or both, in a number of industries. These comprise surface and air transportation, long-distance telecommunications, securities brokerage, and bank deposits. In one important case—oil—maximum price regulation came and went within a decade. For nearly a century it had appeared that each new peacetime regulatory initiative was essentially permanent. That historical pattern was now decisively broken.

These deregulation initiatives are particularly interesting to economists. Had they been put to a vote of the American Economic Association membership, all the initiatives would have passed with large majorities. Probably not since the rise of free trade in the nineteenth century has so broad a professional consensus been so well reflected in policy. The reason for this consensus is economists' belief that deregulation enhances efficiency. This naturally raises a question about the current status of the NPT. Has it been resuscitated because of deregulation? Though the full answer requires evaluation of the alternative ET, deregulation hardly seems like a striking confirmation of the NPT. The main reason has to do with timing. The P, or positive, part of the NPT implies two reasons for deregulation: (1) technological or demand changes eliminate the market failure, or (2) regulation is revealed to have been a mistake by the light of the N, or normative, part of the theory. Most of the examples of deregulation would fit into the second category. The difficulty for the NPT is that these were recognizable as mistakes long before deregulation corrected them. The most obvious problems for the NPT are those cases not discussed here, because deregulation has not yet occurred. For example, the continued licensing of a myriad of professions, such as barbers and beauticians, looks like a continued mistake by the light of the theory. Of the cases I discuss, at least two, ceilings on bank deposit rates and minimum brokerage rates, were normative mistakes from the start, about forty years before deregulation. In transportation, the normative argument for truck regulation had also been dubious from the beginning (1935). As for rail and air transport, the normative case for at least some easing of regulatory constraints on competition goes back at least to the early 1960s. When the exit required by the theory takes twenty or forty years or has yet to occur, the theory can hardly be deemed powerful. Among the cases I discuss, the only one where deregulation seems to have followed reasonably promptly after the normative basis of the regulation became obsolete is long-distance telecommunications.

The relevant question is whether the ET looks any better than the NPT from today's vantage point. My overall answer is that it does, though the ET has its share of failures and unanswered questions. I should point out that the same question and roughly the same answer can be found in an article by Theodore Keeler.[18] His analysis is more narrowly focused on transportation than mine, and it is couched in terms of a synthesis between the NPT and ET. So, though I place more emphasis on the differences between the two theories than he does, there is inevitable overlap. I begin this evaluation of the ET by first summarizing what the theory says about deregulation. Then in the following sections I proceed case by case to summarize the 'facts' surrounding deregulation and show how these facts are or are not consistent with the ET explanation of deregulation. I then try to draw general conclusions about the state of the political economy of deregulation.

My discussion of the entry model implicit in the ET points to two general sources of pressure for deregulation: changes in the 'politics' and changes in the 'economics' of the regulated industries. Political change includes such things as shifts in the relative political power of contending groups and changes in the underlying organization and information technologies. Anything that, for example, made it cheaper to organize or inform the broad mass of consumers about the adverse consequences of regulation in a structurally competitive industry would increase the political pay off to deregulation. Here I ignore these political factors, partly because economists have so far had limited success in pinning them down, but mainly because the more familiar terrain of the economic factors is sufficiently fertile. In the Peltzman and Becker versions of the ET, two kinds of economic change are conducive to deregulation: (1) the gap between the regulated equilibrium and the one plausibly characterizing deregulation of the industry narrows, so continued regulation becomes pointless, or (2) the wealth available for redistribution becomes too small to provide the requisite political payoff to regulation.[19] These two forces can be related. For example, a lower demand for the regulated industry's product may bring the regulated price closer to marginal cost, and it will lower the potential producer rents from regulation. However, I argue that the second force—decreases in available wealth—is empirically more important.

To see how a reduction in available wealth can lead to deregulation, consider the simple case of a constant-cost industry that experiences increased input prices. That reduces the available sum of producer and consumer surplus. In Peltzman's analysis the first-order regulatory response is to distribute the loss across producers and consumers with a price increase less than the cost increase. But this reduces the producer rents that must pay the organizational and information costs that politically support regulation. If the cost increase is large enough, the producer rents may no longer be sufficient to generate the requisite political support for continued regulation.[20] In Becker's framework the loss of rents reduces the pressure for continued regulation of this industry relative to other industries, and the higher price increases the counter-pressure from consumers. Suppose further that the cost increase has in fact been induced by regulation. Then the deadweight losses emphasized by Becker become especially important. There is now not only attenuated support for continued regulation but also the potential for major gains in political utility from deregulation. These would come from the elimination of the cost increase attributable to regulation. For a structurally competitive industry, the lower costs would translate into higher producer and consumer surplus in the short run and higher consumer surplus in the long run, thus raising the possibility that the coalition pushing for deregulation would include some producers.

Railroads

Since the railroad industry was already mature and arguably overbuilt when the Interstate Commerce Act of 1887 was passed, the important features of regulation are control of rates and exit from the industry. The industry technology exhibits increasing returns to density and length of haul, which is also important in understanding the regulatory history.

The regulatory system that was to govern the industry until the late 1970s was not fully developed until the Transportation Act of 1920. That act, as implemented by the Interstate Commerce Commission, had the following results:

—A rate structure characterized by cross subsidies to the high-cost, light-density, and short-haul shippers from long-haul shippers on high-density routes. As nonrail passenger modes developed and rail passenger densities fell, the cross subsidy was extended to rail passenger service.

—Commodity-based price discrimination was superimposed on this rate structure. Goods with a high value per ton and presumably less-elastic demands for freight (because transportation costs represented a smaller share of final product cost) tended to have the higher rates. Railroads could also collude on rate proposals.

—Exit control. Abandonment of freight and passenger service required ICC approval, and the ICC acted to slow the process—even to the point of discouraging applications—more than what the industry would have liked.

This structure is not, of course, wholly consistent with the earliest version of the ET, which mainly emphasized the producer interest. That interest is recognizable here only in the value-of-service rate structure (supplemented by collective ratemaking). But the basic structure of railroad regulation provides a good illustration of what is central to later versions of the ET—the spreading of rents to nonproducer groups. Producers got something—protection from competition and (at least temporarily) profitable price discrimination. Then these gains were partly shared with other groups through cross subsidies. Because these cross subsidies would otherwise induce exit from the industry, implementation of the scheme required restrictions on exit.

However, if this structure represented an equilibrium balance of forces in 1920, that equilibrium came under pressure almost immediately. Unregulated nonrail alternatives became increasingly viable as the highway and inland waterway networks spread. Trucks, in particular, began drawing some of the railroad's high-value, high-rate, primarily manufactured goods traffic. The resulting erosion of the rents that funded the political equilibrium was, of course, greatly exacerbated by the Great Depression. The first line of political defense was to bring the trucks under the regulatory tent in 1935.

The Motor Carrier Act of 1935 established minimum rate and entry controls on common-carrier trucks. If the first effect of this was to slow the erosion of railroad rents, subsequent developments rendered the regulatory system a mixed blessing for the railroads. The system now had two producer interests to contend with, and the trucking interest was soon to be aided by the unionization of the vast majority of common-carrier truck drivers. Though the contribution of regulation is debatable, the fact is that the shift of traffic, particularly the high-margin manufactured goods, from rails to trucks continued over the ensuing decades. The corresponding shift in the political weights of the two ICC constituencies gradually weakened the railroads' stake in continued regulation. Empirically, their best response to the declining demand conditions they faced would have been exit.[21] But maintenance of excess capacity was necessary to preserve the politically optimal system of cross subsidies. So, here, continued regulation could only hurt the railroads. Another margin of response to declining demand was price reductions. These sometimes elicited political opposition from the motor carriers, and this opposition now had to be paid heed. Thus important elements of the regulatory system undermined the railroad's battle to preserve their eroding rents.

Those rents would have been eroding without regulation, given the decline in demand and the long-lived, specialized nature of railroad capital. The plausible effect of regulation was to alter the time profile of the declining rents in a way that ultimately undercut the basis for the regulation. The elements of producer protection—the value-of-service rate structure, the constraints on intramodal competition—worked to make the initial level of the rents higher than otherwise. But the wealth-spreading elements, manifested by the slowing of exit in the face of declining demand, and the need to serve the increasingly important producer interests of other modes, speeded the rate of decline of the rents. Over time the second effect came to predominate, so that the net effects of regulation on rail owners became unfavorable.[22]

In retrospect, the turn of the political tide toward deregulation can be traced to a spate of railroad bankruptcies in the early 1970s. The bankrupt roads were located in the Northeast, which bore heavily the cross subsidy to short-haul and passenger traffic, and in the upper Midwest, where the cross subsidy to light-density traffic was important. These bankruptcies were a signal that the rents required to support the system created in 1920 were no longer available. The first political response was to nationalize the cross subsidies through Conrail and Amtrak. Given the railroads' continued secular decline, the choice facing Congress and the railroads was now clear: further nationalization or deregulation of exit and rates. The rail-roads chose deregulation and they essentially got it by 1980.[23]

This brief history fits the ET's deregulation scenario very well. The rents supporting the political equilibrium eroded, partly because of the incent-ives created by the value-of-service rate structure and partly because of the enforced provision of below-cost service. Support for the regulation eroded along with the rent. The organized producer interest ultimately favored and got deregulation. And the deregulation occurred not long after the economic and political forces turned decisively against regulation.

A major unanswered question in this story—which I return to but do not answer in my discussion of air transport—concerns labor rents. As an organized producer interest, it is plausible that unionized railroad workers shared in any rents generated by regulation.[24] The magnitude of these rents and the degree, if any, to which they were eroded before or after deregulation remains uncertain. This uncertainty should not, however, obscure the basic message provided by the industry's financial difficulties: the old coalition of producers and consumers was no longer sustainable under the established regulatory framework.

Trucking

If rail deregulation is a victory for the ET, truck deregulation is a resound-ing defeat. In generating producer rents, trucking regulation was a signal and long-lasting success. Comparing wages of unionized workers in truck-ing with the wages of nonunionized trucking employees, Thomas Moore estimated a wage premium due to regulation exceeding 30 percent and showed that the premium was growing over time. From the analysis of transactions in operating rights, he was able to estimate that the total value of operating rights represented rents roughly equal to those of workers. Using more sophisticated statistical techniques than Moore, Nancy Rose basically confirmed the magnitude of the regulation-induced wage premium.[25]

Where would the ET have us look for sources of pressure for regulatory change in this industry? The answers would include the following.

—Growing labor rents. These may have been symptomatic of a drift away from the political equilibrium. The cost of that drift would include the accelerating deadweight losses emphasized by Becker.

—Dissipation of owner rents. The operating rights were not output quotas. On multifirm routes the minimum price regulation gave each firm an incentive to expand its market share, which led to cost-increasing service rivalry. Also, the entry control led to circuitous routing: a firm denied permission to enter the A-B market could get in if it bought an A-C and a C-B operating right, but then it had to move the freight through C. (Since these cost-increasing elements of the regulation raised the demand for labor, they would not be inconsistent with growing labor rents.)

—Deregulation of the railroads. This had the potential for lowering the present value of rents in trucking by more than the corresponding gain in total railroad surplus. The difference would be due to the inefficient traffic allocation engendered by rail deregulation when truck prices remained regulated: that is, rails could draw traffic when their marginal cost exceeded the truck cost by less than the regulated price-cost markup in trucking.

None of these possibilities can save the ET here. The reason is empirical rather than logical.

—The growing rents would suggest perhaps some easing of entry control to restore equilibrium. Instead, the regulatory rents have been entirely eliminated. The still-required operating rights are worthless, and according to Rose's estimate, the labor rent has vanished.

—According to Moore's comparison of the price effects of regulation with the observed rents, no more than one-fourth of the potential industry rent was being dissipated by such things as service rivalry and route circuitry. And even if that estimate is not exactly right, the dissipation had to be far from complete, since operating rights of substantial value became worthless overnight because of deregulation.

—The importance of rail regulation as a source of rent for the regulated truckers has long been debated. And the excess capacity maintained by rail regulation worked to reduce rents in trucking. All this aside, however, there is a crude test that shows why rail deregulation cannot have been an important reason for truck deregulation. If it had been important, the trucking industry would have split politically. Those owners and Teamster locals facing especially close rail competition would at least have supported rate deregulation once rail deregulation was in the wind. That did not happen. The opposition of the American Trucking Association and the Teamsters to deregulation seems to have been monolithic and vigorous to the bitter end (too vigorous in the case of the president of the Teamsters, who was jailed for attempted bribery of the chairman of the Senate committee considering the deregulation bill).

Here then is an industry in which substantial and sustainable rents received the fullest measure of organized support from the beneficiaries. There is simply no way I know of to square the wholesale elimination of these rents by political action with any current version of the ET.

Airlines

The formal structure of airline regulation was essentially identical to that of trucking. Minimum rate and entry controls were combined with wide latitude for concerted industry action. But in terms of generating producer rents, airline regulation did not work as well as trucking regulation, and it worked conspicuously less well in the period just before deregulation. Table 2.2 provides some background. It shows the industry's operating cash flow (operating profits plus depreciation) as a percentage of revenues. In the parlance of the empirical industrial organization literature, it is an estimate of the industry's price-cost margin. I use cash flow rather than, say, accounting profits to allow for the possibility that rents may have been hidden in depreciation charges.[26] Though any such accounting data are always to be treated gingerly, the story they tell is not fundamentally different from that found in more detailed analyses, such as those by Keeler, Douglas and Miller, and Jordan.[27]

These authors did not have the benefit of hindsight. However, if one takes the 1980s' data as typifying an unregulated equilibrium, the evidence suggests that regulation was generating some producer rents—maybe 10 cents per dollar of revenues—until the late 1960s. Then a process of erosion set in lasting up to the dawn of deregulation in 1978. In fact, erosion of potential rents seems to have had a longer history. Keeler estimated that around 1970 the average ratio of price to 'competitive marginal cost' was about 1.5 for thirty routes. That translates into a price-cost margin of 33 percent. Note that the figures in Table 2.2, which make no allowance for capital costs, never approach that height. Why not, and why the decline in the decade preceding deregulation? The answer

Table 2.2. *Airline Operating Cash Flow per Revenue Dollar, 1950–86*[a]

Period	Operating cash flow/revenue[b]	Period	Operating cash flow/revenue[b]
1950–54	23.2	1970–74	13.3
1955–59	18.2	1975–80	9.8
1960–64	14.9	1980–86	7.1
1965–69	17.7		

Sources: U.S. Bureau of the Census, *Historical Statistics of the United States: Colonial Times to 1970*, vol. 2 (Department of Commerce, 1975), p. 770; and *Statistical Abstract of the United States, 1976*, p. 612; *1986*, p. 616; and *1988*, p. 592.

a. Operating cash flow = operating profits (that is, before interest expenses and taxes) = depreciation.
b. Depreciation of ground assets is not reported before 1961. I estimated this at 4 percent of revenues for 1950–60, the difference between the reported 1960 and 1961 ratios of depreciation to revenues. Data are for domestic operations.

seems to lie in cost-increasing service rivalry induced by the structure of regulation. The industry's technology is characterized by economies (in terms of costs per quality-constant passenger mile) in distance and route density. The Civil Aeronautics Board fare structure imperfectly reflected the distance economy and ignored the density economy. Thus it contained elements of cost-based cross subsidization—from the low-cost, high-density long-haul markets to the low-density short-haul markets. But even many of the latter were potentially profitable.

Cost-increasing service rivalry, most notably from increased flight frequencies, had always been a source of rent erosion on nonmonopoly routes. It became increasingly important in the 1960s after the widespread introduction of jet-powered aircraft. This technology widened the scope for nonstop service in long-haul markets. The regulated fare structure made securing nonstop authority in such markets lucrative, especially in the high-density markets.

Throughout its history the CAB had assiduously resisted all pressure for entry by outsiders. But it was now faced with a shift in the distribution of wealth among its constituents that favored those with long-haul, nonstop authority. It responded in a manner consistent with Peltzman's wealth-spreading result. The poorer constituents were cut in on the lucrative routes. As a result, by the late 1960s most important routes were served by several carriers. Service rivalry thus grew more pervasive, so that wealth dissipation became the handmaiden of wealth spreading. One symptom of this phenomenon was the behavior of load factors. In the 1950–59 decade the average domestic load factor was 63 percent. In the next decade it was 53 percent. By the early 1970s (1970–73) this figure had fallen to 48 percent. By this time, it appeared that most of the industry rents had been dissipated by the quality competition.[28]

The CAB responded to these events with a celebrated domestic passenger fare investigation. This led to a number of administrative steps in the early 1970s, such as elimination of the distance cross subsidy, toward greater efficiency. In hindsight, these can be seen as the precursors of deregulation in 1978. As far as consistency with the ET is concerned, the story here was roughly the same as for the railroads, except that the dissipation of rents was more clearly related to the working of regulation. By the 1970s the regulation had rendered too many routes too competitive for minimum rates to generate the rents required to sustain support for regulation—a fact clearer in hindsight than it was when deregulation became live politically. Most of the industry opposed deregulation, but important fissures developed. For example, the largest airline (United),

Table 2.3. *Wages in Transportation Relative to Those in Manufacturing, 1980, 1984*

Industry	Relative wage (1975 = 100)[a]		Percent change, 1980–84
	1980	1984	
Railroads	109	116	6
Trucking	101	92	−9
Air transport	108	109	1

Source: Bureau of the Census, *Statistical Abstract of the United States*, 1986, pp. 412, 414, 620.

a. For railroads, trucking, and all manufacturing, the wage is average hourly earnings; for air transport it is the Air Transport Association labor cost index.

which had borne a heavy cost from the CAB's wealth-spreading policy on internal entry, supported deregulation.

As with railroads and trucks, an important question about the effect of regulation concerns labor rents. These played no important role in the academic literature on the subject.[29] But the air transport unions opposed deregulation, and deregulation has brought visible pressure on union wages. This casual evidence suggests that regulation may have been sustaining labor rents. Less casual, but very crude, evidence is not so clear. Table 2.3 shows the evolution of wages in the three transportation industries, relative to the average manufacturing wage, over the period spanning deregulation. From 1975 to 1980 wages in all three industries were rising at least as fast as wages elsewhere. But only in trucking was that tendency decisively broken in the early 1980s. In this respect, the crude data are consistent with what we already know from Rose's work about the demise of labor rents in trucking from deregulation. They are not consistent with a similarly pervasive erosion of labor rents due to deregulation of air and rail transport.[30]

Pending more systematic evidence on labor, it is best to be somewhat tentative about the details of the effects of airline regulation on producer rents. What can be said is that at least one side of the producer interest—the owners—had essentially lost their stake in continued regulation. And the deadweight losses of regulation had opened the possibility that they could now gain from deregulation.[31]

Long-Distance Telecommunications

Up to the 1960s intercity telephone service was provided by a regulated monopoly, AT&T, whose subsidiaries also provided most of the local service. The prevailing wisdom was that both types of service were natural monopolies, and though the regulatory authority was fragmented, both were regulated accordingly. The formal structure was maximum rate-of-return regulation. Since local and long-distance service shared common facilities, any statement about cross subsidies is tenuous. But two kinds of cross subsidy seemed to emerge from the regulation. Long-distance rates subsidized local service, and long-haul, high-density intercity service subsidized thin short-haul service.[32] The latter is another example of cost-based cross subsidies, since the traditional long-distance technology is subject to substantial economies of density and distance. This rate structure combined with new technology to undermine the regulation.

Microwave technology developed rapidly after World War II. Unlike in the traditional technology, there are no important density economies in microwave technology. In addition, microwave costs came down over time, and by the 1960s they were below those of the traditional technology over a wide range of output. Thus comparatively small microwave systems were now cost-competitive with AT&T, and the rents built into long-distance rates provided a further lure for actual competition.[33] The first symptom of growing competition was the growth of private microwave systems, which carried signals for their owners. These private systems did not by themselves siphon off enough long-distance volume to threaten the continued viability of regulation. But the threat was obvious. Consider XYZ, Inc., which operated a private microwave system between its facilities in A and B. It was now possible for XYZ and even its employees and their friends in A to place a local call there to be transported by XYZ's microwave system to B, where another local call would carry it to anyone in B. The total cost of this maneuver, including the two (subsidized) local calls, would be less than AT&T's high long-distance rates. Thus the regulated rates and the new technology were providing an incentive for large users to build their own systems. They were also providing an incentive for these private systems to arbitrage the difference between AT&T's rates and the private system's costs for third parties.

How far and how quickly such arbitrage would have spread in the absence of regulatory change is debatable. Until 1969 it was illegal for private microwave systems to offer long-distance service to the general public. Thus the relevant counterfactual (what would have occurred if regulation had not changed) turns on the costs of getting around this legal restriction. Had these been suitably modest, a fairly rapid unraveling of the regulated rate structure becomes a credible part of the counterfactual. This scenario—a rapid dissipation of rents through competition from private networks—would then provide a basis for deregulation consistent with the ET.

This scenario never took place. And that fact, in my view, is not congenial to an ET-based explanation of the actual events. What happened was that the owner of a private microwave system, MCI, applied for permission to provide public long-distance service by interconnecting with the local networks. This permission was granted in 1969. That decision was the beginning of the end of regulation in long-distance telecommunications. There are now essentially no regulatory constraints on entry, and much of the proverbial cream has been skimmed from long-distance rates. Some formal rate regulation still exists, largely in the form of the rates charged the long-distance carriers for access to the now independent local networks.

The difficulty in viewing this history through the lens of the ET lies in the heavy weight one must give to the foresight of the regulators. One has to argue that they saw as imminent such a rapid erosion of the long-distance rents from the new technology that the present value of the political gains derivable from those rents had, in some sense, become negative by 1969. This kind of argument does not sit well with the experience in airline and railroad deregulation, already reviewed, or in financial services, discussed below. In all those industries considerable actual rent dissipation preceded deregulation. Also, though we will never know the counterfactual time path of the long-distance telecommunication rents, we do know that the United States is still, twenty years after the crucial regulatory change, the main exception to a worldwide rule of entry restriction in this market. That fact at least suggests that U.S. regulators could have resisted new entry for some time after they permitted it. Accordingly, if one had to choose between the ET's explanation and the NPT's—that deregulation follows the demise of natural monopoly conditions—the latter is simpler and thus more appealing.[34]

Stock Brokerage

Though the history is somewhat murky, it appears that until twenty years ago a cartel of New York Stock Exchange (NYSE) members had been setting minimum brokerage rates since 1792. In the 1930s this cartel came within the ambit of the Securities and Exchange Commission (SEC). However, the SEC sanctioned minimum rates at least up to 1968. The interaction between the SEC and the NYSE cartel never acquired a formal institutional structure. But the rates bore the familiar imprint of cost-based cross subsidization: brokerage costs per share (or dollar) decrease as the size of the transaction increases, and these economies of size were incompletely translated into rates. The result was that profits on large trans-actions subsidized losses on small transactions.[35]

Gregg Jarrell has already invoked the ET in explaining the industry's transition to deregulation, and I can do little more than paraphrase him here.[36] The precursor to deregulation was the rise of institutional trading in the 1960s. These large-block traders doubled their share of NYSE trading volume between 1960 and 1976, accounting for nearly half the volume at the latter date. Given the rate structure, this event increased the potential rent available to NYSE members. But that potential was not realized. The rent dissipation took many shapes, the most obvious being nonprice competition in the form of 'free' ancillary services (research) provided to large institutional traders. Also, institutional traders began arranging trades off the NYSE floor, either through their own newly formed brokerage subsidiaries or through specialists that were not NYSE members. These leakages created a split within the cartel. The larger NYSE member firms, which wanted to compete for institutional business, were increasingly hobbled by the need to use inefficient methods to counteract the straight discounts offered by nonmembers. They ultimately supported rate deregulation (and, according to Jarrell, benefited from it).

Formal deregulation of brokerage rates came through congressional action in 1975. But beginning in 1968, a series of regulatory changes pushed in the same direction—more competition and consequently lower rates on large transactions. So far, the brokerage story resembles the airline or railroad story: potential rents from regulation eroded to the point where the supporting coalition was undermined. There is, however, a twist in the story congenial to the ET. It lies in the growth of institutional trading, which touched off the forces leading to deregulation. The institutions had the attributes making for political success in Stigler's explana-tion—compact numbers with large per capita stakes. Jarrell, however, emphasized the purely economic aspects of the institutions' growth as embodied in Peltzman's version of the ET. The institutions were the relatively elastic demanders of NYSE brokerage services, especially after they began integrating vertically and arranging off-board trades. In Peltz-man's multi-interest model, higher demand elasticities shift the equilib-rium toward lower prices. So even if the consumers' political ability had not increased, the SEC would have faced pressure to weaken regulation.

Bank Deposits

The formal regulation of deposit rates is one of the series of regulatory reforms enacted in the wake of the widespread bank failures of the 1930s.

But it took another thirty years for the regulation to have any substantial effects. The original regulation prohibited payment of interest on demand deposits and set a 2.5 percent maximum rate on time deposits in commercial banks. The latter was nonbinding for many institutions until the 1950s, and then was raised to 3 percent in 1957, the first move in a delicate balancing act that was to be played out in the ensuing years.

From the onset of regulation, ninety-day Treasury-bill yields never averaged over 4 percent in any year until 1966. In such a world the marginal effect of the interest ceilings was modest. They moved in the direction of providing some rents to the commercial banks and fostering the growth of savings and loan associations, whose rates were not then regulated. In this sense the regulation served some important organized interest groups—the commercial banks and the S&Ls and their allies, the homebuilding industry. The banking rents were partly dissipated by various forms of nonprice and near-price competition, such as forgone service charges on demand deposits and competition in locational convenience (branching). But regulation of bank entry, state restrictions on branching, and prohibition of S&L competition for demand deposits all acted to restrain the competitive rent dissipation.

This equilibrium could not withstand the dramatic increase in the level and volatility of interest rates that began in the late 1960s and became especially important in the inflation of the 1970s. The first symptom that the equilibrium was unraveling was the extension of maximum rates to the S&Ls in 1966. As interest rates rose, the unregulated S&Ls began drawing time deposits from the commercial banks. In 1966 the S&Ls were allowed to pay only a fixed premium above the maximum rates for bank time deposits. This attempt to preserve the distribution of rents did not, however, work well. In the interest-rate environment of the time, fixed rate differentials exacerbated the volatility of the flow of funds between institutions.

Even more important cleavages were created by the unregulated capital markets' response to the regulation in this interest-rate environment. This response acquired a generic name—disintermediation. When market interest rates could quickly exceed the regulated rates by 500 basis points, depositors were motivated to look for close substitutes for deposits, and suppliers were encouraged to offer them. The first to benefit were the large depositors. Their major close substitute heretofore had been Treasury paper. Now, in the late 1960s and early 1970s, the commercial paper market grew rapidly and non-U.S. banks (joined by offshore subsidiaries of U.S. banks) began issuing dollar-denominated deposits, all at rates beyond the reach of the regulators. By 1970 it was clear that rate regulation on large time deposits was no longer viable, and these were deregulated. As monetary instability grew, the stage was set for new competition for the smaller depositors' business. Mutual funds arose that held the unregulated large-denomination deposits (and/or T-bills, commercial paper, Euro-dollar deposits, and so forth) and sold shares to the broad public. The average fee for this service is about 70 basis points per dollar of deposit, which was no longer enough to stifle their growth given the interest rates of the 1970s. When short-term rates rose into double digits, these funds came of age. From next to nothing in 1978, their assets grew to more than $200 billion by 1982 (or to roughly 15 percent of total time deposits of all financial institutions). An interesting wrinkle was that these funds typically allowed shares to be 'sold' by a check drawn on the fund's bank account. The implications for the future of non-interest-bearing checking accounts were clear.

The rise of the money market funds made it clear that monetary instability and technology had rendered interest-rate regulation obsolete. It also tore apart what remained of the political coalition supporting the regulation. There had long been a large bank-small bank conflict about the regulation. On balance, the larger institutions were net losers because the regulation hindered their ability to compete against money market instruments for large time deposits. Now their 'retail,' or smaller deposit, base was being eroded by the growth of the money market funds. More important, the rate regulation was a threat to the future growth of the larger institutions. The same technology—telephones, computers, advertising, and so on—that permitted the funds to gather $200 billion in a few years made it clear that the geographic balkanization of financial markets was ending. Many of the larger institutions saw their future in the retail market linked to geographic expansion. This meant ultimately attracting the customers of the smaller institutions as well as the relatively sophisticated and demonstrably mobile patrons of the money market funds. Much of the retail base of the smaller institutions consisted of customers who wanted locational convenience and who preferred an insured bank account to the new, unfamiliar money funds. They could be attracted, but not if the large banks had to pay the same rates as small banks. Accordingly, the large banks now openly supported deregulation.

In 1980 and 1982 Congress enacted legislation that, details aside, provided for phased deregulation of all deposit rates except business checking accounts. Given the history just outlined, the life of the latter anomaly may be brief. That history repeats a familiar scenario. A regulation once capable of generating rents was undermined by incentives—in this case to product innovation—created by the regulation that resulted in dissipation of the rents.

Oil

The history of oil-price regulation is brief and complex. I will ignore the complexities and, in the process, shove some arguably important interest groups into the background. Stripped to essentials, the facts are these. Maximum prices were set on domestically produced oil in the early 1970s. Price increases initiated by the Organization of Petroleum Export Countries (OPEC) in 1973 and 1979 pushed world prices substantially above the regulated domestic prices—roughly by a factor of two. The price ceilings were eliminated in 1980, and a windfall profits tax was imposed in their place. This excise tax was a specified fraction of the difference between the transaction price and some stipulated base price for the oil. The tax was to be phased out beginning in 1988, but the base prices have exceeded market prices since 1985. So the effective tax has been zero since then.

The way in which the rents captured from domestic oil producers were distributed is a matter of some controversy, which I will not join. It is sufficient to say that some were captured by intermediaries (refiners, wholesalers), some were captured by certain consumers, and some were dissipated in inefficiency induced by the detail of the regulation (most notably in the building of small, 'tea-kettle,' refineries). The weaseling here about consumers has to do with the uncertain effects of the regulation on product prices at those times—the majority—when there was no obvious queueing, and the uncertain benefits of the queue-inducing prices to typical consumers. To simplify, then, I will henceforth call all the downstream users of oil and refined products 'consumers.'

These consumers lost their benefits in 1980, but the industry was not deregulated. Instead, a new, arguably more efficient, method of collecting producer rents with a new beneficiary—the Treasury—replaced the old method. Accordingly, my focus here is not on the change in 1980, important as that may be in its own right, but on the larger question of why the producer rents were taxed in the first place.

The answer to that question, within the context of the ET, is fairly simple. It is to be found in the earlier history of regulation of the industry. Until the 1970s federal regulatory policy created producer rents. It sanctioned output quotas in the 1930s and enforced import quotas beginning in the 1950s. Both policy initiatives occurred in the wake of events (the Depression, the discovery of prolific fields in the Middle East) that reduced producer rents. Thus the producer interest had received its most active political support at times when rents were threatened. This is consistent with the aspect of the ET that emphasizes the role of regulation as a buffer against shifts in the distribution of wealth. Until OPEC increased prices in the 1970s, the important shifts were going against producers, and these were, as the theory predicts, offset by political action.

OPEC's actions, of course, resulted in a dramatic shift in the opposite direction. The rise in world oil prices generated a massive increase in the demand for domestically produced oil. In the absence of intervention, that would have generated a correspondingly large shift of wealth toward producers, thereby upsetting the politically optimum distribution of wealth. In these circumstances the theory predicts an offsetting tax on producer wealth, which is precisely what happened. The price ceilings and windfall profits tax would, in this theory, help to restore the politically optimum distribution as did the oil import quotas and production quotas in their day.

Thus the ET seems capable of telling a coherent story about regulatory policy both before and after the price increases. The about-face from generating to taxing rents did not represent some unintelligible loss of political power by the producers. (They were left with considerable rents from the OPEC price increases.) Instead, regulatory policy had to accommodate to a large outside shock, and the accommodation required just the sort of change in policy that occurred. The importance of this rent-buffering aspect of regulation is attested to by the fact that when price deregulation occurred, it was accompanied by an explicit tax on the resulting rents. The action of other countries in this period also tends to corroborate the importance of political rent-buffering. Those countries that had negligible domestic production (continental Europe, Japan), and consequently no domestic producer interest, allowed domestic prices to rise to world levels. Those that had substantial domestic production (Canada, Mexico), and would consequently, according to the ET, face the need to balance the interests of producing and consuming sectors, did just what the United States did. They kept domestic prices below world prices during the 1970s.

If the ET provides a unified explanation for oil regulation, it also suggests a corollary for the future. The current real price of oil remains about double the pre-1973 level. Any substantial decline to or below that level should produce pressure for revival of rent protection—through import quotas, tariffs, or other means. Any substantial increase, say to or above the 1973 or 1979 levels, would produce pressure for renewed taxation of the rents.

Summary

The ET was born in a wave of enthusiasm for the notion that regulatory agencies are captured by producers. That notion left little room for deregulation: as long as an industry is viable producers can benefit from regulatory restraints on competition. The ET, however, has evolved away from those origins toward an emphasis on the coalitional aspects of politics. Here the need to balance pressures emanating from competing interests plays a central role. This formulation leaves much more room for deregulation. As long as deregulation benefits some part of the relevant coalition, it cannot be ruled out as a viable policy option. When the deregulation benefits become large relative to the associated losses, the probability that the option will be exercised rises. This situation is more likely to occur if the regulation itself has generated inefficiencies, so that shedding the inefficiency through deregulation provides a potential source of benefits.

Indeed, if there is a model of regulatory entry and exit implicit in the ET, a few simple notions can provide its outlines. Regulation occurs when there is a wide discrepancy between the political balance of pressures and the unregulated distribution of wealth. The regulation (of, say, price) then creates incentives for wealth dissipation (through, say, cost increases), which ultimately make restoration of the preregulation status quo more attractive than continuing regulation. In such a model deregulation is not the correction of some belatedly recognized policy error. It is the last stage in a process about which, in principle, all the actors could have had perfect foresight at the beginning. In practice, of course, there can be mistaken entry into regulation, but none of the industries I have discussed are obviously in this group. Airline regulation, for example, lasted four decades, and the others lasted longer. Few private sector enterprises would be deemed mistakes, even in hindsight, if they survived so long. The point here is that erosion and ultimate elimination of profits, either of the political or monetary kind, is not a reasonable criterion for evaluating the success of a venture. Some attention has to be paid to how durable the profits are and how quickly any requisite exit from the activity occurs. Indeed, if a model with 'endogenous deregulation' proves a useful extension of the ET, it may help illuminate the selective character of entry into regulation. One reason for not regulating an industry would be the prospect that, for example, quality competition would erode rents so quickly that the upfront investment in political pressure required to implement regulation is not worthwhile.

Whether the deregulation is the predictable consequence of regulation or not, any explanation for deregulation derived from the ET has to look for some dissipation of the wealth upon which the political equilibrium in the theory is based. If there is only trivial wealth to redistribute, the ET finds no rationale for continued regulation.

I have examined some of the notable recent examples of deregulation to see how closely they fit the scenario implicit in the ET. Specifically, is there evidence of erosion of the wealth base on which the regulatory equilibrium was plausibly based? I also paid attention to magnitude and timing. Is the erosion plausibly large enough to suggest a crisis in which continued regulation would be unviable? Did the deregulation occur more or less promptly after the crisis?

The answers to these questions were mixed, but in the main followed the pattern implied by the ET. Two cases did not follow this pattern. Trucking was de facto deregulated when substantial rents were being earned by owners and workers who formed the heart of the relevant political coalition. Not only were the rents substantial, but there was no evidence of any serious erosion of them. Entry into long-distance tele-communications was deregulated after the technological threat to existing rents became clear but before substantial erosion took place. This is a less spectacular failure of the ET than trucking, but it has to be counted a failure nevertheless.

All the other cases follow more or less closely the pattern suggested by the ET. The railroads were deregulated after a long decline in demand that eroded the rents spread among producers and high-cost shippers. The precipitating crisis was the widespread bankruptcy and subsequent nationalization of important parts of the industry. Airline deregulation was preceded by a dissipation of regulatory rents because of service competition induced by the regulation. The dissipation followed promptly upon increased internal entry in the 1960s and was fairly complete by the 1970s when deregulation occurred. In the stock brokerage business, a sharp increase in institutional trading in the 1960s created the crisis leading to deregulation in 1975. This shift in trading patterns provoked increased service rivalry and bypassing of the stock exchange, which dissipated rents and upset the intra-industry allocation of rents. In banking, the inflation of the 1970s bred the crisis leading to deregulation of deposit rates. The accompanying rise in nominal interest rates and in their variability allowed good substitutes for bank deposits to draw funds from the banks, and, as with the brokerage industry, exacerbated a divergence of interests within the industry. The last case I examined, petroleum, is somewhat special in that price deregulation was supplanted by an excise tax, which I interpreted as the last in a series of moves consistent with maintaining the optimum distribution of rents. Accordingly, I argued that obituaries for petroleum regulation may be premature.

Even though the ET can tell a coherent story about most of the examples of deregulation, it still cannot answer some important questions about them. Specifically, some of the examples raise questions about the design of institutions and their adaptability that have so far eluded the grasp of economists. Airline regulation is probably the best case in point. When it became clear in the early 1970s that service rivalry was dissipating rents, the CAB encouraged limited, voluntary output quotas. This tentative move was quickly abandoned. A more vigorous, possibly compulsory, system of quotas seems never to have been discussed, though it held the potential for preserving some rents and enhancing efficiency at the same time. The same ends could have been served earlier by a less relaxed policy on internal entry combined with more flexibility on interfirm transfers of operating rights than the CAB evinced. (Interfirm route transfers could be accomplished only through merger.) The then flourishing lightly regulated market in truck operating rights provided a potential role model. In short, obvious measures to stem the forces leading to deregulation seemed available but went unused.

Similar questions are raised by the history of railroad regulation. Here the government provided a flexible political response to the crisis of the 1970s. It nationalized the bankrupt railroads and passenger service and replaced the previous cross subsidies with substantial explicit subsidies. These can be viewed as a substitute for regulation in distributing wealth. For railroads, subsidies are in fact the mode of choice in most of the world for achieving roughly the same distributive goals as American railroad regulation did. But, except for passenger subsidies, the American rail subsidies were terminated by the end of the 1970s. If the ET succeeds in explaining the end of railroad regulation, it is obviously not sharp enough to explain why the alternative is deregulation here and subsidies in other countries.

These examples illustrate why the deregulation wave came as such a surprise to most economists. It was one plausible response to forces that called for regulatory change. But it was not, in many instances, the only plausible response. Indeed, in some cases, like those just cited, more or different regulation would have been an equally plausible response. To show the difficulty here, one need only consider an important contemporary regulatory problem—how to respond to the massive losses in the savings and loan industry. It is utterly implausible that the dissipation of upward of $50 billion in public funds on unproductive investments and random transfers to impecunious borrowers is the low-cost method of serving this industry's political constituency. Accordingly, it requires only modest courage to predict that the current regulatory system will not survive much longer. Given our current state of knowledge, however, it requires a courage bordering on foolhardiness to predict the precise nature of the regulatory change that this particular crisis will breed. Policy options ranging from less regulation (such as reducing the scope of deposit insurance) to more regulation (such as increased capital requirements or restrictions on assets) would be consistent with resolving the crisis.

Twenty years ago economic theory faced the challenge of providing a basis for understanding the behavior of regulatory agencies. The ET was a modest step toward meeting that challenge. I have argued here that it also gives some insight into the forces that strain the institutional underpinnings of regulation. But so far a full analysis of the scope and form of these institutions remains unwritten.

Notes

I am grateful to Gary Becker and George J. Stigler for their valuable comments. I am also grateful to the Center for the Study of the Economy and State, Graduate School of Business, University of Chicago, for financial support.

1. George J. Stigler, 'The Theory of Economic Regulation,' *Bell Journal of Economics and Management Science*, vol. 2 (Spring 1971), pp. 3–21.
2. Richard A. Posner, 'Taxation by Regulation,' *Bell Journal of Economics and Management Science*, vol. 2 (Spring 1971), pp. 22–50, and 'Theories of Economic Regulation,' ibid., vol. 5 (Autumn 1974), pp. 335–58; Sam Peltzman, 'Toward a More General Theory of Regulation,' *Journal of Law and Economics*, vol. 19 (August 1976), pp. 211–40; and Gary Becker, 'A Theory of Competition among Pressure Groups for Political Influence,' *Quarterly Journal of Economics*, vol. 98 (August 1983), pp. 371–400.
3. My focus here is on de jure deregulation—that is, the institutional changes which would require new legal initiatives to reverse. The plausible role of arguably exogenous or temporary political shifts would grow if the administration of basically unchanged legal institutions were part of the inquiry. Changes in administration and, consequently, administrators can change the regulatory 'output' temporarily. It remains uncertain how many of Reagan's purely administrative initiatives, such as the reduced enforcement of the antitrust laws and of occupational health and safety laws, will survive the Bush administration. Evaluation of those initiatives is therefore premature.

4. Paul L. Joskow and Roger G. Noll, 'Regulation in Theory and Practice: An Overview,' in Gary Fromm, ed., *Studies in Public Regulation* (MIT Press, 1981), pp. 1–65.

5. See, for example, John R. Meyer and others, *The Economics of Competition in the Transportation Industries* (Harvard University Press, 1959); and Richard E. Caves, *Air Transport and Its Regulators: An Industry Study* (Harvard University Press, 1962).

6. George J. Stigler and Claire Friedland, 'What Can Regulators Regulate? The Case of Electricity,' *Journal of Law and Economics*, vol. 5 (October 1962), pp. 1–16.

7. William A. Jordan, 'Producer Protection, Prior Market Structure and the Effects of Government Regulation,' *Journal of Law and Economics*, vol. 15 (April 1972), pp. 151–76.

8. For example, Marver H. Bernstein, *Regulating Business by Independent Commission* (Princeton University Press, 1955).

9. 'Theory of Economic Regulation.'

10. Anthony Downs, *An Economic Theory of Democracy* (Harper, 1957); and Mancur Olson, *The Logic of Collective Action: Public Goods and the Theory of Groups* (Harvard University Press, 1965).

11. In a recent attempt to extend the ET by filling in some of the missing institutional structure, Weingast and Moran argue that, at the federal level, congressional oversight committees are the crucial intermediary between the regulatory agency on the one hand and the congressmen and their constituents on the other. They show that policy changes by the Federal Trade Commission were related to changes in the policy preferences of the oversight committee. This evidence, according to the authors, is inconsistent with the view that agencies are essentially unconstrained by legislatures and thus can pursue their own policy agenda. Barry R. Weingast and Mark J. Moran, 'Bureaucratic Discretion or Congressional Control? Regulatory Policymaking by the Federal Trade Commission,' *Journal of Political Economy*, vol. 91 (October 1983), pp. 765–800.

12. 'Taxation by Regulation.'

13. Most economists, for example, favor increased use of taxes and tradable pollution rights in environmental regulation and regard the reluctance of the regulators to adopt these techniques as an exception to the NPT. The history of antitrust is replete with restrictions—on price discrimination, vertical mergers, resale price maintenance, and so on—whose anticompetitive potential was first recognized by economists and more recently by judges and the enforcement agencies.

14. 'Toward a More General Theory of Regulation.'

15. Gary Becker, 'Comment,' *Journal of Law and Economics*, vol. 19 (August 1976), pp. 245–48, and 'Theory of Competition among Pressure Groups.'

16. There are, of course, modes of intervention other than rate or entry regulation that, in principle, are within the purview of the ET. Such measures as tariffs,

taxes, subsidies, and product standards have distributive implications that generate incentive for political pressure. On the broadest view, therefore, every industry is 'regulated' to some degree. This view, however, still begs a question about magnitudes: a handful of structurally competitive industries seem singled out for unusually large departures from competitive equilibrium.

17. Harold Hotelling, 'The General Welfare in Relation to Problems of Taxation and of Railway and Utility Rates,' *Econometrica*, vol. 6 (July 1938), pp. 242–69.

18. Theodore E. Keeler, 'Theories of Regulation and the Deregulation Movement,' *Public Choice*, vol. 44, no. 1 (1984), pp. 103–45.

19. The first type of change—convergence of the regulated and deregulated equilibriums—would also produce deregulation in the NPT. The difference between the two theories rests on how the convergence occurs and where the regulatory equilibrium is. In the NPT, convergence would occur because the source of market failure is removed by a change in technological or demand conditions. Then the market could be relied on to prevent a wedge between price and marginal cost. Since the ET equilibrium entails a *regulated* wedge between price and marginal cost, convergence occurs because the wedge that optimally allocates available rents differs trivially from the unregulated wedge.

20. The producers will continue to support regulation, because it promises some rents. But if the rents are too small to finance *politically effective* support, the political process will seek greener pastures. Producer requests for a free or even cheap lunch will not be honored.

21. Richard C. Levin, 'Regulation, Barriers to Exit, and the Investment Behavior of Railroads,' in Fromm, ed., *Studies in Public Regulation*, pp. 181–224.

22. Levin provided one measure of the magnitude of the unfavorable effect. He estimated that unrestricted abandonment would increase 1975 railroad profits by $1.4 billion. This was about one-tenth of industry revenues at the time, or roughly the same fraction of revenue as *total* industry profits in the best postwar years. He also estimated that, even with these added profits, the industry's rate of return on assets would be less than 9 percent, a figure that is still plausibly lower than the (deregulated) industry's cost of capital. Thus, even after the response to unrestricted abandonment is complete, continued secular decline in the industry's capital stock can be expected. Ibid., p. 192.

23. This came in two stages, the Railroad Revitalization and Regulatory Reform (4R) Act of 1976 and the Staggers Rail Act of 1980. These eased constraints on mergers and abandonments and provided a wide band (a variable-cost) floor and (1.8 × variable cost) ceiling within which individual railroads could set rates to all but 'captive' shippers without regulatory review. The net effect is to allow much more room for the railroads to abandon money-losing traffic and to compete with trucks and barges.

24. See Theodore E. Keeler, *Railroads, Freight, and Public Policy* (Brookings, 1983).

25. Thomas Gale Moore, 'The Beneficiaries of Trucking Regulation,' *Journal of Law and Economics*, vol. 21 (October 1978), pp. 327–44; and Nancy L. Rose,

'Labor Rent Sharing and Regulation: Evidence from the Trucking Industry,' *Journal of Political Economy*, vol. 95 (December 1987), pp. 1146–78.

26. The airlines had the usual tax incentives to overdepreciate. These were enhanced by the CAB's use of rate-of-return targets as part of its rate regulation procedures.

27. Theodore E. Keeler, 'Airline Regulation and Market Performance,' *Bell Journal of Economics and Management Science*, vol. 3 (Autumn 1972), pp. 399–424; George W. Douglas and James C. Miller III, *Economic Regulation of Domestic Air Transport: Theory and Policy* (Brookings, 1974); and William A. Jordan, *Airline Regulation in America: Effects and Imperfections* (Johns Hopkins Press, 1980).

28. See, for example, Keeler, 'Airline Regulation and Market Performance.'

29. Keeler calculated his competitive marginal cost on the assumption that unregulated carriers would face the same labor costs as regulated firms. Ibid.

30. Card's analysis of airline mechanics' wages also finds little obvious impact of deregulation on this worker group. David Card, 'The Impact of Deregulation on the Employment and Wages of Airline Mechanics,' *Industrial and Labor Relations Review*, vol. 39 (July 1986), pp. 527–38.

31. That possibility appears to have been realized. According to Morrison and Winston, deregulation has produced gains of $2.5 billion a year for the owners. Steven Morrison and Clifford Winston, *The Economic Effects of Airline Deregulation* (Brookings, 1986).

32. Leonard Waverman, 'The Regulation of Intercity Telecommunications,' in Almarin Phillips, ed., *Promoting Competition in Regulated Markets* (Brookings, 1975).

33. Waverman compares an estimated microwave cost function to AT&T's cable costs. He finds that microwave average costs flatten at an output that is a trivial fraction of total output on typical high-density routes. He also finds that the minimum cost for microwave dominates the average cost of cable at any cable output level. Ibid.

34. The role of numbers, which Stigler emphasized and which I have so far ignored, may be more important here than in the other cases. Stigler argued that the politically dominant group would be neither too small to count politically nor too big to overcome free riding and rational ignorance. Depending on one's view AT&T may have been too small (one firm) or too big (3 million stockholders) to dominate the compact group (large users and private system operators) that would benefit from deregulation of entry. See Stigler, 'Theory of Economic Regulation.'

35. See Gregg A. Jarrell, 'Change at the Exchange: The Causes and Effects of Deregulation,' *Journal of Law and Economics*, vol. 27 (October 1984), pp. 273–312.

36. Ibid.

Comments and Discussion

Michael E. Levine

I agree that Peltzman's subject is an important area of exploration. In 1981 it occurred to me that the airline deregulation I had just finished designing and implementing at the Civil Aeronautics Board was not predicted either by my own earlier work or that of others. So I began to examine the implications of what I had just been through for the economic theory of regulation, which I, along with most scholars, took very seriously at the time.[1]

The strategy of my paper was, in effect, to say, 'Well, the economic theory didn't predict airline deregulation or trucking deregulation or many of the other deregulations (communications, banking, securities) under way at the time, and therefore it was possible that the public interest theory was still alive.' Perhaps public interest motives explained what Sam Peltzman has called regulatory exit. Since there was no evidence that the economic theory was dead (a great deal of regulation continued that could best be explained by that theory), I suggested in my paper that we needed some kind of meta-theory to reconcile regulation, which could be predicted by the economic theory, and deregulation, which seemed to be motivated by public interest considerations. We needed a theory that could predict when one might expect deregulation and when one might not. Or, more generally, we needed a theory to explain when one could expect government action oriented toward special interests as opposed to government action oriented toward mass interests, which at the time I conflated with the public interest. (I have rethought that since.)

We must now get the question right, as well as attempt an answer. I think the question is not, as Peltzman puts it, which of the two competing theories is the theory that explains regulation. One can find regulatory examples that seem perfectly consistent with the economic theory of regulation, as Peltzman does here, and find examples that do not seem consistent with that theory, as Peltzman does here, though I will question his classification.

One way to look at this paper is as an interesting attempt to challenge my 1981 assumption that the economic theory has been disproved and to prove it can be reconciled with the deregulation of the 1970s. Peltzman concludes that maybe it can and maybe it cannot. I tried to add up the score: it is hard to tell whether out of the seven cases he presents Peltzman won four or five or fewer. I admire his attempt to be fair, but I think he may have been too generous to the economic theory. I think it did less well than he claims, though I do believe in its continuing vitality as one model of regulatory origin and conduct.

In these comments I want to focus on two quite different points. First, I want to examine more closely the case I know most about, which is airlines, and suggest that Peltzman misinterprets the evidence, partly because he omits—deliberately in one case and inadvertently in some others—important benefits of airline regulation to special interest groups and partly because he does not, I think, characterize regulatory facts and institutions correctly. Airline regulation and deregulation are complex; Peltzman treats them rather cursorily. Second, when Peltzman decides to ignore the politics of the regulated industries in favor of the economics, I believe he turns away from the most promising avenue of exploration: attempting to reconcile the 1970s' deregulation with both the economic theory and the public interest theory.

Let me start with airline deregulation. I would argue there is no real evidence of systematically declining rents from airline deregulation. There is even perhaps some evidence of renewed *increase* in rents at the time deregulation began to occur. I base that argument on several points.

For one thing, accounting profits are very difficult to use as a measure of what rents were being accrued in the airline industry. We now recognize that the airline business had hidden assets in the form of leases on gates and historical leases on hangars, as I discovered when I tried to expand service and to repair New York Air's airplanes at the airport (LaGuardia) where that airline was based. Complex questions often arose about aircraft depreciation and valuations. And large unrealized gains and gains unrecognized by the accounting system were buried in airline balance sheets. For example, in 1979 or 1980 one airline that was having a particularly bad year recorded its only significant item of profit by writing off a DC-10 in an accident at Los Angeles. The gain from insurance payments compared with the book value of the aircraft was so large that it outweighed a considerable operating loss the airline had incurred that year. Any account of rents being taken from regulation must, I think, consider the accumulation of those kinds of assets and effects.

At the same time enormous information assets were being developed, what could loosely be called good will, but what I have recently argued are important effects that take advantage of information economies of scope and scale to produce market positions which turn out, in retrospect, to have been well protected from new-entrant competition.[2] The value of that protection has proved to be considerable and was not reflected in the analysis Peltzman cites.

In addition, accumulated regulatory rents can be found in the certificate values that existed before deregulation and in the going-concern value of firms that have lost money consistently since deregulation, when certificate values dropped to zero. Because of positions they acquired and occupied under regulation, many airlines developed positive value in the face of continued operating losses. Pan Am's and Eastern's ability to continue in business while regulated and suffering large accounting losses on the operating side was paralleled after deregulation by their ability to continue to lose large sums of money under the discipline of market competition and to cover those losses by converting hidden assets to cash. This process has revealed the magnitude of the hidden assets built into those balance sheets: they were enormous, literally billions of dollars.

Furthermore, Peltzman consciously excludes labor rents. They were extremely significant, as I argued in a 1976 paper.[3]

There were also very large cross-subsidy benefits built into the system, whether one is talking about the political advantages of funding nonstop service between Portland and New York (which could not sustain nonstop service, except in the particular conditions of regulation and jet service in the late 1960s and early 1970s) or about the political benefits of relatively equal fares on high-density and low-density routes. Those were all substantial benefits to groups that were being maintained by regulation.

Peltzman overlooked some of these rents, I think, partly because the traditional setting of airline regulation was different from the description given in his paper. The CAB treated the fare structure rather inconsistently over the history of regulation until the 1970s, when I lost a court case based on the arbitrariness of the fare system. Before the DPFI (domestic passenger fare investigation) decisions of the early 1970s it did not systematically favor low-density over high-density routes. The fare structure was a product of old airmail regulation, and the amounts needed to make up the difference between operating losses and federal subsidies changed by increments over time as varying factors affected different routes and types of service.

Congressman John E. Moss and Ralph Nader brought the lawsuit that forced the board to explicitly consider the fare structure in the early

1970s. The board responded with the DPFI, which did institutionalize distance and density cross subsidies as well as rents built into the system that clearly affected the population of those who would be willing to continue to support regulation. In economic theory terms, the DPFI should have created a substantial constituency for continued support of regulation.

There was also really no change over the years in the government's willingness to encourage extra capacity in the industry. Industry over-capacity was a fact of life from early in the history of regulation. It is not important, really, whether it was or was not profitable for airlines; what is more important is that it did not change much over time. Probably from the early 1930s until deregulation, there were biases built into the system that did not change in magnitude.

Because the industry was cyclical, the forces producing overcapacity changed periodically through the years. Jets were introduced and were larger than the units they replaced. These introduced indivisibilities into the system, which exaggerated profit swings. The jets lowered load factors from 1958 to 1963, but they had enormous service advantages that produced a surge of market growth with the prosperity of the middle and late 1960s. Load factors came back up and airlines acquired large earnings.

Since service competition was allowed, the airlines that were doing well in 1964–69 ordered wide-body planes. These were delivered just as the economy turned down. So airlines did not do well in the early 1970s. They were just beginning to do better when the oil shock hit, inducing the recession of 1973–74. But by the mid-1970s, when deregulation fever was at its highest, the airlines were beginning to do very well again. They were beginning to fill all those aircraft that had been ordered and that had been a millstone around their necks in the early part of the decade.

The jets and DPFI lowered average load factors. Contrary to what Peltzman says in his paper, the DPFI *institutionalized* (not eliminated) distance cross subsidy, but the degree to which this system was generating or not generating rent did not fundamentally change. Neither the govern-ment nor the industry cartel ever limited service competition and capacity competition, because such restrictions were prohibited by the Civil Aeronautics Act of 1938 and its successor, the Federal Aviation Act of 1958.

I think it is important to have some theoretical understanding of why prohibitions on control of capacity or service were built into a statute that everyone characterizes—including me, certainly, in my earlier work—as creating a cartel. If Congress was trying to design a cartel statute, that is an odd loophole to have left in.

The airline business was *not* institutionally almost identical to the trucking business, as the Peltzman paper suggests. The airlines were allowed much less explicit collusion. The CAB allowed airlines to ineffectively negotiate rates with other airlines through filings but did not allow them rate-bureau-type meetings on their own. And the board zealously enforced its version of the antitrust law. Many of us believed its version was not very procompetition, but the CAB did enforce it, often over airline protests, which the Interstate Commerce Commission certainly never did. Moreover, there were many fewer airlines than trucking firms. And airlines had consumer customers, whereas trucking had producer customers, a distinction that, I believe, is politically relevant.

Finally, producer and geographic opposition to deregulation was genuine and persistent. As a victim of that opposition, I can say it was personally vicious. At one point, in a strange political twist on Adam Smith, I was called a communist for favoring airline deregulation.

Only United Airlines favored deregulation until the end when it became clear that the regulatory system as operated by Alfred Kahn and our colleagues was no longer providing anybody protection. Then people scrambled to get rid of the CAB because they didn't care for the uncertainty of leaving it around. But up to that point only United favored deregulation, and the opposition of the others was clearly not related to their profitability. Many of the opponents were money losers and had always been money losers, and others had made money through the regulated period.

Let me turn briefly to what I think are the analytical opportunities lost in this paper on the political side. Why some deregulations and not others fit the economic theory needs to be explained. As I said in my earlier paper, we need to look for a meta-theory. For that, we should probably look in the area Peltzman leaves unexplored by deliberate choice—the political economy of institutional change. We should look for answers using the recent literature that involves the modern economics of information and agency and examine not only coordination costs, which the traditional economic theory focuses on, but the costs to consumers and producers of monitoring the process and the complex relations among consumers, producers, legislators, their own committees, and agencies. If the results of theories that ignore these dimensions perplex us when we look at problems that are rich in the same dimensions, then it makes sense to look for answers among that complex web of relationships.

We need to deal in our models with the stubborn fact that inefficient regulatory structures persist over very long periods of time, contrary to what Gary Becker and Peltzman believe. But I do appreciate Peltzman's candor in noting that the 'length of the run' matters in evaluating the theory. We must deal with institutions like agricultural regulation and occupational licensure. And we need to deal with the fact that CAB regulation was identified as inefficient as a theoretical matter in a book by Lucille Keyes in 1951, was revealed to be inefficient as an empirical matter by Richard Caves in 1962, and was shown to be inefficient as a comparative matter in a study I made in 1965. Yet this process survived for more than forty years.

The ICC and its progeny lasted largely undisturbed from 1920 on. It was forty years in the making and sixty years in the ascendancy before it was dealt with in the Staggers Act and other revisions of the late 1970s and early 1980s. The CAB, as I have said, persisted for forty years. We need some theory to explain why these agencies all ran out of gas in one five-year period in the late 1970s.

Since the answers are more likely to be found in the modern political economy of agency and information, they will be heavily influenced by the peculiar economics of information, including its public-good character and economies of scope. Answers will also be found in the incentives and effects of policy entrepreneurs, 'economists on white horses,' politicians looking for issue labels that will position them clearly and effectively, and journalists looking for headlines that will capture viewers and readers. It is in these areas, I think, that we will begin someday to reconcile the economic theory and the public interest theory of regulation.

Roger G. Noll

Peltzman examines whether what he calls the economic theory of regulation accounts for the deregulation movement of the 1970s and early 1980s. He sees the issue as a race between two contenders. The alternative he calls the normative-as-positive theory, which he uses as something of a straw man to be knocked down by positive economic analysis.

In my view a more apt name for the economic theory of regulation as described by Peltzman is the Chicago theory of government. In one sense his ET is narrower than the economic theory of politics, for it either ignores or only partly incorporates several other important contributions to the economics of political behavior. In another sense, it is broader than a theory of regulation, for most of the papers cited by Peltzman seek to explain much more than economic regulation.

The Chicago theory of government has three essential components. One is that changes in the opportunities for using the coercive power of the state to capture rents lead to institutional change. Initially, the theory focused on using regulation to increase the imperfection of markets in order to capture monopoly rents. But the theory is symmetric. Peltzman focuses on how the erosion of opportunities for monopoly rents can lead to deregulation.

A second component is that the costs of effective political organization differ among economic interests and so affect who is likely to be the winning bidder in the competition for the use of the coercive power of the state to generate rents. In particular, producer interests are more likely to have lower organization costs and hence to be favored by regulation. Peltzman acknowledges that Mancur Olson has made the biggest contribution to this line of argument; however, the Chicago theory, as I explain more fully later, has not incorporated very much of the theory of mobilization bias as developed by Olson and others. In fact, none of the early Chicago theory papers cites Olson except for George J. Stigler's classic article, and there the reference is only to one idea: that organizations already organized for other purposes (such as the provision of private goods to members) have a natural advantage in the political process. In general, Chicago theory models collapse the theory of mobilization bias into a variable called political power, which sometimes is a parameter and sometimes a function of the size and economic stake of an interest group.

The third main component of the Chicago theory, emphasized more by Gary Becker and Richard A. Posner than by Peltzman or Stigler, is the convergence of policy toward efficiency. That is to say, over the long run economic institutions, broadly defined to include aspects of the economic system that are controlled by government, tend to be efficiency enhancing. The reason, of course, is that inefficient institutions leave potential rents uncollected, so that in principle all parties to a policy can find a Pareto improving change to which they can agree. The limitation to the convergence to efficiency is simply the transactions cost of identifying the change and organizing to acquire it from government.

These three ideas about how policy changes constitute the theory that Peltzman tests against the normative-as-positive theory. My point of departure with Peltzman is to propose that other economic theories of government exist and ought to be considered. To avoid silly paternity debates about contemporary concepts of the economics of politics, I focus on economic arguments first stated before the publication of Stigler's 1971 article. My aim here is to describe some other economic theories of government and the predictions they make about the possible causes of deregulation.

Three Alternative Economic Theories

The first alternative theory I call Arrow I (after Kenneth J. Arrow), or social choice theory. It emphasizes the fundamental indeterminacy of democratic political systems. Originally the focus was on policy instability, a line of research that ultimately led to chaos theory, as promulgated by Linda Cohen, Steven Matthews, and Richard McKelvey. Chaos theory demonstrates that literally any policy outcome can be obtained from some form of agenda in a simple majority-rule democratic process; the primary lesson is that policies are inherently unstable and transitory.

The economists and political scientists who pursued this first wave of social choice theory were not satisfied with its implications about such remarkable instability, in part because in reality political systems are obviously not chaotic. Consequently, in the mid-1970s research in this area sought to determine why politics is stable. Today the leading explanation is the theory of structure-induced equilibrium, as originally proposed by Kenneth A. Shepsle and Barry Weingast. In essence, participants in the political process, recognizing its propensity for chaotic behavior and being risk averse (and hence valuing stability in its own right), construct constraints on policy change that increase the difficulty and cost of upsetting the status quo. Examples are bicameral legislatures, separation of powers between the legislative and executive branches of government, and the committee structure and rules of procedure in Congress.

Recently several scholars have applied this theory to study regulatory policy. One conclusion emerging from their research is that deregulation usually took place only where much of it could be accomplished without changing legislation; a regulatory agency could thus upset the status quo without obtaining any but the president's approval. Another conclusion is that sometimes the courts upset the status quo by interpreting statutes in ways not contemplated by Congress or the regulatory agency at the time the legislation was passed. In both circumstances subsequent legislative action was reactive: Congress lagged behind actual policy and was forced into action by the reality of the new status quo it had inherited from either the agency or the courts.[4]

Another recent offshoot of Arrow I is William Riker's theory of political entrepreneurship. A political entrepreneur is a person who invents a way to undo structure-induced stability. He or she discovers how to take advantage of the fundamental instability of majority rule within the constraints imposed by the institutional arrangements designed to induce stability. In the regulatory sphere, Alfred E. Kahn and his colleagues at the Civil Aeronautics Board, and Darius Gaskins and friends at the Interstate Commerce Commission, subscribed to this theory.[5] Essentially, these officials discovered how to accommodate a policy innovation within the proregulatory legal structure in which they operated. Their initial actions redefined the status quo and thereby changed the equilibrium legislative outcome in Congress, leading to legislative ratification of their initiatives after the fact.

The second alternative economic theory might be called Arrow II, because it is rooted in Arrow's early contributions to the economics of uncertainty in general equilibrium. Anthony Downs, however, was the first to relate these ideas to politics, so a fairer designation would be the Arrow-Downs theory. The basic conception is to apply state-preference theory and the theory of incomplete markets to the political sector. In particular, one might expect that some political contingencies are not freely traded in markets; the technical term is, I believe, bribery. Also, changes in information alter the choice of political strategies and outcomes.

Downs's line of analysis emphasized the relationship between voters and candidates for office; perhaps his most influential contribution was the theory of rational ignorance among voters. Because a single vote is both a weak indicator of preferences in multipolicy elections and an almost inconsequential act for outcomes, voters have essentially no incentive to devote effort or resources to becoming informed about the comparative merits of candidates. This concept has important implications for the role of interest groups in the political process, as argued initially by Downs and developed more thoroughly by Olson. Specifically, it introduces two means of political influence other than formal organizations: supplying free (and easy to digest, perhaps entertaining) information to voters that motivates their participation in the political process, and providing political saliency, a major national issue that commands attention and motivates action in the absence of political organization. It also introduces another variable affecting the costs of organized participants—the costs of becoming sufficiently informed to take rational political action. So presumably organization costs will enter more heavily in areas of policy where information is voluminous and arcane than in areas where one can readily become informed.

Politicians can take advantage of salient issues by being the source of free information to voters on an important issue of the moment. An example from the early and middle 1970s was stagflation; the free information was inefficiency in regulated industries. Indeed a fairly common complaint was that 'excessive regulation' was undermining business performance. Rationally ignorant voters, concerned about macroeconomic performance, could be expected to respond to this information by favoring economic deregulation, even though a fully informed analysis might conclude that economic regulation had only a trivial effect on national economic performance. Moreover, the simplicity of the point with respect to economic regulation—'prices are too high'—may explain why regulatory reform was far more successful in that area than in many other areas where it was proposed, such as drug regulation, environmental regulation, and workplace safety and health regulation.

The third contending economic theory of regulation I call Leviathan. It is associated with the public choice scholars, such as James M. Buchanan, William A. Niskanen, and Gordon Tullock. This theory says essentially that the coercive power of the state is monopolized by those in power and that they exploit it to their own benefit. Hence political actors—elected officials and bureaucrats—extract the rents from coercion, not the interest groups or other citizens affected by the policies. According to this view, for example, airline regulation would not be expected to benefit airlines, pilots, and flight attendants except incidentally, owing to a technical inability of government to extract all the rents. Instead the primary beneficiaries would be officials of the Civil Aeronautics Board, as a monopoly supplier of airline regulation, or the president and members of Congress, as monopoly providers of coercive power to the CAB, or both.

The Leviathan theory predicts change in either of two circumstances. First, exogenous changes may cause political actors to be presented with new ways to enrich themselves. Second, citizens may gain control over government by forcing constitutional change, using instruments ranging from the initiative to revolution. Buchanan is an advocate of several constitutional changes to limit the size of government and the scope of its authority in economic policy. Obviously deregulation was not a result of constitutional change. Thus only the first reason holds: government officials enriched themselves through deregulation.

The discussion thus far has led to a more interesting horse race, for there are now five entrants instead of two. The next task is to see how each stacks up against the facts of the 1970s and 1980s. But before proceeding with that analysis, I went to explore more thoroughly the strengths and weaknesses of the Chicago entrant.

Critique of the Chicago Theory

Critics of the early Chicago theory claimed it bordered on tautology, in that (1) government actions surely redistribute wealth in some fashion, and (2) the relatively simple version of mobilization bias in the theory failed to predict who would win the bidding for a policy and seemed capable of explaining almost any regulatory outcome. Of course, the second point is much like the Arrow I conclusion of chaos, but the Chicago papers were written as though the equilibrium in regulation were unique and stable. Hence part of the criticism was that the theory assumed away the Arrow paradox.

Peltzman's important contribution was to provide a partial answer to both points, and in so doing to make the theory more complex. He does so by using the 'can opener' assumption, a form of cheating ubiquitous in economic theorizing. Specifically, he takes a generalized function (here, 'power') to serve as the vehicle for making comparisons among claimants to policy rents in terms of their political influence. Power is, in turn, determined by organization costs. Positing the right power function gives the model an equilibrium and permits comparative statics on its parameters.

Peltzman's theoretical trick implicitly assumes away the Arrow paradox and the Arrow-Downs uncertainty problems. Basically it amounts to collapsing the policy area to one dimension, measured in dollars. By implication, the theory takes complete markets for granted and condenses all of politics to a single dimension in which median voter theorems can be invoked. Insofar as a model of elections and voter behavior underpins the Chicago theory, it is the unidimensional median voter equilibrium.

Becker and Stigler proposed another way to counteract criticism of the Chicago theory, by assuming that, deep down, everybody has the same preferences. If so, majority-rule voting does not need to overcome differences in ideal points in the policy area and has an equilibrium—indeed, a unanimous equilibrium—at our collective bliss point. Rational ignorance is not a problem either, because social decisions can be delegated to a single informed expert whose self-interest coincides with society's interest.

Both means of avoiding the Arrow paradox and uncertainty problems leave one large issue unresolved, even if one accepts the core of the arguments. That issue is the decision about the distribution of wealth. Even if society can decide unanimously what should be produced, the problem of how to divide it has no equilibrium unless society adopts decision rules that predetermine the outcome.

Becker's recent work illustrates the preceding argument quite elegantly. Becker assumes that a differential incidence of transactions costs among citizens simultaneously determines political power and solves the divide-the-pie problem. But that requires also assuming something that in principle, as a theoretical matter, is false, namely that the allocation of relative power (for example, voting strength) can solve the impossibility theorem problem without creating a dictator. Becker shows that his assumption allows society to approach an efficient equilibrium, limited by the transactions cost of policy change.

What Becker's work demonstrates, beyond the kind of assumptions necessary to derive his conclusions, is the observational equivalence of the Chicago theory of government and the normative-as-positive theory. If the powerful need to create inefficiency to collect their rents, they ought to be able to orchestrate a mutually beneficial transaction with the unpowerful, essentially going public with their power. The constraint on such behavior is the transactions cost of selling out. As regards deregulation, the ultimate result should be greater efficiency, with at least as much wealth in the hands of the former beneficiaries as there was under regulation. The act of deregulation would allow an exogenous, unpredicted change that lowered the transactions costs or increased the potential efficiency gains of selling out.

Peltzman tends to emphasize only one of the possible paths to deregulation that is consistent with the Chicago theory. He focuses on exogenous changes that made maintaining the cost of the regulatory system unattractive. In essence, he argues that industries lost the rents accruing from regulation for one of two reasons. Either the costs of keeping other powerful interests in the supporting coalition became too great, or changes in the industry's costs and demand made the total amount of rent that could be extracted lower than the costs of maintaining the regulatory system. I will not comment on the cases he describes except to point out that his discussion leaves several unsolved puzzles.

—If railroad deregulation came because the costs of keeping trucks, small towns, and passengers in the coalition began to exceed the rents accruing to the railroads, why did regulation last so long? Before the railroad bankruptcies of the 1970s the industry suffered two decades of losses. If economic scholars figured out that railroads were the long-term net losers from regulation fifteen years before deregulation began, cannot we invoke rational expectations to postulate deregulation at least that early, if not earlier? Moreover, in the other cases of economic deregulation in transportation, the bankruptcies tended to follow deregulation, not precede it. Why were railroads different?

—Although the timing issue is also important in telecommunications, two other issues stand out. First, deregulation took place when AT&T's rents from regulation—and the subsidy for rural telephone service—were growing, not decreasing. This coalition was profiting handsomely, not suffering declining fortunes as the railroad industry was. Obviously the Chicago theory should not predict deregulation in two circumstances: when rents are growing and when rents are declining. Second, telecommunications deregulation did not occur in the states—at least, not yet. Should not at least the large states, which are microcosms of the national political economy, respond more or less in the same way as the federal government? And if Chicago theory predicts they will, why is the process so slow?

—Why did the deregulation of stock brokerage occur roughly simultaneously with the regulation of futures trading? The former is explained by a rising elasticity of demand for brokerage services. Is it plausible to believe that exactly the opposite shift in demand elasticity was taking place in another type of brokerage?

Peltzman is disarmingly critical of the Chicago theory's ability to explain some cases of deregulation. Yet, if anything, he leaves still other loose ends like those mentioned above. But these are insufficient data to call the horserace. How do the other theories compare in their explanatory power?

Evaluation of the Several Economic Theories

Leviathan predicts that the rents went to the government. I think this idea can be laughed off, though Michael Levine's postregulatory career gives me pause. Nevertheless, one can safely dismiss the idea that the decline in rents accruing to the airline industry and its employees was not transferred to Michael E. Levine, Alfred E. Kahn, Elizabeth E. Bailey, Jimmy Carter, and Edward M. Kennedy. It does not stand to reason that the CAB maximized its profits by putting itself out of business. Thus the Chicago theory beats Leviathan by many lengths.

Arrow I argues that policy change is random and cyclic and does not require underlying changes in its prospective benefits and costs. But in the later versions that invoke structure-induced equilibrium, it also predicts that policy change will be infrequent—and slow to respond to exogenous changes that might occur in its underlying economics. The emphasis is on entrepreneurs who discover ways to upset an old equilibrium to their own political advantage. Stephen Breyer tells us that Edward Kennedy played this role in the airline case; later Kennedy failed in his attempt to play the same role in reforming drug regulation, even though the potential efficiency benefits there seem to be comparable in magnitude. Presumably the Chicago distinction between the two cases would be that airline interests, but not drug interests, had lost a stake in maintaining regulation. But the counterpart to 'service competition' in airlines is the dramatic increase in the cost of drug research and development brought about by the 1962 amendments to the statutes governing drug regulation. Is the Chicago view plausible? Or is this an example of unpredictability: Edward Kennedy and Alfred Kahn proved to be a more effective entrepreneurial team than Edward Kennedy and Donald Kennedy, then the commissioner of the Food and Drug Administration. Certainly a valuable exercise for the interested student is to examine the failures of reform as well as the successes and to check out which explanation seems to work in both instances.

Finally, the Arrow-Downs-Olson school of imperfect information and mobilization needs to be examined. It comports with one puzzling fact: in the 1970s and 1980s several political candidates did link regulation with the overall performance of the economy, causing the issue to become sufficiently visible for several economists to respond by estimating how much of the problems of rising inflation and declining productivity could be attributed to regulation. Even the Business Roundtable weighed in, financing an expensive study to document these costs. Now why political actors attached plausibility to the argument that regulatory reform was an effective way to 'whip inflation now' remains something of a mystery, but the kind of mystery that fits nicely with the branch of the economic theory of politics that emphasizes imperfect information. Moreover, the steam seems to have run out of the regulatory reform movement roughly coincidentally with the end of the stagflation period, late in the first half of the Reagan administration. Our interested student could spend profitable hours examining this explanation in more detail too.

The various economic theories of deregulation also make different predictions about the future. As I read it, the Chicago theory predicts movement toward marketlike solutions to the problems of environmental regulation, no reversal in economic deregulation, and state deregulation in areas where the federal government has already deregulated. Arrow I would not predict that any of these changes are more likely than any other. But under that theory, some reregulation will happen eventually, when some political entrepreneur figures out how to disrupt the existing state of policy for his or her own selfish ends. Arrow-Downs might predict reregulation as the salient national issue of sagging economic performance wanes, and so interest group politics regains its former significance in this domain of policy.

In my estimate the research is still inconclusive as to the relative merits of the various economic approaches to politics. The main inference to be drawn from my arguments is that all the approaches have something to contribute.

The Chicago theory has brought out the importance of the magnitude and distribution of the economic outcomes in explaining political change and, even more significant, has shown that political actors have more rents to distribute if they can arrange for an industry to operate efficiently. In the 1960s and 1970s economists probably overreacted to the waste that their research uncovered in virtually all areas of regulatory policies. As a result, they underestimated the power of economic efficiency arguments. The relation between the Chicago theory and the normative-as-positive theory is actually its strength, not its weakness, even if, as I believe, the connection may lead to Panglossian conclusions.

The weakness of the Chicago theory is that it has not yet adequately taken into account the important lessons from Arrow I and Arrow-Downs. Arrow I recognizes that institutional arrangements matter, for they lend stability and probably define the direction of feasible policy changes that might upset the preceding coalition. Arrow-Downs emphasizes the role of informational imperfections and the significance of incomplete political markets. The general theory of regulation that will be taught in the year 2100 will be an amalgam of these major ideas of Chicago, Arrow I, and Arrow-Downs.

General Discussion

The paper left many participants disappointed that a 'meta-theory' has not emerged which can adequately explain when, and in what sectors, regulation is put into place and when and where it is dismantled. Consequently, participants defended a variety of eclectic or special case theories and offered various macroeconomic or economic disturbance explanations for the deregulation movement of the 1970s. Nancy Rose suggested that regulatory action takes place when there are substantial disruptions in the national economy. Many of the regulations that have recently been dismantled had their origins during the Depression and accompanying economic disruptions of the 1930s, she noted. Likewise, the industries that have recently been deregulated were in many instances industries that were severely affected by two major disruptive economic events of the 1970s: the surge in oil prices (airlines, trucking, natural gas, petroleum, and electric utilities) and the increase in volatility and levels of interest rates (banking and financial markets).

Robert Hall agreed, noting that 'depression and war give us high taxes and regulation,' whose burdens must then be worked off gradually over time. He observed that the recent period of deregulation preceded only slightly the large tax cuts of 1981, and suggested that the two events represented the final working off of the consequences of the Depression and World War II. Paul Joskow commented that economic disruptions often change the distribution of political power and create opportunities for public policy entrepreneurs to rearrange things to their advantage. He favors a theoretical approach that considers the interactions among economic dislocations of many kinds and integrates aspects of the economic theory of regulation with the other theories. In the case of airlines and trucks, he feels the entrepreneurial influence of Alfred Kahn and Elizabeth Bailey cannot be overstated. They and the other regulators had a policy agenda and used the administrative process, and the lags in the administrative process, to their advantage to accomplish certain changes. The process gave them a 'window of time, perhaps a year when the public had a chance to see what some of the benefits of deregulation would be to them,' Joskow observed. This enabled them to identify a constituency for their proposed reforms, which made it more likely that the reforms would be ratified by legislation and the courts.

Alfred Kahn agreed that what he called the 'demonstration effect' is important. He suggested that changes in the economic conditions of the industry, together with a macroeconomic environment of stagflation, set up conditions for deregulation in the airlines, where there were weak unions and most of the rents had already been dissipated. Deregulation in trucking then followed partly because the lessons learned from airline deregulation were transferred to trucking by the same political coalition, consisting of '[Edward] Kennedy, Ralph Nader, the Consumer Federation of America, Common Cause, the National Association of Manufacturers, and the National Federation of Independent Small Businesses.'

William Nordhaus also stressed political factors, arguing that the bunching of regulation or deregulation movements across different sectors of the economy within short periods of time suggests that the ideology of the policymakers in power is an important influence. But that is tempered by the efficiency considerations that operate if the efficiency losses from political action get too large relative to the rents being redistributed. That explains why wartime price controls and allocation mechanisms are always quickly dismantled, he said.

Robert Crandall noted that an overall political or economic theory of regulation must be able to explain why regulation was expanding at such a rapid rate in areas like health, safety, and environmental regulation at the same time that regulatory constraints were being relaxed in other areas. And it should also be able to explain international anomalies, such as the fact that many other countries still do not allow private microwave businesses to compete with the primary providers of long-distance telecommunications service.

Notes

1. Michael E. Levine, 'Revisionism Revised? Airline Deregulation and the Public Interest,' *Law and Contemporary Problems*, vol. 44 (Winter 1981), pp. 179–95.
2. Michael E. Levine, 'Airline Competition in Deregulated Markets: Theory, Firm, Strategy, and Public Policy,' *Yale Journal of Regulation*, vol. 4 (Spring 1987), pp. 393–494.
3. Michael E. Levine, 'Financial Implications of Regulatory Change in the Airline Industry,' *Southern California Law Review*, vol. 49 (May 1976), pp. 645–64.
4. See John Ferejohn and Charles Shipan, 'Congress and Telecommunications Policy Making,' in Paula R. Newberg, ed., *New Directions in Telecommunications Policy*, vol. 1: *Regulatory Policy* (Duke University Press, forthcoming); and Matthew D. McCubbins, Roger G. Noll, and Barry R. Weingast, 'Structure and Process; Politics and Policy: Administrative Arrangements and the Political Control of Agencies,' *Virginia Law Review*, vol. 75 (March 1989), pp. 431–82.
5. Much of the descriptive material about how deregulation actually happened stresses the importance of specific iconoclasts within the reforming agencies. See, for example, Martha Derthick and Paul J. Quirk, *The Politics of Deregulation* (Brookings, 1985).

Organizing Regulatory Space

L. HANCHER AND M. MORAN

Introduction

Regulation is virtually a defining feature of any system of social organization, for we recognize the existence of a social order by the presence of
rules, and by the attempt to enforce those rules. Whether the matter
concerns the control of sexual morality, the flow of traffic, the licensing of
drugs, or the imposition of taxation, the core of the activity remains
constant: it involves the design of general rules, the creation of institutions
responsible for their implementation, the clarification of the exact meaning of a general rule in particular circumstances, and the enforcement of
the rule in those circumstances. As a large and rich literature testifies,[1]
there is much to be gained from exploring these common features of
regulation, and from comparing the experience of rule-making and implementation in different settings.

Within the broad field of regulation, however, a special place is occupied
by the processes which are the subject of the preceding chapters: the
regulation of economic activity in Western capitalist societies, where organization on market principles is combined with a high level of industrial
development. Economic regulation under advanced capitalism has several
distinctive features, and these features in turn shape the character of regulatory activity. The purpose here is to explore the more important implications for the connections between capitalism, culture, and regulation.

We begin by identifying the most distinctive features of economic
regulation; go on to suggest that regulation is best understood through
the analytical device of 'regulatory space'; and then sketch how national
political and legal settings, historical timing, organizational structure, the
character of markets, and the nature of issue arenas all influence the shape
of regulatory space and the allocation of power within that space.

Regulation and Economic Regulation

The most striking single feature of economic regulation is that it is
dominated by relations between large, sophisticated, and administratively

complex organizations performing wide-ranging economic and social tasks. Such bodies obviously include the various agencies of the state—government departments, quangos, and specialized regulatory bodies—but they also encompass organized interest groups, trade unions, and firms. The importance of the large firm in the regulatory process is particularly notable. Indeed an important theme is the central place of the large, often multinationally organized, enterprise as a locus of power, a reservoir of expertise, a bearer of economic change, and an agent of enforcement in the implementation process. Understanding economic regulation, then, means understanding a process of intermediation and bargaining between large and powerful organizations spanning what are conventionally termed the public and private domains of decision-making. But this understanding points to an important, related, feature. The economies of advanced capitalist societies have been universally marked by a high level of state intervention. Regulation is embedded in the practices of the interventionist state. The aims of regulation are commonly only explicable by reference to the wider structures and more general aims of the interventionist system. The French Government's attempts, for instance, to intervene in the affairs of Thomson can only be understood in the context of its wider sectoral policy ambitions.

Economic regulation under advanced capitalism—its formation as much as its implementation—invariably involves interdependence and bargaining between powerful and sophisticated actors against a background of extensive state involvement. But the particular character of the individual nation-state adds two other distinctive features, the first to do with the role of law, the second with the allocation of sovereign authority. Nations with advanced capitalist economies are almost universally governed, or claim to be governed, according to some principles of constitutional democracy. The exercise of public power, in other words, rests on legal authority, and this legal authority is made legitimate in turn by appeal to popular will. Of course by no means all economic regulation is cast in the form of legal rules, but the central importance of the principle of constitutionalism means that the range and form of regulation is deeply influenced by the particular conception of the scope and purpose of law which prevails in any particular community at any particular time. To put the point more technically, the purpose and character of economic regulation is in part a function of the nature of the surrounding legal culture.

Conceptions of the proper role of law are in turn intimately connected with notions about the appropriate allocation of sovereign authority. Economic regulation is practised in a highly developed form in societies combining organization on market principles, domination of many sectors by giant firms, and political rule according to formally democratic principles. The combination of these three features sets up great tensions in the regulatory process, a tension reflected in much of the literature on the subject. Democracy, especially in the Anglo-Saxon tradition, is closely associated with parliamentarianism: that is, with the assumption that a monopoly of legitimate authority flows from the command of popular and legislative majorities. Regulation, on this conception, is a process by which popular and public control is exercised over the workings of private power in the market-place. The idea was well expressed by one of the most eloquent defenders of American regulation under the New Deal, when he spoke of the regulatory agencies created in that period as 'the outposts of capitalism' designed to control the market-place 'lest capitalism by its own greed, fear, avarice and myopia destroy itself.'[2]

The notion that economic regulation is a process by which sovereign public authority disciplines and controls private interests has exercised a particularly strong influence over American thinking about the subject. Since the literature on regulation, in the English language at least, is largely American inspired, the notion has in turn deeply influenced debates about the historical development of economic regulation and about its proper place in modern democratic systems. The most important consequence has been an instinctive belief that 'private' influence over the regulatory process is illegitimate. If regulation is assumed to be an activity in which some ideal of the public interest is pursued at the expense of the private, then evidence that private interests benefit from regulation, or that they exercise a strong influence over the regulatory process, is naturally treated as a sign that the purpose of the activity has been distorted.

These notions are particularly marked in the long-running debate about 'capture' in regulation. The very idea of 'capture' betrays an assumption that there is a sphere of public regulatory authority which ought to be inviolate from private influence. Both Kolko's historical interpretation of regulation as a response to the needs of powerful corporate interests, and the vast literature 'exposing' particular instances of regulatory capture, are united by the belief that the practise of regulation has involved the subordination of public authority to sectional interest.[3] Likewise the most influential critique of the interventionist regulatory state produced by a political scientist—Lowi's *End of Liberalism*—rests on the argument that there once existed, and should exist again, a liberal constitution possessing an inviolable public core, bounded by law, and clearly distinct from the private sphere.[4] Even observers sceptical of 'capture' theories have shared the assumptions of their opponents: debate has typically turned on attempts to rebut the empirical accuracy of capture theory, rather than on attempts to question the assumption that there should indeed exist an inviolable public sphere.

It is undoubtedly the case that arguments about the capture or otherwise of the regulatory process raise important issues of both constitutional principle and substantive outcome. Questions about who benefits from regulation, and who is allowed to shape the decisions made by regulatory agencies, are plainly central to understanding and evaluation. Yet to couch the discussion in terms suggesting the necessity of identifying and defending a clearly delimited sphere of public authority is unhelpful. It rests on the culturally restricted constitutional assumption that the roles of 'public' and 'private' in the regulatory process can be authoritatively distinguished. But as we explore below, there actually exist significant national variations in how the public–private divide is conventionally drawn. More seriously, the 'capture' debate obscures perhaps the single most important feature of economic regulation under advanced capitalism: that the most important actors in the process are organizations, and organizations which, regardless of their formal status, have acquired important attributes of public status. Of the formally 'private' organizations with public status, none is more important than the large firm.

The role of the large firm is unique. Whereas the regulation of the behaviour of individual 'private' actors is concerned with the imposition of a public or general will on private citizens, large firms cannot be described as private 'takers' of regulation in this sense. They have acquired the status of 'governing institutions'.[5] As Lindblom has argued, in a market economy firms carry out functions of an essentially public character. Their decisions on investment, employment, and output have important allocational and distributional implications which resonate in the 'public' sphere.[6] As we have seen time and time again in this volume, the corporate strategy of individual firms is a major determinant of the direction of the regulatory process. Public governmental agencies do not merely act upon firms as, so to speak, external agents. Corporations are major centres of expertise, and they constitute significant independent social and administrative hierarchies. Their integration into the implementation of regulation is very often a precondition of its success. This is so even where the ownership structure of a firm is independent of a (state) public agency; but the fusion of private and public ownership is actually now a common feature of advanced capitalist economies.

Economic regulation of markets under advanced capitalism can thus be portrayed as an activity shaped by the *interdependence* of powerful organizations who share major public characteristics. In the economic sphere no clear dividing line can be drawn between organizations of a private nature and those entitled to the exclusive exercise of public authority. The fusion is made more complete by one of the features remarked on earlier: economic regulation is an integral part of the activities of the modern interventionist state. While much economic regulation does indeed involve the making of rules and the enforcement of standards, this occurs within a framework of much more diffuse intervention, concerned with a wide range of often unstated and even contradictory objectives. Economic rule-based regulation is not a distinct activity; it is woven into a larger fabric of intervention. The overall pattern is marked by a high level of social and administrative complexity. In regulation much of the most important activity consists in the routinized application of general principles, which may be devised by the regulatory authority or alternatively may be little more than the company's standard operating procedures, officially endorsed as general principles. Hence we say that certain ways of doing things become 'institutionalized'. At the same time, however, organizational alliances are constantly forming and reforming without any reference to a conventional public–private divide. Parties bargain, co-operate, threaten, or act according to semi-articulated customary assumptions. The allocation of roles between rule makers, enforcers, and bearers of sectional interests constantly shifts, again obeying no obvious public–private dichotomy. In such a world firms are not bearers of some distinct private interest which is subject to public control; they are actors in a common sphere with other institutions conventionally given the 'public' label.

Economic regulation under advanced capitalism is therefore best conceived as an activity occurring in economies where the public and private are characteristically mixed, where the dominant actors are powerful and sophisticated organizations, and where the biggest firms have taken on many of the features of governing institutions. In this world the language of regulatory capture is largely devoid of meaning. Questions about who participates in and benefits from regulation are certainly important: explaining the complex and shifting relationships between and within organizations at the heart of economic regulation is the key to understanding the nature of the activity. But little can be gained by depicting the relationship in the dichotomous language of public authority versus private interests. On the basis of the evidence collected in this volume we can see that different institutions have come to inhabit a common regulatory space. The critical question for the analyst of the European regulatory scene is not to assume 'capture', but rather to understand the nature of this shared space: the rules of admission, the relations between occupants, and the variations introduced by differences in markets and issue arenas. The character of regulatory space is our next theme.

Public Space and Regulatory Space

Framing the problem in this way mirrors the approach recently adopted by Crouch in his attempt to make sense of different national configurations in the place given to organized interests in the policy process. Crouch begins with the notion that it is possible in any particular community at any particular time to identify a 'public space', which he describes as the 'range of issues over which general universal decisions are made within a given political unit.'[7] He then explores the historical experiences which have, in different European countries, allowed different groups of participants into this public space. We can likewise speak of a 'regulatory space' whose dimensions and occupants can be understood by examining regulation in any particular national setting, and by analysing that setting in terms of its specific political, legal, and cultural attributes.

The concept of 'regulatory space' is an analytical construct. It is defined, to adapt Crouch's language, by the range of regulatory issues subject to public decision. A number of obvious consequences follow from this. First, precisely because it is a space it is available for occupation. Secondly, because it is a space it can be unevenly divided between actors: there will, in other words, be major and minor participants in the regulatory process. Thirdly, just as we can identify a general concept of regulatory space in operation in a particular community we can also speak of specific concepts of regulatory space at work in individual sectors: in pharmaceuticals, for instance, issues of safety and price control are subjects, or potential subjects, of regulatory activity, whereas in the automobile sector only the former set of issues are included. Fourthly, because 'regulatory space' is an image being used to convey a concept, it can be augmented by similar images: thus because an arena is delineated space we sometimes speak of a 'regulatory arena'. The boundaries which demarcate regulatory space are defined in turn by a range of issues, so it is sensible to speak of regulatory space as encompassing a range of regulatory issues in a community. In these terms regulatory space may be furiously contested. Its occupants are involved in an often ferocious struggle for advantage. Any investigation of the concept involves examining the outcomes of competitive struggles, the resources used in those struggles, and the distribution of those resources between the different involved institutions. In other words, the play of power is at the centre of this process.

Discovering who has power in regulation involves paying close attention to the relations between the organizations which at any one time occupy regulatory space. But the idea of a space also directs us to a far more important aspect of power. It encourages us not only to examine relations between those who enjoy inclusion, but also to examine the characteristics of the excluded. That the structure of power is shaped by modes of exclusion from any political process is an elementary truth. In the case of economic regulation, however, the observation has a particularly sharp point. When we speak of the politics of economic regulation under advanced capitalism we are speaking of a set of power relationships dominated by large organizations. These complex organizations—the biggest firms, representative associations, regulatory agencies, central departments of state—are organized in administrative hierarchies whose method of doing business is shaped by standard operating procedures. Institutional procedure, that is, the routine application of established practices, rather than individual choice, is the dominant influence in deciding who is taken into, or kept out of, regulatory space. Since the rules of organizational life have a routinized character, exclusions tend to be systematic. Understanding who is in, and who is out, is therefore particularly vital, and depends crucially on analysing the customary patterns of organizational relationships in any particular regulatory space.

If groups can be organized into, or organized out of, regulatory space, the same can be said of issues. There are no obvious natural limits of boundaries to regulation. Notions of what is 'regulatable' are plainly shaped by the experience of history, the filter of culture, and the availability of existing resources. The fact that economic regulation is predominantly regulation by and of large organizations means, however, that notions about appropriate scope are routinized, and are embedded in organizational procedures. Understanding why some issues are prioritized, included, or excluded, at different times and in different places, thus demands an exploration of how organizations become committed to, and maintain a commitment to, particular definitions of the scope of regulatory space. Likewise, understanding changes in the notion of what issues should be included demands attention to the shifting balance of power within and between institutional actors inside the common regulatory space.

The factors determining the shape of this space, and the relative position of its occupants, are many and complex. Here only a sketch of the main influences can be offered. But the gist of understanding lies in one simple observation: the most important relationships in economic regulation are relationships between organizations. Thus the key matters requiring explanation—inclusion and exclusion, the relative power of the included, the scope of regulatory issues—will be illuminated in terms of the characteristics of the operating organizations: the cultural environment within which they work, their standard operating procedures, the customary assumptions which govern their interaction, and the resources at their disposal. Understanding economic regulation therefore involves understanding the terms under which organizations enter regulatory space, and defend their position within it. This is in turn heavily influenced by the prevailing general political attitudes and legal traditions existing in any community to the place of organized interests in the policy process. In other words, *place* matters in determining the nature of regulation, an insight also central to Crouch's exploration of national peculiarities and public space. We therefore next sketch the importance of place.

National Peculiarity and Regulatory Space

The central problem examined in Crouch's analysis is the character of the transition from competitive to organized capitalism—from economies marked by comparatively unregulated competition between a large number of actors to economies where a small number of organizations dominate a closely regulated economic environment. The political response to this transformation has been highly varied: in some communities the legitimacy of certain actors, including peak associations, unions, and large corporations, in policy-making is largely denied; in others their incorporation, though thorough, is accomplished informally; in others there still exist developed, statutorily based forms of incorporation. These variations are largely a reflection of national differences in the strength of what Maier calls the 'parliamentary parenthesis': that episode in the history of political development when state institutions claimed a monopoly of authority legitimized by command of parliamentary majorities.[8] Crouch explores the varying strength of the parliamentary parenthesis, tracing the differing capacities of individual states to command a continuing monopoly over 'public space' to a range of deeply rooted historical experiences: the character of pre-capitalist group organization, the timing and incidence of the transition to capitalism, the route taken to organized capitalism, and the varying legacies of fascism.

Our sketch only gives the outline of Crouch's subtle argument, but it serves to highlight one key feature: although the economies of advanced capitalist nations exhibit similar patterns of extensive regulation dominated by a small number of large organizations, there exist significant national variations in the political and constitutional responses to these similarities. Different national traditions conceive of the public-private authority in different ways; and different national traditions likewise allow access to regulatory space to different constellations of actors. The differences are summed up in the importance given to concepts of legal and political culture. Though some argument exists about the independent explanatory power of cultural variables, there can be no doubt that they are at the very least important in mediating the influence of historical experiences. Recognizing the significance of cultural variations means recognizing, in Hayward's words, 'the operation of culturally based dominant values that inhibit or preclude some kinds of arrangements but favour others'.[9]

In regulation, culturally formed assumptions about the purpose and role of law are particularly significant. These assumptions can determine whether regulation happens at all, its scope, how far it is embodied in statute or formal rules, and how far the struggles for competitive advantage which are a part of the regulatory process spill over into the Courts. The variables grouped under the umbrella of legal culture have been well summarized by Friedman, who speaks of

the values and attitudes which bind the system together and determine the place of the legal system in the culture of society as a whole . . . Do groups or individuals willingly go to court? For what purpose do they make use of lawyers? . . . What is the relationship between class structure and the use or non-use of legal institutions? What informal special controls exist in addition to or in place of formal ones? Who prefers which kind of controls and why?[10]

One of the most striking illustrations of the significance of these kinds of variables is provided by a comparison of Anglo-American and European conceptions of public law. In the Anglo-American tradition, where a legal concept of the state is either absent or only weakly present, public law has been essentially concerned with the pragmatic control of public power, especially of the kind of discretionary power which is embedded in the process of economic regulation. In the UK especially, law has not been viewed as the great interpreter of politics. The continental European tradition, more firmly rooted in Roman law, by contrast assigns a central place to the state both as idea and as institution. This establishes the 'unique character of public authority in terms of sovereignty and/or function.'[11] The jurisprudence of public law, enforced through a distinct and specialized court structure in France and West Germany, is developed independently of private law norms, whereas in the United Kingdom and the United States the control of public authority has been characteristically secured through the ordinary courts.[12]

Within these broad traditions, distinct national configurations abound. Vogel has recently explored the striking differences produced by British and American attitudes to the relevance of litigation in the regulatory process, contrasting the detailed rules and adversarial enforcement common in the United States with the discretionary guidelines and co-operative implementation characteristic of so much British regulation.[13] Within the European tradition very different national patterns also exist. In France the ideal of a unitary state and the 'paternalistic conception of a state prerogative police power, conceived as the general regulation of French society for the public good' still permeates public law theory and practice.[14] The constitution is viewed, not so much as a source of legit-imate authority, but rather as an expression of the idea of the unity of the state. In such circumstances, especially in the sphere of economic regula-tion, administrative courts are considered to be of relatively limited value in challenging the rulings of administrations 'addicted to discretionary adaptation of the rules to suit the political convenience of governments'.[15] This truncated approach to constitutional values is reflected in public law procedures and norms. The administrative courts may review the legality of a decision but will not, except in very unusual circumstances, substitute their own evaluation of the facts for that of an administration. The Council of State—the highest administrative 'court'—has indeed consistently refused to interfere in economic decisions involving the exercise of dis-cretion.[16]

The place of the constitution and constitutional values in shaping the practise of regulation in West Germany stands out in sharp contrast. The Basic Law of 1949 is viewed as embodying a juristic idea of the state. When combined with Roman law traditions of deductive legal reasoning from a unified set of principles, this has meant that the 'constitution has acquired an imperative character and policy has become highly judicialised'. The West German Constitution is seen 'not just as a general framework establishing a minimum consensus about certain principles'—in the manner of, for instance, the American Constitution—but as a 'political programme containing particular substantive goals'.[17] This commitment to legalism and formalism has limited the exercise of executive power and given the Courts a prominent role in controlling the scope of regulatory activity and the range of regulatory discretion. Equipped with highly generalized constitutional principles such as the right to equal treatment, the freedom to own property, and the freedom to pursue a profession, the German Courts have not hesitated to invalidate both administrative regulation and legalisation.

This sketch illustrates some of the important ways in which the character of a legal culture mediates the regulatory process, fixing the scope of regulatory space and influencing who gains entry and on what terms. Variables attributable to distinctive legal cultures may also determine the ability of 'excluded' interests to challenge the existing distribution of power within the common regulatory space. Legal culture may further operate as an important variable in determining the way in which the different rules interact to create a regulatory framework. For instance, the interplay of rules established by collective bargaining and the rules established by statute or common law in the regulation of labour markets, varies considerably between the large European democracies. Similar variations exist in financial regulation: some disclosure practices which are simply the standard operating procedures of large firms in the UK have become 'juridified', or expressed as legally binding rules, in the USA.

A similar observation can be made about the more general influence of political culture, conceived as the prevailing set of beliefs and assumptions about the nature of political authority in a community. As an explanatory tool, however, political culture is most useful when disaggregated into its constituent parts: in other words, when we examine the attitudes to such matters as the role of law and the Courts, the place of organized interests, and the appropriate terms for the exercise of legitimate authority.

It might be thought that an emphasis on the mediating power of cultural assumptions overstates the consensual and stable character of regulatory practise, at the expense of the bitter struggles and often rapid changes which can occur in regulatory arenas. But this danger only occurs, first, if culture is indeed assumed to have a changeless, timeless character, and secondly, if we fail to appreciate the sectoral specificity of regulatory arenas. In reality, a consideration of the changing impact of culture on the shape and occupation of the common regulatory space can be particularly illuminating. In the United Kingdom many of the most important regulatory arrangements—for instance, in the financial community and in the professions—were evolved in a political culture marked by a deferential attitude on the part of mass publics towards authority, and by a preference for informal and private regulation on the part of élite groups. These factors ensured that regulation was conducted inside enclosed regulatory communities shielded from the attention of democratic politics. This is what the characteristic British preference for 'self-regulation' amounted to. In the last couple of decades the deferential and secretive character of the political culture has been subjected to some strain, as a result of a combination of government policy failures, changes in social structure, and wider alterations in the character of popular values. One of the most important consequences—illustrated to perfection by the experience of the financial services industry—has been the invasion of regulatory space by organizations (such as central departments of state and highly organized pressure groups) previously excluded under the assumptions of a deferential and secretive culture.

Regulation occurs, it is a truism to observe, in particular places, and therefore place matters. The most important delineation of place is provided by the boundaries of the nation-state. Nations arrange their regulatory spaces in distinctive ways. Yet it is also plain that national peculiarities are by no means the whole story. Within particular countries the characters of different regulatory communities show great variety. Many influences shape these variations, but one of the most important is time—for regulation is practised in time as well in space. The historical timing of regulatory initiatives and development can thus be critical. To this we now turn.

Historical Timing and Regulatory Space

Why is the British insurance industry subject to much tighter statutory regulation than is banking in the United Kingdom? Why are banks in the United States much more tightly controlled by law than are securities firms? Why was a model of central banking regulation initially evolved in the UK during the middle and later decades of the nineteenth century later widely copied in different national settings? The observations prompting these questions illustrate the importance of historical timing in the shaping of regulatory space.

The significance of timing arises from an elementary characteristic of regulation as an activity: it has to be organized. Without appropriate institutional arrangements implementation simply does not take place. The act of organization in turn demands resources: the knowledge to create or to copy regulatory institutions; the money and people to run those institutions; the expertise to devise rules, and to monitor and police their enforcement. The organization that controls these resources will dominate regulatory space; and the organization that commands the necessary resources at the historical moment when regulation is initiated has a good chance of exercising a continuing dominant influence. (For example, the British ABPI has been able to retain continuing control over the regulation of profits on the sale of its member companies drugs to the NHS, stemming from its initial historical domination.) The significance of timing is emphasized by the nature of regulation itself. Regulation is largely a matter of organizational routine, of institutionalized procedures, punctuated by occasional crises, economic or political. Such crises serve the function of inducing change, or at least initiating a search for alternative institutional arrangements. In between periods of crisis, the more dominant organizations can retain and consolidate their position of superiority, so that alternative mechanisms of regulation are ignored or suppressed. The moment of historical origin of regulation can thus be of the utmost significance.

Regulation almost always happens because some sense of crisis is precipitated, but the crisis can occur at very different historical moments: extensive national regulation of banking in the United States began in the critical atmosphere of the American Civil War; extensive national regulation of the British banking industry had to wait for the atmosphere created by the international banking collapse of the 1970s. The balance of institutional forces at the moment of crisis is plainly of enduring importance. In some sectors at the crucial initial moment the state commands the necessary regulatory resources, and its own agencies or actors dominate the process. In the creation of new institutional frameworks to regulate telecommunications, for instance, the state has been the major actor in the United Kingdom. In others—the examples of pharmaceuticals and securities illustrate the point—the control of expertise and personnel gives the regulatory initiative decisively to firms. The key analytical point is that understanding regulatory arrangements in the present depends on understanding the historical configuration out of which they developed.

It will be plain that, in respect both of nations and of particular sectors, there are 'early' and 'late' regulators. This simple fact of historical timing has profound implications for regulatory arrangements, because it intimately affects the international diffusion of regulatory forms. The most casual acquaintance with any important substantive area of regulation soon reveals that institutions and rules are widely imitated. Copying is obviously an economical way of solving the problem of regulatory design. Since regulation typically is begun under pressure of time, or in conditions of crisis, the incentive to imitate is great. The result is that 'early' regulators often provide a model for countries following later along the regulatory road. De-regulators follow a similar path as the 'export' to Europe of many American de-regulatory models illustrates.

The process by which regulatory design is diffused internationally is little understood, but it is apparent that models emanating from countries exercising great economic and political power are most likely to be the objects of emulation. This is part of the explanation for the widespread diffusion in the past of the English model of central banking. Likewise, the United States is a world leader in control of emissions standards. In her study of telecommunications regulation and deregulation Hills has identified a similar pattern, involving the export of American standards and market practices to the industries of competitors.[18]

Regulation takes place in particular places and in particular times, and these two factors have an immense influence on the shape of regulatory space. But there exists a further important consideration. Regulatory space is dominated by organizations. The implications of this are examined in our next section.

Organizational Structure and Regulatory Space

Economic regulation is predominantly regulation by and through organizations. In any particular arena the character of these organizations will vary; the variations in turn influence the nature of the activity. The most fundamental effect governs who or what exercises any power in the regulatory process. The everyday practise of regulation of course involves dealings between individuals. But these individuals characteristically only enjoy access to regulatory space because they have some organizational role: as employees of firms, as the voice of an organized interest, as servants of the state. Private citizens rarely have a significant legitimate role in the formulation and implementation of regulatory policy. Intellectuals may occasionally contribute to the shaping of regulatory ideologies, though even in such cases their influence depends heavily on their identification with the organizational bearers of scholarly knowledge, such as universities and professional associations. Individual political entrepreneurs like Nader in the United States can likewise periodically intervene, though as the history of Nader's campaigns indicates continuing influence depends heavily on the ability to embody activity in organizational form.

Organizational status is thus the most important condition governing access to regulatory space. Private individuals who do not perform organizational roles, or who are not bearers of organizational interests, enjoy limited and usually temporary success in any attempt to intervene. Citizens are 'takers' of regulation; organizations are makers and shapers. Very occasionally private citizens may succeed in mounting a successful legal challenge to a regulatory programme, but sustained or permanent participation is precluded.

The organizations typically dominant in regulatory space, whether they are conventionally labelled 'private' or 'public', share important characteristics. They are usually big—in the case of the state and the largest firms very big indeed—and are marked by the elaborate internal division of administrative labour and extended administrative hierarchies. These features impose both co-operative and conflictual elements on the practise of regulation. When regulatory space is dominated by large, hierarchical bodies regulation inevitably becomes a co-operative matter, because only by such a means can it be accomplished. Almost nothing of significance is done in regulation as the result of the actions of any single individual or simple organizational entity. The regulatory task is subjected to an elaborate and elongated division of labour. Even the design and implementation of comparatively simple standards (like the introduction of transparency guidelines to advise doctors on prescribing) depends on co-operation between large numbers of individuals occupying very different roles in the hierarchies of different organizations. This observation merely serves to reinforce one of our earlier points: that the big firms who are major occupiers of regulatory space can in no sense be pictured as mere 'takers' of regulation. Even if they are not explicitly involved in the formal process of rule-making, nothing would happen to promulgated rules without their extensive co-operation.

In economic regulation, therefore, the most important parties are bound together in relations of exchange and interdependence. But the co-operation enforced by the division of administrative labour should not conceal the way the organizations who inhabit regulatory space are riven by competition and conflict. Indeed the essence of regulatory politics is the pursuit of institutional advantage: the pursuit of advantage in the market-place, measured by indices like market share and profit; and the pursuit of command over the regulatory process itself, as measured by the right to make rules and to command their means of implementation. Regulation—and the rules and distribution of power through which it operates—is always a 'stake' of industrial or political struggle.

Organizational status as a condition of access to regulatory space; large-scale, extended hierarchies; a refined division of administrative labour; enforced co-operation in the implementation of regulation; the relentless

pursuit of institutional advantage: these are the most important consequences of the organizational character of economic regulation under
advanced capitalism. But of course these shared institutional characteristics still allow for considerable diversity, and this diversity influences not
only the allocation of power within the regulatory space but also perceptions about what should be regulated, and how the necessary tasks should
be accomplished. Four influences are particularly important: the way
organizational procedures impose different views about the substance of
regulation; the variations introduced by governmental structure and structure of ownership; variations in the internal cohesion of firms; and variations in the social and cultural cohesion and economic strength of
industries and sectors.

Powerful organizational structures not only dictate, through their standard operating procedures, how things are to be done; they also impose
beliefs about what *can* be done. As Hall expresses it, organizational
structures 'tend to impose certain perceptions, responsibilities and interests on the actors'.[19] The most distinctive feature of organizations is, of
course, precisely that they are indeed formally organized. But organization
involves not only a set of procedures for taking decisions; it also involves
customary assumptions, often barely articulated, about the substantive
purposes of the activities which are being pursued. Understanding economic regulation thus demands not only an examination of national
cultural traits; it also necessitates an exploration of the distinctive subcultures within leading organizations in the regulatory process. For instance,
the phenomenon of *pantouflage* (the career movement of civil servants out
into industry) has produced precisely such a distinctive subculture in
France.

These variations in organizational subculture are obviously linked to
national variations in institutional structures, that is, to routinized forms of
rule-making and rule application. The nature of these structures in any
particular regulatory space will be in part a product of external factors. In
political systems like that of the United States, for instance, where government structures are highly fragmented, the same pattern of fragmentation
tends to be repeated inside individual regulatory arenas. The results
include perpetual contests for authority between different Federal agencies, and constant demarcation disputes between Federal and state agencies. The structure of governmental agencies often in turn imposes a
particular organizational pattern on an industry or an industry's peak
association because, especially in respect of the formal organization of
interest groups, there is a pronounced tendency for such arrangements to

mirror those of the state. The fragmented, competitive pattern of state organization in the United States is thus likewise reflected in the balkanized character of pressure group organization.

Intervention in regulation by international or supranational agencies such as the European Commission has, contrary to what may be commonly assumed, exacerbated the patterns of fragmentation and competition within the state. In some sectors, such as consumer electronics, the process of internationalization has weakened the regulatory capacity of national governments and enhanced the importance of self-regulation by the firms as they make their own response to market pressures. In the extreme case of the capture of a state agency by a firm such as Thomson, a firm in nominal state ownership, this can amount to the regulation of government by the firm.

In an equally obvious way the structure of ownership in a regulated industry also shapes the nature of its organizational world. Since firms are among the key actors in regulatory space, the degree of concentration of ownership is critical. The domination of industries by a small number of giant firms is one of the commonest features of market organization in advanced capitalist economies, but the extent of this domination varies significantly between industries. There is a pattern varying from comparative dispersion (in the securities industry) to oligopoly (automobiles and pharmaceuticals) to monopoly (telecommunications).

Nor is the degree of concentration of market power the only way in which firms shape the organizational character of regulatory space. The internal political character of individual firms, though little investigated, is also a crucial variable. In some firms hierarchical control is strong and the regulatory response of the institution is co-ordinated in a unified fashion. In others formal organizational unity only conceals deep differences between functional divisions, or even between warring factions. It is perfectly possible for separate divisions to operate independently of, and indeed in competition with, each other in the struggle for regulatory advantage.

It will be plain that the internal social and political cohesion of the biggest firms in an industry is an important influence on the kind of organizational life which develops in a particular regulatory arena. The same observation may be made about the social character of an industry as a whole, for different parts of the economy plainly vary greatly in their social cohesion. Some—like the banking industries of many advanced industrial nations—exhibit high social and cultural unity. Such industries are typically dominated by a social élite, enjoying shared life experience and social origins, and often bound by similar ties to élites in state institutions. The possibility that this sort of social cohesion can add cement to organizational structures is plainly contingent on the economic and social history of particular parts of economies.

Economic regulation under advanced capitalism is largely transacted through big organizations. The structure of these organizations, their internal cohesion and their capacity to co-operate with each other, is a function of a wide range of factors in their environment. But one final important consideration should be noticed. Although the organization of a particular regulatory space can plainly only be understood by reference to the social structure of industrial and state élites, it is not simply a product of these features. Patterns of organization can themselves be self-sustaining, and thereby institutionalized. In economic regulation control of the means of organization is itself a major resource. This is in part due to the instrumental resources—of money, information, and personnel—which organizations command. But it is also due to the special legitimacy which attaches to institutional status in regulatory worlds where the key transactions are those involving organizations. Institutions develop their own independent interests and, in the world of economic regulation, have powerful means of ensuring their continuing defence. The history of the regulation of British industrial relations, for instance, is inexplicable without reference to the fragmented and dispersed character of British trade-union organization, and to the capacity of the numerous unions to defend their institutional autonomy. This process of fragmentation is exacerbated in labour markets, so that for trade unions external exclusion is an organizational prerequisite for building internal solidarity. Likewise in the American financial services industry, the historical fragmentation of markets, and the equally dispersed nature of the organizations involved in regulation, are explicable only in terms of the capacity of competing institutions to maintain the existing fragmented structures.

Understanding the nature of the regulatory process in advanced capitalist economies involves, above all, understanding the character of the organizational forms dominant in regulatory arenas. Our sketch shows that the allocation of power and influence within regulatory space is influenced both by legal tradition and by a wide range of social, economic, and cultural factors. But the character of the transactions between organizations is also affected by a more immediate set of influences: by the particular kinds of issues which arise in regulation and by the particular areas where those issues are dealt with. Common issues and common arenas bind actors together in relations of interdependence. Analysis of the process of regulation from the perspective of interdependence is by no means new, but the concept of regulatory space offers additional insights into the character of interdependence.

Interdependence and Regulatory Space

Over two decades ago Lowi developed the notion that patterns of politics were in part determined by the kinds of policies which were at issue—in other words, that 'policies make politics'.[20] He also identified a particular pattern associated with the politics of regulation. Within such a broad schematic framework, however, in any particular regulatory arena there exists a diversity of organizations which interact through a range of networks or linkages of varying density of formality. As we have observed, these linkages may be articulated in terms of formal, binding legal rules, standard operating procedures, or indeed in the form of mere conventions. The range of those involved in the regulatory process will not only vary from issue to issue but will also be deeply influenced by convention or constitutional practice, or by prior patterns of regulatory practice. Inter-organizational linkages are the subject of a large, existing literature on network theory which demonstrates the significance of policy communities and networks within which 'élite coalitions' allocate issues to particular arenas, manage the policy agenda, and control the range of participants allowed into decision-making.[21]

The plurality of the regulatory process, its openness to a variety of actors, is itself a function of bureaucratic and legal traditions and of past regulatory practice. Network analysis offers useful insights into the impact of such traditions on the organizational aspect of regulation. Its aim is to identify or map patterns of dependent relations between key personalities, but it takes as a central premiss the notion that these relations are predicated upon the acceptance of certain internal 'rules of the game' which evolve within stable communities.

One advantage of approaching the subject of interdependence through the concept of 'regulatory space' is that it alerts us to the problem of defining the character of the social relations between the occupants of that space. The notion of a 'regulatory space' focuses attention not only on who the actors involved in regulation are, but on structural factors which facilitate the emergence and development of networks and which contribute to the institutionalization of linkages. In taking the nature of the links between actors as the starting-point of analysis, it offers the chance of

developing a systematic comparison of their character in different industrial sectors and within different national settings.

Network analysis offers the undoubted advantage of highlighting the
functional importance of informal links between actors. It plainly can be
misleading to assume that formal regulatory arrangements are the only
kind of institutionalized relationships. Indeed formal arrangements may
not be institutionalized at all: notwithstanding the plethora of formal rules
on representation and the various substantive rights enshrined in the legal
code, French industrial relations have remained fragmented and the
unions have been unable to exert sufficient economic power to mobilize
their legal rights.

Our sketch shows that the allocation of power and influence within
regulatory space is influenced both by legal tradition and by a wide range
of social, economic, and cultural factors which go beyond narrow 'rules of
the game'. But the character of the transactions between organizations is
also affected by a more immediate set of influences: by the particular kind
of issues which arise in regulation and by the particular areas where those
issues are dealt with. This is what we next examine.

Issues, Arenas, and Regulatory Space

While it is a truism to say that the nature of a regulatory issue intimately
affects the range of those who participate in its resolution, it is plain that
the nature of any single issue is not 'given'. The definition of the character
of a regulatory issue is itself an important part of the process by which it is
allocated to the domain of certain organizations and removed from the
domain of others. Most problems in economic regulation are both complex in their intrinsic character and wide ranging in their social and
economic consequences. It is thus rare for an issue to be 'obviously' in a
particular domain. For instance, does the regulation of work practices
belong to 'industrial relations' or, since it affects the health of the economy,
should it be assigned to the sphere of economic management? The very
process of issue definition will itself be heavily influenced by different
national conceptions as to the legitimate exercise of regulatory power. As
this process of defining or 'labelling' an issue develops, the policy network
to which it is appropriate may become evident.

A second and equally important act of definition involves the distinction
between what are in everyday language loosely described as 'technical' and
'political' issues. The distinction is particularly crucial in the field of regulation, where much of the most important activity consists in the routinized

application of general principles to particular circumstances. The distinction between technical and political issues is also typically a distinction between a 'high' and 'low' politics of regulation. Where an issue is identified as technical, it is commonly consigned for resolution to a very different organizational network from that concerned with resolving 'political' issues held to involve questions of principle. The separation can be crucial in determining who controls the regulatory process. The point is vividly illustrated by the regulation of financial services, where matters critical to the wider economic health of the community—entry into markets, the degree and kind of competition in those markets, the standards of honesty demanded of market participants—have traditionally been defined as technical problems of market control, and thus safely assigned to the 'low politics' of regulatory routine. The identification of the issue, and its allocation to a particular organizational arena are not the subject of constant debate in the regulatory process. On the contrary: issue identification and definition are done largely unthinkingly as a result of customary assumptions and organizational routine. It could not be otherwise because, were it necessary to argue at length about the appropriate identification of every new issue, the activity of regulation would simply grind to a halt. Institutional inertia, the shaping power of professional ideologies, and the underlying force of customary assumptions about what is, and is not, 'political' are all vital to ensuring some continuing routine in the regulatory process.

Expressed thus, our account conveys the importance of custom and convention in deciding how regulatory issues are to be processed—and thus in deciding which organizations are to have the largest say in their resolution. But there is another face to regulation under advanced capitalism. The most highly developed market economies are also extraordinarily dynamic. Since the end of the Second World War they have been marked by historically high rates of growth, profound structural change, and rapid innovation in both technology and market practices. This has far-reaching consequences for the character of regulatory issues, and for the arenas in which they are settled.

One of the most striking recent changes is the redefinition of these issues as involving 'high' politics and their reassignment to new arenas, disrupting the old policy networks. In the second place, rapid change may erode the narrow basis of legitimation on which 'technical' or bureaucratic regulation rests, thus forcing regulatory issues (once again) into the political arena.

The dynamic nature of the market economy disturbs the routine processing of issues and their routine assignment to particular spheres.

Growth, innovation, and structural change all magnify the complexity of the issues which arise in economic regulation. This growth in complexity has three dimensions: intellectual, social and administrative. The growth of intellectual complexity happens because economic innovation typically involves the application of the most advanced technical and scientific processes to the creation and marketing of products. One of the most striking features of regulatory debates is the growing extent to which they are expressed in languages of technical complexity and legal discourse often far removed from everyday lay political argument.

The growing intellectual complexity of the issues at the heart of economic regulation is in many respects matched by the growth in social complexity. The economies of advanced capitalist nations are character- ized by relations of interdependence, at the root of which is the ever more refined and elaborate division of labour. The result in the sphere of regulation is that decisions cannot be made, let alone implemented, by involving only a small group in the regulatory process. Social complexity ensures that effective regulation typically demands the co-operation of countless interdependent social actors, often including those well beyond the boundaries of any conventionally defined regulatory community. (The recent intervention of the European Community in the regulation of subsidies to car manufacturers is a case in point.)

Administrative complexity is in many respects a mirror of this growing social complexity. It refers not only to the substance of rules—though these can be dauntingly elaborate—but also to the administrative appara- tus which increasingly surrounds the activity of regulation. Regulatory space is dominated by organizations, many of which possess elaborate internal hierarchies and numerous points of decision, linked in a network to the numerous points of decision in the other organizations populating regulatory space.

The innovative nature of markets under advanced capitalism therefore constantly disturbs the routine identification of regulatory issues, and their ready assignment to organizational domains. But there is also a more profound sense in which the delineation of regulatory arenas is disrupted. Economic innovation means, quite simply, the invention of new products, and new means of manufacture and marketing. The new products can be anything from a new drug to a novel financial instrument. Innovations in market practice can range from the adoption of a single new sales tech- nique to the creation of whole new social arenas and new social institu- tions. In financial services, for instance, the innovations span the gamut from 'cold calling'—a marketing device made popular and effective by the spread of telephone ownership—to the invention of whole new markets, like those in financial futures. Every innovation in turn raises two immediate problems: is it to be regulated, and by whom? In regulatory politics most of the contests for authority to settle issues surround newly invented products or marketing forms, for which some regulatory arena has to be found.

The connection between the effects of structural change and innovation, and the determination of regulatory domain, is particularly well illustrated by attempts to regulate the most advanced parts of market economies, those organized on a multinational scale. Some early accounts of the significance of the development of multinational institutions, especially of multinational business corporations, suggested that institutions had been created which reduced the nation-state to insignificance. But this is far from the case: national governments are major players in the multinational arena. Nevertheless, this particular regulatory space has two distinctive characteristics, concerning the character of authority and the nature of the parties to regulation. The rules of decision and the lines of authority in the regulatory process are even less clear than is the case within national regulatory communities. Inside nations the sovereign authority of the state is, as we showed earlier, often closely circumscribed by the realities of organized power. Nevertheless, there does characteristically exist some sovereign authority able to act as a 'tie breaker' in disputes, and able to provide a fountain of legitimacy for the exercise of regulatory authority. No such sovereign centre exists in multinational regulatory space; what cannot be bargained is for the most part deadlocked.

The parties to bargaining also have special characteristics. If domestic economic regulation is dominated by organizations, the same is even more emphatically the case in the multinational arena. The only realistic mode of entry into regulatory debates is as a bearer of organizational interests— indeed, usually of the interests of corporations or government departments. These actors have structural and cultural features which, though present in many domestic regulatory arenas, exist in the multinational sphere in particularly highly developed forms. All organizations involved in regulation are bearers of complex arrays of interests, but this feature is especially notable when the organizations are themselves governments trying to distil some national interest out of the wide range of conflicting domestic forces to which they are subject. All domestic regulatory arenas are likewise marked by a degree of cultural diversity, but in the supranational sphere the range of diversity and the consequent potential for clashes is greatly magnified, while the pressure for compromise is weaker.

The connection between issues, arenas, and the character of economic regulation is shaped by both ideological and structural factors. Regulatory 'issues' are in an important sense ideological constructions: their recognition depends on social actors construing the world in a particular way; their allocation to a particular regulatory arena is likewise the result of a process of ideological construction. But these acts of issue recognition and definition are underpinned by the structural forces at work in the economy. The most important of these forces is provided by the dynamic character of the economy of advanced capitalism, which constantly creates new regulatory problems, new regulatory arenas, and new organizations ready and available to compete in those arenas.

Conclusion

Economic regulation is, we have stressed, predominantly regulation by and through organizations. The analyst of contemporary regulation is confronted with the task of understanding the networks of interdependence in the arenas of negotiation and compromise—in a phrase the patterns of power brokerage. The study of regulation thus involves the concepts traditionally central to the disciplines of law and of politics. In this chapter we have argued that the study of regulatory power cannot be furthered by an artificial division between 'public' and 'private' spheres. An organizational perspective on regulation allows us to go beyond 'capture' theory, to examine the process by which powerful organizations, both state and non-state, gain, maintain, and sometimes lose their dominant positions within regulatory space. It also highlights in a new way some very traditional concerns of both law and political science—the definition of the legitimate scope of power, and the quest for meaningful accountability on the part of regulatory institutions. Indeed the problems of accountability and legitimacy can only be fully addressed if the process of power brokerage between powerful institutions in advanced capitalism is made central to the analysis. We have drawn attention to some of the themes emerging from current work on regulation, in the hope that they will serve as pointers for future study and analysis.

Notes

1. For a bibliographic survey see e.g. B. Mitnick, *The Political Economy of Regulation* (New York: Columbia University Press, 1980).
2. J. Allen (ed.), *Democracy and Finance: The Addresses and Public Statements of William O. Douglas* (New Haven: Yale University Press, 1940), 244.

3. G. Kolko, *Railroads and Regulation 1877–1916* (Princeton: Princeton University Press, 1965); and G. Kolko, *The Triumph of Conservatism* (New York: Free Press, 1963). The capture literature is critically examined in G. Wilson, 'Social Regulation and Explanations of Regulatory Failure', *Political Studies*, 32 (1984), 203–25.

4. T. Lowi, *The End of Liberalism: The Second Republic of the United States* (New York: Norton, 1979).

5. The phrase is from R. K. Middlemas, *Politics in Industrial Society* (London: Deutsch, 1979).

6. C. Lindblom, *Politics and Markets* (New York: Basic Books, 1977).

7. C. Crouch, 'Sharing Public Space: States and Organised Interests in Western Europe', in J. Hall (ed.), *States in History* (Oxford: Basil Blackwell, 1986), 177–210. The quotation is on p. 180.

8. C. Maier, ' "Fictitious Bonds . . . of Wealth and Law": On the Theory and Practice of Interest Representation', in S. Berger (ed.), *Organising Interests in Western Europe* (Cambridge: Cambridge University Press, 1981).

9. J. Hayward, 'Institutional Inertia and Political Impetus in France and Britain', *European Journal of Political Research*, 4 (1976), 341–59.

10. L. Friedman, 'Legal Culture and Social Development', *Law and Society Review*, 6 (1969), 19–46 at p. 19.

11. K. Dyson, *The State Tradition in Western Europe* (Oxford: Martin Robertson, 1980), 207.

12. See generally C. Harlow and R. Rawlings, *Law and Administration* (London: Weidenfeld and Nicholson, 1983).

13. D. Vogel, *National Styles of Regulation* (Cornell: Cornell University Press, 1986).

14. J. Hayward, *Governing France: The One and Indivisible Republic*, 2nd edn. (London: Weidenfeld and Nicholson, 1983), 133.

15. Ibid. 134.

16. A. Bockel, 'Actualité et perspective du contrôle de l'interventionisme économique', *Actualité juridique du droit administratif*, 8 (1985), 8–21.

17. Dyson, *The State Tradition in Western Europe*, p. 213.

18. J. Hills, *Deregulating Telecoms: Competition and Control in the United States, Japan and Britain* (London: Frances Pinter, 1986).

19. P. Hall, *Governing the Economy* (Cambridge: Polity Press, 1986), 265.

20. T. Lowi, 'Four Systems of Policy, Politics and Choice', *Public Administration Review*, 32 (1972), 298–310.

21. For a survey see e.g. S. Wilks and M. Wright, *Comparative Government—Industry Relations: Western Europe, the United States, and Japan* (Oxford: Clarendon Press, 1987).

In and Out of the Revolving Door: Making Sense of Regulatory Capture

T. MAKKAI AND J. BRAITHWAITE

ABSTRACT

The concept of regulatory capture is multidimensional according to data from Australian nursing home inspectors. There are three empirically distinct forms of capture: identification with the industry, sympathy with the particular problems that regulated firms confront in meeting standards, and absence of toughness. Inspectors who have prior senior management experience in the industry tend to be less tough in their attitudes to regulatory enforcement. For the other two types of capture, it is not coming in the revolving door (from an industry job), but aspirations to go out of the revolving door (to an industry job) that predicts capture. Captured regulatory attitudes and revolving door variables have little power, however, in explaining the toughness of actual enforcement practices. We do find that over time tougher inspectors are more likely to leave the regulatory agency than softer inspectors. These data are used to inform a policy analysis of capture and corruption. It is concluded that there is limited analytical merit in a conception of capture as an enduring unitary character trait that is structurally determined by a history of interest group affiliations. Capture, we attempt to show, is instead a situational problem that requires situational solutions. Constraining the free movement of the revolving door by restricting regulatory appointments from or to the regulated industry is an example of a flawed policy grounded in an overdrawn structural determinism.

Regulatory Capture

Capture is an influential concept in debates about why regulatory agencies persistently fail to enforce the law against business offenders. It has a long pedigree in American political science, in particular dating from Marver Bernstein's (1955) notion that regulatory agencies go through a 'life cycle' that sees the public interest progressively subordinated to the interests of the regulated industry.[1] In the 1970s Ralph Nader popularised the idea that regulatory agencies become captives of industry because former business executives take influential positions in government agencies whose job it is to regulate business, but perhaps more fundamentally because regulators are seduced by prospects of moving to more lucrative employment in the industries they were regulating. This phenomenon was called the revolving door.

The empirical fact of the revolving door is beyond dispute (Clinard and Yeager, 1980: 106–9). Lawyers in the antitrust division of the U.S. Justice Department or the Federal Trade Commission are essentially trainees getting the experience that will enable them to grab the jobs that bring in big bucks working for business. For 31 of the 96 Australian business regulatory agencies studied by Grabosky and Braithwaite (1986), a majority of inspectors, investigators or complaints officers were recruited from industry.

The interesting question is whether the fact of the revolving door leads to capture. Systematic work on voting by US federal communications' commissioners has produced mixed and ultimately fairly weak support for the revolving door effects on pro-industry decisions (Gormley, 1979; Cohen, 1986). Similarly, Quirk's (1981) empirical work on the US FTC, CAB, FDA and NHTSA finds limited support for the revolving door on capture. More fundamentally, we must ask: What does capture mean in the context of the revolving door? Is capture an analytically useful concept for understanding the failure of regulatory enforcement?

We will seek to answer these questions using unique data on nursing home regulation in Australia. True to the fact of the revolving door, 48 per cent of the regulators in our study had worked in the nursing home industry prior to becoming a nursing home inspector and 23 per cent had aspirations of a future job in the industry. In this paper we will test the separate effects on capture of going into and coming out of the revolving door of nursing home regulation.

Using data from 173 Australian nursing home inspectors[2] and from inspections of 410 nursing homes, we will: (1) explore the structure of regulatory attitudes that might be described as captured through a factor analysis of questionnaire items; (2) test the effect of coming from a nursing home industry background on capture; (3) test the effect of plans to move in future to a nursing home industry job on capture; (4) test the effect of coming into and planning to go out of the revolving door and the effect of capture on how tough inspection teams are in ratings of compliance with the law; (5) combine these findings with the understanding derived from our fieldwork observing nursing home inspections in the U.S. and Australia to inform a policy analysis of capture.

The Capture Domain

Questionnaires were posted to persons who worked as inspectors between 1987 and 1990 on an Australian government programme to ensure the compliance of nursing homes with mandatory national standards. The job of these inspectors (called standards monitors) is to visit nursing homes in teams of two or three and rate their compliance with 31 standards. When nursing homes fail to comply with the standards, the inspectors negotiate an agreed action plan to be implemented within an agreed time frame. Inspectors return to check that the action plan is implemented. If it is not, the inspection team may recommend enforcement actions including financial penalties and closure.

The 31 national standards were introduced in 1987 after a series of scandals rocked the industry. Consumer groups took up the cause of residents found lying for hours in urine-soaked sheets, suffering from pressure sores the size of a fist, under-nourished, and denied a variety of basic human rights. The new standards cover health care; the social independence, freedom of choice, privacy and dignity enjoyed by residents; the environment of the nursing home; the variety of experience available to residents; and safety (including risks from fire, violence, infection, and the use of restraints).

A list of names of all inspectors and managers who worked on the standards monitoring programme between 1987 and 1990 was supplied by the Federal government and self-completion questionnaires were mailed out in May 1990. Two follow-ups by letter were sent in August 1990. Those who had not responded by this time were contacted by telephone and asked to complete the schedule. No further attempts were made to contact those who had refused to participate or whose questionnaire was 'return to sender'. The original list consisted of 258 inspectors. Of these, 14 refused to participate, 32 were return to sender, 21 failed to return the questionnaire and 191 returned usable schedules. Eighteen of these have been excluded from the analyses that follow as they were managers who had had no prior experience as inspectors in the monitoring programme.

Included in this questionnaire were a series of attitude items designed to measure capture. These items were taken from two sources: (1) a previous Australian study designed to assess capture among business regulators across 96 agencies (Grabosky and Braithwaite, 1986: 192–3); and (2) additional items designed specifically to measure capture in the context of Australian nursing home inspection. The latter items were informed by extensive fieldwork (Braithwaite *et al.*, 1990) observing Australian nursing home inspections and interviewing regulatory officials. The results suggest that nursing home inspectors are more 'captured'[3] than top managers (generally heads or second-in-command) of 87 other Australian business regulatory agencies (Grabosky and Braithwaite, 1986: 192–3). For example, 73 per cent of the nursing home inspectors compared to 49 per cent of top managers of other Australian regulatory agencies agreed with the statement: 'It is better to seek to persuade companies [nursing homes] to comply with regulations voluntarily even at the risk of being considered "soft".' If Australian business regulators are, as Grabosky and Braithwaite say, 'of manners gentle', nursing home inspectors are even gentler.

Capture—An Unidimensional or Multidimensional Concept?

The first question we must ask is whether capture is a unidimensional construct. It is conceptually meaningful to speak of capture as a coherent and enduring character trait of regulators? When capture is spoken about in the regulatory context it is assumed that it is unidimensional—either you are captured or you are not. In this study, Australian nursing homes inspectors were asked the extent of their agreement with nineteen attitude items which had been *a priori* defined as measuring capture.

To explore the dimensionality of capture, a principle component analysis followed by a varimax rotation was undertaken. Simple structure was best approximated through extracting and rotating three factors based on the inter-correlations between the items. Factor loadings appear in Table 4.1. This exploratory analysis of the capture items shows that capture may be a more complex notion than has been suggested to date. The first factor was dominated by attitudes that are sympathetic to the problems the home confronts in coming into compliance with the standards. It taps the notions of 'responsiveness' (Ayres and Braithwaite, 1992) or 'regulatory reasonableness' (Bardach and Kagan, 1982) in the conduct of inspections. Capture does not sit comfortably as a description of this dimension since it is arguable that these are positive rather than negative attributes for regulators. The second factor is composed of seven items that indicate identification with the industry. There is a distinction between the second factor and the first. We have found that it is possible to strongly identify as a part of the nursing home industry (the second factor) without being especially sensitive to the difficulties faced by those whom one regulates

Table 4.1. *Principle component analysis of capture items*[a]

	Factor 1	Factor 2	Factor 3
Sympathetic to the home's problems in meeting the standards			
Standards Monitoring Teams should try to get agreement on the best action plans that are practicable in terms of cost	.69	.05	−.00
You can't just demand that certain things be done without first understanding the problems the nursing home is confronting	.64	.17	.03
Where I can, I try to help the nursing home to come up with less costly ways of meeting the standards	.51	.12	.09
Part of being an effective Standards Monitor is being able to sympathize with the point of view of the nursing home	.55	.03	.05
As a general rule, I like to give the nursing home the benefit of the doubt	.57	−.17	−.34
A good Standards Monitor takes account of the difficulties nursing homes must overcome to meet the standards	.44	.15	.03
It is better to seek to persuade nursing homes to comply with standards voluntarily even at the risk of being considered 'soft'	.36	.03	−.22
Identify with the industry			
As a Standards Monitor I feel I am an important part of the nursing home industry rather than an adversary to it	.10	.66	.28
Mostly I have great respect for the people I work with in the nursing home industry	.27	.64	−.12
Standards Monitoring Teams are more interested in catching nursing homes for doing the wrong thing than in helping them	.16	−.64	.28
The relationship of my Team to the nursing homes which we oversee may best be described as adversarial	.16	−.62	.13
I see my work as making a contribution to improving the reputation of the nursing home industry in the community	.20	.55	.15
The last thing I want to do is something that will harm the nursing home industry	.31	.51	−.09
The relationship of my Team to nursing homes is based on negotiation, mutual accommodation, and compromise	.35	.46	−.00
Tough			
It is better to be a tough enforcer of standards, even at the risk of being considered punitive	−.18	.04	.65
I don't care how much it costs to comply with a standard; my job is to get compliance whatever the costs	−.16	−.01	.65
If you want to be judged a success in this job, you are best to err on the side of demanding that the nursing home do more than is really required to meet the standards	.17	−.13	.60
A large number of enforcement actions is a sign that a regulatory agency is doing its job	.01	−.22	.35
The Department of Community Services and Health can't do much if a nursing home decides to defy it	−.16	−.18	−.30
Percent of variance explained	17.4	10.2	9.4

a Respondents were asked to indicate the extent of their agreement with the items. Responses could range from strongly agree, agree, neither agree nor disagree, disagree to strongly disagree.

(the first factor); and it is possible to feel no identification with the industry yet be sympathetic to the practical difficulties nursing homes face in coming into compliance with the law. The third factor is composed of 5 items that refer to being tough with the industry over compliance with the standards.

The goal of the principle component analysis is to maximise the common variance of the items within factors, while minimising the variance across the factors. The first component extracts the maximum amount of variance. In this analysis, sympathy with the industry accounts for 17 per cent of the variance in the total analysis, while identifying with the industry and toughness account for 10 per cent and 9 per cent respectively.

Scales were developed from these factors by summing across the items. When summing the items, each individual item was scored so that a high score consistently indicated strong agreement with the attitudinal direction of the scale.[4] In order to gauge the effectiveness of the analysis in separating the item set into three distinct components alpha reliability coefficients were calculated for each scale together with the correlations between scales. Table 4.2 shows the correlations between the scales, the alpha reliability coefficients for each scale in the diagonal of the matrix, and the means.

As would be expected, identification with the industry and sympathy with the home's problems are positively correlated, while toughness negatively correlates with both these dimensions. The correlations, although significant in two of the three cases, are not high, suggesting that these constructs are related but not to such an extent that they could reasonably be construed as one dimension. The alpha reliabilities also indicate that the items within the scales form reasonably cohesive constructs. The rotated factor solution and the lack of strong correlations between the scales indicates that capture is indeed a multidimensional concept.

Table 4.2. *Inter-correlations and alpha reliability coefficients for capture scales*

	Sympathise	Identify	Tough	Mean
Sympathise with the home's problems	.65			6.18
Identify with the industry	.24**	.69		6.18
Tough	−.13*	−.10	.55	4.42

Statistically significant at *$p < .05$; ** $p < .01$

Does the Revolving Door Explain Capture?

Three common explanations for why capture can occur are explored here. The first is that regulators who come from the industry find their first loyalty is to the industry rather than to the goals of the regulatory organisation. The second involves time as the important factor in the life cycle of a regulatory regime. Recalling Bernstein's theme of a regulatory life cycle, a number of inspectors and regulatory managers expressed the view that 'New surveyors go in like gangbusters, but they mellow eventually' (American state government manager). Hence, we hypothesise that the longer an inspector has been in the regulatory game, the more likely they are to become captured. Over time they increasingly sympathise and identify with the industry. A final explanation is that inspectors who look to the industry as a future career option are less tough and more understanding in regulating that industry. These inspectors are more concerned with their future career options; they often view their time in the regulatory organisation as a training ground for a more lucrative future involvement in the industry. In Table 4.3 we test the extent to which moving in and out of the revolving door affects their levels of capture.[5]

Table 4.3. *Predicting capture for standards monitors*[a]

	Identify with industry		Sympathise with home's problems		Tough on home	
	b	(beta)	b	(beta)	b	(beta)
Control variables						
Age	.03**	(.20**)	.01	(.03)	.03	(.11)
Gender	−.14	(−.04)	.16	(.04)	−.70	(−.16)
Length of time as inspector						
Number of standards monitoring visits	.01	(.14)	−.01	(−.06)	(−.00)	(−.03)
Months worked as a standards monitor	.01	(.09)	.02	(.12)	−.03*	(−.16)*
In the revolving door						
Prior nursing home experience	.28	(.10)	−.01	(−.00)	.36	(−.09)
Prior director or deputy director of nursing home	−.10	(−.03)	.20	(.05)	−1.20**	(−.22**)
Out of the revolving door						
Like to work in nursing homes in the future	.21**	(.17**)	.28*	(.20*)	−.15	(−.09)
Constant	4.35		4.85		4.65	
Adj R-square	.09		.01		.05	

a There were 15 directors of nursing who were co-opted from the industry to participate actively in some inspections.

Statistically significant at * $p < .05$; ** $p < .01$; one-tailed test.

A variety of background control variables were included in the initial model. These variables were the age and sex of the respondent, the number of qualifications held by the respondent, whether the respondent was a registered nurse, and whether the respondent had ceased work as an inspector. Most of these were deleted from the final model presented in Table 4.3 as neither their inclusion or exclusion affected the variables of theoretical interest. In the robust model only two control variables were included—age and gender. Moving into the revolving door is measured by prior experience working in a nursing home and prior experience in a senior management position in the industry (as a director of nursing or a deputy director running a nursing home). Plans to move out of the revolving door are measured by the item 'I would like to work in nursing homes at some time in the future'.

Only one of the six 'in the revolving door' effects is statistically significant.[6] Prior nursing home industry experience effects none of the capture dimensions and previous experience as a senior executive in the industry effects toughness but not the other two dimensions. Even the significant effect on toughness can be called into question, since it ceases to be significant when the 15 current directors of nursing who were co-opted from the industry to serve on the teams are excluded from the analysis. The significant effect of industry background on toughness may be notably about the *current* industry appointments of these co-opted inspectors rather than their *prior* industry background.

While the capture effect, thus qualified, of coming in the revolving door is on toughness alone, aspirations to go out the revolving door into an industry job have no effect on toughness, but have significant effects on the other two capture dimensions—identification with the nursing home industry and sympathy with the home's problems in meeting the standards. These effects remain after excluding the inspectors co-opted from current industry appointments from the analysis. Months worked as an inspector, like industry background at a management level, is significantly associated with toughness, but not the other two dimensions of capture.

Toughness eroding with time supports the prediction derived from Bernstein's life-cycle hypothesis. However, the predicted life-cycle effect does not hold up when number of inspections rather than number of months in the job is used as the predictor. While only four of the predicted 15 relationships are statistically significant, these findings lend glimmers of support for the hypothesis that moving in and out of the revolving door is associated with aspects of capture. However, the effects are modest as is evidenced by the amount of variance explained by the models. It is only toughness that is effected by moving into the revolving door an effect that disappears with the deletion of the inspectors who are currently employed in the industry, while it is the other two dimensions of capture that are affected by a desire to move out of the revolving door.

Does Capture Explain Regulatory Behaviour?

This paper so far has shown that capture is a more complex notion than has been developed to date. The analysis has also shown that there are modest revolving door and life cycle effects explaining capture. However, the ultimate utility of the capture dimensions depends on their explaining actual regulatory behaviour rather than just regulatory attitudes. If the level of capture does not significantly affect the toughness of the behaviour of regulators in their dealings with the industry then capture theory has no practical explanatory utility.

Four hundred and ten nursing homes were inspected in regions surrounding four large metropolitan centres—Sydney, Melbourne, Brisbane and Adelaide. Selection of homes occurred in two ways. Sixty per cent of them represent a proportionate stratified random sample within each sampling region, while the remainder are a supplementary sample of all other nursing homes inspected in the Sydney, Brisbane and Adelaide sampling regions during the period of the study. Analyses elsewhere have shown that there are no significant differences between the samples on a range of important variables. For this reason the samples have been combined.[7]

Each of these homes was visited by a standards monitoring team and their compliance with 31 Commonwealth Outcome Standards assessed. The name of each member of the standards monitoring team that visited the home was recorded. Teams ranged from a minimum of 2 people to a maximum of 8. Using this information, it was possible to match the inspectors' questionnaires to each home that an inspector visited. Across the 410 inspections, 249 different combinations of team members occurred with the largest number of homes visited by a particular team being 15.

To determine whether capture affects compliance, the level of analysis moves from the individual inspectors to the inspection teams that visited the 410 nursing homes. The matching process resulted in 397 homes or inspections for which we had information for at least one member of the team. These homes can in turn be broken down into those where we had returned questionnaires for all team members (n = 187) and those where we had returned questionnaires on 50 per cent or more of the team members (n = 169).

To match the individual team members to the homes, an average score across the individuals that form a team was computed and then matched to the home that the team visited. We could choose to restrict our analysis to those homes where we had information on all team members (full teams), those where we had information on fifty per cent or more of the team (partial teams) or on those for which we had information on at least one team member. A series of analyses were undertaken to determine whether there was any significant difference between full and partial teams.[8] These analyses indicated that the most significant difference between teams occurred across the sampling regions. Full teams were more likely to have come from the Melbourne sample and less likely to have come from the Adelaide sample. If the sample was restricted to full teams then there would be the serious possibility that the inspections would reflect the Melbourne sampling region rather than all the sampling regions. On this basis, we chose to use all available information (that is, to take the 397 homes for which we had information on at least one inspector for the team who visited the home) and enter a variable indicating whether a full or partial team was involved in the inspection process. Hence, we can examine the effect of the independent variables controlling for the proportion of the team for which we had questionnaire data.

Table 4.4 shows the direct effect of capture and our in and out revolving door measures on compliance ratings given by the 410 inspections. As we have already noted there are 31 government standards with which Australian nursing homes have to comply. Each standard has three levels of compliance—met, met in part, or not met. These ratings have been summed: a high score (31) indicates that the team assesses the nursing home as perfectly in compliance and a low score (0) total non-compliance.[9]

There are only two significant predictors of the toughness of compliance ratings—teams for which we had questionnaire data for all inspectors and identification with the industry. The data show that as the average level of inspectors' identity with the industry increases, then higher compliance ratings are given. This is the only significant affect predicted by capture theory.

None of the in and out of the revolving door measures significantly impact on the level of nursing home compliance nor do the length of time measures derived from Bernstein's life cycle and capture theory. However, full data on teams is a significant predictor of compliance, net of a variety of possible confounding influences, including sampling region. Clearly there is something different about teams for which we have questionnaire

Table 4.4. *How important is capture in explaining compliance*[a]

	Compliance-government ratings	
	b	(beta)
Length of time in regulation		
Number of standards monitoring visits	−.00	(−.01)
Months worked as a standards monitor	−.06	(−.10)
In the revolving door		
Prior nursing home experience	−.00	(−.00)
Prior director or deputy director of nursing experience	.01	(.04)
Out the revolving door		
Like to work in nursing homes in the future	−.09	(−.02)
Full data on teams		
Full team[b]	−.84*	(−.11*)
Capture scales		
Identify with the industry	.39*	(.11*)
Sympathise with the home's problems	−.06	(−.02)
Tough on the home	.07	(.03)
Constant	16.06	
Adj R-square	.32	

a This model controls for a variety of factors; ownership type, size of home, age of home, percent of residents female, percent of residents married, mean disability level of residents, number of inspectors on team, geographic location of home, director of nursing's level of control in the home. As the average age of the team and percent of females on the team did not significantly contribute to the model they have been excluded from the analysis for reasons of parsimony.

b Full team is defined as those teams for whom we have data on all members of the team.

data on all inspectors who made up the team. This suggests an inherent selection bias with the inspectors we located. Although the sample was designed to include both prior and current inspectors, success with former inspectors was limited to the extent that names and addresses could be provided by the regulatory agency.

Although there were only 14 outright refusals, if the return to senders and losses are included, the total 'non-response' group amounts to 26 per cent. Most of our losses were therefore not refusals but people who had left the programme who we could not find.

The implication is that those who left the programme were tougher than their peers who remained in the programme. There is support for this interpretation from our qualitative fieldwork. Inspectors who left the agency did complain of lack of agency support to take tough action against recalcitrant nursing homes. If our hypothesis is that inspectors who are tough leave the programme earlier, then we would expect that length of time on the programme and a scale measuring toughness would correlate. The correlation would be weak because we have already lost long-term tough inspectors, yet we still have tough short term inspectors. The correlation should also be negative. The correlation between length of time in the regulatory programme and toughness is both weak and negative:—.10. We would argue that this measure is a proxy for a life cycle effect—tough inspectors have a shorter lifespan in the regulatory programme and for those inspectors who stay in the programme, the longer they stay the less tough they are; this is indeed what our data in Table 4.3 show. There is a significant negative effect for length of time on the team and toughness lending some support for Bernstein's life cycle effects on the regulatory practice of inspectors.

Living with the Revolving Door

What we have shown is that capture is not an especially coherent, unitary concept; rather, it is multidimensional in a way that might cause us to question the usefulness of the capture concept as a unitary negative evaluation of regulators. We have found that going into the revolving door effects only one of three types of capture while going out of the revolving door effects the other two. Only one of the three types of individual capture has an effect on collective regulatory behaviour. None of these effects are especially strong. The most important capture effect may be the serendipitous finding that tough inspectors are more likely to leave the regulatory agency. So we have found that the story of the revolving door and capture is not completely false. But the true story is more complicated than that advanced by capture theorists and it is a story of weak effects.

Indeed the effects are sufficiently weak that we will argue that it would be misguided public policy to put any limits on recruitment from the industry or on leaving the regulatory agency to work for the industry. These conclusions are somewhat similar to those drawn by Quirk (1981:188–91) for certain US regulatory agencies. The only concern would be the narrowing of perspectives that would arise where almost all of the regulators were recruited from the regulated industry, a predicament that should only arise in special circumstances that require special remedies (e.g. judges hearing complaints against lawyers brought by Bar association disciplinary committees). 'Let the revolving door spin for all its worth' would be our general policy prescription. Restricting the revolving door would address only weak capture effects and might eliminate some reverse capture effects—industry employees who take the regulations seriously because at some future time they may be interested in getting a 9 to 5 job as a government regulator; regulators who take into the industry a regulator's perspective on why compliance is important.

Moreover, as has been argued elsewhere (Ayres and Braithwaite, 1992: chapter 3), not all capture is bad. It surely is bad for regulators to believe that 'what's good for General Motors is good for America'; but it is also undesirable for regulators to believe that 'what's bad for General Motors is of no consequence to America'. In a sense, the best regulatory culture is one where regulators are tough and absolutely committed to maximising the policy objectives that lie behind the law while at the same time being flexible—open to ways of achieving those policy objectives that are less costly for business. If mutual understanding by each side of the legitimate concerns of the other is the stuff of a healthy regulatory culture, then the revolving door might have positive effects.

The most important point, however, is that inspectors who come from the industry bring with them not only some special insight into the difficulties the industry faces, but they also bring special insight into the tricks of the trade used to get out of those difficulties. Industry experience can be helpful in finding the skeletons in the corporate closet. Admittedly, inspectors take the tricks of the regulatory trade across to the industry as well. But it is clearly the government that gets the better of this particular exchange. This is because most of the regulator's job involves dealing with industry, while only a little of the business person's job will concern dealing with regulators, unless she becomes a regulatory affairs specialist in a large firm.

Does all of this mean that capture is something we should not worry about as a public policy concern? No, it simply means that generalised capture effects arising from the revolving door are a sufficiently weak problem as to be outweighed by the advantages of the revolving door for good government. We should still be concerned about more particularised revolving door effects. It is most unwise to send an inspector in to assess the compliance of her old workplace; it risks a more situationally powerful form of capture; it risks unreasonable toughness by an inspector determined to prove she will not be captured; and it risks the perception of procedural injustice by regulated actors who perceive that they 'never got on' with the inspector who is now out to 'settle the score'. This leads us into the kind of more situational analysis of capture which we think is of the greatest policy import.

Toward a Situational Analysis of Capture

In this research we have found limited analytical value in a conception of capture as an enduring unitary character trait that is structurally determined by a history of interest group affiliations. Moreover, such a conception leads to misguided policy analysis. From fieldwork in Australia, the United States and England, we have identified many situational pressures that do cause capture of a worrying sort.

First, it is worth asking if there were any forms of capture of which we did not see much evidence. One of these is corruption, the most insidious form of capture. Corruption means capture on the basis of a bribe. Corruption is a serious problem of business regulation in Australia, more so in some types of regulatory agencies than in others (Braithwaite, Grabosky and Rickwood, 1986). We know of no case where bribery has occurred in nursing homes. This does not mean that it has not occurred, yet in the thousands of interviews in Australia, no one has expressed a suspicion that these inspectors can be bribed, though three industry respondents did raise this as a suspicion about nursing home inspectors from one state government. There has been some corruption in nursing home inspection in the United States, though our strong sense here is that this is not one of the more corrupt fields of business regulation in America. In all the fieldwork interviews with key regulatory players and observing inspections in 24 U.S. states, we learned of only one case where a state government inspector was alleged to have demanded a pay-off, and only one case where an inspector claimed to have been offered a bribe. In some states, however, there were suggestions that bribes were paid over the heads of inspectors. We also encountered repeated allegations that, at least in the past, city inspectors and Aldermen in Chicago demanded and received bribes. We even spoke with a nursing home administrator who claimed that the main reason he had moved to another state was that he was fed up with the demands for pay-offs from Chicago city officials.

It is instructive to contemplate both the generally low level of corruption among nursing home inspectors and particular areas where there is some serious suggestion of corruption occurring. Corruption is probably rare at the level of inspection teams because the fact that they are teams makes pay-offs situationally difficult. What is the use of bribing one inspector if there is a risk that their colleagues will mention that they have seen what the bribed inspector has been paid not to see, with this being mentioned in an exit conference attended usually by more than ten people? The only inspector who had been offered a bribe (in fact presented with a briefcase stuffed with $50,000) was given this in relation to discretion unrelated to the inspection team's function of assessing compliance with quality of care regulations.[10] The instances of Chicago bribery described above concerned individuals being bribed. When allegations of bribery above state teams were made, it was allegations of individual supervisors, heads of agencies or prosecutors. Hence, corruption is a form of capture situationally contained by team inspections where the teams are required to account for their findings in an open forum. In the United States in recent years, the open forum of the exit conference has become even more exposed by the attendance of Ombudsmen and representatives of Residents' Councils at exits.

With lesser forms of capture than corruption, however, we see in fieldwork notes persistent recurrence of specific pressures that cause situational capture. The most intense recurrent pressure in Australia, the United States and Britain is an acute shortage of beds in a locality, causing inspectors to believe that they cannot recommend the closure of a facility that continuously fails to reach minimum standards.

Another recurrent situational pressure for capture in both Australia and the United States is that if the team finds serious problems of noncompliance, it increases its workload. Finding a lot of serious deficiencies will require at least one follow-up inspection and, at worst, appeal hearings and a time-consuming and anxiety-provoking court case.

There are ways of reducing all of these situational pressures. The pressure from bed shortages can be eased by granting planning approval for more beds so that there is spare capacity in the system. Another solution is to make alternative remedies to closure easier to implement. The latter include: (a) installing a receiver to run the nursing home, (b) a government-appointed monitor to work full-time at the home, or (c) freezing new admissions as a stepping stone to closure. The pressure on teams to avoid the extra work and angst entailed in reporting serious deficiencies can be reduced by assigning specialist 'SWAT teams' (as they are lovingly known in two American states) to take over tough cases that are detected by the regular teams.

A number of the different types of situational pressures toward capture can be countered by granting participation rights to third parties during the inspection process. The state of Oklahoma has long granted nursing home Ombudsmen (some are community volunteers, others state employees) the right to be present at any time during nursing home inspections; U.S. federal law since October 1990 granted representatives of Residents' Councils the right to participate in exit conferences where regulatory negotiation occurs following an inspection. Inspectors from both the U.S. and Australia commented that one factor that keeps them on their mettle is the fear that something they miss will be the subject of a complaint that is investigated by their department's separate (and somewhat independent) complaints unit.

The contingency of pressures to capture is well illustrated by the highly variable political culture of American states on the question of political interference in nursing home regulatory enforcement decisions. In some states (e.g. Oklahoma, Georgia, Illinois, Indiana, Louisiana) political interference in nursing home regulatory enforcement has been a serious problem for a long time. Indeed this is an understatement. Once in the early 1980s a Georgia legislator prevented the regulatory agency from entering a nursing home to take enforcement action by literally barring the door! More than one agency head in these states has been fired for failing to fix cases for influential politicians.

In other states (e.g. Colorado, Tennessee, Virginia, Massachusetts) a remarkably disparate array of inside informants said political interference was a non-problem at the time of the interviews in 1988/1989. Some differences were starkly confirmed by informant regulators who had moved from apolitical regulatory cultures to highly politicised states, and vice versa. Moreover, the fact that there are remedies to the pathology of political favours subverting regulatory enforcement is illustrated in states where the problem was rife, but where politicians shifted to a more hands-off approach after colleagues got their fingers burnt interfering in nursing home enforcement decisions. Texas and Missouri are states where whistle-blowing or tip-offs to consumer groups have caused interfering politicians grief, thereby helping to create a more political nursing home regulatory culture. Cautionary tales in these states have become a resource that heads of agencies use, as one of them put it, to 'share back with politicians the liabilities they would have to assume' (e.g. pointing out that if the nursing home burns after the fire safety enforcement decision is relaxed, it won't be just me who will go down). The shock waves of such cases have also been felt in other states where capture was once much more mediated by political interference, such as North Carolina, where one senior state bureaucrat said: 'People are more cautious today because there have been political interference scandals around the country where people have been burnt.' None of this means that politicised capture has been removed in these states. The comments of a Texas regulator suggest it may have taken a more subtle, yet still less harmful, form: 'Now politicians are more careful about defending nursing homes. They'll call and ask questions rather than try to exert pressure.'

The implication we draw is that even forms of capture that seem matters of deeply ingrained political culture are in fact contingent and malleable. They can be resisted wherever there are vocal advocacy groups or aggressive investigative journalists who can run with anonymous tip-offs from a single insider with a modicum of courage or spite. There is no structural inevitability about political capture, even in a state where the Governor owns a nursing home that is subjected to tough punitive action by state inspectors, e.g. Tennessee at the time of our fieldwork.

The path to a positive policy analysis of capture does not lie with conceptualising capture as a generalised predisposition that is structurally determined by interest configurations. Rather it lies with an analysis of the range of situational pressures toward capture that are institutionally contingent within particular regulatory contexts. Specific policies then need to be designed to alleviate each of those institutional pressures. In addition, there may be some general countervailing pressures (such as consumer empowerment through advocacy groups) that can have effects across a range of the situational causes of capture. Needless to say, this view implies that what we find true of nursing home regulation may be false in other regulatory domains, and different analyses of capture can be required for different regulatory agencies (Quirk, 1981).

While coming in the revolving door from the industry has an effect on one of the capture dimensions, toughness, hopes of going out the revolving door to an industry job have no effect on this dimension of capture, but do effect the other two dimensions, identification with the industry and sympathy with the nursing home's problems. The variance explained by these revolving door effects is small. Finally, we found that of the three capture dimensions, only identification with the industry has a significant effect on the toughness of regulatory practices. The revolving door variables have no significant effects on actual regulatory behaviour.

These data indicate little support for the theory that regulatory enforcement is under the hegemony of the private interests from which so many regulators come—or to which they hope to go. The deceptively simple idea of the revolving door provides an unsatisfactory basis for analysing such hegemony. What our data do suggest is some support for a version of Bernstein's life cycle theory. Quite simply, tougher inspectors leave the programme earlier, while less tough peers stay on as regulators.

Notes

This project has enjoyed the funding support of the Australian Commonwealth Department of Health, Housing and Community Services, The Australian Research Council, the American Bar Foundation, and the Australian National University. The authors are indebted to their colleagues on the Nursing Home Regulation in Action Project — Valerie Braithwaite, Diane Gibson, David Ermann and Miriam Landau.

1. For commentaries on Bernstein's thesis, see Anthony Downs (1972); P. Freitag (1983); Paul J. Quirk (1981); Paul Sabatier (1975).
2. This also includes 15 directors of nursing who were co-opted onto the programme for short periods to participate in the inspection process.
3. If indeed 'capture' is the right term for the items we use. Responsiveness, as we shall discuss later, may be a better term.
4. To ensure that no one item dominated the scale with a large variance, each item was divided by its standard deviation prior to summation. As the resulting scales have no natural metric they have been rescored from 0 to 10.
5. Ordinary least squares (OLS) regression is the technique employed in the multivariate analyses. This method assumes that the relationships between the variables are reasonably linear and additive (Berry and Feldman, 1985). Two types of regression coefficients are presented in the tables—unstandardised and standardised. Unstandardised coefficients are a parameter estimate of the average amount of increase or decrease in the dependent variable for a one unit difference in the independent variable, controlling for the other independent variables in the model (Lewis-Beck, 1980). Beta or standardised coefficients represent the average standard deviation in the dependent variable for a one standard deviation change in the independent variables, *ceteris paribus*.
6. The t-distribution is used to test for the significance of the relationship between the dependent and independent variables. Where the hypothesis has been determined *a priori* one-tailed tests of significance are employed; in those cases where there is no theoretical rationale for determining the nature of the relationship is unclear or subject to competing interpretations that predict opposite directional effects two tailed tests are utilised.
7. For a more detailed discussion of the sampling regions and samples readers are referred to Braithwaite, John *et al.* (1990).
8. Analyses indicated that there were no significant differences between partial and minimum teams and hence the issue is not considered further. The analyses are not presented here but have been documented and are available from the authors on request.
9. Factor analytic work elsewhere (Braithwaite, John *et al.*, (1990)) have justified the adding of scores from all standards rather than taking clusters of standards or treating the standards individually.

10. It concerned transfer of a 'Certificate of Need' (government planning approval of need for the beds in the locality) following purchase of church home by a private operator which meant that the Certificate of Need no longer applied to the new owner.

References

AYRES, I. and J. BRAITHWAITE (1992). *Responsive Regulation: Transcending the Deregulation Debate*, New York: Oxford.

BARDACH, E. and R. A. KAGAN (1982). *Going by the Book: The Problem of Regulatory Reasonableness*, Philadelphia: Temple University Press.

BERNSTEIN, M. H. (1955). *Regulating Business by Independent Commission*, Princeton: Princeton University Press.

BERRY, W. and S. FELDMAN (1985). *Multiple Regression in Practice*, Sage University Paper no. 50, Beverly Hills and London: Sage Publications.

BRAITHWAITE, J., P. GRABOSKY and D. RICKWOOD (1986). 'Research Note: Corruption Allegations and Australian Business Regulation', *Australian and New Zealand Journal of Criminology*, 19: 179–86.

BRAITHWAITE, J., T. MAKKAI, V. BRAITHWAITE, D. GIBSON and D. ERMANN (1990). *The contribution of the standards monitoring process to the quality of nursing home life: a preliminary report*, Canberra: DCSH.

CLINARD, M. B. and P. C. YEAGER (1980). *Corporate Crime*, New York: Free Press.

COHEN, J. (1986). 'The Dynamics of the "Revolving Door" on the FCC', *The American Journal of Political Science*, 30, 4, 689–708.

Commission on California State Government Organization and Economy (1983). *The Bureaucracy of Care: Continuing Policy Issues for Nursing Home Services and Regulation*, Sacramento: Commission on California State Government Organization and Economy.

DOWNS, A. (1972). 'Up and Down with Ecology: The Issue Attention Cycle', *Public Interest*, 14: 38–50.

FREITAG, P. (1983). 'The Myth of Corporate Capture: Regulatory Commissions in the United States', *Social Problems*, 30: 480–91.

GORMLEY, W. T. (1979) 'A Test of the Revolving Door Hypothesis on the FCC', *American Journal of Political Science*, 27, 1: 86–105.

GRABOSKY, P. and J. BRAITHWAITE (1986). *Of Manners Gentle: Enforcement Strategies of Australian Business Regulatory Agencies*, Melbourne: Oxford.

LEWIS-BECK, M. (1980). *Applied Regression*, Sage University Paper no. 22, Beverly Hills and London: Sage Publications.

QUIRK, P. J. (1981). *Industry Influence in Federal Regulatory Agencies*, Princeton: Princeton University Press.

SABATIER, P. (1975). 'Social Movements and Regulatory Agencies: Toward a More Adequate—and Less Pessimistic—Theory of "Clientele Capture"', *Policy Science*, 6: 301–42.

The Rise of the Regulatory State in Europe

G. MAJONE

Abstract

Privatization and deregulation have created the conditions for the rise of the regulatory state to replace the dirigiste state of the past. Reliance on regulation—rather than public ownership, planning or centralised administration—characterises the methods of the regulatory state. This study examines the growth of regulation in Europe, at the national and Community levels. It stresses the advantages of this mode of policy making, but also recognises its problems. It is suggested that political accountability can be ensured by a variety of substantive and procedural controls, among which judicial review is especially important. Executive oversight and coordination may be improved by using new tools of public management like the regulatory budget or the regulatory clearing house.

Regulation and the Redrawing of the Borders of the State

A paradoxical consequence of the international debate about privatization and deregulation has been to focus the attention of European policy makers and scholars on regulation as a distinctive mode of state intervention in the economy and society. In the words of a legal scholar, regulation has become the new border between the state and the economy, and the battleground for ideas on how the economy should be run.[1] A political scientist observes that regulation is a pervasive and widely accepted phenomenon in all advanced countries.[2] According to an economist, the regulation issue—what, how, and at what level of government to regulate—is the core of the compromise between the European Community and its member states that made the Internal Market programme possible.[3]

This consensus on the significance and distinctiveness of regulation is a relatively new phenomenon. Until recently, European scholars devoted little attention to the special features of regulation that distinguish it from other modes of policy making. Thus, while the American deregulation movement was preceded and prepared by decades of intensive research on the law, economics and politics of the regulatory process, in Europe the terms 'deregulation' and 'privatization' gained sudden currency—even in Great Britain the words were scarcely heard of before 1978—with hardly any intellectual preparation.

The academic and political debate in the United States has been greatly facilitated by the fact that the meaning of regulation is fairly clear within the framework of American public policy and administration (see below). By contrast, European scholars tend to identify regulation with the whole realm of legislation, governance, and social control. Such a broad use of the term makes the study of regulation almost coextensive with the study of law, economics, political science, and sociology. If it is true that reductionism is a necessary condition of scientific progress,[4] it is not surprising that the analysis of regulation as a particular type of policy making is still in its infancy in Europe.

The relative neglect of regulatory analysis in the past corresponded to the low visibility of regulatory activities. While in the United States the tradition of regulation by means of independent agencies combining legislative, administrative, and judicial functions goes back to the Interstate Commerce Act of 1887—and even earlier in states like Wisconsin, Massachusetts and New York—the tendency in Europe has been to treat regulatory issues as either purely administrative, and so tasks for central departments or ministries, or as judicial, and so matters for determination by courts or court-like tribunals. In Britain, for example, tribunals like the Railway Commission (created in 1873),

proved so common that by 1933 the regulation of British public utilities was viewed by some as considerably impaired by this reliance on the quasi-judicial method and by the resulting failure to develop the administrative commission. What was absent was a powerful agency that applied a special expertise, employed its own secretariat and regulated (in the sense of imposing a planned structure on an industry or social issue). Regulators, instead of instituting action, responded to the competing proposals of private interests.[5]

Even these timid beginnings of an autonomous regulatory function were forgotten in the era of nationalisations and municipalisations. In most countries of Europe, public ownership of key industries such as railways, telecommunications, electricity, gas, water and other natural monopolies was supposed to protect the public interest against powerful private interests. In this respect, nationalisations and municipalisations were the functional equivalent of American-style regulation. Indeed, at one level, this equivalence is so close that it is possible to establish a one-to-one correspondence between typical forms of 'regulatory failure' and certain well-known problems of public ownership, as shown by Table 5.1.[6]

Table 5.1. *Comparing Two Types of Government Failure*

Failures of Economic Regulation	Failures of Nationalised Industries
Capture of regulators by regulated firms	Capture of public managers by politicians and trade unions
Overcapitalisation (so-called Averch-Johnson effect)	Overmanning
Anticompetitive regulation	Public monopolies
Vague objectives ('regulate in the public interest')	Ambiguous and inconsistent goals given to public managers
Poor coordination among different regulators	Poor coordination among different public enterprises
Insufficient political accountability of independent regulatory agencies	No effective control over public enterprises by Parliament, the courts, or the sponsoring minister

Because of these analogies, it has been argued that there is no great difference between public monopolies, like the European Post and Telecommunications Ministries, and privately owned but publicly regulated monopolies like the American Telephone and Telegraph Company before deregulation. However, this argument overlooks one important point: the purpose of public ownership was not simply to regulate prices, conditions of entry and quality of service, but also to pursue many other goals including economic development, technical innovation, employment, regional income redistribution, and national security. While nationalisations and other traditional forms of direct state intervention were thus justified by appealing to a variety of often conflicting goals, regulation has a single normative justification: improving the efficiency of the economy by correcting specific forms of market failure such as monopoly, imperfect information, and negative externalities.

Because regulation is more narrowly targeted, and because many of the traditional goals of nationalisations have become obsolete or can be pursued more efficiently by other means, privatisations tend to strengthen, rather than weaken, the regulatory capacity of the state. The British experience, for all its imperfections, is quite instructive in this respect. Paralleling the sale process of industries such as British Telecommunications and British Gas has been the development of a whole new regulatory structure.[7] This structure rests on a body of economic law involving

specific obligations and license conditions placed on the privatized industries, and on a new breed of regulatory agencies—the regulatory offices
(ROs). The ROs combine several functions: they regulate prices; they
ensure that the privatized firms comply with the terms of their licenses;
they act as a channel for consumer complaints and as promoters of
competition in the industry they regulate. Detected instances of monopoly
abuse are referred to the Office of Fair Trading and to the Monopolies and
Mergers Commission (MMC).

Thus, privatization has led to a considerable widening of the scope of
agencies to promote competition. Now the MMC has a direct role in the
regulation of utilities, while prior to privatization it did not have
the competence to examine the potentially anti-competitive practices of
the nationalised industries. Regulation of the competitive behaviour of the
privatized industries is further strengthened by the availability of
the competition law of the European Community (EC) which offers
considerably more powerful remedies than are available under British
law.[8] Similarly, in America newly deregulated industries have lost their
pre-existing statutory immunity from anti-trust laws, and despite major
changes in the telecommunications sector, important segments of the
industry remain regulated.[9] In sum, neither privatization nor deregulation
have meant a return to *laissez-faire* or an end to all regulation. Privatization
changes the role of the state from a producer of goods and services to that
of an umpire whose function is to ensure that economic actors play by the
agreed rules of the game. Deregulation often means less restrictive or rigid
regulation: a search for ways of achieving the relevant regulatory objectives by less burdensome methods of government intervention, as when
command-and-control methods are replaced by economic incentives.
Thus, neither American deregulations nor European privatizations can
be interpreted as a retreat of the state, but rather as a redefinition of its
functions. What is observed in practice is a redrawing of the borders of the
public sphere in a way that excludes certain fields better left to private
activity, while at the same time strengthening and even expanding the
state's regulatory capacity in other fields like competition or environmental and consumer protection.

Normative and Positive Theories of Regulation

In order to explain the sudden growth of administrative regulation, as well
as the lateness of its arrival on the European political stage, it is important
to specify more precisely the basic characteristics of this mode of policy

making. As noted above, within the framework of American public policy and administration, regulation has acquired a meaning which is often imperfectly understood in Europe. To use Philip Selznick's formulation,[10] regulation refers to sustained and focused control exercised by a public agency over activities that are socially valued. The reference to sustained and focused control by an agency suggests that regulation is not achieved simply by passing a law, but requires detailed knowledge of, and intimate involvement with, the regulated activity. This requirement will necessitate, sooner or later, the creation of specialised agencies entrusted with fact-finding, rule-making, and enforcement.

The emphasis on socially valued activities excludes, for example, much of what goes on in the criminal justice system: the detection and punishment of illegal behaviour is not, *per se*, regulation in the sense in which the term is used here. On the other hand, market activities can be 'regulated' only in societies that consider such activities worthwhile in themselves and hence in need of protection as well as control. If the first part of Selznick's definition reminds us of the different institutional traditions of the United States and Europe, and specifically of the lack of a tradition of independent regulatory bodies in Europe, the second part reminds us of important ideological differences in the past. As discussed above, nationalisations may be viewed, in important respects, as the functional equivalent of American-style regulation. The fact remains that nationalisations were not undertaken in order to support the market by improving its efficiency, but rather to replace market criteria by political and administrative ones. The first wave of nationalisations coincided with the first worldwide depression of the capitalist economy (1873–96) which shattered popular and elite support of the market for almost one century. The late Peter Jenkins[11] exaggerated only slightly when he wrote in 1988 that only now, for the first time in this century, the governing classes of Europe no longer assume that socialism in some form is what history has in store.

By contrast, the American rejection of nationalisation as an economically and politically viable option expressed a widely held belief that the market works well under normal circumstances and should be interfered with only when it does not function properly. The normative theory of regulation expresses this belief in analytic terms. According to this theory, public regulation of economic activity is justified only when the market is incapable of producing a social (Pareto) optimum. This occurs when some form of market failure is present: monopoly power, negative externalities, inadequate or asymmetrically distributed information, public goods. Regulation should be used to increase the efficiency of the economy by correcting market failures, but not for other purposes, however legitimate. For example, income redistribution should be achieved through social policy, not through regulation. An important recent development is the recognition that market failures provide only a *prima facie* case for intervention, since the costs of public intervention may exceed the benefits. Hence 'regulatory failure' must also be considered (see Table 5.1).

A frequent criticism of the market-failure approach is precisely that it is a normative, not a positive, theory. It provides a basis for identifying situations where the government ought to do something, tempered by considerations of regulatory failure. Many political scientists and economists argue that analysts should focus their attention not on normative issues but on describing the consequences of government programmes and the nature of the political processes that produce such programmes. Normative analysis, it is said, is irrelevant since policy outcomes depend, not on norms or ideas of the public interest, but on factors such as the rules of the political process, the incentives facing various participants in the process, and the changing configurations of power and interests in society.

According to the positive theory, as formulated by George Stigler among others, regulation is not instituted in the public interest, that is, for the protection and benefit of the public at large or some large subclass of the public, but is acquired by an industry and is designed and operated primarily for its benefit.[12] How else could one explain the price and entry regulation of basically competitive industries such as airlines, trucking, banking and telephone services, or the anti-competitive licensing of so many professions and trades? The positive theory has greatly enriched our understanding of the regulatory process, but has not made the normative theory obsolete. As always in the social sciences, the distinction between normative and positive is much less sharp than positivists used to think.[13]

In a useful survey paper on 'Regulation in Theory and Practice', Joskow and Noll call 'normative analysis as a positive theory' (or NPT) the theory which regards market failure as the motivating reason for the introduction of public regulation.[14] The characterisation is appropriate, since the normative theory is often successful in explaining the origin and development of many regulatory policies. As Peltzman[15] writes:

If there is an empirical basis for the NPT's continuing attraction for economists, it is probably its apparent success as an entry theory. Consider Hotelling's classic statement in 1938 of the natural monopoly version of the NPT. In this purely theoretical piece, railroads and utilities are presumed, without much evidence, to be the main real-world examples of natural monopoly. They also occupied most of the regulatory (including public ownership) effort when Hotelling wrote. The correspondence between the NPT and the real-world allocation of regulatory effort seems striking. Now consider the postwar expansion of regulation. In terms of the resources involved, the biggest single chunk is probably accounted for by environmental regulation, where the externalities aspect of the NPT scores another success.

In Europe, too, as we shall see in the following pages, much of the recent growth of regulation can be explained in normative, public-interest, terms. But even when regulation is best explained by the political or economic power of groups seeking selfish ends, those who attempt to justify it must appeal to the merits of the case. Legislators, administrators, scholars, and the public at large wish to know whether the regulation is justified. All of them seek standards against which to judge the success of a policy and the merits of specific programmes initiated within the framework of that policy.

The Growth of Regulation in Europe

Administrative regulation—economic and social regulation by means of agencies operating outside the line of hierarchical control or oversight by the central administration—is rapidly becoming the new frontier of public policy and public administration throughout the industrialised world. The absence of an efficient regulatory framework is increasingly seen as a major obstacle to modernisation. Thus, as a 1993 issue of *The Economist* points out, one of the serious problems of privatization in Russia is that there is no regulatory system to control trading in vouchers or shares. This 'regulatory black hole' has already claimed many victims among uninformed investors, and creates an irresistible temptation for any swindler.[16]

The growth of administrative regulation in Europe has greatly accelerated during the last two decades. In France, for example, the expression 'autorité administrative indépendante' was used for the first time by the law of 6 January 1978 creating the Commission Nationale de l'Informatique et des Libertés, but several independent regulatory agencies already existed prior to that date: the Commission de Contrôle des Banques created in 1941 and transformed into the Commission Bancaire by the law of 24 January 1984; the Commission des Opérations de Bourse (1967), whose powers have been significantly extended by the law of 2 August 1984; the Commission des Infractions Fiscales (1977); the Commission des Sondages (1977); the Médiateur (1973), the only single-headed regulatory agency created so far in France. Today there are almost 20 independent agencies including, in addition to those already mentioned, the Commission d'Accès aux Documents Administratifs (1978), the Commission de la Sécurité des Consommateurs (1983), the Conseil de la Concurrence (1986), and the Commission de Contrôle des Assurances (1989).[17]

In Britain, too, the 1970s have been a period of significant innovation, especially in the area of social regulation. The Independent Broadcasting Authority (1972), the Civil Aviation Authority (1972), the Health and Safety Commission (1974), the Equal Opportunities Commission (1976), and the Commission for Racial Equality (1976) are only some of the regulatory bodies created in this period.[18] Despite the hostility of Conservative governments toward any kind of 'quangos', regulatory agencies were set up in the 1980s and early 1990s, partly because it was realised that in many cases privatization would only mean the replacement of public by private monopolies unless the newly privatised companies were subjected to public regulation of profits, prices, and entry and service conditions. Hence the rise of a new breed of regulatory agencies, the regulatory offices: Office of Telecommunications (1984), Office of Gas Supply (1986), Office of Water Services (1989), Office of Electricity Regulation (1990).

Parallel, if slower, institutional developments are taking place in all other European countries, and the reasons given for the rise of the independent agencies are strikingly similar from country to country. These functional explanations are also strongly reminiscent of the arguments of earlier American writers. Thus it is said that agencies are justified by the need of expertise in highly complex or technical matters, combined with a rule-making or adjudicative function that is inappropriate for a government department or a court; that an agency structure may favour public participation, while the opportunity for consultations by means of public hearings is often denied to government departments because of the conventions under which they operate; that agencies' separateness from government is useful whenever it is hoped to free government administration from partisan politics and party political influence. Agencies are also said to provide greater continuity and stability than cabinets because they are one step removed from election returns; and the exercise of a policy-making function by an administrative agency should provide flexibility not only in policy formulation but also in the application of policy to particular circumstances. Finally, it is argued that independent agencies can protect citizens from bureaucratic arrogance and reticence, and are able to focus public attention on controversial issues, thus enriching public debate.[19]

The growth of administrative regulation in Europe owes much to these newly articulated perceptions of a mismatch between existing institutional capacities and the growing complexity of policy problems: policing financial markets in an increasingly interdependent world economy; controlling the risks of new products and new technologies; protecting the health and economic interests of consumers without impeding the free flow of goods, services and people across national boundaries; reducing environmental pollution. It is sufficient to mention problems such as these to realise how significant is the supranational dimension of the new economic and social regulation. Hence the important role of the European Community (now Union) in complementing the regulatory capacities of the member states.

The European Community as Regulator

Apart from competition rules and measures necessary to the integration of national markets, few regulatory policies or programmes are explicitly mentioned in the Treaty of Rome. Transport and energy policies which could have given rise to significant regulatory activities, have remained until lately largely undeveloped. On the other hand, agriculture, fisheries, regional development, social programmes and aid to developing countries, which together account for more than 80 per cent of the Community budget (see Table 5.2), are mostly distributive or redistributive rather than regulatory in nature.

This budget of almost ECU 47 billion represents less than 1.3 per cent of the gross domestic product (GDP) of the Community and less than 4 per cent of the central government spending of member states. Given such limited resources, how can one explain the continuous growth of Community regulation, even in the absence of explicit legal mandates? Take the case of environmental protection, an area not even mentioned by the Treaty of Rome. In the two decades from 1967 to 1987, when the Single European Act finally recognised the authority of the Community to legislate in this area, almost 200 directives, regulations, and decisions were introduced by the Commission. Moreover, the rate of growth of environmental regulation appears to have been largely unaffected by the political vicissitudes, budgetary crises, and recurrent waves of Euro-pessimism of the 1970s and early 1980s. From the single directive on preventing risks by testing of 1969 (L68/19.3.69) we pass to 10 directives/decisions in 1975, 13 in 1980, 20 in 1982, 23 in 1984, 24 in 1985 and 17 in the six months immediately preceding passage of the Single European Act.

Table 5.2 *The EC Budget by Major Categories of Expenditure (1990, ECU)*

Administration—Total	1,529,765,860
Operations	
Agricultural market guarantee	26,452,000,000
Guidance (agricultural structures)	2,073,475,000
Fisheries	376,100,000
Regional development and transport	5,209,700,000
Operations in the social sector	3,672,885,000
Energy, technology, research, nuclear safeguards, information market and innovation	1,763,478,000
Repayments and aid to member states	2,335,091,812
Co-operation with developing countries	1,503,590,000
Other expenditures	1,000,000,000
Operations—Total	44,386,319,812
Commission—Total	45,916,085,672
Other institutions	847,661,982
Grand Total	46,763,747,654

Source: *The Community Budget: The Facts in Figures*—1990 edn., Luxembourg: Office for Official Publications of the European Communities, p. 62.

The case of environmental regulation is particularly striking, partly because of the political salience of environmental issues, but it is by no means unique. The volume and depth of Community regulation in the areas of consumer product safety, medical drug testing, banking and financial services and, of course, competition law is hardly less impressive. In fact, the hundreds of regulatory measures proposed by the Commission's White Paper on the completion of the internal market[20] represent only the acceleration of a trend set in motion decades ago. The continuous growth of supranational regulation is not easily explained by traditional theories of Community policy making. At most, such theories suggest that the serious implementation gap that exists in the European Community may make it easier for the member states, and their representatives in the Council, to accept Commission proposals which they have not serious intention of applying. The main limitation of this argument is that it fails to differentiate between areas where policy development has been slow and uncertain (for example, transport, energy or research) and areas such as environmental protection where significant policy development has taken place even in the absence of a clear legal basis.

Moreover, existing theories of Union policy making do not usually draw any clear distinction between regulatory and other types of policies. Now, an important characteristic of regulatory policy making is the limited influence of budgetary limitations on the activities of regulators. The size of non-regulatory, direct-expenditure programmes is constrained by budgetary appropriations and, ultimately, by the size of government tax revenues. In contrast, the real costs of most regulatory programmes are borne directly by the firms and individuals who have to comply with them. Compared with these costs, the resources needed to produce the regulations are trivial.

It is difficult to overstate the significance of this structural difference between regulatory policies and policies involving the direct expenditure of public funds. The distinction is particularly important for the analysis of Community policy making, since not only the economic, but also the political and administrative costs of enforcing EC regulations are borne by the member states.[21] As already noted, the financial resources of the Community go, for the most part, to the Common Agricultural Policy and to a handful of distributive programmes. The remaining resources are insufficient to support large-scale initiatives in areas such as industrial policy, energy, research, or technological innovation. Given this constraint, the only way for the Commission to increase its role was to expand the scope of its regulatory activities.

Another important element in an explanation of the growth of Community regulation is the interest of multinational, export-oriented industries in avoiding inconsistent and progressively more stringent regulations in various EC and non-EC countries. Community regulation can eliminate or at least reduce this risk.

A similar phenomenon has been observed in the United States, where certain industries, faced with the danger of a significant loss of markets through state and local legislation, have strongly supported federal regulation ('preemptive federalism'). For example, the American car industry, which during the early 1960s had successfully opposed federal emission standards for motor vehicles, abruptly reversed its position in mid-1965: provided that the federal standards would be set by a regulatory agency, and provided that they would preempt any state standards more stringent than California's, the industry would support federal legislation.

Analogous reasons explain the preference for Community solutions of some powerful and well-organised European industries. Consider, for example, the 'Sixth Amendment' of Directive 67/548 on the classification, packaging, and labelling of dangerous substances. This amending Directive does not prevent member states from including more substances within the scope of national regulations than are required by the Directive itself. In fact, the British Health and Safety Commission proposed to go further than the Directive by bringing intermediate products within the scope of national regulation. This, however, was opposed by the chemical industry, represented by the Chemical Industries Association (CIA) which argued that national regulation should not impose greater burdens on British industry than the Directive placed on its competitors. The CIA view eventually prevailed.

Similarly, German negotiators pressed for a European-wide scheme that would also provide the framework for an acceptable regulatory programme at home, wanted a full and explicit statement of their obligations to be defined at the EC level. Moreover, with more than 50 per cent of Germany's chemical trade going to other EC countries, German businessmen and government officials wished to avoid the commercial obstacles that would arise from divergent national regulations.[22]

The European chemical industry had another reason for supporting Community regulation. In 1976 the United States, without consulting their commercial partners, enacted the Toxic Substances Control Act (TSCA). The new regulation represented a serious threat for European exports to the lucrative American market. A European response to TSCA was clearly needed, and the Community was the logical forum for fashioning such a response. An EC-wide system of testing new chemical substances could serve as a model for negotiating standardised requirements covering the major chemical markets. In fact, the 1979 Directive has enabled the Community to speak with one voice in discussions with the United States and other Organization For Economic Co-operation and Development (OECD) countries, and has strengthened the position of the European chemical industry in ensuring that the new American regulation does not create obstacles to its exports. There is little doubt that the ability of the Commission to enter into discussions with the USA has been greatly enhanced by the Directive, and it is unlikely that each European country on its own could do so effectively.[23]

Explaining Regulatory Policy Making in the EC

In the preceding section I have considered three variables that are clearly important for explaining the growth of EC regulation: the tightness and rigidity of the Community budget; the desire of the Commission to increase its influence by expanding its competencies; and the preference of multinational firms for dealing with a uniform set of rules rather than with 12 different national regulations. However, these variables are not sufficient to explain the willingness of the member states to surrender important regulatory powers to supranational institutions, nor the ability of the Commission to introduce significant innovations with respect to the policies of the member states.[24]

As already suggested, available theories of policy making in the Community do not explain why the member states would be willing to delegate regulatory powers beyond the level required by an integrated market; nor can they explain the policy entrepreneurship of the EC Commission. This is because such theories stress the dominant role of the member states in all stages of the policy process, from initiation (which comes from the heads of state or governments in the European Council) to formal adoption (the prerogative of the Council of Ministers), to implementation (in the hands of the national administrations).

A model capable of explaining the above mentioned phenomena must come to grips with two issues that have been overlooked by the traditional theories: first, problems of 'regulatory failure' in an international context, which limit the usefulness of purely inter-governmental solutions; and, second, the fact that regulation, as a very specialised type of policy making, requires a high level of technical and administrative discretion.

To start with the first issue, market failures with international impacts, such as transboundary pollution, could be managed in a co-operative fashion without the necessity of delegating powers to a supranational level, *provided* that national regulators were willing and able to take into account the international repercussions of their choices; that they had sufficient knowledge of one another's intentions; and that the costs of organising and monitoring policy co-ordination were not too high. These conditions are seldom, if ever, satisfied in practice. Experience shows that it is quite difficult to verify whether or not inter-governmental agreements are being properly kept. Because regulators lack information that only regulated firms have, and because governments are reluctant, for political reasons, to impose excessive costs on industry, bargaining is an essential feature of the process of regulatory enforcement. Regardless of what the law says, the process of regulation is not simply one where the regulators command and the regulated obey. A 'market' is created in which bureaucrats and those subject to regulation bargain over the precise obligations of the latter.[25] Because bargaining is so pervasive, it may be impossible for an outside observer to determine whether or not an international regulation has been, in fact, violated.

When it is difficult to observe whether governments are making an honest effort to enforce a co-operative agreement, the agreement is not credible. For example, where pollution has international effects and fines impose significant competitive disadvantages on firms that compete internationally, firms are likely to believe that national regulators will be unwilling to prosecute them as rigorously if they determine the level of enforcement unilaterally rather than under supranational supervision. Hence the transfer of regulatory powers to a supranational authority like the European Commission, by making more stringent regulation credible, may improve the behaviour of regulated firms. Also, because the Commission is involved in the regulation of numerous firms throughout the Community, it has much more to gain by being tough in any individual case than a national regulator: weak enforcement would destroy its credibility in the eyes of more firms. Thus it may be more willing to enforce sanctions than a member state would be.[26] In fact, the Commission has consistently taken a stricter pro-competition stance than national authorities such as the British Monopolies and Mergers Commission, the German Bundeskartellamt, or the French Conseil de la Concurrence.

In short, the low credibility of inter-governmental agreements explains the willingness of member states to delegate regulatory powers to a supranational authority. At the same time, however, governments attempt to limit the discretion of the Commission by making it dependent on the information and knowledge provided by national bureaucrats and experts. We must now explain how the Commission often manages to overcome these limitations.

The offices of the Commission responsible for a particular policy area form the central node in a vast 'issue network' that includes not only experts from the national administrations, but independent experts (also from non-EU countries), academics, public-interest advocates like environmentalists and leaders of consumer movements, representatives of economic and professional organisations and of regional bodies. Commission officials listen to everybody—both in advisory committees, which they normally chair, and in informal consultations—but are free to choose whose ideas and proposals to adopt. They operate less as technical experts alongside other technical experts, than as policy entrepreneurs, that is, as 'advocates who are willing to invest their resources—time, energy, reputation, money—to promote a position in return for anticipated future gain in the form of material, purposive, or solidary benefits'.[27]

In his study of policy innovations in America, Kingdon identifies three main characteristics of successful policy entrepreneurs: first, the person must have some claim to be taken seriously, either as an expert, as a leader of a powerful interest group, or as an authoritative decision maker; second, the person must be known for his political connections or negotiating skills; third, and probably most important, successful entrepreneurs are persistent.[28] Because of the way they are recruited, the structure of their career incentives, and the crucial role of the Commission in policy initiation, Commission officials usually display the qualities of a successful policy entrepreneur to a degree unmatched by national civil servants. Actually

the Commission officials' typical motivational structure is quite different from that of the average national government official. While the staff of the national governments is often recruited from persons who tend to be—compared with their peers who choose an industrial career—solid, correct, security-oriented, conservative, risk-averse and often somewhat narrow-minded, the Commission recruits its staff from people who are highly motivated, risk oriented, polyglot, cosmopolitan, open-minded and innovative . . . From the beginnings in the 1960s and up to the present, it has indeed been officials of a special type who chose to leave the relative security of their national administrations to go to Brussels to do there a well-paid but extremely challenging job . . . The structural conditions of recruitment and career favour a tendency to support new ideas and to pursue a strategy of innovative regulation which attempts to go beyond everything which can presently be found in the Member States. [29]

Because of this tendency to favour innovative regulatory solutions, even national experts may find the Community a more receptive forum for their ideas than their own administration. A 1989 directive on the safety of machinery (89/392/EEC) offers a striking example of this phenomenon. The crucially important technical annex of the directive was drafted by a British labour inspector who originally sought to reform the British regulatory approach. Having failed to persuade the policy makers of his own country, he brought his innovative ideas about risk assessment to Brussels, where they were welcomed by Commission officials and eventually became European law.[30]

Moreover, what is known about the *modus operandi* of the advisory committees suggests that debates there follow substantive rather than national lines. A good deal of *copinage technocratique* develops between Commission officials and national experts interested in discovering pragmatic solutions rather than defending political positions. By the time a Commission proposal reaches the political level, first in COREPER (the committee of permanent representatives of the Member States) and then in the Council of Ministers, all the technical details have been worked out and modifications usually leave the essentials untouched. The Council may, of course, delay a decision or reject the proposal outright, but these options are becoming increasingly problematic under the qualified majority rule and the 'co-operation procedure' between the European Parliament and the Council introduced by the Single European Act. Fitting together all the variables introduced in this and the preceding section—budget constraints, bureaucratic and economic interests, the poor credibility of purely intergovernmental arrangements and, last but not least, the highly technical nature of most regulatory policy-making—we begin to understand not only the origin and growth of Community regulation, but also its increasingly innovative character.

The Problem of Political Accountability

We just noted the significance of administrative and technical discretion for EC policy-making. Of course, regulatory discretion has important institutional and political implications also at the national level. One obvious consequence is the creation of specialised agencies such as the French *autorités administratives indépendantes* and the British regulatory offices mentioned above. Such agencies are independent of the central administration, and hence of civil service rules, and often combine legislative, judicial, and executive powers—rule making, adjudication, and enforcement, in the terminology of American administrative law—in more or less narrowly defined areas of policy making.

As already suggested, such institutional arrangements represent an important departure from European constitutional and administrative traditions. The implicit, and in some cases explicit, model is the American independent regulatory commission (IRC). The IRCs were created by Congress to ensure agency independence from presidential control and short-term political considerations. Although they cover an extremely wide range of administrative activities—from the control of prices, routes and service conditions of railway companies by the Interstate Commerce Commission created in 1887 to the licensing of nuclear power plants by the Nuclear Regulatory Commission created in 1975—all IRCs share some organisational characteristics that are meant to protect their decisional autonomy: they are multi-headed, having five or seven members; they are bipartisan; members are appointed by the president with the consent of the Senate and serve for fixed, staggered terms. Unlike the single-headed line agencies, the IRCs operate outside the presidential hierarchy in making their policy decisions. As the US Supreme Court asserted in *Humphrey's Executor* vs. *United States* (1935) commissioners can be removed from office only for official misbehaviour, not for disagreement with presidential policy.

In the course of their century-old history, IRCs have been often criticised for violating the principle of separation of powers, for their lack of political accountability, and for an alleged tendency to be captured by private interests. Not surprisingly, the same criticisms are heard now in Europe. Here, regulatory agencies are still seen as 'constitutional anomalies which do not fit well into the framework of controls, checks and balances',[31] even as challenges to basic principles of democracy and of the *Rechtsstaat*.[32] To be sure, it is no easy task to fit the new institutions into the constitutional framework of countries where the diffraction of state power is seen as a direct challenge to parliamentary sovereignty and to the principle of a rigid separation of powers. Expressed in traditional terms the dilemma is: either the regulatory agencies are part of the state administration, and then they cannot be independent; or else they are independent, but in this case to whom are they accountable?

It is impossible to escape this dilemma without questioning the relevance of traditional notions such as the constitutional axiom of the tripartite separation of powers, or the political principle that governmental policy making ought to be subject to control only by persons accountable to the electorate. It is certainly not a coincidence that similar issues are being raised in the ongoing debate about the proper scope of judicial review and judicial policy making. The rise of judicial review in Europe shows that the triad of government powers is no longer considered an inviolable principle. At the same time, courts find their policy making role enlarged by the public perception of them as guarantors of the substantive ideals of democracy when electoral accountability in all spheres of government seems to be waning.[33] What connects the discourse about administrative regulation with that about judicial review and policy making is the issue of the role of non-majoritarian institutions in democratic societies. Again, it is no mere coincidence that the same country has developed both the most advanced system of judicial review and the most extensive network of regulatory institutions.

The American experience shows that a highly complex and specialised activity like regulation can be monitored and kept politically accountable only by a combination of control instruments: legislative and executive oversight, strict procedural requirements, public participation and, most importantly, substantive judicial review. Measured against these standards, regulation in Europe is seen to be highly discretionary, suffering from weak accountability to Parliament, weak judicial review, absence of procedural safeguards, and insufficient public participation.[34]

The issue of the political accountability of regulators, who are neither elected nor directly responsible to elected officials, is particularly visible at the EU level precisely because of the central importance of regulatory policy-making in the Community system. However, the remedies should not compromise the effectiveness of the supranational institutions. The comparative advantage of EU regulation lies mainly in the relative insulation of Community regulators from the short-run political considerations and pressures which tend to dominate national policy-making. As was noted above, the Commission has more to gain by being tough in any individual case than a national regulator. This is because the Commission is involved in the regulation of firms throughout the Community, so that weak enforcement would destroy its credibility in the eyes of more firms. For the same reason, the Commission is less likely to be captured by a particular firm or industry than a national regulator. In the language of James Madison, the insulation of the Commission from day-to-day politics is an important safeguard against national and sectoral 'factionalism'.

In fact, as I have shown elsewhere,[35] many of the arguments developed along Madisonian lines by the American advocates of an 'independent fourth branch of government'—the regulatory branch—apply, *mutatis mutandis*, in the context of the European Union and its member states. These writers acknowledge that government by judges and technocratic experts raises serious issues for democratic theory, but point out that government by elected officials, too, suffers from defects. For example, in seeking re-election legislators engage in advertising and position taking rather than in serious policy making, or they design laws with numerous opportunities to aid particular constituencies. Thus, re-election pressures have negative consequences for the quality of legislation. On the other hand, pro-regulation scholars ask, if the courts require the regulatory process to be open to public inputs and scrutiny and to act on the basis of competent analyses, are the regulators necessarily less accountable than elected politicians?[36]

The procedural remedies suggested here are also relevant to the problem of the 'democratic deficit' of the EU. For example, it is well known that the Treaty of Rome does not structure the executive power of the Community in a single way, applicable to all instances of legislation needing further execution. Instead, it has been left to the Council, in its capacity as legislative decision maker, to organise, case by case, the executive process.[37] This ad hoc approach is the very negation of the idea of transparency which plays such a large role in the current discussion of regulation. The adoption of something like an Administrative Procedures Act for the European Union could do more to make public accountability possible than the wholesale transfer of traditional party politics to Brussels. Any progress along such lines at Union level would have positive spillovers for the member states where, as we saw, the accountability of regulators is still an open issue. The fact that regulation is relatively more important at EU than at national level, makes the Union an ideal laboratory for the study of the problems of the regulatory state. This can be seen also by examining the issue of co-ordination and executive control—the second key issue of regulatory policy-making.

Co-ordination and Control

An important characteristic of regulatory policy making is the absence of a regulatory budget procedure. Because, as was shown above, the size of regulatory programmes is not significantly constrained by legislative appropriations and by the level of tax revenues, as in the case of non-regulatory programmes, no mechanism exists for regulation that requires policy makers throughout the government to solve the two-level budget problem—how much to spend during a given period and then how to allocate this total amount among alternative uses—which is addressed by any government in its direct expenditure activities. The result is both economic inefficiency and inadequate political oversight.

These defects of the regulatory process are, again, particularly evident in the case of EU rule-making. Thus budgetary discipline is even weaker than at the national level since the burden of implementing Union regulations is carried by the governments of the member states. Also, because of the absence of a central political authority, regulatory issues are dealt with sector by sector, with little attempt to achieve overall policy coherence. Even within the same sector it would be difficult to maintain that regulatory priorities are set in a way that explicitly takes into consideration either the urgency of the problem or the benefits and costs of different proposals. The piecemeal procedure of the Commission in proposing new regulatory measures has resulted in directives in areas where harmonisation is a low priority, while neglecting other areas which need a considerable amount of harmonisation.

Since the lack of budgetary discipline is a basic reason for the structural defects of the regulatory process, one should attempt to create control mechanisms similar to those traditionally used in the case of direct public expenditures. This simple idea has led several analysts of the American regulatory process to propose the introduction of a *regulatory budget*. In its basic outline the regulatory budget would be established by Congress and the President for each agency, perhaps by starting with a budget constraint on total private expenditures mandated by regulation, and then allocating the budget among the different agencies. By setting a budget constraint on mandated private expenditures, the regulatory budget would clarify the real costs to the economy of adopting a regulation and encourage cost effectiveness. The knowledge that agencies would be competing against each other would lead them to propose their 'best' regulations in order to win presidential and congressional approval. Simultaneous consideration of all new regulations would permit an assessment of their joint impact on particular industries and the economy as a whole.[38]

Serious technical difficulties (e.g., estimating the full social cost of regulations, especially when the regulations restrict outputs or behaviour rather than merely requiring outlays for compliance) have to be resolved before the regulatory budget could actually be implemented. Nevertheless, because the budget is such a useful analogy for highlighting the defects in the current regulatory process, a promising approach consists in developing methods of regulatory oversight and control that incorporate budget concepts in a workable fashion.

One possible model suggested by the analogy with the budgetary process, deserves special investigation: a *regulatory clearing-house*. In the EU context, such a clearing house should be located at a sufficiently high level in the Union bureaucracy, possibly in the office of the President of the Commission. Directorates-General would be asked to submit annually draft regulatory programmes to the clearing house for review. When disagreements or serious inconsistencies arise, the President or a 'working committee on regulation' would be asked to intervene. By extending centralised control over the regulatory agenda of the Directorates-General, this review process would help the Commission shape a consistent set of regulatory measures to submit to the Council and the Parliament. The usefulness of the procedure as a tool of managerial control could be increased by co-ordinating the regulatory review with the normal budgetary review, thus linking the level of budgetary appropriations to the cost-effectiveness of the various regulatory programmes.

One key function of such a clearing-house system, in addition to providing for greater coherence, would be to flesh out the concept of subsidiarity: only through systematic review of all proposals put forward by the various Directorates-General will the Commission be able to determine when action by the Union is necessary. Obviously the idea of a regulatory clearing-house system would be useful also for the member states, as one way of reducing the negative consequences of the diffraction of state power which is one of the significant characteristics of the regulatory state.

Conclusion: The Paradoxes of Privatization, Deregulation and Re-regulation

At the beginning of this analysis we noted that European scholars and policy makers began to recognise regulation as a distinct mode of policy making only after deregulation became a popular theme of political discourse. This is only one of several paradoxes, real or presumed, that seem to characterise the development of regulation in Europe during the past two or three decades. Thus, the privatization and/or deregulation of potentially competitive industries have not meant the end of all regulation; on the contrary, they have created the conditions for the rise of a regulatory state to replace the *dirigiste* state of the past. Where competitive conditions did not yet exist, as in the case of telecommunications, only public regulation could ensure that privatization did not simply mean the replacement of public monopolies by private ones.

Often, deregulation is only a first step towards re-regulation, that is, regulation by other means—economic incentives instead of administrative rules, statutory instead of self-regulation—or at different levels of government—for example, at Community rather than national level. This paradoxical combination of deregulation and re-regulation is what is usually meant by regulatory reform.

On the other hand, the experience of countries such as Britain shows that old habits of secretiveness and ministerial interference, characteristic of the management of nationalised industries, continue to persist even after privatization. Serious flaws in the design of institutions to regulate the newly privatized industries can be detected in the choice of a non-participatory model, with none of the public hearings and other procedural characteristics of US regulation; in the creation of a system of agencies linked to particular industries, rather than the pattern of commissions regulating a range of utilities in order to reduce the risk of agency capture; and in the fact that government departments still preserve important regulatory powers, so that the operations of agencies are often dependent on prior decisions of the minister laying down the principles to be applied. The danger, Tony Prosser concludes, is that these powers of direction 'could be abused to exert behind-the-scenes pressure on the regulation in much the same way as pressure was put on the nationalised industries by government, precisely the situation which the privatization programme is supposed to render impossible'.[39]

Also the stupendous growth of EU regulation has a certain paradoxical quality. By imposing a tight and rigid budget, the member states no doubt wished to restrict as much as possible the competencies and decisional autonomy of the Commission. Accustomed to think of state power primarily in terms of the power of taxing and spending, national leaders did not apparently realise that regulatory activities cannot be controlled by means of the traditional budget constraints: only a 'regulatory budget' could introduce the necessary discipline. In the absence of a regulatory budget procedure, the rule-making power of the Union has proved well-nigh irresistible. Moreover, the growth has been qualitative as well as quantitative. As noted above, in some areas of economic and social regulation EU directives go beyond the levels achieved by the legislation of the most advanced member states. This is another paradox, at least for theories claiming that member states control all stages of Union policy making.

Finally, the terms of the debate about the 'democratic deficit' of the Union are often paradoxical when not simply hypocritical. Problems of political accountability can be perceived most clearly at Union level precisely because regulation is at the core of EU policy making. Yet the frequent criticisms that Union institutions lack direct democratic legitimacy also apply to many national institutions, including courts and independent regulatory agencies. The problem of a 'democratic deficit' concerns all regulatory states, not just the Union. The problem has no simple solution, but it can be mitigated by a variety of substantive and procedural means ranging from judicial review to the 'regulatory budget'. The shift to regulation at the national and supranational level is an attempt to improve the procedural and substantive rationality of public policy in a dramatically changing world. However, the changing role of the state raises new conceptual and practical issues that are still poorly understood, let alone resolved.

Notes

1. Cento Veljanovski, 'The Regulation Game', in Veljanovski (ed.), *Regulators and the Market* (London: Inst. of Economic Affairs, 1991), pp. 3–28.
2. Kenneth Dyson, 'Theories of Regulation and the Case of Germany: A Model of Regulatory Change', in Dyson (ed.), *The Politics of German Regulation* (Brookfield, VT: Dartmouth, 1992), pp. 1–28.
3. Jacques Pelkmans, 'Regulation and the Single Market: An Economic Perspective', in H. Siebert (ed.), *The Completion of the Internal Market* (Tübingen: J.C.B. Mohr, 1989), pp. 91–117.
4. Jon Elster, *Explaining Technical Change* (Cambridge: CUP, 1983).
5. Robert Baldwin and Christopher McCrudden, *Regulation and Public Law* (London: Weidenfeld, 1987).

6. Giandomenico Majone and Antonio La Spina, 'Lo Stato Regolatore', *Rivista Trimestrale di Scienza dell' Amministrazione* 13/3 (1991), pp. 3–62.

7. Cento Veljanovski, *Selling the State* (London: Weidenfeld, 1987).

8. Ibid., pp. 165–73.

9. Giandomenico Majone, 'Introduction' in G. Majone (ed.), *Deregulation or Re-Regulation?* (London: Pinter Publishers, 1990), pp. 1–6.

10. Philip Selznick, 'Focusing Organizational Research on Regulation', in R. G. Noll (ed.), *Regulatory Policy and the Social Sciences* (Berkeley and Los Angeles: Univ. of California Press, 1985), pp. 363–7.

11. Peter Jenkins, *Mrs. Thatcher's Revolution* (Cambridge, MA: Harvard UP, 1988).

12. George J. Stigler, 'The Theory of Economic Regulation', *Bell Journal of Economics and Management Science*, 6/2 (1971), pp. 114–41.

13. Giandomenico Majone, *Evidence, Argument and Persuasion in the Policy Process* (New Haven, CT: Yale UP, 1989).

14. Paul J. Joskow and Robert G. Noll: 'Regulation in Theory and Practice: An Overview', in G. Fromm (ed.), *Studies in Public Regulation* (Cambridge, MA: MIT Press, 1981), pp. 1–65.

15. Sam Peltzman, 'The Economic Theory of Regulation after a Decade of Deregulation', in *Brookings Papers in Economic Activity* (Washington, DC: The Brookings Instn., 1989), p. 17.

16. *The Economist*, 27 Feb. 1993, pp. 89–90.

17. Marie-José Guédon, *Les Autorités Administratives Indépendantes* (Paris: Librairie Générale de Droit et de Jurisprudence, 1991).

18. Baldwin and McCrudden (note 5).

19. Catherine Teitgen-Colly, 'Les Autorités Administratives Indépendantes: Histoire d'une Institution', in Claude-Albert Colliard and Gérard Timsit (eds.), *Les Autorités Administratives Indépendantes* (Paris: Presses Universitaires de France, 1988); Giulio Vesperini, 'Le Funzioni delle Autorità Amministrative Indipendenti', *Diritto della Banca e del Mercato Finanziario*, 4/4 (1990), pp. 415–19; Baldwin and McCrudden (note 5), pp. 4–9; Guédon (note 17), pp. 16–27.

20. Commission of the European Communities, *Completing the Internal Market*, COM(85)310, final, (Luxembourg: Office for Official Publications of the European Communities, 1985).

21. Giandomenico Majone, 'Market Integration and Regulation: Europe after 1992', *Metroeconomica* 43/1–2 (1992), pp. 131–56, and, 'Regulatory Federalism in the European Community', *Government and Policy*, Vol. 10 (1992), pp. 299–316.

22. Ronald Brickman, Sheila Jasanoff, Thomas Ilgen, *Controlling Chemicals* (Ithaca, NY: Cornell UP, 1985).

23. Ibid., p. 277.

24. Giandomenico Majone, 'The European Community between Social Policy and Social Regulation', *Journal of Common Market Studies* 31/2 (1993), pp. 153–70.

25. Alan Peacock (ed.), *The Regulation Game* (Oxford: Basil Blackwell, 1984).

26. Kristos Gatsios and Paul Seabright, 'Regulation in the European Community', *Oxford Review of Economic Policy,* 5/2 (1989), pp. 37–60.

27. John W. Kingdon, *Agendas, Alternatives and Public Policies* (Boston: Little, Brown, 1984), p. 188.

28. Ibid., pp. 189–90.

29. Volker Eichener, *Social Dumping or Innovative Regulation?* Working Paper SPS No. 92/28 (Florence: Eur. Univ. Inst., 1992).

30. Ibid., p. 52.

31. Veljanovski, *Regulators and the Market* (note 1), p. 16.

32. Teitgen-Colly (note 19), p. 49.

33. Mary L. Volcansek, 'Judges, Courts and Policy-Making in Western Europe', *West European Politics* 15/3 (July 1992), p. 5.

34. Tony Prosser, 'Regulation of Privatized Enterprises: Institutions and Procedures', in Leigh Hancher and Michael Moran (eds.), *Capitalism, Culture and Economic Regulation* (Oxford: Clarendon Press, 1989), pp. 135–65; Baldwin and McCrudden (note 5); Veljanovski (note 1).

35. Giandomenico Majone, 'Controlling Regulatory Bureaucracies: Lessons from the American Experience' in Hans Ulrich Derlein, Ita Gerhardt and Fritz W. Scharpf (eds.), *Systemnationalität und Partiellintereste* (Baden-Baden: Nomos, 1994), pp. 291–314.

36. Susan Rose-Ackerman, *Rethinking the Progressive Agenda* (NY: The Free Press, 1992).

37. Koen Lenaerts, 'Some Reflections on the Separation of Powers in the European Community', *Common Market Law Review,* Vol. 11 (1991).

38. Robert E. Litan and William D. Nordhaus, *Reforming Federal Regulation* (New Haven, CT: Yale UP, 1983).

39. Prosser (note 34), p. 147.

Part II
Standard Setting and Rule Choices

The Optimal Precision of Administrative Rules

C. S. DIVER

A state judge enjoins a liquor licensing board from denying future license applications until it adopts written rules to flesh out a vague 'public interest' standard.[1] A federal court orders the Federal Communications Commission to entertain requests for waivers from its 'clear channel' rules, noting that 'a system where regulations are maintained inflexibly without any procedure for waiver poses legal difficulties.'[2] A congressional committee studying federal bank chartering by the Comptroller of the Currency assails the Comptroller's 'reliance on vague standards [which accord him] unbridled discretion in the chartering process.'[3] Meanwhile, two political scientists lament the increasing 'imposition of uniform regulatory requirements in situations where they do not make sense.'[4]

The common thread that connects these dissimilar complaints is dissatisfaction with the precision of administrative rules, because of either administrative underprecision or excessive regulatory rigidity.[5]

This Article attempts to bring into sharper focus the assumptions and concerns about regulatory precision implicit in these diverse opinions about administrative policymaking. Those who take it upon themselves, by choice or obligation, to judge the quality of administrative rules must determine the degree of formal precision to demand from their authors. They need, to paraphrase Judge Skelly Wright, a 'standard for standards.'[6] The purpose of this Article is to fashion such a 'standard for standards' and to illustrate its applications and limitations.

The Article begins by defining the concept of rule 'precision.' Using an example based on the FAA's mandatory retirement rule, I distinguish three elements of regulatory precision—'transparency,' 'accessibility,' and 'congruence'—and explore the relationships among them. In Section II, I develop criteria to determine the appropriate degree of regulatory precision. I apply this analytical framework in Section III to the evaluation of four very different administrative policies: the FAA's retirement rule, the Comptroller of the Currency's standards for chartering national banks, the

Social Security Administration's grid rule for determining disability, and the Immigration Service's criteria for granting permanent resident status for nonimmigrant aliens.

Section IV explores the model's applicability to administrative policy-making. This section discusses the two kinds of 'administrative failure'—imperfect information and the divergence of social and private preferences—that seem most likely to cause poorly drafted regulations. The Article concludes by drawing lessons from this model for reviewing courts faced with challenges to the precision of administrative rules.

I. The Concept of Rule Precision

One would naturally expect the concept of rule precision to occupy a central place in any coherent philosophy of law. Yet legal philosophers differ considerably in both the relative significance they attach to formal rules and the attributes of rules with which they are most concerned. Commentators have identified a wide variety of parameters to describe legal rules: generality and clarity,[7] comprehensibility,[8] accuracy of prediction,[9] determinacy,[10] weight,[11] value,[12] and consistency with social purpose.[13] Before we can begin to make useful prescriptions about the precision of administrative rules, we must give the concept some added precision of its own.

A. Three Dimensions of Rules

The success of a rule in effecting its purpose largely depends on the words a draftsman uses to express his intentions.[14] A rational rulemaker will therefore be attentive to the probable effect of his choice of words upon the rule's intended audience. First, he will want to use words with well-defined and universally accepted meanings within the relevant community. I refer to this quality as 'transparency.'[15] Second, the rulemaker will want his rule to be 'accessible' to its intended audience—that is, applicable to concrete situations without excessive difficulty or effort.[16] Finally, of course, a policymaker will care about whether the substantive content of the message communicated in his words produces the desired behavior.[17] The rule should, in other words, be 'congruent' with the underlying policy objective.[18]

One can see each of these objectives at work in contemporary debates about the precision of legal rules. Transparency is the virtue chiefly celebrated in the 'void-for-vagueness' doctrine,[19] as well as in judicial and scholarly attacks on unconfined legislative delegation[20] and administrative discretion.[21] The asserted defect of an academic 'misconduct' standard, for instance, was its failure to provide a sufficiently clear guide for students' behavior.[22] The desire to make legal rules more accessible motivates recurrent calls for 'simplification' of convoluted regimes like the tax code.[23] This urge also animates proposals to expand the use of per se rules to resolve complex issues of antitrust law.[24] On the other hand, the concern primarily evoked by 'irrebuttable presumption'[25] and 'required waiver'[26] claims is congruence. A rule that makes eligibility for disability insurance turn on one's birth date, the argument runs, fails adequately to discriminate between those who are capable and those who are incapable of supporting themselves.[27] Since any criterion for evaluating the 'precision' of administrative rules should include these three values, it would be tempting simply to define as 'precise' a rule that combined the virtues of transparency, accessibility, and congruence. But two formidable obstacles lie in the path of such a venture—measurement and tradeoffs.

B. *The Problem of Measurement*

We must ask initially how to translate the goals of transparency, accessibility, and congruence into usable criteria for evaluating specific rules. To sketch the dimensions of that task, I offer a simple illustration.[28] Imagine a policymaker who must establish certification criteria for commercial aircraft pilots. One aspect of that task is to define the circumstances under which a pilot, once certified, should no longer be eligible to serve in that capacity. Let us suppose our lawmaker has a rough idea of a policy objective: pilots should retire when the social cost of allowing them to continue, measured as the risk of accidents that they might cause multiplied by their consequences, exceeds the social benefit, measured as the costs avoided by not having to find and train a replacement. But how can the lawmaker capture this idea in a legal standard?

Let us initially offer three alternative verbal formulations for such a rule:

Model I: No person may pilot a commercial airplane after his sixtieth birthday.

Model II: No person may pilot a commercial airplane if he poses an unreasonable risk of an accident.

Model III: No person may pilot a commercial airplane if he falls within one of the following categories. (There follow tables displaying all combinations of values for numerous variables, including years and level of experience, hours of air time logged, age, height, weight, blood pressure, heart rate, eyesight, and other vital signs, that would dis-qualify a pilot from further eligibility to pilot aircraft.)[29]

Which formulation is most transparent? The answer is easy: Model I. Everyone knows exactly what the words 'sixtieth' and 'birthday' mean. The crucial concept of Model II—'unreasonable' risk—seems, by contrast, susceptible to widely varying interpretations. Suppose, however, that among the rule's intended audience, the term 'unreasonable risk of accid-ent' had acquired a very special meaning: namely, 'older than 60.' In that case, the two rules would be equally transparent. That contingency, however implausible here, nonetheless reminds us of the danger of judging a rule's transparency without looking beyond its words to its actual impact.

The danger inherent in facial evaluation is even more evident in apply-ing the other two criteria. Is the rule of Model II or Model III more accessible? The former is shorter and more memorable. It also apparently requires only a single judgment—the 'reasonableness' of the risk. That judgment, however, may well rest on a set of subsidiary inquiries as numerous and complex as those encompassed within Model III's more explicit set of tables.

Similarly, our intuition that Model II is more congruent than, say, Model I, may be unreliable. The facial resemblance between Model II and the rulemaker's ultimate objective depends on the unverifiable assumption that 'unreasonable' connotes 'economically inefficient.'

It might be possible to assess these alternatives by reducing our three values to some empirically measurable form. We could, for example, conduct an experiment in which we present a series of hypothetical questions to a random sample of a rule's intended audience and require them to apply it to specific situations.[30] We might measure the rule's congruence by the ratio of agreement between the respondents' answers and the rulemaker's desired answers. We could use the ratio of internal agreement among respondents to measure the rule's transparency. Finally, we could construct an index of the rule's accessibility by assessing the average time (or money, in a more realistic experiment) that respondents invest in arriving at their answers. These measures, however, are at best only expensive proxies for the values that underlie them.

C. The Problem of Tradeoffs

Assuming that we could make reliable measurements along each of the three dimensions, we would still have to find a way to aggregate them in an overall evaluation. If transparency always correlated closely with accessibility and congruence, this would present no difficulty. Our three models of a pilot retirement rule, however, suggest that it does not. Each formulation has something to recommend it, but each also presents obvious difficulties. Model I may indeed be amenable to mechanical application, but it will undoubtedly ground many pilots who should continue flying and may allow some to continue who should be grounded. Even if we concede that Model II is simple and faithful to our policymaker's intentions, it generates widely varying interpretations in individual cases. Model III is commendably objective and may even discriminate accurately between low and high risks. But it achieves this latter objective only at the cost of difficulty in application.

Attempting to escape from these tradeoffs with a fourth option seems hopeless. Suppose we begin with Model I's 'age 60' version. Since this rule's greatest flaw is its apparent incongruity, we might try to soften its hard edges by allowing exceptions in particularly deserving cases.[31] We could, for example, permit especially robust sexagenarians to continue flying. But this stratagem merely poses a new riddle: how should we define the category of exempt pilots? There are, of course, many choices, but all of them seem to suffer in one degree or another from problems of opacity (e.g., 'reasonably healthy'), incongruence (e.g., 'able to press 150 pounds and run five miles in 40 minutes'), or inaccessibility (Model III's tables).

Similarly, starting from Model II's 'unreasonable risk' standard, we could increase its transparency by appending a list of the components of 'unreasonable risk'—for example, 'taking into consideration the person's age, physical condition, mental alertness, skill and experience.' Yet such laundry lists add relatively little transparency when both the meaning and relative weights of the enumerated terms remain unspecified. Providing the necessary specification, however, makes the standard less congruent or accessible.

II. The Optimal Degree of Regulatory Precision

The observation that various verbal formulations are likely to involve differing mixes of transparency, accessibility, and congruence offers little solace to a regulatory draftsman. Tradeoffs may be inevitable, but not all tradeoffs are equally acceptable. What our rulemaker needs is a normative principle for comparing formulations.

Invocation of moral values like fairness, equity, or community offers little promise. Each dimension of regulatory precision implicates important moral principles. Transparent rules help to assure equality by defining when people are 'similarly situated'[32] and divorcing the outcome of an official determination from the decisionmakers. An accessible rule, by contrast, promotes communal and 'dignitary' values by enabling members of its audience to participate in its application to their individual circumstances.[33] Congruence directly fosters the law's substantive moral aims by promoting outcomes in individual cases consistent with those aims.

These principles frequently work at cross-purposes, however, precisely because tradeoffs occur along the three dimensions of precision. A perfectly transparent rule ('no person with a surname ending in a vowel may be a pilot') may assure similar treatment of categorically similar cases, but it may also fail to provide defensible applications. A morally congruent rule ('immorality is prohibited') can be too vague to satisfy the moral imperatives of fair warning and meaningful participation. A perfectly transparent and congruent rule may be so cumbersome as to deprive its audience of fair warning.

A. An Efficiency Criterion for Rule Precision

Since tradeoffs among values are unavoidable, the morally sensitive rulemaker must reduce those conflicting values to some common denominator. One candidate is the currency of welfare economics—'social utility.'[34] A social utility-maximizing rulemaker would, for any conceivable set of rule formulations, identify and estimate the social costs and benefits flowing from each, and select the one with the greatest net social benefit. Subject to a constraint on his rulemaking budget or authority, the rulemaker would continue adding to his stock of rules so long as the marginal social benefit of the last increment exceeded its marginal cost.[35]

We can use our pilot retirement rule to sketch the dimensions of this task. Suppose our hypothetical policymaker wants to decide whether Model I or Model II is socially preferable. Several considerations argue in favor of Model I. It may, for example, produce a higher level of voluntary compliance, since the rulemaker can more readily charge pilots with its enforcement. For this reason, pilots are less likely to evade or sabotage the rule.

Model I also seems cheaper to enforce. Since it increases accuracy of prediction, there will be fewer requests for interpretation. Since it increases the level of compliance, there will be fewer violations to process. And since it is highly objective, the enforcement agency can quickly and accurately resolve the disputes that do arise. Model II, by contrast, will generate numerous and expensive conflicts. In the absence of clear stand-ards, factfinding and offers of proof will range far and wide. The rule's audience will expend effort in interpreting the meaning of the standard and in making successive elaborations of its meaning in individual cases.

The increased compliance and reduced litigation are counterproductive, however, if a rule induces the wrong result. The age-60 rule will deprive society of the services of safe, experienced sexagenarians. Even the claim that Model I has lower transaction costs must be tempered with skepticism. Arbitrary rules invite demands for modification. Proponents of Model I will spend their days defending the rule and may in the end accede to some exceptions. Processing petitions for waiver will consume many of the same social resources required for the administration of Model II.

Varying the degree of precision with which a rule is expressed can have an impact on both the primary behavior of the rule's audience and the transaction costs associated with administering the rule.[36] Refining these concepts further, one can identify four principal subcategories of potential costs and benefits:

1. *Rate of Compliance.*—Increased precision may increase compliance and decrease evasion or concealment costs. First, it will reduce the cost of determining the rule's application to an actor's intended conduct. Second, the ease of enforcing transparent rules discourages would-be violators from making costly (and, from society's viewpoint, wasteful) efforts to avoid compliance. Increasing a rule's transparency may, however, eventually reduce compliance by increasing the cost of locat-ing and applying the applicable provision, i.e., increasing the rule's inaccessibility and incongruence.

2. *Over- and Under-Inclusiveness.*—Increasing the transparency of a rule may increase the variance between intended and actual outcomes. The rulemaker may be unable to predict every consequence of applying the rule or to foresee all of the circumstances to which it may apply. While the rulemaker presumably can change the rule after learning of its incongruence, the process of amendment is costly and gives rise to social losses in the interim. On the other hand, a more opaque rule, though facially congruent, may be under- or over-inclusive in applica-tion, because its vagueness invites misinterpretation. Increasing a rule's transparency may therefore substitute errors of misspecification for errors of misapplication.

3. *Costs of Rulemaking.*—Rulemaking involves two sorts of social costs: the cost of obtaining and analyzing information about the rule's probable

impact, and the cost of securing agreement among participants in the rulemaking process. These costs usually rise with increases in a rule's transparency since objective regulatory line-drawing increases the risk of misspecification and sharpens the focus of value conflicts. Yet, greater initial precision can also reduce the need for future rulemaking by leaving fewer policy questions open for later resolution by amendment or case-by-case elaboration.

4. *Cost of Applying a Rule.*—The cost to both the regulated population and enforcement officials of applying a rule tends to increase as the rule's opacity or inaccessibility increases. Transparent and accessible rules can reduce the number of disputes that arise and simplify their resolution by causing the parties' predictions of the outcome to converge.

Having identified the costs and benefits associated with alternative rule formulations, the optimizing rulemaker computes the net social cost or benefit of each and selects the version generating the greatest net benefit.

B. Balancing the Factors

Classifying the consequences of alternative rules in this way helps identify situations in which *one factor may exert especially strong pressures* for *transparency, accessibility, or congruence.* The rate of compliance, for example, is an especially important consideration in the analysis of rules regulating socially harmful conduct. This factor supports use of highly transparent and accessible standards. By 'strictly' construing the language used in criminal statutes according to its most widely accepted meaning, for example, courts enhance the transparency of the criminal law.[37] One would similarly expect a high degree of transparency in the rules used to define easily concealable regulatory offenses such as unsafe transportation of hazardous chemicals,[38] unauthorized entry into the country,[39] or over-harvesting fisheries.[40]

Concerns about over- or under-inclusiveness dominate *when errors of misclassification are particularly costly.* The First Amendment 'over-breadth' doctrine, for example, reflects a belief that speech often has a higher value to society than to the individual speaker.[41] Similarly, the Supreme Court's concern about excessively rigid death penalty statutes reflects the very high cost it assigns to erroneous executions.[42] Less dramatic examples also abound in administrative regulation. For example, the social impact of discharging a given quantity of a pollutant into a stream can vary widely from industry to industry (because of variations in costs of prevention) or from stream to stream (because of variations in harm caused).[43] Where the costs of over- or under-inclusiveness are high, rational policymakers will favor highly flexible or intricate regulatory formulas.

The costs of applying rules often loom especially large in the formulation of standards designed to govern a large volume of disputes. In these situations a desire to minimize litigation costs by using bright-line rules may outweigh countervailing considerations. Thus, agencies with particularly crowded enforcement dockets tend to adopt the most transparent rules.[44] A related transaction cost is incurred in controlling the behavior of persons charged with a policy's enforcement. Numerous scholars have documented the difficulties of controlling the behavior of police officers and other officials applying law at the 'street level.'[45] In occupational safety and health regulation or administration of the tax laws, which depend on large decentralized enforcement staffs, the costs of applying rules often push rules to a highly transparent extreme.[46]

The cost of rulemaking may assume particular saliency in a collegial rulemaking body such as a legislature or multi-member independent agency.[47] The larger the number of participants and the more divergent their values, the greater will be the cost of reaching agreement. One would therefore expect collegial rulemakers to favor formulas like Model II, which minimize the range of agreement required. This effect is especially pronounced if the subsequent process of elaborating such open-ended rules has fewer participants.

The implication of this analysis is that optimal precision varies from rule to rule. The degree of precision appropriate to any particular rule depends on a series of variables peculiar to the rule's author, enforcer, and addressee. As a consequence, generalizations about optimal rule precision are inherently suspect. Nonetheless, one can use this framework to draw some general inferences about the relative precision of different types of rules. In the remainder of this section, I offer three illustrations based on distinctions between external and internal rules, between liability and sanctioning standards, and between prohibitory and licensure rules.

C. *Internal vs. External Rules*

Administrative rulemakers typically promulgate two kinds of rules: 'external' rules addressed principally to the regulated public, and 'internal' rules, addressed to persons charged with the enforcement of the external rules.[48] There is often a substantial difference in the content of the two types of rules. Sometimes an internal rule directly contradicts an external rule.[49]

More commonly, internal rules seek to establish priorities for the allocation of resources to the enforcement of facially absolute commands.

Since they are addressed to different audiences and serve different
functions, the two types of rules would be expected to have a different
degree of precision. Because internal standards are fashioned to allocate
resources,[50] concerns about incongruity will weigh heavily in the rule
formulation. The socially optimal allocation of scarce prosecutorial
resources, for instance, is a monumentally complicated matter, turning
on a wide variety of factors.[51] Simple, transparent rules may, therefore,
grossly misallocate resources.

The putative gains from using transparent language, moreover, are
likely to be smaller in the context of internal rules. Agency personnel
are typically more homogeneous than the regulated public. The selection,
training, and socialization of enforcement staff reduce the need to rely on
internal standards to supply the education and motivation often provided
by external standards. Since the audience for internal rules is also subject
to more continuous and intensive supervision, the compliance-inducing
function of rule precision is similarly less important.

These considerations provide support for the judiciary's customary
reluctance to interfere with the 'internal management' of administrative
agencies.[52] Courts have displayed a great tolerance toward opaque prosecutorial policies,[53] for example, despite frequent academic calls for
reform.[54] Our analysis cautions us not to be dismayed at this condition.
It also suggests a basis for explaining occasional deviations from this
deferential posture. The Supreme Court has, for instance, required most
investigative agencies to establish relatively transparent policies for the
conduct of regulatory inspections.[55] Although such policies allocate internal investigative resources, they also regulate external conduct by instruct-
ing inspectors what to inspect and by advising regulated entities what to
make available for inspection. Because most inspectors' work occurs at
remote locations, moreover, close personal supervision is not a practical
substitute for detailed written guidance.[56]

D. Sanctioning vs. Liability Rules

Rules defining standards of criminal conduct tend to be relatively precise,[57]
while rules for determining appropriate punishment tend to be opaque.[58]
A similar divergence has been observed in civil regulation.[59] Our framework suggests a basis for both this disparity and for the extreme deference
that reviewing courts have accorded to administrative sanctioning decisions.[60]

First, many policymakers feel that encouraging compliance—an important function of precision—has little application to sanctioning standards. This sentiment in part reflects the modest range of most regulatory sanctions. When the range of options is known to be small, the marginal benefit of greater precision is commensurately small. Indeed, many regulators believe that imprecision is a better deterrent than precision, where actual penalties are modest.[61]

Drafters of sanctioning standards also face problems with congruence. The imposition of sanctions may serve several different objectives simultaneously such as general deterrence, special deterrence, compensation, retribution, incapacitation, or rehabilitation.[62] Tailoring a standard to fit the relevant mix of objectives is often difficult. Even if one accepts general deterrence as the sole objective, the task is not greatly simplified. Effective deterrence demands a penalty based on the perceived probability of detection and conviction, the net gain to the violator from his violation, and the nonpenalty cost of violation.[63] The same act, committed by different actors under different circumstances, may warrant widely divergent sanctions. Any transparent rule, therefore, is likely to produce both underdeterrence (by generating too low a penalty in many cases) and overdeterrence (by generating too high a penalty in others).

The distinction between liability rules and sanctioning rules is most apparent, however, in the area of transaction costs. Liability rules must be interpreted by the regulated population as well as persons involved in every level of enforcement. Since sanctioning rules apply only after a preliminary finding of liability, they are typically applied by a smaller group of officials (prosecutors and arbiters) and in a drastically reduced number of cases. As a consequence, the cost of applying sanctioning rules is smaller than the cost of applying liability rules.

The foregoing analysis suggests that, as a general rule, drafters of sanctioning rules will be less willing to compromise congruence to attain transparency and accessibility than drafters of liability rules. The analysis also suggests the proper characteristics to look for in seeking exceptions to this general tendency. For example, the larger the number of enforcement officials involved in the sanctioning process—and the greater the resulting cost of policing their conduct—the more transparent one would expect sanctioning rules to be. This helps to explain why agencies with huge caseloads and a highly decentralized enforcement process, like the Occupational Safety and Health Administration[64] or the Mine Safety and Health Administration,[65] have detailed penalty standards.

E. Licensure Standards vs. Prohibitory Rules

A third type of disparity explained by our analysis is the tendency of policymakers to formulate less transparent standards for issuing licenses than for direct prohibitions or commands.[66] Licensure rules do not primarily deter or influence conduct. Rather, they seek to facilitate predictions about future conduct. They are, in this sense, addressed more to licensing officials than to the regulated population.

Licensure rules, moreover, are likely to pose greater difficulties in attaining congruence than liability rules because they tend to address relatively large and complex phenomena—such as the entry of a new competitor into an existing market—rather than isolated acts or omissions. Accurate estimation of social impact is bound to be correspondingly complex in scope and difficulty. Some licensing rules, moreover, seek to facilitate relative, rather than absolute, judgments. The question is not simply, 'Is A socially beneficial?' but rather, 'Which, among A, B, C, etc., is most socially beneficial?' Simple, transparent rules seem particularly prone to error in sorting out such calculations.[67]

A comparison of transaction costs in licensing and direct-conduct regulation yields an indeterminate result. Licensure cases are relatively infrequent because they deal with much lumpier issues. Yet such cases typically involve substantial individual stakes, because foreclosure from the licensed activity may involve substantial opportunity costs in foregone earnings.

These factors should induce drafters of licensing standards to give more weight to congruence and less to transparency and accessibility than do the authors of prohibitory rules. One would expect the strongest pressure for transparency in matters like occupational licensure or licensing motor vehicle operators, which involve a large volume of individual determinations, each having small social significance. In these settings, pressure to reduce transaction costs would push standards more in the direction of transparency, notwithstanding the cost in over- or under-inclusiveness.

III. Four Case Studies of Rule Precision

The foregoing categorical comparisons illustrate the insights that one can derive by using an efficiency model to evaluate rule precision. But insights at so high a level of generality provide little useful guidance to rulemakers and their overseers. The acid test for the efficiency criterion is its ability to support confident judgments about the precision of particular regulatory formulations.

To test the utility of our 'precision calculus' as an evaluative framework, I apply it in this section to four specific administrative rules: the Federal Aviation Administration's retirement policy for commercial pilots, the Comptroller of the Currency's criteria for chartering national banks, the Social Security Administration's 'grid' rules for disability determination, and the Immigration and Naturalization Service's standards for awarding permanent resident status to nonimmigrant aliens. The first three illustrate the three prototypical models sketched in Section I. Although the relative precision of each has been the subject of considerable public controversy, my analysis suggests that each represents a rational response to the particular demands of its regulatory context. The fourth case study, by contrast, highlights an administrative standard whose flaws fall into clear relief under the light of the precision framework.

A. The Pilot Retirement Rule

The Federal Aviation Act of 1958 authorized the Federal Aviation Administration (FAA) 'to promote safety of flight of civil aircraft,' giving 'full consideration to the duty resting upon air carriers to perform their services with the highest possible degree of safety in the public interest.'[68] Among the more specific charges, the law instructed the FAA to develop '[r]easonable rules and regulations governing, in the interest of safety, the maximum hours or periods of service of airmen...'[69] The Act evinced a single-minded concern for the safety of air transportation.

As part of its program to implement the Act, the FAA promulgated the 'age 60 rule' in 1959: 'No individual who has reached his 60th birthday shall be utilized or serve as a pilot on any aircraft while engaged in air carrier operations.'[70] In explaining the basis for the rule, the FAA Administrator expressed concern about the 'progressive deterioration of certain important physiological and psychological functions.'[71] Although the agency conceded that 'available data do not permit any precise determination of the specific age at which continued activity as a pilot can be said conclusively to constitute a hazard to safety under normal or emergency conditions of flight,'[72] it chose a cutoff at age 60 for lack of any more defensible alternative.[73]

The rule has drawn recurrent criticism for its overinclusiveness. The rule's earliest and, until recently, most persistent critic was the Air Line Pilots Association (ALPA). After unsuccessfully opposing the rule's initial adoption,[74] ALPA turned to the courts for relief. Its challenge to the rule's rationality in *ALPA* v. *Quesada*[75] failed, however, producing instead this characteristically deferential judicial response: 'It is not the business of courts to substitute their untutored judgment for the expert knowledge of those who are given authority to implement the general directives of Congress.'[76] Subsequent efforts to enlist judicial support in the attack on the rule have proved equally unavailing. Encouraged by a suggestive footnote in the *Quesada* case,[77] several pilots petitioned the FAA for exemption from the retirement rule pursuant to a statutory provision that authorizes the Administrator to 'grant exemptions ... if he finds that such action would be in the public interest.'[78] The FAA has, however, promptly denied all petitions for exemption without hearing and has been uniformly upheld on appeal.[79]

Having failed to secure relief from the agency or the courts, ALPA approached Congress. After a decade of unsuccessful lobbying, ALPA finally persuaded Congress to direct a study of the rule's medical justification by the National Institutes of Health.[80] But the study panel's report, released two years later, concluded that the rule should be retained.[81] After examining a wide array of medical and performance simulation tests, the panel found none able to predict loss of function with sufficient accuracy to replace the simple age criterion.[82]

The age 60 rule is pure Model I: almost perfectly transparent and elementally simple. Model I formulations are likely to seem especially attractive when enforcement is particularly difficult or costly. This consideration might have motivated the FAA in 1959, even though its official explanation for the rule makes scant mention of it.[83] Involuntary retirement can exact a heavy toll on the unwilling pilot in forgone income[84] and loss of professional satisfaction or self-esteem. Many pilots might go to considerable lengths to avoid the rule. A bright-line retirement standard offers a promising way to minimize the costs of combatting evasion.

In fact, however, the risk of evasion could not have appeared substantial. Piloting commercial aircraft is a visible activity, and the FAA could count on the carriers to help it police any reasonable retirement policy.[85] The transaction-cost savings argument is more telling. Disqualification from piloting commercial aircraft is a sufficiently severe deprivation to warrant a hearing of contested issues. Enforcement of a discretionary retirement standard, consequently, could generate expensive proceedings involving a high proportion of the pilots to whom it was applied. Although the number of commercial pilots approaching retirement in 1959 was small, the FAA correctly foresaw a substantial increase in their numbers.[86]

Set against this modest saving in enforcement costs, one must consider the incongruity losses occasioned by the use of a sharp dividing line. Prematurely grounding healthy pilots can involve two complementary forms of social cost: (1) the cost of training replacements, and (2) the additional accidents caused by insufficiently trained replacements. At the time of the rule's adoption, these costs did not appear particularly great. The airline industry was beginning to introduce turbojet aircraft into commercial aviation on a large scale in the late 1950's. Operation of the new aircraft, even by experienced pilots, required extensive training. In fact, far from being concerned about the cost of replacing experienced pilots, the FAA expressed doubt whether any amount of retraining could break senior pilots of old habits completely enough to assure proper response in emergencies.[87]

A second reason for the FAA's apparent disregard of incongruity costs was the lack of any discriminant better than age.[88] Granted, the FAA seemed to agree that age is only a crude proxy for incapacitating conditions. But it does no good to bemoan the crudeness of that proxy unless a better predictor can be found.

If the case for the rule's original adoption rests heavily on the introduction of turbojet aircraft and the infancy of medical science, what factors justify the rule's retention in 1983? The calculus clearly has changed. Transaction costs provide an even weightier argument for a Model I rule now, with 500 to 1000 airline pilots reaching 60 each year.[89] Yet the potential losses occasioned by a hard-and-fast age discriminant have also increased. No dramatic revolution in aircraft technology threatens the present generation of senior pilots with obsolescence. At an estimated cost of $250,000[90] to train a new pilot, the replacement tradeoff begins to look less favorable than it did in 1959.

Time has also eroded the 'lack of alternatives' argument. Much progress has been made in developing reliable measures for many important physiological functions.[91] Yet, as testing techniques have become more sophisticated, so has our appreciation of the conditions for successful pilot performance. There remain more critical functions, especially intellectual and psychological ones, for which no better discriminant than age has been found.[92] Recent progress in developing testing procedures, in short, cannot guarantee the reduction in the volume of unnecessarily grounded pilots that a more individualized screening process might ordinarily generate.

The ultimate balance is not easy to strike.[93] One can say with assurance only that in the twenty-four years since 1959, the stakes have risen on both sides of the dispute. The number of skilled pilots languishing in premature retirement is unquestionably much greater today, but, then, so is the number of lives that a more individualized screen would unavoidably entrust to aging pilots with undetectable risks. In the weighing of such imponderables, even a modest saving in transaction costs is justification enough to retain the present rule.

B. National Bank Chartering Standards

Compared to the FAA's retirement rule, the criteria used by the Comptroller of the Currency to charter national banks are a study in ambiguity. The Comptroller of the Currency derives his authority to grant charters to national banks from the National Bank Act of 1864.[94] Throughout the period since the Act's adoption, Comptrollers have made very little effort to confine their virtually unrestricted statutory discretion by articulating more precise criteria for chartering decisions. Prior to 1976, the Comptroller's published policy statements merely listed five factors that would be investigated in the course of processing an application:

(1) The adequacy of the proposed bank's capital structure;
(2) The earning prospects of the proposed bank;
(3) The convenience and needs of the community to be served by the proposed bank;
(4) The character and general standing in the community or [sic] the applicants, prospective directors, proposed officers, and other employees, and other persons connected with the application or to be connected with the proposed bank; and
(5) The banking ability and experience of proposed officers and other employees.[95]

Virtually no 'common law' of bank chartering evolved, moreover, since Comptrollers furnished little or no explanation for their decisions.[96]

This state of extreme regulatory opacity led Professor Kenneth Scott, in a 1975 study, to criticize the Comptroller for failing to 'provide a clear and consistent explanation of what he is doing.'[97] Based on Scott's report, the Administrative Conference of the United States recommended that the bank chartering agencies, including the Office of the Comptroller of the Currency (OCC), 'undertake to provide a full statement of their objectives in approving or denying applications for charters . . . and . . . in concrete terms the standards to be applied.'[98]

On June 4, 1976, the Comptroller responded by publishing in the *Federal Register* a document entitled 'Policy Statements on Corporate Activities.'[99] The statement articulated an overarching policy goal for bank chartering—'to maintain a sound national banking system without placing undue restraint upon entry into that system.' The statement imposed several constraints on the pursuit of this goal: avoiding the chartering of 'so many banks that none can grow to a size sufficient to offer a full range of needed services,' admitting 'only those qualified applicants that can be economically supported and profitably operated,' and protecting the 'viability' of newly chartered independent banks.

The policy statement went on to enumerate four 'banking factors' ('income and expenses,' 'management,' 'stock distribution,' and 'capital'), five 'market factors' ('economic condition and growth potential,' 'primary service area,' 'location,' 'population,' and 'financial institutions'), and several 'other factors' to be considered in evaluating an application. Although the guidelines included a few objective tests for stock distribution and adequacy of capital,[100] most of the relevant factors were expressed in highly conclusory terms with no indication of their relative weights.[101]

Predictably, the 1976 policy statement did not still the Comptroller's critics. The Senate Banking Committee concluded in 1980 that: 'OCC's reliance on vague chartering standards...[has] exposed the chartering process to charges of favoritism and arbitrary decision making.'[102] To support its characterization, the study cited the high rate of disagreement among internal OCC reviewers and alleged inconsistencies in handling specific cases.[103] Finding OCC's economic projections to have been wide of the mark in several instances, the committee concluded that the 'community need' criterion 'is a poor indicator of a new bank's likely prospects'[104] and proposed greater reliance on factors relating to organization and management.

Almost simultaneously with release of the Committee report, the Comptroller issued a revised policy statement. The statement spoke of 'clarifying' previous policy and 'facilitat[ing] applicant and public understanding,'[105] but its principal function was to announce a shift toward a more competitive bank entry policy.[106] As an exercise in policy 'clarification,' the 1980 statement accomplishes little. While the sheer volume of words has increased since 1976, the few earlier per se rules relating to stock ownership and capitalization have been replaced with vague rule-of-reason language (e.g., 'sufficient' capital,[107] 'wide distribution of stock'[108]). Aside from lowering the 'community need' barrier to entry,[109] the policy statement provides little guidance to individual applicants.

The Comptroller's persistent reliance on an opaque Model II approach should neither surprise nor dismay us. First, the likelihood that per se rules will produce costly incongruities seems high, if one assumes—as Comptrollers emphatically have—that the overriding purpose of entry restrictions is to maintain public confidence in the banking system by reducing the risk of failure. The likelihood that new entry will cause economic dislocation and erosion of confidence—either through the entrant's failure or by weakening an incumbent—seems to depend on a host of variables relating to the entrant's capabilities, its competitors' positions, and market conditions. These factors will vary widely from market to market, and the history of chartering suggests that they can change markedly with shifts in economic conditions.[110]

Encouraging compliance, moreover, seems largely irrelevant here. Chartering standards are not aimed at modifying behavior. Their sole function is to guide the selection of applicants who are qualified to be admitted to the banking industry. It is true, of course, that the relative transparency of standards may influence the rate of applications and, consequently, the rate of entry. More precise criteria would reduce uncertainty and might encourage applications from those dissuaded by the high costs of compiling the necessary economic data. During a time of perceived inadequacy of banking services, this factor might exert a stronger pull toward greater transparency.

The evidence does not support this thesis, however. The 1976 policy statement—the high-water mark of OCC charter rule precision—is far more protectionist in tone than the 1980 rules, and was issued by a Comptroller whose charter approval rates were the lowest in the decade. Furthermore, Comptrollers who wish to encourage new entry can often encourage applications far more efficiently by making procompetitive public statements than by issuing rule changes.[111]

Transaction costs similarly offer little support for a high degree of precision. The costs of applying the rules are not substantial. The Comptroller received, on average, only about 120 formal charter applications per year during the 1970's. The process for deciding cases is highly informal, usually consisting of only a field examination and several internal reviews. While organizers often have a sufficient stake in the outcome to demand far more elaborate procedures, the courts and Congress have resisted pressures to impose them.[112] The opportunity for applicants to reapply or to seek entry through the state regulatory system undoubtedly mitigates those pressures. Furthermore, the decision making is highly centralized. Even after receiving blanket legislative authority in 1980 to delegate any power vested in his office by law,[113] the Comptroller has maintained tight central control over chartering decisions.[114] This longstanding tradition of centralized decision making has substantially reduced the pressure to use clear rules to control agency decision makers.

The cost of rulemaking similarly cuts against increased transparency. If it is true that the risks of incongruity are serious, the cost of developing a transparent, yet congruent, rule would be quite high. Preliminary efforts by staff economists to produce more rigorous models for predicting economic impact have been discouraging.[115] Nor does the Comptroller face as great a tradeoff between *ex ante* and *ex post* policymaking costs as other agencies, given the informality of the charter decision making process and the minimal explanation for rejections demanded by reviewing courts.

In sum, the degree of precision with which Comptrollers have articulated charter policy, especially since 1976, seems fully consistent with the context in which they operate. This is not to say that the substantive policy assumptions or the procedural informality associated with the regulation of bank entry are necessarily defensible.[116] But in a system built on these features, a substantial increase in charter rule precision would probably not produce benefits justifying its cost.

C. The Disability Insurance 'Grid' Rule

The Social Security Disability Insurance (DI) Program pays benefits to wage earners and their dependents enrolled in the Social Security programs who lose their jobs as the result of a 'disability.' Since the program's inception in 1957, the definition of a 'disability' has undergone repeated administrative revision and elaboration.[117] This evolution culminated in 1978 with adoption of the so-called 'grid' rule—a complex formula that specifies how various physical and vocational attributes of claimants are to be integrated into the ultimate disability determination.[118] As a prototypical Model III rule, the grid rule has drawn intense criticism for its alleged incongruity and inaccessibility.[119]

The Social Security Act of 1956 defined 'disability' quite simply as 'inability to engage in any substantial gainful activity by reason of any medically determinable physical or mental impairment which can be expected to result in death or to be of long-continued and indefinite duration.'[120] Although the statutory formula has been revised several times,[121] it still delegates primary responsibility to the Social Security Administration (SSA) to elaborate the meaning of 'disability.' Before 1978, SSA devoted most of its attention to 'physical and mental impairment,' developing detailed guidelines for measuring impairments and defining several 'per se disabling' conditions.[122] The nonmedical criteria for determining 'inability to engage in substantial gainful activity,' however, remained clouded in imprecise verbiage.[123] Congress amended the Act in 1968 to require SSA to consider the applicant's 'age, education, and work experience' in making the disability determination.[124] Until 1978, however, the assessment of these factors was consigned to the judgment of claims processing officials, who relied heavily on the professional opinion of vocational experts.[125]

The grid rule substituted a mechanical formula for the previously individualized process in a large number of disability cases.[126] The grid specifies the relationships among four independent variables (the claimant's 'exertional capabilities,' 'education,' 'age,' and 'previous work experience') and the dependent variable ('disability').[127] Each of the independent variables can take several possible values—for example, there are four 'age' categories ('advanced,' 'closely approaching advanced,' 'younger (45–49),' and 'younger (18–44)'), and three 'experience' groupings ('unskilled or none,' 'skilled or semiskilled—skills not transferable,' and 'skilled or semiskilled—skills transferable'). For each combination of these variables, the rule specifies the ultimate decision ('disabled'/'not disabled').

The grid rule is the latest stage in a relentless progression toward transparency and complexity in the disability standard. The factor most obviously responsible for this trend is transaction costs.[128] The volume of determinations is immense and was, until recently, growing at a rapid rate. The number of hearings is still growing.[129] Moreover, although the average cost of processing all DI claims is modest ($171 in 1978[130]), the cost per contested claim is a good deal higher.[131] The total administrative cost of the disability insurance system in 1978 was $327 million.[132]

Raw numbers like these fail to do full justice to the importance of transaction costs. A 'hidden' transaction cost in any benefits system is the impact of delay on deserving applicants. The 551,500 applicants who received a favorable decision in 1976, for example, had to wait an average of 105 days for the award.[133] The human costs of anxiety and deprivation from such delays are enormous.

A second hidden transaction cost is the difficulty of controlling subordinate decisionmakers. A substantial degree of *de facto* decentralization is unavoidable in so enormous an operation. But the structure of the DI program promotes decentralization with a vengeance. Initial decisions (which become final determinations in the eighty-five percent of cases not appealed to SSA) are made by officers of fifty autonomous state agencies who are subject only to indirect supervision by SSA.[134] These state agencies themselves are often administratively decentralized and rely heavily on consulting physicians and vocational experts.[135] Within SSA, decisions are made by a cadre of about seven hundred fiercely independent Administrative Law Judges (ALJ's) who preside at hearings where there are usually no representatives of SSA present.[136] Any decision making apparatus so fragmented—especially one which affects such large sums of money and so many people—cries out for tight, centralized control. Recent studies documenting inconsistencies among state agencies and ALJ's have intensified pressures for reform.[137]

Demands for tighter supervision naturally focus attention on the clarity of substantive standards. The utility of conventional management control devices like reporting systems, performance appraisal, and quality review[138] ultimately depends on the transparency of the underlying standards to be applied.[139] It is one thing to document inconsistency in results by comparing two individuals' resolutions of a hypothetical case.[140] But it is very difficult to remedy that inconsistency without having clear criteria. Without the dramatic increase in regulatory objectivity, SSA's massive quality control program and its impressive quantitative[141] gains would be almost unthinkable.

Transparency is usually bought at the price of incongruity or *ex ante* rulemaking costs. To take the latter first, the development of SSA's elaborate scheme has undoubtedly been costly. But failure to develop generic criteria would merely postpone, not avoid, rulemaking costs in a program that has always required elaborate justification for individual decisions. Disappointed recipients are entitled to increasingly thorough and coherent explanations at successive levels. Formal hearing procedures (at the ALJ stage)[142] and searching judicial review[143] together impose a particularly rigorous justificatory burden on those who deny claims at the appellate stage. A legalistic system for processing claims will reward heavy initial investment in *a priori* rulemaking by reducing the cost of meeting its subsequent explanatory obligation.

The incongruity argument is more troublesome. The current rules undoubtedly miss their target with some frequency.[144] Can it be true, for example, that no person in his late 40's who is unskilled, uneducated, and limited to sedentary work, can be 'disabled'?[145] Yet, despite such troubling examples, the true cost of misclassifying a case depends on how close the case is to the boundary between 'disabled' and 'not disabled.'[146] A regime that misclassifies 100,000 healthy malingerers or immobile quadriplegics is far more costly to society than one that misclassifies 100,000 potentially handicapped persons. The latter, if granted benefits, may forgo only limited productive effort, and, if denied benefits, may have some hope for independent support. The relevant question then becomes whether the unavoidable incongruities of a bright-line rule cluster near the dividing line or near the extremes. As Professor Jerry

Mashaw shows, under SSA's current regime, the incongruities cluster near the dividing line.[147] SSA's decision rule uses simple, transparent tests to eliminate the easy cases at both extremes, reserving the closer cases for resolution under more refined criteria.[148] Intuitively, at least, the grid seems to embrace within the company of the disabled the most deserving cases.

Moreover, while the rule contains many more bright lines than before, it still contains strategically located discretionary judgments, such as the threshold severity-of-impairment determination,[149] the 'medical equivalence' test for unusual medical impairments,[150] and the classification of a claimants' 'residual functional capacity.'[151] The flexibility afforded by these assessments enables decision makers to avoid egregiously unjust applications of the rule. On this impressionistic level, the SSA rules seem to hold incongruity costs within tolerable limits.

This brings us back to transaction costs, since the rules achieve their objective only at the cost of enormous complexity. Does not the sheer difficulty of the decision rule compensate, in added fact-finding and interpretive efforts, for the savings effected by increased transparency? The answer here seems to be, 'No.' First, because the rule does not announce a standard of behavior,[152] its complexity has no adverse effect on private planning. Second, most of the effort currently expended on gathering medical and vocational information in processing a claim would still be required under a superficially simpler standard. And since most cases raise only a few contestable issues, the overall complexity of the rules is less important than their accessibility and transparency. In these latter respects, SSA's rules receive a high score.

D. INS Change-of-Status Policy

Until 1952, aliens visiting the United States on non-immigrant visas who wished to remain had to return to their native lands to obtain an immigrant visa from the United States Consul.[153] To relieve the burden of that requirement, Congress authorized the Attorney General, 'in his discretion' and 'under such regulations as he may prescribe,' to adjust the status of some aliens to that of 'an alien lawfully admitted for permanent residence.'[154]

To qualify for adjustment of status, the applicant must meet several statutory criteria, including immediate eligibility for an immigrant visa under applicable quotas.[155] These threshold criteria are either facially transparent or well articulated by a history of interpretation. The additional 'discretionary' element of the determination, however, is neither transparent nor well articulated. In delegating his authority to the Immigration and Naturalization Service (INS), the Attorney General made no effort to clarify the statute's 'discretionary' residue.[156] The INS has taken only very modest steps in that direction. Its published regulations under section 245 of the Immigration and Nationality Act[157] provide no extra-statutory criteria for exercising discretion.[158] The Service's Operations Instructions merely state a 'policy that the application should not be denied as a matter of discretion when substantial equities exist.'[159] The published decisions of the INS District Directors and the Board of Immigration Appeals (BIA) yield only a list of undefined and unweighted 'adverse factors' (e.g., preconceived intent to seek permanent residence at the time of entry, misrepresentations made in the application, petty criminal conduct, illegal employment) and 'equities' (e.g., bona fide marriage, substantial difficulties in resettling in or returning to one's native land, candor in dealing with the Service).[160]

The Service has frequently been criticized for the opacity of these standards. Professor Abraham Sofaer, for example, presented compelling statistical and anecdotal evidence of inconsistencies in the Service's exercise of discretionary authority.[161] Discretionary denials, he observed, were considerably more susceptible to political intervention and administrative reversal than denials based on the more explicit statutory criteria.[162] While most courts have upheld section 245's discretionary power,[163] a few judges have voiced concern about its breadth. Dissenting in *Ameeriar* v. *INS*,[164] Judge Freedman characterized the Service's exercise of discretion as 'an utterly unguided and unpredictable undertaking. Only the inevitable necessity of disposing of the case is specified, like a result without a cause. What is the desired goal and what guides should channel the course to it receive no recognition.'[165]

In 1979, the Service proposed a rule establishing standards for changing the status of aliens.[166] The stated purpose of the rule was 'to assure that all applicants and petitioners receive fair and equal treatment before the Service.'[167] The rule listed six adverse and five favorable factors, required adjustment in the absence of adverse factors, and stated a strong presumption against adjusting the status of any alien who had evaded the normal immigration process.[168]

While one might be tempted to dismiss these proposed rules as a mere codification of existing practice, they make more visible and mandatory what had hitherto been largely implicit. Even this modest degree of policy clarification was too much for the INS. In a terse order issued on January 21, 1981, the INS withdrew the proposed rule, stating:

[I]t is impossible to foresee and enumerate all the favourable or adverse factors which may be relevant and should be considered in the exercise of administrative discretion. Listing some factors, even with the caveat that such list is not all inclusive, poses a danger that use of guidelines may become so rigid as to amount to an abuse of discretion.[169]

At least the Service is consistent: its explanations are no more transparent than its rules. In order to fathom the rejection of the proposed rule, we must look behind the official explanation. Several INS district officials feared increased litigation. One particularly colorful comment predicted:

[T]he proposals embodied in this draft would subject the Service to a constant barrage of spurious appeal [sic] by Immigration attorneys on the basis of the semantics proposed to be injected into the regulations. They subvert Government to the vagaries of attorney dilatory tactics and would appear to tie our hands completely in the cobwebs of endless liturgical [sic] dialogue.[170]

It is hard to take such an assertion seriously. If anything, transaction costs cut in the opposite direction. The sheer volume of status-adjustment cases is staggering.[171] Moreover, most individual applicants have a sufficient interest in the outcome to expend considerable effort in the process.[172] The Sofaer study showed that the Service eventually reversed over ninety percent of the initial denials appealed.[173] Professor Sofaer thus regarded the savings in transaction costs from clearer rules as substantial.[174]

Greater clarity would, of course, entail additional *ex ante* rulemaking costs. But that investment would undoubtedly be repaid by the reduced explanatory burden on individual adjudicators. The INS Operations Instructions require that a discretionary denial not governed by applicable precedent be accompanied by a 'full discussion of the favorable and unfavorable factors' considered.[175] Clearer rules could facilitate the search for applicable precedent and shrink the residual category of decisions requiring elaborate ad hoc justification.

Another current form of *ex post* rulemaking by the Service is the selection of precedents for publication. The Service publishes only about a hundred of the thousands of status-adjustment decisions made each year by its district directors.[176] The very act of selection constitutes a form of rulemaking that could be displaced by issuing clearer *ex ante* guidelines.

Transparent rules could achieve additional savings in transaction costs by facilitating internal quality control. Decisionmaking in status-adjustment cases is unavoidably decentralized. In most cases,[177] initial decisions are rendered by 'Immigration Examiners' assigned to the

Service's thirty-six district offices.[178] To control the work product of this far-flung corps of adjudicators, the INS relies primarily on two devices. The weaker instrument is an exhortation in its Operations Instructions to decisionmakers to review the selected precedents periodically published by the agency.[179] The stronger control is the system of hierarchical review. A superior district officer must review all discretionary denials and any discretionary approvals involving adverse factors.[180] In fact, according to one former General Counsel, district directors personally review and issue all status adjustment decisions.[181] In addition, unsuccessful applicants may request review at the district level by a motion to reopen or to reconsider, and may obtain a new evaluation of their application at a deportation hearing.[182] More transparent decision rules would enable the Service to reduce its reliance on this elaborate system of quality control.

Clearer rules may also encourage greater compliance with the immigration laws. Every year thousands of illegal aliens seek residence in the United States. Ambiguous criteria for changing the status of non-immigrant visitors may encourage would-be immigrants to evade proper immigration channels. Clear standards cannot, of course, discourage evasion if physical remoteness or cultural barriers block their communication to aliens. But aliens affected by status-adjustment standards are already sufficiently familiar with immigration procedures to obtain a non-immigrant visa, enter the United States, and apply for status adjustment. They are therefore likely to be aware of INS policy.

Measuring the potential costs of the incongruity produced by a more transparent standard is difficult. It is unclear what Congress intended by inserting a discretionary element. The statutory eligibility conditions seem to address the most obvious concerns (e.g., excluding 'misfits' or preventing an evasion of quotas). One can imagine three possible reasons for further limiting access to status adjustment: (1) to prevent the circumvention of normal immigration channels; (2) to assure harmony between status-adjustment policy and our relations with foreign countries; and (3) to limit status adjustment to persons likely to contribute to society. The first of these purposes surely lends itself to a reasonably transparent rule. The second justifies at most a separate rule (or exception from the standard approach) for nationals of countries with whom our bilateral relations require a distinct policy.

The third hypothesized statutory objective provides the most plausible justification for resisting rule clarification. Assessing a person's prospective contribution to society, so the argument runs, is a holistic judgment that cannot be reduced to a formula. In the words of one INS official: '[T]he diversity of human activities tends to continually generate new factors and issues which should logically affect the exercise of discretion.'[183] At times, in fact, the Service seems to treat discretion as an *advantage*, rather than an absence of law.[184] Perhaps the Service is following a notion akin to Professor Tribe's 'structural due process' model[185] or Professor Mashaw's 'moral judgment' model.[186] Central to these models is the injunction that the state must permit persons with whom it deals to participate in the articulation of the very standards to be applied to their case. Reliance on a transparent antecedent rule effectively precludes that participation.

But status adjustment fails to satisfy the prerequisites specified by Mashaw and Tribe. The change-of-status case is rarely a contest of relative 'deservedness' or a determination of 'culpability.'[187] Nor is it usually the focal point of a clash of fundamental values.[188] While outcomes occasionally turn on the applicant's moral character,[189] most of the reasons for discretionary grant or denial could be subjected to greater anterior specification without offending an applicant's humanity.

IV. Administrative Failure and Suboptimal Rule Precision

The 'precision calculus' illustrated in Section III is a normative model, not a behavioral model, of administrative rulemaking. Even if one accepts my favorable assessment of the age-60, bank chartering, and disability rules, one must still ask whether it is reasonable to expect policymakers systematically to investigate the consequences of their linguistic choices. Selecting the optimally precise form for a given rule would seem to require qualities beyond the reach of many administrators: a selfless concern for the public good, consistent goals, comprehensive vision, and accurate foresight. Real policymakers, by contrast, are ordinary mortals burdened with incomplete knowledge, imperfect vision, and selfish desires. Governmental rule-making is plagued with 'administrative failures' as numerous and stubborn as the 'market failures' it theoretically seeks to correct.[190]

These characteristics may prevent the attainment of perfect rationality, but they need not foreclose a tolerable approximation, or 'bounded rationality.'[191] Herbert Simon long ago pointed out that 'administrative man' does not optimize, he 'satisfices.'[192] He proceeds incrementally, testing marginal deviations from the status quo against a slowly shifting threshold of acceptable performance.[193] To borrow a metaphor from the 'cybernetic' theorists, decisionmakers adopt thermostat mechanisms to test policies against an uncertain and changing environment.[194] These adaptive responses to imperfect information do not prevent errors, but they do promise that errors will be corrected.[195] Where these processes work effectively, we would expect even poorly drafted administrative rules to evolve toward the optimally precise formulation.

A. Communication of Social Costs and Benefits

This theory of error correction rests on two crucial assumptions: (1) that the social costs of excessively incongruent, inaccessible, or opaque rules will be effectively communicated to rulemakers; and (2) that rulemakers will respond to those costs. The first assumption incorporates the plausible premise that those with the most to lose (gain) from the promulgation of a particular rule will invest the most in efforts to defeat (enact) it.[196] Thus, in the pilot retirement example, if aging pilots stand to lose more (in reduced income) from adoption of an 'age-60' rule than younger pilots stand to gain (from more rapid advancement), one would expect an organization representing the pilots to lobby against its adoption.[197]

One cannot, however, logically equate the intensity of the response to a policy decision with the magnitude of the costs and benefits generated by the decision. The cost of sending signals of equivalent intensity may not be the same for each of the interests affected. The most vociferous lobby need not have the highest stake in the outcome; it may simply have the lowest organization costs.[198]

The FAA's decision to adopt the age-60 rule, for example, was greeted by intense criticism from the pilots' association and silence from the flying public. Yet the FAA should not necessarily have relaxed the rule. The net safety benefits to the public from retaining the rule might have greater value than the pilots' lost income. Yet the cost of organizing the public to lobby on behalf of the rule is much greater than the cost of organizing pilots to lobby for its relaxation,[199] and pilots can communicate their views far more efficiently than airline passengers.

Of course, reality is not as clear-cut as my example. Other well-organized factions, such as airlines and enforcement officials, may efficiently champion interests neglected by the pilots or shared by the traveling public. But the example does make the point that widely dispersed costs or benefits are less effectively represented in policymaking than concentrated costs or benefits.[200] Thus we would expect error-correction to favor interests championed by enforcers and regulated firms and to undervalue interests of unorganized beneficiaries of government programs.

The effect of disparity in organization costs on the precision of particular rules is not immediately obvious. Large, unorganized groups have no intrinsic preference for transparent rules. Beneficiaries of regulatory programs, for example, are as likely to object to the over- or under-inclusiveness of bright-line rules as to the evasion and misapplication of opaque rules. On occasion, however, the interests of regulated producers will diverge sufficiently from those of consumers to affect the precision of rules. Incumbent licensees, for instance, may have a powerful interest in maintaining especially vague or complex licensing standards as a barrier to entry by competitors.[201] The interest of consumers, by contrast, might be better served by clearer, more accessible standards that reduce the transaction costs of obtaining licenses. If the incumbents can organize and lobby the rulemaker more cheaply than consumers or potential entrants, the signals received by the rulemaker will be biased in favor of a Model II formulation.

Television station licensing provides a classic illustration. The standards employed by the Federal Communications Commission (FCC) for broadcast licenses have long been regarded as a model of administrative opacity.[202] In thirty years of television licensing, these standards have stubbornly resisted significant clarification.[203] It seems eminently plausible that this resiliency reflects an imbalance between the power of incumbent broadcasters and that of viewers and potential entrants. Because major market television franchises have enormous value[204] and because new entry into that market usually displaces an existing licensee, incumbents wish to maintain high barriers to entry. Both the enormous cost of contested renewal proceedings[205] and the infrequency of challenges to incumbents[206] indicate that the incumbents have established such barriers by preserving the Commission's opaque renewal standards. Moreover, the affiliation of many television licensees with one of the three major networks[207] decreases their organizational costs far below those of viewers or potential entrants. Consequently, neither the networks' opposition to more transparent entry criteria,[208] nor the acquiescence of the networks' opponents should surprise us.

Recipients of public assistance programs, by contrast, may have a stronger voice in policymaking than beneficiaries of regulatory programs. The process of individualized application, eligibility review, and termination theoretically gives recipients more direct access to policymakers than regulatory beneficiaries possess. If the stakes in individual cases frequently justify the expense of litigation and appeal,[209] recipients' interests slighted at the rulemaking stage will be asserted in the adjudication of claims. Repeated efforts by individual claimants to circumvent bright-line rules will alert policymakers to their incongruity costs, just as repeated efforts to exploit ambiguities in open-textured standards will dramatize the transaction and misapplication costs.

One cannot, however, always count on beneficiary self-help to cleanse impurities in the formulation of public assistance eligibility standards. Beneficiaries, as individuals, may lack the necessary knowledge, access, or incentive. Disappointed applicants for scarce public housing units, for example, may be too demoralized to demand clarification of vague selection standards.[210] Native Americans[211] or aliens[212] may be handicapped by cultural or linguistic barriers from effectively counteracting either the patronizing opacity or insensitive rigidity of their would-be bureaucratic benefactors.

B. *Divergence of Public and Private Interests*

The receipt of accurate signals about social costs and benefits is a necessary, but not sufficient, condition for optimal precision of rules. As mentioned earlier, a second condition is that the rulemaker be responsive to those signals. He must act to maximize social benefit or minimize social cost.

In today's intellectual climate that assumption may seem quaintly heroic. Most contemporary students of administrative behavior reject an earlier generation's faith in the public-spiritedness of governmental officials as hopelessly naive.[213] The revisionists claim that administrators pursue strictly personal objectives like wealth, power, and fame.[214] Rather than seeking to maximize social benefit, administrators will seek to maximize 'budgets,'[215] 'votes,'[216] or 'power.'[217] Of course, they may also enjoy promoting 'the public good.'[218] But actions motivated by a mix of selfish desires and idiosyncratic notions of social welfare will only incidentally correspond with the social optimum.

This view invites us to think of administrative policymakers as profit-maximizing entrepreneurs who manufacture standards. As such, the agency will select that mix of transparency, congruity, and complexity[219] that maximizes its net income. Like other profit-maximizing producers, it will consider only internal costs and benefits.

Using this analysis to predict the precision in particular standards requires us to separate the various costs and benefits enumerated earlier[220] into 'internal' and 'external' categories. The proper assignment of costs and benefits depends, of course, on the rulemaker's utility function. What is 'external' to one rulemaker may be 'internal' to another. A regulator seeking to maximize 'votes,'[221] for instance, will probably respond to a broader segment of the public than a regulator seeking only to maximize his own future income.[222] Let us initially adopt the most restrictive assumption—that 'internal' effects are only those that have a direct impact on the rulemaker's budget. In the next section we will examine the implications of relaxing that assumption.[223]

A policymaker concerned only with the direct fiscal impact of his actions would choose a rule that minimizes the sum of his rulemaking and enforcement costs. He would ignore its adverse consequences for private transaction costs, noncompliance, or incongruent behavior. Rules promulgated under these conditions would frequently deviate from the optimal amount of precision.

To illustrate this point, let us return to our earlier distinction between external and internal rules.[224] The 'externalities' hypothesis predicts that external rules will generally deviate farther from the social optimum than internal rules. An agency internalizes most of the costs and benefits associated with the precision of internal standards. An incongruent rule for assigning staff, for example, misallocates agency resources. Similarly, the unnecessary transaction costs from insufficiently transparent internal rules are borne by the agency. If an excessively vague prosecutorial guideline repeatedly forces agency prosecutors to seek interpretations from supervisors, the agency pays in lower staff productivity. Conversely, if clear staff instructions enable the agency to discipline uncooperative staff without protracted grievance hearings, the agency benefits.

A larger share of the burden inflicted by suboptimally precise external rules, by contrast, falls on persons outside the agency. Over-inclusive occupational safety standards, for example, burden employers, while under-inclusive standards permit excessive injury to workers. An agency less responsive to these external costs than to its internal costs of applying rules may favor rigid, bright-line formulations over more flexible alternatives. This may help to explain the frequently observed tendency of health, safety, and environmental regulators to adopt highly specific, inflexible standards.[225]

Similarly, the confusion and evasion generated by regulatory vagueness may burden the regulated or benefitted public far more than the regulator. Our broadcast licensing example of the previous section provides an illustration.[226] As I suggested there, vague licensing standards discourage challenges to incumbents by driving up the cost and increasing the uncertainty of comparative licensing proceedings. Yet the burden of this adverse consequence falls primarily on the viewing public and potential entrants. Those consequences of the strategy that the rulemaker bears are lower rulemaking costs and fewer hearings. From the perspective of the rulemaker's narrowly defined fiscal self-interest, the tradeoff is decidedly favorable.

To some rulemakers, rule enforcement costs are external. The purest example is a legislative body, but most administrative agencies rely to some extent on the courts, other agencies, and the public to enforce their rules. The more extreme the separation, the more appealing Model II formulations are likely to appear. The rulemaker captures the benefit of Model II rules (low initial rulemaking investment) while exporting their costs (high enforcement costs) to someone else. This analysis helps to explain why legislatures customarily use open-ended language to embody their substantive commands.[227]

The costs and benefits associated with competing formulations also have a temporal dimension. Some options, like Model III, involve a heavy initial rulemaking effort while others, such as Model II, necessitate substantial future rulemaking. Rational decisionmakers frequently encounter problems of intertemporal comparisons, of course, and routinely cope with them by discounting. By applying a suitable discount rate, the analyst converts streams of costs and benefits into present values and simply selects that option having the greatest present value.[228] The same method should be used to select the optimally precise formulation of a standard.

The self-interested policymaker, however, may have an internal discount rate different from the optimal social discount rate. Whereas the social discount rate should reflect the opportunity cost of capital generally prevailing in the society,[229] an administrator's individual discount rate reflects the opportunity cost of personal capital (time and effort) invested in the enterprise.[230] Most political appointees, for example, have a short tenure in office and are therefore likely to assign a high opportunity cost to the investment of their time.[231] Thus their discount rate will greatly exceed the social discount rate.

Socially suboptimal time horizons are a universal problem in a political system such as ours, and thus one might expect all administrative policy to be suboptimally precise. But in many agencies, the nearsightedness of political appointees is powerfully counterbalanced by strongly entrenched career bureaucrats.[232] In general, older agencies will exhibit this characteristic while newer agencies are more likely to be dominated by short-termers.[233] The head of a new agency may want to show immediate results. This desire creates a strong pressure for regulatory formulae that can be enacted quickly and enforced mechanically, although a more flexible approach might achieve a better balance of social values. Shortly after its creation, for example, the Occupational Safety and Health Administration uncritically adopted thousands of detailed standards, originally developed as voluntary guidelines by private industry groups, as mandatory occupational safety standards. Only much later did OSHA begin to wrestle with the glaring incongruities produced by this strategy.[234]

C. Internalization of Social Costs and Benefits

The classification of costs and benefits on which the previous argument rests is, of course, grossly oversimplified. Not even the most self-serving bureaucrats ignore the costs they inflict or the burdens they impose on persons outside their agencies. Virtually every objective commonly assumed to motivate administrators—future income, reputation, power—depends on a larger political process.[235] That political process, operating through the mechanisms of authorization, appropriation, appointment, and oversight, transforms private benefits and costs into administrative resources or burdens.[236] Airline pilots, for example, have repeatedly petitioned Congress to pressure the FAA to change its retirement rule.[237] While successful to date, the FAA's defense against these attacks cannot have been costless to the agency.

If the political process faithfully converted social costs and benefits into administrative costs and benefits, we would not be concerned about externalities. While pursuing private gain, administrators would accomplish social good. But, of course, the process does not always work that way. Various features of our electoral process—such as the equal weighting of votes,[238] the two-party system,[239] and the districting of most legislatures[240]—distort the communication of private preferences to the political branches.[241] Other imperfections, such as the cost of effectively monitoring and controlling bureaus,[242] further distort the communication of elected officials' preferences to administrative agencies.

At a minimum, therefore, one would expect external effects to lose intensity in the process of political conversion. Consequently, agencies will tend to value the direct effects (on transaction costs) of their rulemaking decisions more than their indirect effects (on compliance rate and incongruity effects). To that extent, at least, the predictions advanced in the preceding section should hold true.

Political conversion often obscures the magnitude of private costs and benefits. Generally, one would expect difficulty of estimation to increase with the intensity of conflict in the political arena. The more intense the conflict, the more confused and unintelligible will be the signals received by the administrative policymaker. Estimation of the political consequences of alternative strategies will become more difficult, and the perceived political costs of selecting the wrong alternatives will rise. Faced with this dilemma, the risk-averse policymaker will tend to favor Model II formulations. Transparent rules tend to spotlight a value choice. Opponents of that choice will attack the agency's action, forcing the agency to expend its own resources for defense. Rules having low transparency thus become more attractive, since they conceal value choices.

Beyond these general observations, predictions about the effect of political distortions are difficult. Once again, public choice theory provides some guidance.[243] In the distribution of political influence in the larger governmental arena—as at the administrative level—organizational costs are a crucial factor: groups with lower organizational costs will outbid those with higher costs. To the extent that the resulting distribution of administrative costs and benefits misrepresents the distribution of social costs and benefits, rules made by self-serving rulemakers will deviate from the optimally precise form.

V. Conclusion: Administrative Rule Precision From the Judicial Perspective

We began this journey at the courthouse, and it is time to return. Rule precision has importance not simply to administrative policymakers and their critics but to the courts as well. As the case studies and anecdotes illustrate, courts are repeatedly drawn into controversies about the appropriate precision of administrative rules as they review the legality of actions predicated upon them. What they need to discharge that function is neither philosophizing nor modelmaking, but hardheaded guidelines for adjudicating disputes between the government and the public. When is a rule so opaque that its application denies a person 'due process of law'?[244] When is it an 'abuse of discretion' to ground actions on an accretion of ad hoc rationales rather than on a more comprehensive directive?[245] When does the application of a rule become so mechanistic that it denies an individualized hearing guaranteed by statute?[246] At what point does its application to borderline cases become arbitrary and capricious[247] or deny equal protection of the law?[248]

To a large degree, answers to these questions depend on the peculiar statutory or doctrinal context in which they arise. Regulatory incongruities that impair speech[249] or disadvantage suspect minorities[250] will receive far less tolerance, for instance, than those that burden economic interests.[251] Some statutory schemes will display greater legislative concern for individualized treatment[252] or clarity of regulatory exposition[253] than others.

But even after allowing for such doctrinal or statutory peculiarities, there still remains an irreducible core of legal controversy about rule precision that yields only to an indwelling jurisprudential principle of fairness or propriety. The point of this Article has been to elaborate such a principle—one based on the norm of efficiency—and to explore its application as both an evaluative criterion and predictive model. It is not by any means the only way to think about rule precision, nor perhaps always the best way. Controversies about the transparency and congruity of certain rules are perhaps best resolved by a 'moral judgment,'[254] 'structural due process,'[255] or a 'libertarian'[256] model. But in the messy relativistic world of most administrative policymaking, the tensions between accountability and responsiveness,[257] accuracy and fraternity,[258] and individualism and altruism[259] will not often yield to resolution by deontological fiat. Courts, as much as politicians, must throw competing values on the scales and somehow total the score.

It is not an easy task, especially for courts. As Jerry Mashaw has forcefully argued in a different context, courts are ill-equipped for 'social-cost accounting,'[260] particularly when looking over an administrative policymaker's shoulder. Not only do courts lack the administrator's presumed investigative resources, analytic competence, and technical literacy, but they view social policy issues through the refracting prism of judicial review. Resolving competing claims about the precision of rules in the context of enforcement proceedings requires courts to extrapolate from a single known application of a rule to a universe of imagined applications. Even in a pre-enforcement challenge, the restricted, party-centered empiricism of appellate review consigns the court to deciphering that artifact of litigation known as the 'administrative record.'[261]

The difficulty of the task counsels broad deference to administrators' choice of rule formulations. Not only are administrators better equipped for 'social-cost accounting,' but, as the case studies in Section III suggest, the political 'marketplace' can often be relied upon to restrain administrative excesses. Courts, however, cannot wholly escape their editorial responsibility, precisely because the formal dimensions of a rule are so intertwined with its substantive and procedural legality. If the framework presented in this Article cautions against excessive judicial intervention, it also points the way to more productive interventions. Courts should, first of all, reserve their closest scrutiny for rules least likely to be subject to effective political discipline. As organization-cost disparities progressively skew the 'reinternalization' of 'external' effects, the need for judicial oversight grows. Our earlier discussion suggests that courts should be most sensitive to the plaint of the unorganized beneficiary of regulatory protection and the adversarially disadvantaged public assistance recipient.

When courts are drawn into disputes about regulatory precision, they should be sensitive to the inevitable tradeoffs among transparency, accessibility, and congruence. They should look for evidence of the factors that drive rules toward one extreme or the other—for example, the high social costs of misspecification error associated with rules of reason, the large rule application costs and quality control problems associated with per se rules. Prohibitory rules should presumptively be more transparent than licensure rules, liability rules more transparent than remedial rules, external rules more transparent than internal rules. Incongruent outcomes should be more tolerable when they appear to cluster near the boundary than at the extremes. In many ways, of course, homilies like this misrepresent the complexity of the subject. But they serve to remind us that 'social-cost accounting,' for all its intimidating connotations, is really the sophisticated and sensitive application of common sense. As applied to the art of regulatory rulewriting, it is a business too important to leave entirely to the accountants.

Notes

This Article is based in part on a report prepared by the author for the Administrative Conference of the United States. The author acknowledges with gratitude the assistance of the members and the staff of the Conference. Portions of the Article are part of a larger study of administrative policymaking supported by a grant from the Russell Sage Foundation. The author is, however, solely responsible for the contents of this Article.

1. Sun Ray Drive-In Dairy, Inc. v. Oregon Liquor Control Comm'n, 16 Or. App. 63, 517 P. 2d 289 (1973); *see also* Megdal v. Oregon State Bd. of Dental Examiners, 288 Or. 293, 320–21, 605 P.2d 273 (1980) (Board of Dental Examiners had no grounds to revoke dentist's license because 'unprofessional conduct' was not defined in statute and no rule forbade conduct).

2. WAIT Radio v. FCC, 418 F.2d 1153, 1157 (D.C. Cir. 1969).

3. Majority Staff of Senate Comm. on Banking, Housing & Urban Affairs, 96th Cong., 2d Sess., Majority Staff Study on Chartering of National Banks 4 (Comm. Print 1980) [hereinafter cited as Majority Staff Study].

4. E. Bardach & R. Kagan, Going By the Book: The Problem of Regulatory Unreasonableness 58 (1982).

5. Throughout this Article, I use the term 'rule' broadly, to refer to the linguistic formula used by an administrative agency to express its governing policy. The term should not be confused with the much narrower meaning assigned to it by the Administrative Procedure Act § 2(c), 5 U.S.C. § 551(4) (1976).

6. Wright, *Beyond Discretionary Justice* (Book Review), 81 YALE L.J. 575, 587 (1972) (reviewing K. DAVIS, DISCRETIONARY JUSTICE (1969)) ('We need, in short, some standards for when we should require standards.')

7. L. FULLER, THE MORALITY OF LAW 46–49, 63–65 (1964).

8. H.L.A. HART, THE CONCEPT OF LAW 121 (1961).

9. J. FRANK, LAW AND THE MODERN MIND 118–19 (1930).

10. R. DWORKIN, TAKING RIGHTS SERIOUSLY 24–26 (1977).

11. *Id.* at 26–28; Raz, *Legal Principles and the Limits of Law*, 81 YALE L. J. 823, 832–33 (1972).

12. *See, e.g.,* R. POSNER, ECONOMIC ANALYSIS OF LAW 419–21 (2d ed. 1977); Landes & Posner, *Legal Precedent: A Theoretical and Empirical Analysis*, 19 J. L. & ECON. 249, 263–64 (1976).

13. *See* Friedman, *Legal Rules and the Process of Social Change*, 19 STAN. L. REV. 786, 822–24 (1967).

14. Implicit in this assertion is a rejection of the 'nihilist' view that legal texts have any meaning that the reader chooses to assign to them. *See* Levinson, *Law as Literature*, 60 TEX. L. REV. 373, 373–77 (1982); Fish, *Interpretation and the Pluralist Vision*, 60 TEX. L. REV. 495, 503 (1982). I assume, at a minimum, that the addressees of most administrative rules are a 'community' whose shared experiences or values can give objective (if not wholly deterministic) meaning to such texts. *See* P. BERGER & T. LUCKMANN, THE SOCIAL CONSTRUCTION OF REALITY: A TREATISE IN THE SOCIOLOGY OF KNOWLEDGE 34–46 (1966); White, *Law as Language: Reading Law and Reading Literature*, 60 TEX. L. REV. 415, 415–16 (1982).

15. Jerry Mashaw uses the term 'transparency' to describe a similar idea. Mashaw, *Administrative Due Process: The Quest for a Dignitary Theory*, 61 B.U.L. REV. 885, 901 (1981). It is presumably this same notion that Hart has in mind when speaking of rules 'which multitudes of individuals could understand,' H.L.A. HART, *supra* note 8, at 121, that Fuller has in mind when speaking of a rule's 'clarity,' L. FULLER, *supra* note 7, at 63–65, and that Kennedy describes as 'formal realizability,' Kennedy, *Form and Substance in Private Law Adjudication*, 89 HARV. L. REV. 1685, 1687–88 (1976).

16. *See* G. TULLOCK, TRIALS ON TRIAL: A PURE THEORY OF LEGAL PROCEDURE 180 (1980); Brodley, *In Defense of Presumptive Rules: An Approach to Legal Rulemaking for Conglomerate Mergers*, in THE CONGLOMERATE CORPORATION: AN ANTITRUST LAW AND ECONOMICS SYMPOSIUM 249, 255–60 (1981).

17. For a graphic representation of this point, see Tussman & tenBroek, *The Equal Protection of the Laws*, 37 CALIF. L. REV. 341, 346–49 (1949) (discussing passage of a hypothetical law for sterilization of suspected hereditary criminals); *see also* Cabell v. Chavez-Salido, 454 U.S. 432, 440 (1982) (defining 'specificity' of a classification as its degree of 'over or underinclusive[ness]' in serving legitimate political ends).

18. I use the term 'congruent' in a sense similar to that used by Paul Brest. P. BREST, PROCESSES OF CONSTITUTIONAL DECISIONMAKING: CASES AND MATERIALS

478, 480 (1975); *cf.* L. FULLER, *supra* note 7, at 81 (using 'congruence' to refer to the fit between the law as written and the law as applied).

19. *See generally* Note, *The Void-for-Vagueness Doctrine in the Supreme Court*, 109 U. PA L. REV. 67 (1960) (examining cases where void-for-vagueness doctrine was invoked).

20. *See* Schechter Poultry Corp. v. United States, 295 U.S. 495, 551 (1935) (Cardozo, J., concurring).

21. *See* K. DAVIS, DISCRETIONARY JUSTICE: A PRELIMINARY INQUIRY 52–96 (1969).

22. Soglin v. Kauffman, 418 F.2d 163, 168 (7th Cir. 1969).

23. *See, e.g.,* Bittker, *Tax Reform and Tax Simplification*, 29 U. MIAMI L. REV. 1, 5–7 (1974); Brannon, *Simplification and Other Tax Objectives*, in FEDERAL INCOME TAX SIMPLIFICATION 191 (C. Gustafson ed. 1979); Woodworth, *Tax Simplification and the Tax Reform Act of 1969*, 34 LAW & CONTEMP. PROBS 711, 711, 713 (1969).

24. *See* Posner, *The Next Step in the Antitrust Treatment of Restricted Distribution: Per Se Legality*, 48 U. CHI. L. REV. 6, 23 (1981) (arguing for per se legality of vertical restraints in distribution absent inter-retailer cartels).

25. *See generally* Note, *The Irrebuttable Presumption Doctrine in the Supreme Court*, 87 HARV. L. REV. 1534 (1974) (examining constitutional underpinnings of irrebuttable presumption doctrine).

26. The required waiver cases examine the extent to which agencies may use bright-line rules to close off an individual's right to a hearing. *See* Aman, *Administrative Equity: An Analysis of Exceptions to Administrative Rules*, 1982 DUKE L.J. 277. Early decisions upheld the practice, but implied that agencies had to afford adversely affected persons an opportunity to seek a waiver from their terms. Although the Supreme Court has refused to read that implication as a universal requirement, FPC v. Texaco, Inc., 377 U.S. 33, 40–41 (1964); United States v. Storer Broadcasting Co., 351 U.S. 192, 205 (1956); National Broadcasting Co. v. United States, 319 U.S. 190, 224–25 (1943), the struggle to accommodate individual justice with mechanical rules continues, *see e.g.,* Matlovich v. Secretary of Air Force, 591 F.2d 852, 857 (D.C. Cir. 1978) (requiring greater flexibility in Air Force disciplinary rules); National Petroleum Refiners Ass'n v. FTC, 482 F.2d 672, 689–91 (D.C. Cir. 1973) (requiring greater flexibility in FTC trade regulations), *cert. denied*, 415 U.S. 951 (1974); WAIT Radio v. FCC, 418 F.2d 1153, 1157–59 (D.C. Cir. 1969) (requiring greater flexibility in FCC clear channel rules).

27. *See* Broz v. Schweiker, 677 F.2d 1351, 1360 (11th Cir. 1982) (absence of scientific support for age-based regulations supports case-by-case determination of physical ability to do job).

28. The illustration is drawn from the 'age-60' pilot retirement rule, 24 Fed. Reg. 9776 (1959), *upheld*, Airline Pilots Ass'n, Int'l v. Quesada, 276 F.2d 892, 898 (2nd Cir. 1960). The current rule is virtually identical to the original: 'No person may serve as a pilot on an airplane engaged in [commercial] operations . . . if that person has reached his 60th birthday.' 14 C.F.R. § 121.383(c) (1982).

29. For a review of some possible parameters, see NAT'L INST ON AGING, DEP'T OF HEALTH AND HUMAN SERV., REPORT OF THE NATIONAL INSTITUTE ON AGING PANEL ON THE EXPERIENCED PILOT STUDY (August 1981) [hereinafter cited as NIA REPORT]. For promulgated illustrations of such tables, see 20 C.F.R. subpt. P, app. 2 (1982) (Social Security Administration grid rule for determining disability); 28 C.F.R. § 2.20 (1982) (U.S. Parole Commission parole release guidelines).

30. For a discussion of intelligibility, see Ross, On Legalities and Linguistics: Plain Language Legislation, 30 BUFFALO L. REV. 317, 334–35 (1981).

31. For a detailed account of the difficulties inherent in administering an exceptions policy, see Schuck, When the Exception Becomes the Rule: Regulatory Equity, the Exceptions Process, and the Formulation of Energy Policy (Feb. 16, 1983) (Discussion Draft Report to the Admin. Conf. of the U.S.) (exceptions to federal petroleum price and allocation rules).

32. But see Western, The Empty Idea of Equality, 95 HARV. L. REV. 537, 543–48 (1982) (equal treatment of equals constitutes a tautology).

33. See Tribe, Perspectives on Bakke: Equal Protection, Procedural Fairness, or Structural Justice?, 92 HARV. L. REV. 864, 869–70 (1979); Tribe, Structural Due Process, 10 HARV. C.R.-C.L. L. REV. 269, 283–88, 295–98 (1975) [hereinafter cited as Tribe, Structural Due Process]. On 'dignitary' values, see Mashaw, supra note 15; Saphire, Specifying Due Process Values: Toward a More Responsive Approach to Procedural Protection, 127 U. PA L. REV. 111, 117–25 (1978).

34. On the conceptual difficulties in measurement of social utility, see Coleman, Efficiency, Utility, and Wealth Maximization, 8 HOFSTRA L. REV. 509 (1980); Posner, Utilitarianism, Economics, and Legal Theory, 8 J. LEGAL STUD. 103, 112–17 (1979).

35. See G. TULLOCK, supra note 16; Ehrlich & Posner, An Economic Analysis of Legal Rulemaking, 3 J. LEGAL STUD. 257 (1974).

36. The classification used here is based loosely on that used by Ehrlich & Posner, supra note 35. See also Gifford, Communication of Legal Standards, Policy Development, and Effective Conduct Regulation, 56 CORNELL L. REV. 409, 466 (1971) (discussing 'three-way relationship between resource expenditures, effectiveness of control, and substantive standards').

37. See Dunn v. United States, 442 U.S. 100, 112–13 (1979); Hall, Strict or Liberal Construction of Penal Statutes, 48 HARV. L. REV. 748, 756–62 (1935).

38. See COMPTROLLER GEN. OF THE U.S., PROGRAMS FOR ENSURING THE SAFE TRANSPORTATION OF HAZARDOUS MATERIALS NEED IMPROVEMENT (Nov. 4, 1980); COMPTROLLER GEN. OF THE U.S., FEDERAL ACTIONS ARE NEEDED TO IMPROVE SAFETY AND SECURITY OF NUCLEAR MATERIALS TRANSPORTATION (May 7, 1979).

39. See COMPTROLLER GEN. OF THE U.S., PROSPECTS DIM FOR EFFECTIVELY ENFORCING IMMIGRATION LAWS (Nov. 5, 1980).

40. See COMPTROLLER GEN. OF THE U.S., ENFORCEMENT PROBLEMS HINDER EFFECTIVE IMPLEMENTATION OF NEW FISHERY MANAGEMENT ACTIVITIES (Sept. 12, 1979);

Comptroller Gen. of the U.S., Progress and Problems of Fisheries Management Under the Fishery Conservation and Management Act (Jan. 9, 1979).

41. *See, e.g.,* Central Hudson Gas v. Public Serv. Comm'n, 447 U.S. 557, 565–66 (1980); Gooding v. Wilson, 405 U.S. 518 (1972); *cf.* Monaghan, *Overbreadth,* 1981 Sup. Ct. Rev. 1 (discussing overbreadth as specific instance of challenge to third-party effects of rules).

42. *See* Woodson v. North Carolina, 428 U.S. 280, 305 (1976); Black, *Due Process for Death,* 26 Cath. U.L. Rev. 1, 12 (1976); Radin, *Cruel Punishment and Respect for Persons: Super Due Process for Death,* 53 S. Cal. L. Rev. 1143, 1150 (1980).

43. *See, e.g.,* Harrison, *Regulation and Distribution,* in Attacking Regulatory Problems 185, 188–91, 200–1 (A. Ferguson ed. 1981); Spence & Weitzman, *Regulatory Strategies for Pollution Control,* in Approaches to Controlling Air Pollution 199, 204–11 (A. Friedlaender ed. 1978).

44. *See* Diver, *The Assessment and Mitigation of Civil Money Penalties by Federal Administrative Agencies,* in Admin. Conf. of the U.S., Recommendations and Reports, 1979, at 203, 223–83 (of four agencies studied, the Mine Safety and Health Administration, with the largest caseload, had the most transparent penalty standard).

45. *See, e.g.,* M. Lipsky, Street Level Bureaucracy 145–46, 163–69 (1980) (private goal definition and unaccountability of police); J. Prottas' People Processing: The Street-Level Bureaucrat in Public Service Bureaucracies (1979) (describing behavior in welfare departments, public housing offices, hospitals, etc.); J. Wilson, Varieties of Police Behavior 57–82 (1968) (discussing police administration of patrolmen).

46. *See* Nichols & Zeckhauser, *Government Comes to the Workplace: An Assessment of OSHA,* Pub Interest, Fall 1977, at 39, 49; Smith, *Protecting Workers' Health and Safety,* in Instead of Regulation: Alternatives to Federal Regulatory Agencies 311, 313–14 (R. Poole, Jr. ed. 1982).

47. *Cf.* Ehrlich & Posner, *supra* note 35, at 267.

48. *See id.* at 261; *cf.* H.L.A. Hart, *supra* note 8, at 77–96 (distinguishing 'primary' from 'secondary' rules).

49. *Cf.* R. Katzmann, Regulatory Bureaucracy 155–56 (1980) (FTC de-emphasis of Robinson-Patman Act prosecutions).

50. *See* A. Downs, Inside Bureaucracy 59–63 (1967).

51. *See* Diver, *A Theory of Regulatory Enforcement,* 28 Pub Policy 257, 286–91 (1980); Rabin, *Agency Criminal Referrals in the Federal System: An Empirical Study of Prosecutorial Discretion,* 24 Stan. L. Rev. 1036, 1044–72 (1972).

52. Natural Resources Defense Council v. SEC, 606 F. 2d 1031, 1046 (D.C. Cir. 1979) (dictum); *see, e.g.,* Greater New York Hosp. Ass'n v. Mathews, 536 F.2d 494, 497–98 (2d Cir. 1976) (noting unreviewability of HEW Secretary's decision to change mode of reimbursement for Medicare services rendered by hospitals); Kletschka v. Driver, 411 F. 2d 436, 444 (2d Cir. 1969) (noting unreviewability of Veterans Administration research grant).

53. *See, e.g.,* Linda R.S. v. Richard D., 410 U.S. 614 (1973) (refusing to require prosecution of parent for failure to support illegitimate child); FTC v. Universal-Rundle Corp., 387 U.S. 244 (1967) (holding FTC's refusal to withhold enforcement of cease-and-desist order did not constitute patent abuse of discretion). *But cf.* Adams v. Richardson, 480 F.2d 1159 (D.C. Cir. 1973) (en banc) (requiring HEW enforcement of Title VII against educational institutions); American Pub. Health Ass'n v. Veneman, 349 F. Supp. 1311 (D.D.C. 1972) (requiring FDA to release reports on efficacy of drugs and set deadlines for completion of further evaluations of efficacy).

54. *See, e.g.,* K. DAVIS, *supra* note 6, at 162–87; Vorenberg, *Decent Restraint of Prosecutorial Discretion,* 94 HARV. L. REV. 1521, 1560–72 (1981).

55. *See* Marshall v. Barlow's, Inc., 436 U.S. 307, 323 (1978) (search must be 'pursuant to an administrative plan containing specific neutral criteria'); *see also* See v. City of Seattle, 387 U.S. 541 (1967) (requiring administrative subpoena to inspect warehouse); Camara v. Municipal Court, 387 U.S. 523 (1967) (requiring search warrants for nonemergency building inspection).

56. *See, e.g.,* K. HAWKINS, ENVIRONMENT AND ENFORCEMENT chs. 7–8; J. WILSON, THE INVESTIGATORS: MANAGING FBI AND NARCOTICS AGENTS 25 (1978).

57. *See* R. POSNER, *supra* note 12, at 425.

58. *See, e.g.,* M. FRANKEL, CRIMINAL SENTENCES: LAW WITHOUT ORDER (1973); P. O'DONNELL, M. CHURGIN & D. CURTIS, TOWARD A JUST AND EFFECTIVE SENTENCING SYSTEM: AGENDA FOR LEGISLATIVE REFORM 3 (1977).

59. Diver, *The Assessment and Mitigation of Civil Money Penalties by Federal Administrative Agencies,* 79 COLUM. L. REV. 1435, 1457–59 (1979).

60. *E.g.,* Butz v. Glover Livestock Comm'n Co., 411 U.S. 182 (1973); Professional Air Traffic Controllers Org. v. Federal Labor Relations Authority, 54 AD. L. REP. 2d 1, 58 (D.C. Cir. 1982); Nowicki v. United States, 536 F.2d 1171 (7th Cir. 1976), *cert. denied,* 429 U.S. 1092 (1977).

61. *See* Abrams, *Internal Policy: Guiding The Exercise of Prosecutorial Discretion,* 19 U.C.L.A. L. REV. 1, 29 (1971); Sofaer, *Judicial Control of Informal Discretionary Adjudication and Enforcement,* 72 COLUM. L. REV. 1293, 1297 (1972).

62. *See* F. ZIMRING & G. HAWKINS, DETERRENCE 71–90 (1973).

63. *See* Becker, *Crime and Punishment: An Economic Approach,* 76 J. POL. ECON. 169 (1968); Polinsky & Shavell, *The Optimal Tradeoff Between the Probability and the Magnitude of Fines,* 69 AM. ECON. REV. 880 (1979); Stigler, *The Optimum Enforcement of Laws,* 78 J. POL. ECON. 526, 530 (1970).

64. *See* OSHA FIELD OPERATIONS MANUAL 81–93.

65. *See* 30 C.F.R. § 100.3 (1982); Diver, *supra* note 59, at 1447–52.

66. *See* Breyer, *Analyzing Regulatory Failure: Mismatches, Less Restrictive Alternatives, and Reform,* 92 HARV. L. REV. 549, 575–76 (1979).

67. *See* G. CALABRESI & P. BOBBITT, TRAGIC CHOICES 72 (1978).

68. 49 U.S.C. § 1421 (a)–1421(b) (1976).

69. *Id.* § 1421 (a)(5).

70. 24 Fed. Reg. 9773 (1959). For the current version, see *supra* note 28.

71. 24 Fed. Reg. 5247 (1959) (notice of proposed rulemaking).

72. *Id.* at 5249.

73. *Id.* at 9772.

74. *See* Comment, *Mandatory Retirement of Airline Pilots: An Analysis of the FAA's Age 60 Retirement Rule,* 33 HASTINGS L.J. 241, 245–46 (1981).

75. 276 F.2d 892, 898 (2d Cir. 1960).

76. *Id.*

77. *Id.* at 898 n. 10.

78. 49 U.S.C. § 1421(c) (1976).

79. Keating v. FAA, 610 F.2d 611 (9th Cir. 1979); Gray v. FAA, 594 F. 2d 793 (10th Cir. 1979); Starr v. FAA, 589 F. 2d 307 (7th Cir. 1978); *see also* O'Donnell v. Shaffer, 491 F.2d 59 (D.C. Cir. 1974) (finding no requirement for adjudicatory hearing in denying petitions to revoke age 60 rule).

80. Pub. L. No. 96–171, 93 Stat. 1285 (1979) (codified at 49 U.S.C. § 1421 (Supp. V 1980)).

81. NIA REPORT, *supra* note 29. The report acknowledged that 'there is no convincing medical evidence to support age 60, or any other specific age, for mandatory pilot retirement.' *Id.* at 2. But it did conclude, from examining 'available actuarial and epidemiological data,' that the probability of 'accident attributed to acute or subtle incapacitation' of pilots would increase with pilot age. *Id.*

82. *See id.* at 4, 7.

83. 24 Fed. Reg. 9772–73 (1959).

84. Today, pensions average about 50% of pre-retirement salaries. For captains employed by major airlines, the resulting loss of income ranges from $30,000 to $50,000. NIA REPORT, *supra* note 29, app. C, at C-73 to C-74 (statement of Air Transport Ass'n). The financial impact of retirement in 1959 was more severe since pensions were relatively less generous.

85. Air carriers, which generally wish to maintain good relations with the FAA, have consistently supported mandatory retirement at age 60. *See id.* at C-51 (statement of Air Transport Ass'n).

86. *See* 24 Fed. Reg. 5248 (1959) (80 airline pilots expected to reach age 60 by 1962). In the 1980's, 'between 500 and 1000 airline pilots will reach age 60 each year.' *Report of the Institute of Medicine, Airline Pilot Age, Health and Performance: Scientific and Medical Considerations* (Mar. 1981), in NIA REPORT, *supra* note 29, at F-32.

87. 24 Fed. Reg. 9773 (1959).

88. *Id.*

89. *See supra* note 86.

90. NIA REPORT, *supra* note 29, app. C, at C-37 (statement of Air Line Pilots Ass'n).

91. *See id.,* app. F, at F-23 to F-26.

92. *Id.* at F-20.

93. For that very reason, the FAA's recent decision to reopen the issue for more systematic reappraisal is most welcome. *See* 47 Fed. Reg. 29,782 (1982) (advance notice of proposed rulemaking).

94. Act of June 3, 1864, ch. 106, 13 Stat. 99 (codified in relevant part at 12 U.S.C. §§ 21–27 (1976)). The only substantive standard for bank chartering in the Act is:

> If ... it appears that such association is lawfully entitled to commence the business of banking, the comptroller shall give to such association a certificate ... But the comptroller may withhold from an association his certificate authorizing the commencement of business, whenever he has reason to suppose that the shareholders have formed the same for any other than the legitimate objects contemplated by this chapter.

12 U.S.C. § 27 (1976).

The Federal Deposit Insurance Act of 1935, 12 U.S.C. § 1816 (1976), augmented this sparse language modestly. Since national banks must have deposit insurance, a charter applicant must satisfy the Act's standard for insurability. But this standard merely enumerates six factors to be considered by the Comptroller: the financial history and condition of the bank, the adequacy of its capital structure, its future earnings prospects, the general character of its management, the convenience and needs of the community to be served by the bank, and whether its corporate powers are consistent with the purpose of the act.

95. 12 C.F.R. § 4.2(b) (1974).

96. Scott, *In Quest of Reason: The Licensing Decisions of the Federal Banking Agencies*, 42 U. Chi. L. Rev. 235, 261–68 (1975).

97. *Id.* at 268.

98. Admin. Conf. of the U.S., Recommendation 75–1(1), 1 C.F.R. § 305.75–1(1) (1977).

99. 41 Fed. Reg. 47,964 (1976).

100. Two examples are a limit of 10% stock ownership by any one person and minimum capital of $1,000,000. *Id.* at 47,965.

101. For example, the applicant's officers must have 'reputations evidencing honesty and integrity. They should have employment and business histories demonstrating success, and should be responsible in financial affairs.' *Id.* at 47,964–65.

102. Majority Staff Study, *supra* note 3, at iv.

103. *Id.* at 18–19, 33.

104. *Id.* at 55.

105. 45 Fed. Reg. 68,603 (1980).

106. Statistics on the Comptroller's charter approval rate show that this policy shift had occurred well before the 1980 policy statement. The approval rate, which had fallen below 50% in 1977, increased to 88% in 1980. *See* Office of the Comptroller of the Currency, 1980 Annual Report 240

(1980); OFFICE OF THE COMPTROLLER OF THE CURRENCY, 1977 ANNUAL REPORT 7 (1977).

107. 12 C.F.R. § 5.20(c)(3)(iii) (1982).

108. *Id.* § 5.20(c)(3)(iv)(B).

109. For an empirical demonstration that the 'need' criterion 'significantly reduced the entry rate into banking,' see Peltzman, *Entry into Commercial Banking*, 8 J. L. & ECON. 11, 48 (1965).

110. Edwards & Edwards, *Measuring the Effectiveness of Regulation: The Case of Bank Entry Regulation*, 17 J. L. & ECON. 445, 452 (1974). OCC's charter approval rate has fluctuated from lows of 18% in 1965 and 1967, to a high of 66% in 1973, then down to a low of 45% in 1977, and again dramatically upward since then. *See* OFFICE OF THE COMPTROLLER OF THE CURRENCY, 1973 ANNUAL REPORT 5, 7 (1973); OFFICE OF THE COMPTROLLER OF THE CURRENCY, 1967 ANNUAL REPORT 8 (1967); OFFICE OF THE COMPTROLLER OF THE CURRENCY, 1965 ANNUAL REPORT 22 (1965); *supra* note 106.

111. For an asserted illustration, see MAJORITY STAFF STUDY, *supra* note 3, at 7–8 (Comptroller James Saxon at the beginning of his tenure in 1962–1963).

112. *See* Scott, *supra* note 96.

113. 12 U.S.C. § 4a (Supp. V 1981).

114. *See* 12 C.F.R. § 5.3 (1981).

115. Interview with John Schockey, former OCC General Counsel (Jan. 10, 1981) (notes on file with author).

116. *See, e.g.*, Alhadeff, *A Reconsideration of Restrictions on Bank Entry*, 76 Q.J. ECON. 246 (1962); Tussing, *The Case of Bank Failure*, 10 J.L. & ECON. 129 (1967). The policies behind these regulations show no signs of yielding.

117. For a more detailed account, see J. MASHAW, BUREAUCRATIC JUSTICE: MANAGING SOCIAL SECURITY DISABILITY CLAIMS 103–23 (1983).

118. 43 Fed. Reg. 55,366 (1978) (codified at 20 C.F.R. subpt. P app. 2 (1983)).

119. Litigation concerning the validity and application of the grid rules has been prolific. Most circuits have upheld the rules. *See* Rivers v. Schweiker, 684 F.2d 1144 (5th Cir. 1982); McCoy v. Schweiker, 683 F.2d 1138 (8th Cir. 1982); Torres v. Secretary of Dep't of Health & Human Servs., 677 F.2d 167 (1st Cir. 1982); Santise v. Schweiker, 676 F.2d 925 (3d Cir. 1982); Cummins v. Schweiker, 670 F.2d 81 (7th Cir. 1982); Frady v. Harris, 646 F.2d 143 (4th Cir. 1981). The Supreme Court reversed the two circuits that had partially invalidated the rules. Heckler v. Campbell, 103 S. Ct. 1952 (1983) (reversing Campbell v. Secretary of Health & Human Servs., 665 F.2d 48 (2d Cir. 1981)); Heckler v. Broz, 51 U.S.L.W. 3857 (U.S. May 31, 1983) (vacating Broz v. Schweiker, 677 F.2d 1351 (11th Cir. 1982)).

120. Act of Aug. 1, 1956, ch. 836, § 103(a), 70 Stat. 807, 815 (codified as amended at 42 U.S.C. § 423(d) (1976)).

121. Act of Sept. 13, 1960, Pub. L. No. 86–778, § 401(a), 74 Stat. 924, 964; Act of July 30, 1965, Pub. L. No. 89–97, § 303(a)(2), 79 Stat. 286, 367; Act of Jan. 2, 1968, Pub. L. No. 90–248, § 158(b), 81 Stat. 821, 868.

122. 22 Fed. Reg. 4362 (1957); 26 Fed. Reg. 5572 (1961); 33 Fed. Reg. 11,749 (1968).

123. Only the earnings test is reasonably transparent. See 26 Fed. Reg. 11,049, 11,051 (1961) (codified as amended at 20 C.F.R. § 404.1574–1575 (1982)).

124. Act of Jan. 2, 1968, Pub. L. No. 90–248, § 158(b), 81 Stat. 821, 869 (inserted in 42 U.S.C. § 423(d)(2)(A) (1976)).

125. For a description of the handling of claims, see R. Dixon, Social Security Disability and Mass Justice 24–30 (1973).

126. The rule applies only to disability claims grounded on 'exertional' incapacity. After eliminating claims based on per se disabling conditions (e.g., blindness, loss of limbs), most claims fall within this category.

127. 20 C.F.R. subpt. P app. 2 (1983).

128. Since the rules are intended solely to characterize a status resulting from an unexpected and presumably unwanted cause, their evolution cannot plausibly be related to any compliance-related goals. Their only possible behavioral objective would be to discourage malingerers from filing claims, an effect that would be reflected in a reduction of transaction costs.

129. Staff of Senate Comm. on Finance, 97th Cong., 2d Sess., Staff Data and Materials Related to the Social Security Disability Insurance Program 20–29, 69–72, 145–46 (Comm. Print 1982). From 1974 to 1981, DI applications dropped slightly from 1.33 million to 1.23 million, id. at 21–22, while hearing requests increased from 121,504 to 281, 700, id. at 69–70.

130. Social Sec. Admin., 1978 SSA Year in Review: Administration of Social Security Program 12 (1978).

131. One study estimated the cost per hearing at $500 to $1000. J. Mashaw, C. Goetz, F. Goodman, W. Schwartz, P. Verkuil & M. Carrow, Social Security Hearings and Appeals 15 (1978).

132. H.R. Rep. No. 100, 96th Cong., 1st Sess. 19 (1979).

133. Social Sec. Admin., 1977 SSA Annual Report 20 (105-day mean processing time for allowed claims as of October 1976); Staff of Senate Comm. on Finance, supra note 129, at 21 (number of claims awarded).

134. Social Sec. Admin., supra note 133, at 52.

135. See R. Dixon, supra note 125, at 35–40.

136. See Bloch, Representation and Advocacy at Non-Adversary Hearings: The Need for Non-Adversary Representatives at Social Security Disability Hearings, 59 Wash. U.L.Q. 349, 356–66 (1981).

137. See J. Mashaw, C. Goetz, F. Goodman, W. Schwartz, P. Verkuil & M. Carrow, supra note 131, at 3–4; Champagne & Danube, An Empirical Analysis of Decisions of Administrative Law Judges in the Social Security Disability Program, 64 Geo. L.J. 43 (1975).

138. SSA's quality-control system is described in J. MASHAW, *supra* note 117, at 145–68 and Chassman & Rolston, *Social Security Disability Hearings: A Case Study in Quality Assurance and Due Process*, 65 CORNELL L. REV. 801 (1980).

139. *See* R. DIXON, *supra* note 125, at 51.

140. This technique was used in *Secretary of Health & Human Servs., Implementation of Section 304(g) of Public Law 96–265, 'Social Security Disability Amendments of 1980'* (January 1982) ('The Bellmon Report'), *reprinted in* STAFF OF SENATE COMM. ON FINANCE, *supra* note 129, at 133.

141. For example, processing time has dropped steadily in recent years. The mean time for initial awards dropped from 110 days in 1976 to 85 days in 1978. SOCIAL SEC. ADMIN., *supra* note 130, at 12. Mean processing time for ALJ hearings fell from 249 days in 1976 to 145 days in 1979. SOCIAL SEC. ADMIN., 1979 SSA ANNUAL REPORT 59 (1979). The 'productivity index,' SSA's overall measure of productivity in processing DI cases, increased from 100 in 1967 to 145 in 1976. SOCIAL SEC. ADMIN., *supra* note 130, at v.

142. *See* Mathews v. Eldridge, 424 U.S. 319, 339, 349 (1976) (post-termination evidentiary hearing adequate safeguard of claimants' rights).

143. *See* Echevarria v. Secretary of Health & Human Servs., 685 F.2d 751, 756 (2d Cir. 1983) (reversing SSA's denial of benefits because ALJ did not fulfill his 'special duty to pro se claimants').

144. *See* Goldhammer, *The Effect of the New Vocational Regulations on Social Security and Supplemental Security Income Disability Claims*, 32 AD. L. REV. 501, 502–03 (1980) (discussing omissions from SSA's list of impairments).

145. 20 C.F.R. subpt. P app. 2, § 201.17 (1983); *see* Broz v. Schweiker, 677 F.2d 1351 (11th Cir. 1982) (criticizing mechanistic use of grid regulations but approving their use as burden-shifting tool), *vacated and remanded sub nom.* Heckler v. Broz, 51 U.S.L.W. 3857 (U.S. May 31, 1983).

146. *See* Mashaw, *How Much of What Quality?: A Comment on Conscientious Procedural Design*, 65 CORNELL L. REV. 823, 824–28 (1980) (discussing relationship between closeness of case and its cost).

147. *See* Mashaw, *Administrative Due Process as Social-Cost Accounting*, 9 HOFSTRA L. REV. 1423, 1441 (1981).

148. 20 C.F.R. § 404.1520 (1983).

149. *Id.* § 404.1520(c).

150. *Id.* § 404.1520(d).

151. *Id.* § 404.1545–.1546.

152. *See supra* note 128.

153. These aliens had to return to their country even if they were immediately eligible for such a visa. *See* Sofaer, *The Change-of-Status Adjudication: A Case Study of the Informal Agency Process*, 1 J. LEGAL STUD. 349, 350–51 (1972).

154. Immigration and Nationality Act of 1952, ch. 477, § 245(a), 66 Stat. 163, 217 (current version at 8 U.S.C. § 1255(a) (1976)).

155. 8 C.F.R. § 245.1(g) (1981).

156. *See id.* § 2.1.

157. Immigration and Nationality Act of 1952, ch. 477, § 245, 66 Stat. 162, 217 (current version at 8 U.S.C. § 1255 (1976)).

158. 8 C.F.R. § 245 (1981).

159. INS Operations Instructions § 245.5d(5), *reprinted in* 4 C. GORDON & H. ROSENWELD, IMMIGRATION LAW AND PROCEDURE 23–532 (1983). For assistance in determining whether 'substantial equities' exist, the District Director is referred to another discretionary determination ('voluntary departure'), the published standards for which are equally opaque. *See id.* § 242.10, *reprinted in* 4 C. GORDON & H. ROSENWELD, *supra*, at 23–488.

160. *See* 2 C. GORDON & H. ROSENWELD, *supra* note 159, § 7.7d, at 790–95; Orlow, *Adjustment of Status of Lawful Permanent Resident*, in TENTH ANNUAL IMMIGRATION AND NATURALIZATION INSTITUTE 151, 156–68 (A. Fragomen, Jr. ed. 1979).

161. Sofaer, *supra* note 153, at 365–93.

162. *Id.* at 385–93.

163. *See, e.g.*, Faddah v. INS, 580 F.2d 132, 133 (5th Cir. 1978) (finding that obtaining temporary visas by aliens intending to remain permanently is sufficient to support discretionary refusal to adjust status of aliens under § 245); Ameeriar v. INS, 438 F.2d 1028, 1032 (3d Cir. 1971) (no abuse of discretion where alien was denied permanent resident status for bypassing normal procedures and entering country on visitor's visa with intent to remain).

164. 438 F.2d 1028 (3d Cir. 1971).

165. *Id.* at 1042.

166. 44 Fed. Reg. 36, 187, 36, 191 (1979) (proposing 8 C.F.R. § 245.8). The rules also proposed standards for the exercise of several other discretionary functions.

167. *Id.* at 36,187.

168. *Id.* at 36,191.

169. 46 Fed. Reg. 9119 (1981).

170. Memorandum from [name and position deleted], INS, to Lionel J. Castillo, Commissioner, INS (Sept. 12, 1978), at 1.

171. In fiscal year 1977, INS received 90,450 applications and granted 54,523. 1977 INS ANNUAL REPORT 8 (1977). In fiscal year 1978, the number of status adjustments granted rose to 101,397. 1978 INS ANNUAL REPORT 8 (1978).

172. It is true that an alien whose application is denied for discretionary reasons can still apply for an immigrant visa at the American Consulate in his native land. But this option may entail considerable costs, including round trip transportation for the alien and his family, the delay, the risk of erroneous denial by the Consul, and in some cases exposure to military service or imprisonment at home.

173. Sofaer, *supra* note 153, at 396–97.

174. *Id.* at 421.

175. INS Operations Instructions §245.5d(2), *reprinted in* 4 C. GORDON & H. ROSENWELD, *supra* note 159, at 23–531 to −532.

176. Interview with Paul Schmidt, Acting General Counsel, INS, in Washington, D.C. (Dec. 17, 1980) (notes on file with author).

177. Nonimmigrant aliens may first apply for change of status at a deportation hearing. In that event, the initial determination is made by a Special Inquiry Officer ('immigration judge'). *See* 2 C. GORDON & H. ROSENWELD, *supra* note 159, § 7.7e, at 7–98.

178. Sofaer, *supra* note 153, at 357 n. 25. Most examiners are non-lawyers. Sofaer, *Judicial Control of Informal Discretionary Adjudication and Enforcement*, 72 COLUM. L. REV. 1293, 1299 (1972).

179. INS Operations Instructions § 245.5d(1), *reprinted in* 4 C. GORDON & H. ROSENWELD, *supra* note 159, at 23–531.

180. *Id.* § 245.5d(3), (4), *reprinted in* 4 C. GORDON & H. ROSENWELD, *supra* note 159, at 23–532.

181. Letter from Charles Gordon, INS General Counsel, to James Orlow, Esq. (Feb. 25, 1972) at 1.

182. *See* Orlow, *supra* note 160, at 165–67. Denial by an immigration judge (at the deportation stage) is appealable to the Board of Immigration Appeals and a Court of Appeals. *Id.* at 167.

183. Memorandum from [name and position deleted], INS, to Lionel J. Castillo, Commissioner, INS (Sept. 15, 1978) at 1.

184. *See* 46 Fed. Reg. 9119 (1981).

185. Tribe, *Structural Due Process*, *supra* note 33.

186. Mashaw, *Conflict and Compromise Among Models of Administrative Justice*, 1981 DUKE L.J. 181, 188–90.

187. *Id.* at 188–89.

188. Tribe, *Structural Due Process*, *supra* note 33, at 310–14.

189. *See* Matter of Francois, 10 I. & N. Dec. 168 (1963).

190. *See* Wolf, *A Theory of Nonmarket Failure: A Framework for Implementation Analysis*, 22 J. L. & ECON. 107, 107 (1979); *see also* O. WILLIAMSON, MARKETS AND HIERARCHIES 20–40 (1975) (speaking of 'organizational failures').

191. *See* March, *Bounded Rationality, Ambiguity and the Engineering of Choice*, 9 BELL J. ECON. 587, 590–91 (1978).

192. H. SIMON, ADMINISTRATIVE BEHAVIOR 79 (3d ed. 1976); H. SIMON, MODELS OF MAN 198 (1957).

193. *See* Diver, *Policymaking Paradigms in Administrative Law*, 95 HARV. L. REV. 393, 399–400 (1981).

194. *See* W. ASHBY, AN INTRODUCTION TO CYBERNETICS 24–41 (1956); J. STEINBRUNER, THE CYBERNETIC THEORY OF DECISION 51 (1974).

195. *See* D. BRAYBROOKE & C. LINDBLOM, A STRATEGY OF DECISION 71–77 (1963); Lindblom, *The Science of 'Muddling Through,'* 19 PUB AD. REV. 79 (1959).

196. This is the premise of various theories of democracy, including pluralism, *see* R. DAHL, A PREFACE TO DEMOCRATIC THEORY 134–35 (1956), and 'economic theories,' *see, e.g.*, Posner, *Theories of Economic Regulation*, 5 BELL J. ECON.

335, 344–50 (1974); Stigler, *The Theory of Economic Regulation*, 2 Bell J. Econ. 3, 10–13 (1971).

197. In fact, the Air Line Pilots Association abandoned its longstanding opposition to the age-60 rule in 1980, citing its success at adjusting pilots' salaries and pensions to the age 60 retirement date. NIA Report, *supra* note 29, app. C, at C-39 to -40.

198. *See* M. Olson, The Logic of Collective Action 46–47 (1965).

199. Pilots are fewer in number than airline passengers, their individual stakes in the decision are much greater, and they have already been organized for other purposes. In addition, pilots have access to the policymaking process—the right to a hearing in individual decertification actions—denied to the general public.

200. R. Noll, Reforming Regulation 39–42 (1970); W. Riker, The Theory of Political Coalitions (1962).

201. On the use of regulation to create barriers to entry in general, see B. Owen & R. Braeutigam, The Regulation Game 2–9 (1978).

202. *See, e.g.*, Anthony, *Towards Simplicity and Rationality in Comparative Broadcast Licensing Proceedings*, 24 Stan. L. Rev. 1, 39 (1971); Geller, *The Comparative Renewal Process in Television: Problems and Suggested Solutions*, 61 Va L. Rev. 471, 500–03 (1975); Schwartz, *Comparative Television and the Chancellor's Foot*, 47 Geo. L.J. 655, 678–89 (1959).

203. The FCC has launched several abortive efforts to clarify its policies. *See, e.g.*, Policy Statement Concerning Comparative Hearings Involving Regular Renewal Applicants, 22 F.C.C.2d 424 (1970), *struck down in* Citizens Communication Center v. FCC, 447 F.2d 1201 (D.C. Cir. 1971); Notice of Inquiry, In the Matter of Formulation of Policies Relating to the Broadcast Renewal Applicant, Stemming from the Comparative Hearing Process, 27 F.C.C.2d 580 (1971), *terminated without action*, Report and Order, 66 F.C.C.2d 419 (1977), *aff'd sub nom.* National Black Media Coalition v. FCC, 589 F.2d 578 (D.C. Cir. 1978).

204. *See* Cass, *RKO: A Special Kind of Lottery*, 9 Media L. Notes 2, 3 (No. 4, 1982).

205. *See* Citizens Communications Center v. FCC, 447 F.2d 1201, 1205 n.7 (D.C. Cir. 1971) (citing 1969 figure of $250,000 to prepare an application for major-market television license).

206. From 1961 through 1978, there were 17 comparative television hearings. Central Florida Enters. Inc. v. FCC, 598 F.2d 37, 61 (D.C. Cir. 1978).

207. R. Cass, Revolution in the Wasteland 8–12 (1981).

208. *See* In the Matter of Policies Relating to the Broadcast Renewal Applicant, Stemming from the Comparative Hearing Process, FCC Broadcast Docket No. 81–742, in response to Notice of Inquiry, 88 F.C.C.2d 21 (1981) (Comments of CBS, NBC, and ABC).

209. Jerry Mashaw estimates the average DI claim to be worth $30,000 to the claimant. J. Mashaw, *supra* note 117, at 81. The number of hearings

demanded exceeded 300,000 in 1982. STAFF OF SENATE COMM. ON FINANCE, *supra* note 129, at 70.

210. *See, e.g.,* Holmes v. New York City Hous. Auth., 398 F.2d 262 (2d Cir. 1968).

211. *See* Morton v. Ruiz, 415 U.S. 199 (1974).

212. *See* Asimakopoulos v. INS, 445 F.2d 1362 (9th Cir. 1971).

213. *See* Posner, *supra* note 196, at 336–41. Some recent accounts of airline deregulation rely on 'public interest' explanations for administrative actions in support of deregulation. *See* S. BREYER, REGULATION AND ITS REFORM 317 (1982); Levine, *Revisionism Revised? Airline Deregulation and the Public Interest,* 44 LAW & CONTEMP. PROBS. 179, 182 (Winter 1981).

214. W. NISKANEN, BUREAUCRACY AND REPRESENTATIVE GOVERNMENT 36–42 (1971); Niskanen, *The Peculiar Economics of Bureaucracy,* 58 AM. ECON. REV. PAPERS & PROCS. 293, 296–98 (1968). For a critique of Niskanen's assumptions, see Breton & Wintrobe, *The Equilibrium Size of a Budget-Maximizing Bureau: A Note on Niskanen's Theory of Bureaucracy,* 83 J. POL. ECON. 195 (1975).

215. Peltzman, *Toward a More General Theory of Regulation,* 19 J. L. & ECON. 211 (1976).

216. *See* Wilson, *The Dead Hand of Regulation,* 25 PUB. INTEREST 39 (Fall 1971); Wilson, *The Rise of the Bureaucratic State,* 41 PUB. INTEREST 77 (Fall 1975).

217. *See* Hilton, *The Basic Behavior of Regulatory Commissions,* 62 AM. ECON. REV. PAPERS & PROC. 47 (1972); Manne, *Individual Constraints and Incentives in Government Regulation of Business,* in INTERACTION OF ECONOMICS AND LAW 23 (B. Siegan ed. 1977).

218. *See* Eckert, *On the Incentives of Regulators: The Case of Taxicabs,* 14 PUB CHOICE 83, 85–88 (Spring 1973).

219. *Cf.* Magat & Estomin, *The Behavior of Regulatory Agencies,* in ATTACKING REGULATORY PROBLEMS, *supra* note 43, at 101 ('quality' of regulations includes 'clarity of interpretation' and 'ease of enforcement').

220. *See supra* pp. 224–5.

221. *See* Peltzman, *supra* note 215, at 211–14.

222. *See* Eckert, *The Life Cycle of Regulatory Commissioners,* 24 J.L. & ECON. 113 (1980).

223. *See infra* pp. 250–1.

224. *See supra* pp. 227–8.

225. *See* E. BARDACH & R. KAGAN, *supra* note 4.

226. *See supra* pp. 246–7.

227. *See* Posner, *Economics, Politics, and the Reading of Statutes and the Constitution,* 49 U. CHI. L. REV. 263, 288–90 (1982); Stewart, *The Reformation of American Administrative Law,* 88 HARV. L. REV. 1669, 1695–96 (1975).

228. *See* E. STOKEY & R. ZECKHAUSER, A PRIMER FOR POLICY ANALYSIS 159–76 (1978).

229. *See* Baumol, *On the Social Rate of Discount,* 58 AM. ECON. REV. 788 (1968); Marglin, *The Social Rate of Discount and the Optimal Rate of Investment,* 77 Q.J. ECON. 95 (1963).

230. *See* W. NISKANEN, *supra* note 214, at 114–23 (bureaucrat's personal discount rate a function of expected tenure in office).

231. *See* Eckert, *supra* note 222; Hilton, *supra* note 217.

232. *See* M. DERTHICK, POLICYMAKING FOR SOCIAL SECURITY (1979).

233. M. BERNSTEIN, REGULATING BUSINESS BY INDEPENDENT COMMISSION 74–95 (1955).

234. *See* Zeckhauser & Nichols, *The Occupational Safety and Health Administration—An Overview,* in SENATE COMM. ON GOV'TAL AFFAIRS, 95TH CONG., 2D SESS., STUDY ON FEDERAL REGULATION, APP. TO VOL VI: FRAMEWORK FOR REGULATION 169, 200–01 (Comm. Print 1978).

235. *See, e.g.,* R. ARNOLD, CONGRESS AND THE BUREAUCRACY: A THEORY OF INFLUENCE (1979); L. DODD & R. SCHOTT, CONGRESS AND THE ADMINISTRATIVE STATE (1979).

236. For illustrations, see W. CARY, POLITICS AND THE REGULATORY AGENCIES (1967); THE FEDERAL TRADE COMMISSION SINCE 1970: ECONOMIC REGULATION AND BUREAUCRATIC BEHAVIOR (K. Clarkson & T. Muris eds. 1981); Parnell, *Congressional Interference in Agency Enforcement: The IRS Experience,* 89 YALE L. J. 1360 (1980).

237. *See To Eliminate Age Limitations Presently Imposed on Certain Pilots of Aircraft: Hearings Before the Subcomm. on Aviation of the House Comm. on Public Works and Transp.,* 96th Cong., 1st Sess. 160–64 (testimony of Pilots' Rights Association Panel), 367–69 (1974) (submission of John Young, legislative vice president, Pilots' Rights Association).

238. *See, e.g.,* W. RIKER, DEMOCRACY IN THE UNITED STATES 61 (2d ed. 1965). Inability to weigh votes by relative intensity of voter preferences is one of the conditions that produces the problem of cyclical majorities. *See* A. MACKAY, ARROW'S THEOREM: THE PARADOX OF SOCIAL CHOICE 26–27, 42–48 (1980).

239. *See* A. DOWNS, AN ECONOMIC THEORY OF DEMOCRACY 136 (1957) (noting tendency of candidates in a two-party system to converge on the midpoint of the voter frequency distribution).

240. *See* Weingast, Shepsle & Johnsen, *The Political Economy of Benefits and Costs: A Neoclassical Approach to Distribution Politics,* 89 J. POL. ECON. 642 (1981).

241. For an extreme view, see E. NORDLINGER, ON THE AUTONOMY OF THE DEMOCRATIC STATE (1981).

242. *See* J. SUNDQUIST, THE DECLINE AND RESURGENCE OF CONGRESS 318–24 (1981); W. NISKANEN, *supra* note 214, at 24–35.

243. *See supra* pp. 245–7.

244. *See, e.g.,* White v. Roughton, 530 F.2d 750 (7th Cir. 1976) (use of unwritten personal standards in determinations of general assistance eligibility violates due process); Holmes v. New York City Hous. Auth., 398 F.2d 262 (2d Cir. 1968) (due process requires that selections among applicants for public housing be made in accordance with 'ascertainable standards').

245. *See, e.g.*, Bahat v. Sureck, 637 F.2d 1315, 1317 (9th Cir. 1981) (INS adjudication found inconsistent with agency regulations); Ruangswang v. INS, 591 F.2d 39, 46 (9th Cir. 1978) (agency cannot create new standard and apply it in context of adjudicatory process).

246. *See* Heckler v. Campbell, 103 S. Ct. 1952 (1983).

247. *See* WAIT Radio v. FCC, 418 F.2d 1153, 1157 (D.C. Cir. 1969).

248. *See, e.g.*, Ambach v. Norwick, 441 U.S. 68, 72–74, 80–81 (1979) (addressing permissible statutory classifications of aliens); Nyquist v. Mauclet, 432 U.S. 1, 7–11 (1977) (same); Sugarman v. Dougall, 413 U.S. 634, 641–44 (1973) (citizenship restriction in municipal civil service 'sweeps indiscriminately').

249. *See* Broadrick v. Oklahoma, 413 U.S. 601, 611–15 (1973).

250. *See, e.g.*, Graham v. Richardson, 403 U.S. 365, 370–73 (1971) (alienage); Loving v. Virginia, 388 U.S. 1 (1967) (race).

251. *See* Williamson v. Lee Optical, 348 U.S. 483 (1955); United States v. Carolene Prods., 304 U.S. 144, 153–54 (1938).

252. *See* National Petroleum Refiners Ass'n v. FTC, 482 F.2d 672, 675 (D.C. Cir. 1973), *cert. denied*, 415 U.S. 951 (1974).

253. *See* Rockbridge v. Lincoln, 449 F.2d 567, 569–71 (9th Cir. 1971).

254. Mashaw, *supra* note 186, at 188–90.

255. *See* Tribe, *Childhood, Suspect Classification and Conclusive Presumptions: Three Linked Riddles*, 39 LAW & CONTEMP. PROBS 8 (Summer 1975); *supra* note 33.

256. F. HAYEK, THE CONSTITUTION OF LIBERTY 205–14 (1960); F. HAYEK, THE ROAD TO SERFDOM 72 (1944).

257. *See* Nonet, *The Legitimation of Purposive Decisions*, 68 CALIF. L. REV. 263, 274–77 (1980).

258. *See* Michelman, *Formal and Associational Aims in Procedural Due Process*, in DUE PROCESS NOMOS XVIII, at 126 (1977).

259. *See* Kennedy, *supra* note 15.

260. Mashaw, *supra* note 147, at 1435–36, 1447–49; *see also* Mashaw, *The Supreme Court's Due Process Calculus for Administrative Adjudication in* Mathews v. Eldridge: *Three Factors in Search of a Theory of Value*, 44 U. CHI. L. REV. 28 (1976).

261. *See* Auerbach, *Informal Rule Making: A Proposed Relationship Between Administrative Procedures and Judicial Review*, 72 Nw. U.L. REV. 15 (1977); Pedersen, *Formal Records and Informal Rulemaking*, 85 YALE L.J. 38 (1975); Verkuil, *Judicial Review of Informal Rulemaking*, 60 VA. L. REV. 185 (1974).

Uncertainty and the Producer Strategy

The Case for Minimizing Type-II Errors in Rational Risk Evaluation

K. SHRADER-FRECHETTE

In 1973, U.S. assessors established that the fungicide ethylene dibromide (EDB) is carcinogenic. Gathering epidemiological data and following the procedures required for regulation, however, took more than a decade. Meanwhile, EDB began showing up in bread, flour, and cereal products in such quantities that risk assessors predicted that, based on lifetime consumption, EDB would cause up to 200,000 cases of cancer per year in the United States. Immediately after the Environmental Protection Agency announced regulations limiting its presence in food, industry switched to using methyl bromide instead. The main benefit of the new chemical is that it is unregulated, although it is a very close chemical relative of EDB and almost certainly highly carcinogenic. Policymakers expect it to take another decade to develop regulations to cover methyl bromide. Meanwhile, it is being used in bread, flour, and cereal products.[1]

Apart from whether industry ought to have regulated itself and not begun use of methyl bromide after EDB was banned, this case raises another question. What is appropriate risk behavior when methyl bromide carcinogenicity is not absolutely certain? In situations of uncertainty, especially those involving potential catastrophes, policymakers ought to act so as to avoid the worst case. In this fungicide instance, the worst case is probably something like 200,000 annual cancers caused by the chemical. In order to avoid the 'worst case,' we might need to protect the public from high-consequence technological dangers that are less likely to occur than more ordinary, lower-consequence events. But—because it is more expensive to protect against improbable, worst-case accidents than against more likely ones—this higher level of protection typically leads to potential financial losses for industry and to the possibility that a certain technology will be rejected on grounds of safety.[2]

All this indicates that choosing a maximin strategy, in cases of uncertainty, typically minimizes public risk (to citizens) and maximizes industry risk (to those responsible for the dangerous technology). But this raises the question of whether, in a situation of uncertainty where we must do one or the other, we ought to minimize industry risk or public risk. This chapter argues that *rational* risk evaluation and management often requires us to minimize public risk.

Type-I (Industry) Risks and Type-II (Public) Risks

The concepts of industry and public risks are related to those of type-I and type-II statistical error. In a situation of uncertainty, errors of type I occur when one rejects a null hypothesis that is true; errors of type II occur when one fails to reject a null hypothesis that is false. Statistics dictates that we make assumptions about the size of each of these types of error that can be tolerated, and, on this basis, we choose a testing pattern for our hypothesis. This concept of *significance*, for example, is often defined in terms of a type-I risk of error of either 0.01 or 0.05, where there is not more than a 1 in 100 or a 5 in 100 chance of committing the error of rejecting a true hypothesis.

Determining significance, however, is not a sufficient basis for answering an important question. Given a situation of uncertainty, which is the more serious error, type I or type II? An analogous issue arises in law. Is the more serious error to acquit a guilty person or to convict an innocent person? In assessing technological impacts, ought one to minimize type-I risk, which Churchman terms the 'Producer Risk,' or ought one to minimize type-II risk, which he calls the 'Consumer Risk'? (I also call the producer risk and the consumer risk, respectively, 'industry risk' and 'public risk.') That is, ought one to run the risk of rejecting a true null hypothesis, of not using a technology that is really acceptable and safe; or ought one to run the risk of not rejecting a false null hypothesis, of using a technology that is really unacceptable and unsafe? To decrease industry risk might hurt the public, and to decrease public risk might hurt industry.[3]

Why Risk Assessors Tend to Minimize Industry Risk

Just as most experts (risk assessors) probably tend to pursue the dominant Bayesian strategy, even in situations of uncertainty, they also probably tend to minimize producer or industry risk and to maximize consumer or public risk.[4] This tendency likely arises because preferences for type-II errors and for minimizing type-I risks appear more consistent with scientific practice. Hypothesis testing in science operates on the basis of limiting false positives (assertions of effects where none exists), or limiting incorrect rejections of the null hypothesis. In order to minimize type-I errors, scientists design studies to guard against the influence of all possible confounding variables, and they demand replication of study results before accepting them as supporting a particular hypothesis. They apply tests of statistical significance, which reject results whose probability of occurring by chance (whose p value) is greater than, for example, 5 percent. Moreover, it is difficult to see how the scientific enterprise could function without such rigorous reluctance to accept positive results. As Abraham Kaplan put it: 'The scientist usually attaches a greater loss to accepting a falsehood than to failing to acknowledge a truth. As a result, there is a certain conservatism or inertia in the scientific enterprise, often rationalized as the healthy skepticism characteristic of the scientific temper.'[5]

The preference for type-II errors (for consumer or public risks) and for minimizing type-I errors (industry risks) is also consistent with the standards of proof required in criminal cases, as opposed to cases in torts. Our law requires the jury in a criminal case to be sure beyond a reasonable doubt that a defendant is guilty before deciding against him; standards of proof in criminal cases thus also reveal a preference for type-II error, a preference for accepting the null hypothesis or innocence, a preference for the risk of acquitting a guilty person. In a case in torts, however, our law requires the jury to believe only that it is more probable than not that the defendant is guilty; standards of proof in civil cases thus reveal no preference for either type-I or type-II error.

As Judith Jarvis Thomson points out, 'our society takes the view that in a criminal case, the society's potential mistake-loss is very much greater than the society's potential omission-loss.'[6] Presumably, this difference in the standards for proof in civil and criminal law stems at least in part from the fact that the consequences to the defendant in the criminal case are more likely to lead to grave harms (such as death or life imprisonment) than are the consequences to society.[7] Moreover, the state needs to protect its moral legitimacy by minimizing type-I risks in criminal cases. If it fails to convict the guilty, the state commits wrong in a more passive (less reprehensible) sense than if it errs by convicting the innocent. For these reasons, if standards of proof in cases of industry (or type-I) risks were analogous to those in criminal cases, then this analogy might provide a good reason for minimizing industry, rather than public, risk. (As the next section of this chapter will argue, however, they are analogous neither to hypothesis testing in pure science nor to determination of guilt in criminal cases.)

Preferences for type-II error or public risk might also arise from the fact that many risk assessments and impact analyses are done by those who are closely associated with the technology being evaluated and who are therefore sympathetic to it and to those who implement it.[8] In such cases, assessors typically underestimate risk probabilities,[9] at least in part because it is difficult to identify all hazards, and because unidentified risks are usually assumed to be zero. Minimizing industry risk probably also arises because technical experts almost always use widely accepted Bayesian decision rules based on expected utility and subjective probabilities, rather than the maximin principle.[10] As a result, even when everyone agrees that the probability of a high-consequence impact is uncertain but low, using a Bayesian decision rule typically generates a choice in favor of the potentially catastrophic technology or environmental impact, whereas using a maximin principle likely produces a verdict against the technology or environmental impact.[11]

Why Analogies from Scientific Practice and Criminal Law are not Applicable

Contrary to most assessors, I shall argue that there are prima facie grounds for minimizing public, rather than industry, risk. Before doing so, however, I will attempt to explain why standards of proof in assessing technological and environmental risks under uncertainty are analogous neither to hypothesis testing in pure science nor to determination of guilt in criminal cases. If my explanation is correct, then neither science nor criminal law provides arguments for minimizing industry, over public, risk.

Researchers doing pure science apparently prefer to minimize type-I error and to risk type-II error (consumer or public risk) because it is a more conservative course, epistemologically speaking, than is risking type-I error (industry risk). It is more conservative in the sense that it avoids positing an effect (e.g., that a substance causes cancer above a given level). Instead, it presupposes that the null hypothesis is correct (e.g., that a substance causes no cancer above a given level). Hence, it is reasonable to claim that one ought to follow a model of 'epistemological rationality,' rationality concerned with maximizing truth and avoiding positive error, when one is engaged in pure science.

Societal decisionmaking under uncertainty, however, is arguably not analogous to decisionmaking in pure science. 'Epistemological rationality' is an insufficient basis for making decisions about whether to minimize industry and public risks affecting the welfare of many people. This is because judgments about societal welfare involve 'cultural rationality,' and hence an assessment of the democratic justifiability of the risk imposition. Individual risk cases, or cases of purely scientific decisionmaking, might involve a *substantive* concept of epistemological rationality; but cases involving societal risk decisions require a *procedural* concept of rationality, one able to take account of a process for recognizing ethical and legal obligations. When one moves from pure science to applied science affecting policy, the question of what is rational moves from epistemological considerations to both ethical and epistemological ones. Therefore, the fact that pure scientists minimize type-I errors provides no compelling reasons for arguing that societal decisionmakers ought to minimize type-I errors.

Likewise, the legal system provides no strong reasons for minimizing type-I errors. For one thing, civil law exhibits no preference for minimizing type-I errors. Although criminal law does reveal such a preference, it does not appear to be analogous to the societal situation of technological or environmental risk under uncertainty. In protecting the accused criminal, presupposing his innocence, and therefore minimizing type-I errors, the criminal law is protecting the most vulnerable person. Since an accused criminal is more vulnerable than his potential or alleged societal victims, harm to him is more serious than harm to society, in the event of a mistake. In a case of societal risk from technology, however, harm to the public is more serious than harm to industry. If decisionmakers err in assuming that a given technology is safe, then this type-II error could result in loss of life by members of the public. However, if decisionmakers err in assuming that a given technology is harmful and therefore err in rejecting it, then the main losses for industry are economic. Hence, if the aim of decisionmaking under risk is to avoid the more serious harms, this case is not analogous to that of the criminal being tried, since in the risk case the greatest threat is to the public, and in the criminal case the greatest threat is to the defendant.

Moreover, if Thomson is correct in claiming that criminal law shows a presupposition in favor of minimizing type-I error, industry risk, because alleged criminals are more vulnerable than are societal victims of criminals, then this reason also shows that the criminal case and the societal risk cases are disanalogous. The public is far more vulnerable than are industrial producers and users of risky technologies. The public is privy to less information about the alleged risks, and the public typically has fewer financial resources to use in avoiding the risks. Also, it is extremely difficult for victims of societal/industrial hazards (for example, people who have cancer) to exercise their due-process rights, since such an exercise requires that they prove causality in the case of a technological risk.[12] Hence, if the public is more vulnerable than industrial producers of risk, protecting the more vulnerable persons requires that one minimize public or type-II risks (rather than the type-I risks minimized by the criminal law).

The Prima Facie Case for Minimizing Public Risk

In arguing that there are prima facie grounds for reducing public (rather than industry) risk, I intend to show that, all things being equal, one ought to take this approach. Obviously, however, the decision to minimize either public or industry risk must be decided in part on a case-by-case basis (so that, for example, the particular benefits at stake are considered). Arguing that there are prima facie grounds for reducing public risk therefore amounts to arguing that the burden of proof (regarding risk acceptability) should be placed on the person wishing to reduce industry, rather than public, risk. If that person cannot provide evidence to the contrary, one ought to minimize public risk.

There are at least eight different reasons for holding that assessors' prima facie duty is to minimize the chance that an unsafe technology is implemented; that is, to minimize public risk. The first five arguments stress that the dangers faced by the public (rather than by industry) represent the *kind* of risk most deserving of reduction. The last three arguments focus on the public as the *locus* of decisionmaking regarding societal hazards, since laypeople typically argue for reducing public risk.

Arguments for Minimizing Public Risk as a Kind of Risk

Minimizing false positives, judgments that an unsafe technology is acceptable, is prima facie reasonable on ethical grounds. That is, it is more important to protect the public from harm than to provide, in some positive sense, for welfare, because protecting from harm seems to be a necessary condition for enjoying other freedoms.[13] Bentham, for instance, in discussing an important part of liberalism, cautioned, much as Nozick and others might, that 'the care of providing for his enjoyments ought to be left almost entirely to each individual; the principal function of government being to protect him from sufferings.'[14] In other words, Bentham established protection from harm as more basic than provision of enjoyments.

Admittedly, it is difficult to draw the line between providing benefits and protecting from harm, between positive and negative laws. Nevertheless, just as there is a basic distinction between *welfare* rights and *negative* rights,[15] there is an analogous relationship between welfare laws (that provide some good) and protective laws (that prohibit some infringement). Moral philosophers continue to honor distinctions similar to this one; indeed, they distinguish not only between welfare-enhancing laws and protective laws but also between closely related concepts, such as letting die versus killing, and between acts of *omission* and acts of *commission*.[16] Given such distinctions, it is arguably more important to protect from harm or to avoid committing wrong than it is to provide some good or to avoid some omission. It therefore seems more important to protect citizens from public hazards than to attempt to enhance their welfare by implementing a risky technology. Also, industrial producers, users, and implementers of technology, not the public, receive the bulk of benefits from it. Because they receive most of the benefits, they ought to bear most of the risks and costs.[17]

There are likewise prima facie grounds for limiting public, rather than industry, risk because the public typically needs more risk protection than does industry. The public usually has fewer financial resources and less information to deal with the societal hazards that affect it, and laypersons are often faced with bureaucratic denials of public danger. Their vulnerability in this regard is well established in a number of cases of environmental risk. When the toxic polybrominated biphenyl (PBB) was accidentally used in cattlefeed in Michigan, for example, it was the most widespread, least reported, chemical disaster ever to happen in the Western world. There was strong evidence of contamination in September 1973, but detailed articles on the problem did not appear, even in the local papers, for two more years. Larger newspapers, such as the *Detroit Free Press* and the *Detroit News*, did not examine the crisis until four years after it was evident. The problem was ignored for this length of time because the local bureaucrats denied the claims made by the farmers. Typically, a reporter would interview the owner of a contaminated farm and then check with the Michigan Farm Bureau and the Michigan Department of Agriculture, both of which would claim that the farmer's allegations were false. Because of all this bureaucratic denial, industry indifference, and isolation of the afflicted, PBB led to the deaths of tens of thousands of farm animals and to the contamination of nine million people who ate contaminated meat.[18]

Likewise, in 1976, after repeated bureaucratic denials of risk, a poisonous cloud of dioxin escaped from a chemical plant at Seveso, Italy, contaminating an area of 18 million square meters, killing thousands of animals and causing numerous cases of disfiguring skin disease in children. A similar situation occurred in Japan, where the dangers of mercury poisoning were identified in 1940, deaths were reported in 1948, and the famous Minimata poisoning occurred in 1953. Because of industry indifference, however, it was not until the 1960s that public awareness of the problem caused officials to take action against mercury contamination. These and similar instances of whistle-swallowing (rather than whistle-blowing), in cases involving asbestos, biotechnology, and chemical dumps, suggest that new public risks very likely will also be ignored. Hence, there is reason to believe that the public, rather than industry, has a greater need for protection.[19]

Another reason for minimizing public risk, especially in cases of uncertainty, is that laypersons ought to be accorded legal rights to protection against industrial decisions that could threaten their health or physical security. These legal rights arise out of the consideration that everyone has both due-process rights and rights to bodily security.

The problem of protecting the consumer against the extended effects of industrial decisions typically addresses three general kinds of protection: prevention, transferral of loss, and retention of the risk. When citizens protect themselves against losses (resulting from the decisions of others) by maintaining enough assets to sustain damages caused by those decisions, they protect themselves by *retention* of the risk. When they use mechanisms like insurance and legal liability to transfer the risk or loss, they are protecting themselves by *transferral* of the majority of the loss to someone else—namely, the insurer or the liable party. The practical advantage of risk transfer over retention is that it does not require one to retain as many assets, idle and unproductive, as a way of guarding against damages. The moral advantage is that, if the harm itself is caused by another legal/moral 'person,' an industry, then that person—and not the individual harmed—is liable. And if the 'person' causing the damage is liable, then there are practical grounds for using this moral responsibility as a basis for the individual or his insurer to remove the financial responsibility from the victim. Insurance is probably a better vehicle for risk transfer than is liability, since insurance (unlike liability) does not typically require the victim to use legal remedies to obtain protection or compensation.[20]

Prevention, of course, is the most thorough way for members of recipient populations to protect themselves against losses resulting from the decisions of others. By eliminating the sources of the risk, the potential victim has more to gain, practically speaking, than by using risk transfer or retention as means of protection. This is because prevention does not tie up any of the potential victim's assets. The moral grounds for prevention are that, in cases where those responsible or liable cannot redress the harm done to others by their faulty decisions, risk should be eliminated. When industrial decisionmakers cannot adequately compensate or insure their potential victims, surely these incompensable risks should not be imposed on those who fail to give free, informed consent to them.

Thomson describes 'incompensable harms' as harms so serious that no amount of money could possibly compensate the victim. By this definition, death, at least, is an obviously 'incompensable harm,' since there is no way to compensate a dead person. As Thomson puts it, speaking of another case, 'however fair and efficient the judicial system may be, . . . [those] who cause incompensable harms by their negligence cannot square accounts with their victims.'[21] Clearly, anyone who imposes a significant risk of death on another, without free, informed consent, is imposing an incompensable, and therefore morally unjustifiable, harm. But how do we know when someone is imposing a significant risk of death on another, without free, informed consent?[22]

Although the boundary cases would be difficult to decide, potentially catastrophic technologies such as nuclear power do appear to impose a significant risk of death on another. As has been mentioned, even the government admits that a nuclear accident could kill 150,000 people, and that the core-melt probability, for all existing and planned U.S. commercial reactors, is 1 in 4 during their thirty-year lifetime. To the degree that this hazard is imposed on citizens without their free, informed consent, then to that extent is the risk both unjustified and incompensable. Moreover, as was also mentioned earlier, U.S. citizens are prohibited by law from obtaining full compensation from the negligent utility, in the event that there is a commercial nuclear catastrophe.[23]

Other cases of incompensable harm seem to arise most often in connection with potentially catastrophic, involuntarily imposed technologies whose risks are uncertain (for example, specific lethal pesticides or liquefied natural gas facilities). Precisely because these technologies are catastrophic, and have the potential for causing incompensable and involuntarily imposed harm, one might argue that the risks they impose are unjustifiable. This is all the more true if the probability of harm is uncertain, because the person imposing the risk is unable to know how grave a danger he is imposing. Moreover, harm can be imposed, or discrimination justified, only when it leads to greater good for all, including those most disadvantaged by it. If there is uncertainty about the level of the harm, then it would also be difficult (if not impossible) to prove that imposing such a risk would lead to greater good for all.

An Objection: Does Economic Well-Being Justify Minimizing Industry Risk?

In response to all these arguments for minimizing public (not industry) risk, it might be objected that assessors have a duty, for the good of the *economy* (which allegedly maximizes overall welfare), to minimize industry, not public, risk.[24] To defend this point, however, the objectors would have to show that their position does not amount to violating a basic ethical rule prohibiting the use of persons (the public) as means to the ends of other persons (industry and society as a whole). Both tort law and the Fifth and Fourteenth Amendments to the U.S. Constitution arguably presuppose this rule.[25] It would probably be quite difficult to show that minimizing industry risk, on grounds of economic efficiency, would not violate both this rule and the right to bodily security.[26]

Proponents of economic efficiency would also have to show that, contrary to what conflicting hazard assessments suggest, risk probabilities as calculated by experts provide a reliable basis from which to assess and pursue economic efficiency and societal welfare. If Kahneman, Tversky, and others are right, this point might be hard to prove, since there is strong evidence that experts have as many heuristic biases in estimating probabilities as laypeople.[27] Therefore, especially since expert opinion on risk may err, we ought to minimize public risk so as to protect the public's right to security.

Obviously, no one is eager either to cripple technology or to set back the economy in order to minimize public risk. Many potentially catastrophic technologies, however, are in principle able to 'set back' the economy. Nuclear technology, for example, has 'set back' the economy in the sense that it could not have survived without protection from normal market mechanisms. If there were no government-guaranteed liability limit for catastrophic accidents involving commercial nuclear fission, then no major U.S. atomic interests would ever have gone into generation of electricity. Even the major pronuclear lobby, the Atomic Industrial Forum (AIF), admits this.[28] The upshot is that, although nuclear utilities have been relieved of the burden of competing in an open market, including the liability market, they nevertheless have the potential to cripple the economy with a dangerous accident that could (on the government's own estimates) wipe out an area the size of Pennsylvania. Because the industry risk is minimized, while the public risk from nuclear power is maximized, the liability limit could easily contribute to massive economic harm.[29]

Hazardous technologies could also 'set back' the economy in the sense that many of the most dangerous industries (in the sense of high public risk and high public risk aversion) are also among the most capital intensive. Because they are so capital intensive, they threaten the flow of available money for other societal projects and hence jeopardize the economic well-being of society. This is particularly the case with nuclear technology.[30]

These argument sketches suggest that insistence on the operation of the free market (free from regulations to minimize public risk and free from liability limits to minimize industry risk) might be just as threatening to dangerous technologies as to members of the public who are risk averse. They also suggest that proponents of maximizing public risk and minimizing industry risk are inconsistent; often they wish to interfere with the market so as to *protect industry*, but they complain when risk regulation interferes with the same market in order to *protect the public*. Given this inconsistency, it is unclear why incompensable risks should be borne only by their victims (which seems to be the intention of the Price-Anderson Act), rather than also by their perpetrators.[31]

There are other problems, however, with the basic argument that one ought not to mandate high levels of public safety because this would hurt the economy or 'progress.' Such a line of reasoning sounds vaguely like several others: 'We can't abolish slavery, because this would destroy the economy of the South.' Or 'We can't pass the ERA, because women won't stay home and take care of their children, and this would hurt the family.' All these arguments pit important values, such as family and economic well-being, *against* moral values, such as citizen safety or abolishing racism and sexism. The arguments are troubling because they force us to choose between two goods. Thomson's response to such arguments—those that force us to choose between risking our life versus starving, for example—is simple. 'It is morally indecent that anyone in a moderately well-off society should be faced with such a choice.'[32]

Moreover, these three arguments—about technology, slavery, and women's rights—all propose using humans—whether citizens at risk from technology, or blacks who are victims of slavery, or women who are disadvantaged by sexism—as *means* to some economic or social *end*. But humans ought never be used as means to some end sought by other persons, especially not if all humans have equal rights and equal dignity. We do often have to weigh the interests of one group in society over those of another, and we do often discriminate. Yet the only grounds justifying discrimination, the failure to treat one person as equal to another, as Frankena has pointed out, is that the discrimination will work to the advantage of everyone, including those discriminated against. Any other attempt to justify discrimination fails because it would amount to sanctioning the use of some humans as means to the ends of other humans.[33]

Applied to technological risk assessment and type-I and type-II risks, this insight about justified discrimination suggests that a necessary condition for discriminating against members of the public who prefer conservative health and safety standards would be to prove that rejecting conservative standards would work to the advantage of everyone, including the public. In other words, the burden of proof is on the industry attempting to put the public at risk. And if the burden ought to be on industry, then this is grounds for minimizing public risk.

Arguments for Giving the Public the Power to Make Risk Decisions

In addition to the five reasons already given, there are also several arguments for minimizing public risk by means of giving potential victims the power to make risk decisions affecting them. For example, one could argue, on grounds of democratic process and procedural rationality, that there ought to be no imposition of risk without the free, informed consent of those who must bear it. This dictum holds true in medical experimentation, and it could easily be shown to have an analogue in risk management.[34] Likewise, there are strong *economic* grounds for minimizing public risk whenever this minimization is consistent with public preferences. Consumer sovereignty in matters of risk is not justified merely by reference to the alleged unseen hand controlling economic events, but by a revered economic and political principle: 'No taxation without representation.' Welfare economics, in particular, establishes the convenience and efficiency of consumer sovereignty, and citizens themselves, as Schelling notes, have safeguarded it by means of 'arms, martyrdom, boycott, or some principles held to be self-evident. . . . [I]t includes the inalienable right of the consumer to make his own mistakes.'[35]

Minimizing public risk, in the name of consumer or citizen self-determination, is also consistent with most ethical theories about situations in which paternalism is or is not justified. In his classic discussion of liberty, Mill makes clear that it is acceptable to override individual decisionmaking only to protect others or to keep someone from selling himself into slavery. Any other justification for a limitation on individual freedom, claims Mill, would amount to a dangerous infringement on individual autonomy.[36] But if Mill is correct, then there are no paternalistic grounds for overriding the hesitancies of the public about accepting a particular technological risk. This is because, in arguments to minimize industry risk at the expense of the public, experts are arguing that citizens are over-protective of themselves. The assessors want to provide the public with less, not more, protection, and largely for the benefit of industry. Hence, their paternalism is suspect.

Consider, for example, what happened in 1987 when the U.S. Environmental Protection Agency (EPA) proposed new standards to protect the public (living near steel mills) from coke-oven emissions. One of the greatest hazards caused by the emissions was lung cancer, both among steelworkers and nearby residents. As soon as the EPA issued its proposed standards, risk assessors employed by the steel industry developed a hazard analysis critical of the EPA study. In defending less stringent emissions standards to protect public health, the industry assessors (working under a taxpayer-funded National Science Foundation grant) made a number of arguments, none of which was directed at protecting the public health and safety. The industry assessors criticized the EPA standards on grounds that they 'would weaken the [steel] industry' and that 'the cost to reduce exposure under the EPA standard is very high.'[37]

The self-interested nature of the industry assessment of coke-oven emissions was even more apparent when the assessors argued that the EPA was 'unjustified' in proposing regulations that could save one person in one thousand from cancer induced by emissions from the nearby steel mills. They wrote:

Even if the population were subjected to exposures that produced an increase in cancers equal to the upper bound risk calculated by the EPA, an increase of one cancer per 1000 residents over their lives, this represents only a 2 percent increase in the cancer rate. This rate is too small to detect using epidemiology. In a 2 percent or smaller increase in the lung cancer rate for the most exposed population worth all the effort of an EPA regulation? ... The EPA approach is an arbitrary one in the name of prudent public protection.... The EPA's proposed regulation seems unjustified.[38]

This reasoning of industry risk assessors appears seriously flawed. They assume that, in order to benefit steel manufacturers financially, it is acceptable to cause the death of one person in a thousand. Moreover, the government typically regulates all risks above the level of one fatality in one million. This means that the industry risk assessors are trying to impose a steel-emissions risk on the public that is three orders of magnitude *greater* than those typically *prohibited*. Moreover, since government epidemiologists typically discover risks of one in one million, it is simply false for the two industry assessors to claim that the rate (one in one thousand) 'is too small to detect using epidemiology.' (See quotation above.) Finally, despite their admission that failure to adopt the new EPA standards could result in an increase of one cancer per thousand members of the public, the industry risk assessors never gave any ethical or political rationale for rejecting the standards. They ignored issues of consent, compensation, and equity, but justified the standards on the basis of industry's economic interest. Hence, as this example illustrates, those who wish to increase public risks often tend to make self-serving arguments.

At this point, industry might object that the public wants the benefits associated with technological hazards, and hence that those arguing for reducing public risk must bear the charge of behaving paternalistically toward those who do not want public risk minimized. There are at least two responses to this objection. For one thing, there is substantial social scientific and philosophical evidence that those bearing high levels of public risk have not given free, informed consent to imposition of the hazards.[39] Another response is that economists have long recognized that risk imposition represents a diminution in welfare for those who bear the hazards.[40] Since industry imposes risks on the public, industry ought to bear the burden of proof in justifying the imposition, particularly since the public typically has not given free, informed consent.

Minimizing public risk is also defensible because it might be less likely to lead to social and political unrest than minimizing industry risk. Although developing this point fully is not possible in this chapter, there might be pragmatic and political, as well as ethical and economic, grounds for following public preferences to minimize public risk. As many risk assessors have pointed out, effective hazard management requires the cooperation of many laypeople; otherwise, accidents, costly publicity, and civil disobedience may result. The long controversy over the Seabrook (New Hampshire) nuclear facility illustrates the need for such cooperation between industry and the public. Both industry and members of the public must agree to do without some things and to accept substitutes for others. They must vote sensibly, act reasonably, and engage in much give-and-take over regulations and standards. If they do not, then a hazardous technology could be crippled. Moreover, 'even if the experts were much better judges of risk than laypeople, giving experts an exclusive franchise for hazard management would mean substituting short-term efficiency for the long-term effort needed to create an informed citizenry.'[41]

Notes

1. H. Otway, 'Regulation and Risk Analysis,' in *Regulating Industrial Risks*, ed. H. Otway and M. Peltu (London: Butterworths, 1985), pp. 10–11.

2. This point is made, for example, by L. Lave and B. Leonard, 'Regulating Coke Oven Emissions,' in *The Risk Assessment of Environmental and Human Health Hazards*, ed. D. J. Paustenbach (New York: Wiley, 1989), pp. 1064–1081. See also C. Starr, R. Rudman, and C. Whipple, 'Philosophical Basis for Risk Analysis,' *Annual Review of Energy* 1 (1976): 629–662.

3. C. W. Churchman, *Theory of Experimental Inference* (New York: Macmillan, 1947). See S. Axinn, 'The Fallacy of the Single Risk,' *Philosophy of Science* 33, nos. 1–2 (1966): 154–162.

4. J. Harsanyi, 'Can the Maximin Principle Serve as a Basis for Morality? A Critique of John Rawls's Theory,' *American Political Science Review* 69, no. 2 (1975): 594. Admittedly, some risk decisions minimize both industry and public risk, and some maximize both industry and public risk. The dilemma arises when only one can be minimized, so that a choice must be made between the two.

5. A. Kaplan, *The Conduct of Inquiry* (San Francisco: Chandler, 1964), p. 253.

6. J. J. Thomson, *Rights, Restitution, and Risk* (Cambridge, Mass.: Harvard University Press, 1986).

7. Grave harms, for both plaintiffs and defendants, are also likely to be greater in the criminal case; hence the tougher standard of proof. There likewise appears to be a greater potential for abuse in the criminal law than in civil or tort law, since all crimes are potentially political crimes, especially in a tyrannical society. This may arise from the fact that criminal law enforces the power of the *state*, whereas civil-tort law merely enforces the power of the legal *individual*.

8. Two industry risk assessors concluded, for example, that the risk of cancer to the public because of a waste site contaminated with chromium was 'insignificant' (see R. Golden and N. Karch, 'Assessment of a Waste Site Contaminated with Chromium,' in Paustenbach, *Risk Assessment*, pp. 577–598). Likewise, two risk assessors employed by Procter and Gamble analyzed the danger posed by a chemical widely used in laundry detergents made by their company. Assessing the chemical, nitrilotriacetic acid, they said that, although it is highly toxic, the chemical 'causes no environmental problems' and 'no risk to humans' because the average dose received by humans is below the level required to initiate cancer (see R. Anderson and C. Alden, 'Risk Assessment for Nitrilotriacetic Acid,' in Paustenbach, *Risk Assessment*, pp. 390–426).

9. For an example of a risk assessment performed by industry analysts, who likely underestimated the risks, see H. Leung and D. Paustenbach, 'Assessing Health Risks in the Workplace,' in Paustenbach, *Risk Assessment*, pp. 689–710. In their study, Leung (who works for Syntex Corporation) and Paustenbach (who works for McLaren Company) claimed that, despite their exposure to dioxin and despite their having residual chloracne for twenty-six years, Dow

Uncertainty and the Producer Strategy 285

Chemical workers and Monsanto workers showed 'no significant differences in a variety of clinical parameters.' However, the assessors did not mention (1) for how long a period the exposed workers were studied, (2) how many workers were studied, or (3) which 'clinical parameters' were examined for the exposed workers. Failure to detect harms to the exposed workers hence could be a result of (1) too short a time for the study, (2) too few workers being studied, and (3) inappropriate or incomplete clinical parameters being investigated. For all these reasons, the industry risk assessors likely underestimated the hazard from dioxin. See R. M. Cooke, 'Risk Assessment and Rational Decision Theory,' *Dialectica* 36 (no. 4), 334. See also note 8 above.

10. See Harsanyi, 'Maximin Principle'; M. Resnick, *Choices* (Minneapolis: University of Minnesota Press, 1987), pp. 26–37.

11. See Cooke, 'Risk Assessment,' pp. 341–342.

12. Regarding the difficulty of proving causality, see, for example, P. Ricci and A. Henderson, 'Fear, Fiat, and Fiasco,' in *Phenotypic Variation in Populations*, ed. A. Woodhead, M. Bender, and R. Leonard (New York: Plenum, 1988), pp. 285–293. See also J. W. Falco and R. Moraski, 'Methods Used in the United States for the Assessment and Management of Health Risk Due to Chemicals,' in *Risk Management of Chemicals in the Environment*, ed. H. M. Seip and A. B. Heiberg (New York: Plenum, 1989), pp. 37–60; and L. Cox and P. Ricci, 'Risk, Uncertainty, and Causation,' in Paustenbach, *Risk Assessment*, pp. 125–156.

13. See, for example, H. Shue, 'Exporting Hazards,' in *Boundaries: National Autonomy and Its Limits*, ed. P. Brown and H. Shue (Totowa, N.J.: Rowman and Littlefield, 1981), pp. 107–145; J. Lichtenberg, 'National Boundaries and Moral Boundaries,' in Brown and Shue, *Boundaries*, pp. 79–100.

14. J. Bentham, *Principles of the Civil Code*, in *The Works of Jeremy Bentham*, ed. J. Bowring (New York: Russell and Russell, 1962), 1:301.

15. See, for example, L. Becker, 'Rights,' in *Property*, ed. L. Becker and K. Kipnis (Englewood Cliffs, N.J.: Prentice-Hall, 1984), p. 76. For a discussion of the flaws in this view of rights, see A. Baier, 'Poisoning the Wells,' in *Values at Risk*, ed. D. MacLean (Totowa, N.J.: Rowman and Allanheld, 1986), pp. 49–74.

16. See, for example, J. Bentham, *Principles of Morals and Legislation*, in Bowring, *Works*, 1:36; J. Feinberg, *Social Philosophy* (Englewood Cliffs, N.J.: Prentice-Hall, 1973), pp. 29, 59; J. Rachels, 'Euthanasia,' in *Matters of Life and Death*, ed. T. Regan (New York: Random House, 1980), p. 38.

17. See L. Cox and P. Ricci, 'Legal and Philosophical Aspects of Risk Analysis,' in Paustenbach, *Risk Analysis*, pp. 22–26. See also W. Hoffman and J. Fisher, 'Corporate Responsibility,' in Becker and Kipnis, *Property*, pp. 211–220.

18. See M. Peltu, 'The Role of Communications Media,' in Otway and Peltu, *Regulating Industrial Risks*, p. 132.

19. Ibid., pp. 132–136.

20. See A. C. Michalos, *Foundations of Decisionmaking* (Ottowa: Canadian Library of Philosophy, 1987), pp. 202 ff.; and H. S. Denenberg et al., *Risk and Insurance*

(Englewood Cliffs, N.J.: Prentice-Hall, 1964). See also Cox and Ricci, 'Legal and Philosophical Aspects,' p. 1035.

21. Thomson, *Rights*, p. 158.

22. For the centrality and importance of consent in risk evaluation, see D. MacLean, 'Introduction' and 'Risk and Consent,' in MacLean, *Values at Risk*, pp. 1–16, 17–30.

23. See K. S. Shrader-Frechette, *Nuclear Power and Public Policy* (Boston: Reidel, 1983), pp. 74–78.

24. Harsanyi, in 'Maximin Principle,' uses this argument, as does L. Maxim, 'Problems Associated with the Use of Conservative Assumptions in Exposure and Risk Analysis,' in Paustenbach, *Risk Assessment*, pp. 539–555. Other risk assessors who use this argument include, for example, Lave and Leonard, 'Coke Oven Emissions,' pp. 1068–1069.

25. See Shrader-Frechette, *Nuclear Power*, pp. 33–35.

26. See W. Frankena, 'The Concept of Social Justice,' in *Social Justice*, ed. R. Brandt (Englewood Cliffs, N.J.: Prentice-Hall, 1962), pp. 10, 14; Shue, 'Exporting Hazards'; and Lichtenberg, 'National Boundaries.' See also Cox and Ricci, 'Legal and Philosophical Aspects.'

27. D. Eddy, 'Probabilistic Reasoning in Clinical Medicine,' in *Judgment under Uncertainty: Heuristics and Biases*, ed. D. Kahneman, P. Slovic, and A. Tversky (Cambridge, England: Cambridge University Press, 1982), p. 267.

28. Shrader-Frechette, *Nuclear Power*, chap. 1.

29. See P. Huber, 'The Bhopalization of American Tort Law,' in *Hazards: Technology and Fairness*, ed. R. Kates et al. (Washington, D.C.: National Academy Press, 1986), pp. 94–95, 106–107. See also Shrader-Frechette, *Nuclear Power*, chap. 4.

30. See, for example, A. B. Lovins and J. H. Price, *Non-Nuclear Futures* (New York: Harper and Row, 1975). See also C. Flavin, *Nuclear Power: The Market Test* (Washington, D.C.: Worldwatch Institute, 1983).

31. See Cooke, 'Risk Assessment,' pp. 345–347.

32. Thomson, *Rights*, p. 172.

33. For discussion of this argument, see Frankena, 'Concept of Social Justice,' p. 15.

34. For analyses of collective strategies whereby consumers might exercise their sovereignty, see K. S. Shrader-Frechette, *Science Policy, Ethics, and Economic Methodology* (Boston: Reidel, 1985), pp. 286–312. See T. Schelling, *Choice and Consequence* (Cambridge, Mass.: Harvard University Press, 1984), pp. 145–146.

35. Schelling, *Choice and Consequences*, pp. 145–146.

36. See, for example, J. S. Mill, *On Liberty* (Buffalo, N.Y.: Prometheus Books, 1986), esp. p. 16.

37. Lave and Leonard, 'Coke Oven Emissions,' pp. 1068–1069.

38. Ibid., pp. 1071–1078.

39. B. Emmet et al., 'The Distribution of Environmental Quality,' in *Environmental Assessment*, ed. D. Burkhardt and W. Ittelson (New York: Plenum, 1978),

pp. 367–374; J. Egerton, 'Appalachia's Absentee Landlords,' *The Progressive* 45, no. 6 (June 1981): 43 ff.; and K. S. Shrader-Frechette, *Risk Analysis and Scientific Method* (Boston: Reidel, 1985), pp. 97–122. See also MacLean, 'Risk and Consent.'

40. C. Starr, 'General Philosophy of Risk-Benefit Analysis,' in *Energy and the Environment*, ed. H. Ashley, R. Rudman, and C. Whipple (Elmsford, N.Y.: Pergamon Press, 1976), p. 16. See Cox and Ricci, 'Legal and Philosophical Aspects.'

41. Slovic, 'Facts vs. Fears,' p. 488.

Law As Last Resort

K. HAWKINS

I. Prosecution in Extremis

A central concern of this book has been the role of law in regulation. My intention has been to portray the formal process of prosecution as a kind of *éminence grise*, a shadowy entity lurking off-stage, often invoked, however discreetly, yet rarely revealed. Why is it so little used and by what principles are particular cases selected for prosecution? In general, what explains enforcement behaviour in this arena of legal control?

Though the water authorities only employ prosecution *in extremis*, this is not to suggest that law is not central to their concerns. Law provides the mandate and the context for agency activities. And field staff themselves are legal actors, implicitly defining every day the reach of the law. Practical criminal law—the enforcement of the norms embodied in that branch of the law—is, to paraphrase Matza (1964: 176), founded not so much on the substantive acts it deems unlawful, but rather on principles that define its proper realm and procedure. In pollution control the conditions under which formal intervention is deemed to be morally and organizationally permissible are very narrowly construed indeed. The irony is that the adoption of strict liability does not expedite formal enforcement of the law, for taking advantage of strict liability is regarded as being 'unreasonable': '[The agencies' predecessor authorities] were expected to act reasonably by prosecuting only for flagrant and careless breaches of consent conditions.' (Agency document.)

Discussions about the role of formal enforcement in regulation are, in general, of two kinds. Behind both lurks an implied complaint about a rate of prosecution that is too low. One argument is couched in economic terms. Resources are inadequate, it runs, with the apparent implication that agencies would prosecute more vigorously if only they could afford the personnel or time (e.g. Cranston, 1979; Conklin, 1977). Thus it has been claimed in the United States that the 'greatest handicap to the successful enforcement of agency regulations' is limited agency budgets and inadequate staff (Clinard *et al.*, 1979: 35).

Financial impediments, it is held, drive agencies into a conciliatory posture. The enforcement of standards against individual polluters, 'may be quite inefficient in terms of time, money, and results, and bargaining with violators may often be necessary' (Davies, 1970: 176). This suggests an economically rational view of prosecution, one which ignores the moral component at its heart and the social context in which enforcement is conducted. The allocation of resources does, of course, impose its own ultimate constraints on what an enforcement agency can do (Long, 1979), but there is no evidence to suggest that the water authorities' present prosecution rate is one inhibited by lack of resources. Indeed, the director of one agency suggested that a doubling of its annual prosecution rate could be absorbed without any noticeable impact on the work of its legal department or senior staff, while the head of his legal department claimed he could 'mount three or four times the amount of prosecutions . . . without any difficulty'.[1]

Another group of explanations is framed in terms of the relative power of the regulator and the regulated. Capture theory is the best known example of this species. In another version, the low rate of formal enforcement is testimony to the power of corporations (Nader, 1970: viii). But there is little evidence from the present research to support this argument, whether or not it is true of the American position. Many polluters comply, or try to comply, generally as a matter of principle; besides, the water authorities are in a rather strong position when deciding whether to prosecute, and possess a virtual monopoly of the information on which a prosecution will be based. Despite their apparently modest legal penalties the agencies enjoy a variety of practical powers which are seemingly rather effective in the personal encounters where enforcement work is done. Large companies, indeed, were frequently portrayed by field men as nervous of agency authority. Little reliable evidence came to light to suggest that such companies attempted to use excessive muscle or influence upon the agencies beyond that which would be considered appropriate in establishing a negotiating position. Here again, the field man's typical portrait of industry emphasized a defensive posture.

Another version of the explanation centred on power emphasizes social status.[2] This suggests that the reluctance of regulatory agencies to prosecute more vigorously can be understood in terms of deference to social status (Mileski, 1971). Agencies tend to process high-status offenders by administrative rather than legal means, the argument runs, particularly where complainants are of low status. This sort of explanation may be relevant where agencies have identifiable complainants as third parties in the enforcement relationship (as in housing code violations) but there is little evidence of its validity in pollution control work where complainants are seldom involved directly, and where those open to prosecution possess no kind of homogeneous social status.

In this chapter I want to put forward a different view about the strategies employed in enforcing regulation, emphasizing the role of formal legal processes. In essence, the argument is that regulatory enforcement is a symbolic matter, reflecting intimately the conjunction of privately-held (but shared) values with organizational interests in enforcing a secular code of conduct about which there is a high degree of social and political ambivalence. I stress again that the discussion is about regulatory enforcement strategies in general, even though for convenience it takes the place of prosecution for its focus.

Any treatment of the problem must address two questions: first, what prompts the level of prosecutions mounted? Secondly, what are the properties which mark out certain cases as worth prosecuting? In considering the former question I shall rest the argument on an analysis of prosecution as a public act and on a recapitulation of the features promoting a compliance strategy. The more elaborate discussion on the interconnected question about the selection of particular cases deemed deserving of prosecution necessarily involves a measure of overlap but for clarity is dealt with separately in discussions of efficiency and justice.

Why is there such sparing use of prosecution? The pollution control agencies, like other regulatory bodies, operate in a public environment. They are public bureaucracies, publicly funded, exposed to a measure of scrutiny, and vulnerable to public criticism. Their audience and their image matter. No organization exists in a vacuum, as Selznick (1966: 10) reminds us. 'Large or small, it must pay some heed to the consequences of its own activities (and even existence) for other groups and forces in the community.' Thus, as an area man put it, 'the preservation of public confidence in the authority is a relevant factor in the consideration of legal action'. As public bodies the water authorities are sensitive to the conflicting demands of the two competing and potentially critical constituencies representing the 'environmentalist' and 'business' perspectives. In their use of the formal legal process the agencies express the nature of their relationship to their environment, while the divergent views represented by the constituencies themselves suggest the extent of the ambivalence surrounding the conduct to be controlled. Selecting cases for prosecution is in large part a consequence of the organizational need to manage appearances before these two ill-defined, but none the less real constituencies with an interest in agency work. The necessity is to satisfy the demands of the environmentalists for action, while achieving the quiescence of the business constituency.

Enforcement work in pollution control, like police work, is bound up with the management of appearances. Prosecution is a symbolic act, 'the dramatization of the moral notions of the community', as Thurman Arnold (1935: 153) put it. It isolates a target group, 'shows it to be vulnerable, and implies that the problem it represents is controlled by such symbolic action' (Manning, 1977: 248). Prosecution is visible evidence of the commitment of an agency to its legal mandate, for, in the words of a senior man, 'the authority's not seen to be doing its job unless it does prosecute'. However lowly the setting, however feeble the sanction, prosecution for pollution is a ceremonial statement of what is desirable in the public interest (Gusfield, 1967). The agencies feel exposed to public attention in the exercise of their authority—to endorsement of their policy or to the risk of public criticism of bullying or extravagance.[3] Prosecution transforms the enforcement of regulation from a private ordering of relations between the polluter and the agency in which the nature of control has been shaped by bureaucratic and moral constraints, into an open contest based on the principles of formal legal control, in which the agency publicly seeks to establish and sanction the polluter's rule-breaking. For these reasons the agencies have a strong incentive to prosecute only those who are likely to offer guilty pleas, thus merely reserving the question of sanction for independent adjudication.

Prosecution also brings regulatory deviance to public view, modest though the publicity of the local newspaper or the trade journals might be. Publicity makes possible the vindication of the agency as a credible enforcement authority. Public enforcement visibly displays regulatory rule-breaking as the law's business, dramatizing the success and effectiveness of the agency, and enhancing such deterrence as resides in the criminal process. *The need to dramatize a measure—but a carefully controlled measure—of activity is the more acute given the lack of substantial consensus about the agencies' mandate.* For this reason the large majority of the pollutions which agencies handle—the routine cases—possess too few symbolically significant features to make them worthy of public enforcement (Manning, 1977: 249). The issue here, ultimately, is one of organizational self-preservation, for organizations are very human institutions which behave in very human ways. 'Prestige and survival are not normally accepted as legitimate ends of administrative behavior,' Selznick writes (1966: 65). '... But prestige and survival ... are real factors in decision. ...' The management of appearances towards potentially critical constituencies imprints agency prosecution policy with a concern for self-preservation.

Yet the agencies lack workable indices of impact and success which may be conjured up to display their effectiveness. Success in regulation in fact is often less visible than failure (Diver, 1980: 274). A policy of fuller enforcement expressed in a swelling prosecution rate cannot be employed as an indicator of efficiency, for in an environment of ambivalence this risks being treated as evidence of agency harassment. It is, rather, in the careful and sparing selection of cases for prosecution, that the agency is best able to protect its own interests by showing that 'something is being done': 'MPs, local councils, anglers, members of the public, pressure groups, from time to time have to see that the authority is doing something. . . . And if it's not doing what it should be doing then it's quite deservedly open to criticism.'

The environment of regulatory control is one riddled with ambiguity and ambivalence. The very notion of 'regulatory justice' is itself the embodiment of ambiguity, while ambivalence about the nature of regulatory control is central to the adoption of strategies of compliance. Legal rules are not generally enforced in court because the regulators and the regulated have a mutual interest in not enforcing them in this way. Agencies paradoxically believe their efforts to attain the wider goals of their legislative mandate to be *facilitated by the extensive (formal) non-enforcement of the specific offences*. The degree to which an agency turns to the formal procedures of the law depends on its perception of the relative strengths of its significant constituencies. Since the perceived social and political environment is a shifting thing, regulatory agencies may be expected to shift accordingly in the extent of their commitment to a strategy of compliance on the one hand, and a sanctioning strategy on the other.

In pollution control work discretion is moulded by an imperative to conciliate, for officials seek to put problems right or to prevent recurrence of damaging or hazardous events. Compliance implies continuity. The open-ended enforcement relationship creates a context in which an officer judges individuals, acts, events, or incidents. His discretion, informed by such continuity, and exercised over a small and stable segment of the population, is expressed in longitudinal perspective, on the basis of what is 'known' over a period of time and what might need to be done in the future.

Pollution control work is adaptive, given to serial enforcement by negotiation, and to incrementalism, with the gradual application of pressure and, if necessary, ever more ominous threats. Flexible control is made possible by time, bargaining, and privacy. A range of tactical options is available. Earlier decisions may be revised, and the timetable of compliance stretched or tightened. For the deviant's part, even scant display of remedial efforts may be enough morally to foreclose *for the time being* the possibility of sanctioning on the grounds of unco-operativeness or non-compliance. To display willingness to work towards conformity with legal standards frees the deviant from imputations of blame. But such a compliance strategy stems from the symbiotic character of the enforcement relationship and is only possible where there is little recourse to law.

These features serve in fact only to emphasize the similarities in the behaviour of the police and regulatory officials. Where the police deal with states of affairs (cf. Bittner, 1967) and with a familiar population (Gardiner, 1969; Whyte, 1943; Wilson, 1968) their enforcement in less serious cases also takes on a conciliatory character:

The officer emphasizes non-legal solutions to problems rather than legal ones as he progressively becomes more involved in interactions with the people with whom he has to deal. A working norm for the uniformed officer in situations such as these is perhaps best expressed as limited enforcement, arrest is used only in cases of flagrant violations. (Petersen, 1968: 206–7)[4]

Similarly, the pollution control officer confronted with a flagrant pollution incident is likely to think in terms of a penal rather than a conciliatory response. A strategy of compliance is only possible where rule-breaking is not weighty. In all but the most massive pollutions, it is the component of moral disreputability—of wilful or negligent rule-breaking or persistent disregard for the enforcement agent's authority—which can make deviance serious.

In pollution control and other regulatory enforcement work the behaviour subject to control is also significant in another sense. Pollution treatment processes involve chemical, biological, and technological applications whose functioning and maintenance are sometimes only imperfectly understood. Unless negligence or malice are readily apparent, deviance and control in this context tend to be regarded by enforcement agents—at least at the outset of a relationship—as essentially 'technical' or 'scientific' in character, lending themselves readily to a judgment that they may lie beyond the immediate practical control of the discharger, and sometimes beyond his economic capacity. Often harms are not readily determined and victims are diffuse. This again prompts a compliance strategy. But where suggestions of culpability or lack of co-operation enter the picture, however, the problem, once more, is much less likely to be designated as 'technical' or 'inevitable', for here matters are most certainly regarded as preventable. Blameworthy conduct is punishable conduct.

In the more familiar areas of behaviour embraced by the traditional criminal law, compliance usually means refraining from an act. But in pollution control compliance often requires a positive accomplishment, sometimes with major economic implications. Time and money have to be spent in one form or another, in planning, buying, building, and maintaining compliance. Money is not always immediately available; planning and consultation can be time-consuming; equipment is often long in the delivery; facilities are not quickly designed and built; erratic treatment processes take time to settle down. To insist on instant compliance is an affront to moral sensibilities about what is reasonable. Compliance in practice usually means time, for compliance is not often, and cannot normally be, instant:

> 'you've got to give people time to do it. It's not "You mustn't do it today, and if you do it again tomorrow I'll smack your legs," you know. It's not like speeding. . . . I can instance a discharge in [one town] that is not consented that's been discharging for two hundred years. . . . The factory's been there for two hundred years and making this discharge for two hundred years. You can't suddenly leap in—it's not like a motoring offence. . . .'

The result of all of this is that pollution control staff must display patience and tolerance, rather than legal authority, for their goal is not to punish but to secure change. After all, the only alternatives to graduated compliance are often more appealing in theory than in practice, for they involve immediate stoppage of a discharge (which could shut down a factory) or disposal of the effluent elsewhere (which with anything but a very small volume discharge could impose crippling costs). Since both alternatives have far-reaching implications for employment and the economic position of a company, common sense at field level dictates that such measures are beyond the polluter's control.

If the consequence of all this is a working presumption against use of the formal processes of law, in what kinds of case will prosecution actually be employed?

II. Efficiency

Strategies of control are shaped by the continuing need for what enforcement agents regard as effective pollution work. A notion of efficiency is of central concern at both field-officer and agency level, acting as a constraint against too ready a commitment to a sanctioning strategy. Legal bureaucracies, like others, are preoccupied with issues such as the maintenance of internal and external relationships and the management of work. These concerns have major implications for the kind of justice dispensed. Highly selective use of the formal processes of law is implicit in regulatory control founded upon compliance since to use prosecution in any but the most serious cases is regarded as counter-productive. Negotiation is the effective way of achieving results.

The thoroughly pragmatic approach to pollution control work shared by field men is expressed in the primacy accorded to 'getting the job done' through the maintenance of relationships with their client population. The high discretion each officer enjoys is operationally efficient; he is the only person who 'really knows' the dischargers, their problems, and their negotiating styles. The field man's conception of effective work calls for the active co-operation of those whose behaviour he is regulating, and the cultivation of good relationships eases the task now and in the future. Though a legalistic view of regulatory enforcement might contemplate the use of prosecution as an efficient tool for an enforcement agent (presumably serving the ends of deterrence), I have stressed that field staff in practice regard it in all but a few cases as obstructive (cf. Macaulay, 1963). It is inimical to the attainment of compliance, the overriding goal of regulation, and incompatible with effective discovery and detection: 'The trouble is, once you've prosecuted somebody it leaves a sour taste in the mouth, and it's very difficult to ... be on good friendly terms with them thereafter. . . . [T]hey don't forget it, and you've lost that influence— that friendly influence—that you had before.' Or, as agency policy has it:

Experience shows that a general strict application of the letter of the law is not conducive to effective pollution control. Practical realities [are] to be taken properly into account. . . . [I]t is generally more important that pollution should be prevented and recurrence avoided, than it is that polluting acts be penalized . . . (Unpubl. agency document)

The result, in the words of an agency head, is that '. . . the authority determines a low level of enforcement, and it's really that it has at the back of its mind that this is the *best* level of enforcement, because you can upset people. You can get so much done by not upsetting people.' (His emphasis.) To prosecute a case in which the polluter does not acknowledge the agency's interpretation of his behaviour will be seen as undeserved and resented. Regulatory law in these circumstances does not intimidate so much as alienate. If prosecution is to be employed, therefore, it must be with a high degree of selectivity. Sparing and judicious use of the power is further underpinned by recognition that going to law is disruptive to the essential work of the organization. 'Of course prosecutions are a lot of work,' said a senior man. 'Normally we don't do any more than we have to. And it's largely unproductive work so far as pollution prevention is concerned.' In enforcement of regulation, then, the handling of routine cases is informed by organizational norms of efficiency. It is in the exceptional case where the norms of justice deserve conspicuous display.

In the field, intransigence may normally be avoided by practice of the officer's art of 'common sense', eschewing too precipitous a shift to an adversarial stance which threatens his control over the private management of enforcement. Negotiation confers control over the rules of the game: the timing and choice of tactics are the officer's, and the grounds on which compliance is defined and sought are his also. The adaptive nature of negotiating helps preserve the semblance of the control which is a major preoccupation of enforcement agents committed to a compliance strategy, and which, when competently managed, almost always pre-empts the disruption of prosecution. There is virtually no opportunity—since the stage is hardly ever reached—for the deviant to escape the legal sanction, to 'get off'. It is precisely when a deviant appears to be 'getting away with it' that recourse to the law is had, the ceremony of the law only entering the picture when the enforcement agent has exhausted the tactical possibilities and has effectively lost personal control: 'We don't take people to court just like that. It's a history of problems. We've tried everything with them: negotiation, discussion, etc. When we take them to court, it's like saying all the other methods have failed.' In these cases field staff have nothing more to lose. Where too ready a resort to the law would once have been counter-productive, the deviant now presents himself *in a way recognizable to himself and others* as deserving of legal sanction for his obduracy. It is not the continued deviance which prompts the response, so much as the persistence which signifies wilfulness. The non-compliance is transformed by it into wrong-doing of the same order as the deliberate pollution incident, where field staff feel they have everything to lose by not prosecuting. The persistent rule-breaker deserves sanctioning for his intent, constructive or actual. Here compliance strategy yields to a sanctioning strategy.

A relationship based on bargaining lends itself to a certain stability, assisting efficiency by enhancing predictability and the organization of behaviour. While efficiency at field officer level is expressed in terms of a desire to negotiate and protect relationships, at agency level it is transformed into an imperative to portray the authority as all-powerful. Where, in routine cases at field level, efficiency is a constraint against use of the formal process, the most serious incidents of pollution are a matter for general agency concern. Here efficiency positively demands prosecution. Such incidents possess features which make prosecution appear a rational and reasonable response, even—very occasionally—in the apparently complete absence of culpability. Prosecution here not only furthers general deterrence, it also serves to display publicly the agency carrying through its legal mandate as a credible enforcement agency, an important recognition of the interests of its environmentalist constituency in salient cases. Furthermore, such a show of strength may help convince those polluters whose inclination is to comply that they will not be commercially disadvantaged by their deviant competitors (Kagan and Scholz, 1979).

But agencies, like individual field men, are also reluctant to yield control over the handling and disposal of a case. The high degree of selectivity in the cases which go to court reflects in part anxieties about the surrender of control to the lay judgment of magistrates who will dispose of the case by principles which are by no means similar to the principles employed in everyday administrative behaviour. If the agencies cannot play on their pitch, by their rules, with their referee, they can at least choose their opponents and decide whether or not to go through with the fixture. The caution is striking, given that the agencies have a strict liability law at their disposal. To lose a case, however, is held to be extremely inefficient from a deterrence standpoint (see Rabin, 1972). Such a prospect is too severe a blow to contemplate. In surrendering control over the adjudication and disposal of a pollution prosecuted, the agency is at the same time yielding to procedures which create a salient case. However much the odds are stacked in their favour prosecution remains a gamble for agency administrators. Losing the gamble risks proclaiming to the agency's clientele that ultimately it is not omnipotent. The mystique of the law and the legal process cultivated at field level risks exposure, for there the threat of prosecution may no longer be the trump card.

Achieving what agencies perceive to be optimum efficiency in use of the formal law demands a balance be struck. Some degree of formal enforcement is necessary for symbolic purposes. After all, a weapon which is never used may provoke doubts about the will of those who possess it to use it:

Doubtless, enforcing some rules may have a self-defeating property. However, most rule enforcement persists as a practical option because it is useful for enforcement agencies. [It protects] law enforcement organizations from the appearance of laxity. By setting more severe public symbolic standards, they may be able to attain modest levels of control or deterrence ...

(Manning, 1977: 248)

From the pollution control agency's point of view, to sum up this part of the argument, there are two types of case where efficiency decrees prosecution to be the most appropriate response. First, where persistent, noticeable failure to comply is concerned, belief in individual and general deterrence demands public sanctioning. The formal legal process is employed here to enable the agency and its field staff to preserve their credibility for the conduct of future negotiations. Secondly, where a pollution incident which causes substantial and noticeable damage, hazards water supplies, or involves the agency in heavy expenditure takes place, the response will again be to prosecute. Here the agency is compelled publicly to declare the fulfilment of its legal mandate. Given a sufficiently grave pollution, this will be the case even if there is no evidence of blameworthy behaviour on the polluter's part, for the scale of the pollution itself will help shield the agency from the appearance of vindictiveness. On the contrary, prosecution will be demanded: 'It should be borne in mind that [in] special cases of occurrence, or grave risk, of massive pollution damage, or of great public outcry, the taking of a prosecution may be necessary, irrespective of the other practical circumstances of the case.' (Unpubl. agency document.) Not to be seen to be taking action against such a striking breach will invite criticism that the agency is failing in its duty, while the sheer gravity of the pollution will serve to mute any complaints from the business constituency: 'OK if there's . . . a lot of damage, no-one seems to mind very much.' Such cases possess particular potential for dramatizing the agency's prowess as an enforcement authority.

But it must be a grave pollution for such action to be taken against the blameless; agencies are extremely reluctant to announce publicly the moral status of one who may not be blameworthy, for the use of the apparatus of criminal trial is intimately bound up with the suggestion of moral disreputability. The gravity of the harm is the key factor in this kind of case, outweighing any complaints that morally blameless behaviour is being stigmatized as criminal by the enforcement of a strict liability statute. Such cases demand a symbolic display of agency authority. It must act in 'big' cases. The environmentalist constituency will expect action, while its opponents can hardly object in the face of such conspicuous harm. Thus it was entirely appropriate for the water authority which prosecuted the company in the chromate pollution case to take the very unusual step of having it tried in the Crown Court, where greater public attention to the proceedings could be expected and where legal sanctions were higher. Senior staff expressed considerable satisfaction with the outcome of the trial, and were also delighted with the fact that BBC television cameras had been filming stretches of the river on the day of the prosecution in preparation for a news story on the case.

III. Justice

I have argued that moral judgments play a central part in the use of enforcement discretion. Where agents deal with persistent problems and compliance is delayed, moral inferences may be drawn of the polluter's responsiveness to the enforcement process, leading to sanctioning of the unco-operative on the grounds that they had a choice in the matter. A prosecution here represents a failure of compliance strategy, and is needed for purposes of credibility and deterrence. Where specific acts or incidents of pollution are concerned, however, moral evaluations of the act are of crucial importance in establishing whether it involves blameworthy behaviour by the polluter worthy of sanction. The moral content of the act makes any prosecution deserved, for this rule-breaking resembles more familiar forms of traditional crime. Here prosecution acquires an expressive character. In these circumstances blame is crucial in the public enforcement of the law, for to display publicly an indifference to the question of intent would, in Holmes' words, 'shock the moral sense of any civilized community' (1881: 50; also Matza, 1964: 71).

There is little explicit moral content relating to intent in the pollution control legislation, in keeping with most offences crudely categorized as 'strict liability'.[5] Yet although in the setting of standards equity is a guiding principle, and in their enforcement moral judgments are all-pervasive, there is in practice, paradoxically, a marked ambivalence about use of the formal machinery of criminal law to sanction pollution. The values society seeks to protect in regulating economic activity occupy a morally problematic position, as the existence of the two competing 'environmentalist' and 'business' constituencies suggests. The police, in contrast, are often portrayed as enforcing norms about which for the most part a high degree of social consensus exists. Traditional crime is a symbolic assault upon a society's fundamental moral integrity demanding repressive enforcement. Pollution—and doubtless other forms of regulatory misconduct—enjoy no such status.[6] Indeed, the behaviour of regulatory agencies should be understood as a response to the lack of consensus about the values society wishes to advance (Stone, 1975: 97).

In seeking to promote social interests, regulation burdens productive behaviour. It imposes costs on industrialists and agriculturalists which must ultimately be borne by the public, while constraining activities which are not widely regarded as morally beyond the pale. In pollution control work, field men deal with behaviour which is possibly 'illegal' but hardly ever 'criminal'. The ambivalence is also reflected in the pollution legislation (and, indeed, in other forms of regulatory legislation) which defines conduct as criminal in strict liability terms but provides for rather modest amounts of punishment (in contrast with those sanctions available—and sometimes meted out—for breach of traditional criminal law). In regulation we see a compromise: the criminal law is given a wide potential reach but little sanctioning power. Strict liability offers ready enforceability, but the penalties impose little cost. Yet in practice, the perception of an illegal act as a 'problem' rather than a 'crime' leads to a substantial proportion of cases being defined by regulatory agents as outside the proper province of criminal law (cf. Clinard, 1952: 298; Lane, 1954: 94–5). The reluctance of officials to link much regulatory misconduct with blameworthiness is a persistent feature:

Violators of the laws the agency administered were looked upon as honest businessmen who had inadvertently engaged in practices that conflicted with some of the complex legal regulations. The agent was expected to understand their predicament and to help them correct their mistakes. To be sure, violators were ordered to cease their illegal practices, but only a very small proportion of them—typically wilful, repeating offenders—were brought into court to be penalized for having broken the law.

(Blau, 1963: 190)

It has been argued that such reluctance is partly due to the recency of the legislation carving regulatory deviance out of behaviour which used to be perfectly legitimate. The implication of this, so far as breaches of the Factories Act are concerned, is that 'Thieves, the penal system's closest equivalent to the alleged white-collar criminal, violate rules of conduct which, whatever their origin, are by now a traditional part of our culture; the factory-occupier seldom contravenes such rules even though he may break the criminal law.' (Carson, 1970: 397). In effect offences against regulation have not been culturally absorbed and do not invite the same condemnation as breaches of the traditional code—except

where hazardous behaviour is the result of negligent or deliberate misconduct.

Use of the formal law is heavy with meaning for the pollution control
agency. Criminal trial stigmatizes, setting up an internal constraint against
extensive use of prosecution, since the agencies and their field staffs will
not countenance prosecution in any but the most blatantly culpable cases;
a more legalistic policy of enforcement, a senior officer said, would lead to
the courts being 'full of morally fairly innocent people'. In effect those
moral features in any pollution case which make prosecution undeserved,
serve in traditional crime merely to mitigate punishment. But there is also
an external constraint, as a significant segment of the public is regarded as
intolerant of stigmatizing economically productive activity as criminal,
except where clearly blameworthy behaviour is involved:

'We're dealing with legislation in matters which the general public doesn't *really*
consider to be part of the criminal law.... They don't consider themselves
criminals because they've discharged an effluent containing one part per
million more BOD than they ought.... And also... because these minor transgres-
sions of... applying for consent don't in fact, in many cases, actually *do* any
damage. If someone hasn't applied for consent, what he hasn't done is comply
with an administrative requirement of the Act. But he hasn't in fact *done*
anything.... So in fact to *prosecute* him for not having applied for the right piece
of paper in this country doesn't go down too well. And so—I think this is the real
thing, that people just don't consider that they are criminal acts....' (His emphasis)

To enforce the law against the blameless is to diminish the moral authority
of that law.

But where blameworthy behaviour is concerned, the regulators' moral
mandate can be made clear. Thus law is used where enforcers can rely on
what they perceive to be a consensus of values. The legal process here is a
morality play, a symbolic vindication, censuring blameworthy conduct
and preserving shared social bonds. It is this concern for culpability
which forecloses the possibility of significant criticism from the anti-regula-
tion constituency. *What is really being sanctioned is not pollution, but deliberate
or negligent law-breaking and its symbolic assault on the legitimacy of the
regulatory authority.* This is where the agencies see a consensus. In securing
their salient enforcement activity in a recognizable framework, regulatory
agencies are anchoring their behaviour in pervasive, deeply-held norms.

Commonsense conceptions of criminality shared by the general public
and enforcement agents alike hold blameworthiness to be the essential
ingredient in a decision to invoke the law, hence the emphasis given to
selecting those cases which have violated commonsense principles of

justice. While being highly selective about prosecution, field men are still enforcing a code of behaviour which somehow corresponds with their perceptions of the moral sentiments of the community. Most pollution cases yield few instances of unambiguously blameworthy behaviour. At field level, pollutions are not often defined as being the result of calculated or purposive behaviour or indeed the consequence of a deliberate unwillingness to spend money to comply. While agency staff regard their standards as generally attainable without extravagant cost, causing pollution is viewed more often as the inevitable consequence of physical impediment, limited economic means, or the result of carelessness or inefficient management, or of accident. And where there is a suggestion of culpability it must be clear-cut, with noticeable consequences. 'If it's a relatively minor offence,' said an older officer, 'it goes against the grain that people should be prosecuted or fined.' Furthermore, the technological problems involved and the complex industrial setting in which many pollutions take place often make it very difficult for an agent satisfactorily to establish cause and allocate blame. Hence it is a relatively small proportion of culprits for whom the formal process and its stigmatizing consequences accord with the agency staff's moral view of just deserts. In formulating and enacting prosecution policy senior staff are extremely sensitive about avoiding the appearance of vindictiveness. As one senior man put it: 'Public authorities—the big risk on publicity is that they will be castigated in the press as the big heartless bureaucracy victimizing the private citizen.' The risk is particularly acute in compliance systems where a problem has been corrected in the time necessary to mount a prosecution. Negotiating an outcome to a problem need not be concerned with such questions.

Two kinds of culpable misconduct invite the regulatory agency's ultimate sanction. In serious one-off pollutions where officials can be satisfied that the incident was the result of culpable misconduct, prosecution will be regarded as deserved. 'Desert' is a concept very carefully construed in practical terms by the water authorities. While desert may be relevant in private transactions at field level in shaping routine responses, it must be handled with restraint if there is a chance of prosecution, because public sanction almost always means public condemnation. However, there is a nagging uncertainty in potential prosecution cases as to the target for public condemnation. While an unequivocally blameworthy regulatory offender becomes indistinguishable from the traditional criminal when convicted and punished, there is a risk that in the absence of clear desert the condemnation will be directed towards his accusers.

In visiting their personal conceptions of justice and desert onto a formal law which is indifferent (so far as cause is concerned) to *mens rea*, administrative officials inevitably narrow the field of incidents deserving of prosecution. Though I have emphasized the importance of efficiency in structuring enforcement behaviour aimed at securing compliance, the demands a field man makes of a persistently non-compliant polluter and his response to intransigence—the other kind of culpable misconduct—are ultimately also geared to a moral appreciation of the deviant's co-operativeness. There is a clear preference to take only 'obvious cases' of moral disreputability. If a polluter does not see himself at fault or the public cannot infer fault from the damage done and what it knows about the discharger's behaviour, the prosecution of that discharger may again be the occasion for public criticism. *Such constraints demand prosecution of 'the bad' cases:* the malicious, the negligent, and the conspicuously obdurate who have resisted the legitimate efforts of the agency to enforce its legal mandate. Here, again, the agency can be confident of expressing shared values, for the most fervent opponent of regulation can hardly complain about the vindictiveness of an authority which prosecutes those who flout the law. Industrialists, it seems, share the same values as agency staff as to what warrants punishment (Brittan, 1984).

IV. Postscript

The formal processes of the law will be employed only where a regulatory agency can be sure they rest upon the secure foundation of a perceived moral consensus. In the vast majority of cases of regulatory deviance a confusion of interests and values exists, manifested in doubts about whether agencies are protecting the public good when sanctioning behaviour which is a consequence of economic activity beneficial to the public. *In an environment of ambivalence what is mutually recognizable assumes immense importance.* Conduct placed within a moral framework possesses just such recognizability. The formal machinery of the law is appropriate therefore only in those 'big' and 'bad' cases where the gravity or moral offensiveness of a breach renders the confusion of interest minimal. The agencies are demonstrably doing something while offending few. This is deeply-entrenched behaviour in pollution control work and perhaps a major reason for the persistence and consistency of the patterns of enforcement behaviour to be observed in a wide variety of areas of regulation. To regard a compliance strategy of enforcement at field level, or the formulation of prosecution policy at headquarters as symptomatic of the capture of the regulators misses the point. The practice of regulatory enforcement expresses an identity of moral values which transcends the regulator-regulated relationship.

While rules are enforced by human beings, the rule and its breach will always be set in their social contexts, leading to judgments about desert or equity. Regulation may be contemplated by the law as the dispassionate sanctioning of misconduct by the even-handed application of a criminal law unconcerned for the niceties of *mens rea*, but regulation in practice, mediated as it is by a bureaucracy in which people have to exercise their discretion in making judgments about their fellows, is founded upon notions of justice. Pollution control is done in a moral, not a technological world.

Notes

1. Another senior man suggested his agency could increase its prosecution rate without difficulty 'because the more you do, the easier they get, so far as the evidence is concerned, 'cause the people know what they're doing'. Similarly, lack of resources is not thought a constraint in American antitrust enforcement. Weaver (1977: 138) quotes an Assistant Attorney-General as saying 'I don't really know what we'd *do* with many more men.' (Emphasis in original)
2. An argument possibly adopted from the white-collar crime literature: see Newman, 1958; Sutherland, 1949.
3. This has also been observed in the enforcement of factory legislation: thus where 'arguments put to the court might show the [Factory] Inspectorate in an unfavourable light, for instance, in having failed in its duty of enforcement or in prosecuting an employer long after the required standards have been achieved, authorization of proceedings is likely to be withheld' (Law Commission, 1969: 27).
4. Thus Banton (1964: 136–7) has argued that informal controls (that is, a strategy of compliance) are more likely to be employed in areas of high social integration.
5. This is not to suggest, however, that the environmentalism which prompted the legislation is not a largely moralistic movement, or that strict liability does not express the view that those who pollute are morally obliged to be vigilant.
6. Newman (1957) showed that the public views adulteration of food, drugs, and cosmetics as more akin to traffic offences than to burglary. Perpetrators are 'law-breakers' rather than 'criminals'.

References

Arnold, Thurman W. (1935) *The symbols of government* (New Haven, Conn.: Yale University Press, repr. Harcourt Brace and World, 1962).

Banton, Michael (1964) *The policeman in the community* (London: Tavistock).

Bittner, Egon (1967) 'Police discretion in emergency apprehension of mentally ill persons' *Social Problems* 14: 278–92.

Blau, Peter M. (1963) *The dynamics of bureaucracy. A study of interpersonal relations in two government agencies* (Chicago: University of Chicago Press, rev. ed.).

Brittan, Yvonne (1984) *The impact of water pollution control on industry: a case study of fifty dischargers* (SSRC Centre for Socio-Legal Studies, Oxford).

Carson, W. G. (1970) 'White-collar crime and the enforcement of factory legislation' *British Journal of Criminology* 10: 383–98.

Clinard, Marshall B. (1952) *The black market. A study of white collar crime* (New York: Holt, Rinehart and Winston Inc., repr. Patterson Smith, NJ, 1969).

Clinard, Marshall B., Peter C. Yeager, Jeanne Brissette, David Petrashek, and Elizabeth Harries (1979) *Illegal corporate behavior* (Washington DC.: National Institute of Law Enforcement and Criminal Justice).

Conklin, John E. (1977) *'Illegal but not criminal'. Business crime in America* (Englewood Cliffs, NJ: Prentice-Hall).

Cranston, Ross (1979) *Regulating business. Law and consumer agencies* (London: Macmillan).

Davies, J. Clarence (1970) *The politics of pollution* (Indianapolis: Bobbs-Merrill).

Diver, Colin S. (1980) 'A theory of regulatory enforcement' *Public Policy* 28: 257–99.

Gardiner, J. A. (1969) *Traffic and the police* (Cambridge, Mass.: Harvard University Press).

Gusfield, Joseph (1967) 'Moral passage: the symbolic process in public designations of deviance' *Social Problems* 15: 175–88.

Holmes, Oliver Wendell (1881) *The common law* (Boston: Little, Brown).

Kagan, Robert A. and John T. Scholz (1979) 'The criminology of the corporation and regulatory enforcement strategies', paper presented to the Symposium on Organizational Factors in the Implementation of Law, University of Oldenburg, May.

Lane, Robert E. (1954) *The regulation of businessmen* (New Haven, Conn.: Yale University Press).

Law Commission (1969) *Strict liability and the enforcement of the Factories Act 1961*, a report by members of the Sub-Faculty of Law at the University of Kent at Canterbury to the Law Commission, December, Working Paper no. 30.

Long, Susan B. (1979), 'The Internal Revenue Service: examining the exercise of discretion in tax enforcement', paper presented to 1979 Annual Meeting of the US Law and Society Association, San Francisco, May.

Macaulay, Stewart (1963) 'Non-contractual relations in business: a preliminary study' *American Sociological Review* 28: 55–67.

Manning, Peter K. (1977) *Police work: the social organization of policing* (Cambridge, Mass.: MIT Press).

Matza, David (1964) *Delinquency and drift* (New York: Wiley).

Mileski, Maureen (1971) 'Policing slum landlords: an observation study of administrative control' Ph.D. dissertation, Yale University.

Nader, Ralph (1970) Foreword to Esposito (1970).

Newman, Donald J. (1957) 'Public attitudes toward a form of white collar crime' *Social Problems* 4: 228–32.

——(1958) 'White-collar crime' *Law and Contemporary Problems* 23: 735–53.

Petersen, David M. (1968) 'The police, discretion and the decision to arrest' Ph.D. dissertation, University of Kentucky.

Rabin, Robert L. (1972) 'Agency criminal referrals in the Federal System: an empirical study of prosecutorial discretion' *Stanford Law Review* 24: 1036–91.

Selznick, Philip (1966) *TVA and the grass roots. A study in the sociology of journal organization* (rev. ed.) (New York: Harper and Row).

Stone, Christopher D. (1975) *Where the law ends. The social control of corporate behavior* (New York: Harper and Row).

Sutherland, Edwin H. (1949) *White collar crime* (New York: The Dryden Press).

Weaver, Suzanne (1977) *Decision to prosecute: organization and public policy in the Antitrust Division* (Cambridge, Mass.: MIT Press).

Whyte, William Foote (1943) *Street-corner society. The social structure of an Italian slum* (Chicago: University of Chicago Press).

Wilson, James Q. (1968) *Varieties of police behavior. The management of law and order in eight communities* (Cambridge, Mass.: Harvard University Press).

The Optimal Structure of Law Enforcement

S. SHAVELL

Consistency of Observed and Theoretically Optimal Law Enforcement

I will now consider the five methods of law enforcement described in the tableau—tort law, criminal law, safety regulation, the injunction, and corrective taxation—and for each ask whether its actual use is consistent with theoretically optimal law enforcement. That is, for each method of law enforcement, I will ask whether its characteristics—in terms of the stage of legal intervention, the form of sanction, and the public and private role in enforcement—make sense given the nature of the acts that method of enforcement apparently aims to control. My discussion will be frankly speculative in many respects, but I will still come to the conclusion that these methods of enforcement can be explained as rational in a broad and very approximate sense by the hypothesis that they represent optimal law enforcement.

A. Tort Law

I have characterized tort law as the method of law enforcement that employs harm-based monetary sanctions which are awarded to individuals who suffer harm and report it when they bring suits. Now I want to explain why the method of enforcement with these characteristics should be employed to control the harmful activities that tort law does control. What are those activities? They are virtually all the activities of everyday life and business enterprise, for any of them can cause accidents—slips and falls, collisions involving moving vehicles, product injuries, harms caused by explosions and fires, and the like.[1] Of course, acts causing accidents are controlled not only by tort law but also by regulation and other means of law enforcement, as I shall discuss later; for now, however, my focus is on tort law and acts for which these other methods of law enforcement are not of substantial influence. For concreteness, the reader might keep in mind an act like lighting a grill in one's backyard, which could result in a fire that would destroy a neighbor's property, or running to catch a bus, in the course of which one might knock into someone and injure him.[2]

Stage of Intervention. Consider first the issue of the stage of legal intervention. Why do we not employ prevention rather than sanctions to control the acts of concern, and why should we use sanctions triggered by harm rather than by commission of undesirable acts?

As to why not prevention, my response is simply that this would be impractical. As mentioned, to control driving behavior through prevention, enforcement agents would have to be sitting alongside drivers; and to prevent people from recklessly chasing after buses or from grilling in a dangerous manner, enforcement agents would have to be present to police behavior of people around bus stops and in their backyards. That a regime in which all this were to be done strikes one as fanciful only reflects the fact that prevention as a general instrument of control of unwanted behavior would be inordinately expensive.

Consideration of the knowledge of the social authority also argues against prevention. How would an enforcement agent (assuming that he were present) know that a person was about to make an improper left turn before it was actually done, or that a person was going to run for a bus until he or she actually did so? In many situations, an enforcement agent would not have the information to prevent an undesirable act before it happened.

Thus, the use of sanctions rather than prevention seems necessary to control the broad category of acts with which tort law is concerned, but now we must say why harm-based sanctions rather than act-based sanctions are applied. The answer, I think, again lies in part with enforcement costs. The sheer number of acts that can cause harm is great; to hope to employ sanctions whenever acts appear dangerous would thus be very expensive. It would seem far better on administrative cost grounds to focus on the small-by-comparison number of acts that turn out to result in harm. Moreover, the actual doing of harm furnishes us with some information about the dangerousness of acts; that they did harm means that they were probably dangerous. Hence, harm-based sanctions seem generally best as the method for the law to employ to control behavior giving rise to what we call torts.

Form of Sanctions. But why should the form of sanction for torts be a money sanction rather than imprisonment? The explanation is that money sanctions work tolerably well, so that society usually need not resort to the more expensive form of sanction of imprisonment.

In most accident situations that we describe as torts, the likelihood of the responsible party having to pay, if liable, is fairly high (at least relative to what will be described in certain other contexts, such as where criminal acts are committed). If my grill causes a fire and damages my neighbor's home, he will be likely to know how the harm came about and who was responsible; if I run into someone while trying to catch a bus, that person will ordinarily obtain my name (if I run, my act may become criminal, as I will later discuss).

With regard to ability to pay for harm, although there may be a problem, it is often not one of significance. The damage to my neighbor's home might be limited, and in any case I am likely to have liability insurance sufficient to cover it. Moreover, the fact that the likelihood of my having to pay for harm is large means that the magnitude of the sanction necessary to deter me will not be inflated. Hence, it seems that the ability to pay the sanctions needed to deter undesirable acts should be reasonably good as a general matter (but see the qualifications in the comment below).

An additional factor to be noted in this regard is that under the negligence rule, which is the dominant rule of liability in tort, an individual will be induced to exercise proper care even if his assets are lower than the harm he might cause and plausibly substantially below it. For instance, if a person would cause harm of $100,000 with probability 2 percent and could reduce this risk to 1 percent by an expenditure of $10, must his level of wealth be near $100,000 for him to be induced to make the expenditure? The answer is that, even if his wealth were only, say, $10,000—far less than $100,000—he would make the $10 expenditure to avoid liability, for if he does not, his expected liability would be 2 percent × $10,000 or $200. Under the negligence rule, in other words, the incentive to take adequate precautions is sharp since one thereby avoids all liability for harm.[3]

Turning next to the expected harm caused by acts, recall that this is relevant because of the consequences of failure to deter. If the expected harm is low, then failure to deter is not as socially costly than if expected harm is high. Now most acts creating risks of accidents do not create very large risks, even though the size of the harm, if it eventuates, may be large. When I make an improper left turn, an accident usually will not occur as a result, and if I run after a bus, usually I will not bump into someone and cause serious injury. The problem, therefore, due to occasional failure to deter such acts is not nearly as serious as is failure to deter other types of acts, notably those called criminal, that we shall discuss.

Public versus Private Enforcement. Finally, what can be said about the private nature of enforcement in tort law? It seems quite reasonable, in that victims of tortious harm will usually know the identity of injurers. Thus private enforcement is best, and allowing victims to collect rewards—their tort damages—should supply them with incentives to come forward with their information. Were we instead to rely on enforcement agents of the state to report tortious harms, we would be spending our resources needlessly.

Also, recall that it was observed that agreements between victims and liable parties not to go to court do not dilute incentives when rewards to reporting parties equal the sanctions of liable parties (for then bargained-for payments should reflect sanctions). This is the situation in tort law, for what the liable party pays is what the party who sues successfully receives. Hence, we can see as rational that settlements between victims and potentially liable parties are allowed in the tort context.

Comment. This review of the typical tort has left out, among other things, some important qualifications concerning situations in which deterrence is apparently weakened. In such situations, what we would expect, and what we find, is that the legal system responds so as to remedy the problem of insufficient deterrence.

One type of situation where deterrence might be inadequate is where an injurer tries to conceal his identity, the classic example being hit-and-run accidents. Here, the response of the legal system is often to deem the act that would otherwise only be a tort a criminal act as well, allowing for the application of additional nonmonetary sanctions to alleviate problems with deterrence. Another response of the legal system in such cases is to permit imposition of punitive tort damages; implicitly, these can reflect the probability of escape from liability and offset the underdeterrence problem.

It is also possible that an injurer would find that he is not identified because of circumstance rather than design. For instance, a firm's product may not be seen as the cause of disease because of other possible causes of the disease or because other firms sold the same product and the victim cannot say which he had purchased. In this case, the law could, and in fact does sometimes, relax the normal causation requirements that force the plaintiff to establish a clear connection between his harm and a particular injurer. Under the market-share theory, notably, any firm that could have caused harm will be liable, but damages will be only in proportion to the likelihood that it was the cause. This tends to solve the problem of dilution of deterrence.

There are other examples that could be mentioned, but the point should be clear. The reaction of the tort system to situations in which deterrence would be compromised is along the lines of what would be predicted, namely, some step to bolster deterrence.

B. Criminal Law

To control the acts to which criminal law applies—theft, robbery, rape, murder, treason, and so forth—it was observed that the law intervenes at all three stages, imposes nonmonetary as well as monetary sanctions, and relies on public enforcement agents along with private parties. The question to be addressed here is why criminal law has these characteristics.

Stage of Intervention. The heart of the answer as to why legal intervention in criminal law occurs at all three stages is that deterrence is weak for the acts of concern, meaning that it is desirable for society to avail itself of all opportunities to control the acts.

Deterrence of criminal acts is poor for several reasons. One is that the likelihood of apprehending and convicting offenders is low, often significantly less than 50 percent.[4] That the probability of apprehension and punishment of criminal acts is generally small is not surprising since such acts frequently are carried out with a view toward escaping sanctions. A person who plots a crime, like murder or treason or theft, will generally execute it in such a way as to avoid responsibility. A robber can search for a lone person in a deserted area at night, and in a neighborhood where he would be unlikely to be recognized.[5]

Deterrence is weak in the criminal realm not only because the likelihood of sanctions is low, but also for two other important reasons. First, many of those who commit crimes are poor, making monetary sanctions ineffective. Second, the benefits that individuals tend to obtain when they commit criminal acts are large, making the sanctions necessary to deter high. I will elaborate on these below when I discuss the form of sanctions.

The weakness in deterrence means, as I said, that society wants to take all opportunities to control the acts in question. In particular, we endeavor to prevent people from committing criminal acts because we cannot rely on sanctions imposed on those who commit such acts to discourage them. Likewise, we punish people for committing undesirable acts even if they do no harm because we cannot rely on sanctions imposed on those who succeed in their harmful acts to adequately deter. Thus, we impose sanctions on those who shoot at others and miss, who pick empty pockets—generally, those who attempt crimes but fail. And, of course, we punish those who succeed in doing harm, for this is our final way of augmenting deterrence.

Although we intervene at every stage in the criminal context, we usually impose lower sanctions the earlier the stage. If a person is caught when he is planning to commit an act or is interrupted in an attempt, the sanction is generally less than if he commits the act but fails, that is, engages in a complete but unsuccessful attempt. And if he engages in a complete attempt and fails, his sanction is often less than if he succeeds in his act. This pattern of sanctions is consistent with the point that the state ordinarily possesses less evidence of the harmfulness of acts at earlier stages.

Form of Sanctions. Turning now to the form of sanction, the main point to be dealt with is why monetary sanctions are generally not adequate to deter. One factor is that those who commit crimes tend to be poor; notably, statistics show that the inmate population is composed of people who have very little income prior to arrest.[6] Why should the poor display a greater tendency to commit crime? Most obviously, they will often commit crimes that are economic in character because they have a greater need for money. In addition, lack of wealth is associated with substandard education, drug and alcohol abuse, and social alienation, all of which makes those with low wealth less likely to respond to extralegal influences that would channel their conduct in desirable directions. For these various reasons, then, criminality is associated with low wealth and, thus, with our being unable to accomplish deterrence with monetary sanctions. Having little to lose, the poor need to be deterred through imposition of nonmonetary sanctions.

A second factor suggesting that use of monetary sanctions alone will not be enough to accomplish deterrence is the low probability of apprehending and punishing those who commit crimes. I explained above why the probability is low, and consideration of an example will illustrate the inadequacy of deterrence were we to employ solely monetary sanctions. Suppose that the probability of punishment for motor vehicle theft is about 5 percent[7] and that the value of a vehicle to a thief is $500. Then the monetary sanction needed to deter would be in the range of $10,000, an amount substantially exceeding the ability to pay of the many thieves who have essentially no liquid assets and few possessions with market value. Similar calculations for many other crimes make it evident that reliance on monetary sanctions would not be nearly adequate to deter.

A third factor is that the benefits people obtain from committing the acts that we call criminal are frequently large, which makes them difficult to deter. One of the defining elements of a crime is intent, which often has to do with a person's purpose. Those who commit acts like murder or rape or treason will usually obtain a substantial private benefit from success, which is something that will be relatively likely given their desire not to fail in their acts.[8]

A fourth factor is that the expected harm done by criminal acts is, in an average sense, substantial. Most obviously, the magnitude of harm associated with acts that we classify as criminal is often great. But this is not always true (as when a person steals a small amount), and at the same time the harm due to many noncriminal acts may be significant (people may be killed due to negligence). What I believe to be the main reason that crimes are more costly socially is that they are more likely to cause harm than noncriminal acts. When a person tries to steal, or to rape, or to kill, he is going to succeed with a relatively high probability. In fact, we ordinarily *define* crime in a way that implies the probability of doing harm will be high: the legal meaning of 'intent,' usually necessary for a criminal conviction, is either that a person acted with the purpose of causing harm— meaning that harm would be likely—or, if not, that harm was, from outward appearances of the act, very likely (as when someone acts with extreme recklessness). Hence, the expected consequences of failure to control the acts we call crimes seem large, and this makes it socially worthwhile to employ the more costly nonmonetary sanction of imprisonment to control the acts.

One more point may be added about imprisonment, namely, that it prevents further bad acts by incapacitating individuals. This is significant because those who commit acts have revealed themselves not to have been deterred by the threat of sanctions. Hence, they constitute a subpopulation whose behavior we often can control only by prevention, and this is accomplished by imprisoning them. Alternative nonmonetary punishments, like whipping or branding, would not prevent further crimes because they do not incapacitate.

Finally, let me comment on situations in which criminal sanctions do not include imprisonment but involve criminal fines. Such sanctions tend to be observed when crimes are not of the most serious nature. In these cases, one suspects that money sanctions coupled with the nonmonetary sanction of humiliation are enough to deter reasonably well, and thus that society need not invest in the more expensive sanction of imprisonment. Also, it may be that the need to prevent further acts is not great, so that the incapacitative benefit of imprisonment is not significant.

We might ask, however, if society does not impose imprisonment as a punishment, why should it categorize an act as criminal? A chief reason may be that this serves as a socially inexpensive way to increase deterrence. The classification of an act as criminal stigmatizes the person subject to sanction and thus may add to the humiliation just mentioned that accompanies criminal conviction. Indeed, for corporations, this may be one of the only reasons for classifying certain acts as criminal, for corporations cannot be imprisoned. The strength of the stigmatizing effect, however, is limited by, among other factors, the scope of acts labeled 'criminal.' As the range of such acts expands, the stigma will be diluted, for society will no longer view a criminal offense as signaling the commission of such an undesirable act.

Public and Private Enforcement. The explanation for the use of public enforcement agents to control and identify those who commit crimes is clear. Victims of crimes frequently do not know who has harmed them. A great deal of effort is often required to find those who have committed criminal acts. Hence a corps of enforcement agents is needed. Moreover, in cases where individuals can identify those who have harmed them, the criminals will often flee, so that enforcement agents will be needed to locate them. In addition, where the victims know who have harmed them and could report this, there is the issue of reprisal by the criminals. This problem is made more serious by the severity of criminal sanctions and the character of people who commit criminal acts and, thus, may call for enforcement agents to play a role even where the victims know who have harmed them and those people have not fled.

Private parties do, however, play a role in reporting criminal acts. They often notify the police when they have been victimized or when someone has attempted to harm them. Sometimes they do this to prevent further harm, as when they fear that the person wants to harm them in particular; other times they may make reports to satisfy a retributive urge, out of a feeling of social responsibility, or in order to collect insurance proceeds.

In any case, a private party is not allowed to make a bargain with a criminal not to report his crime, even if the private party is the victim of the crime. The reason that this makes sense is that allowing such bargains would dilute deterrence. The most that the criminal could give the victim is the criminal's wealth, so the cost to the criminal of such a bargain is at most this amount. But the criminal sanction will generally include imprisonment, so that the sanction that the state would impose will be higher. Accordingly, unlike in the tort context, private agreements would result in substantially lower costs to offenders and would weaken deterrence. In addition, one supposes that allowing private settlements would encourage criminals to threaten victims with harm unless they settled, further reducing deterrence.

C. Safety Regulation

As discussed earlier, by safety regulation I refer to control of behavior by means of prevention, such as by refusing or removing licenses to operate equipment or businesses, as well as by imposition of act-based monetary sanctions, that is, fines for violation of rules.[9]

Stage of Intervention. Why should the stage of legal intervention for the behavior controlled by safety regulation be before harm comes about? The reason is essentially that use of sanctions for harm done might not provide sufficient deterrence. This is plausibly often true where we tend to see safety regulation: in controlling the risks of fire, foods and drugs, or transport of dangerous substances, to take important examples. A fire at a restaurant could harm a large number of people and create losses far exceeding the net worth of its owner. Likewise, the harm caused by contamination of food could be widespread, easily surpassing the assets of the owner. Because parties would not have sufficient assets to cover losses in such cases, they might not be led by the prospect of liability to take adequate steps to reduce risks. In addition, there may be problems due to parties escaping liability for harm done in some areas of regulation. In particular, many health-related and environmental risks are difficult to trace to their origin. Finally, it may be that harm is dispersed, as is often true with pollution-caused losses, so that individual victims might not find bringing suit worthwhile.

Given, then, that deterrence would often be inadequate if harm-based sanctions alone were relied on in areas of safety regulation, there is a need for prevention or act-based sanctions, and this need is what safety regula-tion satisfies. Safety regulation appears to take the form of prevention where that form of legal intervention is administratively easy. A general circumstance in which this is so is where a party is applying for a license to undertake an activity, or for renewal of a license, and where what is regulated is the presence of some physical device, like a sprinkler system in a hotel. In such cases, a regulatory authority can deny the license if the sprinkler system has not been installed. The appeal of prevention over act-based sanctions is that the former by definition stops unwanted behavior, whereas act-based sanctions rely on deterrence. Act-based sanctions, though, are often employed where prevention would be expensive to accomplish. This is frequently true when what needs to be controlled is human behavior, which can be modified from one occasion to the next.

Thus, if there is a regulation concerning the number of people monitoring controls at night in a nuclear power plant, or the clearing of ice from sidewalks in front of commercial establishments, we would expect enforcement to take the form of act-based sanctions.[10]

Consider next the question whether a regulatory authority will have the knowledge needed to formulate good rules. It seems typical of much regulation that its requirements can be justified by common knowledge or something close to it, so that informational demands on regulators are minimal. When regulation calls for trucks carrying explosives not to enter tunnels or for people not to hunt in hiking areas, regulatory authorities can be reasonably confident that their requirements are justified. It is true, though, that regulation sometimes requires substantially more than common knowledge. In such cases, regulatory authorities often develop information on their own, such as where government agencies determine health and environmental risks. In some such instances, the knowledge of a regulator may be superior to that of private parties (and this may provide a reason for regulation independent of inadequate deterrence from harm-based sanctions). When, however, information becomes a problem for a regulator, we may see relaxation of regulatory requirements. Thus, we may see that although fire safety regulation stipulates use of sprinkler systems and fire-retardant materials, it does not go so far as to say exactly what can and cannot be stored in closets, how often kitchen equipment must be cleaned, and so forth. The limits of regulation appear to reflect the quality of information of regulators.

To summarize the discussion here, it is suggested that safety regulation is explained primarily as an answer to the need for control of behavior where harm-based liability might not create proper deterrence. Further, regulation seems to take the form of prevention rather than act-based sanctions when the former is administratively simpler, and it appears that regulatory rules are sensitive to the adequacy of information possessed by regulators.

Form of Sanctions. Let us turn now to the question why enforcement of safety regulation through act-based sanctions is by means of money sanctions, that is, why criminal sanctions are not needed. The reasons why money sanctions usually work well enough are several. First, because the sanctions are act-based and therefore may be applied whether or not harm comes about, they can be effective even if their size is relatively small. If, for example, regulation calls for a party to spend $50 on an exit sign to warn people how to escape a public place should a fire occur, a fine of only $100 would suffice if the probability of checking for fire exit signs is

50 percent. (In contrast, under *harm-based* sanctions, sanctions would be imposed only if a fire actually occurred, and if this is unlikely, the size of the sanction necessary to induce installation of the sign could be far larger.)[11]

Another factor helping to explain why monetary sanctions will ordinarily be enough to lead to adherence to safety regulation is that the benefits obtained by violating regulations are often, like those in the area of tort, the savings from not taking precautions, like that from not purchasing an exit sign. In particular, the benefits seem lower than the gains often obtained by persons committing criminal acts. An additional factor is that regulated parties often have substantial wealth, especially when they are corporations.

These arguments notwithstanding, imposition of monetary sanctions sometimes is not enough to enforce safety regulation, and when so, we tend to observe two things. On one hand, we may see resort to prevention. Thus, if in some area of regulation, expected harms are large and a firm's assets are insufficient to pay fines for violations, we may see the firm shut down unless and until it satisfies regulatory requirements. On the other hand, we may see regulatory violations punished under criminal as well as civil law.

Public versus Private Enforcement. Finally, let us ask why enforcement of safety regulation is primarily public in nature. The answer seems to be mainly that private parties cannot be counted on to be aware of risks. If a restaurant kitchen is unclean yet I do not get sick when I go to the restaurant, how will I know about the status of the kitchen? If a nuclear power plant is not following proper procedures, it is unlikely that I will be aware of this. If a person fails to vaccinate his dog against rabies, there is no way for me to be aware of it in the normal course of events. Thus, the absence of harm seems a generally strong factor explaining why, in regulated areas, we would not expect people to be aware of who needs to be sanctioned for violating regulations or of how to prevent their violation.

Nevertheless, it could, of course, be the case that someone becomes aware of a regulatory infraction. A person might have occasion to go into a restaurant kitchen, hear about kitchen conditions from a restaurant employee, or be an employee himself. In these cases, the person might have a motive to report, which might be that the person wants to prevent harm to himself or the community or that he would be rewarded by the state for so doing. But it does not seem that people have nearly enough information for us to rely generally on private enforcement in regulated areas. Society thus needs to make an effort to discover violations of regulation and therefore needs public enforcement agents.

D. Injunction

The injunction is the legal device whereby private parties may enlist the power of the state to prevent harm. Injunctions may be brought in the context of the general class of nuisances, for example, to stop an activity that generates noxious odors, like maintaining a compost heap in a suburban neighborhood, or to make someone chain a vicious dog. Injunctions may also be brought to prevent activities that hold the risk of large harms, not normally called 'nuisances,' such as where people enjoin a factory from continuing its operations because they fear that it is introducing a carcinogen into the water supply.

Stage of Intervention. Prevention is the mode of legal intervention where the injunction is employed for reasons that are in some respects similar to those offered in relation to safety regulation. On one hand, where the injunction is used, our knowledge of the undesirability of the acts in question is often good; and on the other hand, use of sanctions might not accomplish deterrence, though, as I shall indicate, the relevance of this latter factor is not entirely clear.

With regard, first, to a social authority's knowledge, consider the typical nuisance. It will be obvious, virtually by definition of a nuisance, that the behavior is undesirable. Moreover, when a party seeks an injunction, the harm will often be ongoing—as in the case of a compost heap that is already producing foul odors—so that little need be demonstrated to prove that more harm will eventuate in the future. Or, if the harm is not ongoing, there will frequently have been past harm. In the case of a vicious dog, there will frequently have been previous incidents of problems with the dog; indeed, this may well be a prerequisite for obtaining an injunction concerning the dog. With regard to injunctions secured in situations other than that of nuisance, similar arguments can be made; sometimes, there is ongoing harm, and generally, courts insist on having clear evidence of future danger before granting injunctions.

Consider next the question whether the use of sanctions would not accomplish deterrence. Would sanctions fail to deter in the typical nuisance situation? Is it unlikely that imposition of damages would dissuade a person from maintaining a compost heap or from keeping a vicious dog? I can imagine factors that would reduce the deterrent of liability in such situations, such as difficulty in proving that a particular dog bit a child, but most do not seem to me to constitute a general basis for favoring prevention by means of injunctions. A factor that may be of significance, though, is difficulty in determining the proper level of damages.[12] In any event, in some instances where injunctions are granted, there are fairly clear arguments supporting the view that liability would not adequately deter. In the case of a firm that is polluting the water supply with a carcinogenic substance, that might be true. The possibility that the firm would not be able to pay for the cancers caused or that the firm could not be linked to the cancers could explain lack of confidence in deterrence and the utility of an injunction.

Public versus Private Enforcement. Why is the injunction a privately employed device to prevent undesirable behavior? The answer is evidently that the injunction is used where private parties themselves become aware of dangers. When this is so, it is socially desirable, for society to use their information. And giving private parties the legal right to prevent the harm that they themselves would suffer provides them with an incentive to supply information.

When we think of nuisances, we can see that it is indeed the case that private parties have information about harms that may come about. Maintenance of compost heaps in backyards and the keeping of vicious dogs are practices whose dangerous characteristics are ordinarily obvious to private parties. Outside the area of the typical nuisance, it may also happen for one reason or another that private parties become aware of a risk. For instance, a neighborhood organization concerned about the safety of the water supply may test the water and discover that a firm is discharging a carcinogen into it. However private parties come on their information, providing them an opportunity to prevent harm is helpful to society since it makes use of their information.

E. Corrective Taxation

The corrective tax—a tax equal to the expected harm caused by an activity—is, recall, a tool usually described in economics textbooks as one of the most important for the control of harmful activities. The corrective tax is an act-based sanction because it is not related to harm actually done but to predicted harm. The corrective tax for emitting a pollutant into the atmosphere is set equal to the harm that is estimated to be done by the pollution, not to the harm actually done by the pollution.

Despite its prominence in economic literature, the corrective tax is in fact rarely employed to control undesirable activities; its use is restricted to a few instances of polluting activities. For the most part, society relies on regulation, liability, the injunction, or criminal law for controlling undesirable acts. After the rationality of use of the tax to control pollution is examined, I will briefly address the question why use of the tax is so infrequent.

Stage of Intervention. Let us first ask why a harm-based sanction may not be desirable to control pollution. The general answer is that it may be difficult to identify and link harm caused by pollution to responsible parties. The ways in which pollution can cause harm are manifold and complicated, and harm may take years to eventuate. If, for these reasons, polluters would often escape liability for harm, deterrence from harm-based sanctions would be diluted.

If harm-based sanctions would not perform well to cure pollution problems, why should the corrective tax be employed rather than fines for violation of regulations? And why should a corrective tax be preferred to prevention? A tax may be preferable to regulation because a tax requires less information to apply. To determine the proper corrective tax a social authority needs only to know the expected harm due to the activity. If the authority sets the tax equal to the expected harm, the taxed party will engage in an activity if and only if his benefit exceeds the expected harm, which is to say, if and only if the activity is socially desirable.[13] By contrast, to formulate proper regulation, a social authority must know not only the expected harm due to the activity but also the benefit from the activity, for the authority has to compare benefits with expected harm to determine whether the activity is socially undesirable and should be disallowed. Similarly, a social authority must know benefits as well as expected costs to know when to intervene and prevent an act. Hence, both regulation and prevention require the social authority to know more than it needs to know to impose a tax, making a tax potentially superior.

Another issue of relevance concerns the cost of enforcing a tax. If the activity to be taxed is fairly easily monitored, and the expected harm is approximately equal to a simple multiple of the scale of the activity, then the tax will be easy to administer. This is plausibly the case for many pollutants, such as the quantity of an effluent that is released into the atmosphere.

Form of Sanctions. Since the corrective tax is set equal to the expected harm caused by an activity rather than to the actual harm, the tax will often be lower than the actual harm and more likely to be within the capacity of the taxed party to pay than liability for harm. Also, since taxed parties are often corporations, they usually will have assets sufficient to pay the taxes. This is not to deny that nonmonetary sanctions might be necessary to increase deterrence. It is rather to say that in the few situations in which taxes are employed, they seem to be within the capability of parties to pay.

Public versus Private Enforcement. That the corrective tax for pollution should be publicly enforced seems easily explained. Private citizens will not naturally have the information about the amount of pollutants that firms or individuals are discharging. Hence, enforcement agents must obtain the information.

Limited Use of Taxation. Having attempted to say why the corrective tax seems to work particularly well in many cases of pollution, I now want to comment on the question why the tax would not be advantageous in much greater realms. Consider why the tax would not work well in the classic area of tort. Why not tax people for running after buses without looking where they are going or for leaving flower pots dangerously close to the edge of balconies? That is, why not tax negligent behavior or, for that matter, all behavior on the basis of the expected losses? The explanation may lie in the enormous administrative expense that would entail. In contrast, the tort system, as I have emphasized, is administratively cheap, for it is employed only in the relatively few cases in which harm comes about.

Administrative expense also appears to explain why the corrective tax may often be inferior to regulation where regulation is used. Consider, for instance, regulations requiring the display of exit signs in buildings to which the public has access, or regulations concerning the number of lifeboats carried by large vessels. To enforce such regulations, there will only have to be a transaction involving money when regulations are violated, which is to say, only when the number of exit signs or of lifeboats is inadequate. Under corrective taxation, however, there will be transactions involving payments of taxes by all owners of public places and of ships. Hence, tax collection may well be more expensive to administer than regulation. This disadvantage of taxation may offset its informational advantage over regulation.[14]

Concluding Remarks

Although the theme in this section has been explanatory, the general theory of enforcement discussed here also suggests ways of altering the current system toward greater efficiency. For example, it may well be that where private parties have information about violations, we should more vigorously reward the reporting of violations. There are usually people in large organizations who become aware of violations of regulations, yet my impression is that 'whistle-blower' rewards are not common and that protection of the identity of informants is not a well-developed strategy. It also appears to me that use of the corrective tax could be expanded. There must be additional areas where it would be administratively feasible to impose a tax based on expected harm, such as for purchase of noisy machinery.

I want also to acknowledge a basic omission from the analysis, namely, that there are sometimes important extralegal influences on behavior— market forces and social sanctions such as loss of reputation in the community. These may serve to varying degrees as substitutes for legal sanctions. If, for instance, a firm sells tainted food, consumers will be likely to decide to take their business elsewhere, so the need for control by the legal system will be reduced. Or the prospect of loss of face were a person negligently to cause a fire that harms his neighbors may help to make him careful. Although these factors reduce the need for legal sanctions, they do not seem to do so generally, for they require that private parties be aware of the identity of wrongdoers. Hence, market forces and informal social sanctions are unlikely to be of much help where public enforcement agents would be needed to enforce the law.

Notes

This is a revised version of a paper presented at the John M. Olin Centennial Conference in Law and Economics at the University of Chicago Law School, April 7–9, 1992. The author is Professor of Law and Economics, Harvard Law School. I wish to thank Gary Becker, Louis Kaplow, A. Mitchell Polinsky, and David Rosenberg for comments and Jesse Fried and Abraham Wickelgren for able research assistance.

1. I am restricting myself in this discussion to unintentional torts.
2. In neither of these cases is it likely that regulation or another form of legal intervention would play a real role.
3. The observation that incentives to take care are sharp under the negligence rule is first developed by John Summers, The Case of the Disappearing Defendant: An Economic Analysis, 132 U. Pa. L. Rev. 145 (1983); see also the discussion in Steven Shavell, Economic Analysis of Accident Law (1987), at 167.
4. According to Federal Bureau of Investigation, U.S. Department of Justice, 1990 Uniform Crime Reports, Crime in the United States, table 20, p. 165, the probability of an arrest following a reported offense was 21.6 percent, when averaged over all offenses. For specific types of offense, the probabilities of arrest were as follows: 45.6 percent for violent crimes; 67.2 percent for murder

and nonnegligent manslaughter; 52.8 percent for forcible rape; 57.3 percent for aggravated assault; 18.1 percent for property crimes; 24.9 percent for robbery; 13.8 percent for burglary; 20.5 percent for larceny-theft; 14.6 percent for motor vehicle theft; and 14.9 percent for arson. But offenses are not always reported, and arrests do not necessarily result in convictions, so that these probabilities overstate the true probabilities of conviction. According to U.S. Department of Justice, Bureau of Justice Statistics, Report to the Nation on Crime and Justice (1988), at 34, the probability of reporting is 48 percent for violent crimes, 26 percent for property crimes, 69 percent for motor vehicle theft, 49 percent for household burglary, and 25 percent for household larceny. Also, certain states report statistics on the probability that arrests for serious crimes result in conviction, at 60; this probability is 61 percent in California, 69 percent in Minnesota, 68 percent in Nebraska, 67 percent in New York, 50 percent in Ohio, 56 percent in Pennsylvania, 79 percent in Utah, and 61 percent in Virginia. If I assume for simplicity that 60 percent is the likelihood of an arrest resulting in a conviction for all types of offense, the probability of punishment for violent crimes becomes 48 percent × 45.6 percent × 60 percent = 13.1 percent rather than 45.6 percent; that for property crimes becomes 26 percent × 18.1 percent × 60 percent = 2.8 percent rather than 18.1 percent; that for motor vehicle theft becomes 69 percent × 14.6 percent × 60 percent = 6 percent rather than 14.6 percent; and so forth.

5. In contrast, note, the typical tort occurs (as the word 'accident' suggests) at an unpredictable time and place, and thus only by chance can the responsible party easily avoid being identified. Moreover, since the tort is often connected with one's everyday behavior, it may naturally occur in circumstances such that those who observe it will know who caused it: if I leave my sidewalks covered with ice, any accident that occurs will automatically be known to be linked to me.

6. For example, in U.S. Department of Justice, Bureau of Justice Statistics, Report to the Nation on Crime and Justice (1988), at 49, it is reported that the median income of inmates is lower than the poverty level and that almost half of male inmates had been unemployed prior to incarceration.

7. See n. 4 *supra*.

8. Note that the situation is altogether different in the context of the typical tort, where the private benefit an actor usually obtains from acting improperly is avoiding the cost of a precaution, like saving the effort of removing oily rags that could cause a fire. It requires a much smaller penalty to induce a person to give up this sort of gain than it does to induce a person to give up the likely gains from murder, which may involve large sums of money or great personal satisfaction.

9. Although in fact violation of regulations sometimes results in criminal sanctions, I will focus here, as I indicated earlier, only on regulations punished by civil monetary sanctions.

10. There is, though, a complication that should be noted. If a commercial establishment has failed to clear ice from the sidewalk, it can be prevented from doing this in the future by having its license to operate removed. Analysis of this issue would involve the following points. If an activity like operating a store is prevented, then there may be a loss in social welfare exceeding that associated with preventing a particular unwanted act, like failing to clear ice. Hence, one would expect that act-based sanctions would be preferred to removal of licenses unless the regulatory violations were sufficiently serious and it was decided that act-based sanctions would not function reasonably well in the future.

11. If a fire would occur with probability .05 percent for instance, then the sanction necessary to induce installation of the $50 sign would be at least $100,000 since .05 percent × $100,000 is $50.

12. When components of loss (such as disutility due to a noxious odor) are hard to calculate, courts often exclude them from tort damages, leading to dilution of deterrence and to the appeal of the injunction. This notion is consistent with the fact that to obtain an injunction, it must usually be true that the damage amount cannot be adequately proved.

13. Also, the party will be led to take appropriate precautions to reduce harm, given that he engages in his activity, but I omit this point for simplicity.

14. Martin Weitzman, Prices vs. Quantities, 41 Rev. Econ. Stud. 477 (1974), offers another argument in favor of regulation over taxation that does not involve administrative costs, but it rests on the assumption that a tax must be of a simple form, namely (in the context of pollution), the quantity of an effluent multiplied by a per unit tax. If, as here, it is assumed that the tax equals expected harm—which may be a nonlinear function of the quantity of effluent—the tax is unambiguously superior to regulation, in the absence of administrative cost considerations.

Moving Backstage

Uncovering the Role of Compliance Practices in Shaping Regulatory Policy

N. REICHMAN

Sutherland's address (1940) before the American Sociological Society focused attention on the significance of 'white-collar' criminality. Since then we have sought to identify ways in which white-collar offenses and offenders can be distinguished from their street-level counterparts. We have identified the criminogenic characteristics of particular industries in an effort to explain why violations are located there. We also have come some distance in understanding our responses to white-collar crime, its detection, prosecution, and sanctioning. Yet there is still much to be done to develop an appreciation of how business discourse and practice actively participate in the construction of regulatory violations and pattern their distribution.

I offer this essay as one effort to explicate the business sector's influence on the definition and distribution of white-collar crime within specific regulatory contexts. I argue that business actors influence the distribution of white-collar crime not only through their influence on the enactment and administration of law, but also through their relative abilities to define what regulatory law is, how it is violated, and enforced. Typically, when studies have considered private-sector influence on the behavior of law, they have examined how business interests and activities affect the detection of offenses, the application of sanctions, and the potential deterrent effect of enforcement initiatives.

To fully understand patterns of regulatory behavior, including the patterns of violations and sanctions we observe, we must move 'backstage' in the regulatory drama to explore how everyday business transactions organize a firm's compliance with regulatory rules. Legal action is not simply a reaction or alternative to the threat of a legal sanction (see also Yeager, 1990). Regulatory enforcement policy emerges out of the informal arrangements, tacit agreements, and pressures for conformity that provide legal significance to behavior quite apart from regulatory action. Thus, we must extend the criminological program to look beyond the relationship between regulator and regulated, and locate regulatory policy and practice within the complex networks of clients, legal and accounting personnel, and market competitors that offer authority and legitimacy for business activity (see Stone, 1975; Vaughan, 1983; Stenning et al., 1990; Manning, 1987; and Yeager, 1990 for different discussions of how regulatory law is embedded in the complexity of social life). And, most importantly, once we have identified the inter- and intra-organizational correlates of business authority, we must begin to consider how variation in the organization of compliance affects the observation of regulatory violations and the distribution of regulatory enforcement actions.

I argue here that the shape of regulatory policy, including the distribution of regulatory violations, can be linked to the patterns of cultural authority that develop within a particular business sphere. Following Starr (1982, p. 13), cultural authority is defined as the authority to construct reality through definitions of fact and value. It is the ability to interpret, diagnose, and persuade, not necessarily the ability to command action (the latter he refers to as 'social authority'). One manifestation of cultural authority is the ability to assign legal significance to business activities. I call this kind of cultural authority 'regulatory authority.' Regulatory authority relates to the relative power of firms to embed their compliance in larger social networks that allow them to authenticate their actions while marginalizing and discrediting the actions of others. It is the authority to set the rules, to define the winners and losers, and to change the definitions of the regulation game (Meidinger, 1987, p. 357). Business firms acquire regulatory authority through the accumulation of juridical capital (Bourdieu, 1987). They build legitimating social networks by purchasing the 'legal' authority of other professional groups—for example, lawyers and accountants. Regulatory authority converts into business privilege when the norms, values, beliefs, and justifications associated with a particular regulatory culture become status indicators that differentiate core and periphery firms.

Efforts to model variation in compliance practice and the construction of regulatory authority offer to elaborate arguments of systematic bias in regulatory law enforcement. Observations of bias (systematic differences in the amount and type of enforcement) have been linked to the characteristics of offenses, the technical abilities and interests of regulatory agencies (Shapiro, 1984),[1] the situational 'politics' of regulatory action (Bardach and Kagan, 1982), as well as to the attributes of the regulated entities themselves (for example, their size, economic clout, technical prowess (Yeager, 1987), personal background (Shover, 1980), and legal competence (Galanter, 1974)).[2] I suggest that neither the situated politics of regulatory actions, nor the attributes of parties to the regulatory process are sufficient for understanding systematic variation in regulatory practice. Patterns of enforcement cannot be understood without attending to structural differences in the inter- and intra-organizational relationships that provide meaning for regulatory compliance (and, thus, its non-compliance). Understanding variation in how regulated firms and their employees 'manage' or negotiate the substance of law—that is, a firm's regulatory authority—may tell us a great deal about where we might expect to find rule-breaking behaviors.

In the remainder of this essay, I weave a model of regulatory authority and its effect on regulatory policy and practice around the context of deal making in the securities industry. The mobilization of regulatory law in the securities industry depends on a vast inter-organizational net-work of stock issuers, brokers, independent gatekeepers (lawyers, account-ants, and the like), regulators, and investors who transcend the form and content of their constituent agencies to create a shared, albeit temporary and contingent, 'regulatory authority.' I hypothesize that this authority has significant influence on the interpretation of business practice as conform-ing or not conforming to regulatory law. (See the discussion of legal networks in O'Malley (1989) or regulatory communities in Meidinger (1987).)

The Construction of Regulatory Meanings

As observers of the regulatory process have shown time and again, regulatory rules, despite (or because of) the minutia of detail, command wide discretion in their application. A certain amount of rule ambiguity is necessary because of the nearly impossible task of standardizing perfor-mance (Bardach and Kagan, 1982), an acute problem in many business contexts where innovation and outperformance is the *raison d'etre*.[3] The vast case law associated with regulatory programs provides continuing testimony for the need to interpret regulatory rules. Rule ambiguity is considered to be an important factor in regulatory accommodation. (See, for example, Diver's (1989) discussion of the effect of rule imprecision on, among other things, compliance with regulatory rules.)

Indeed, the past decade of regulatory scholarship has sought to show how regulatory policy is situationally constructed in the context of regulatory rule ambiguity (Hawkins and Thomas, 1984; 1989). Studies have shown how regulators cajole, persuade, and negotiate compliance with regulatory rules (Bardach and Kagan, 1982; Lynxwiler, Shover, and Clelland, 1983; Hawkins, 1984; Scholz, 1984; Braithwaite et al., 1987; Ayres and Braithwaite, 1989; Hawkins and Thomas, 1989). Kenneth Mann's (1985) study of attorneys who represent white-collar crime defendants offers a different twist on the dilemma of ambiguity. His work shows how attorneys, through a variety of information strategies, retroactively structure facts and reinterpret rules so that behavior is seen as fitting within the law. In this way, ambiguity limits the reach of formal legal process.

The regulatory agency/law enforcement perspective that has organized much of the regulatory scholarship about the consequences of rule ambiguity produces a somewhat myopic vision of regulatory practice. While we recognize that regulated entities may transform regulations by pressuring legislatures and regulatory agents to pass laws and enforce them in particular ways, we often overlook how the day-to-day activities of regulated actors shape and modify the rules that organize and provide meaning for business practice.[4] As Manning (1989, p. 51) observed, it is 'interpreted meaning, not information, [that] is the basis for regulation.' Legal interpretation arises not only in response to, or in the context of, official legal action, but out of the interpretations of behavior and organizational constraints offered by the networks of social agents and institutions in which everyday transactions are embedded.[5] Organizations regulated by law collectively create, modify, and undermine the very regulatory structures through which their work is organized. It is in this sense that we can define organizations as dual creations, governed by rules yet transformed from within as organizational actors adapt and reconstruct the regulations that constitute organizational life (see Giddens's (1986) conceptualization of structures as creations and constraints of social action and Burk's (1988) description of regulated financial markets).

Extending the white-collar crime paradigm to include the day-to-day compliance practices and the social construction of legal meaning is consistent with a movement in the sociology of law to understand how law is shaped by, and in turn shapes, social phenomena (Merry, 1989; Harrington and Merry, 1988; Yngvesson, 1988; Silbey and Sarat, 1987, as well as many others). The 'force of law' (Bourdieu, 1987) is not simply imposed by external agencies. It is 'simultaneously separate and immanent, imposed and participatory' (Yngvesson, 1988, p. 412), a product and producer of conflicts over authorized or legitimized interpretations of legal texts and regulatory practice.

As described by Rafter (1990), this constructionist approach to legal 'meanings' should not be equated with more subjective accounts of negotiated order in which individuals' rule-breaking behavior is explained in terms of the way largely atomistic actors construct symbolic understandings of themselves and the situations they face. The constructionist approach to legal behavior advanced here recognizes that legal meanings are powerful ideologies that both reflect and reinforce relations of power, conditions of hierarchy, and historical circumstance. Our task then is to

illustrate how particular ways of seeing the world come to be constituted, how they achieve hegemony through particular practices and discourses, what institutional conditions and social forces serve to maintain such discourses as authoritative, and how people cope with and represent to themselves their ongoing *struggle* to make the world conform to their conventional understandings and expectations of it.

(Coombe, 1989, p. 111)

As we move the criminological focus to include the constitution and reproduction of regulatory meanings through organizational practice, we bring organizational theory into the study of white-collar crime in ways that it has not been in the past. Typically, when white-collar crime theorists bring organizational theory into their work they focus on the criminogenic characteristics of organizational structures, in particular, their goals and opportunity structures. Organizational environments, including regulatory environments, enter into these models as constraints on organizational action, which create pressures to violate the law or opportunities to neutralize social controls. (See the discussions by Vaughan, 1983, and Kramer, 1982.)

A different view of organizational environments and their relationship to white-collar crime considers the environment, including state regulatory policy as enacted by organizations. According to this perspective, regulation is not simply a constraint on organizational action. Organizations interact with their regulatory environments—shaping as well as being shaped by them.[6] And because organizations do not operate in political or social vacuums, 'The structure of relations rather than the individual organizations are the units of analysis' (Mizruichi and Schwartz, 1987, p. 3).

Organizational theorists use the term 'organizational field' to describe the set of organizations that constitute a recognized area of institutional life. Within fields there is a tendency for 'institutional isomorphism,' a kind of structural and cultural convergence that provides a 'map' for behavior (DiMaggio and Powell, 1983). Specifying the organizational fields that influence or 'map' the regulatory program is an important step in developing theory about business influence on regulatory policy. Nonetheless, as Fligstein (1990) observed, it is important that as we do so we also remember that

> organizational fields are not generally benign and cooperative arrangements held in place by a sense of duty or honor, although the rhetoric and ideology of their proponents might lead one to think so. Instead, they are set up to benefit their most powerful members. These firms have often organized the rules and have the power to enforce them. The most important determinants of that power are the size of the firms and the ability of actors in them to prevent other organizations from entering their fields. (p. 6)

Although Fligstein sees the common barriers to entry in terms of the economic factors of production (patents, technologies, investments, and the like), we might also ask whether firms use their abilities to influence regulation and construct cultural (or normative) barriers as well. If so, this might help predict where business influence on regulatory programs is most likely to occur.

Borrowing from the insights of the organizational theory outlined above, I suggest that businesses influence regulatory policy not only through pressure on legislation and the administration of justice, but by their participation in the organizational fields that 'enact' regulatory policy through daily practice. In short, organizational policies and practices constitute and reproduce regulatory meanings and structures. And since firms differ in their position and power within fields, it may be possible to distinguish firms by the amount of regulatory authority they can generate.[7] Firms with high levels of regulatory authority may take command of the rules of the game in ways that marginalize, if not discredit, the actions of more subordinate members of their field. If so, the organization of compliance may be linked to the definition of regulatory meanings and the distribution of white-collar crime.

In the following section I use aspects of the securities business to illustrate why the study of business influence on regulatory process requires a deep understanding of the networks of interpersonal and organizational relations in which compliance activities are embedded.

The Securities Case

To illustrate the importance of moving to the 'backstage' of compliance (that is, to the ordinary transactions where law 'happens'), I draw from my preliminary observation of regulatory compliance in the securities industry. The securities industry provides a particularly apt arena for studying the organizational dimensions of compliance. It is hard to think of another setting in which so many different interests, agency relationships, and gate-keeping functionaries are required to intersect. Nor can one think of a business arena where the compliance function has been so clearly institutionalized, in part a response to the myriad conflicts of interests and risks of agency relationships that are found there. And, at no other time is the effort to link our understanding of white-collar crime and regulatory processes more important. The stock market 'crashes' in 1987 and 1989, and insider-trading scandals have raised public fears about the fates of individual investors in a market that appears rigged against them.

Regulatory Context

The corpus of statutory rules regulating the market is vast, technically complex, and enjoys a complicated history (see, for example, Seligman, 1982; and Burk, 1988, as well as others). The Securities Act of 1933, the Securities Exchange Act of 1934, and the Investment Company Act of 1940 lay the foundation for half a century of rule making in the securities industry.[8] These rules, among other things, (1) established a reporting protocol for disclosure of 'material' information, (2) constructed barriers to participation that protected individuals from manipulative and fraudulent agents, (3) prohibited market manipulations, (4) bolstered procedures for maintaining an orderly market, (5) set limits on outright speculation, and (6) insulated participants from the effects of market collapse. A regulatory agency, the Securities and Exchange Commission, was created to ensure that these objectives were met.

Rules that mandate disclosure of 'material' information about a securities offering have been cornerstones of SEC enforcement activities for decades, and thus are useful foci for our understanding of how compliance practices shape enforcement action. They are rules that tend to get enforced. Shapiro (1984) found, for example, that misrepresentations and registration violations were the most 'popular' offenses in her sample. More importantly, these rules have been a source of normative debate (and substantive ambiguity) from their inception. They are important texts for regulatory interpretation.[9]

Disclosure rules require stock issuers to file a registration statement with the SEC and to use a particular circular, a prospectus, for offering their stock. These rules provide a set of explicit conventions by which actors can make judgments about their investments. The keystone to these regulations is the revelation of all matters 'material' to an investor's decisions (Howell, Allison, and Hentley, 1985, p. 1109). Registration statements include, among other things information about the organization, financial structure and nature of the business, balance sheets, and profit-and-loss statements for a three-year period, as well as discussion about the significant risks facing the industry and the particular organization. Continuous updating of registration statements with annual and quarterly reports (10-Ks and 10-Qs, respectively) is mandatory. Although the SEC evaluates the sufficiency and accuracy of statements made in the registration and prospectus, it does not rule on the merits of the offering. Federal rules merely provide a reporting protocol to aid investors as they attempt to sort out the worthiness of stock offerings. Some states include a merit review as part of their regulatory program as well.

Compliance Networks

Even an overly simplified illustration of how securities products are 'made' and then distributed to the public can demonstrate why our understanding of regulatory behavior needs to expand beyond the sights of regulatory agencies to include a wide range of actors and activities that directly and indirectly participate in generating meaningful compliance with rules about disclosure. A diagram of the actors that will be described can be found in Fig. 10.1.

As the term is conventionally used, 'security' refers to the legal representation of the right to receive some prospective benefit (or loss) from corporate activities. It is, in essence, the corporation's promise of a future 'piece of the action,' given in return for an investor's willingness to provide capital today (Sharpe, 1985).[10] Securities are issued to raise capital. A family-owned manufacturing company. Jones Inc., that wishes to expand its widget-making capabilities but cannot finance the expansion on its own, might decide to open up ownership of the company by *issuing* a type of security—common stock or public shares of ownership.

Having made their decision to 'go public,' the Jones family chooses an investment bank to help structure and finance their stock offering. *Investment bankers* mediate the flow of assets between *issuers*, those who want to sell pieces of their action, and potential *investors*, companies, institutions, and individuals who wish to purchase a piece of it.[11] The prospectus that describes the 'deal,' or security offering, is constructed by an investment

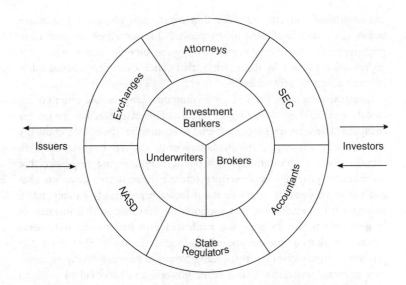

Fig. 10.1. Constellation of Actors Creating and Selling Security Products

bank's team of lawyers, accountants, and bankers, and a similar team of legal and financial professionals hired by the company issuing stock. As noted earlier, Securities and Exchange Commission rules, state regulations, and the rules of self-regulatory organizations mandate full disclosure of material facts about the corporation and its stock offering. Still, there is plenty of room for interpretation as issuers and investment bankers haggle over exactly what details should appear in the prospectus and precisely what language should be used to describe them. Lawyers and accountants might debate whether certain items, such as outstanding lawsuits against a company, qualify or not. In the case of outstanding litigation against Jones Inc., for example, lawyers might provide opinions about the likelihood of a judgment against Jones, and accountants might debate whether the penalties that would accrue are material to Jones's future operation. Whatever the outcome of the negotiations between the investment bank and the issuing corporation, decisions about whether and what to disclose must still pass muster with the SEC, the state regulators, stock exchanges, and professional standards boards—each providing an arena for further debate and negotiation.[12]

Additional (local) counsel may be brought in to negotiate the special 'issues' associated with gaining approval from the geographically and organizationally diverse agencies that must 'sign off' on a prospectus before it can be distributed to the public. One securities attorney commenting on the use of local counsel for gaining 'blue-sky' (state regulatory) approval for a deal said, for example, that 'Their existence is based solely on their ability to schmooze.'

Investment bankers also engage accountants, lawyers, and other professionals to aid in their 'due diligence,' a formal investigation into the issuing company. These reviews are conducted to ensure that the issuing company has sufficient accounting and management procedures to meet the additional reporting requirements of a public company and to ensure that information provided in a security offering is accurate. Case law that establishes an investor's right to sue if losses arise because bankers failed to perform this important duty supports the expectation that investment bankers will probe for mis- and malfeasance in the issuer's statements before distributing the securities products.[13] Similarly, SEC Rule 2(e) provides a mechanism for suspending from practice before the commission lawyers, accountants, and other professionals who fail to perform reasonable due diligence, fail to comply with GAAS and GAAP (government accounting standards), or fail to uncover and disclose material facts about an issuer.

In many cases, investment bankers also *underwrite* the offering. This means that they agree to purchase some or all of the securities and then distribute them. Underwriters can be thought of as the wholesalers of the securities product. It is their job to establish the price of the offering. In our example, ABC Securities helps Jones, Inc., construct an offering to sell one hundred shares of stock, and then buys the one hundred shares for future sales. In another case involving a larger distribution of the securities product, it might be necessary to assemble a syndicate of underwriters to purchase the security for later distribution to the public.

The possibility of deal syndications creates an additional web of entanglement and obligations that may induce an investment bank to conform to its peers at the expense of either its clients' or regulators' interests. Bankers must price a security so that it sells *and* provides sufficient revenue for the interests involved in its distribution. Underwriting, thus, creates different and sometimes contradictory risks (to a firm's reputation as well as its finances) for investment banks and their clients.

Finally, the actual trading of stock is realized by brokers. *Brokers* are agents who effect transactions for the account of other investors. Thus, if I wanted to purchase Jones, Inc. stock, I would ask my broker to purchase it for me at a particular price. Institutions (mutual funds, pension plans, corporations) use special brokers to place their market orders. In some cases, these institutional investors trade directly in the marketplace. As agents for investors, brokers are bound by the law of agency and SEC rules that say, among other things, that they must know their clients, know their products, and trade fairly (refrain from, for example, manipulating the price of stocks, churning accounts, using bait-and-switch tactics, selling unregistered securities, and the like). As employees of securities firms, brokers are bound by the organizational constraints of their firms. As commission salespersons, they are out to make a sale.

In short, creating and distributing a securities product combines a diverse set of actors and organizations into a single network organized around a particular, regulated product. Each actor has to be both responsive to the deal and also to the larger constellation of actors that embed his or her work. My preliminary research suggests that firms organize these relationships in different ways. Explicating these differences and their effect on compliance practice and the distribution of regulatory violations is of great theoretical import.

Observations of structural bias in SEC enforcement action raise important questions about how variations in compliance practices might affect regulatory law enforcement. Shapiro (1984), for example, notes that 'the organizations subject to SEC investigation are not corporate giants that have been around for a long time; they are very young and very small' (p. 41). Further support for enforcement bias can be found in Ewick's (1985) study of SEC sanctioning. She found that, in the case of organizational offenders, the most severe sanctions were reserved for firms that were financially or organizationally moribund.

Similarly, task force reports (for example, NASAA, 1989) supporting increased enforcement of penny-stock fraud suggest that there are important industry differences between the compliance practices of firms that specialize in penny stocks and the practices of firms that offer more prestigious stock products. Regulatory processes, standard in other markets, apparently do not reach the penny-stock market, and, if they do, fail to meet their control objectives.[14] The persistence of fraud is often implicitly linked to the attributes of those who sell penny stocks. While not entirely discounting the 'bad apple' theory of lawbreaking, I think it is important to ask whether differences in the social production of compliance (or noncompliance) have a more structural foundation.[15] Small, penny-stock firms may find themselves more likely to be classified as violators because they cannot 'authoritatively reinterpret (within limits) what the rules mean' (Clegg, 1989).[16] Regulatory traditions that reify the marginality of penny-stock trading may relegate that sector of the market as the one where delinquency is 'allowed' to flourish, and, in effect, privilege other sectors. This may occur because regulatory programs leave the interpretation of regulatory rules to the networks of regulated entities, only some of which have the power to make those interpretations, and only some of which are listened to when they do.

Toward a Model of Regulatory Authority and White-Collar Crime

In this section of the essay, I offer a model of regulatory authority that may help explicate differences in compliance practices and their effect on regulatory process. Once again, regulatory authority refers to the ability to assign legal significance to one's action, to set the rules of the game, and to define winners and losers in regulatory negotiations. The model is speculative and should be understood as a framework for future empirical work.

Faced with regulatory ambiguity, securities firms and their agents play important roles in constructing meaning for their deal-making activities. Regulatory compliance is a fluid process (Hawkins, 1984) that involves negotiated interpretations of both rules and facts. From the perspective of the regulated entity, rule-oriented negotiations involve efforts to show that the rules don't apply, or don't apply in traditional ways, to the deals that investment bankers construct. For example, an investment banking firm might try to convince the SEC that the acquisition of a failed savings and loan institution is not the acquisition of an ongoing business, and, thus, should not be subject to historical financial disclosure. In this case, the jurisdiction of the rule is the subject of the negotiation. Fact-oriented negotiations involve efforts to change deal facts to fit within accepted rule structures. Attempts to construct deals so that they fit within the rule parameters or decisions to omit deal facts on the deal prospectus might be so regarded. To avoid complex regulatory requirements, for example, companies issuing a limited partnership might choose not to specify the assets that the partnership intends to purchase.

Regulators respond to these efforts at interpretation in a number of ways that depend on the gap between the regulators' impression of the rules or facts and the interpretation offered by the regulated entity, and on regulators' judgments about the motives for interpretation. (For an excellent discussion of the variegated response to suspected deviance, see Hawkins, 1984.) Regulators may reject all efforts at interpretation, in essence playing the game 'by the book,' regardless of the situation and contingencies encountered. Regulators may accept the interpretation as legitimate or purposeful from a public policy point of view. Or, finally, regulators may perceive the interpretations as wilful attempts to get around the rules and, thus, regard them as legally implausible readings of the situations at hand.

I suggest that regulatory response is shaped by (and in turn shapes) the regulatory authority of regulated entities. Firms mobilize their power to shape regulatory response by embedding their activities within a network of interorganizational relations that authenticate and legitimate their actions. I hypothesize that three aspects of embeddedness condition the interplay of regulatory authority and regulatory response: (1) professional embeddedness, (2) structural embeddedness, and (3) cultural embeddedness. Each will be briefly discussed below.

1. *Professional embeddedness* refers to the ability to embed compliance practices within an inter-professional coalition that offers different legitimizing perspectives on compliance practice. Business organizations that can embed their compliance activities within the legitimation structures of other professional groups are more likely to exercise authority over the regulatory process than business organizations that cannot situate their activities within a professional network. As noted earlier, Bourdieu (1987) argues that the 'force of law' relates to ongoing professional struggles over the legal significance of everyday behavior. Regulatory authority flows to those who can accumulate the greatest number of these professional resources. The professional groups that are pivotal in the case of securities work are accountants, lawyers, and even regulators who can form coalitions of regulatory practice and meaning. There are two methods for securing professional embeddedness. The first involves purchasing professional authority by contracting with the 'big' law firm or accounting firm to take advantage of its authority and influence. The second way to secure professional legitimation is through the transfer of personnel. This form of professional embeddedness includes actions such as bringing in a former SEC enforcement attorney to head the compliance department for a firm, or hiring in-house counsel with previous SEC experience. Whichever way it is accumulated, the more professional 'capital' a firm acquires, the greater its regulatory authority and the more influence it will have on defining regulatory practice and policy.

2. *Structural embeddedness* refers to the contextualization of economic exchange in patterns of ongoing interpersonal relations (Granovetter, 1985). This kind of embeddedness is important for its perceived social

control (self-regulatory) benefits. Researchers have argued that the reciprocal obligations of 'doing deals' and threats to reputation offer important social constraints in modern business contexts (Macaulay, 1963; Granovetter, 1985; Leifer and White, 1987; Eccles and Crane, 1988; as well as others). To the extent that regulatory policy incorporates this notion, firms that can build their compliance activities within such networks (for example, incorporating continuing relationships with clients or other financial institutions in compliance programs) may be less carefully scrutinized by regulatory agents. The assumption here is that an organization's business reputation is a reasonably reliable source of control and that state attention should be reserved for more marginal firms that do not offer this alternative, that is, where customers or suppliers are less likely to monitor the activities of firms.

3. *Cultural embeddedness* refers to the extent that firms can participate in constructing the collective understandings that shape more general economic strategies and goals. (See the discussion in Zukin and DiMaggio, 1990.) Here the concern is with a firm's ability to participate in shaping definitions of integrity, reasonableness, success, fairness, and justice. It is not simply that 'the *subcultures* of Wall Street rationalize exploitative behavior as that which made America great,' as Braithwaite (1992) suggests (my emphasis). To the extent that businesses participate in perpetuating general cultural values such as 'greed is good,' they may also play significant roles in constructing the normative agenda for regulatory programs. Firms that can achieve this kind of cultural embeddedness are likely to be those with access to media (popular culture) and those that can locate their actions within a 'tradition of service' by placing key personnel on professional task forces, presidential commissions, and the like that 'investigate' industry wrongdoing. Cultural embeddedness provides a way to control the normative agenda, but does so in ways that mask the power and authority of key players.

The regulatory authority built by embedding the practice of social compliance within structured inter-organizational networks can be linked to the definition and distribution of regulatory enforcement actions in two ways. Regulatory authority, derived from the organization of compliance practice, is positively correlated with the likelihood that regulated entities will offer rule-centered interpretations of their behavior and with the likelihood that these interpretations will be accepted as legitimate. Regulatory acceptance reproduces regulatory authority for regulated entities. The following hypotheses are proposed.

The greater the regulatory authority of a given firm, the more likely that regulatory negotiation will focus on rules rather than facts.

When firms can locate their compliance practices within a complex inter-organizational network of attorneys and accountants, they will be more likely to offer rule-centered negotiations than fact-centered ones. This is because they are able to mobilize the necessary inter-organizational alliances to challenge the rules of the game. But it is also because interpretations of fact may be too visible and costly. These are the firms whose actions are most actively scrutinized by other professional organizations, clients, and investors, and, thus, discrepancies in deal facts may be regarded as too blatant or obvious. More subtle, yet more powerful, rule interpretations may be preferred. (See the discussion in Gross, 1980, that refers to the effect of organization set on organizational misconduct.) By way of contrast, the more marginal firms who cannot mobilize the resources to change the rules may be more likely to engage in fact-centered negotiations. The activities of these small firms may be less keenly scrutinized by their peers and their clients, so some manipulation of fact may be possible. (Although, for this reason, they may be more subject to regulatory enforcement initiatives.)

The greater the regulatory authority of a given firm, the more likely that its interpretations of rules and facts will be accepted as legitimate exercises of public policy.

Hawkins (1984, p. 127) argues that the issue of compliance is ultimately evaluated in moral terms. The perception of the regulated entity as reasonable is a predictor of a regulator's willingness to negotiate interpretations. (See also, Ayres and Braithwaite, 1989; Kagan and Scholz, 1984; and Shover et. al., 1984.) The construction of regulatory authority is an important component of the image of a regulated entity as a moral, reasonable actor. Firms that have a significant amount of regulatory authority, therefore, are more likely to find that their interpretations of facts and rules are accepted as legitimate public policy. Firms with limited regulatory authority are more likely to find their interpretations perceived as wilful, self-interested manipulations of fact and law.

Conclusion

I have proposed that our understanding of regulatory behavior, including the definitions and distribution of regulatory violations, would benefit from efforts to extend the criminological enterprise to the everyday practices that set regulatory programs into motion. Compliance is a process that deserves our attention, not simply as an alternative or corrective to the activities of regulatory agencies, but as an important regulatory process in its own right. I have suggested that we must examine how regulated actors interpret, implement, and modify regulatory rules. Looking at regulation from the backstage of compliance promises a more contextual understanding of regulatory behavior since it permits us to consider how regulated firms structure the interpretation of their behavior.

I have introduced the concept of regulatory authority to describe how business firms influence the regulatory program. Regulatory authority, I have argued, is a product of the social organization of compliance. Firms that accumulate significant amounts of juridical capital (for example, by buying the cultural authority of different professional groups) and that can embed their compliance practices within ongoing networks of professional and social relations are likely to exercise significant regulatory authority. They use that authority to define the shape of regulatory programs. I have suggested that regulatory authority might determine when, how, to what extent, and with what consequences regulators scrutinize business transactions. Understanding differences in firms' abilities to construct regulatory authority, that is differences in the social organization of compliance, may provide insight into how business influences the definition and distribution of white-collar crime. Firms that can command high levels of regulatory authority are most likely to take control of the rules of the game in ways that authenticate their actions at the same time that they marginalize, if not discredit, the actions of more subordinate members of their community.

Notes

1. Shapiro (1984) notes that 'the social organization of illicit activities determines the way they are detected, and, therefore, . . . different strategies of intelligence catch different kinds of securities offenses' (p. 167). Strategic choices about appropriate intelligence gathering, therefore, are important determinants of the enforcement 'catch.'

2. Regulatory bias is actualized in a number of ways. First, regulatory law favors larger business that can better afford the increased costs of compliance (Barnett, 1981). Indeed, historically, large firms have 'welcomed' regulation and have even influenced the drafting of regulatory rules. This is because regulations can provide the modicum of certainty necessary for business development. The higher unit costs of compliance imposed on smaller firms has the positive benefit of reducing competition from those firms. A second manifestation of bias is seen in the situational contexts of regulatory action. Powerful

corporate offenders are better able to mobilize sufficient political, economic, technical, and legal resources to thwart or neutralize regulatory action than their smaller counterparts (Shover et al., 1984). In this paper I suggest that regulatory bias is due not only to the static attributes of regulated firms, but also to their 'organizational place' and the constellations of roles, interests, and liabilities that compete and interact with law to constrain organizational life (Stone, 1975).

3. The ambiguity of rules creates a variety of problems for regulatory agents, often discussed in terms of regulators' legal risks, that is, uncertainty of successful prosecution should official legal action be invoked (see, for example, Hawkins, 1989).

4. Braithwaite's (1985) interviews with coal-mining company executives about the characteristics of their internal compliance systems and his study of the pharmaceutical industry (1984) are some of the important exceptions. See also Yeager's (1990) suggestion to 'extend the conventional criminological paradigm . . . by inspecting the ways in which rules of morality are perceived and enacted in corporate bureaucracies.'

5. Moving to the backstage of regulatory activity—that is, to the patterned interactions that construct regulatory policy—implies an expanded notion of state power. As Cohen (1985) notes, locally produced understandings of law-abiding or non-law-abiding behavior can increase the reach and intensity of state control. (See Silbey (1990) for a related discussion.)

6. For a discussion of how financial institutions 'enact' their regulatory environments, see Burk (1988) and Abolafia and Kilduff (1988).

7. Baron and Bielby (1980, 1984) argue that firms within an industry sector are stratified by the degree of task differentiation, the vitality of internal labor markets, and types of control systems that operate. I am suggesting that the organization of compliance may be another important status indicator.

8. State governments were responsible for the early statutory regulation of securities trading. Laws of incorporation set conventions by which potential investors could assess their risk by requiring certain kinds of financial disclosures. Commissions were established to review new stock issues (Nash, 1964). In 1911 Kansas enacted the first so-called 'blue-sky' law that required state licensing of securities sold within a state. 'The objective was to curb fraudulent securities transactions by refusing licenses for worthless securities and to the swindlers willing to peddle them' (Burk, 1988, p. 170). The states continue to play an important, albeit quite variable, role in securities regulation today.

9. A cursory review of business and legal periodicals reveals that there is substantial debate about the normative utility of disclosure rules. At one end of the debate are those who argue that the market itself provides incentives for corporations to voluntarily disclose information sufficient to protect all but the most gullible investors. (For a classic statement see Stigler, 1964.) Others argue that disclosure rules are important to maintain adequate disclosure and

historically have served the investor and the market well (Seligman, 1983). For contemporary refinements and elaboration of the debate, see 'Fifty Years of Federal Securities Regulation' (1984).

10. In theory, those who purchase stock become the 'owners of the corporation,' or the owners of the corporation's assets. In practice, this is hardly the case (Glasberg and Schwartz, 1983).

11. Eccles and Crane (1988) offer one of the few systematic studies of investment banking activities. Their work examines the management system that coordinates the flexible and changing network structure of investment banks. Interestingly, regulation and regulatory networks are not discussed as part of the internal and external ties that require strategic management.

12. Note that the criteria for approval may not be the same.

13. Because of their role as mediator between issuers and investors, bankers often stand in an uneasy relationship with their clients. As one investment banker told me, 'Entrepreneurs expect to give up some control of their company to their public shareholders. What they don't expect is that they also give up control to the brigade of legal, accounting, and financial experts who must approve every step they now take.' Bankers have to create a product that will sell, and thus, they have to be concerned with the regulatory, marketing, and retail aspects of their deals as well as the interests of their clients.

14. One reason for this market's vulnerability to fraud and abuse is that neither penny-stock investors nor regulators can effectively monitor the price quotations. The computer-guided market surveillance that watches other equity markets does not reach here.

15. Another explanation for penny stock fraud locates the problem in the character of the market itself. 'The stocks have no chance of going up (in the absence of manipulation), because there are too many shares outstanding ... the amount of buying that would have to take place in these companies is almost impossible, and therefore the stocks can't rise. If they rise, it's done artificially' (NASAA, 1989, p. 29).

16. Although we may observe both more violations *and* more enforcement in a particular sector, it is not clear that we see more enforcement *because* there are more violations. The same social processes that breed opportunities to violate may also engender more opportunities and/or incentives to mobilize formal legal actions.

References

Abolafia, M. Y., and Kilduff, M. (1988). Enacting market crisis: The social construction of a speculative bubble. *Administrative Science Quarterly, 33*, 125.

Ayres, I., and Braithwaite, J. (1989). Tripartism, empowerment and game-theoretic notions of regulatory capture. Paper presented at the annual meeting of the Law and Society Association, Madison, Wisconsin.

Bardach, E., and Kagan, R. A. (1982). *Going by the book: The problem of regulatory unreasonableness.* Philadelphia: Temple University Press.

Barnett, H. C. (1981). Corporate capitalism, corporate crime. *Crime & Delinquency,* 3, 171.

Baron, J. N., and Bielby, W. B. (1980). Bringing the firms back in: Segmentation and the organization of work. *American Sociological Review,* 45, 737.

—— and —— (1984). The organization of work in a segmented economy. *American Sociological Review,* 49, 454.

Bourdieu, P. (1987). The force of law: Toward a sociology of the juridical field. *Hastings Law Journal,* 38, 805.

Braithwaite, J. (1984). *Corporate crime in the pharmaceutical industry.* London: Routledge & Kegan Paul.

—— (1985). *To punish or persuade: Enforcement of coal mining safety.* Albany: State University of New York Press.

—— (1992). Poverty, power, and white-collar crime: Sutherland and the paradoxes of criminological theory. In K. Schlegel and D. Weisburd, eds. *White-collar Crime reconsidered,* 78–107. Boston: Northeastern University Press.

Braithwaite, J., and Fisse, B. (1987). Self regulation and the control of corporate crime. In C. Shearing and P. Stenning, eds. *Private Policing,* 221–247. Beverly Hills: Sage.

Braithwaite, J., Walker, J., and Grabosky, P. (1987). An enforcement taxonomy of regulatory agencies. *Law and Policy,* 9, 323.

Burk, J. (1988). *Values in the marketplace: The American stock market under federal securities laws.* New York: Walter de Gruyter.

Clegg, S. (1989). *Frameworks of power.* Newbury Park, Calif.: Sage Publications.

Cohen, S. (1985). *Visions of social control: Crime punishment and classification.* New York: Basil Blackwell.

Coleman, J. W. (1992). The theory of white-collar crime: From Sutherland to the 1990s. In K. Schlegel and D. Weisburd, eds. *White-collar Crime reconsidered,* 53–77. Boston: Northeastern University Press.

Coombe, R. J. (1989). Room for maneuver: Toward a theory of practice in critical legal studies. *Law and Social Inquiry,* 14, 69.

DiMaggio, P., and Powell, W. W. (1983). The iron cage revisited: Institutional isomorphism and collective rationality in organizational fields. *American Sociological Review,* 48, 147.

Diver, C. S. (1989). Regulatory precision. In K. Hawkins and J. Thomas, eds. *Making regulatory policy,* 199–232. Pittsburgh: University of Pittsburgh Press.

Eccles, R. G., and Crane, D. B. (1988). *Doing deals: Investment banks at work.* Boston: Harvard Business School Press.

Ewick, P. (1985). Redundant regulation: Sanctioning broker-dealers. *Law and Policy,* 7, 423.

Fifty years of federal securities regulation: Symposium on contemporary problems in securities regulation (1984). *Virginia Law Review,* 70, (entire).

Fligstein, N. (1990). *The transformation of corporate control*. Cambridge, Mass.: Harvard University Press.

Galanter, M. (1974). Why the 'haves' come out ahead: Speculation on the limits of legal change. *Law and Society Review, 9, 95*.

Giddens, A. (1986). *The constitution of society*. Berkeley: University of California Press.

Glasberg, D., and Schwartz, M. (1983). Ownership and control of corporations. *Annual Review of Sociology, 9, 311*.

Granovetter, M. (1985). Economic action and social structure: The problem of embeddedness. *American Journal of Sociology, 91, 481*.

Gross, E. (1980). Organizational structure and organizational crime. In G. Geis and E. Scotland, eds. *White-collar crime: Theory and research, 52–77*. Beverly Hills: Sage.

Gunningham, N. (1987). Negotiated non-compliance. *Law and Policy, 9, 69*.

Harrington, C., and Merry, S. (1988). Ideological production: The making of community mediation. *Law and Society Review, 22, 709*.

Hawkins, K. (1984). *Environment and enforcement: Regulation and the social definition of pollution*. New York: Oxford University Press.

——(1989). 'FATCATS' and prosecution in a regulatory agency: A footnote on the social construction of risk. *Law and Policy, 11*.

Hawkins, K., and Thomas, J. M. (1984). *Enforcing regulation*. New York: Kluwer-Nijhoff Press.

Hawkins, K., and Thomas, J., eds. (1989). *Making regulatory policy*. Pittsburgh: University of Pittsburgh Press.

Howell, R. A., Allison, J. R., and Hentley, N. T. (1985). *Business law*. New York: Dryden Press.

Kagan, R. A., and Scholz, J. T. (1984). The criminology of the corporation and regulatory enforcement strategies. In K. Hawkins and J. M. Thomas, eds. *Enforcing regulation, 67–95*. New York: Kluwer-Nijhoff.

Kramer, R. C. (1982). Corporate crime: An organizational perspective. In P. Wickman and T. Daily, eds. *White-collar and economic crime, 75–94*. Lexington, Mass.: Lexington Books.

——(1992). The space shuttle *Challenger* explosion: A case study of state-corporate crime. In K. Schlegel and D. Weisburd, eds. *White-collar crime reconsidered, 214–243*. Boston: Northeastern University Press.

Leifer, E. M., and White, H. C. (1987). A structural approach to markets. In M. S. Mizruichi and M. Schwartz, eds. *Intercorporate relations: The structural analysis of business, 85–108*. New York: Cambridge University Press.

Lynxwiler, J., Shover, N., and Clelland, D. A. (1983). The organization and impact of inspector discretion in a regulatory bureaucracy. *Social Problems, 30, 425*.

Macaulay, S. (1963). Non-contractual relations in business: A preliminary study. *American Sociological Review, 28, 55*.

Mann, K. (1985). *Defending white-collar crime: A portrait of attorneys at work.* New Haven: Yale University Press.

Manning, P. K. (1987). Ironies of compliance. In C. Shearing and P. Stenning, eds. *Private policing*, 298–316. Beverly Hills: Sage.

——(1989). The limits of knowledge: The role of information in regulation. In K. Hawkins and J. N. Thomas, eds. *Making regulatory policy*, 49–87. Pittsburgh: University of Pittsburgh Press.

Meidinger, E. (1987). Regulatory culture: A theoretical outline. *Law and Policy, 9,* 355.

Merry, S. E. (1989). *Getting justice or getting even.* Chicago: University of Chicago Press.

Mizruichi, M. S., and Schwartz, M. (1987). *Intercorporate relations: The structural analysis of business.* New York: Cambridge University Press.

Nash, Gerald D. (1964). Government and business: A case study of state regulation of corporate securities, 1860–1933. *Business History Review, 38,* 144.

North American Securities Administrators Association (NASAA) (1989). The NASAA report on fraud and abuse in the penny stock industry. Washington, D.C.: NASAA.

O'Malley, P. (1989). Legal networks and domestic security. A paper presented at the annual meeting of the Law and Society Association, Madison, Wisconsin.

Palay, T. M. (1985). Avoiding regulatory constraints: Contracting safeguards and the role of informal agreements. *Journal of Law, Economics, and Organization, 1,* 155.

Rafter, N. H. (1990). The social construction of crime and crime control. *Journal of Research in Crime and Delinquency, 27,* 376.

Reichman, N. (1989). Breaking confidences: Organizational influences on insider trading. *The Sociological Quarterly, 30,* 185.

Scheppele, K. L. (1988). *Legal secrets: Equality and efficiency in the common law.* Chicago: University of Chicago Press.

Scholz, J. T. (1984). Cooperation, deterrence and the ecology of regulatory enforcement. *Law and Society Review, 18,* 179.

Seligman, J. (1983). The historical need for a mandatory corporate disclosure system. *Journal of Corporation Law, 9,* 45.

——(1982). *The transformation of Wall Street: A history of the Securities and Exchange Commission and modern corporate finance.* Boston: Houghton Mifflin Company.

Shapiro, S. P. (1984). *Wayward capitalists: Targets of the Securities and Exchange Commission.* New Haven: Yale University Press.

——(1987a). The social control of impersonal trust. *American Journal of Sociology, 93,* 623.

——(1987b). Policing trust. In C. Shearing and P. Stenning, eds. *Private policing,* 194–220. Beverly Hills: Sage.

——(1990). Collaring the crime, not the criminal: Reconsidering white-collar crime. *American Sociological Review, 55,* 346.

Sharpe, W. F. (1985). *Investments.* Englewood Cliffs, N.J.: Prentice Hall.

Shover, N. (1980). The criminalization of corporate behavior: Federal surface coal mining. In G. Geis and E. Stotland, eds. *White-collar crime*, 98–125. Beverly Hills: Sage.

—— Lynxwiller, J., Groce, S., and Clelland, D. (1984). Regional variation in regulatory law enforcement: The Surface Mining Control and Reclamation Act of 1977. In K. Hawkins and J. Thomas, eds. *Enforcing regulation*, 121–146. New York: Kluwer-Nijhoff.

Silbey, S. S. (1990). On the relationship of state theory to sociolegal research: The example of minor dispute processing. In S. S. Silbey and A. Sarat, eds. *Studies of law, politics and society*, 67–75. Greenwich, Conn.: JAI Press.

—— and Sarat, A. (1987). Critical traditions in law and society research. *Law and Society Review, 21*, 165.

Starr, P. (1982). *The social transformation of American medicine*. New York: Basic Books.

Stenning, P., Shearing, C., Addario, S., and Condon, M. (1990). Controlling interests: Two conceptions of order in regulating a financial market. In M. L. Friedland, ed. *Securing compliance: Seven case studies*, 88–118. Toronto: University of Toronto Press.

Stevenson, R. A., and Jennings, E. H. (1984). *Fundamentals of investments*. New York: West Publishing Company.

Stigler, G. (1964). Public regulation of the securities market. *Journal of Business, 37*, 37.

Stone, C. D. (1975). *Where the law ends: The social control of corporate behavior*. New York: Harper & Row.

Sutherland, E. H. (1940). White collar criminality. *American Sociological Review, 5*, 1.

Vaughan, D. (1983). *Controlling unlawful organizational behavior: Social structure and corporate misconduct*. Chicago: University of Chicago Press.

—— (1992). The macro-micro connection in white-collar crime theory. In K. Schlegel and D. Weisburd, eds. *White-collar crime reconsidered*, 124–148. Boston: Northeastern University Press.

Yeager, P. C. (1987). Structural bias in regulatory law enforcement: The case of the U.S. Environmental Protection Agency. *Social Problems, 34*, 330.

—— (1990a). *The limits of law: The public regulation of private pollution*. New York: Cambridge University Press.

—— (1990b). Realms of reason: Notes on the division of moral labor in corporate behavior. Paper presented at the Edwin Sutherland Conference on White-Collar Crime: Fifty years of research and beyond. Bloomington, Indiana.

Yngvesson, B. (1988). Making law at the doorway: The clerk, the court, and the construction of community in a New England town. *Law and Society Review, 22*, 409.

Zukin, S., and DiMaggio, P. C. (1990). Introduction. In S. Zukin and P. C. DiMaggio, eds. *Structures of capital: The social organization of the economy*, 1–36. New York: Cambridge University Press.

PART III
Varieties of Regulatory Styles and Techniques

Legal Measures and Their Analysis

T. DAINTITH

We will proceed to the identification of the legal and other formal measures adopted by States for the achievement of the objectives over the period covered by our investigation (1973–82), or adopted previously and in active operation during the period. These measures provide the basic data for analysis and comparison. Analysis has been conducted according to a standard scheme with six main elements: the general or specific character of the measure; its duration; its source in the legal hierarchy (broadly conceived to include not only Parliament, government, Ministers etc., but also courts, regional or local authorities, the European Communities, as well as non-legal measures); its unilateral or bilateral character; its content (in terms of whether it is purely declaratory, whether it creates duties and how it sanctions them, whether it creates powers, transfers funds or property etc.); and finally the procedures associated with its operation.

On the basis of this analysis we are able to say what is the incidence of general as against specific legal measures, of short-term as against long-term ones, what is the frequency of amendment and substitution of legal measures (at least over our rather restricted period of inquiry), what is the incidence of 'high-source' (Parliament) as against 'low-source' (departments, Ministers) measures, and so on; and to compare these profiles of legalisation as between one country and another.

Policy Instruments

This information has considerable intrinsic value in so far as it provides up-to-date empirical evidence to support or refute the various impressionistic descriptions of trends in instrumental law which have fed the debates on this subject. By itself, however, it can do little to explain why instrumental legislation should assume particular forms or why particular sources should be favoured, nor why such preferences should vary from one country to another. To obtain such explanations we need to introduce into our analysis a typology of *means* of economic policy (here termed economic policy *instruments*). Such instruments form the link between the objectives of economic policy, on the one hand, and the specific legal measures of implementation, on the other. Only by introducing some such intermediate concept can we take account of the fact that the very existence of *legal* measures of implementation of economic policy results not from economic policy alone but from the fact of pursuing such a policy *within the framework of a given legal system*—that framework being understood to include both the constellation of legally protected private rights, duties and freedoms, and a constitutional structure for the exercise of all State power. If we are to understand how such a legal system determines the incidence of legal, as opposed to non-legal, implementation of policy, and how it shapes the relevant legal measures, we need some non-legal standard by reference to which we may observe and compare national variations in legal implementation. This we do by making each legal measure appear as the operationalisation, according to the demands of the national legal system, of one of a range of possible instruments of policy.

A variety of typologies of policy instruments have been offered, both by economists[1] and by political scientists.[2] Mayntz's classification, in particular, into regulative norms, financial transfers and incentives, public provision, procedural regulation, and persuasion, has considerable intuitive appeal.[3] Rather than simply adopt it, however, it seems desirable to attempt to trace out the steps through which a typology of instruments can be derived *a priori*, without relying on inferring a categorisation from examination of the characteristics of implementing measures: we need to avoid the circularity implicit in defining instruments by reference to legal measures and then comparing measures by reference to instruments. We may then check our results against the categories already proposed by others.

The first step is to consider the nature of the economic objectives which form our starting point. Kirschen has defined such objectives as 'the economic translations of political aims into concepts which can be given some quantification'.[4] While he had in mind objectives of a more general character than those we have picked out here, quantifiability remains a key characteristic even of such highly specific objectives as development of domestic energy supplies, or job maintenance or creation. Performance in relation to these objectives is likewise quantitatively assessed. Progress in job maintenance or creation will obviously be measured by the number of jobs created or maintained; in domestic energy development, by quantities of production or reserves. Even for objectives which might seem harder to quantify, such as diversification of imported energy supplies or efficient manpower adjustment, some numerical measures are normally available and used, such as the number of suppliers of a given energy source and the proportion of needs met by the largest supplier; or for manpower, the composition of the labour force, particularly by reference to age, the length of waiting periods between jobs, and so on. Non-quantifiable elements are in most cases relegated to a secondary position.

Without too much distortion, therefore, one can treat the essence of economic policy as being the attempt by government to influence the movement of a range of economic quantities or indicators, by promoting movement in a preferred direction or toward specified targets. Though the popular vocabulary of economic management suggests the capacity of government, by itself, to secure such results—we speak of government 'creating jobs', 'restricting imports', 'boosting investment'—its ability to do this by direct action is in fact restricted by reference to the economic resources and activities which it has under its immediate control. Outside this area its means of influencing economic quantities must be indirect, in the sense that they operate on the actions and decisions of persons outside the government, whose aggregated results determine the level of the relevant economic indicators. This distinction between direct and indirect action forms the first element of an instrument typology.

Governmental self-management is clearly an instrument of policy in so far as government uses its direct control over its own finances, labour, property, equipment and so on for the purpose of advancing policy objectives. Government may, for example, be able to make a worthwhile contribution to energy saving by ordering a reduction of working temperatures in its offices, schools and barracks. The size of the contribution will depend on the extent to which central government *directly* controls the provision of public sector activities; where there has been diffusion of responsibility for such activities to separately-constituted bodies, even within the public sector, such changes may be beyond the reach of government managerial power, and may require the use of the same kinds of instruments as are used to affect the behaviour of actors in the private sector. The public character of the bodies may, however, lead to those instruments being operationalised in such cases in a distinctive way. At the same time non-government public sector bodies may be made the object of legal (or non-legal) measures simply in order that they may serve as a transmission mechanism, through which the aim of affecting the behaviour of private sector actors is attained. The position of public sector banks and credit institutions offers an example of this type. This means that delineation of the instrumental role of the public sector as a whole is a highly complex matter.[5] On balance it seems best to take, as an instrument-type, the whole phenomenon of 'public sector management', understood as comprising both governmental self-management in the strict sense of direct, hierarchical control, and the distinctive application of policy instruments to public sector bodies outside central government.

Outside the scope of its managerial powers, government action in pursuit of economic policy goals involves attempting to change other people's behaviour,[6] the 'others', in the public sector as well as in the private, who charge prices, pay wages, export and import goods, invest capital, borrow and lend money, make take-over bids, purchase goods and services. It is their actions which in aggregate or on average make up the greatest part of all the quantities which government is trying to manipulate; their actions, therefore, which must be made different from what they would have been in the absence of the policy. More precisely, *some* of those actions, *some* of that behaviour, must be different: zero and 100 per cent are not necessarily the only quantities that government aims at. A government that wants a rising birthrate for economic reasons may not wish every wife to bear an extra child. Government would appear to possess a bewildering variety of means for use in this enterprise, ranging from criminal sanctions to mentions in the Honours List, but it is possible to order their discussion and inter-relation by resort to two reference concepts: of the *costs* of behaviour, and of the *resources* of government.

All behaviour choices involve a weighing of the costs of the alternative courses of action, measured not just in money but also in terms of time, of satisfactions foregone, of self-esteem, of reputation and so on. Government's aim is that such choices should, so far as is possible and necessary, be compatible with its policy objectives. This involves changing choices, either by showing the decision-makers that they are misguided as to their own balance of costs, or by altering those balances. The first approach will be realised simply by the presentation of appropriate information to those confronted with choices—as by indicating to householders how much in heating bills they may save by installing roof insulation. To change the relative costs of different choices requires stronger measures, which may be aimed either at increasing the costs of the choices which are incompatible with the government's programme—as by fining builders who do not install roof insulation—or reducing the costs of choices which are compatible with it—as by offering subsidies to householders who do install insulation. All government measures which are addressed to third parties, whether legal or non-legal, formal or informal, can be analysed in terms of this relative cost concept. To be sure, the kinds of costs imposed or relieved will vary: a criminal prohibition backed by imprisonment creates costs in terms of loss of liberty and reputation, while heavy taxes impose money costs. This difference in nature does not, however, make them non-comparable. In their daily decision-making economic actors balance bundles of costs including these different elements; they may discount such costs by reference to the likelihood of detection, prosecution and conviction for a criminal offence no less than they may calculate the likelihood of successful evasion of taxes.

Viewing policy implementation, including legal implementation, in terms of the relative costs of economic actors' decisions helps to elucidate two important points, which tend to be disguised by differences in legal technique.

First, it is implicit in the relative costs concept that the individual decision-maker always retains a choice as to whether he will align his conduct with the demands of government policy, no matter what instrument government deploys. One may imagine—though it is much harder actually to find—situations in which the physical control and supervision exercised by governmental agents is so tight as to eliminate even the possibility of non-compliance, so that choice is absent and non-compliance beyond price. The rarity of such cases, however, serves essentially to emphasise the element of choice existing in all normal cases, even in the face of express prohibitions. The point is worth stressing, not least because there is a tendency among writers who set out to assess the costs and benefits of using different kinds of instruments, in fields such as pollution policy, to assume that people always obey mandatory legal rules.[7] On this basis regulatory standards are argued to be inflexible and productive of sub-optimal results, in contrast to 'market-type' instruments such as taxes, subsidies, or tradeable pollution entitlements. These are said to leave sufficient discretion to the individual to permit him to adjust his activity in a way which is capable of achieving the best available balance of compliance costs and policy benefits. Behaviour in response to mandatory rules is in fact much more complex than this model allows for in the economic sphere, at least, calculated and negotiated non-compliance are common phenomena, and are based on the same kind of cost-benefit analysis as is explicitly demanded by the use of 'market-type' instruments.[8] There may still be very good reasons for preferring, in a given case, a tax-based to a regulation-based scheme (for example, greater economic transparency or the reduction or administrative discretion): but the evaluation must take account of the individual's 'discretion to disobey',[9] as well as the capacity of regulatory schemes to offer more satisfying protection to certain kinds of non-economic values than can taxation.

Second, and in some sense a corollary to the above point, the idea that a government measures work by changing relative costs reminds us of the essential imprecision of much government action. If government is dealing with small numbers of actors, it may acquire the necessary information about the effect of proposed measures by such means as bilateral discussion and negotiation, and operate with some degree of precision. The attractiveness of working in this way is an obvious reason for government encouragement of private interest associations. But many areas of economic life obstinately remain as unorganised, large-number situations. Here government moves in a fog: it cannot know the individual cost balances of the large numbers of economic actors it addresses, and can only judge the likely impact of its measures by observation of the effects of past measures, by sampling, and other aggregative techniques. In consequence it is unrealistic for government to think in terms of obtaining precise results from its measures, and in fact it seldom does so; yet if it uses legal measures shaped by the private rights model—such as criminally sanctioned prohibitions—precise and uncompromising drafting will be required. Thus what appears from a reading of the statute book of the Official Gazette to be a clear and unqualified prohibitory measure may from the standpoint of government policy be the means of effecting a reduction of uncertain extent in the incidence of the prohibited behaviour, an element of an implementation programme which may yield different results depending upon such variables as the strength of economic counter-forces and the resources devoted to enforcement. The persistence of prohibited conduct does not, therefore, *necessarily* denote a failure of implementation or the 'symbolic' character of the prohibition; government may be satisfied with the results it is getting. There is here an important but seldom-remarked conflict between lawyers' and policy-makers' pictures of instrumental law. Lawyers see hard-edged individual obligations, which should be uniformly observed and impartially applied;[10] policy-makers see a change in the general conditions of decision-making, whose aggregate results can be guessed at but whose effects on any given individual are both unknowable and uninteresting. The conflict disappears only when individuals get big enough to matter to policy-makers.

Turning back to the development of an instrument classification, then, the relative costs concept suggests a broad division into cost-revealing instruments (information), and cost-altering instruments. For the moment we may simply divide the latter group into cost-increasing instruments, directed to the reduction or elimination of behaviour incompatible with policy, and cost-reducing instruments, directed to the promotion of compatible behaviour. To break the group down further, we need to take into account the different *resources* on which government may be able to rely for the purpose of effecting changes in relative costs.

Three types of resources may be distinguished. First, there is the physical force which is at the disposal of government; normally, the threat of exercise of such force in response to undesired behaviour—as by imprisonment or confiscation of property—is all that is needed to induce its renunciation. Second, there is the wealth of government, in the sense of its capacity to use offers of money or other forms of property as an inducement to economic actors to behave in desired ways. Third, there is the respect it may enjoy as a recognised or duly constituted government, as a legitimate repository of secular authority. Each of these resources may be possessed in varying degrees by different governments; their possession and use are not dependent upon the existence of any particular form of legal or constitutional system, though obviously their deployment is shaped by the characteristics of the legal system actually obtaining in any given State. In relating these resources with the alteration of economic actors' costs, one might at first sight assume a pairing between force and the increasing of costs the paradigm case being a force-backed prohibition of undesired behaviour, and between wealth and cost-reduction (through grants and subsidies for desired behaviour). In fact, if one considers not a hypothetical initial position, but the situation of economic actors within an existing policy framework at a given moment, one sees that each resource may be used either 'positively', for cost-reducing purposes, or 'negatively', for cost-increasing purposes. Thus a threat to withdraw government benefits previously enjoyed may discourage undesired behaviour as may a new prohibition; a reduction of taxes, or the relaxation of a prohibition, may encourage a specific course of desired behaviour just as may a financial reward. From the standpoint of the economic actor, in fact, government's resources appear as positive and negative sanctions.[11]

Instruments appear within this framework of impacts and resources as distinctive ways of employing resources to produce impacts. The threat of force is used to increase costs both through regulations (including prohibitions) and through taxes, both through the unilateral imposition of regulations and through their consensual acceptance. As well as underpinning different instruments in this way, resources may be recombined within a given instrument: thus the incentive to make consensual arrangements with government which are restrictive of private behaviour may derive both from the fear of imposed regulations backed by force or from the fear of withdrawal of existing benefits, or both. In the light of these possibilities of differentiation and recombination, and of the need to be able to relate specific legal and other implementing measures to instrument-types in an unambiguous way, the following typology of instruments has been adopted for the study:

1. Unilateral regulation
2. Taxation
3. Consensual constraints, i.e. control of activity through contractual and other agreements with government
4. Removal or relaxation of regulations
5. Removal of taxation or the granting of tax exemptions
6. Public benefits, e.g. subsidies and other financial assistance, provision of public services and other forms of assistance in kind
7. Public sector management
8. Information.

The similarity to Mayntz's list is obvious. Apart from some differences of grouping of instruments, which are not important here, the main element in her scheme not represented is that of procedural regulation, which she defines as 'norms establishing decision and conflict resolution procedures for private parties'.[12] She argues that particular significance attaches today to this instrument by reason of the degree to which the State relies upon private organisations for participation in the formulation and implementation of policy, under the banner of self-regulation. Procedural regulation is the means by which the State creates or ratifies the structures of internal decision-making within, and of inter-relationship between, such organisations. Self-regulation is undoubtedly an important modern phenomenon: for Schmitter and Streeck it is an element of an 'associative' model of social order equal in significance to the established 'community', 'market' and 'State' models;[13] for Teubner it is part of a style of 'reflexive' law which offers *the* way out of an otherwise unavoidable 'regulatory trilemma'.[14] Why then does it not figure in our analysis?

The short answer is that self-regulation *does* figure; but it appears as an area for discovery, rather than as a tool for analysis. Our perspective is that of the way in which the State deploys its resources in aid of policy implementation: and the resources which the State may use to create, and then to control, self-regulatory capacity are not different in kind from those which it may use for purposes of 'direct' policy implementation.

Regulation, benefits, bargains all play their part. What is distinctive is the content of the measures employed (conferment of competences structured by procedural limitations) in conjunction with the nature of the actors addressed (economically powerful organisations). An empirical enquiry like this, whose starting point is the analysis of measures, may therefore enable us to discover the extent of the complex phenomenon of self-regulation in the fields examined and to understand its supports, by identifying the occasions on which competences are conferred on private bodies or rules promulgated for the discharge of such bodies' functions and powers. It appears, in fact, that explicit reliance upon self-regulation as a vehicle of policy is almost unknown in the field of energy policy, but much commoner in the manpower field, where collective agreements, sometimes with regulatory extension, play a major role in the furtherance of particular policy objectives or sub-objectives[15] and where labour subsidy programmes may be confided to autonomous bipartite or tripartite organisations. Explicit reliance, however, by no means exhausts the scope and significance of self-regulation in these sectors.

Two further remarks may be made about self-regulation in the context of this study. First, the measures employed by the State to create and structure self-regulatory capacity offer the clearest example of the determination and revision of 'private' legal rights by means adopted from public law: the determination of competences, and the creation of decisional structures for their exercise, are key functions for public law. The self-regulation phenomenon is one of deliberate and explicit organisation or ratification by the State of a diffusion of economic power. It is precisely where economic power is accumulated within private sector organisations (whether by reason of such diffusion, of industrial concentration, of trade unionism or any other cause) that we may expect to encounter legal implementation which draws in some measure on 'collective interest' as opposed to 'private rights' legal models.

Second, the instrument typology here can be linked with self-regulation in the sense that it is no less applicable to the implementation functions of the organisation than to those of the State itself. Its basic concepts are equally relevant to private power holders, who may also deploy a range of resources in order to change the relative costs of behaviour by others— normally their individual members—the results of whose actions are of concern to them. Essentially the same kinds of resources are available, though the monopoly of legitimate force reserved to the State by most modern legal systems means that the threat of force will usually be available only by delegation from the State or on an illegitimate basis.

Both kinds of situation are common. Further pursuit of this application is beyond the scope of this study, but the typology could serve, among other things, to facilitate comparison of the operation of private interest organisations of widely differing types, or to identify ways in which different legal systems affect the governance capacities of similar organisations in different countries.

Hypotheses and Results

The elaboration of a typology of instruments completes the methodological apparatus of our inquiry. The triple typology of measures, instruments and objectives immediately engenders a series of questions, essentially about the relationships of these three elements of policy, among themselves and with national legal systems, which have structured our examination of the mass of legal and other data collected and whose answers may help to pinpoint the key elements in the law/policy relationship and to indicate the extent and seriousness of the problems present there. In the following paragraphs of this section I look at these relationships and attempt to draw together a number of specific findings reported in the thematic contributions to this volume.

A. The Design of Measures

I consider first the influences bearing on the design of measures. The key question is whether the shape of legal measures varies according to the nature of the instrument that they operationalise. To some extent this is bound to be so, in that certain characteristics of instruments are replicated in the typology of legal measures we use: thus consensual constraints will obviously be operated by bilateral legal norms, regulations by unilateral ones; measures implementing subsidy instruments will have as their substantive content the transfer of funds or property, those implementing regulations the imposition of duties; and so on. But there are many points in which the measures operationalising the same instrument might vary (as to scope, or period, or source, for example), and the process of tracing such variations should permit the making of empirically-based comments about assertions of the changing shape of instrumental law, of its move away from the 'private rights model', both in general terms—is this true?—and in a more discriminating way, by indicating in relation to which instruments, if any, the phenomenon is particularly marked. We might guess that if there are such correspondences, then it is measures which implement the instruments least likely to bear on private rights—

relaxations of regulations and taxes, public benefits, information, maybe public sector management also—which are most likely to be temporary, non-general, low level, etc. We might be wrong. Among other things, the guess is dependent upon there in fact being regularities in the relationship between instruments and measures across a number of legal systems. It cannot be assumed, *ex ante*, that these will be found. It may be that demands of the national legal system are a stronger determinant of the shape of legal measures than are the characteristics of the instruments they implement, and that these demands are diverse enough to make all measures from a given system resemble each other more than they resemble the measures from each other system operationalising the same instrument. Despite the fact that Western European legal systems, at least, are said to resemble one another greatly in fundamentals,[16] and that the Hungarian system has abandoned less of its private law under-pinnings than one might at first sight assume,[17] the variety of approach to the instrumental law issue by scholars of different nationalities gives some initial credence to this latter hypothesis.

In thinking about the ways in which national legal systems may bear upon the shape of legal measures, we have had in mind not only the formal and explicit constitutional requirements of the system, but also two other sources of influence which, while properly labelled 'legal' as opposed to 'political' or 'economic', are not capable of such precise expression. The first may be termed legal *style*: the historical evolution of a given legal culture may dictate or encourage certain choices—in terms of 'ways of doing things'—which are not easily referable to the effects of constitutional or other rules. One example might be the Anglo-Saxon preference for procedural rules and safeguards as a guarantee of fair administrative action, contrasted with the French reliance on judicial review of administrative action on substantive grounds. Another example is afforded by the contrast between the German and Dutch preference for the use of general rules of corporation law as the means of structuring and controlling public enterprise activity, and that of the French, Italians and British for a specialised legal regime for this purpose.[18]

The second influence, which might be termed legal *substance*, is that furnished by the existence, at the time when policy is being formulated or relevant bodies of substantive law, whose adaptation or development may provide one means of achieving the objective at hand. In such a situation the policy-maker may be more likely to resort to an instrument which draws on such a body of law than to one which requires the creation of quite new legal arrangements; and if he does, the shape of the measures he uses will be dictated by the terms in which the existing legal scheme is expressed. In so far as such substantive norms are seen as accidental, as responses to past policy needs rather than as core elements of the legal system, their influence, or lack of it, tells us little about the relationship between a given legal system and modes of implementation of policy therein: but a demonstration of the relevance of existing substantive provisions to the policy-maker's choice of instruments and measures would provide support for incrementalist theories of policy formation and implementation.[19]

Having set out these considerations, let me try to assess their influence by looking briefly at some of the characteristics of the measures examined which seem important from the point of view of a critical evaluation of instrumental law: principally their scope, temporal dimension, source, and certain features of their contents. The task is simplified by the fact only a part of the instrument range needs to be taken into account: taxation measures, relaxations of regulations and pure information measures were all encountered too rarely in our survey to permit the making of significant findings about them. I consider below the possible reasons for this. In relation to the remaining instrument-types—regulations, consensual constraints, subsidies, and public sector management—it has been hard to identify consistent cross-national relationships between instrument-types and characteristics of measures. At some times legal system influences seem to prevail, at others the characteristics of the policy field may have a direct influence on the shape of measures.

One thing at least is clear: that the law is not dissolving into a 'wilderness of single instances', of individual measures of limited duration. Outside the field of public sector management, individual measures are rare,[20] and are even then often connected to the foundation of public bodies which will carry on activities like subsidy distribution. The finding requires qualification in that instruments may be operationalised by a series of measures, issued at descending levels of the legal hierarchy, of increasing degrees of particularity, and individual measures at the lowest level may be invisible to the reviewer of formal or published acts of government; but it is still important to notice the determination of lawmakers to express their precepts—even in fields like territorial or sectoral job creation or maintenance—very largely in general and objective terms.

As for the temporal element, there is considerable complexity in the demands addressed by policy-makers to the legal system in this respect. Different time-scales are involved in the attainment of the various objectives examined, varying between the need to be permanently ready to act quickly and (if possible) briefly to cope with energy supply disturbances, and the need to make steady efforts over a long but not necessarily indefinite period of time to attain a satisfactory national standard in fields like energy conservation. The nature of the time element in measures may therefore depend more on the character of the objective pursued than on either the type of instrument involved or the demands of a particular national legal system, so that it may be misleading to generalise about this particular instrument-measures relationship. Some specific remarks can however be made.

The first is that measures expressed to be of permanent or indefinite duration predominate over the whole field of our inquiry. The most important usage of temporary measures occurs in the field of response to energy disturbances, where substantial numbers of short-term regulatory measures are found; these, however, are normally second-level measures, whose authorisation is found in permanent legislation containing broad powers for dealing with energy crises. (The exception is Italy, which has relied largely on the constitutional emergency power to introduce, by governmental fiat, *decreti-leggi* which lapse after 60 days unless converted into Parliamentary legislation.) The explicit time-limitation in this sphere should be seen rather as an expression of respect for democratic concerns about unusually broad delegations of regulatory power to cope with crisis conditions, than as a simple reflection of the expectation that those crisis conditions will sooner or later cease. Temporary measures also predominate in the field of manpower (but not energy) subsidies, though even here we frequently encounter open-ended measures, notwithstanding the fact that the conditions attacked may be expected to be of temporary duration.[21] This is true, for most countries, of subsidy policy in the areas of job maintenance and facilitation of movement between jobs. This preference for open-endedness perhaps reflects the fact that schemes in these fields are *reactive*, offering a response to a situation whose duration government cannot predict, as opposed to *pro-active* (as in the job creation field), seeking to secure a once-and-for-all shift in behaviour, a shift whose period of accomplishment can be estimated (not necessarily accurately, of course) in advance. Yet while a contrast of this kind also appears in the energy sector between the objectives of energy conservation (reactive) and alternation of consumption patterns (pro-active), open-ended subsidy schemes dominate in both these fields.

A second, perhaps obvious remark is that measures expressed to be permanent, or of indefinite duration, have no guarantee of a lifespan greater than that of temporary measures. Frequent variation of measures expressing ordering policies might give us more cause for concern than equivalent variation of process policy measures, but we did not in fact find much evidence of such variation outside the field of process policies like price control in the energy sector. Frequent variation is most widespread in Hungary, doubtless because regulation assumes much of the burden elsewhere carried by flexible market relations.

A characteristic of measures which, we thought, might correspond in a more regular way with different instrument-types is that of their source (Parliament, central government, individual Ministers etc.), since national constitutions may allot these bodies law-making competences which vary in some degree with the characteristics of different instruments.[22] In fact, subsidies and regulations, the instrument-types to which the great majority of measures refer, do not appear very distinctive in terms of sources. In the Western states examined,[23] parliamentary participation in the process of making regulations appears in general to be rather more regular and intensive than is the case with subsidies. Subsidies, in their turn, have a higher legal profile, in terms of formal legal expression and the source thereof, than do measures of public sector management.

The more striking differences, however, relate to the practice of individual states and to the subject-matter treated. As to national differences, Jarass notes that Germany is three times as likely to use Parliamentary legislation as a vehicle for regulation as is France, and that this sort of discrepancy can be found between the two countries in relation to subsidies also. In this respect a fairly consistent ordering appears among countries, with the United Kingdom next following Germany in 'Parliament-mindedness' and the Netherlands and Italy occupying an intermediate position above France and Hungary. Less easy to predict, perhaps, is the significance of subject-matter in this respect. Particularly in the field of regulatory measures, Parliament, in all the Western states, holds a much more important position, as law-maker, in the manpower sector than in the energy sector. This greater involvement in one of the two sectors examined may be explained by reference to three factors, which overlap: the greater constitutional or political importance attached to the situation of workers than to energy problems; the fact that labour law and relations are (unlike energy) a recognisably distinct subject matter in terms of established law, which is unlikely to be capable of regulation by the use of executive powers (e.g. of price control or rationing) conferred by legislation for use in a variety of sectors; and, finally, the fact that, among regulatory techniques, the adjustment of individual rights is much more important in the manpower sector than in the energy field.

This third factor is directly evidenced by the data collected in this study about the content of measures. An important dichotomy, within the instrument of regulation, is that which opposes regulation by the adjustment of individual rights, legally enforceable on the initiative of the holders of those rights, and regulation through the conferment of control powers on government, utilisable on the initiative, and often at the discretion, of government itself. In the first case the task of securing compliance with regulatory policy is left to interested individuals, in the second government keeps it in its own hands.[24] The former approach predominates in such fields as job maintenance and labour market adjustment, through the legislative conferment of basic or supplementary employment security rights on employees. (There are of course exceptions, such as the long-established administrative control of dismissals operating in the Netherlands, more recently introduced in France also.) The second is much more frequently encountered in areas like energy conservation, and typically takes the form of legislation empowering administrative authorities to lay down rules or standards breach of which may be visited with criminal or, more commonly, administrative penalties. The contrast is not surprising: there is a high degree of congruence between individual interests in job security and a State policy of job maintenance, and a high capacity for effective enforcement of individual worker rights based on trade union support. Both of these factors are absent in the energy sector. While long-term similarity of interest may exist as between the State and the large enterprises which make up the supply side of the industry, it is only rarely that such interests may be furthered by the enlargement of the enterprises' 'private' rights, and even where this is the case (in relation, for example, to the compulsory acquisition of land for oil terminals, pipelines, generating stations etc.) the State will normally exercise some control, *ex ante*, of the use of these rights.

The influence of characteristics of the policy field is also reflected in a complex way in the extent to which measures *confer powers* on central government or other public authorities. The conferment of *regulatory* powers is, as noted above, the antithesis of the direct adjustment of individual rights, and we consequently find many more examples of such power-conferment in the energy sector than in the manpower sector. At the same time there is a high degree of centralisation of such control powers in the energy sector: delegation of rule-making power to local regional, or functionally specialised bodies is unusual, occurring only where (as in Italy in relation to aspects of energy conservation) a group of functions touching on one of the objectives is constitutionally confided to a sub-national level of government. The exercise of policing functions at the local level may, of course, be more common. Centralisation of power in the hands of a politically responsible government seems appropriate to the situations of disturbance, or even crisis, which will trigger many of the regulatory schemes in the energy sector; but in relation to less dramatic objectives, such as energy conservation or development of domestic resources, we may find the explanation rather in the domination of energy supply by powerful enterprises (or even monopolies) operating on a national scale, and a relative lack of organisation of consumer interests.

In the manpower sector, the conferment of powers is notable rather in the operation of *subsidy* schemes than of regulation. Here, however, it is associated with a decentralisation of the administration of such schemes, normally through bodies with a specialised competence in this sector like the Manpower Services Commission in the United Kingdom, the *Bundes-anstalt für Arbeit* in Germany. This diffusion of power to often tripartite (workers/employers State) quasi-autonomous bodies reflects the same congruence of policy goals between State and economic actors as is manifested in the strength of individual rights enforcement in the regulatory mode. The decentralised approach to policy implementation in this field is emphasised and extended by the occurrence of collective agreements, at various levels, which may interlock with or substitute for State action, and under which benefits may be made available to particular groups of workers in aid of objectives similar to those of State policy: examples are afforded by agreements favouring early retirement of workers in the Netherlands, or redistribution of industrial investment in Italy.

B. The Choice of Instruments

The extent to which instrument choices are determined by idiosyncracies of national legal systems, as opposed to being a function of objectives and of the social and economic context in which they are pursued, is again a question for which an answer may be suggested by the empirical enquiries we have pursued. At the same time hypotheses about cross-national regularities in relationships between objectives and instruments can be tested. Mayntz, for example, suggests that problems whose solution depends on the positive motivation and voluntary collaboration of the target population—the people whose behaviour the policy-maker wants to change—are better tackled through incentive (benefit) or information instruments than through regulation.[25] A number of the energy and manpower policy objectives picked out in the study are responses to problems of this type—energy conservation and job creation, for example—so that the data should show how far governments follow out this logic.

A strong negative motivation, on the part of the population, towards the behaviour desired by government is not a necessary condition for the use of regulations, but where innovative behaviour is required, regulations are much less likely to be employed: the relative incidence of regulations, in the manpower sector, for job creation as opposed to job maintenance, and in the energy sector, for alteration of consumption patterns as opposed to restriction of consumption, alike attest to this. Further the difficulty of using regulations in situations where innovation or initiative are needed is one of sufficiently specifying the behaviour which is required. This thinking reflects the 'private rights' model of instrumental law, whereby hard-edged rules, not vague precepts, are sought after in cases where private rights are to be affected.

At this point the apparent interpenetration of the public and private sectors within State and economy, occasioned by the concentration of economic power in State and private enterprise and other organisations, suggests the introduction of another hypothesis, relating to the size and degree of organisation of the target population. Does the private rights model, as represented by formal general regulations or subsidy schemes containing clearly formulated rules of application or eligibility, assume greater importance where the State addresses a large and unorganised population? The study offers evidence in support of this possibility: on the supply side of the energy industry, where a few powerful actors are involved, regulations are encountered less frequently than on the generally less well organised demand side, being replaced by more flexible and individualistic instruments such as consensual constraints, public sector management, and individualised subsidies. By such means the State may oblige individually powerful actors, as a matter of contractual or statutory duty, to undertake courses of innovative behaviour to which it may only encourage larger groups (like employers, or house-owners, or builders) by means of general subsidy schemes of uncertain effect.

Another idea which receives support from the study data is that of the variable impact of different instruments. The heavy preponderance of regulations in the field of short-term responses to energy supply difficulties is mainly attributable to the desire of governments to achieve a rapid effect and to manifest a strong and incisive governmental reaction to crisis; these needs are not present to the same degree in any other area. A different kind of point about impact in relation to subsidies in the manpower sector, is that by reason of their indirect or non-coercive impact they correspond better than do regulations to a fundamental characteristic of the policy field, that is, the idea of freedom to choose one's work, which in some of the countries studied is the object of constitutional guarantee.[26]

The relationship between regulations, in general, and public benefits, in general, is a complex one, in that a variety of factors appear to combine together to affect the policy-maker's choice as between these two types of instrument. The difficulty of drawing broad distinctions is indicated by the fact that regulations and subsidies are often found in close proximity, occupying complementary or mutually reinforcing roles in relation to a given objective. An example from the energy sector is the promotion of energy conservation by regulatory standards for the construction of new buildings, coupled with subsidies for the conversion of old ones; from the manpower sector, that of the provision of a public service of job place-ment, coupled with the regulation of private employment agencies, where these are permitted at all. Overall, however, the incidence of regulations, in relation to that of subsidies, is much greater in the energy sector than in manpower. The idea of innovation is probably of greater general import-ance in manpower policy and especially significant in the field of job creation (where regulations are very few), but the different kinds of impact of the two instruments, the impact of subsidies on the choices of actors (especially individual workers or unemployed) being—legally speaking at least—non-coercive whereas that of regulations is coercive, may also be stressed.

As between subsidies and regulations the size of target population does not seem to be an important variable, in that general subsidy schemes are frequently encountered in both sectors. There are, however, limits to the capacity of such schemes: they respond rather to situations of local or sectoral difficulty, than to needs for global economic adjustments. Clearly a problem the State confronts in the latter type of situation is that of the sheer cost—and of the highly visible nature of such cost—of national subsidies which are not tightly defined in terms of their beneficiaries or of the occasions of benefit. In such circumstances it may be easier to load the costs of behaviour changes on to the actors concerned by means of regulation—so long as they have the capacity to bear such costs. Con-siderations of how best to allocate the costs of compliance with policy may do much to explain the rarity of tax measures in the fields we have examined, and even the relative rarity of tax exemptions which, to work effectively, require that the target population be in good enough economic health to be actually paying the relevant tax.[27] Differing capacities to bear regulatory costs may also explain some national variations in the use of instruments in particular policy fields: thus only in the United Kingdom and the Netherlands, with successful indigenous oil and gas industries, do we find regulations (or consensual constraints), as opposed to public benefits, used to guide indigenous energy development along the paths preferred by the State.

With the occasional exception of situations of this type, which are attributable more to variations in social or economic context than to legal systems, the factors we have identified as relevant to instrument choices appear to operate in much the same way in all West European legal systems.[28] One should not deduce from this that the demands of the legal system cannot influence the choice of instruments: feedback from the legal system is certainly possible, in that it may install links between particular kinds of instruments and particular characteristics of implementing measures, which may make some instruments more attractive to the policy maker and some less so, other things being equal. An example will illustrate the point. If regulation to restrict the level of wage increases would require Parliamentary legislation, a government which is short of Parliamentary time or of a stable majority may prefer to achieve the same purpose by threatening withdrawal of public benefits from firms granting excessive increases, if this can be done by simple decree.[29] The example also demonstrates the error of assuming that the choice of an instrument to attain an objective, and of a measure to put that instrument into operation, are necessarily separate and independent steps. While the concept of a policy instrument is more than a mere analytical construct, but reflects real choices about ways of achieving policy ends, the policy-maker may often pass directly from objectives to a specific type of measure which seems 'natural', without perceiving that quite different instrument choices are in principle available.[30]

What emerges, therefore, from our survey is that West European legal systems are, at least in terms of their broad effects,[31] similar enough not to cause, through the operation of this kind of mechanism, significant discrepancies in instrument choices between the different States involved. Far more important are the differing characteristics of the policy fields which also may have a direct influence on the shaping of legal measures. That this is not a trite or trivial finding is shown by the strong contrast that the United States case offers us. There, legal system factors seem strongly determinative both of instrument choices and of their realisation in the shape of legal measures, and produce profiles of instrument choice and measure design which differ from the European ones. Among instruments, at least at Federal level, regulation dominates. While the existence in the United States of economic and political pressures for regulation reflect concerns similar to those voiced in Europe, the influence of the special constitutional features of the American polity may be stressed: the separation of Executive and Legislature, which deprives Congress of direct concern with the implementation of the measures it enacts, and the Federal-State separation, which limits the scope of Congress to use direct modifications of private rights as a means of policy implementation. The first feature helps to explain Congressional preferences for broad regulatory standards to be implemented and enforced by agency action, even to serve functions, like the promotion of new technology, which in Europe would more readily be assigned to other instruments like subsidies: Congressmen get the political credit and the agency, beset on every side by interest groups, courts, and budget officials, does the detailed and ungrateful implementation work. The second separation operates directly on the content of regulation: since adjustment of rights as between individuals is seen as primarily and traditionally the concern of the States, direct modification of such rights by Congress as a tool of policy is ruled out in all but a few established areas, leading to the dominance of control-type regulation even in areas where the congruence of private interests and public policy might suggest other methods.

Conclusion

The study has postulated three interlinked determinants of the ways in which law might be used in implementation of policy: the characteristics of the policy field (here subdivided by sector and by objective); the nature and mode of operation of the resources available to government (here represented by the notion of instruments); and the demands of the national legal system itself. Of these three, it is the first that appears the most powerful: patterns of legal implementation, as traced by our scheme of analysis of measures, vary more strongly according to the policy field—energy or manpower—in which measures are deployed than according to the legal system which deploys them. Cross-national generalisation across a number of policy fields thus appears unpromising. Together, the influence of these two factors, policy field and legal system, leaves relatively little scope for regularities between instruments and measures (other than necessary ones like the relationship between the subsidy instrument and measures transferring funds) across the boundaries of legal systems and broad policy sectors. In West European countries at least, legal systems appear to be a rather weak cause of differentiation of legal implementation of policy, producing, outside the area of *sources* of law (where they are important), only occasional significant disparities which correspond mainly to differences in pre-existing bodies of national law. This finding offers some encouragement to further comparative reflection on instrumental law. Before considering what kind of contribution the study makes to such reflections, a puzzle must be confronted: why should national perceptions of the problems and virtues of instrumental law vary so, if different national law-makers respond in largely consistent ways to policy stimuli?

The subjective differences between academic lawyers may provide a part of the answer, but it hardly seems satisfactory to stop at that. In terms of specific countries, the study does suggest that there are major system-related differences between legal implementation in the United States and in Western Europe, which might (subject to what is said in the next paragraph) go some way to explain distinctive American attitudes to instrumental law and which should, in any event, counsel caution about the transposability of American experience and solutions into the European context.[32] Examination of the Hungarian case shows that comparisons with socialist experience are likewise risky, not because the legal profile of implementation is necessarily radically different, but because the background against which economic objectives are formulated may, in some cases at least, offer little resemblance to that in the West.

These points apart, it should in general be remembered that this study has concentrated on the formal, *ex ante* aspects of legal implementation, taking as its primary data the laws and other published measures through which policy instruments have been put into operation. Equally important, however, to the observer's sense of how the legal system operates may be the government's capacities for administrative operation and enforcement of the rules it makes. Excessively detailed legal regulation may be much more irksome in Germany, where it is likely to be efficiently enforced, than in Italy, where this is less likely. Another factor, not considered in the study save in so far as it might feed back into implementation strategies, is that of judicial power to review and correct legally defective measures. This may cut both ways. Where such powers are limited as in the United Kingdom, broad delegations of rule-making or administrative power are treated with concern as occasions of arbitrariness and excessive discretion. Where such powers are strong, their application in relation to similar kinds of general implementing measures may induce a spiral of regulatory complexity. Complaints of excessive legalisation result.

While these possibilities may deserve further investigation, they remain on the margins of our inquiry. Having suggested that one can, in Western Europe, generalise about legal implementation of policy, across legal systems but within, rather than across, well-defined fields like energy policy and manpower policy, the more important question is what principle, or principles, should be adopted as a guide for further comparative investigation, whether of a purely critical or of a policy-oriented kind. Two relationships suggested by the study's findings seem to be particularly powerful in this respect.

The first is that of *congruence of public policy and private interest*. This is an hypothesis worthy of use by lawyers both for the purpose of understanding why they are confronted with particular phenomena of instrumental law, such as regulation (or why it should be absent), and for that of evaluating and criticising the specific legal arrangements that are made. Consideration of exactly what congruence exists, what is the nature of the relevant private interests, who holds or represents those interests and how great is their economic power, may permit the researcher to determine where schemes of self-regulation represent mere abnegation of authority on the part of government, or where they are cosmetic devices to hide a loss of control; or to say what legal devices should be sought for the protection of those whose interests conflict with the ones enjoying this happy state of congruence. It may also help to explain contrasting national choices between, say, control-type regulation and regulation through the adjustment of individual rights, and to suggest what consequences might follow from a switch from one to the other.

The second relationship may be barely stated as that between *the size of a target population and the form of the legal (and other) measures directed at it*. The study shows that there is no straightforward correspondence between regulatory measures and respect for what I have called the 'private rights' model of law. In particular, public benefit laws may, at least in form, answer just as well to the demands of this model as may their regulatory counterparts, especially where general subsidy schemes are concerned. But there is a correspondence, cutting across the categories of instruments we established, between all (or most) instruments as applied to small groups of actors, or large individual actors like public enterprises, and legal forms which are more individualised, more variable, more flexible, more like what I call the 'collective interest' model of legislation. In studies, whether national or comparative, of specific policy fields, the detailed tracing of this relationship may elucidate just what functions law is fulfilling in such 'small numbers' situations: whether, in particular, the legal forms used for the various instruments deployed—tax exemptions, for example, or public sector management—are anything more than expressions of an essentially contractual or bargained arrangement between government and the economic actors involved, or whether they do offer additional protection for the public interest through the procedures for decision and opportunities for review which are associated with their use. In this way we may be able to develop a constructive critique of the use and design of law in such situations, one which takes account of its potential for new applications such as the promotion of values like openness in discussion, rather than being limited to envisaging, with the aid of a traditional but partial model of law, a bleak dichotomy of tighter regulation or the withdrawal of law.

Given that a bargaining approach may be easiest where there is some congruence of public policy and private interest, and that this congruence may be most easily perceived where small numbers of powerful actors, like trade unions or banks, operate as representatives of or intermediaries for large numbers of individuals, there may clearly be an overlap between these two relationships. Each, however, seems to me to be worthy of exploration, in both national and comparative contexts, as a means of comprehending the bewildering variety of legal expressions of economic policy, and of determining in which cases the more unusual among these expressions represent unfortunate distortions of law as opposed to ingenious adaptations to its modern control tasks.

Notes

1. The most elaborate is perhaps that of Kirschen, developed in E.S. Kirschen et al., *Economic Policy in our Time* (3 vols., 1964, Amsterdam), and in E.S. Kirschen, ed, *Economic Policies Compared: West and East* (2 vols., 1974, Amsterdam).
2. R. Mayntz, 'The Conditions of Effective Public Policy: A New Challenge for Policy Analysis' (1983) 11 *Policy and Politics* 123; C. Hood, *The Tools of Government* (1983, London).
3. Mayntz, *supra* note 2, pp. 127–128.
4. See *Economic Policy in Our Time* (1964), vol. 1 at p. 17.
5. See L. Hancher, 'The Public Sector as Object and Instrument of Economic Policy' in T. Daintith (ed.), *Law as an Instrument of Economic Policy* (1988).
6. With the arguable exception, on the margins of our subject, of social welfare policy for such ends as the relief of poverty, where transfer payments by government may *in themselves* meet the policy goal, without any need for behavioural change on the part of recipients. But even social assistance schemes usually have *some* elements designed to affect behaviour, to encourage obtaining of work, retraining, etc.

7. For an example see S. Breyer, 'Analyzing Regulatory Failure: Mismatches, Less Restrictive Alternatives, and Reform', (1979) 92 *Harvard Law Review* 549, at 581: 'The very fact that taxes do not prohibit an activity, or suppress a product *totally*, means that those with special needs and willingness to pay may obtain it. Taxes thus lessen the risk, present with standard setting, of working serious harm in an unknown special case.'

8. For some evidence in a United Kingdom context see D. Storey, 'An Economic Appraisal of the Legal and Administrative Aspects of Water Pollution Control in England and Wales', in T. O'Riordan and G. D'Arce, ed, *Progress in Resource Management and Environmental Planning*, vol. 1 (1979, New York), ch 9. For a contrary view of the general point made here see R. Cooter, 'Prices and Sanctions', (1984) 84 *Columbia L. Rev.* 1523.

9. The phrase, but not the thought, is borrowed from M. R. Kadish and S. H. Kadish, *Discretion to Disobey: a study of Lawful Departures from Legal Rules* (1973, Stanford).

10. This expectation does not, of course, extend to instrumental changes to private law rules, where the discretion of the right holder to invoke, or not to invoke, the (changed) rule is assumed: cf D. Black, 'The Mobilization of Law' (1973) 2 *Journal of Legal Studies* 125.

11. Cf. V. Aubert, *In Search of Law: Sociological Approaches to Law* (1983, Oxford), at pp. 159–169.

12. *Supra* note 2, at p. 128.

13. W. Streeck and P. C. Schmitter, '*Community, Market, State—and Associations? The Prospective Contribution of Interest Governance to Social Order* (EUI Working Paper No. 94, 1984, Florence).

14. G. Teubner, 'Juridification: Concepts, Aspects, Limits, Solutions' in G. Teubner (ed), *The Juridification of Social Spheres* (1987).

15. For example, their use for the purpose of creating job opportunities in particular areas or sectors, or for facilitating early retirement from the labour market.

16. See e.g. R. David, *Les Grands Systèmes du Droit Contemporain* (8me ed 1982, Paris, by C. Jauffret-Spinosi), pp. 25–26.

17. Hungary has not, for example, adopted a code of economic law, as have Czechoslovakia and the German Democratic Republic.

18. In France and Italy, though not in the United Kingdom, this preference is reinforced by formal constitutional requirements: French Constitution, art. 34; Italian Constitution, art. 43.

19. Leading exponents include D. Braybrooke and C. E. Lindblom see their *A Strategy of Decision* (1963, New York), esp. ch 5.

20. Note though that in the nuclear field, individual measures dominate even where the industry is privately run, as in Germany. This seems to result from governmental pursuit of subsidy policies in an industry with few actors.

21. Note that though a scheme may be of indefinite duration, the period for which assistance may be enjoyed by any particular recipient is likely to be limited.

22. See T. C. Daintith, 'Legal Analysis of Economic Policy—I' (1982) 9 *Journal of Law and Society* 191.

23. In Hungary parliamentary involvement is limited to legislative approval of medium term plans, which are implemented by collective or individual ministerial decrees.

24. Legal systems vary in the extent to which they offer facilities for concerned individuals and groups to compel, through legal process, the due exercise of governmental control powers of this type, or to act themselves in the event of governmental default.

25. Cf. Mayntz, *supra* note 2, at p. 138.

26. See art. 12 of the German Basic Law, art. 4 of the Italian Constitution.

27. Such tax exemptions as have been encountered often relate to non-progressive taxes like social security payments or fuel duty, rather than to variable income or corporation taxes.

28. More important variations from the general pattern observed in the use of subsidies and regulations occur in Hungary. Not only is there a higher incidence of regulations than in any West European State, which may be readily assumed to reflect a more dirigiste style of economic management, there are also a few interesting inversions of this tendency, as where subsidies are used to encourage firms to employ handicapped workers, whereas several Western States impose quotas or other regulatory obligations (United Kingdom, France, Italy). In both the general and the special case economic structures and situations appear to be at the root of the difference. Notwithstanding recent moves towards the diffusion of market-type incentives, the highly structured and centralised nature of the Hungarian economy and the overwhelming predominance of State and co-operative enterprise therein continue to call for regulatory measures where less centralised economies may rely on market forces or, in dealing with their public sector enterprises, on less formal measures. Instrument choices in the manpower sector need to be seen against the background of labour shortages and output targets faced by firms.

29. As occurred in the United Kingdom: for details see Ganz, Comment, 1978 *Public Law* 333; R. Ferguson and A. C. Page, 'Pay Restraint: The Legal Constraints' (1978) 128 *New Law Journal* 515.

30. Cf. Mayntz, *supra* note 2, at pp. 129–131.

31. Obviously, specific instances of legal system feedback can be found. A good case is furnished by the different ways in which the European Community obligation to hold certain levels of oil stocks has been translated into the national laws of Member States: see G. P. Levy, 'The Relationship between Oil Companies and Consumer State Governments in Europe 1973–82', (1984) 2 *Journal of Energy and Natural Resources Law* 9, at pp. 14–17.

32. Compare I. Harden and N. Lewis, 'Regulation, De-Regulation and Privatization: Some Anglo-American Comparisons', (1983) 34 *N. Ireland Legal Qly* 207.

Rethinking Self-Regulation

A. OGUS

'Britain', it has been said, 'appears to be something of a haven for self-regulation'.[1] The phenomenon has come under increased scrutiny in recent years and it has been subjected to a greater degree of formalization and the imposition of external controls. Nevertheless, self-regulation remains as the principal controlling device for a wide range of activities including, notably, advertising, financial services, and the practice of a large variety of professional occupations.

Unsurprisingly, self-regulation has been the subject of severe criticism from lawyers and other social scientists. While much of the criticism (which I shall summarize in section II of the paper) is well-founded in relation to some forms, insufficient attention has been given to the wide range of institutional arrangements which may properly be labelled 'self-regulation' (section III) and particularly to new forms which have been emerging. I focus on two models; one based on consensual bargaining (section IV), the other involving competition between self-regulatory regimes (section V). I argue that when combined with some measure of external constraint each has the potential, at least in some contexts, to meet the traditional criticisms and to generate outcomes which may be superior to those emanating from conventional public regulatory forms. First, however, it is necessary to consider briefly the conventional justifications and explanations for self-regulation.

I Justifications and Explanations for Self-Regulation

Put succinctly, the public interest justification for self-regulation in a particular context is based on three conditions being fulfilled: first, that the activity is afflicted by some form of market failure, notably externalities or information asymmetries; secondly, that private law instruments are inadequate or too costly to correct the failure; and, thirdly, that self-regulation is a better (cheaper) method of solving the problem than conventional public regulation. I will focus on the last of these conditions, since the first two go beyond the scope of this paper and are, in any event, fully analysed in the standard literature on regulation.[2]

What then are the advantages traditionally claimed for self-regulation over public regulation?[3] First, since self-regulatory agencies (hereafter SRAs) can normally command a greater degree of expertise and technical knowledge of practices and innovatory possibilities within the relevant area than independent agencies, information costs for the formulation and interpretation of standards are lower. Secondly, for the same reasons, monitoring and enforcement costs are also reduced, as are the costs to practitioners of dealing with regulators, given that such interaction is likely to be fostered by mutual trust. Thirdly, to the extent that the processes of, and rules issued by, SRAs are less formalized than those of public regulatory regimes, there are savings in the costs (including those attributable to delay) of amending standards. Fourthly, the administrative costs of the regime are normally internalized in the trade or activity which is subject to regulation; in the case of independent, public agencies, they are typically borne by taxpayers.

It would, however, be naïve to assume that public interest justifications provide an exclusive explanation for the existence of self-regulatory regimes. Obviously, private interests that are threatened by regulation may gain considerable benefits if they are allowed themselves to formulate and enforce the relevant controls. From the abundant literature on public choice theory[4] which treats legislation as a response to the competing demands of interest groups, there emerges the hypothesis that regulation serves mainly to confer rents (supra-competitive profits) on the regulated firms.[5] If regulatory rule-making remains with the legislature or an independent agency, groups representing such firms have the task of exerting influence on those institutions and diverting them away from public interest goals or other, competing, private interest claims. Of course, delegation of the regulatory powers to SRAs relieves the groups of this task and the relative absence of accountability and external constraints maximizes the possibilities of rent-seeking—'with self-regulation, regulatory capture is there from the outset'.[6]

II Traditional Criticisms of Self-Regulation

Lawyers and economists have been equally scathing in their criticisms of self-regulation. From a legal perspective, it is seen as an example of modern 'corporatism', the acquisition of power by groups which are not accountable to the body politic through the conventional constitutional channels.[7] The capacity of an SRA to make rules governing the activities of an association or profession may itself constitute an abuse if it lacks democratic legitimacy in relation to members of the association or profession.[8] The potential for abuse becomes intolerable if, and to the extent that, the rules affect third parties.[9] Further, if—as often occurs—the SRA's functions cover policy formulation, interpretation of the rules, adjudication and enforcement (including the imposition of sanctions) as well as rule-making, there is a fundamental breach of the separation of powers doctrine.[10] Finally, irrespective of theoretical considerations, SRAs are claimed to have a poor record of enforcing their standards against recalcitrant members.[11]

In line with the rent-seeking hypothesis described in the last section, economists have developed models to predict how firms will benefit from self-regulatory regimes;[12] and numerous studies have been published which purport to validate empirically the prediction. Thus SRAs with exclusive power to issue licences authorizing the practice of a profession or occupation have used that power to restrict entry and thereby to enable incumbent practitioners to earn supra-competitive profits.[13] So also their formulation of ongoing quality standards has enabled them to protect anti-competitive practices: for example, fee regulation and restrictions on advertising which limit price competition;[14] and 'professional ethics' which may serve the well-being of practitioners rather than their clients and mask prohibitions on cost-saving innovation.[15]

III The Nature of Self-Regulation

One problem with the traditional criticisms of self-regulation is that they are based on a narrow, stereotyped conception of the phenomenon. There is, in fact, a multitude of institutional arrangements which can properly be described as 'self-regulation'[16] and, as we shall argue, it is wrong to tar them all with the same brush.

To appreciate the range of possibilities, it may be helpful to identify some key variables.[17] Take, first, the question of autonomy. There is no clear dichotomy in this respect between 'self-regulation' and 'public regulation', but rather a spectrum containing different degrees of legislative constraints, outsider participation in relation to rule formulation or enforcement (or both), and external control and accountability.[18] Thus, at one extreme, rules may be private to a firm, association or organization; at the other, they may have to be approved by a government minister or some independent public authority. Secondly, the rules or standards issued by the SRA may have varying degrees of legal force: they may be formally binding, codes of practice which presumptively apply unless an alleged offender can show that some alternative conduct was capable of satisfactorily meeting the regulatory goals,[19] or purely voluntary. Thirdly, regimes may differ according to their degree of monopolistic power. They may apply to all those supplying a relevant market; alternatively they may be adopted only by a group of suppliers (or even a single supplier) who compete with others in the market. This has important implications for the arguments deployed later in the paper, since it gives rise to the possibility of competition between self-regulatory regimes.

IV Self-Regulation and Consensual Bargaining

This rich choice of forms can be exploited in the pursuit of models of self-regulation which retain the advantages traditionally attributed to the latter but which also meet the criticisms summarized above. The first such model which we will explore derives its inspiration from the Coase Theorem.[20]

The Theorem demonstrates that, subject to transactions costs, allocative efficiency will be achieved by voluntary market transactions, however the law is formulated. Transactions costs are, of course, important. In relation to some areas where regulation proliferates, they are prohibitively high. For example, environmental pollution generates widely spread externalities and bargaining between polluting firms and the affected parties is generally not feasible. This is not simply because large numbers are involved; it is also because of the heterogeneity of the pollutees—they are likely to have diverse interests in environmental amenity and therefore will not easily reach agreement on what is desirable.

By way of contrast, let us consider a situation where the affected group is relatively homogeneous and externalities are largely absent. Occupational health and safety may be considered to be such, provided that the effects are predominantly restricted to the workforce. Presumptively, we might here expect Coasian bargaining to provide the optimal solution: following negotiations, employers will agree to provide employees, in return for their labour, with a combination of a prescribed level of care and wages. The cost of the package to the employer will reflect the marginal value of the employees' work and the relative levels of care and wages will reflect how the employees value the benefits of care.[21]

Thus a system may be envisaged in which legislation lays down general regulatory goals but specific standards are resolved by 'self-regulatory' negotiation at shop-floor level, with a public agency playing only a residual role, monitoring agreements to ensure that they are consistent with the statutory goals and, if necessary, enforcing them.[22] The history of occupational health and safety regulation in Britain provides an illustration of evolution towards such a system.

The nineteenth-century working conditions in factories and mines presented a classic case for centralized regulation, given particularly the problems concerning information flows, restrictions on private law remedies and the absence of effective labour organization. The creation of specialized agencies, such as the Factory Inspectorate, served to inject an almost unstoppable momentum into the expansion of public regulatory law.[23] The growth of technology and its attendant risks created a need for detailed standards. But with more detail came inevitably loopholes and the possibility of avoidance behaviour. To meet these, further detailed rules would be formulated and the cycle would be repeated, perhaps indefinitely.

When the Robens Committee reviewed the law in 1972, it could observe thousands of rigid specific standards prescribed, often in considerable pedantic detail, for a huge variety of processes, leaving employers little or no choice as to the method of compliance.[24] The defects of such a system were clear.[25] The law was highly complex and difficult to assimilate. The standards rapidly become outmoded and created no incentive for the employer to find cheaper ways of meeting the relevant goals. Formulating, monitoring and enforcing the standards gave rise to huge administrative costs, much of which fell on the taxpayer.

What emerged in the Committee's recommendations, and in the Health and Safety at Work etc Act 1974 which largely implemented those recommendations, was something akin to our model of consensual self-regulation.[26] At the heart of the new approach lies the notion that compliance with the general regulatory goals[27] should primarily be achieved by agreement between employer and employees, in practice trade union safety representatives (TUSRs) and safety committees.[28] Consensualism plays its part not only in the consultation and negotiation which precede the issuing of the formal regulations and the publication of Authorized Codes of Practice and guidance notes by the Health and Safety Commission (or Executive) but also in the formulation by each employer (with more than four employees) of a health and safety policy.[29] The information asymmetry problem is met by imposing on employers an obligation to obtain and communicate to TUSRs adequate information on the workplace risks.[30] There is a public agency, the Health and Safety

Executive, with ultimate powers of control and enforcement, but its role is a residual one.[31]

The advantages of the new approach are that the resulting standards should be better tailored to the localized circumstances, the parties from whom the protection is devised are themselves involved in standard-setting, and incentives to devise better (cheaper) means of meeting the risks are preserved. Some important limitations to the consensual model should, however, be noted.

In the first place, it may not be the optimal form of regulation in relation to risks which give rise to particularly drastic consequences or those for which information is less readily available or controversial. Here, economies of scale may be achieved by centralized agencies accumulating and processing the information; agreements between employers and employees may be harder to reach, especially where there is some uncertainty regarding the nature of the risk; and the risks may affect third parties—in other words, there are significant externalities. These considerations help to explain why, for example, the regulatory framework governing the control of hazardous substances qualifies consensualism by some reliance on the more traditional forms of public regulation.[32]

Secondly, a more general problem arises from what one writer has referred to as the 'consensual paradox': consensual regulation 'is aimed at the well-informed, well-intentioned and well-organized employer who would present few problems if left wholly to self-regulate. But many hazards relate to the ill-informed, ill-intentioned and ill-organized employer...'[33] Empirical studies of the new regime confirm that it does not adequately deal with the latter.[34]

V Competitive Self-Regulation

Consensual self-regulation is feasible only where bargaining can take place between the risk-creators and the potential victims at relatively low cost. Our second model of self-regulation is potentially applicable in a wider context and relates more directly to instances, such as the regulation of the professions, which have attracted so much criticism. It has its source in a simple observation: if the principal objection to SRAs is that they are able to exploit their monopolistic control of supply so as to enable practitioners to earn rents, then why not force SRAs to compete with one another, so that the rents will be eliminated?[35] Such competition would obviously prevent SRAs creating barriers to entry. But it should also constrain SRAs to formulate standards which meet consumer preferences at lowest cost

since, assuming consumers have adequate information to make appropriate comparisons, they will choose the combination of price and self-
regulatory standards which most closely corresponds to those preferences.

Competition in this context can bear different meanings. We shall
examine successively three forms: *(1) unconstrained market competition;
(2) agency-assisted competition;* and *(3) ex-ante competition for ex-post monopoly.*

(1) Unconstrained Market Competition

Competition between self-regulatory systems is more prevalent than is
often supposed.[36] In the ordinary markets for products and services,
suppliers compete to attract consumers by the quality (as well as the
price) of their products and services. Quality is, to some extent at least,
a consequence of standards and other forms of control imposed internally
by the management of a firm. The standards may reflect public regulatory
requirements but more often they are voluntary, representing the firm's
response to assumed consumer demand and, in some cases, incorporating
industry-wide practices. Although such competition can generate a variety
of quality-price trade-offs to match different consumer preferences, there
are two reasons why it may prove to be inadequate. First, there may be an
externality problem: inferior quality may have adverse effects on parties
not involved in the purchasing decision. Secondly, it is often difficult for
suppliers to communicate quality (and therefore the voluntary standards)
to consumers in a way that they can easily comprehend and use as the basis
for comparison.[37] If prices are easily compared but quality remains hidden,
competition will have the perverse effect of forcing traders to lower the
latter.[38]

(2) Independent Agency-Assisted Competition

How then can these problems of externalities and information be solved?
Where significant externalities arise, there may be no alternative to the
imposition of public regulation, requiring that suppliers meet appropriate
minimum quality standards. As regards information, it may be possible for
an independent agency to devise some form of scoring system, points
being awarded for compliance with different quality standards[39]—the
grading by motoring associations and local tourist authorities of hotels
furnishes a well-known example.[40] In the large majority of cases, however,
the costs of reaching agreement on appropriate criteria and applying them
to a large range of heterogeneous products would be enormous. In
relation to most types of services, the difficulties are compounded by

the fact that quality typically involves a multi-dimensional set of attributes and often requires the supplier to adapt to the specific needs of the purchaser.

An alternative, if also inferior, solution is available if suppliers submit their products or services to SRAs for some form of accreditation or certification.[41] For the reasons given in the last paragraph, the conditions for obtaining such accreditation or certification are likely to involve a single threshold quality standard. Nevertheless, if there is genuine competition in the relevant market, in the sense notably that supply is not limited to those who obtain a single SRA's mark of approval, then the system can provide information signals to consumers on different quality standards.

At its simplest, this may generate a choice between an uncertified product and one certified under a single self-regulatory regime, such as the system of 'Kitemarks' issued by the British Standards Institution.[42] But suppliers who aim at higher quality standards, and have difficulty in communicating that fact to consumers, will have an incentive to establish a rival certification system. Competing self-regulatory regimes may thus emerge.

An instructive analogy to this notion of competitive self-regulation can be located in European Community Law. Divergent national mandatory standards can, of course, constitute barriers to freedom of trade between Member States. The original, ambitious aim of solving this problem by harmonized standards has, to a significant extent, been abandoned.[43] The emphasis is now on limiting harmonization to 'essential safety requirements (or other requirements in the general interest)',[44] what in terms of our analysis may be deemed necessary to control externalities. To meet these requirements, Member States can continue to use and develop their own sets of national standards and it is to be presumed that such standards satisfy the requirements and thus should be the subject of mutual recognition.[45] The corollary is that, for the purposes of intra-Union trade, suppliers can select the national regulatory regime with which they wish to comply. Correspondingly, provided that they are informed as to the relevant national compliance certificate, consumers can choose between the different quality standards imposed by the national systems in accordance with their own preferences.[46] In short, there is competition between national regulatory regimes which should induce standard-setters to meet those preferences.[47]

Within a single legal system, the generation of competitive self-regulation may be difficult where existing SRAs occupy a monopoly position. But, as the recent history of the regulation of the legal professions in England and Wales reveals, it is not impossible.[48] Prior to the Courts and Legal Services Act 1990, the two principal legal professions (solicitors and barristers), each with its own SRA and regulatory regime, enjoyed monopoly rights over certain legal processes (e.g. conveyancing, probate, rights of audience). In principle, and in broad terms,[49] the 1990 Act abolished the monopolies and 'authorized bodies' representing other professions or practitioners may apply for the rights to be exercisable by their members. The prospect is, then, that the consumer who needs to be represented at court will, in due course, be able to choose between (say) a barrister, a solicitor and perhaps a newly-designated professional (a 'court-litigator'?) and competition between the relevant self-regulatory regimes will emerge.[50]

Hitherto, we have proceeded on the crucial assumption that consumers (or, more accurately, marginal consumers)[51] are able to identify the differential impact of competing regulatory regimes. Where, as will sometimes be the case, this assumption is not justified, price variance will prevail over quality variance in determining consumer choice and a 'race to the bottom' may ensue leaving predominantly low-cost/lax-standards combinations.[52] Supplier rents may disappear but they will be replaced by significant welfare losses—the inability of at least some consumers to choose higher-cost/stricter-standards combinations.

To remedy this problem, some public institutional intervention may be desirable. The Courts and Legal Services Act provides some ideas for how such intervention may be designed, in so far as it requires SRAs to submit their regulatory regime for approval by independent, public agencies which, thus, constitute a second tier of regulation.[53] Ideally, the public agency would be mandated to carry out a dual function.[54] On the one hand, it would promote competition between SRAs by searching for evidence of, and if necessary eliminating, cartelization. On the other hand, it would meet the 'race to the bottom' problem by itself laying down minimum quality standards which the SRA regimes must presumptively satisfy. As such, it would act as a proxy for insufficiently informed consumers.

(3) Ex-Ante Competition for Ex-Post Monopoly

The creation of an independent, public agency to exercise residual control over SRAs can be used to demonstrate that allowing an SRA monopoly power does not necessarily exclude the possibility of competitive self-regulation. Inspiration can here be drawn from the much-discussed regulation of natural monopolies.[55]

A natural monopoly arises in relation to products (notably utilities) for which it is economically preferable to have a single supplier, rather than some or many. Conventionally, the undesirable consequences of monopoly have been controlled by placing supply under public ownership or, particularly recently, allowing the monopoly rights to be exercised by private firms but subjecting them to price and quality regulation. Economists have for long recognized that competition for public franchises is a viable, and often superior, alternative to the latter.[56] Briefly put, the argument is that competitive tendering can be used as a substitute for conventional market competition: to enjoy the monopoly right ex post, the supplier must engage in competition ex ante to secure that right. Such competition should, it is contended, force firms to supply their goods or services on terms which are consistent with the public interest. Competing applicants can obviously be required to include their self-regulatory rules as part of the bid. The terms of the successful bid then become conditions of the franchise which, like any other contract, governs the on-going behaviour of the supplier.

What distinguishes this system from our previous examples is that, ex hypothesi, there is no competition during the currency of the franchise contract. Given that the latter is generally of a long-term duration, and that suppliers cannot predict with certainty all the contingencies which will affect supply (and demand) over the period, there is the problem that the suppliers will be under no pressure to adapt their self-regulatory standards to meet the contingencies once they have acquired the monopoly right. Against this, it may be argued that if suppliers fail to adapt their standards they may prejudice their chances of having the franchise renewed when it expires. But, of course, if they do not seek renewal, the appropriate incentive will disappear. It thus seems inevitable—and the institutional arrangements for public franchising endorse this[57]—that the franchise-awarding agency should retain some residual on-going regulatory powers.

VI Conclusions

In this paper I have explored two models of self-regulation, both of them markedly different from that which has been the object of so much criticism. The first of them envisages a regime based on Coasian bargaining and is appropriate only where there are no significant externalities or information asymmetries. The second, which has a more general applicability, crucially requires there to be competition between self-regulatory agencies. Each retains the advantages traditionally associated with self-regulation—notably lower information and enforcement costs, and greater flexibility—while dealing with the traditional objections of rent-creation and other forms of abuse. Under the first model, the latter phenomena are controlled by the need to secure agreement with representatives of the principally affected parties. Under the second, they are overcome by effectively enabling consumers to choose between competing self-regulatory regimes. Under both, there is a much-reduced, residual role for independent agencies.

I must not be taken as here arguing that these models of self-regulation are universally preferable to other forms of intervention (or indeed non-intervention). Where externalities are widespread, as in the case of pollution, a conventional centralized regulatory regime may reduce both information and enforcement costs. My principal concern has been to correct the stereotyped image of self-regulation and to suggest ways in which it may be combined with a limited degree of centralized control to provide a viable solution to problems of market failure.

Notes

1. R. Baggott, 'Regulatory Reform in Britain: The Changing Face of Self-Regulation' (1989) 67 Pub Admin 435, 438.
2. E.g. S. Breyer, Regulation and Its Reform (1982), ch. 1; A. Ogus, Regulation: Legal Form and Economic Theory (1994), ch. 3.
3. Cf. P. Cane, 'Self Regulation and Judicial Review' (1987) 6 Civil Justice Q 324, 328–33.
4. For an overview, see D. Mueller, Public Choice II (1989).
5. G. Stigler, 'The Theory of Economic Regulation' (1971) 2 Bell J Econ 3; R. A. Posner, 'Theories of Economic Regulation' (1974) 5 Bell J Econ 335; S. Peltzman, 'Towards a More General Theory of Regulation' (1976) 19 J Law & Econ 21, and, more generally, C. K. Rowley, R. D. Tollinson and G. Tullock (eds), The Political Economy of Rent-Seeking (1988).
6. J. Kay, 'The Forms of Regulation', in A. Seldon (ed), Financial Regulation—or Over-Regulation (1988), 34.
7. P. C. Schmitter, 'Neo-Corporatism and the State', in W. Grant (ed), The Political Economy of Corporatism (1985), 32 62; N. Lewis, 'Corporatism and Accountability: The Democratic Dilemma', in C. Crouch and R. Dore (eds), Corporatism and Accountability: Organized Interests in British Public Life (1990), ch 3.
8. A. C. Page, 'Self-Regulation: The Constitutional Dimension' (1986) 49 Mod LR 141, 163.
9. Cane, above, n 3, 325–6; and see R v Panel on Take-overs and Mergers, ex parte Datafin plc [1987] QB 815, 838, per Sir John Donaldson MR.

10. I. Harden and N. Lewis, *The Noble Lie: The British Constitution and the Rule of Law* (1986), ch 6.

11. R. Cranston, *Consumers and the Law* (2nd edn, 1984), 60–2; R. Abel, *The Legal Profession in England and Wales* (1988), 250–8; J. Fishman, 'A Comparison of Enforcement of Securities Law Violations in the UK and US' (1993) 14 *Co Law* 163.

12. E.g. A. Shaked and J. Sutton, 'The Self-Regulating Profession' (1981) 47 *Rev Econ Stud* 217.

13. See, esp: M. Friedman and S. Kuznets, *Income from Independent Professional Practice* (1945); A. Maurizi, 'Occupational Licensing and the Public Interest' (1974) 82 *J Pol Econ* 399; W. Gellhorn, 'The Abuse of Occupational Licensing' (1976) 44 *U Chi LR* 6; L. Shepard, 'Licensing Restrictions and the Cost of Dental Care' (1978) 21 *J Law & Econ* 187; W. D. White, 'Dynamic Elements of Regulation: The Case of Occupational Licensure' (1979) 1 *Res Law & Econ* 15; J. K. Smith, 'Production of Licensing Legislation: An Economic Analysis of Interstate Differences' (1982) 11 *J Legal Stud* 117; R. Van den Bergh and M. Faure, 'Self-Regulation of the Professions in Belgium' (1991) 11 *Int Rev Law & Econ* 165; M. Faure *et al.*, *Regulation of the Professions* (1993).

14. S. Domberger and A. Sherr, 'The Impact of Competition on Pricing and Quality of Legal Services' (1989) 9 *Int Rev Law & Econ* 41; Van den Bergh and Faure, above, n 13, 174–6.

15. H. Gravelle, 'Economic Analysis of Health Service Professions: A Survey' (1985) 20 *Soc Sci Med* 1049, 1052; H.-M. Trautwein and A. Rönnau, 'Self-Regulation of the Medical Profession in Germany: A Survey' in Faure *et al.*, above, n 13, 289–99.

16. Page, above, n 8, 144–8; Cane, above, n 3, 324–8.

17. Cf. Baggott, above, n 1, 436–8. For more extensive discussion, see: E. Bardach and R. A. Kagan, *Going by the Book: The Problem of Regulatory Unreasonableness* (1982), ch. 8; R. E. Cheit, *Setting Standards: Regulation in the Public and Private Sectors* (1990).

18. See above, n 8, 144.

19. Cf. Health and Safety at Work etc Act 1974, s 17.

20. R. H. Coase, 'The Problem of Social Cost' (1960) 3 *J Law & Econ* 1.

21. W. Y. Oi, 'On the Economics of Industrial Safety' (1974) 38 *Law & Contemp Prob* 669.

22. See, to similar effect, Bardach and Kagan, above, n 17, and J. Braithwaite, 'Enforced Self-Regulation: A New Strategy for Corporate Crime Control' (1982) 80 *Mich LR* 1466.

23. O. MacDonagh, 'The Nineteenth-Century Revolution in Government: A Reappraisal' (1958) 1 *Historical J* 52.

24. Report of the Committee on Safety and Health and Safety at Work (Cmnd 5034), esp para 29.

25. Ibid, paras 28–9, 138.

26. R. Baldwin, 'Health and Safety at Work: Consensus and Self-Regulation', in R. Baldwin and C. McCrudden, *Regulation and Public Law* (1987), ch 7.

27. Notably, 'the provision and maintenance of plant and systems of work that are, so far as is reasonably practicable, safe and without risks to health': Health and Safety at Work etc Act (hereafter HSWA) 1974, s 2(2)(a).

28. HSWA 1974, s 2(6)–(7). See, further, The Safety Representatives and Safety Committee Regulations, SI 1977/500.

29. HSWA 1974, s 2(3) and the Employers' Health and Safety Policy Statements (Exception) Regulations, SI 1975/1584.

30. Safety Representatives and Safety Committees Regulations, SI 1977/500, Reg 7(2), and, more generally, HSWA 1974, s 2(2)(c).

31. Baldwin, above, n 26, 148–52.

32. See the Control of Substances Hazardous to Health Regulations, SI 1988/1657.

33. Baldwin, above, n 26, 153.

34. H. Genn, *Great Expectations: the Robens Legacy and Employer Self-Regulation* (1987, unpublished); id, 'Business Responses to the Regulation of Health and Safety in England' (1993) 15 *Law & Pol* 219; R. Baldwin, 'Why Rules Don't Work' (1990) 53 *Mod LR* 321.

35. Cf. J. Kay and J. Vickers, 'Regulatory Reform: An Appraisal', in G. Majone, *Deregulation or Re-regulation: Regulatory Reform in Europe and the United States* (1990), 239–41.

36. Ibid, 239; Bardach and Kagan, above, n 17, 219 23.

37. The problem is partly alleviated by suppliers over time accumulating the consumers' trust in their reputation and brand name (see P. Nelson, 'Information and Consumer Behavior' (1970) 78 *J Pol Econ* 311) but this is of no value in one-off transactions.

38. G. A. Akerlof, 'The Market for Lemons: Qualitative Uncertainty and the Market Mechanism' (1970) 84 *Q J Econ* 488.

39. See generally on this and analogous devices, H. Beales, R. Craswell and S. Salop, 'The Efficient Regulation of Consumer Information' (1981) 24 *J Law & Econ* 491, 523–7.

40. The powers conferred by the Development of Tourism Act 1969, s 17, on the English Tourist Board to institute a compulsory system of registration and grading of hotels have not been exercised.

41. Bardach and Kagan, above, n 17, 220–1. For the widespread use of such systems in relation to consumer products, see: B. Harvey and D. Parry, *The Law of Consumer Protection and Fair Trading* (4th edn, 1992), 54–6; L. Krämer, *EEC Consumer Law* (1986), ch. 3. And for the certification of professional and other occupations, see: P. Moore, 'The Purpose of Licensing' (1961) 4 *J Law & Econ* 93, 104–6; B. Shimberg, *Occupational Licensing: A Public Perspective* (1982), 15–18.

42. Harvey and Parry, above, n 41, 55.

43. See generally G. Majone, 'Market Integration and Regulation: Europe After 1992' (1992) 43 *Metroeconomica* 131, 140–6.

44. Council Resolution of 7 May 1985 on a New Approach to Technical Harmon-isation and Standards (1985) OJ C/136/01, Annex II.

45. Mutual recognition may, in any event, be required by the principles adum-brated in the *Cassis de Dijon* case: *Rewe-Zentrale AG v Bundesmonopolverwaltung für Branntwein* [1979] 3 CMLR 494, on which see S. Weatherill and P. Beau-mont, *EC Law* (1993), ch 17.

46. A. McGee and S. Weatherill, 'The Evolution of the Single Market—Harmon-isation or Liberalisation' (1990) 53 *Mod LR* 578, 584–5.

47. Kay and Vickers, above, n 35, 244.

48. Cf. A. Ogus, 'Regulation of the Legal Profession in England and Wales' in Faure *et al.*, above, n 13, 307–29.

49. The incumbent professions retain certain advantages. For details, see Ogus, above, n 48, 310–11.

50. In December 1993, rights of audience in the higher courts were granted to solicitors in private practice: *Legal Action*, January 1994, 4. An Institute of Commercial Litigators, representing especially quantity surveyors, has been created and it has applied for a further extension of the rights: *Law Society Gazette*, 19 January 1994, 4.

51. Cf. A. Schwartz and L. Wilde, 'Intervening in Markets on the Basis of Imperfect Information: A Legal and Economic Analysis' (1979) 127 *U Penn LR* 630, 636.

52. R. Stewart, 'Pyramids of Sacrifice? Problems of Federalism in Mandating State Implementation of National Environmental Policy' (1977) 86 *Yale LR* 1196; McGee and Weatherill, above, n 46, loc cit; O. Brouwer, 'Free Movement of Foodstuffs and Quality Requirements; Has the Commission Got It Wrong?' (1988) 25 *Common Market LR* 237. For theoretical analysis, see Akerlof, above, n. 38.

53. Different committees determine the rights to provide different services: see ss 19, 29, 34. Another example is to be found in the Financial Services Act 1986 in which a general public agency (the Securities and Investments Board) overviews the regimes operated by five SRAs (the Securities Association, the Association of Future Brokers and Dealers, the Investment Management Regulatory Organisation, the Life Assurances and Unit Trust Regulatory Organisation and the Financial Intermediaries, Managers and Brokers Regulatory Associa-tion). However, it should be noted that though the jurisdiction of these SRAs overlap, there is not the degree of competition between them envisaged in the model. See, generally, on this, A. Page, 'Financial Services: The Self-Regulatory Alternative' in Baldwin and McCrudden, above, n 26, ch 13.

54. The decisions of 'second tier' agencies created by the Courts and Legal Services Act 1990 are subject to a general statutory objective (s 17 (1)), the first limb of which—'the development of legal services ... by making provision for new or better ways of providing such services and a wider choice of persons providing them'—incorporates the competition function, and the second limb

of which—'while maintaining the proper and efficient administration of just-ice'—by implication incorporates the minimum standards function.

55. See, generally: C. Foster, *Privatization, Public Ownership and the Regulation of Natural Monopoly* (1992); Ogus, above, n 2, chs. 13–15.

56. The theory can be traced back to E. Chadwick, 'Research of different principles of legislation and administration in Europe of competition for the field as compared with competition within the field of service' (1859) 22 *J Royal Stat Soc (Series A)* 381. The leading modern exponents are: H. Demsetz, 'Why Regulate Utilities?' (1968) 11 *J Law & Econ* 55; and R. Posner, 'The Appropriate Scope of Regulation in the Cable Television Industry' (1972) 3 *Bell J Econ* 98. See also S. Domberger, 'Economic Regulation Through Franchise Contracts', in J. Kay, C. Mayer, D. Thompson, *Privatisation and Regulation: The UK Experience* (1986), ch. 14.

57. See, e.g., in relation to the broadcasting franchising systems, Broadcasting Act 1990, s 2, and T. Gibbons, *Regulating the Media* (1991), 142–9.

Juridification: Concepts, Aspects, Limits, Solutions

G. TEUBNER

I. Introduction

Juridification is an ugly word—as ugly as the reality which it describes. The old formula used to describe the excess of laws, *fiat justitia, pereat mundus*, at least had the heroic quality of a search for justice at all costs. Today we no longer fear that the proliferation of laws will bring about the end of the world but we do fear 'legal pollution' (Ehrlich, 1976). The bureaucratic sound and aura of the word juridification indicate what kind of pollution is primarily meant: the bureaucratization of the world (Jacoby, 1969; Bosetzky, 1978: 52). To put it in the language of sociology: law, when used as a control medium of the welfare state, has at its disposal modes of functioning, criteria of rationality and forms of organization which are not appropriate to the 'life-world' structures of the regulated social areas and which therefore either fail to achieve the desired results or do so at the cost of destroying these structures. The ambivalence of juridification, the ambivalence of a guarantee of freedom that is at the same time a deprivation of freedom, is made clear in the telling phrase 'the colonialization of the life-world', which was coined by Habermas. Social modernization at the expense of subjection to the logic of the system and the destruction of intact social structures is the essence of this idea (Habermas, 1981: 522; 1985: 203).

Expressed in this extreme, dramatic form, juridification describes a reality which is not merely a problem of jurists, nor a national phenomenon. *Verrechtlichung* does not only spring from the well-known Teutonic tendency towards overregulation, so the discussion of the problem is not confined to German jurisprudence. Although national divergences exist (see Daintith, 1987) the phenomenon is universal, and the debate international and interdisciplinary. In the United States in particular a lively debate is going on about the 'legal explosion', the 'regulatory crisis' and 'delegalization'—a debate in which not only lawyers and jurists but sociologists and economists are particularly involved.[1] If one attempts—and this is the aim of this introductory essay—to bring together some of the different strands in this discussion, the results may be instructive for all who participate in the debate. National peculiarities will then be able to be seen in the light of their universal elements. Sociological generalizations can be corrected when viewed from within the laws if they are set against specific legal material. On the other hand a dynamization of the strictly juristic perspective could be hoped for if extralegal modes of interpretation are actually taken up and not simply dismissed. However, one must remain sceptical about the possibility that such learning processes will actually lead to perspectives for solutions. The problem of 'juridification' is too abstractly formulated for this and as such is perhaps even insoluble. What *can* be achieved is tentative answers to three questions: How and to what extent is the expansion of law into the social environment contingent and reversible or necessary and irreversible, and how is it connected to wider societal developments? How and where are the limits of legal growth becoming apparent? And can guidelines for a kind of legal growth which is less damaging to the social environment be given? For each of these complexes of questions a proposition can be elaborated. The first complex concerns the *definition of the problem* of juridification. In the current debate, the term has come to designate so many diverse phenomena that it must be carefully delimited before any sensible pronouncements can be made about it at all. It is scarcely illuminating to subsume all tendencies towards proliferation of law or all legal evolution under the heading 'juridification'. In such a case one would have to be content with a mere stock-taking of contradictory and heterogeneous developments under the relatively arbitrary heading 'Developments in Law in the World of Industry, Work and Social Solidarity'. The phenomenon of juridification becomes a subject which is analyzable, interpretable and strategically appropriate only when—and this is the first proposition—it is identified with the type of modern *'regulatory law'* in which law, in a peculiar fashion, seems to be both politicized and socialized. This type of law must then be related to Max Weber's concept of *'materialization of formal law'*. This will provide an analytical framework in which both naive delegalization recommendations of the 'alternatives to law' movement and politically motivated 'de-regulation' strategies can be adequately and critically assessed. Here the changes which law itself, in its function, legitimacy and structure, has undergone in the process of juridification also become clear.

The second complex of questions relates to limits to the growth of regulatory law. Is it possible to discern fundamental limits of juridification in so far as certain juridification processes prove inadequate in the face of regulated social structures and/or constitute an excessive strain on the internal capacities of law? The argument I would like to propose here is that this is not merely a problem of the implementation of law, nor of the use of state power, nor merely of the efficiency of law in terms of the appropriateness of means to ends, but it is a problem of the *'structural coupling'* of law with politics on the one hand and with the regulated social fields on the other. Once the limits of this structural coupling have been overstepped, law is caught up in an inevitable situation which I propose to examine more closely under the heading *'regulatory trilemma'*.

If, thus, the 'regulatory crisis' is adequately interpreted, the third question that arises is how to assess the various proposed therapies and alternative strategies. Are there alternatives to juridification which at the same time do justice to the social guidance requirements of politics, the special properties of the respective social areas and the inner capacities of law? The proposition I would like to put forward here is that neither the various suggestions on improvements in the implementation of law nor the numerous recommendations on delegalization take adequate account of the problem of structural coupling. Intellectual attention and institutional energies should be concentrated on a series of conceptions which go beyond materialization and reformalization and amount to more abstract, more indirect control by law. What these conceptions have in common is that they look for models of 'socialization of law'. Among the relevant terms here are: 'semi-autonomous social fields' (Moore, 1973: 719), 'negotiated regulation' (Harter, 1982: 1), 'officially sponsored indigenous law' (Galanter, 1980: 26), 'proceduralisation of law' (Wiethölter, 1982a: 38, 1982b: 7; 1985), 'ecological law' (Ladeur, 1984), 'reflexive law' (Teubner, 1983: 239ff., 1985: 299ff., 1986b), and 'relationing programmes' (Willke, 1983a: 62); in short: *legal control of self-regulation* (Teubner, 1983: 239ff.). This term refers to different legal programs which, sometimes more, sometimes less explicitly, define structural coupling as 'legal self-restraint' and which, therefore, are appropriate as a means of reducing legal pollution.

2. Concepts

A precise use of terms and definitions is necessary, especially in the case of juridification, not just for the sake of terminological clarity but, as already indicated, to create a working framework in which to examine the complex phenomenon of juridification. Furthermore, when we are using a term as polemical as juridification it becomes clear that the term not only enables us to make definitions but also provides options. Options are empirical analyses of the historical situation on the basis of which evaluative assessments are made, strategies chosen and decisions taken (Luhmann, 1981: 118; Rottleuthner, 1985: 9ff.). Notions of juridification always contain a theory of the conditions in which it developed, an evaluation of its consequences and a strategy for dealing with it. A clarification of the term would therefore have to lay bare these three elements in the different ways in which the term is used. At the same time it would have to state the reasons why one of the options is finally chosen.

2.1 Legal Explosion

In legal discussion juridification is described primarily as a growth phenomenon.[2] Fear-laden terms such as 'flood of norms' or 'legal explosion' (Barton, 1975: 567) underline the disquieting effect which the rapid expansion of law has had on the legal profession and the general public alike. Especially in those areas of the law which cover the world of industry, labor and social solidarity—labor law, company law, antitrust law and social security law—the enormous quantitative growth of norms and standards is noted and criticized. From a certain threshold onwards, those involved are overtaxed. The enforcement of law is damaged, credibility suffers and a high level of dogmatic mastering of legal material becomes impossible (Heldrich, 1981: 814). In all four areas of law it can be observed from a comparative perspective that consistency control of norm and decision making material as well as the construction of conceptual structures—the two classical tasks of legal doctrine—is giving way to a new mode of thinking—'case-law-positivism' as Zoellner polemically terms it. This style of legal thinking is content to analyse developments in judicial decisions and to produce ad-hoc criticism of their 'policies'. As an observer from outside has noted: 'The disastrous state of modern positive law lies in the incoherence of large numbers of norms which are produced procedurally in response to a particular situation and are then lumped together in disordered heaps. No adequate means of coping with this material intellectually has been developed' (Luhmann, 1972: 331; cf. also Hegenbarth, 1983: 67).

Of course with a term like juridification, if it is geared towards a crisis of growth, the therapy is implicitly contained in the term itself. Growth itself must be combatted. The prescription reads as follows: rationalize legislation, reduce the number of regulations, thin out the stock of laws—in short, simplify the law.[3] However, scepticism based on historical experience with such appeals is not unjustified, and perhaps makes one more receptive to the cynical proposal to try the exact opposite remedy: 'growth-boosting hormone injections'. The experiment has already been tried with weeds: acceleration of growth beyond an optimum level is a sure means of extermination (Luhmann, 1981: 73).

Yet it still seems too narrow an approach to concentrate on the expansion of legal material, on the extension and intensification of law. The current criticism of juridification processes under the general heading 'flood of norms' scarcely seems an appropriate starting point because it limits the discussion in several respects. The term 'flood of norms' merely stresses the quantitative aspect of the increase in legal material—a problem which could certainly be combatted by technical improvements in legislation. In fact, qualitative aspects are more important: what changes in the content of legal structures has the (alleged?) crisis of juridification brought about? The term 'flood of norms' is also historically unspecific—throughout the centuries complaints have been made about the proliferation of laws and their intricacy (Nörr, 1974). Juridification processes should in fact be analysed in terms of the specific conditions of the modern social state, 'the interventionist state'. This at the same time excludes the law-centered and lawyer-centered perspective of the 'flood of norms' school, which concentrates exclusively on the legal material as such. The problem to be addressed is broader in scope: the political and social appropriateness of juridification processes in various social areas (labor, market, company, and social security law). Finally, an attempt should be made to abstract from the national peculiarities of the flood of norms and, adopting a comparative perspective, to bring out the universal features of juridification processes and the problems which result from them.

2.2 Expropriation of Conflict

If one attempts to correct the myopia of the legal perspective by means of the optics of legal sociology juridification suddenly appears in a quite different light. The 'politics of informal justice' in the U.S. and its European equivalent, 'alternatives to law', come to the fore while problems of growth recede into the background (Abel, 1980: 27; Blankenburg *et al.*, 1980). Sociologists of law describe juridification as a process in which human conflicts are torn through formalization out of their living context and distorted by being subjected to legal processes. Juridification, as it were, is the expropriation of conflict. Christie (1976: 12) even uses the expression 'conflict as property'. This is certainly an extreme formulation, but it clearly indicates the direction of the analysis. Doubt is cast on whether law can fulfil what is generally regarded as its major function, the resolution of conflicts. Numerous socio-legal studies have pinpointed factors which constitute 'obstacles to the adequate conflict resolution through law: barriers to access, fear of going to court, the length and cost of proceedings as well as processual inequality of chances of success' (Hegenbarth, 1980: 48). In this view juridification does not solve conflicts but alienates them. It mutilates the social conflict, reducing it to a legal case and thereby excludes the possibility of an adequate future oriented, socially rewarding resolution.

If conflicts are thus expropriated by juridification, the slogan of the delegalization movement is: expropriation of the expropriators.[4] As 'alternatives to law', informal modes of dealing with conflicts are sought, modes which will take conflicts out of the hands of lawyers and give them back to the people. Certainly, the people will achieve a solution to the conflicts in the real social world, not only in the illusory world of legal concepts and procedures.

Institutional proposals and experiments (see Blankenburg, Gottwald, Strempel, 1982) range from reinforcement of the arbitration element in court proceedings[5] to the extension of out-of-court proceedings,[6] to the establishment of 'community courts' in big city neighbour-hoods (Danzig, 1973: 1). Comparative legal and anthropological studies of Kbelle palavers in Africa, of arbitration phenomena in Japan and of social courts under real socialism are the inspiration behind these 'alternatives to law'.

These ideas of 'communal law', as Galanter rightly terms it (Galanter, 1980), have been severely criticized in the socio-legal discussion. Abel provided the ideology-critical, Hegenbarth the conflict-theoretical and Luhmann the social-theoretical variants of this criticism (Abel, 1980, Hegenbarth, 1980; Luhmann, 1985). To put it briefly—a return to 'informal justice' means, under today's conditions, surrendering conflict to the existing power constellations. Secondly, 'alternatives to law' ignore crucial factors in dealing with conflict under modern conditions of role separation. Thirdly, they underestimate an indispensable function of law in functionally differentiated societies—which is to use the possibility of conflict in order to generalize congruent expectations throughout society. They may, of course, be able to formulate useful reform proposals which could certainly increase social potential for satisfactory conflict resolution, but they are scarcely appropriate as a general perspective for interpreting juridification and for developing alternatives to dejuridification. This is ultimately because the current discussion in legal sociology has confined itself to the classical tasks of law (conflict regulation) and has only marginally concerned itself with the really explosive aspects of modern juridification (social regulation). Sociologists of law have concentrated their attacks on the unsatisfactory consequences for a continuation of harmonious social relations when human conflicts are delivered up to the court system. But how relevant is this criticism of the judicial system in face of the far more disquieting tendencies of a politically instrumentalized law, which threatens profoundly to change entire social spheres through its regulatory interventions. In comparison the legal sociological formulation of the question seems somewhat harmless, and almost provincial.

2.3 Depoliticization

In view of these belittling definitions it is perhaps as well to look at the historical origins of the term. The word *Verrechtlichung* (juridification) was first employed as a polemic term in the debate on labor law in the Weimar Republic. Kirchheimer used it to criticize the legal formalization of labor relations, which neutralized genuine political class conflicts (Kirchheimer, 1933: 79). According to Fraenkel, juridification of labor relations means to 'petrify' the political dynamics of the working class movement (Fraenkel, 1932: 255). Critical labor lawyers in West Germany have recently renewed this line of argument. The ambivalence of juridification—the guarantee and the simultaneous deprivation of freedom—is clearly worked out with examples from industrial relations law, codetermination, strikes and lockouts. On the one hand labor law protects and guarantees certain interests of employees and ensures that labor unions have scope for action. Yet on the other, the repressive character of juridification tends to depoliticize social conflicts by drastically limiting the labor unions' possibilities of militant action (Hoffmann, 1968: 92; Däubler, 1976: 29; von Beyme, 1977: 198; Erd, 1978; Voigt, 1980: 170). This kind of ambivalent juridification and its acceptance by labor unions is explained in terms of the interaction of the interests of specific trade union groups with state control interests: juridification reinforces 'cooperative' trade union policies, just as it is reinforced by them. This interaction of course occurs at the expense of 'conflictive' trade union policy (Erd, 1978: 19).

Here too, the counter-strategy is implied. Only when labor union policy changed to 'conflictive' strategies and stressed autonomous representation of interests could juridification processes be reversed and labor conflicts repoliticized (Erd, 1978: 26, 251; Rosenbaum, 1982: 392). In fact this interpretation of the term has clear advantages over the lawyer-centred and judiciary-critical formulation of juridification. It takes account of the effects of the proliferation of laws on regulatory areas, stresses qualitative as well as quantitative aspects of change brought about by law, provides differentiated analyses of the ambivalence of the phenomenon and, with its concept of depoliticization, has certainly pinpointed one of the most important consequences of juridification processes.

Nonetheless, it is in several respects an over-simplification. Simitis has pointed out the, as it were, 'voluntaristic' nature of this concept of juridification. The key role of the 'conflictive/cooperative' alternative implies that the dynamics of juridification are primarily a strategy problem of the labor unions: the concept is restricted to the politics of organised labor. Yet it is also necessary to point out a national limitation in this concept. Because tendencies of 'cooperative' trade union policy are highly marked, especially in Germany, it is tempting to regard 'juridification' as a 'German speciality' (Unterseher, 1972: 190; v. Beyme, 1977: 198). This is a deficit in comparative legal terms, and it shows that the theoretical connection between 'cooperative trade union policy' and juridification is far more relative than it appeared to be. The limitations of this perspective lead finally to a theoretical deficit. The attempt to explain juridification in terms of intra-union preconditions and the collusion between decision-making groups in trade unions with legislation and judiciary (Erd, 1978: 19; Moritz, 1980: 171) can perhaps be accepted as a particular explanation of interests and influences operating in this area, but cannot be regarded as a class theoretical analysis, let alone as a component in a social theory of juridification phenomena.[7] This concept of juridification hardly seems inappropriate, not so much because it is normatively limited to particular social interests but because it is limited to the labor union perspective and abstains from socio-structural explanations.

2.4 Materialization

We have examined and found wanting the juristic view of juridification as a 'flood of norms', the concept of conflict expropriation propounded by sociologists of law and the political science perspective which sees juridification as restricting the room for manoeuvre of social movements and interest groups. So to arrive at an adequate formulation of this problem we will have to go beyond those disciplines and draw on the great theories of legal evolution in the tradition of Marx, Maine, Durkheim and Max Weber, as continued by Parsons, Unger, Nonet and Selznick in the U.S. and by Habermas and Luhmann in Europe.[8] Of course we cannot even begin here to disentangle the complexities of legal evolution. On the contrary, we will merely attempt to take up a few strands from the tangle of theory and to combine them in such a way as to further our comprehension of juridification. And here the distinction introduced by Max Weber between 'formal and material qualities of modern law' will play a crucial role (Weber, 1978: 644ff.).

Firstly, the wider historical context of juridification becomes clear, the context of the development of the modern welfare state. Habermas' analysis (1981: 522; 1985: 203) in particular shows how in the modern era law has responded to global social developments with various thrusts of juridification which in turn have influenced the developments to which they responded. Habermas distinguishes 'in a rough fashion' between four epoch-making thrusts of juridification. The first thrust led to the bourgeois state, which in West Europe developed in the form of absolutism. Law reacted to the differentiation of the two great subsystems—economy and politics—and safeguarded their new autonomy in legal form. Here the modern formal system of civil law originated and formed the common starting point for the later differentiation between 'materialized' areas of civil law such as labor law, antitrust law, company law and social security law. The classical system of civil law was 'tailored to strategically acting legal persons who enter into contracts with one another... This legal order bears the features of positivity, generality and formality, and is constructed on the basis of the modern concept of statutory law as well as the concept of the legal person, as one who can enter into contracts, acquire, dispose and bequeath property. The legal order has to guarantee the liberty and property of the private person, the certainty of the law (*Rechtssicherheit*) and the formal equality of all legal subjects before the law, and thereby the calculability of all legal-normed action' (Habermas, 1985: 205). The three thrusts of juridification which followed, of which the last is of particular interest for us, are described by Habermas as historical counter-movements to the differentiation of the economic and political system, more precisely as their legal, democratic and social constitutionalization. In Habermas's words this is to be understood as follows: 'a lifeworld which was at first placed at the disposal of the market and absolutist rule little by little makes good its claims' (Habermas, 1985: 206). In the first thrust of legal constitutionalization the system of civil law was so coordinated with the exercise of power that the principle of the legality of administration could be interpreted in terms of the 'rule of law'. In a further thrust the democratization of the constitutionalized power of the state was introduced by law. Universal and equal franchise and freedom of organization for political associations and parties legalized the political process. The last thrust of juridification, that which occurred in the social state, is of crucial importance to our subject. There, the juridification of the modern world of industry and labor, the line of freedom-guaranteeing juridification was continued. Juridification in the social state means 'constitutionalization' of the economic system. The social state controls the economic system in a similar fashion to that in which the two previous thrusts of juridification controlled the political system (Habermas, 1985: 208). The collective bargaining system, norms of employee protection, the complicated network of social security protection, the intensification of company constitutions as well as antitrust law interventions in the market are all part of this latest epoch-making thrust of juridification in which the intervening social state uses law as a means of control to constitutionalize the economy.

If this analysis is basically correct then two important conclusions may be drawn. First, our analysis of the problem of juridification should concentrate on the thrust of juridification in the social state.[9] Juridification cannot be usefully analysed as a universal historical phenomenon. Rather the task must be to analyse a specific form of juridification, which can only be understood in its proper historical context. The most pressing problem at the moment is how to cope with the typical thrust of juridification which occurs in the welfare state, one in which law is used as a control medium for state intervention and compensation. The problem becomes one of the 'legitimacy and desirability of state intervention'. In this view, concepts of juridification discussed above appear either too abstract in their approach or as only partial aspects of a wider problem. The proliferation of law, for example, is not a phenomenon which can be analysed or even combatted as such but one which can only be understood in the context of social guidance in the social state. The 'flood of norms' is not primarily a problem for law as such, but one for the interventionist state. Conflict expropriation by law does not come within the framework of analysis chosen here in so far as classical justice is concerned, but it becomes relevant again in so far as these are triggered by typical forms of welfare state intervention. Finally, the restriction of autonomous social groups is reduced to the status of one of several problems of juridification in the welfare state in which the ambivalence of the guarantee of freedom and the deprivation of freedom is expressed.

The second conclusion to be drawn is that—despite political formulae such as deregulation—delegalization cannot be seriously considered as a counter-strategy. If it is correct that juridification in the welfare state is part of an epoch-making thrust of development then it cannot be reversed by mere political decision, let alone by an isolated decision about more law or less law. The 'flood of laws' cannot be stemmed by dykes and dams; at best it can be channelled. Nor can juridification processes in industrial relations be reversed, and certainly not by a shift of trade union policy from cooperative to conflictive strategies. And in the larger perspective of development any delegalization of conflicts is likely to be merely marginal. The already completed functional differentiation of societies with welfare state structures does not permit 'alternatives to law'; at best it permits alternatives within law.

Radical demands for delegalization—which suggest that the juridification process as such could be reversed—are simply illusory. Indeed the juridification versus delegalization alternative should be abandoned completely and replaced by a formulation of the problem which recognizes the juridification thrust within welfare states as a historical fact but also resolutely confronts its dysfunctional consequences. Certainly the problematic results of juridification in welfare states are far clearer to us today than they were when the process began. But this should not blind us to the freedom-guaranteeing function of juridification processes in the intervention state (Voigt, 1980: 15; Habermas, 1981: 530, 1985: 208; Heldrich, 1981: 824). Even from a normative perspective juridification in welfare states should be accepted as such and reforming attention should be directed to compensating for negative side-effects, although of course every compensation inevitably brings dysfunctional results in its train which in turn require correction, and so on and so on.

3. Aspects

In order to examine more closely how law transforms itself in the thrust of juridification in welfare states, it is helpful to take up Max Weber's famous distinction (1978: 653ff.) between formal and material legal rationality. It makes clear what effects are produced when the rule-of-law orientation of classical law is overlaid by a welfare state orientation (1978: 868ff.).

More than half a century ago, Max Weber, whose main sociological interest was the tension between material and formal rationality in the most diverse areas of life, described modern European law, and to a lesser extent Anglo-American law, as formal-rational. The formalization of law is part of the great rationalization process of the modern era analysed by Weber, which developed parallel to the differentiation of economics, politics and science as spheres of action. The legal system is one of formal rationality to the extent that professionally trained lawyers orientate themselves by universal norms, or more concretely, to the extent that in legal procedures, 'in both substantive and procedural matters, only unambiguous general characteristics of the facts of the case are taken into account' (Weber, 1978: 656). In modern legal formalism a conceptually 'increasingly logical sublimation and deductive rigor of law' is paralleled by a procedural element, 'an increasingly rational technique in procedure' (Weber, 1978: 882). Weber analyzed certain processes of legal development in which powerful social interests so influenced the law as to transform its orientation from the primarily material ethical, to the formal conceptually abstract and procedurally rationalized orientation.

Yet at the same time Max Weber also emphasized certain anti-formal elements in modern legal development. In the law of contract for example such rematerialization manifested itself in 'an increasing particularization of law' and an increasing legislative and judicial control of the content of contracts. For Weber this meant a threat to formal rationality by norms of different quality: 'the norms to which substantive rationality accords predominance include ethical imperatives, utilitarian and other expediential rules, and political maxims, all of which diverge from the formalism of the "external characteristics" variety as well as from that which uses logical abstraction.' According to Weber, the inner quality of highly developed legal culture would be damaged; 'the juristic precision of judicial opinions will be seriously impaired if sociological, economic, or ethical argument were to take the place of legal concepts' (1978: 894).

Weber traced this recent particularization of law to various causes. At force here were the 'social demands of democracy' (1978: 886) for interventions of the welfare state. Material demands are made on law by interest groups, especially labor unions. Other interests in industry also bring about different materializations of formal law. And finally lawyers themselves bring about change 'by new demands for a "social law" to be based upon such emotionally colored ethical postulates as "justice" or "human dignity"' (Weber, 1978: 886).

However compared with the extremely powerful processes of the formal rationality of law, Max Weber regarded these material tendencies as all in all only marginal. In modern theories of development these tendencies are assessed very differently. 'Materialization of formal law' today appears as the dominant development trend and evolutionary approaches are brought into play to explain it.[10] The trend towards juridification in welfare states, which expresses itself in the materialization of formal law characterizes large numbers of legal control interventions in areas classically regarded as self-regulating (Hart, 1983: 10) in the world of industry and labor. The main reasons for intervention—and this applies to labor law as well as to company, anti-trust and social security law—are the appearance of phenomena of economic power and/or a societal need for social protection. Juridification in welfare states can be further defined in terms of three processes of change with regard to formal law: change in the function of law, in its legitimation and in its norm structure.[11]

3.1 Function

Compared with classical formal law, materialized law in the industrial world has taken on a new social function. It is no longer tailored only to the normative requirements of conflict resolution but to the political intervention requirements of the modern welfare state. It can be instrumentalized for the purposes of the political system which now takes on responsibility for social processes—and this means the definition of goals, the choice of normative means, the ordering of concrete behavioral programs and the implementation of norms. Instrumentalization is most evident in social security law, in the two dimensions for which Zacher uses the terms externalization and internalization. Here the internalized changes, in which classical formal law is itself transformed for social purposes, are highly instructive. The same applies to individual and to collective labor law, both of which for reasons of social protection were brought into the sphere of political responsibility. Both company law and antitrust law must be seen in more relative terms. Cartel law of course, is also conceived as a state institution to ensure that genuine competition is maintained. The 'visible hand' of the state intervenes in the operations of the market to break up existent market power, to limit market power and to exclude the abuse of market power. But its complete political instrumentalization beyond its function of guaranteeing competition is problematic and in any case controversial. Interventionist instrumentalization seems not very clearly marked in the field of company law either; however, in certain areas such as the legal definition of corporate social responsibility, the norms on publicity and in particular the rules of codetermination and company constitution, the 'activist state' intervenes massively in structures of company law. Perhaps the US-American development of corporation law following four stages of legal evolution—(1) facilitative rules; (2) fiduciary duties; (3) 'soundness' rules; (4) 'consumer protection' (see Clark, 1981)—provides the clearest example of the increasing role of massive public intervention in capitalist activities.

3.2 Legitimation

Materialized law at the same time derives a new inner legitimation from this new function. Whereas formal law clearly viewed itself to be confined to the delimitation of abstract spheres for private-autonomous action[12] material law legitimates itself by the social results it achieves by regulation. 'La justice légaliste-libérale' is replaced by 'la justice normative-technocratique' (Ost, 1984: 46). The legitimation shifts from autonomy to regulation. Even in the still more formally oriented areas of company and antitrust law, the rhetorics of direct regulation are breaking through. In company law an if anything obfuscating 'ethicization' can be observed which basically amounts to regulations for the protection of shareholders and minorities (Wiedemann, 1980b: 147). The regulatory intention is far clearer in the case of regulations on codetermination on the supervisory boards. In antitrust law, legitimation is sought in the area of indirect rather than direct control of economic behavior. Yet here too regulations on market behavior and the abuse of market power are clearly phenomena of result oriented direct control.

3.3 Structure

This transformation of function and legitimation triggered by juridification processes in social states clearly also affects the norm structure and inner order of the law itself. The effects range from a weakening of the idea of generality to changes in methods of interpretation (see Wiethölter, 1985). In labor law, the tendency towards particularization was observable at an early stage. Classical formal law, in using the concept of the legal person, abstracted from socially relevant features and was therefore accused of covering up real power positions or indeed helping to force them through by this means. In contrast modern labor law deliberately extended the class of legally relevant features through its definitions of the employer and employee (Rottleuthner, 1985). Labor law thus made formal law material in the sense that it internalized features that were previously extralegal. This transposition of law from general norms to specific positional roles is probably one of the most significant changes in the course of modern juridification (Rehbinder, 1967: 197; Teubner, 1980: 50; Koendgen, 1981: 192). Here, too, labor and social security law are centrally affected, while the changes in company law and antitrust law are less striking. The counterpart to particularization in antitrust law is the process of gearing to specific market structures in which the same behavior may be judged differently depending on the market situation. In company law too a growth in positionally specific thinking has been noted under the heading of 'role and law' (Lutter, 1982: 565).

A further structural feature of juridification in social states is the unstoppable rise of 'purpose in law'. It is no accident that the teleological method was not included in Savigny's canon of methods: yet its domination over other methods is more or less generally recognized today.[13] Indeed the term 'legal policies' goes even further and legitimates in Continental law too the policy thinking which is so popular in the U.S. (Steindorff, 1973: 217; 1979). Cartel law and company law may be considered two classical areas of the conflict between two modes of legal thinking. In both areas, policy oriented legal thinking is penetrating into areas of classical formal law and leading to difficult problems, such as the relation between codetermination law and traditional company law in Germany (Wiedemann, 1980a: 607; Kübler, 1981: 367) and the conflict between the civil law and the antitrust law concept of contract.

As a general rule it can be said that the predominant rule orientation is being increasingly overlaid by an instrumental orientation. According to Selznick, 'sovereignty of purpose' is the main feature of a responsive law which can only develop in the context of the social state (Nonet and Selznick, 1978: 78). Instead of strictly applying precisely defined legal norms (conditional programs), legal experts now tend to administer ill-defined standards and vague general clauses (purpose programs). This is causing a dramatic shift in the mode of legal thinking, a shift which can be adequately defined by the term 'result orientation'. However, the consequences of this shift for legal doctrine are far from being adequately worked out, let alone solved (Luhmann, 1974, 1987; Teubner, 1975: 179; Unger 1976: 193ff.; Rottleuthner, 1979: 97; Lübbe-Wolff, 1981).

Result orientation leads us to a final consequence of juridification which has been noted with interest and disquiet in recent years. Social science thinking in the widest sense has been observed to exert increasing influence on the formation of legal concepts and on practical decision-making in the courts. This is especially true for antitrust law.[14] This applies not only to academic discussion but also deeply affects the decision-making practices of the regulatory agencies and the courts. Legal argumentation is heavily subsidized by the language of economics, whether the issue is the major ideological question of the function of competition (protection of freedom or economic results) (Reich, 1977: 29; Möschel, 1983: § 3), the issue of whether antitrust law can be instrumentalized for different economic ends, or the solution of technical problems relating to 'as-if' competition in § 22 German Antitrust Statute (Klauss, 1975) and to the definition of market power. Indeed this could scarcely be otherwise, for how could antitrust law credibly demonstrate that it was seeking the maintenance or restoration of competition over and above the concrete case at hand if it disregarded available social science knowledge on the regulatory control of markets?

The situation is the same in the area of company law. In Germany, the great legal-political debates on corporate governance (*Unternehmensverfassung*) in the context of the larger political and economic constitution (*Wirtschaftsverfassung*) simply could not be conducted without the aid of social sciences. Whether explicit borrowings are made from organization theory as with terms such as 'the company as organization',[15] whether efficiency prognoses are made disguised as constitutional law (Badura *et al.* 1977: 123; Kübler *et al.*, 1978: 145, 197), or whether company law, in apparently strict dogmatic style, is rethought in terms of basic concepts such as 'organization' and 'group' (Flume 1977: §§ 1, 4, 7)—theories of the interrelation between organization and market, politics and law, will always be needed. In the U.S., the influence of social science thinking, especially of economic analysis of law, can hardly be over- estimated (see Buxbaum 1984a, 1984b, 1986 for a critique). The everywhere evident opening of legal practice and doctrine to ideas from economics, sociology and political science cannot simply be dismissed as a passing fashion of the unruly sixties and seventies. Of course yesterday critical theory, system theory and 'law and society' were the height of fashion, whereas today the trend is towards economic analysis of law, 'property rights' and 'public choice'.[16] Of course these are fashions, but the reasons for them lie deeper: the opening to the social sciences is closely connected with the phenomenon of juridification itself. For regulatory law regards itself as instrumental law, as a means of social guidance which aims to bring about certain social changes and therefore needs social knowledge.

In the self-image of classical formal law, on the other hand, particular effects were not regarded as significant. Classical formal law saw itself as having to provide only a formal framework within which social autonomy could develop, and no particular control effects were thereby intended. The tenacious survival of formal law can be explained in particular by the fact that it makes itself independent of particular effects on society and if it has any aim at all it is to bring about a state of universal freedom. The crisis of formal law cannot therefore be understood as a crisis of effect. In practice it has functioned splendidly according to its own conception of its identity. It is in terms of this internal model of formal law that Windscheid's confident dictum of the 'lawyer as such' who is 'not concerned with ethical, political or economic considerations' (Windscheid, 1904: 101) becomes plausible—a view that today appears arrogant or unworldly to us. As Max Weber showed, it was only by indirect means, through politics, which developed welfare state conceptions in response to the pressure of social problems and class movements, that formal law began to suffer from a crisis of identity. It was the conflict between political demands for compensation for the results of industrialization and the structures of classical formal law that triggered the crisis of formal law, to which law has responded with materialization tendencies. In contrast, materialized law as an instrument of political guidance regards itself as designed to produce social effects. If these effects are not achieved, this directly affects its legitimacy. Accordingly material law is forced to enlist the aid of implementation analyses. Social sciences therefore become directly relevant in that analyses of effects can shed light on the effectiveness of law. The extent of so-called sociologization of law cannot therefore be arbitrarily modified by lawyers according to intellectual fashion; on the contrary, it is connected with the transformations of law in the welfare state itself.

At this stage we may formulate a *first interim finding*: juridification does not merely mean proliferation of law; it signifies a process in which the interventionist social state produces a new type of law, regulatory law. Only when both elements—materialization *and* the intention of the social state—are taken together can we understand the precise nature of the contemporary phenomenon of juridification.[17] Regulatory law 'coercively specifies conduct in order to achieve particular substantive ends' (Stewart, 1986). Regulatory law, which is characterized by material rationality as opposed to formal rationality, may be defined in terms of the following aspects. In its function it is geared to the guidance requirements of the social state, in its legitimation the social results of its controlling and compensating regulations are predominant. In its structure it tends to be particularistic, purpose oriented and dependent on assistance from the social sciences. As part of a greater historical process juridification cannot be reversed by political decision. The only approach worthy of serious discussion is that which seeks to mitigate dysfunctional problems resulting from juridification.

4. Limits

4.1   Regulatory Trilemma

What then are the dysfunctional problems resulting from juridification?
With such an abstract formulation of the question we will have to concentrate on questions of principle—islands of safety where we can escape
drowning in the flood of norms. Above, we have already discussed important problems resulting from juridification under headings such as proliferation of law, conflict expropriation and depoliticization—the list could
be increased at will. In contrast to these partial aspects of the problem, the
fundamental question is this: are there any signs that regulatory law has
reached insurmountable limits of effectiveness? Has juridification today
already reached its 'limits of growth'?

In order to find our theoretical bearings, we will again draw on Max
Weber's concepts of formal and material rationality of law, but this time
we will examine them from a different angle. Weber (1978: 641ff.)
described two conflicting developmental tendencies. On the one hand
the legal system increases its 'formal' specialization, professionalization
and internal systematization; on the other hand it is exposed to increasing
'material' demands from social interests, to the welfare-state demands of
democracy etc. From the viewpoint of system theory this is to be refor-
mulated as a conflict between the social *function* of law, namely to produce
from conflicts social expectations in which it then specializes more and
more, and the regulatory *performance* which the social environment
demands from law.[18]

This indicates that the materialization of formal law should be reinterpreted as a process in which two conflicting trends are intensified
simultaneously. On the one hand the 'formalization' of law is intensified
in the sense that law partakes of the functional differentiation of society
and develops its autonomy to a point which sociologists today refer
to as autopoietic self-reference.[19] This concept cannot here be analysed
in all its ramifications; a rough explanation will have to suffice. The
official definition is: An autopoietic system of this kind in all its operations
always refers to itself and produces its elements from the relations
between its elements. In the field of law autopoietic self-reference
means that its validity is based solely on legal normativity and that
legal validity has definitively freed itself from all extralegal connections—
politics, morality, science—as well as from justifications in terms of
natural law. Law can therefore only reproduce itself intra-legally
(Luhmann, 1985).

On the other hand, 'materialization' of law increases with, and is indeed caused by, the increase in formalization. The more the legal system specializes in its function of creating expectations by conflict regulation, the more it develops and refines norms and procedures which can be used for future oriented behavior control. This can only be formulated in the following paradoxical terms: *law, by being posited as autonomous in its function—formality—becomes increasingly dependent on the demands for performance from its social environment—materiality*. And in today's conditions this means: autonomous, positive, highly formalized and professionalized law, when instrumentalized for purposes of political control, is exposed to specified demands of politics on the one hand and of regulated areas of life on the other.

This tension between increasing autonomy and increasing interdependence explains the necessity and the problem of modern juridification. The problem lies precisely in the 'contradiction' between increasing autonomy and simultaneously increasing dependence. When certain sectors of society such as economy, politics, law, culture and science become so autonomous that they not only program themselves, but exclusively react to themselves, they are no longer directly accessible to one another. Within its own power cycle, politics produces binding decisions; law reproduces its normativity in the decision-rule cycle and the economy is, so to speak, short-circuited in the money cycle. Reciprocal influences do, of course, occur permanently but they do not operate according to a simple causal scheme. External demands are not directly translated into internal effects according to the stimulus-response scheme. They are filtered according to specific selection criteria into the respective system structures and adapted into the autonomous logic of the system. In terms of environmental influences on law, this means that even the most powerful social and political pressures are only perceived and processed in the legal system to the extent that they appear on the inner 'screens' of legal reality constructions. Conversely, legal regulations are accepted by environmental systems only as external triggers for internal developments which are no longer controllable by law.

One is therefore forced to abandon ideas of effective outside regulation, the notion that law or politics could have a direct goal oriented controlling influence on sectors of society. The effect of regulatory law must be described in far more modest terms as the mere *triggering of self-regulatory processes*, the direction and effect of which can scarcely be predicted. Beer (1975) puts it well, saying that legal regulations do not change social institutions at all, they only offer a new challenge for their autopoietic adaptation. Cyberneticians use the term 'black box' to describe this phenomenon (Glanville, 1979: 35). External influence on areas of social life is possible but—and this is crucial—only within the paths and the limits of the respective self-reproduction. These are described by the *regulatory trilemma*: Every regulatory intervention which goes beyond these limits is either irrelevant or produces disintegrating effects on the social area of life or else disintegrating effects on regulatory law itself (Teubner, 1985).

The matter is further complicated by the political instrumentalization of law. In the activist state legal regulation involves not only the legal system and the respective social area of life but invariably also the political system. However, the legal system and the political system in turn are autonomous self-referential social systems which cannot directly influence each other but can only reciprocally trigger self-regulating processes. This they can only do if they respect the limits of their respective self-regulation. If we adopt this perspective and regard juridification processes as complex relations between three self-regulating social systems, we begin to grasp why 'regulatory failures' must in fact be the rule rather than the exception and that this is not merely a problem of human inadequacy or social power structures but above all one of inadequate *structural coupling of politics, law and the area of social life*.[20]

The unlikely event of a successful structural coupling of political decision-making, legal norm-making and social guidance can only occur if relevance thresholds are successfully crossed and if the respective limits of self-reproduction are observed. If this structural coupling is not achieved, then law inevitably gets caught up in the regulatory trilemma mentioned above. We can now see more clearly that this trilemma of law applies both to the regulated area of life and to politics. For law must first pass through a complicated series of phases, beginning with the build-up of political power and the political guidance decision, moving on to legal norm-making and application and finally to the process of social implementation. First, the guidance decision is 'legalized' in the political process, i.e., politics is translated into law. This first phase of juridification is itself problematic, for it must on the one hand satisfy the relevance criteria of law but on the other must not interfere with the conditions of self-regulation either of law or of politics itself. In the second phase of 'juridification' the social area of life is 'legalized' by regulatory law. Here law must cross social relevance thresholds but must not cross the limits of its own self-regulation nor those of social self-regulation. In other words, the regulatory trilemma exists on both frontiers of the law, that which borders on politics and that which borders on the area of social life. The trilemma exists in three forms: first, as a problem of mutual indifference;

second, as a problem of social disintegration through law; and third, as a problem of legal disintegration through society.

4.2 Mutual Indifference

Robert Fischer, president of the Cartel Senate of the Federal Supreme Court, has criticized the amendment practice of the German Antitrust Statute, arguing that the Law on Restraints of Competition is no longer a law but a novel, that paragraphs covering three pages are not litigable, that political compromises have left the application of law without bearings and that constant amendments have made doctrinal analyses of law obsolete (Fischer, 1978: 6). Fischer's criticisms are a drastic example of how politics can fail to achieve the relevance criteria of law. Hopt describes these normative guidelines of competition policy as one of the major reasons for the growth crisis in antitrust law. The reaction of law to this is an increasing indifference to political guidelines of this kind. The legislature is constantly producing amendments to indicate changes of direction. However, these signals no longer appear on the internal screen of the legal system; they vanish without trace. This indifference of law to politics is not confined to antitrust law. Precisely in the case of other laws designed to control the economy it has been noted that the inadequate litigability of modern legislative decisions on the micro and macro level make traditional legal control and regulation problematic (Brüggemeier, 1980: 80). This is an inevitable conflict in the structure of politics and law as systems with different self-reference. According to Luhmann 'the political selection of legal decision-making premises by parliamentary legislatures is a permanent problem for legal systems' (Luhmann, 1981a: 45).

There are, however, two sides to this indifference. Not only must politics attune its decisions to legal relevance criteria; law too can and must change its relevance criteria with respect to politics. The increasing use of the method of 'interest weighing' and the increasing policy orientation of legal decisions indicate such changes of direction in law itself. Accordingly, in some cases where politics seems to come up against legal indifference it has in fact merely reached relative limits of the coupling of politics and law. Law can change its concrete structures without affecting its self-reproductive organization (for this distinction in general see Maturana and Varela, 1980: 137f.).

In the case of Germany, the conflicts between classical company law and the current laws on codetermination provide a good example of this situation (Wiedemann, 1980a: 607). In the literature it is said that company law has coupling; indeed the result may be a partial disintegration of self-reproduction.

This much criticized effect of juridification will be examined later in greater detail. However, one misunderstanding must be cleared up first (Macaulay, 1983: 114; Reich, 1983). If the present article stresses self-reproduction and self-regulation of social spheres, to which regulatory legal interventions can only remain external, this should not be regarded as taking sides against political instrumentalization of antitrust law and in favor of a position such as that of Hayek, who views competition as a noncontrollable process of discovery which should on no account be interfered with by interventionist constructivism. On the contrary, the purpose is to underline the contradictory nature of juridification (the fact that in many fields of politics juridification must cope with both the political instrumentalization of law and the resistance of self-regulating social systems at the same time); and to show that the essential task is to discover the limits of this improbable combination, with a view to defining the conditions of compatibility, of 'structural coupling'.

4.3   Social Disintegration through Law

'Colonialization of the life-world'—this was the dramatic heading under which Jürgen Habermas (1985: 203) analyzed the dilemma of juridification in welfare states. We have already looked at Habermas' analysis of juridification in social states—he sees it as the political-legal constitutionalization of the economic system. Regulatory law, by delimiting class conflicts and shaping the social state, has a freedom-guaranteeing character. Yet at the same time juridification reveals a dilemma. Tendencies to destroy life-world structures emanate from the very character of juridification itself in the welfare state and cannot be regarded only as undesirable side-effects of this process. Social security law itself is the most important instance of this dilemma. Modern social security certainly represents an improvement on traditional measures for care of the poor, yet bureaucratic procedures and the cash payment of legal entitlements have damaging effects on the social situation, on the self-image of those affected, and on their relations to their social environment. The alien 'if...then' structure of conditional law programs cannot react adequately, let alone preventively, to the causation of the facts requiring compensation. Legal subsumption and bureaucratic procedures subject the concrete life-problem to 'violent abstraction' (Habermas, 1981a: 530–532; 1985: 209–210).

If one attempts to fit this example into our general framework, then the following limit of juridification becomes clear: law intervenes in self-regulating situations in a way which endangers the conditions of self-reproduction. Habermas views this as a general dilemma of juridification in the social state. In social law, family law and educational law it can be observed that juridification endangers the self-reproductive spheres of the life-world, i.e. the areas of socialization, social integration and cultural reproduction in their own conditions of self-reproduction (Tennstedt, 1976: 139; Pitschas, 1980: 50; Habermas, 1981: 540; 1985: 210). Even at the risk of falling short of Habermas' normative intention, we are obliged to pursue the abstraction even further. Dangers to self-organization and self-reproduction from regulatory interventions of law are not confined to the sphere of the 'life-world'. These disintegrating consequences of juridification are also observable in other self-regulating social areas which Habermas classifies as belonging to the 'system'. Fraenkel, for example, wrote that the price of juridification of labor relations would be a 'petrification' of the political class conflict (Fraenkel, 1932). In fact, the above mentioned depoliticization argument leads to the limits of the juridification of politics. Of course, in the modern social state in particular political processes are legalized to a considerable extent, but in such a way that they make possible the build-up of power to produce binding decisions and are not replaced by legally-specific criteria of right and wrong. The same applies to the areas of labor and industry. Simitis has pointed to the dilemmatic structure of norms in juridification on health and safety at work: under the German Work Safety Law and under the American Occupational Safety and Health Act the worker gains increased protection of his health and safety, but he also has to accept the increasing revelation of his personal life area just as he is obliged to accept the consequences for his life style of measures introduced for his safety. The same applies to the extension of constitutional safeguards in the field of labor. If in the case of dismissals, transfers and appointments employers are to be constitutionally bound to objective, verifiable criteria, this can lead to the creating of stereotypes which in turn force employees to conform.

4.4 Legal Disintegration through Society

A third limit of juridification is reached when regulatory law is itself exposed to the disintegrating demands of politics and society. This equally important phenomenon is often overlooked in the course of the debate on juridification, which has concentrated on the social effects of 'creeping legalism'. The juridification of society can have disastrous repercussions on law itself. Political and social demands for regulation push law to the limits of its effectiveness (Mitnick, 1983). This does not mean that the implementation of law is inadequate, quite the contrary. It is the successful attempts to increase the effectiveness of legal control that have repercussions on the internal structure of law, repercussions with which law may no longer be able to cope. Law is so to speak sandwiched—on one side by social state policy, which calls for legal enforcement and thus for the adjustment of law to the logic of political guidance and on the other by the regulated areas of social life, with their autonomous logic with which law must become involved if it is to be successfully implemented. These double demands on law can go so far as to endanger its own self-reproductive organization.

Niklas Luhmann (1985: 111) recently analyzed the paradoxical danger which juridification poses for law in its relation to the political system. He distinguishes between *normative* elements in law as representatives of the self-reference of law in which legal decisions are produced, and *cognitive* elements as representatives of the openness of law, in which law adapts to its environment. Both elements are necessary but they stand in precariously tense relation to one another. Now when law is enlisted for regulatory tasks in the social state, this precarious relation becomes so strained as to endanger the self-referential structure of law. In particular, Luhmann quotes two major instances of political overtaxing of law: the rapidity of change in political decisions on regulation, which do not allow case law and dogmatics sufficient time to develop independently, and the result orientation of political guidance, which burdens law with the problem of controlling its own results. Although one may disagree with Luhmann about whether these are absolute limits of strain or only relative limits—in which case law could adjust more, particularly with regard to result-orientation—one must in principle agree with his analysis. Even if law, by developing its own stop-rules of result control and by more abstract dogmatic concept formulation, can increase its adjustment and learning capacities—and there are signs that this is happening—it will at some stage come up against absolute limits at which normativity as such is in danger. Here too, a clear distinction must be made between structural changes within the framework of self-reproductive organization and changes in this organization itself, although this does not necessarily mean that the structural scope of self-reproductive organization can be defined in advance.

Yet this is only one side of the self-endangerment of law by juridification, that is, the enforced inclusion of political criteria in law. The normativity of law is equally strained by the inclusion of social criteria, by the enforced adjustment of law to the autonomous logic of the regulated social areas. Once more German antitrust law provides a good example. In his study of the control of abuses in §22 of the Law on Restraints of Competition, Möschel has shown how the law on competition, for conceptual and practical reasons, has reached its limits (Möschel, 1981b: §22,4). How is law to maintain its normativity and at the same time become involved in a structure of regulations whose elements are so interdependent that they become, as it were, 'moving targets' when they are defined as aspects of the relevant market, of market power and of abuse, with the result that they completely defy any solid legal subsumption? (Möschel, 1974: 166, 171).

Of course to a certain extent economic analyses may be of assistance here. Cartel law, as already stated, provides a spectacular example of the inroads made by the social sciences into law. The phenomenon applies to a wide range of areas. 'Norm area analyses', to use the term coined by Friedrich Mueller (1966: 168), are required in many areas in order to achieve the regulatory intention. But this 'economization' and 'sociologization' of law also has its limits (see Daintith and Teubner, 1986). In the case of economic analysis of law fears have been expressed that this 'economization' of law could endanger its characteristic feature: its very normativity (Assmann, 1980b: 305). Yet precisely as a partisan of 'sociological jurisprudence' one must examine closely such limits of law, in order to realistically estimate the opportunities and dangers of the opening of law towards the social sciences.

We can now formulate a *second interim finding*: juridification raises many problems, such as inadequate effectiveness of regulation and unintended side-effects, whether in the regulation area or in other social sectors. But these are, so to speak, only the 'everyday' problems of the phenomenon. To find out whether fundamental limits of effectiveness have been reached, one must concentrate on the problem of structural coupling of law with social state policies as well as with various social life areas. The deeper reason for this problem lies in the autonomy of social subsystems, which is so highly developed that as self-referential systems they cannot directly influence one another but can only affect self-regulatory processes that are uncontrollable from outside. The fundamental limits of structural coupling are reached either when relevance criteria are not met or when the conditions of self-reproductive organization are endangered. When juridification processes overstep the limits of structural coupling, law inevitably becomes caught up in a regulatory trilemma. This means: either law, politics and/or the social area of life will be mutually indifferent, or juridification will have disintegrating effects on politics and/or social sectors concerned, or, finally, law itself will be exposed to the disintegrating pressures to conform of politics and/or social sectors.

5.   Solutions

There is no 'solution' of the regulatory trilemma in sight. As already stated, the phenomenon of juridification as such is a partial aspect of societal evolution and cannot therefore be effectively reversed by delegalization strategies. The only approaches which can be taken seriously are those which seek to deal with the dysfunctional consequences resulting from juridification. The solutions proposed are very different, depending on whether juridification processes are regarded as positive or negative and on which problems are perceived as relevant. In the discussion which follows we will take as our criterion how far the various approaches seem capable of avoiding the regulatory trilemma by taking the problem of the structural coupling of law, politics and the area of regulation implicitly or explicitly into account.

5.1   Implementation

Partisans of comprehensive regulation through law will concentrate on the effectiveness of juridification. Their view of the problem has been most clearly formulated in a branch of socio-legal and political research known as 'implementation' research (Mayntz, 1977: 51, 1980, 1983; Windhoff-Heritier, 1980, Sabatier and Mazmanian, 1980: 538). It takes as its starting point an 'enforcement deficit' of regulatory law which is diagnosed again and again, in environmental, consumer protection, and other policy fields. Implementation research aims to pinpoint the causes of this enforcement deficit and to produce political recommendations on how to overcome them. The background theories here are frequently theories of political guidance of society, including guidance through law. The political system takes on overall responsibility for social processes and in particular is responsible for balancing out and compensating for false developments, particularly in economic life.

The problem of structural coupling is then reduced to a problem of technical effectiveness. If political regulation fails, then power resources and funds must be increased and the means of regulation refined to a point that will ensure the desired effects. In the U.S., this view is strongly supported by a new movement for 're-regulation' (Tolchin and Tolchin, 1983). According to this view, the crisis of regulatory law can only be overcome if the instrumental effectiveness of law is increased. Accordingly the task, then, is to reinforce cognitive, organizational and power resources so that law in fact will fulfil its regulatory functions. Thus legal dogmatics will have to shift even more from a primarily law-applying to a legal-political orientation, even in their conceptuality (Nonet and Selznick, 1978). Jurisprudence will definitively come to see itself as one of those social sciences which produce knowledge about social guidance (Ziegert, 1975). Law will then primarily be a matter of socio-technics (Podgorecki, 1974). In the attempt to achieve greater efficiency, economic and socio-logical analyses will have to be drawn on. This means in particular that law will have to take into consideration both its own implementation and its social consequences (Luhmann, 1974; Teubner, 1975: 179; Rottleuthner, 1979: 97; Lübbe-Wolff, 1981).

The boom in implementation research in recent years can be explained precisely in these terms: as the expression of an attempt to respond to the crisis of regulatory law by drawing increasingly on social science methods. Implementation research is based on a clearly instrumental notion of law which sees law as a means of social engineering designed to produce certain social changes. In political processes a goal is defined and translated into a legal program which in turn is meant to bring about changes in behavior among those whom it affects. Implementation research works with a relatively simple causal model: the goal determines the program; the program determines the behavior of the implementors and target groups; this in turn produces the required effect. Implementation research concentrates especially on the last links in this chain and attempts to find out why certain enforcement deficits occur, why certain programs do not result in the desired behavioral changes and the desired changes in the social situation. The major objective here is to increase the effectiveness of regulatory law by clarifying the causal connections in the implementation field, thus making them accessible to social engineering.

Renate Mayntz recently published a first appraisal of the achievements of implementation research in which she points out that the hopes pinned on it cannot be fulfilled and argues that corrections must be made in its basic approach (Mayntz, 1983: 7). These corrections point precisely in the direction of our notion of 'structural coupling'. This relates both to the theoretical and practical mastery of causal connections. Mayntz concludes that the scientific ideal of setting up testable causal hypotheses and developing an axiomatized theory can only be partially realized in implementation research. Instead one must be content with far more modest results: 1) conceptual identification of phenomena and the establishment of categories and typologies; 2) the use of the case-study method, which allows only very guarded generalizations; 3) the taking back of precise individual prognoses on the model of Hayek's pattern predictions, i.e., the mere prediction of general structural patterns. These deficiencies are all explained in terms of the great complexity implementation research faces.

This means quite simply that the most ambitious attempt so far to cope with the crisis of regulatory law by means of social science research on its effects will apparently fail because of the complexity of the subject which it is analyzing. Here again—this time on the basis of practical research experience—the limits of regulatory law become apparent. Social science is not yet capable, and is perhaps fundamentally incapable, of developing sufficiently complex models of reality to check and control in the necessary detail the probable effectiveness of regulatory law in the implementation field. From the standpoint of our approach, this is hardly surprizing. If it is correct that social regulation, because of the autonomy of social systems, can do nothing but trigger uncontrollable self-regulation processes, then simple causal models are inadequate as a means of analyzing and checking the results of legal regulations. In this case both the regulatory claim of law and the analytical claim of the social sciences must be restrained. But does restraint here also mean abandonment of the claim?

The various solutions which Mayntz herself proposes are interesting. Pattern predictions allow only prognoses of very general constellations. In the scientific study of implementation, causal models, it is argued, should be replaced by so-called congruence models. Public policy effectiveness would depend on a 'congruent' relationship between structural properties ('the problem to be solved') on the one hand and contextual variables ('program characteristics') on the other. Regulatory law, in the narrower sense of direct regulation which is described as scarcely appropriate, ought to be replaced by incentive programs and persuasive strategies. Finally, hopes are pinned on the granting of calculated autonomy to implementors and target groups alike. She argues for a specific type of 'procedural regulation' as an intraorganizational and interorganizational device.

5.2 *Deregulation*

Is deregulation then the solution? If an implementation expert such as Renate Mayntz, who is not in principle opposed to state intervention, is fascinated by Hayek's 'pattern predictions', then we are not far from the normative consequence that juridification should be cut back to the classical framework for competition—a self-regulating process of discovery. However, careful distinctions are required if the 'deregulation' movement's criticisms of juridification processes are to be adequately judged and institutional conclusions drawn from them (cf. Mitnick, 1980; Breyer, 1981). We must differentiate between at least three different strands of criticism: 1) cost-benefit analyses, (2) economic versions of 'capture theories', and (3) political criticisms of 'constructive interventionism'.

In the U.S. in particular the regulatory agencies, such as the Securities Exchange Commission, which tackles problems of company law, the Federal Trade Commission which handles questions of antitrust law and the National Labor Relations Board, which deals with problems of labor law, have all been subjected to detailed cost-benefit analyses by economists (McCraw, 1975: 159). The verdicts on this kind of juridification are frank: 'What the regulatory commissions are trying to do is difficult to discover; what effect these commissions have is, to a large extent, unknown; when it can be discovered, it is often absurd' (Coase, 1964: 194). Economic cost-benefit analyses have shown the costs of regulation in many cases to be horrendous: the estimated negative balance of the regulation of inshore water pollution in the U.S. from 1972 to 2000: 107 billion dollars; the regulation of transport goods: 4 to 8 billion dollars per annum; the regulation of medical drugs: 350 million dollars per annum (McCraw, 1975: 172; Feick, 1980: 51). Weidenbaum (1980) estimated that the annual costs of administering federal regulatory programs in the U.S. amounted to 6 billion dollars and the cost of compliance amounted to 120 billion dollars. These cost-benefit analyses are undoubtedly useful and their results should certainly be considered in the debate over the extent to which and the way in which regulatory juridification should take place. But of course economic cost-benefit analyses must be treated with caution and used only as one criterion among others. Economic burdens in the form of costs are relatively easy to measure, whereas the *social* benefits of regulation are often difficult, if not impossible, to quantify. One must be very wary of allowing economic criteria of efficiency to completely replace the legal or political weighing up of interests and values—a method which is usually more complex. Stewart (1986), for example, lists six principles which go beyond considerations of economic efficiency: (1) moral condemnation, (2) distributional equity, (3) noncommodity values, (4) assuming control over outcomes, (5) access to judicial remedies, (6) honoring expectations created by past regulation.

The second strand of arguments for deregulation is found in economic versions of the so-called 'capture theories'. Bernstein (1955), the best known representative of the political 'capture theory', put forward the proposition that regulatory agencies are subject to a typical 'life cycle'. In the first stage of juridification, it is argued, they tackle their regulatory task with public support actively, if not aggressively; in the next phase, however, they degenerate into tired, inert organizations that can be easily captured by the economic interests they are regulating (hence the term 'capture theories'). This thesis, which has been taken up and further developed by political-economic authors such as Kolko (1965), McConell (1966) and Lowi (1969), was surprizingly given further support by leading represent-atives of the Chicago School (Stigler, 1971: 3, 1972: 207, 1975). Stigler, for example, comes to the pointed conclusion that 'regulation is acquired by the industry and is designed and operated primarily for its benefits' (Stigler, 1975: 114). Juridification is regarded as a resource supplied by politics and demanded by the regulated industry. In return for political support, industries interested in regulatory policies can receive the form of juridification which corresponds to their interests. Deregulation strategies based on such analyses do not appear at all unreasonable; they concentrate on dysfunctional consequences of juridification. However they hardly affect the fundamental limits of juridification with which we are con-cerned.

These limits are more likely to be touched on by a politically motivated deregulation strategy. Here, too, Chicago stands in the front line (e.g. Posner, 1974; Stigler, 1976: 17; McCormick and Tollison, 1981). Regulatory state intervention is described as the 'visible paw' of state economic policy, which prevents the invisible hand of market competition from developing its beneficial effects. The goal striven for here is a high degree of self-organization in society through markets. Milton Friedman says he would most like to see a 'completely anarchic world' but he is content with 'completely untrammelled capitalism' (Milton Friedman in *Der Spiegel*, No. 48, 1970: 153). Even clearly recognized deficiencies in the market are preferable to state intervention. The consequence of this philosophy is the demand for complete economic deregulation.

Von Hayek and his school propose a more sophisticated line of argu-ment (v. Hayek, 1972, 1973–1979). Social state intervention through jur-idification is criticized as 'interventionist constructivism'. The criticism has been applied in particular to antitrust law but can also be generalized to cover every area of economic regulation (Hoppmann, 1972). This school holds that the connections which interventionists claim exist between market structures, market behavior and market results are based on inadequate theoretical premises and are not empirically testable. They work from the unrealistic assumption that complicated market processes can be depicted in simple models of causal relations between a few variables, one that is bound to lead to false economic policies. Hayek's school argues that the regulation of market results by interventions in market structures is fundamentally impossible and leads to arbitrary economic interventionism. Instead, the conception of 'competition as a process of discovery' is advocated. Social structures and processes are interpreted as complex phenomena which cannot be reduced to simple so-called economic laws. The market is regarded as a complex, cybernetic system, the elements of which are individuals and companies, which interact spontaneously on the basis of general rules of behavior. The nature of the system is self-regulating, environmentally open and evolutionary.

This means that competition is a dynamic process which cannot be captured in static models. The data and information which go into this process cannot be grasped or pinpointed, so scientifically sound predictions can relate only to the emergence of a general structure but never to specific market results. This need not be a disadvantage, however, because the social institution of competition is consciously brought into play as a process of information, seeking and learning. Competition as a process of discovery is beyond the reach of any scientific method of discovery. It is therefore nonsensical to attempt to define the institutional preconditions of competition on the basis of its results, of the so-called economic competitive functions. The only sensible course is to introduce a system of general rules to guarantee the basic conditions of freedom of competition.

In my view this is a remarkable attempt to tackle the central problem of juridification, that of the structural coupling of juridification and the area of regulation—a remarkable attempt, but one which discredits itself in advance by its normative hypostatization. It is remarkable because it aims to define the absolute limits of effectiveness of juridification: interventionist interference in self-regulating systems cannot in principle be controlled from outside. At the same time an attempt is made to formulate the conditions of the structural coupling of law and competition in the concept of 'pattern predictions' and of law as a system of general rules of the game. Thus, we have the possibility of acting in the political and legal spheres despite the limitations of human knowledge about complex self-regulatory processes. This is also the reason why the concept of pattern predictions is so attractive for implementation research, which has reached its cognitive and organizational limits. This concept of competition as a process of discovery could also be usefully applied to other self-regulating systems which are exposed to legal intervention (Gotthold, 1984b).

However, the manner in which this theory hypostatizes sectoral economic rationality is unacceptable. The absolute primacy of freedom

of competition over other economic, social and political goals is normatively postulated. According to this view, the sole function of legal rules
concerning the economy would be to safeguard freedom of competition.
This is unacceptable to jurists on constitutional grounds alone. In terms
of constitutional law it can be said that goal conflicts cannot be resolved
by the absolute primacy of freedom of competition over other economic and social goals. On the contrary, the constitutional method normally used seems more practicable: the mediation of goals in terms
of 'practical concordance'—a method which allows greater legislative
scope.

For social theory this position is again unacceptable because it hypostatizes the sectoral rationality of the economic system—market and competition—for the whole and refuses to see that it is precisely the task of
juridification in welfare states to bring the rationality of other social
subsystems into play against the economy (Habermas, 1981: 530; 1985:
209; Willke, 1983b). The function of law cannot be reduced to the mere
preservation of self-regulating structures. On the contrary, the fact must be
acknowledged that one important function of law is precisely to coordin-
ate the sectoral rationalities of different self-regulating systems with one
another (Teubner, 1983: 273). This function does not become redundant
because self-regulatory systems defy direct control. It remains necessary—
but is incomparably more difficult.

Our discussion has now reached a point at which the most interesting
alternatives to juridification appear. Solutions to the problem of juridification are sought which assume *both the necessity of the socio-political instrumentalization of law and the necessity of structural coupling with self-regulating
areas of life*. The problem can be formulated as follows: are there ways and
means by which law can change from direct regulatory intervention to
more indirect, more abstract forms of social regulation, i.e. to the politico-
legal control of social self-regulation?

5.3   Control of Self-regulation

As alternative solutions going beyond the formalization and materialization of law, strategies are today being discussed which tend towards more
abstract, indirect regulation by law. Law is relieved of its task of regulating
social areas and is instead burdened with the control of self-regulating
processes (Bohnert and Klitzsch, 1980: 200; Ronge, 1984).

The crisis of regulatory law is here diagnosed as a social immune
reaction to legal interventions. The problems of juridification show that
different social systems operate according to their own inner logic, which

cannot easily be harmonized with the logic of other systems. Material legal programs have at their disposal modes of functioning, criteria of rationality and organizational patterns which are not necessarily adequate to the regulated areas. The background theories on which such ideas are based are frequently macro-theories of society and law, usually variants of system functionalism or critical theory or manifold attempts to combine the two (see Wiethölter, 1985). Normatively, these approaches have highly different perspectives, from the emancipation of man to smoothly functioning system technology, depending on the theoretical context and normative preferences. Yet they all have one problem in common. Is normative integration still possible in a society characterized by inner contradictions, by distintegrating, indeed disruptive conflicts between the specific logic of highly specialized sub-systems? (Habermas, 1981: 334; Luhmann, 1975: 51). They all assume that neither the state nor law is capable of achieving this integration—as Durkheim perhaps envisaged in his notion of organic solidarity. However, politics and law have to bring about important structural preconditions for a new type of decentralized integration of society.

The proposed solution is to move to 'constitutive strategies of law' (Stewart, 1986), i.e., to introduce structural legal frameworks for social self-regulation. The term 'proceduralization', for instance, is used as an overall heading for this function of law, which is to encourage 'social systems capable of learning' (Wiethölter, 1982a, 1982b, 1984, 1985). Essentially three matters are concerned here: 1) the safeguarding of social autonomy by an 'external constitution' (Habermas, 1981: 544f.; 1985: 218f.), a legal guarantee for 'semi-autonomous social fields' (Moore, 1973; Galanter, 1980; 1981); 2) structural frameworks for effective self-regulation, for instance along the lines of 'external decentralization' of public tasks or in terms of internal reflection of social effects (Lehner, 1979: 178; Teubner, 1983: 273; 1987; Hart, 1983; Gotthold, 1984a: 249;); 3) the canalization of conflicts between systems by 'relational programmes' (Willke, 1983a: 62ff., 145) or neo-corporatist mediation mechanisms of 'procedural regulation' (Mayntz, 1983; Streeck and Schmitter, 1985), by 'negotiated regulations' (Harter, 1982; Reich, 1983), by semi-formal modes of procedure in the so-called 'discovery process of practice' (Joerges, 1981: 111), or by legal coordination of different system rationalities (Scharpf, 1979; Assmann, 1980a: 324; 1980b; Ladeur, 1982a: 391; 1982b: 74; 1983: 102; 1984). In short: instead of directly regulating social behavior, law confines itself to the regulation of organization, procedures and the redistribution of competences.

What does this mean in concrete terms? 'Negotiated regulation' is one heading under which such indirect regulations through law are discussed today (Harter, 1982; Reich, 1983). It includes 'dependent bargaining' as well as 'constitutive bargaining' (Stewart, 1986). Antitrust law, for example, contains a wealth of material to illustrate regulation through negotiation, in which solutions are reached through negotiation under the pressure of legal sanctions. The control of company mergers is an important example. Here, with the threat of a ban on the contemplated merger looming in the background, modifications of the merger proposals are worked out cooperatively.

'Bargaining in the shadow of law' describes a mechanism which has been demonstrated in many areas of law (Mnookin and Kornhauser, 1979: 950; Galanter, 1980). The mere existence of substantive law with its threat of sanctions creates negotiating positions for the parties—whether private individuals, organizations or state institutions—which ultimately affect the result of negotiations—an effect which would not have been achieved had the law not existed. The advantages here are clear to see: this method is more likely to lead to flexible, cooperative solutions geared to specific situations as opposed to rigid, approximative and authoritative solutions. The problem of structural coupling is tackled in such a way that the official function of law, which is to decree changes of behavior recedes into the background, whereas its latent function, which is to regulate systems of negotiation becomes crucial.

Numerous studies have analysed how widespread this phenomenon has become (e.g. Treiber, 1983). Events regularly take the following course. First, law is primarily used to bring about a certain kind of behavior by the threat of negative sanctions. However, enforcement deficits appear which oblige the parties concerned to transform the enforcement systems into negotiation systems. One can interpret this by arguing that in this case regulatory law is subject to a latent change of function. As direct regulation of human behavior it soon reaches its limits and is tacitly reinterpreted as a kind of procedural law. The threat potential of legal sanctions is not used. It is not so to say 'liquidated', but in fact survives as a legally guaranteed power of negotiation within the self-regulating system of negotiation. Indeed there are even interpretations of regulatory law which warn against taking the implementation of law too seriously. 'Strict enforcement by the book' often appears unreasonable and endangers the precarious regulation situation (Bardach and Kagan, 1982).

A critical point is reached when not only the parties concerned reinterpret regulatory law more or less openly and more or less legitimately as negotiation regulating law, but law itself abandons direct regulation to concentrate instead on structuring negotiation systems. Of course labor law provides the historical paradigm here (Wiethölter, 1985: 239; Mückenberger, 1980: 241). State legislation on safety at work and the mere regulation of free collective bargaining are, within certain limits, functional equivalents of the goals of employee protection. In many cases indirect regulation of the system of free collective bargaining has been preferred to substantive regulation because of the obvious advantages it brings. Without placing the emphasis on concrete substantive control state law here tends to regulate collective agreements only indirectly—by making legal recognition of negotiating parties dependent on certain structural conditions, by devising procedural norms for the system of negotiation and for disputes, and by extending or restricting the competences of the collective parties. In fact the attempt here is merely to control indirectly the quality of the negotiation results through a balancing of negotiating power. More important than rearrangements of social power by means of law are legal strategies designed to increase the 'public responsibility' of parties involved in industrial disputes. Here I do not mean the rather naive attempts to impose public accountability on both sides of industry through a 'public interest' clause. The development of reflection structures in the system of industrial conflicts, i.e. of structures in which the external social results are taken into account when action is being considered, is more likely to be achieved by institutional influencing of the size of organizations and their internal structures. Comparative empirical studies to a certain extent support the hypothesis that the overall social impact tends to be reflected more within the decision-making processes of the system of collective bargaining when collective labor law systematically favors a centralized 'industrial trade union' as opposed to a decentralized system of shop stewards with professionally oriented trade unions (Streeck *et al.* 1978; Streeck 1979: 206, Groser, 1979: 258). Although here too one should be wary of generalizations, procedural law does show a certain superiority over material law. As Simitis puts it: 'Procedural rules are almost always symptomatic of a phase of juridification in which regulation by material rules is no longer sufficient, if only because of their fundamentally selective approach and their limited adaptability to changing social and economic conditions' (Simitis, 1984: 102).

Of course, the model of collective labor law cannot be universally applied throughout the world of industry and labor. Similar attempts in other areas to establish a system of negotiation based on countervailing power have proved only partially capable of development, especially in the field of consumer law (Hart and Joerges, 1980; Joerges, 1981: 52).

In the U.S. proposals for 'negotiated regulation' have aroused considerable interest (Harter, 1982). As a means of preventing excessive 'lawyering', which only intensifies conflicts, it is proposed that the groups concerned hold negotiations on regulation, to be presided over by a convenor who would mediate between the parties and be vested with certain legal powers. The intention here is clearly to draw on the experience gained in American labor law arbitration. Similar proposals have been made in France in connection with problems of rent and consumer law (Reich, 1983: 28). This generally amounts to the state directed organization of a system of negotiation in which all the relevant interest groups participate. It is intended to lead to 'accords negociés collectivement'. The problematic of the parallel to collective labor law is evident: the organizational capacity of consumer associations are not even remotely comparable with those of trade unions.

Consumer law in particular, but other areas of contract law as well, show that 'external decentralization' fails when social power and information asymmetries reduce legal control of self-regulating processes to a farce. The inevitable consequence is therefore specific legal reinforcement of negotiating power in order to counteract these asymmetries—but the likelihood of this achieving the desired effects must be regarded with scepticism. Functional equivalents, however, may be established if autonomous public institutions are 'artificially' created with state aid—to provide consumer information or to organize effective representation of consumer interests (e.g. the creation of the 'Stiftung Warentest', of consumer centres, state-funded representation of consumers) (Joerges, 1981: 133). Here, too, the role of state law would consist not of the material regulation of market processes but of procedural and organizational pre-structuring of 'autonomous' social processes. Through the ordering of organizational norms, the law forces highly specialized, unilaterally oriented organizations to take the conflicting demands of their social environment into account when making decisions. (The consequence of this perspective in consumer law, which could overcome the weaknesses of direct legal interventionism is described by Joerges, 1983: 57, 65).

'Social contract' is the term used to define a trend in which the role of law is transformed from one of direct regulation of behavior to a more indirect regulation of procedures.[21] The social contract is merely a special case of the many 'neocorporatist arrangements' which are attracting increasing interest internationally.[22] Unlike the pluralistic mediation of interests, in which social groups bring their interests to bear only in the forecourt of state power, the neocorporatist syndrome amounts to a form of voluntary cooperation between the state and social interests, and in particular to a decision-making symbiosis between the state, trade unions and industrial associations. The reasons for this development are essentially found in the increase of power and rationality of sectoral social systems, in the face of which classical legal forms of state regulation break down (Schmitter, 1977: 7; Winkler, 1976: 100). This 'disenchantment of the state' (Willke, 1983a) leads to new forms of juridification, to 'new legal forms of the intertwining of the state and the economy' (Gessner and Winter, 1982). According to Winter, the crucial feature here is the 'avoidance of imperative intervention' through temporary cooperation in which the state gives up part of its domination and industry gives up part of its freedom. This takes the form of the permanent installation of state rationality in private organizations, of the repetition of social conflicts in the sectoral system itself and of the private 'occupation' of state organizations. The concomitant loss of demarcation and generalization of the state apparatus can even lead to a form of intertwining in which the two parties are no longer distinguishable as organizations with structural and functional limits but which instead form a single identity (Winter, 1982: 28).

The term 'relational program' has been introduced into the discussion to describe the new role of law in such neocorporatist arrangements (Willke, 1983a: 10; Teubner and Willke, 1984). It differs from the conditional program of classical formal law and the purpose program of social state regulatory law by being oriented towards organization and procedures for coordinating different rationalities of social sub-systems. It is no longer the classical forms of law—prohibitions and incentives—which predominate, but 'procedural regulations' (Mayntz, 1983) in which the state involves social interests in procedures of program formulation, decision-making and implementation.

The juridification process is not stopped by such trends towards the reduction of direct state influence but merely steered into new channels. As Streeck and Schmitter (1985: 25f.) explain: 'It is true that an associative social order implies a devolution of state functions to interest intermediaries. But this has to be accompanied by a simultaneous acquisition by the state of a capacity to design, monitor, and keep in check the new self-regulating systems' ('procedural corporatism'). There is another phenomenon worth noting here, as well, in connection with which Simitis (infra: 143) talks of a 'second generation of employee protection rules'—but it is a

phenomenon which is generalizable beyond this: the internal organizational consequences of neocorporatism. In the development of American
labor law the duty to bargain has been supplemented by the duty of fair
representation: the employer's duty to negotiate implies the duty of the
trade unions to defend the interests of all their members. This was the
starting point for a wave of juridification which affects the internal organization of trade unions and other organizations representing employees,
which have hitherto been regarded as autonomous (see, e.g., Summers,
1977: 251). Even in Great Britain, Clark and Wedderburn observe, in
regard to the internal conduct of trade union affairs, 'an unambiguous
increase in state intervention in areas which were previously left to
autonomous regulation'. The phenomenon is generalizable from trade
unions to all organized interests which are bound into neocorporatist
negotiation systems. As a result of this binding a large number of social
problems (the coordination of interests, the build-up of legitimation, the
implementation of the policies worked out in negotiation) are shifted to
the inside of the organization itself. This means a shift from 'external'
market coordination to 'internal' political processes of organizations. The
internal structure of the organization thus becomes the 'Achilles' heel of
corporatism'.[23] Thus the internal constitution of private organizations
becomes a central regulatory problem of state law.

This leads directly to the last complex of problems: the role of law in
relation to large private organizations. As Buxbaum, Kübler and Corsi
have demonstrated, there is a tendency in company law towards a materialization of previously neutral formal law. However, state regulation
and judicial control here seem to reach the limits of their control capacity,
not only because of superficial changes in political trends but for structural
reasons as well (Mayntz, 1979: 55). Our approach would not necessarily
lead to a reinforcement of state power resources but rather to a shift
towards more abstract guidance mechanisms: i.e., towards the design
of legal norms which would systematically strengthen the development
of 'reflection structures' within the economic industry. 'Company constitution' and 'neocorporatist systems of negotiation' are the relevant
terms here (see Hopt and Teubner, 1985). The question which remains
unanswered is whether such control mechanisms can be directed in such
a way that they will function effectively as a 'corporate conscience', in
other words, force the economic system or the company to 'internalize'
external social conflicts, and do so in such a way that internal decision-
making processes also take into account non-economic interests of
employees, consumers and the general public. Within the past decades,

economic goal structures within companies have undergone considerable changes, from profit orientation to growth orientation. Is it completely inconceivable that they could change again so as to include problems of ecological balance in their set of goals? Does this have to be, as Christopher Stone (1975) puts it, the point 'where the law ends'? Is it not rather precisely the point at which law receives its institutional opportunity: to bring about the 'reflexive' control of economic behavior, which is capable of transforming external social 'troubles' into internal organizational 'issues' for the micro-policies of the company? Buxbaum points out rightly that the success of such a legal strategy depends mainly on the 'institutional setting' of adequate judicial and bureaucratic structures.

The main goal is not the reduction of power, nor an increase in individual participation in the emphatic sense of 'participatory democracy' but the well-considered design of internal organizational structures which make the institutions concerned—companies, public associations, trade unions, mass media and educational institutions—sensitive to the social effects which their strategies for the maximization of their specific rationality trigger. The major function of such reflexive internal structures would be to replace interventionist state control by effective internal control. The creation of structural conditions for an 'organizational conscience' which would reflect the balance between function and performance of the social system—this, in our definition, would be the integrative role of reflexive law.

These various approaches and development trends appear at first sight to be extremely varied. What they have in common is that they tackle, though in very different ways, the problem of the structural coupling of law, politics and the regulated areas. 'Structural coupling' is a term which could open up further perspectives for future theoretical and practical legal attempts to grasp the phenomenon of juridification. It seems essential for an adequate understanding of the relationship between law and society to draw conclusions from the social autonomy discussed above, or more precisely, from the autopoietic organization of social subsystems. Politico-legal intervention in complex self-reproducing systems would then have to abandon the model of hierarchic control relations and adapt itself to reticular interaction of communication systems with equal status. This refers legal intervention to the indirect method of 'decentral context regulation' (Teubner and Willke, 1984: 4). This form of regulation is made necessary and possible by the high degree of autonomy of social subsystems: regulation impulses are only possible in the form of context conditions, which as observable differences constitute the information basis for the respective basal circularity.

And this means more than regulation in the classical liberal sense of residual context regulation which provides the social subsystems with the basic framework for their freedom of self-organization. What is required is an *internal legal modelling of the autopoietic organization of social subsystems*, with the goal of identifying strategic variables in order to change them and, by influencing them, to institutionalize environmentally appropriate reflection processes. The possibility that this would overtax the internal capabilities of law cannot be ruled out. However, theoretical considerations do not in principle invalidate this form of regulation; on the contrary they support it.

A second possibility of decentral context regulation consists of fully accepting the closure and intransparence of complex social systems as 'black boxes' and concentrating legal regulation solely on the external relations, the interactive relations between the subsystems. The chances of legal effectiveness would then lie in the fact that law would not have to impose its mode of operation on other areas but could confine itself to the norming of the independent interaction systems. In this case no isomorphism of modes of operation would be required but only their 'structural coupling'. The necessary consequence of the social phenomenon of self-reference and self-reproduction is the adjustment of legal theory and legal practice to such concepts.

However, exaggerated hopes must be warned against.[24] It must be assumed that the move from direct legal control to indirect regulation of self-regulation would bring new, serious problems in its wake. 'Inexactness' of legal regulation and increased coordination costs would almost inevitably be side-effects of a 'proceduralization' of law. Finally it must be emphasized that the issue is not one of totally adjusting law to new forms of regulation. Just as classical formal law is not replaced, but at most overlaid, by materialization processes, here too it is only a matter of relative dominance. The most that can be expected is a shift of emphasis in legal regulation towards more flexible strategies. These strategies will not solve all the problems of juridification, nor will they reverse the process of juridification as such. On the contrary, the legal regulation of self-regulation can itself be seen as a continuation of the juridification trend, but— and this would be the crucial step forward—it would help steer the process into more socially compatible channels.

[Translated from the German by Paul Knight]

Notes

1. For previous discussion of 'creeping legalism', cf Fuller, 1969: 3; Shuklar, 1964; Nonet, 1969; Friedman, 1975; Galanter, 1980: 11, 1981: 147; Abel, 1980: 27, 1982; Mitnick, 1980; Wilson, 1980; Breyer, 1982; Stewart, 1985. Cf the results of a German/American conference on regulatory control, Trubek, 1984.

2. Berner, 1978: 617; Boerlin *et al.*, 1978: 295; Hillermeier, 1978: 321; Weiss, 1978: 601; Vogel, 1979: 321; Starck, 1979: 209; Sendler, 1979, 227; Barton, 1975: 567.

3. Ehrlich, 1976: note 1. Cf the references in note 2 supra.

4. A valuable analysis of the different directions in which the movements towards delegalisation is going is offered by Röhl, 1982: 15.

5. E.g., active role of the judge, settlements, negotiations aimed at reaching an amicable agreement: see Giese, 1978: 117; Röhl, 1980: 279.

6. E.g., arbitration courts, courts within companies and associations: see Bender, 1976: 193; Bierbrauer *et al.*, 1978: 141.

7. This is not meant as an overall criticism of the very useful analyses of Erd. It simply seems noteworthy that Erd firstly makes a vehement criticism of the limited nature of rival explanations, and then for his part produces a very limited explanation. Interesting nuances of his explanation are found recently in Erd, 1984.

8. With respect of Parsons' theory of norms, which can only be reconstructed from scattered fragments, cf Damm, 1976. For more recent theories of legal development in the U.S., see Unger, 1976; Nonet and Selznick, 1978; Habermas, 1976: 9, 1981: 322, 522, 1985: 203; Luhmann, 1972; 1981a. For a discussion of theories of evolution of law, see Rottleuthner, 1985.

9. Similar definitions are given in Voigt, 1984: 17; Dreier, 1980; 1983: 101; Ronge, 1984; Werle, 1982: 1.

10. Eder, 1978: 247. For materialization trends in American law, cf Unger, 1976: 192; Trubek, 1972: 11; Turkel, 1980–81: 41. For German analyses of processes of materialization, see Wieacker, 1967: 514; Wiethölter, 1982a, 1985; Assmann *et al.*, 1980.

11. For these dimensions and their application to a third type of law, i.e. reflexive law, cf Teubner, 1983: 252, 1985: 305ff.

12. Kennedy, 1973: 351, 1976: 1685; Unger, 1976: 166; Heller, 1979.

13. For a comparative law study of evolution of methods, cf Fikentscher, 1975; Krawietz, 1978: 86.

14. An example is provided by the discussion between Gotthold, 1981: 286 and Möschel, 1981a: 590.

15. For the German discussion, see Raiser, 1969, 1980: 206. Even the critics cannot help basing themselves on extra-legal theories, cf for example, Wiedemann, 1980a: 307. For the French discussion, see Farjat, 1986.

16. As a more recent thorough survey, cf the introductory essay by Walz, 1983: 1ff.; cf as well, the various approaches of social science to legal analysis in Daintith and Teubner, 1986.

17. With some slight differences, this concept of regulatory control of the social state is at the basis of many of the contributions in these volumes. For example Simitis puts greater emphasis on the control of the social state, whether in the form of direct regulation or in other legal forms, while Kübler emphasizes rather the aspect of mandatory law with direct regulatory action. In my opinion, only the combination of both elements can make something of the difficult problem of regulatory control, i.e. if law is subjected to the combined requirements of political objectives and direct social regulation.

18. For the distinction between function and performance in law, see Teubner, 1983: 272.

19. The terms self-reference/autopoiesis are used in biology as well as in the social sciences in order to identify a system which produces and reproduces the elements of which it is made. See in general, Maturana et al. 1980; Varela, 1979. For an application in the social sciences, cf. Hejl, 1982a, 1982b; Luhmann, 1984. For the legal system, see Luhmann, 1983; 1985; 1987; Teubner, 1984, 1987.

20. On the difficult concept of the structural coupling of autopoietic systems, see the introduction in Maturana, 1982: 20ff. See also Hejl, 1982: 63.

21. For the emergence of different forms of 'Social Contract' see Simitis, Giugni, Clark and Wedderburn.

22. See as an informative introduction, Alemann and Heinze, 1979; Alemann, 1981. For recent proposals in the U.S., see Industrial Policy Study Group, 1984.

23. A discussion of the relationship of neo-corporatist structures and the internal structures of organization is found in Teubner, 1978b: 545, 1979: 487.

24. Blankenburg, 1984, expends a great amount of energy in destroying illusions about 'proceduralized' law, which in fact no one ever had in this form.

References

Abel, Richard L. (1980) 'Delegalization—A Critical Review of its Ideology, Manifestations, and Social Consequences', in E. Blankenburg, E. Klausa, H. Rottleuthner (eds.), *Alternative Rechtsformen und Alternativen zum Recht*. Opladen: Westdeutscher Verlag.

—— (ed.) (1982) *The Politics of Informal Justice*. New York: American Press.

Alemann, Ulrich von (ed.) (1981) *Neokorporatismus*. Frankfurt: Campus.

Alemann, Ulrich von and Rolf G. Heinze (1979) *Verbände und Staat*. Opladen: Westdeutscher Verlag.

Assmann, Heinz Dieter (1980a) *Wirtschaftsrecht in der Mixed Economy. Auf der Suche nach einem Sozialmodell für das Wirtschaftsrecht*. Königstein: Athenäum.

ASSMANN, Heinz-Dieter (1980b) 'Zur Steuerung gesellschaftlich-ökonomischer Entwicklung durch Recht', in H.-D. Assmann, G. Brüggemeier, D. Hart and C. Joerges, *Wirtschaftsrecht als Kritik des Privatrechts*. Königstein: Athenäum.

ASSMANN, Heinz-Dieter, Gerd BRÜGGEMEIER, Dieter HART and Christian JOERGES (1980) *Wirtschaftsrecht als Kritik des Privatrechts*. Königstein: Athenäum.

BADURA, Peter, Fritz RITTNER, and Bernd RUETHERS (1977) *Mitbestimmungsgesetz 1976 und Grundgesetz. Gemeinschaftsgutachten*. München: Beck.

BARDACH, Eugene and Robert A. KAGAN (1982) *Going by the Book—the Problem of Regulatory Unreasonableness*. Philadelphia: Temple University Press.

BARTON, John H. (1975) 'Behind the Legal Explosion', 27 *Stanford Law Review* 567.

BEER, Stafford (1975) 'Preface to "Autopoiesis"', in: H. Maturana and F. Varela (1980) *Autopoiesis and Cognition*. London: Reidel.

BENDER, Rolf (1976) 'Das staatliche Schiedsgericht—ein Ausweg aus der Krise des Zivilprozesses?', 54 *Deutsche Richterzeitung* 193.

BERNER, Georg (1978) 'Inflation im Recht', 24 *Bayrisches Verwaltungsblatt* 617.

BERNSTEIN, Marver (1955) *Regulating Business by Independent Commissions*. Princeton: Princeton University Press.

BEYME, Klaus von (1977) *Gewerkschaften und Arbeitsbeziehungen in kapitalistischen Ländern*. München: Piper.

BIERBRAUER, Günter, Josef FALKE and Klaus Friedrich KOCH (1978) 'Konflikt und Konfliktbeteiligung. Eine interdisziplinäre Studie über Rechtsgrundlage und Funktion der Schiedsmannsinstitution', in Bierbrauer *et al. Zugang zum Recht*. Bielefeld: Gieseking.

BLANKENBURG, Erhard (1984) 'The Poverty of Evolutionism. A Critique of Teubner's Case for "Reflexive Law"', 18 *Law and Society Review* 723.

BLANKENBURG, Erhard, Walter GOTTWALD and Dieter STREMPEL (eds.) (1982) *Alternativen in der Ziviljustiz*. Köln: Bundesanzieger Verlag.

BLANKENBURG, Erhard, Ekkehard KLAUSA and Hubert ROTTLEUTHNER (eds.) (1980) *Alternative Rechtsformen und Alternativen zum Recht*. Opladen: Westdeutscher Vlg.

BOERLIN, Daniel, Gottlieb A. KELLER and Christoph ZUMSTEIN (1978) 'Die Normenflut als Rechtsproblem', in K. Eichenberger, W. Buser, A. Metraux, P. Trappe (eds.), *Grundfragen der Rechtsetzung*. Basel.

BOHNERT, Werner and Wolfgang KITZSCH (1980) 'Gesellschaftliche Selbstregulierung und staatliche Implementation politischer Programme' in R. Mayntz (ed.), *Implementation politischer Programme* I. Königstein: Athenäum.

BOSETZKY, Horst (1978) 'Bürokratisierung in Wirtschaft und Unternehmung', in H. Geissler (ed.), *Verwaltete Bürger-Gesellschaft in Fesseln. Bürokratisierung und ihre Folgen für Staat, Wirtschaft und Gesellschaft*. Frankfurt a.M.: Ullstein.

BREYER, Stephen G. (1981) *Administrative Law and Regulatory Policy*. Boston: Little Brown.

——(1982) *Regulation and its Reform*. Cambridge: Harvard University Press.

BRÜGGEMEIER, Gerd (1980) 'Probleme einer Theorie des Wirtschaftsrechts', in H.-D. Assmann, G. Brüggemeier, D. Hart, C. Joerges, *Wirtschaftsrecht als Kritik des Privatrechts*. Königstein: Athenäum.

BUXBAUM, Richard M. (1984a) 'Corporate Legitimacy, Economic Theory, and Legal Doctrine', 45 *Ohio State Law Journal* 515.

—— (1984b) 'Federalism and Company Law', 82 *Michigan Law Review.*

—— (1986) 'Federal Aspects of Corporate Law and Economic Theory', in T. C. Daintith and G. Teubner (eds.), *Contract and Organization*. Berlin: De Gruyter.

CHRISTIE, Nils (1976) 'Konflikte als Eigentum', *Informationsbrief der Sektion Rechtssoziologie der deutschen Gesellschaft für Soziologie* 12.

CLARK, Robert (1981) 'The Four Stages of Capitalism: Reflections on Investment Management Treaties', 94 *Harvard Law Review* 561.

COASE, Ronald H. (1964) 'Comment', 14 *American Economic Review* 194.

DÄUBLER, Wolfgang (1976) *Das Arbeitsrecht* Bd. 1. Reinbek: Rowohlt.

DAINTITH, Terence C. (1987) 'Law as Policy Instrument: A Comparative Perspective', in T. C. Daintith (ed.), *Law and Economic Policy: Comparative and Critical Approaches*. Berlin: De Gruyter.

DAINTITH, Terence C. and Gunther TEUBNER (eds.) (1986) *Contract and Organisation*. Berlin: De Gruyter.

DAMM, Reinhard (1976) *Systemtheorie und Recht. Zur Normentheorie Talcott Parsons*. Berlin: Duncker und Humblot.

DANZIG, Richard (1973) 'Toward the Creation of a Complementary Decentralized System of Criminal Justice', 26 *Stanford Law Review* 1.

DREIER, Horst (1983) 'Rezension zu Voigt, Verrechtlichung', 4 *Zeitschrift für Rechtssoziologie* 101.

EDELMAN, Murray (1964) *The Symbolic Uses of Politics*. Urbana: University of Illinois Press.

EDER, Klaus (1978) 'Zur Rationalisierungsproblematik des modernen Rechts', 29 *Soziale Welt* 247.

EHRLICH, Thomas (1976) 'Legal Pollution', *New York Times Magazine* (February 8) 17.

ERD, Rainer (1978) *Verrechtlichung industrieller Konflikte. Normative Rahmenbedingungen des dualen Systems der Industrie*. Frankfurt a.M.: Campus.

—— (1984) 'Gesetzgebung oder Machtpoker? Das Beispiel der amerikanischen Gewerkschaften', in R. Voigt (ed.), *Abschied vom Recht?* Frankfurt: Suhrkamp.

FARJAT, Gerard (1986) 'The Contribution of Economics to Legal Analysis: The Concept of the Firm' in G. Teubner and T. Daintith (eds.) *Contract and Organization*. Berlin: De Gruyter.

FEICK, Jürgen (1980) 'Zur Kritik regulativer Politik in den Vereinigten Staaten', 21 *Politische Vierteljahresschrift* 43.

FIKENTSCHER, Wolfgang (1975) *Methoden des Rechts*. Tübingen: Mohr Siebeck.

FISCHER, Robert (1978) 'Kurzinformation', 28 *Wirtschaft und Wettbewerb* 6.

FLUME, Werner (1977) *Allgemeiner Teil des Bürgerlichen Rechtes, Bd. I, Teil 1. Die Personengesellschaft.* Berlin: Springer.

FRAENKEL, Ernst (1932) 'Die politische Bedeutung des Arbeitsrechts', in T. Ramm (ed.) (1966) *Arbeitsrecht und Politik.* Neuwied: Luchterhand.

FRIEDMAN Lawrence M. (1975) *The Legal System. A Social Science Perspective.* New York: Simon and Schuster.

FULLER, Lon L. (1969) 'Two Principles of Human Association'. 11 *Nomos 3.*

GALANTER, Marc (1980) 'Legality and its Discontents: A Preliminary Assessment of Current Theories of Legalization and Delegalization', in E. Blankenburg, E. Klausa and H. Rottleuthner (eds.), *Alternative Rechtsformen und Alternativen zum Recht.* Opladen: Westdeutscher Verlag.

——(1981) 'Justice in Many Rooms: Courts, Private Ordering and Indigenous Law', in M. Cappelletti (ed.), *Access to Justice and the Welfare State.* Alphen: Sijthoff.

GESSNER, Volker and Gerd WINTER (1982) *Rechtsformen der Verflechtung von Staat und Wirtschaft.* Opladen: Westdeutscher Verlag.

GIESE, Bernhard (1978) 'Ansätze zur Tatsachenforschung und Rechtssoziologie des Prozessvergleichs', in G. Bierbrauer *et al. Zugang zum Recht.* Bielefeld: Gieseking.

GLANVILLE, Ranulph (1979) *The Form of Cybernetics: Whitening the Black Box.* Louisville, Kentucky.

GOTTHOLD, Jürgen (1981) 'Neuere Entwicklung der Wettbewerbstheorie', 145 *Zeitschrift für das gesamte Handelsrecht und Wirtschaftsrecht* 286.

——(1984a) 'Privatisierung oder Entbürokratisierung kommunaler Sozialpolitik zur Erfüllung von Aufgaben, die nicht durch Geld und Recht steuerbar sind', in R. Voigt (ed.), *Abschied vom Recht?* Frankfurt: Suhrkamp.

——(1984b) 'Jenseits von Geld und Recht. Chancen und Grenzen kommunaler Sozialpolitik für soziale Brennpunkte', in Krüger and Pankoke (eds.), *Kommunale Sozialpolitik.* München: Beck.

GOTTWALD, Walter (1981) *Streitbeilegung ohne Urteil.* Tübingen: Mohr und Siebeck.

GROSER, Manfred (1979) 'Stabilität und Wandel im System der Arbeitsbeziehungen', 20 *Politische Vierteljahresschrift* 258.

HABERMAS, Jürgen (1976) *Zur Rekonstruktion des historischen Materialismus.* Frankfurt: Suhrkamp.

——(1981) *Theorie des kommunikativen Handelns* Vol. 1 and 2. Frankfurt: Suhrkamp.

——(1985) 'Law as Medium and Law as Institution', in G. Teubner (ed.), *Dilemmas of Law in the Welfare State.* Berlin/New York: De Gruyter.

HART, Dieter (1983) 'Contract and Consumer Protection: Organizing Countervailing Power—On the Development of Substantive and Reflexive Elements in Modern Contract Law', in D. Trubek (ed.), *Reflexive Law and the Regulatory Crisis,* Madison: University of Madison.

HART, Dieter, and Christian JOERGES (1980) 'Verbraucherrecht und Marktökonomie', in H.-D. Assmann, G. Brüggemeier, D. Hart and C. Joerges, *Wirtschaftsrecht als Kritik des Privatrechts.* Königstein: Athenäum.

HARTER, Philip J. (1982) 'Negotiating Regulation: A Cure for Malaise', 71 *Georgetown Law Journal* 1.

HAYEK, Friedrich A. von (1972) *Die Theorie komplexer Phänomene*. Tübingen: Mohr.

—— (1973–79) *Law Legislation and Liberty*, vols. 1–3. London: Routledge & K. Paul.

HEGENBARTH, Rainer (1980) 'Sichtbegrenzungen, Forschungsdefizite und Zielkonflikte in der Diskussion über Alternativen zur Justiz', in E. Blankenburg, E. Klausa and H. Rottleuthner (eds.), *Alternative Rechtsformen und Alternative zum Recht*. Opladen: Westdeutscher Verlag.

—— (1983) 'Selbstauflösung des Rechtssystems', in R. Voigt (ed.), *Abschied vom Recht?* Frankfurt: Suhrkamp.

HEJL, Peter M. (1982a) *Sozialwissenschaft als Theorie selbstreferentieller Systeme*. Frankfurt: Campus.

—— (1982b) 'Die Theorie autopoietischer Systeme: Perspektiven für die soziologische Systemtheorie', 13 *Rechtstheorie* 45.

HELDRICH, Andreas (1981) 'Normüberflutung'. *Festschrift für Zweigert*. Tübingen: Mohr und Siebeck.

HELLER, Thomas C. (1979) 'Is the Charitable Exemption from Property Taxation an Easy Case? General Concerns about Legal Economics and Jurisprudence', in D. Rubinfeld (ed.), *Essays on the Law and the Economics of Local Governments*. Washington D.C.: Urban Institute.

HILLERMEIER, Karl (1978) 'Eindämmung der Gesetzesflut', 24 *Bayrisches Verwaltungsblatt* 321.

HOFFMANN, Reinhard (1968) *Rechtsfortschritt durch gewerkschaftliche Gegenmacht*. Frankfurt a.M.: Europäische Verlagsanstalt.

HOPPMANN, Erich (1972) *Fusionskontrolle*. Tübingen: Mohr Siebeck.

HOPT, Klaus and Gunther TEUBNER (eds.) (1985) *Corporate Governance and Directors' Liability*. Berlin: De Gruyter.

INDUSTRIAL POLICY STUDY GROUP (1984) *Promoting Economic Growth and Competitiveness*. London.

JACOBY, Henry (1969) *Die Bürokratisierung der Welt. Ein Beitrag zur Problemgeschichte*. Neuwied: Luchterhand.

JOERGES, Christian (1981) *Verbraucherschutz als Rechtsproblem*. Heidelberg: Verlagsgesellschaft Recht und Wirtschaft.

—— (1983) 'Der Schutz des Verbrauchers und die Einheit des Zivilrechts', 28 *Aktiengesellschaft* 57.

KENNEDY, Duncan (1973) 'Legal Formality', 2 *The Journal of Legal Studies* 351.

—— (1976) 'Form and Substance in Private Law Adjudication', 89 *Harvard Law Review* 1685.

KIRCHHEIMER, Otto (1933) 'Verfassungsreform und Sozialdemokratie' (1972) in O. Kirchheimer (ed.), *Funktionen des States und der Verfassung*. Frankfurt: Suhrkamp.

KLAUSS, Gerd (1975) *Die Bestimmung von Marktmacht. Eine Untersuchung von Machtkriterien unter Berücksichtigung der Zusammenschlußkontrolle des 'Gesetzes gegen*

Wettbewerbsbeschränkungen' in der Bundesrepublik Deutschland. Berlin: Duncker und Humblot.

KOLKO, Gabriel (1965) *Railroads and Regulation 1877–1916.* Princeton: Princeton U.P.

KÖNDGEN, Johannes (1981) *Selbstbindung ohne Vertrag. Zur Haftung aus geschäftsbezogenem Handeln.* Tübingen: Mohr und Siebeck.

KRAWIETZ, Werner (1978) *Juristische Entscheidung und wissenschaftliche Erkenntnis. Eine Untersuchung zum Verhältnis von dogmatischer Rechtswissenschaft und rechtswissenschaftlicher Grundlagenforschung.* Wien, New York: Springer.

KÜBLER, Friedrich (1981) *Gesellschaftsrecht.* Heidelberg: C.F. Müller.

KÜBLER, Friedrich, Walter SCHMIDT and Spiros SIMITIS (1978) *Mitbestimmung als gesetzgebungspolitische Aufgabe. Zur Verfassungsmäßigkeit des Mitbestimmungsgesetzes.* Baden-Baden: Nomos.

LADEUR, Karl-Heinz (1982a) 'Konsensstrategien statt Verfassungsinterpretation?', 29 *Der Staat* 391.

——(1982b) 'Verrechtlichung der Ökonomie—Ökonomisierung des Rechts?' in V. Gessner, G. Winter (eds.), *Rechtsformen der Verflechtung von Staat und Wirtschaft.* Opladen: Westdeutscher Verlag.

——(1983) 'Politische Ökonomie verwaltungsgerichtlicher Planungskontrolle', in R. Voigt (ed.), *Gegentendenzen zur Verrechtlichung.* Opladen: Westdeutscher Verlag.

——(1984) *Abwägung—Ein neues Paradigma des Verwaltungsrechts.* Frankfurt: Campus.

LEHNER, Franz (1979) *Grenzen des Regierens.* Königstein: Athenäum.

LITAN, Robert E. and William D. NORDHAUS (1983) *Reforming Federal Regulation.* Yale: Yale University Press.

LOWI, Theodore (1969) *The End of Liberalism.* New York: Norton.

LÜBBE-WOLFF, Gertrude (1981) *Rechtsfolgen und Realfolgen.* Freiburg: Alber.

LUHMANN, Niklas (1972) *Rechtssoziologie.* Reinbek: Rowohlt.

——(1974) *Rechtssystem und Rechtsdogmatik.* Stuttgart: Kohlhammer.

——(1975) 'Die Weltgesellschaft', in *Soziologische Aufklärung.* Opladen: Westdeutscher Verlag.

——(1977) *Funktion der Religion.* Frankfurt a.M.: Suhrkamp.

——(1981a) *Ausdifferenzierung des Rechts.* Frankfurt a.M.: Suhrkamp.

——(1981b) 'Selbstreferenz und Teleologie in gesellschaftstheoretischer Perspektive', in N. Luhmann, *Gesellschaftsstruktur und Semantik 2.* Frankfurt: Suhrkamp.

——(1981c) *Politische Theorie im Wohlfahrtsstaat.* München: Olzog.

——(1984) *Soziale Systeme. Grundriß einer allgemeinen Theorie.* Frankfurt: Suhrkamp.

——(1985) 'The Self-Reproduction of the Law and its Limits' in G. Teubner (ed.), *Dilemmas of Law in the Welfare State.* Berlin: De Gruyter.

——(1987) 'The Unity of the Legal System' in G. Teubner (ed.), *Autopoiesis in Law and Society.* Berlin: De Gruyter.

LUTTER, Marcus (1982) 'Rolle und Recht', in *Festschrift für Helmut Coing.* München: Beck.

MACAULY, Stewart (1983) 'Private Government', in D. Trubek (ed.), *Reflexive Law and the Regulatory Crisis*. Madison: University of Madison-Wisconsin.

MARTENS, Klaus Peter (1976) 'Allgemeine Grundsätze zur Anwendbarkeit des Mitbestimmungsgesetzes', 21 *Aktiengesellschaft* 113.

MATURANA, Humberto R., Francisco E. VARELA and R. URIBE (1980) *Autopoiesis and Cognition*. Boston: Reidel.

MAYNTZ, Renate (1977) 'Die Implementation politischer Programme: Theoretische Überlegungen zu einem neuen Forschungsgebiet', 10 *Die Verwaltung* 51.

——(1979) 'Regulative Politik in der Krise?', in J. Matthes (ed.), *Sozialer Wandel in Westeuropa*. Frankfurt: Campus.

——(1980) 'Die Implementation politischer Programme', in R. Mayntz (ed.), *Implementation politischer Programme I*. Königstein: Athenäum.

——(1983) 'Zur Einleitung: Probleme der Theoriebildung', in R. Mayntz (ed.), *Implementation politischer Programme II. Ansätze zur Theoriebildung*. Opladen: Westdeutscher Verlag.

McCONNELL, Grant (1966) *Private Power and American Democracy*. New York: Vintage Books.

McCORMICK, Robert E. and Robert D. TOLLISON (1981) *Politicians, Legislation and the Economy*. Boston: Nijhoff.

McCRAW, Thomas K. (1975) 'Regulation in America, A Review Article', 49 *Business History Review* 159.

MITNICK, Barry (1980) *The Political Economy of Regulation. Creating, Designing and Removing Regulatory Forms*. New York: Columbia University Press.

MITNICK, S. Shep (1983) *Regulation and the Courts. The Case of the Clean Air Act*. New York: Brookings.

MNOOKIN, Robert H. and Lewis KORNHAUSER (1979) 'Bargaining in the Shadow of the Law. The Case of Divorce', 88 *Yale Law Journal* 950.

MÖSCHEL, Wernhard (1974) *Der Oligopolmißrauch im Recht der Wettbewerbsbeschränkungen*. Tübingen: Mohr und Siebeck.

——(1981a) 'Neuere Entwicklungen der Wettbewerbstheorie', 145 *Zeitschrift für das gesamte Handelsrecht und Wirtschaftsrecht* 590.

——(1981b) 'Zu § 22 IV', in U. Immenga and E. J. Mestmächer: *Kommentar zum Gesetz gegen Wettbewerbsbeschränkungen*. München: Beck.

——(1983) *Recht der Wettbewerbsbeschränkungen*. Köln: Heymann.

MOORE, Sally F. (1973) 'Law and Social Change: The Semi-Autonomous Social Field as an Appropriate Object of Study', 7 *Law & Society Review* 719.

MORITZ, Klaus (1980) 'Begrenzung gewerkschaftlicher Politik durch Arbeitsrecht', in R. Voigt (ed.), *Verrechtlichung*. Königstein: Athenäum.

MÜCKENBERGER, Ulrich (1980) 'Der Arbeitskampf als staatlich inszeniertes Ritual' *Blätter für Steuerrecht, Sozialversicherung und Arbeitsrecht* 241.

MUELLER, Friedrich (1966) *Normstruktur und Normativität. Zum Verhältnis von Recht und Wirklichkeit in der juristischen Hermeneutik, entwickelt an Fragen der Verfassungsinterpretation*. Berlin: Duncker und Humblot.

NONET, Philippe (1969) *Administrative Justice*. New York: Russell Sage Foundation.

NONET, Philippe and Philip SELZNICK (1978) *Law and Society in Transition*. New York: Harper.

NÖRR, Dieter (1974) *Rechtskritik in der römischen Antike*. München: Beck.

OST, François (1984) 'Entre jeu et providence: le juge des relations économiques', in A. Jaquemin and B. Remiche (eds.), *Les magistratures économiques et la Crise*. Brussels: CRISP.

OTT, Claus (1972) 'Die soziale Effektivität des Rechts bei der sozialen Kontrolle der Wirtschaft', 3 *Jahrbuch für Rechtssoziologie und Rechtstheorie* 345.

PITSCHAS, Rainer (1980) 'Soziale Sicherung durch fortschreitende Verrechtli-chung?—Staatliche Sozialpolitik im Dilemma von aktiver Sozialgestaltung und normativer Selbstbeschränkung', in R. Voigt (ed.), *Verrechtlichung*. Königstein: Athenäum.

PODGORECKI, Adam (1974) *Law and Society*. London: Routledge and Kegan Paul.

POSNER, Richard (1974) 'Theories of Economic Regulation' 5 *Bell Journal of Economic and Management Science* 335.

RAISER, Thomas (1969) *Das Unternehmen als Organisation: Kritik und Erneuerung der juristischen Unternehmenslehre*. Berlin: De Gruyter.

——(1980) 'Unternehmensziele und Unternehmensbegriffe', 144 *Zeitschrift für das gesamte Handelsrecht und Wirtschaftsrecht* 260.

REHBINDER, Manfred (1967) 'Wandlungen der Rechtsstrukturen im Sozialstaat', in E.E. Hirsch and M. Rehbinder (eds.), *Studien und Materialien zur Rechtssoziologie*. Opladen: Westdeutscher Verlag.

REICH, Norbert (1977) *Markt und Recht*. Neuwied: Luchterhand.

——(1983) 'The Regulatory Crisis: Ideology or Reality?', in D. Trubek (ed.), *Reflexive Law and the Regulatory Crisis*. Madison: University of Wisconsin.

RÖHL, Klaus F. (1980) 'Der Vergleich—eine Alternative zum Recht?' in E. Blanken-burg, E. Klausa and H. Rottleuthner (eds.), *Alternative Rechtsformen und Alter-native zum Recht*. Opladen: Westdeutscher Verlag.

——(1982) 'Rechtspolitische und ideologische Hintergründe der Diskussion über Alternativen zur Justiz', in E. Blankenburg, W. Gottwald, D. Stempel (eds.), *Alternativen in der Ziviljustiz*. Opladen: Westdeutscher Verlag.

RONGE, Volker (1984) 'Entrechtlichung oder äquifunktionale "Alternativen zum Recht" '?, in R. Voigt (ed.), *Abschied vom Recht?* Frankfurt: Suhrkamp.

ROSENBAUM, Wolf (1982) 'Die Wirkungen des Arbeitsrechts auf die Bezie-hungen zwischen Arbeitnehmern und Arbeitgebern im Betrieb', 10 *Leviathan* 392.

ROTTLEUTHNER, Hubert (1979) 'Zur Methode einer folgenorientierten Rechtsan-wendung', *Archiv für Rechts und Sozialphilosophie, Beiheft 13*.

——(1985) 'Theories of Legal Evolution: Between Empiricism and Philosophy of History', *Rechtstheorie Supplement 9*.

SABATIER, Paul and Daniel MAZMANIAN (1980) 'The Implementation of Public Policy: A Framework of Analysis', 8 *Policy Studies Journal* 538.

SCHARPF, Fritz (1979) 'Die Rolle des States im westdeutschen Wirtschaftssystem: Zwischen Krise und Neuorientierung', in v. Weizsäcker (ed.), *Staat und Wirtschaft*. Berlin: Duncker und Humblot.

SCHMITTER, Philippe C. (1977) 'Modes of Interest Intermediation and Models of Societal Change in Western Europe', 10 *Comparative Political Studies* 7.

SELZNICK, Philip (1968) 'Law. The Sociology of Law', 9 *International Encyclopedia of the Social Sciences* 50.

—— (1969) *Law, Society and Industrial Justice*. New York: Russell Sage.

SENDLER, Horst (1979) 'Normenflut und Richter', 12 *Zeitschrift für Rechtspolitik* 227.

SHKLAR, Judith N. (1964) *Legalism*. Cambridge: Harvard University Press.

SIMITIS, Spiros (1984) 'Zur Verrechtlichung der Arbeitsbeziehungen', in H.F. Zacher, S. Simitis, F. Kübler, K. Hopt and G. Teubner, *Verrechtlichung von Wirtschaft, Arbeit und sozialer Solidarität*. Frankfurt: Suhrkamp.

STARCK, Christian (1979) 'Übermaß und Rechtsstaat?' 12 *Zeitschrift für Rechtspolitik* 209.

STEINDORFF, Ernst (1973) 'Politik des Gesetzes als Auslegungsmaßstab im Wirtschaftsrecht', in: *Festschrift für Karl Larenz*. München: Beck.

—— (1979) 'Legal Consequences of State Regulation', 17 *International Encyclopedia of Comparative Law*, Ch. 11. Tübingen: Mohr und Siebeck.

STEWART, Richard (1981) 'Regulation, Innovation and Administrative Law. A Conceptual Framework', 69 *California Law Review* 1263.

—— (1986) 'Regulation and the Crisis of Legalization in the United States', in T. Daintith (ed.), *Law as an Instrument of Economic Policy: Comparative and Critical Approaches*. Berlin: De Gruyter.

STIGLER, George Joseph (1971) 'The Theory of Economic Regulation', 2 *Bell Journal of Economics and Management Science* 3.

—— (1972) 'The Process of Economic Regulation', 17 *Anti-Trust Bulletin* 207.

—— (1975) *The Citizen and the State: Essays on Regulation*. Chicago: University of Chicago Press.

—— (1976) 'The Sizes of Legislation', 5 *Journal of Legal Studies* 17.

STONE, Christopher D. (1975) *Where the Law Ends? The Social Control of Corporate Behaviour*. New York: Harper & Row.

STREECK, Wolfgang (1979) 'Gewerkschaftsorganisation und industrielle Beziehungen', in J. Matthes (ed.), *Sozialer Wandel in Westeuropa*. Frankfurt: Campus.

STREECK, Wolfgang and Philippe C. SCHMITTER (1985) 'Community, Market, State— and Associations?' in W. Streeck and P.C. Schmitter (eds.), *Private Interest Government: Beyond Market and State*. Beverly Hills/London: Sage.

STREECK, Wolfgang, Peter SEGLOW and Pat WALLACE (1978) *Railway Unions in Britain and West Germany. Structural Sources of Crossnational Differences and Similarities*. Frankfurt: Campus.

SUMMERS, Clyde W. (1977) 'The Individual Employee's Rights under the Collective Agreement: What Constitutes Fair Representation?' 126 *University of Pennsylvania Law Review* 251.

TENNSTEDT, Florian (1976) 'Zur Ökonomisierung und Verrechtlichung in der Sozialpolitik', in A. Murswieck (ed.), *Staatliche Politik im Sozialsektor.* München: Piper.

TEUBNER, Gunther (1975) 'Folgenkontrolle und responsive Dogmatik', 6 *Rechtstheorie* 179.

—— (1978a) *Organisationsdemokratie und Verbandsverfassung. Rechtsmodelle für politisch relevante Verbände.* Tübingen: Mohr und Siebeck.

—— (1978b) 'Zu den Regelungsproblemen der Verbände. Neo-Korporatismus und innerverbandliche Opposition', *Juristenzeitung* 545.

—— (1979) 'Neo-korporatistische Strategien rechtlicher Organisationssteuerung', 10 *Zeitschrift für Parlamentsfragen* 487.

—— (1980) 'Kommentierung des § 242', in *Alternativkommentar zum Bürgerlichen Gesetzbuch.* Neuwied: Luchterhand.

—— (1983) 'Substantive and Reflexive Elements in Modern Law', 17 *Law and Society Review* 239.

—— (1984) 'Autopoiesis in Law and Society: A Rejoinder to Blankenburg' 18 *Law and Society Review* 281.

—— (1985) 'After Legal Instrumentalism? Strategic Models of Post-regulatory Law' in G. Teubner (ed.), *Dilemmas of Law in the Welfare State.* Berlin/New York: De Gruyter.

—— (1987) 'Autopoietic Law', in G. Teubner (ed.), *Autopoiesis in Law and Society.* Berlin: De Gruyter.

TEUBNER, Gunther and Helmut WILLKE (1984) 'Kontext und Autonomie: Gesellschaftliche Selbststeuerung durch reflexives Recht', 5 *Zeitschrift für Rechtssoziologie* 4.

TOLCHIN, Susan J. and Martin TOLCHIN (1983) *Dismantling America: The Rush to Deregulate.* Boston: Houghton Mifflin.

TREIBER, Hubert (1983) 'Regulative Politik in der Krise', in D. Trubek (ed.), *Reflexive Law and the Regulatory Crisis.* Madison: University Wisconsin-Madison.

TRUBEK, David (1972) 'Toward a Social Theory of Law: An Essay on the Study of Law and Development', 82 *Yale Law Journal* 11.

—— (1983) (ed.), *Reflexive Law and the Regulatory Crisis.* Madison: University of Madison Press.

TURKEL, Gerald (1980–81) 'Rational Law and Boundary Maintenance', 15 *Law & Society Review* 41.

UNGER, Roberto Mangabeira (1976) *Law in Modern Society.* New York: Free Press.

UNTERSEHER, Lutz (1972) 'Arbeitsrecht—Eine deutsche Spezialität', in O. Jacobi et al. (eds.), *Klassenkampf. Kritisches Jahrbuch.* Frankfurt: Fischer.

VARELA, Francesco J. (1979) *Principles of Biological Autonomy.* New York: Elsevier.

VOGEL, Hans-Jochen (1979) 'Zur Diskussion um die Normenflut', *Juristenzeitung* 321.

VOIGT, Rüdiger (1980) 'Verrechtlichung in Staat und Gesellschaft', in R. Voigt (ed.), *Verrechtlichung.* Königstein: Athenäum.

Voigt, Rudiger (1983) 'Gegentendenzen zur Verrechtlichung. Verrechtlichung und Entrechtlichung im Kontext der Diskussion um den Wohlfahrtsstaat', in R. Voigt (ed.), *Gegentendenzen zur Verrechtlichung*. Opladen: Westdeutscher Verlag.

——(1984) *Abschied vom Recht?* Frankfurt a.M.: Suhrkamp.

Walz, Rainer (1983) 'Sozialwissenschaften im Zivilrecht', in R. Walz (ed.), *Sozialwissenschaften im Zivilrecht*. Neuwied: Luchterhand.

Weber, Max (1978) *Economy and Society*. Berkeley: University of California Press.

Weidenbaum, Murray (1980) *Cost of Regulation and Benefits of Reform*.

Weiss, Hans-Dietrich (1978) 'Verrechtlichung als Selbstgefährdung des Rechts', 31 *Die öffentliche Verwaltung* 601.

Werle, Raymond (1982) 'Aspekte der Verrechtlichung', 3 *Zeitschrift für Rechtssoziologie* 2.

Wieacker, Franz (1967) *Privatrechtsgeschichte der Neuzeit*, (2nd edn.). Göttingen: Vandenboeck und Ruprecht.

Wiedemann, Herbert (1980a) *Gesellschaftsrecht*. München: Beck.

——(1980b) 'Rechtsethische Maßstäbe im Unternehmensrecht', 2 *Zeitschrift für Unternehmensrecht und Gesellschaft* 147.

Wiethölter, Rudolf (1968) *Rechtswissenschaft*. Frankfurt, Hamburg: Fischer.

——(1982a) 'Entwicklung des Rechtsbegriffs', in V. Gessner and R. Geinter (eds.), *Rechtsformen der Verflechtung von Staat und Wirtschaft*. Opladen: Westdeutscher Verlag.

——(1982b) 'Wissenschaftskritische Ausbildungsreform—Anspruch und Wirklichkeit', in R. Francke, D. Hart, R. Lautman and P. Thoss (eds.), *Einstufige Juristenausbildung in Bremen. Zehn Jahre Bremen Modell*. Neuwied: Luchterhand.

——(1985) 'Materialization and Proceduralization', in G. Teubner (ed.), *Dilemmas of Law in the Welfare State*. Berlin: De Gruyter.

Willke, Helmut (1983a) *Die Entzauberung des Staates. Überlegungen zu einer sozietalen Steuerungstheorie*. Königstein: Athenäum.

——(1983b) 'Gesellschaftliche Kritierien ökonomischer Rationalität'. Bielefeld: Manuscript.

Wilson, James (1980) *The Politics of Regulation*. New York: Basic Books.

Windhoff-Heritier, Adrienne (1980) *Politikimplementation. Ziel und Wirklichkeit politischer Entscheidungen*. Königstein: Athenäum.

Windscheid, Bernhard (1904) 'Die Aufgaben der Rechtswissenschaft', in B. Windscheid, *Gesammelte Reden und Abhandlungen*. Leipzig: Duncker.

Winkler, John T. (1976) 'Corporatism', 17 *European Journal of Sociology* 100.

Winter, Gerd (1982) 'Literaturbericht zum Thema', in V. Gessner and G. Winter (eds.), *Rechtsformen der Verflechtung von Staat und Wirtschaft*. Opladen: Westdeutscher Verlag.

Ziegert, (1975) *Zur Effektivität der Rechtssoziologie. Die Rekonstruktion der Gesellschaft durch Recht*. Stuttgart: Enke.

Part IV
Varieties of Regulatory Scale

Regulatory Competition in the Single Market

J.-M. SUN AND J. PELKMANS

Abstract

Although regulatory competition has been hailed in some quarters as a superior alternative to Council-driven harmonization, little empirical investigation has been carried out to demonstrate how regulatory competition might work in actual EC practice, and therefore whether its expected benefits will, in fact, materialize.

We construct a framework stylizing the iterative process of regulatory competition, and illuminate its emergence from five elements of the regulatory strategy of the EC-1992 internal market programme.

The framework presented shows that the process of regulatory competition is a complex and unpredictable one. Two case studies are provided to exemplify the difficulties. These practical limitations severely weaken the case for regulatory competition based on theoretical economic arguments. Moreover, a comparative cost-benefit analysis of regulatory competition and harmonization suggests that, where relevant, regulatory competition and harmonization should be seen as complements, rather than substitutes. The demarcation between the two is best determined on a case-by-case basis according to the principle of subsidiarity.

I. Introduction

Once the EC-1992 process had begun to take shape, a fundamental debate on the optimal regulatory strategy for the single market emerged. Following the advocacy of 'competition among rules' in the Padoa-Schioppa Report (1987), this debate came to be focused on the merits of, and potential for, 'regulatory competition'. There is now an emerging literature on regulatory competition (see, e.g., Hauser and Hosli, 1991; Siebert, 1990; Siebert and Koop, 1990, 1993), which is inspired by the literature on economic regulation and the economics of federalism. Crucial in the former is that regulation can only be economically justified if it remedies a market failure, while minimizing its (regulatory) costs. The latter provides the economic underpinning of subsidiarity, in seeking the optimal economic assignment of regulatory competencies in a multi-layer structure of government.

While much of this literature discusses the supposed attributes of regulatory competition from a theoretical economic perspective, there is scant literature which explains exactly how regulatory competition might work in actual practice. Indeed, the practical application of the policy conclusions drawn by the existing literature would present serious difficulties. The most far-reaching of these conclusions is that regulatory competition should be considered a *substitute* for harmonization, and that the former is a superior substitute on normative economic grounds. This article will show that this generalization is unlikely to hold in the absence of specific caveats, and that it will only exceptionally hold if applied within the context of the EC's single market. This neither means, however, that regulatory competition has no (economic) merits, nor that the EC should not encourage it where possible and desirable.

After briefly setting out what exactly regulatory competition is, and how it emerged from EC-1992 and its regulatory strategy (Section II), we stylize regulatory competition in the single market with the aid of a flow chart (Section III). In Sections IV and V, we provide two case studies. The purpose there is to illustrate a number of difficulties with regulatory competition—for instance, that it is difficult to observe and assess, may take a lot of time or is open-ended, or that it might not occur at all. With the contextual EC framework thus defined, Section VI turns to the relative merits of regulatory competition and harmonization based on a cost-benefit analysis for each. Section VII concludes.

II. The Nature of Regulatory Competition

What is Regulatory Competition?

Regulatory competition is the alteration of national regulation in response to the actual or expected impact of internationally mobile goods, services, or factors on national economic activity.[1] Regulatory competition presupposes some degree of national acceptance of the economic mobilities at stake; the option of blocking or throttling these mobilities is consciously forgone. This acceptance may arise from international obligations, but could also flow from unilateral policy decisions. So for example, there are few (if any) *de jure* obligations on countries to allow the free movement of portfolio capital, yet portfolio capital markets have become global in scope. Given such high mobility (and aided by the removal of cross-border controls), there is a compelling need to adapt regulation (for example) to prevent large capital outflows and consequent hikes in the rate of interest. One can interpret this regulatory adjustment as an attempt to 'compete' for the mobile factor, which will arbitrage across the various existing market opportunities.

In the specific context of the EC's single market, the key elements that may prompt regulatory competition are *free movement* and *mutual recognition*. Free movement implies a right of access to the markets of other Member States and hence the *de facto* irrelevance of intra-EU border controls. But when product, service, or factor markets are regulated, free movement is not a sufficient condition for market access; approximation of economic regulation should be such that cross-border movement is not more costly than intra-national flows.

An important innovation which facilitates free movement is the principle of mutual recognition, which is based around the idea of establishing equivalent regulatory *objectives*. Given such equivalence, regulatory instruments (i.e. specific details, technical specifications, reference to standards) can no longer serve to deny market access. There are, in turn, two distinct sub-principles of mutual recognition. The *judicial* principle has emerged from *Cassis de Dijon* case law: even if Article 36 EC-type essential requirements apply, mutual recognition is compulsory if those requirements are deemed to be equivalent among Member States, to the extent that national essential requirements are maintained.[2] Moreover, measures must be proportional to the objective sought and least restrictive for free movement. In 1985, the White Paper on completing the internal market introduced mutual recognition as a *regulatory* principle: approximation of laws was purposefully limited to the essential requirements, beyond which mutual recognition would henceforth apply.[3]

Judicial mutual recognition has the great merit of removing (or pre-empting) arbitrary requirements which help to protect domestic producers. By eliminating a major category of technical barriers, it exposes producers to EC competition, in spite of (extra or differentiated) regulation. Regulatory mutual recognition plays a complementary role in greatly facilitating the harmonization process. Where applicable, it moves the Community away from the 'all-or-nothing' trap of harmonization. It is also useful from an economic point of view since in many cases there is no economic justification for pursuing such comprehensive EC regulation.

But mutual recognition is a static notion. An importing Member State A has to 'accept' as equivalent the regulatory regime (if any) of B under which the product or service is produced and marketed. No regulatory adjustment is implied. Regulatory competition, on the other hand, is dynamic. Given, or in anticipation of, 'acceptance' or mutual recognition, national regulation is adapted in response to the actual or expected impact of the mobilities induced. As other Member States may do this too, or if initial adjustments were somehow insufficient, iterative processes may develop. It is normally taken for granted that regulatory competition is the result of complex business—government interactions which occur at national level, leading Member States to experiment for such strategic reasons as the 'competitiveness' of local business or the reduction of the adverse effects of its (say, relatively costly) regulations on local business in the single market.

The more radical proposition referred to before can now be stated more precisely. When regulatory competition is a substitute for harmonization, internal market forces would respond to differences in national regulation. The subsequent variations in the flow of goods, services, and factors would force the adversely affected Member States to react. Such an iterative process would eventually bring about a 'market-driven' regulatory convergence. Since market preferences would probably be better revealed by the dynamics of regulatory competition, than by bureaucracy-driven and politicized harmonization in the Council, regulatory competition would further be a superior solution on normative economic grounds.

The Emergence of Regulatory Competition from EC-1992

The potential for regulatory competition in the single market is better understood once it is placed against the backdrop of the Community's regulatory strategy. In the course of the EC-1992 process, a regulatory strategy emerged which consisted of five elements: free movement, minimum harmonization, mutual recognition, subsidiarity, and no internal frontiers (see Pelkmans and Sun, 1994, for elaboration).

First, *free movement* within the internal market is much more secure today as a result of the progressive removal of internal frontiers, as set out in the EC-1992 programme. Free movement has been buttressed by the case law of the European Court of Justice and the widespread application of the minimum harmonization and mutual recognition principles. These last two principles are complementary with one another since, by definition, anything less than total harmonization would require Member States mutually to recognize remaining differences in one another's national regulations, if free movement is to be upheld.

Further, the combination of the free movement imperative and reliance on mutual recognition, provides much greater room to apply the *subsidiarity* principle in a functional way.[4] Given that the four economic freedoms of movement in the internal market are much more secure as a result of '1992', and taking comfort from the Court's consistent protection of the single market's integrity, the European Union can be much more relaxed than in the 1970s about the 'remaining' regulatory powers of Member States. At the same time, mutual recognition provides Member States with a degree of regulatory autonomy which, under the old 'all-or-nothing' perspective, could be retained only by maintaining intra-EU barriers.

Finally, the relationship between subsidiarity, free movement, no-internal-frontiers, and mutual recognition is also interesting from a domestic political perspective. The Community's failure to complete its internal market prior to the EC-1992 programme can be explained in large part by the success of national business in persuading their governments to erect all sorts of protective non-tariff barriers. Post-1992, however, the incentives for national industry to 'capture' its national regulators are severely reduced (or, in the extreme, eliminated). Rather, the imperative of remaining internationally competitive now dictates the reverse: industry should 'capture' or otherwise pressure its national legislators to enact regulations which favour domestic competitiveness. If such pressure results in 'deregulation' (i.e. the removal of heretofore protective regulation), the political influence of the regulated industry should also decline: entry into the domestic market by foreign producers will dilute the power of the domestic industry *vis-à-vis* national regulators.[5] Ultimately, the interaction of these five elements allows national regulatory systems to become exposed to one another. The fact of exposure is a *static* event and is the result of mutual recognition. However, the exposure may also (but need not) prompt a *dynamic* process of regulatory competition. The latter is dynamic because regulations are changed over time in response to the market signals unleashed by mutual recognition. In order for a process of regulatory competition actually to take place, a series of business–government interactions must occur at national level. It is to these interactions that we now turn.

III.   Stylizing Regulatory Competition in the European Union

In this section, we focus on regulatory competition as a means to achieve progressive regulatory rapprochement in the internal market. The flow chart in Fig. 14.1 provides a stylized view of EU processes of regulatory

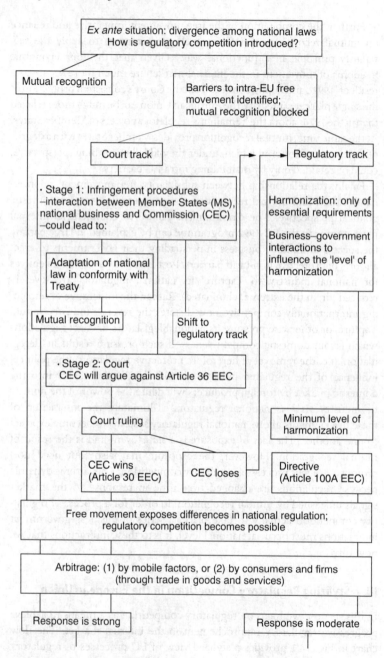

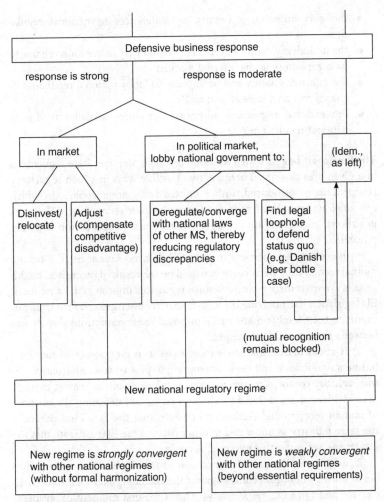

Fig. 14.1 Tracking Regulatory Competition in the EU

competition, post '1992', as we believe they operate. Within these processes, one can identify the 'moments' where business–government interactions can be expected to occur, thereby fuelling the process along. These moments, however, are not uniform; rather, they are opportunities for business behaviour, government behaviour, and their interaction. Whether these opportunities will actually be exploited is a function of a number of factors including:

- the cost differentials implied by differences in national regulations;
- the underlying competitiveness of the industry in question relative to its competitors in the internal market;
- the industry's ability and willingness to lobby national regulators to change national regulations; and
- the national regulatory authority's incentive actually to change national regulations.

The flow chart begins with a situation in which Member State regulations in a given area diverge. There are two possible ways in which regulatory competition is introduced. Either mutual recognition applies, in which case the four economic freedoms of movement are recognized, differences in national regulation are exposed, and regulatory competition becomes possible.

In the other case, barriers to intra-EU free movement exist, blocking mutual recognition. Such barriers would be the result of ostensible 'health or safety' requirements which national regulators impose in the absence of EU legislation harmonizing these 'essential' requirements. A firm trying to export to the Member State which imposed these restrictions can choose between three possible strategies:

(1) It could decide that the export market in question is of marginal business significance and cease attempting to penetrate it. Alternatively, it may actually conform to the national regulations of the export market, thereby incurring additional production costs, and defeating the purpose of mutual recognition.[6] Assuming however, that the firm (and others in the same industry at home and in other parts of the EU) estimate that the export market is worth exploiting, it could:

(2) Lobby the European Commission and/or its home government to begin infringement procedures against the offending Member State (Articles 169 and 170 EEC, respectively). This is the first moment of business–government interaction one can identify, and it occurs within a 'Court track'.

The outcome of these interactions could be a removal of the barrier which originally blocked mutual recognition; an attempt in the Council to establish harmonized minimum essential requirements for the good/service in question (shift to the 'regulatory track'—see below); or an adaptation of the offending national regulation in conformity with the Treaty (i.e. the regulation is adjusted so that it allows free movement and is more 'proportional' to the market failure it seeks to combat). At this stage, business located in the offending regulatory jurisdiction will similarly have an incentive to interact with *its* national regulatory authority.

If none of these solutions is ultimately adopted, the firm/industry will have no choice but to take the case to the European Court of Justice (assuming that the former still believes the case is worth pursuing). At the Court, the defendent Member State will naturally argue that its regulation conforms with Article 36 EC or its rule of reason, or even that Article 30 does not apply; the Commission or prosecuting Member State will argue that the national regulation violates Article 30 EC. If the Court rules in favour of the Commission/prosecuting Member State, the offending national regulation will have to be altered such that imports from other Member States are permitted free access.[7] On the other hand, if the Court upholds the national regulation on the basis of Article 36 EC, it is up to the Council to seek a harmonized level of essential requirements, upon a proposal by the Commission (shift to 'regulatory track').

(3) While the exporting firm could begin infringement procedures, it could equally, from the onset, pressure its national government to get the Council to agree harmonized essential requirements. This is what can be stylized as a 'regulatory track'. At this stage, a second moment of business–government interaction will occur as the exporting firm/industry lobbies its Member State to go for minimum harmonization (or whatever level is most favourable for the national industry), while industry in the country which originally blocked mutual recognition will normally press its government to argue for a higher, more restrictive interpretation of the minimum essential requirements. The level of harmonization ultimately established will manifest itself in the form of a directive, the legal basis of which is Article 100A EC.

At this stage, mutual recognition will be applied, free movement will be recognized, and differences in national regulations will be exposed. How do business–government interactions now fuel the process of regulatory competition?

While mutual recognition, free movement, and differences in national regulations set the stage for regulatory competition, such competition will not actually occur unless economic agents *react to* these differences. There are two ways in which the expected reactions can be understood, both of which rely on the concept of arbitrage.

In the first case, mobile factors of production (capital and, to a much lower degree, labour) can relocate to the jurisdiction whose regulations are most favourable for the factor. Alternatively, arbitrage can occur even if factors of production are immobile. In this scenario, it would be goods and services which, through free movement, could be sold freely across the EC. Consumers and firms would then respond by purchasing the bundle of goods and services which most closely approximates preferences for cost and quality. The scope or 'margin' for either type of arbitrage is a function of the degree to which national regulations diverge. Therefore, if regulatory competition is introduced via a directive which establishes a certain level of harmonization, the scope for arbitrage is correspondingly lower than if free movement had been recognized *without* any prior harmonization.

By engaging in arbitrage, consumers, firms and capital are in effect expressing their preferences for different kinds of regulation. When arbitrage is effected by mobile factors, these preferences are signalled to the authorities which formulate and implement national regulations; when arbitrage opportunities are provided through the free movement of goods and services, the target audience are the businesses involved in producing these goods and services. Business could respond in either of two ways.

Within the internal market, it could either relocate to another Member State whose regulations are more favourable for the firm's operations, or it could 'adjust' by trying to cut costs, or otherwise restructuring its activities so that it can overcome (at least to a certain extent) the immediate competitive disadvantages it faces relative to other firms operating under a lighter regulatory burden. These are reactions which occur in the *economic market*.

However, if industry has incurred large sunk costs to establish itself within a Member State, or if restructuring would involve large reductions in employment, it would probably attempt (first) to lobby its national government; in other words, it would react in the *political market*. Because barriers to free movement can no longer be imposed, the purpose of such lobbying efforts could only be one of two things. Business could either pressure the national government to find a 'legal loophole' with which to defend the status quo and effectively limit free movement, without, however, completely blocking it.[8] On the other hand, business could accept that free movement is now a fact of life, and press its national government to adapt national regulations in a way which reduces regulatory discrepancies and, therefore, the competitive disadvantage faced by national business.

The end result of these cumulative business–government interactions will be 'new' national regulatory regimes across the EC. At one end of the spectrum, a given new regime may be strongly convergent with those of other Member States. The likelihood of this outcome is greater if no prior harmonization *à la* Articles 100 or 100 A was initially established (i.e. regulatory competition was either introduced by mutual recognition, or by a Court ruling on the basis of Article 30 EEC, for goods). At the other end of the spectrum, the new regime may be only slightly different from the former one if the level of minimum harmonization established in a directive under the 'regulatory track' is high, and therefore the scope for arbitrage, and the need for a defensive business response, is low. In this case, national regulators would have little incentive to alter national regulations since the competitive threat to national business would be commensurately lower.

Of course, stylizing such processes may prompt generalizations which may not be valid. Such is the case, for example, with the interpretation of business interests *vis-à-vis* the nature and intensity of regulation. These interests may greatly differ across different firms. Some firms (in some situations) will see regulation as a *restriction* on their ability to manoeuvre, while others in other situations view it as a business *opportunity*. This possibility, however, does not change the fundamental nature of the regulatory competition processes in Fig. 14.1, but merely widens the range of contexts in which business–government interactions can occur. For instance, firms whose core business is the production of environmental technology will benefit from the enactment of certain environmental regulation. On the other hand, firms whose costs would be raised as a result of having to comply with environmental regulation (at least in the short run), would be adversely affected. Both firms should, according to our schema, exert countervailing pressures on their national government. The type of environmental regulation ultimately implemented (or not) will depend *inter alia* on each firm's access to the regulatory authority relative to the other, the political power configurations of the various government ministries involved, and the way in which inter-ministerial conflicts are resolved.

Stylizing regulatory competition in the EU context serves to highlight its constraints and complexities. But, in the absence of a satisfactory behavioural theory of regulatory competition, only case studies can shed further light on these processes. In the following we provide a case study of the goods market and, in Section V, one of the services market. Both are meant to illustrate difficulties and hence are selective (though examples of relatively smooth competitive adoptions of both regulatory and fiscal regimes can be found as well). The typical difficulties illustrated here are that regulatory competition is hard to observe and assess, that it is open-ended or time-consuming, and that it may not transpire at all.

IV.   Case Study I: Upholstered Furniture[9]

This case illustrates the first stages of the flow chart above, namely the business–government interactions within both the 'court' and 'regulatory' tracks.

In 1988, the United Kingdom (UK) enacted national legislation stipulating that any upholstered furniture sold on the UK market must be manufactured with flame retardants, a response to the danger of fires in cinemas, discos, theatres and other public places. The Irish Republic (IRL) also followed suit by enacting similar national legislation that year. Because the other 10 Member States of the EC had no legislation on the matter, a divergence of national laws was created. Moreover, the UK and IRL refused to admit imports from the other 10 Member States if these did not comply with their respective national legislations (though British and Irish upholstered furniture could enter Continental markets). The mutual recognition of continental national regulations was therefore blocked.

Led by the Federal Republic of Germany (D), the 10 continental Member States took the UK and IRL to the European Court of Justice on the grounds that the latter had erected a barrier to the free movement of goods (beginning of infringement procedures under the 'Court track'). While the 10 had the nominal support of the European Commission (CEC), the CEC did not feel that the 10 had a strong case, since the UK and IRL legislations could be justified under Article 36 EEC. Ultimately, in 1990, the UK and IRL persuaded the other 10 to work towards an EC directive harmonizing the essential requirements of upholstered furniture with respect to its fire behaviour (shift to 'Regulatory track').

Within the regulatory track, business–government interactions were intense. For reasons of space, we shall only briefly touch upon the main elements:

- *Business interests* were split into (at least) three active groups: the furniture producers outside the UK and Ireland who wished to level the playing field;[10] the European Flame Retardants Association (EFRA) which formed in September 1990; and a subgroup of these producers which subsequently organized within the European Brominated Flame Retardant Industry Panel (EBFRIP). The formation of EBFRIP was a consequence of heavy political pressure; halogenated flame retardants are believed to be much more dangerous to health, safety and the environment than their non-halogenated counterparts. While EFRA and EBFRIP both pushed for an EC directive, the latter also wished to ensure that the use of halogenated flame retardants would not be excluded.

- Some *national governments* were active in the pre-legislative phase and tried to influence the substance of Commission proposals being drafted in DG III. The question then arises, were these governments 'captured' by local business? It would seem that neither the German nor the Italian government—active though they were—pursued business interests; rather, public safety concerns were primary. Thus, Germany secured a ban on halogenated retardants in the Commission proposal of 1991. As a consequence, German firms, which had not succeeded in persuading the German government to withdraw its opposition to the use of flame retardants, now channelled their lobbying efforts via CEFIC in Brussels (the European Chemical Industry Council). Italy managed to insert an additional test to the original UK and IRL essential requirements, but again, without feeling (any) domestic business pressure. The UK and Ireland pushed for a directive based on their national legislation. This *could* be explained by the fact that, in the UK, most suppliers produce halogenated flame retardants.[11]

- By early 1993, the Commission was set to discuss a proposal for a directive which would have allowed the use of both halogenated and non-halogenated flame retardants in upholstered furniture. It was at this point that Jacques Delors personally withdrew the proposal from the Commission's legislative programme, invoking subsidiarity as a justification. Interestingly, he argued that Member States acting individually could more appropriately enact national legislation. Did he imply that this was true irrespective of mutual recognition, which would clearly be mistaken? Or did he allow for the (indeed, a) possibility that more Member States would legislate on the need for flame retardants and, given the cost advantages, the likelihood that business would no longer sell upholstered furniture without flame retardants in the volume segment of the market? Speculating even further, one could conceive that users (i.e. the market) might 'drive out' the use of halogenated flame retardants, by switching purchases away from furniture produced with such flame retardants, or by demanding that national regulations additionally stipulate the use of non-halogenated flame retardants. The point is that no reliable mechanism exists to gauge whether the *ex post* convergence of regulations or market outcomes is likely to result from these processes (indeed, after Delors' intervention intense lobbying around a potential directive was resumed).

V.   Case Study 2: Banking[12]

Whereas the previous case study focused on the business–government interactions involved in establishing mutual recognition and free movement, the present example begins with a situation in which mutual recognition and free movement prevail at the outset, therefore permitting regulatory competition actually to take place.

The creation of an internal market for banking services from 1 January 1993 is primarily the result of the principle of 'home country control' espoused in the so-called Second Banking Directive (89/646 EEC, 17 December 1989). The principle stipulates that the host country must 'mutually recognize' the regulations of the home country, beyond the harmonized essential requirements.

Given a situation of mutual recognition and free movement, how are differences in national banking regulations being arbitraged by consumers and firms?

One example is given by the French bank Crédit Lyonnais which introduced a high interest deposit account in Belgium before the Second Banking Directive came into effect. Because this type of account is not permitted in Belgium, but can be very advantageous for depositors, Crédit Lyonnais attracted a substantial amount of business away from Belgian banks. Faced with such a competitive disadvantage (i.e. more favourable treatment of foreign banks in Belgium than that of domestic banks), Belgian banks according to our schema should have pressured Belgian bank regulators to alter Belgian law and reduce the regulatory discrepancy.[13] However, Belgian banks have thus far not exerted such pressure on the Belgian authorities. This highlights the difficulty of predicting exactly if, when, and to what degree, business–government interactions will take place.

In a separate, but similar case, Barclays Bank of the UK attempted to introduce interest-bearing current accounts through its subsidiaries in France. However, this effort was blocked by French authorities on the grounds that it would be against the interest of consumers, as it would result in higher fees on deposits for bank customers. The French government consequently enacted legislation banning similar banking products. While our schema predicts (or at least allows for the possibility) that Barclays should have pressured the UK or the CEC to take France to the European Court of Justice, Barclays chose not to do this. Rather, it felt that such a confrontational approach could potentially damage Barclays' future relations with French authorities, and therefore accepted the French ban on their product.

Both of these banking examples demonstrate the limitations of the Court track, or the unwillingness of business more generally to invest resources in order to uphold (as opposed to secure) mutual recognition and free movement.[14] Even more fundamentally, however, these examples underscore the unpredictable and complex nature of business behaviour in a context of regulatory competition. All of these difficulties serve to illustrate that the process of regulatory competition in the EU cannot be generalized by way of overly simplified models.

VI.   Regulatory Competition or Harmonization? A Cost-Benefit Analysis

The schematic representation depicted above shows quite clearly that regulatory competition is a complex, and potentially long, uncertain process. Yet, there is a theoretical economic literature on regulatory competition which claims that it is superior to prior harmonization as a tool for achieving regulatory rapprochement. In this section, we provide a comparative, qualitative cost–benefit analysis for both regulatory competition and harmonization. As the previous section demonstrated, however, due consideration should be paid to institutional and other 'real-world' factors which might decisively impact actual processes of regulatory competition, and therefore the policy choice between regulatory competition and harmonization.

Our main conclusions from such an exercise are twofold: first, the benefits of regulatory competition on theoretical economic grounds may well be outweighed by its practical costs. Second, harmonization is today much more flexible as a result of EC-1992. Therefore, its costs have been dramatically reduced, and in commensurate fashion, so have its disadvantages relative to regulatory competition. A comparative cost–benefit analysis conducted in an EC context therefore casts serious doubt on the general empirical validity of the results from economic theories of regulatory competition.

Regulatory Competition

Broadly speaking, there are three *benefits* of regulatory competition:

1. *Greater choice of regulation.* Given the four economic freedoms of movement, consumers and firms will be able to arbitrage among the differences

in national regulations revealed thereby. With mutual recognition, consumers will be able to choose among the goods and services produced according to various national regulations. To the extent that greater variety increases utility, consumer welfare will be enhanced. Further, when mobility rests with factors of production (capital, and in Europe, to a much lesser degree, labour), these factors can locate within the jurisdiction the regulations of which most closely approximate their preferences; allocative efficiency will be improved, and output will expand.

2. *'Disciplining effect' on national regulatory systems.* With a choice of regulatory regimes, consumer and firm behaviour can serve to tame the 'Leviathan tendencies of government' (Sinn, 1990). According to this reasoning, government officials (politicians and bureaucrats) are self-interested individuals who maximize their utility subject to the constraint of being re-elected/reappointed. Their utility is enhanced by raising tax revenues in excess of what is needed to finance the provision of public goods in their jurisdiction, or by imposing regulation which is socially sub-optimal, but privately beneficial. In a context of fiscal (regulatory) competition, however, governments are forced to provide the public goods demanded by their constituents at the lowest possible tax rate (optimal regulatory burden): if they fail to do this, these constituents might leave the regulatory domain altogether (in which case the tax base of the regulatory domain would be eroded), or they might not re-elect the government. In this way, fiscal (regulatory) competition is said to exert a disciplinary function on government spending (regulation), in the absence of explicit constraints (Hauser and Hosli, 1991).

3. *Strategy for discovery, experimentation, and innovation.* Given a situation of imperfect information among economic agents (including regulators themselves) regarding the most desirable form and content of regulation, regulatory competition provides a market-driven way to 'discover' which regulations offer 'protection' that is demanded by the residents and firms of a given jurisdiction, and which are deemed superfluous. By 'voting with their feet',[15] or by simply substituting purchases of the 'home' good or service with that of a good/service produced according to the regulations of another jurisdiction, consumers and firms will signal their preferences for regulation to their regulatory authority (or, in any event, make explicit the opportunity costs of certain inefficient regulations). Whenever governments recognize that domestic regulations are too costly for citizens or companies—relative to their objectives—they have an incentive (driven by vote maximization, and the fear of tax base erosion due to the relocation of residents) to adapt the system. This makes regulation flexible, and allows

authorities to adopt measures in line with (changing) local preferences. In this way, regulatory competition uses the 'market for regulations' as an exploratory device for finding the best institutional arrangements (Hayek, 1968, quoted in Siebert and Koop, 1993).

On the other hand, there are three types of *costs*:

1. *Open-ended and distortive.* As the case studies illustrate, actual processes of regulatory competition in the EC are very difficult to observe. The iterative process fuelled by business–government interaction can be very time-consuming and fraught with many potential obstacles. While sceptics of regulatory competition often point to the danger of a 'race to the bottom' (implying that jurisdictions involved in the competitive process progressively deregulate until 'zero' regulation is in place; see further, below), it is important to realize that the iterative process *itself* may get 'stuck', leaving regulations unchanged, and the distortions arising from different regulations, in place. In other words, the fear of a 'race to the bottom' presupposes that the competitive process actually proceeds until new regulatory regimes are established. By returning to the flow chart presented earlier, however, it is evident that regulatory competition faces potential obstacles at every step along the way.[16] Assuming free movement (which is itself a problem; see first case study) we will briefly elaborate problems associated with arbitrage and the adaptation of regulation:

Does arbitrage take place?—Imperfect information regarding regulatory differences may prevent arbitrage of these differences. Even if economic agents are aware of regulatory differences, but choose not to arbitrage them, these differences will simply persist. Neither the hoped-for regulatory convergence, nor the creation of a 'level playing field for business' will occur.

Why might regulatory arbitrage not take place? When regulatory competition is seen as a process of arbitrage by mobile factors between locations, two key assumptions are critical: factors are (perfectly) mobile, and they will move in response to differences in regulation. Both of these assumptions, however, are somewhat unrealistic in practice. In the EC, only capital can be said to be mobile, and even then a distinction must be made between portfolio investment (which is highly elastic with respect to net rates of return), and direct investment, which is a function of a variety of factors (including market proximity/transport costs, infrastructure quality and levels, and labour costs relative to skill and productivity levels). Given these caveats, the speed and intensity with which market forces will respond to regulatory divergences will be dulled, and the eventual out-come of the process will therefore be less pronounced.

Another difficulty derives from the role of regulatory preferences. If a given national market exhibits strong regulatory preferences, an entrant to that market (via either local production or exports) may have an economic incentive to produce according to these long-standing national regulatory traditions, rather than to exercise the right, upheld by mutual recognition, of operating according to home-country regulations. This, indeed, is the case illustrated by the banking example above. In such circumstances, the incentive of host-country regulators to adapt national regulations in line with those of the home country is limited, since firms in the host country will feel commensurately lower competitive pressures to adjust.

Will regulation change?—Even if regulatory arbitrage does occur and sends a strong signal to the firms and regulatory authorities involved, the national regulation in question might still not be adapted. To under-stand why this is so, return to the possible ways in which business could respond. In the economic market, for example, the magnitude of any relocation/divestment or adjustment may be too small to cause the regulatory authority to change the regulations. The same argument can be extended to the political market, where firms acting alone or together might not wield the influence necessary to get regulations changed. Recourse to legal loopholes in order to retain barriers to mutual recogni-tion is also an uncertain strategy, as such loopholes will most probably face trial before the European Court.

2. *Sub-optimal regulation.* (a) *Too little regulation*: since regulatory competi-tion exposes costly regulations, one should expect a deregulatory bias in many cases. This introduces the possibility that regulation, justified by existing market failures, will no longer be provided, or will be provided in an inappropriate way. Some of the literature (cf. Siebert and Koop, 1990, 1993; Oates and Schwab, 1988) refutes this proposition. However, the defence of regulatory competition relies on the premise that fiscal and regulatory competition faces similar constraints: with pure *fiscal* competi-tion the potential for a zero or sub-optimal tax rate is reduced if one assumes that the users and payers of public goods are equivalent.[17] Once taxes are reduced beyond a certain level, the marginal costs of such action will outweigh the marginal benefits. In the case of *regulatory* competition, however, the concept of 'equivalence' simply does not apply. Insufficient regulation will allow the re-emergence of the market failure which regula-tion was originally designed to minimize. Take the case of consumers who

cannot immediately, or even *ex post*, observe quality levels (e.g. professional services). This is an example of asymmetric information, and suboptimal regulation would impair the functioning of the market.

(b) Too much regulation: it must be noted that the converse—too high or restrictive regulation—is also a possible outcome of regulatory competition. An example of this is given by the case of registered nurses in the United States. When competition among state licensing rules was allowed to run its course, states followed one another in increasing the restrictiveness of licensing requirements for nurses; inflows of less-skilled nurses from other states provoked a levelling-up, rather than a levelling-down of professional standards (Peltzman, quoted in Pelkmans and Vanheukelen, 1988). In the EU, an analogy is found in the possibility that packaging laws will be made progressively more restrictive in line with the recent German Packaging Ordinance.

3. *National regulatory 'drift'*: national regulatory 'drift' results from the fact that national regulations may be altered several times in the course of 'discovering' which regime is ultimately the most appropriate, with adjustment costs borne by business each time it adapts to new national regulations. Firms will lack the certainty they need in order to plan and execute their business strategies. Thus, in the US insurance market, business is said to suffer from almost permanent regulatory drift at the state level, not least with respect to product liability (see Pelkmans and Vanheukelen, 1988).

Harmonization

There are two *benefits* of harmonization:

1. *Removal of distortions with legal business certainty*: a primary policy goal of European market integration has been to ensure that distortions between the Member States—arising from tariff and non-tariff barriers—were progressively removed, and that free movement would work. Prior to EC-1992, this was achieved via total and detailed *ex ante* harmonization: it was believed that free movement could be permitted only if certain national regulations were replaced by common EC regulation.

Today, approximation concentrates on essential requirements, often with reference to (voluntary) European standards which are 'deemed' to comply with those requirements. Both the old and new approach guarantee the removal of distortions, yet without legislative drift, or the severe problems which would arise from differing national interpretations of the essential requirements. This degree of legal certainty is a benefit to business.

2. *Flexibility through various modes, intensities, and scope:* post-'1992', harmonization more closely resembles the original notion of 'approximation' as used in the Treaty of Rome's text. The quality of legislation and the speed of decision-making have improved, not least as a result of qualified majority voting. Today, approximation is a multi-faceted policy tool: its scope, intensity, and modes are typically varied according to the issue at hand, and this is predominantly a result of the learning process the EC has experienced throughout the course of the EC-1992 programme. Minimum harmonization (i.e. only of the essential requirements), a much greater reliance on framework directives, sunset legislation, and differentiation with the provision of derogations are the different ways in which harmonization has become a resourceful, flexible, and responsive legislative tool for the single market. Also, by reference to voluntary standards, innovative products can still get around standards at only slightly higher costs.

There are two *costs* of harmonization:

1. *Regulation disproportionate to market failure:* because of the 'all-or-nothing' character of the 'old' style of harmonization, EC regulation suffered from a lack of proportionality. Thus, while the EC Court imposes a proportionality requirement on national regulations when they hinder intra-EC trade, EC regulation remained excessive for two reasons: excessive detail, usually accepted so as to attain unanimity; and a lack of confidence in mutual recognition, so that 'minimum harmonization' was unacceptable. Therefore, the costs of the old harmonization were considerable: failure ('nothing') was frequent and accomplishment of harmonization tended to be too heavy-handed ('all').

But both *tendencies* have largely disappeared, and hence the costs of harmonization have come down considerably. Qualified majority voting makes it difficult for recalcitrant Member States to 'extend' minimum harmonization by detailing the 'essential requirements' beyond 'essentials'. Moreover, failing to achieve a blocking minority (which, on essential requirements, is much harder than with total harmonization), forces the minority countries to innovate (i.e. find alternatives which are attractive or superior), compromise, or be overruled. This is likely to upgrade the quality of legislation and lower the costs of harmonization still more.

2. *Regulation difficult to alter once in place:* when unanimity and detailed specifications apply, the *need* to adapt to technical progress is continuous and leads to permanent regulatory 'drift' in technical details.[18] This makes implementation, enforcement, and monitoring more costly. At the same time, the sensitive elements of a given directive become very difficult to

change. However, with qualified majority voting and harmonization only of the essential requirements, the need to adapt to technical progress becomes a minor issue, and when the need does arise, modifications are much easier.

The relative costs and benefits of today's harmonization have therefore changed drastically since the advent of EC-1992. Generally speaking, the costs of harmonization have been significantly reduced. In addition, recourse to different modes and intensities of harmonization has introduced greater flexibility.

It is therefore somewhat disingenuous that the older and costly form of harmonization is often invoked as a *prima facie* justification for the alternative: regulatory competition. To the extent that obsolete examples of the 'old harmonization' are represented as the current reality of harmonization, they are misleading, and their erroneous citation weakens the case for a complete substitution of harmonization with regulatory competition. More important still, it is crucial to understand that the mere threat of regulatory competition as a realistic alternative to recent forms of harmonization disciplines the harmonization process itself. In other words, the potential for prior harmonization to occur at the 'wrong' level (too high or too low) is reduced precisely *because* arbitrage of regulatory differences may occur at a later stage. The use of qualified majority voting in the Council, together with the no-internal-frontiers principle, further enables ministers to 'promote' the regulatory competition alternative.

Given the foregoing comparative cost–benefit framework, the optimal regulatory solution in a given case would combine minimum harmonization of the essential requirements with regulatory competition beyond this level. In other words, when market failures need to be addressed, regulatory competition and harmonization should be seen as complements rather than substitutes, with the demarcation between the two determined on a case-by-case basis according to the principle of subsidiarity.

VII.   Conclusions

Although regulatory competition has been hailed in some quarters as a superior alternative to Council-driven harmonization, little empirical investigation has been made to demonstrate how regulatory competition might actually work in EC practice, and therefore whether its expected benefits will, in fact, materialize.

In this article, we have tried to remedy the gap by stylizing the iterative regulatory competition process in the EC context. The framework presented shows quite clearly that the role of business–government inter-actions in fuelling the process of regulatory competition is a complex and unpredictable one. Moreover, examination of practical cases highlights the difficulties associated with the process at each of the stages described in the schema. More detailed case studies are necessary before any definite conclusions can be drawn on the precise nature of business–government interactions.

The practical limitations of regulatory competition therefore severely weaken the case for regulatory competition based on theoretical economic arguments. Moreover, a comparative cost–benefit analysis of regulatory competition and harmonization suggests that harmonization is much more flexible as a result of EC-1992. Its costs have been dramatically reduced and, in commensurate fashion, so have its disadvantages relative to regulatory competition. Therefore, when regulation is economically justified, regulatory competition and harmonization should be seen as complements, rather than substitutes, to one another, with the demarca-tion between the two determined on a case-by-case basis according to the principle of subsidiarity.

Notes

This is a revised version of a paper presented at the European Community Studies Association (ECSA) Third Biennial Conference, held in Washington D.C., 27–29 May 1993. The authors would like to thank the following persons for helpful comments on earlier drafts: Erik Jones, Kathleen McNamara, and Alberta Sbragia (all visiting fellows at the Centre for European Policy Studies, Brussels, during 1993) and a referee. The usual disclaimer applies.

1. It is to be distinguished from *regulatory emulation* or *imitation*, which need not depend on the competitive or other pressures induced by cross-border move-ments. For instance, if the US changes its health care system by adopting elements of the Canadian system, this is prompted by domestic concerns and not by arbitrage in the health care markets.
2. Note that (as a referee reminded us) *Cassis de Dijon* allows Member States to pursue objectives not specified in Art. 36 (the so-called 'rule of reason'), although this has not been of major importance in actual practice.
3. In fact, a better term would be 'mutual acceptance', since (additional) require-ments in country A have no validity in B. We ignore this point here, however.
4. The application of subsidiarity requires the following question to be tackled: for a given set of objectives, to what level of government should various public economic functions be assigned? Due to problems of information and pre-ference-revelation, as well as regional and local differences in preferences

among voters, central government cannot supply an optimal set of public goods including regulation. Economic federalism therefore assigns such powers to local governments, except when this would be ineffective, inefficient, inimical to others, or demonstrably unnecessary. *Ineffective* local policies can result from positive 'externalities' ('spillovers' to or from an adjacent jurisdiction); *inimical* measures are those of a beggar-thy-neighbour character—in effect, negative externalities; *inefficiency* may result from economies of scale, which make federal regulation more cost-efficient than separate national systems of regulation; local regulation would be *unnecessary* if voter preferences for public policy were, in fact, sufficiently congruent across the entire internal market (Pelkmans, 1990).

5. There are two caveats to the foregoing analysis. First, relations between regulators and regulatees are not exclusively adversarial. Therefore, convergence of interests between the two sides should not always be seen as evidence of 'capture'. Second, the interests of firms *vis-à-vis* the nature and intensity of regulation differ. Some firms in some situations will see regulation as a restriction on their ability to do business, while others will view it as a business opportunity. The implications of this second caveat are discussed further in Section IV.

6. From a practical point of view, it is very important to bear in mind that going to the EU Court or pressing for a directive takes time, money, and other resources which a firm acting alone (or even together with its industry) may not be willing to expend. Adopting a 'confrontational' strategy *vis-à-vis* the offending Member State may also be risky for the firm in the long term, because of the hostility engendered between the two sides. It may thus be less costly for a firm to abandon its efforts to penetrate the market in question, or to conform to the latter's existing national regulations. Of course, if most firms in such situations will not press for mutual recognition, there is no prospect of regulatory competition, and thus no movement towards regulatory rapprochement.

7. Note that the national regulation will still apply to firms producing within the regulatory jurisdiction, until or unless it is changed in response to these firms' lobbying efforts (in the face of competitive disadvantages). Therefore, after the Court ruled in 1987 that the German 'beer purity' law could not be used to block imports of beer from other Member States, beer producers in Germany (of German and foreign nationality) continued to face the purity law (and still do). However, because the demand for beer is not purely a function of price, beer producers in Germany have not been greatly disadvantaged by the ruling.

8. The most prominent example of such a 'loophole' is given by the famous Danish beer bottle case. In 1981, Denmark introduced a law which required that beer and soft drinks be sold in returnable bottles, with a compulsory deposit. Brewers from other EC Member States protested because the cost of recycling bottles made their exports unprofitable. The European Commission

took the case to the Court arguing that the Danes were imposing a disproportionate level of environmental protection, which fragmented the internal
market. In September 1988, the Court sided with Denmark, invoking the
environmental provisions of the Single European Act. The restriction of free
movement resulting from the law was not regarded as disproportionate.

9. The authors are indebted to CEFIC, the European Chemical Industry Council,
Brussels, for background information. Neither CEFIC nor the European
Commission can be held responsible for the interpretation provided in the
text. It is entirely that of the authors.

10. Curiously enough, it was first believed that the British flammability standards
would raise costs, but later it was discovered that upholstering with flame
retardants was actually approximately 20 per cent cheaper.

11. If one assumes that such firms (and the UK government) had a comparative
advantage in lobbying the British chairman of the European Parliament's
Environment Committee (Ken Collins) and the committee's British rapporteur
(Caroline Jackson), this might explain the EP position, in late 1991, that the use
of halogenated retardants would not be excluded from the proposed directive.

12. The following draws from Lannoo and Mortensen (1993).

13. For instance, Belgian banks could have lobbied the Belgian Banking Supervisory Commission to impose additional constraints on Crédit Lyonnais, on
the grounds that the latter's high interest bearing accounts could have endangered the solvency of Belgian banks, and thus the 'general good'.

14. Note that because the bank was a subsidiary rather than a branch, the French
authorities were not strictly required to mutually recognize British regulations.
Therefore, in this case, Barclays faced an additional option: it could have
altered the status of its subsidiaries, making them branches instead, though
this would presumably have entailed costs which Barclays was not willing to
incur.

15. See Tiebout's seminal contribution on the finance of local public goods (1956).

16. We begin our analysis with the 'arbitrage' stage, assuming that free movement
has already been recognized. Of course, there are difficulties associated with
achieving this free movement in the first place, as the first case study above
showed.

17. This is the concept of 'fiscal equivalence', introduced by Olson (1969). For a
careful discussion of the fiscal 'race-to-the-bottom' argument, see Smith (1993).

18. In the pre-1985 'old approach', this adaptation was done via Commission (not
Council) directives, after Member States, in an advisory committee, agreed by
majority.

References

Hauser, H. and Hosli, M. (1991) 'Harmonisation or Regulatory Competition in the
EC (and the EEA)?' *Aussenwirtschaft*, Vol. 46, pp. 265–80.

Lannoo, K. and Mortensen, J. (1993) 'Towards a European Financial Area: Achievements, Implementation, and Remaining Hurdles'. CEPS Research Report No. 13 (Brussels: Centre for European Policy Studies).

Oates, W.E. and Schwab, R.M. (1988) 'Economic Competition among Jurisdictions: Efficiency Enhancing or Distortion Inducing?' *Journal of Public Economics*, Vol. 35, pp. 333–54.

Olson, M. (1969) 'The Principle of "Fiscal Equivalence": The Division of Responsibilities among Different Levels of Government'. *American Economic Review*, Vol. 59, No. 2, May, pp. 479–87.

Padoa-Schioppa, T. *et al.* (1987) *Efficiency, Stability and Equity* (Oxford: Oxford University Press).

Pelkmans, J. (1990) 'Regulation and the Single Market: An Economic Perspective'. In Siebert, H. (ed.), *The Completion of the Internal Market* (Tübingen: Mohr).

Pelkmans, J and Sun, J.-M. (1994) 'Towards an EC Regulatory Strategy: Lessons from "Learning by Doing" '. In OECD Regulatory Cooperation for an Interdependent World (Paris: OECD).

Pelkmans, J. and Vanheukelen, M. (1988) 'The Internal Markets of North America: Fragmentation and Integration in the US and Canada'. *Research on the 'Cost of Non-Europe'*, Basic Findings. Vol. 16 (Brussels: Commission of the European Communities).

Siebert, H. (1990) 'The Harmonisation Process in Europe: Prior Agreement or a Competitive Process?' In Siebert, H. (ed.), *The Completion of the Internal Market* (Tübingen: Mohr).

Siebert, H. and Koop, M.J. (1990) 'Institutional Competition. A Concept for Europe?' *Aussenwirtschaft*, Vol. 45, pp. 439–62.

Siebert, H. and Koop, M.J. (1993) 'Institutional Competition Versus Centralisation: Quo Vadis Europe?' *Oxford Review of Economic Policy*, Vol. 9, No. 1, Spring, pp. 15–30.

Sinn, S. (1990) 'The Taming of Leviathan: Competition among Governments'. *Kiel Working Papers*, Working Paper No. 433, August.

Smith, S. (1993) 'Subsidiarity and the Co-ordination of Indirect Taxes in the European Community'. *Oxford Review of Economic Policy*, Vol. 9, No. 1, Spring, pp. 67–94.

Tiebout, C.M. (1956) 'A Pure Theory of Local Expenditures'. *Journal of Political Economy*, Vol. 64, No. 5, pp. 416–24.

Part V
Variety in Accounting for Regulation

Crisis and Legitimacy in the Administrative Process

A Historical Perspective

J. O. FREEDMAN

> The rise of administrative bodies probably has been the most significant legal trend of the last half-century and perhaps more values are affected by their decisions than those of all the courts, review of administrative decisions apart.
>
> Justice Robert H. Jackson, in *FTC v. Ruberoid Co.* (1952)

When Alexis de Tocqueville published his remarkable study of democracy in America, he expressed a nineteenth-century European's admiration for the ease with which Americans did without government. It is not likely that a contemporary European observer, retracing Tocqueville's footsteps, would be led to express a similar admiration.

The steady growth in the role of the federal government since Tocqueville's time has been one of the most distinctive and important developments in American history. As the role of the federal government in national life has expanded, the center of gravity of the powers it exercises has gradually shifted, from the legislature in the first half of the nineteenth century, to the judiciary in the second half of the nineteenth century, to the executive and administration in the twentieth century. The characteristic pattern that underlies this shift can be seen in the nation's assertion of public control over the railroads, first by the enactment of restrictive legislation, then by emphasis upon judicial remedies, and finally by resort to administrative regulation.

This shift in the center of gravity of governmental powers has become so pronounced that contemporary political scientists, with increasing regularity, describe America as an administrative state. The distinguishing quality of the modern administrative state is its reliance upon the administrative process as a principal instrumentality for the achievement of national policies.

Roots of the modern administrative process

The growth of the administrative process in the United States occurred gradually, as the original thirteen states matured into a continental nation, increasingly industrialized and urbanized, facing economic and social problems that required responses more technologically expert, more institutionally flexible, and more procedurally expeditious than either the Congress or the federal courts could provide. The creation of administrative agencies was designed to supply these institutional deficiencies in the formulation and administration of public policy.

Although the rise of the administrative process is often identified with the presidency of Franklin D. Roosevelt, in fact reliance upon administrative agencies to meet emerging national problems long antedates the New Deal. It is as old as the Republic itself. The First Congress of the United States, meeting in 1789, enacted legislation authorizing administrative officers to 'estimate the duties payable' on imports and to adjudicate claims to military pensions for 'invalids who were wounded and disabled during the late war.' The forerunner of the Patent Office was created in 1790, of the Office of Indian Affairs in 1796. The General Land Office was established in 1812. The administrative process thus has deep historical roots.

Approximately one-third of the federal administrative agencies were created before 1900, notably the Civil Service Commission in 1883 and the Interstate Commerce Commission in 1887. By 1891, the Pension Office of the Department of the Interior, with six thousand employees and more than a half-million cases pending for adjudication, was, according to its commissioner, the 'largest executive bureau in the world.'[1] Still another third of the federal agencies were created between 1900 and 1930, notably the Federal Reserve Board in 1913, the Federal Trade Commission in 1914, and the United States Tariff Commission in 1916. During these same decades, many state governments, responding to the influence of the Granger and Progressive movements, created administrative agencies to regulate banking, bridges, canals, ferries, grain elevators, insurance, railroad freight rates, and warehouses.

Reliance upon the administrative process was thus an established practice by the time that Roosevelt became President in 1933. But it nevertheless seems natural to associate the dominant position of the administrative process in modern government with President Roosevelt because the New Deal radiated a faith in the capacity of the administrative process perhaps exceeding that of any previous administration.

Faced with the devastating consequences of a major depression, the New Deal created a large number of administrative agencies to attack the nation's economic and social problems. These agencies, almost all of which eventually wrought major changes in American life, included the Federal Deposit Insurance Corporation (1933), the Tennessee Valley Authority (1933), the Federal Communications Commission (1934), the Securities and Exchange Commission (1934), the National Labor Relations Board (1935), and the Civil Aeronautics Board (1938).

In 1937, the President's Committee on Administrative Management reported critically to President Roosevelt that Congress had created more than a dozen major independent regulatory agencies since 1887, and went on to complain that 'Congress is always tempted to turn each new responsibility over to a new independent commission. This is not only following the line of least resistance. It is also following a 50-year-old tradition.'[2]

The tradition persists to this day. The demonstrated utility of the administrative process in meeting serious national problems during the New Deal years undoubtedly influenced the decision to create additional administrative agencies to meet the problems of controlling materials, manpower, prices, and production presented by World War II. In the decades since the war, the creation of new administrative agencies to deal with emerging national problems has continued apace. Under Democratic and Republican Presidents alike, Congress has regularly chosen to rely upon administrative regulation—rather than upon civil remedies, criminal penalties, subsidies to the private sector, or the free market, for example—to implement public policies in new and complex areas of federal concern. These areas have included atomic energy (the Atomic Energy Commission, 1946), military conscription (the Selective Service Commission, 1948), space exploration (the National Aeronautics and Space Administration, 1958), shipping (the Federal Maritime Commission, 1961), employment discrimination (the Equal Employment Opportunity Commission, 1965), environmental protection (the Environmental Protection Agency, 1970), occupational safety (the Occupational Safety and Health Review Commission, 1970), and consumer product safety (the Consumer Product Safety Commission, 1972).

The continuing growth in the administrative process has led to a corresponding increase in the prominence of administrative law in the decisions of the Supreme Court. The role of the Supreme Court in the shaping of American administrative law dates at least from the decision in *The Brig Aurora* in 1813.[3] At one time, in 1957, decisions involving review of administrative action constituted the largest single category of cases decided by the Court on the merits, about one-third of the total.[4] In the decades of the 1960s and 1970s, however, the Court considered proportionally fewer administrative law cases as other classes of litigation, particularly those involving criminal procedure and civil rights, assumed a heightened national importance and claimed a greater share of the Court's attention.

By the time of the nation's bicentennial in 1976, the federal administrative process had achieved a considerable status. It embraced more than sixty independent regulatory agencies as well as perhaps several hundred administrative agencies located in the executive departments. Administrative agencies exercised regulatory responsibilities in scores of important and sensitive areas. The decisions rendered by the federal administrative agencies were many times the number rendered by the federal courts and probably affected the lives of more ordinary citizens more pervasively and more intimately than the decisions of the federal courts. In virtually every relevant respect, the administrative process has become a fourth branch of government, comparable in the scope of its authority and the impact of its decision making to the three more familiar constitutional branches.

The United States thus has increasingly become an administrative state. Americans have sought to understand the implications of this fact for the character of American democracy, the nature of American justice, and the quality of American life. These implications have often been troubling— even though the administrative process had deep historical roots, even though its growth has been gradual and evolutionary, and even though that growth has occurred only by deliberative acts of democratic choice. If the United States is to realize the promise and respect the limitations of the administrative process, the quest for understanding its implications must be regularly renewed.

The recurrent sense of crisis

Erik Erikson once wrote that 'in every field there are a few very simple questions which are highly embarrassing because the debate which forever arises around them leads only to perpetual failure and seems consistently to make fools of the most expert.'[5] This observation has particular applicability to the administrative process, where the kinds of questions to which Erikson refers concern the status, the soundness, and ultimately the legitimacy of the administrative process: What justifies the exercise of such extensive lawmaking powers by groups that lack the political accountability of the legislature? What justifies the exercise of such decisive adjudicatory powers by groups whose members lack the tenure and independence of the judiciary? What explains the failure of the administrative agencies, as the recurrent generalization would have it, to achieve a significant measure of effectiveness in performing their regulatory tasks?

Questions such as these have usually been based upon the premise that there is a 'crisis' in the administrative process. Each generation has tended to define the crisis in its own terms, usually by focusing upon a major question that has attracted its attention and reforming impulses.

For many years, the dominant concern was the anomaly of the existence of administrative agencies in a government founded upon a commitment to the separation of powers. That concern later became closely joined to a concern over the constitutionality of the delegation of power. Slowly, these questions gave rise to the creation of a satisfactory explanation in theory, which rationalized the position of the administrative agencies, accommodated their existence to the constitutional structure, and set limits to the powers that might properly be delegated.[6] Thus the initial concerns were stilled for the moment. But they soon were replaced by new ones, each in its own time phrased in the idiom of crisis.

During the early years of the twentieth century, one such concern focused on the role of the courts in reviewing administrative action. As the theoretical responses to this concern became increasingly elaborated, particularly in the magisterial work of John Dickinson,[7] they gained a general acceptance by lawyers, legislators, and citizens. A second question, which followed closely upon the debate over judicial review, involved the procedures by which administrative agencies reached their decisions. No single phrase can capture the variegated procedural styles that the scores of federal administrative agencies followed during the period from 1920 to 1945, when this concern was dominant. But it is surely fair to say that many agencies paid scant attention to the matter at all while others followed ad hoc schemes that departed widely from the judicial-type procedures that traditional theory regarded as the finest fruit of centuries of Anglo-American legal experience. This concern over procedure grew in intensity until it was substantially satisfied by passage of the Administrative Procedure Act[8] in 1946, and by the Supreme Court's increased readiness to enforce the requirements of procedural due process.

There have been other significant areas of concern as well, although none can properly be described as having been dominant during a particular historical period. These are concerns that have been so consistently troubling to those who study and participate in the administrative process that the terms by which they are commonly described have almost become clichés. They include phenomena such as these: the failure of agencies to develop standards that, in Judge Friendly's phrase, are 'sufficiently definite to permit decisions to be fairly predictable and the reasons for them to be understood';[9] the tendency of agencies to become 'captives' of the industries they are charged with regulating; the agencies' lack of demonstrable and relevant expertise; the blight of *ex parte* influence and communication; and the failure of agencies to protect the interests of the consumer. Many of these concerns were captured in the catchphrase of Justice Jackson, who, in a notable dissent, referred to a pervasive 'malaise in the administrative scheme.'[10]

Virtually every President since the period of the New Deal has been sufficiently disturbed by the functioning and status of the federal administrative agencies to order at least one major study seeking recommendations for improvement. President Roosevelt commissioned two such studies: the Report of the President's Committee on Administrative Management, which concluded that the agencies constituted 'a headless fourth branch of government' and should be abolished, with their responsibilities being absorbed by the executive branch; and the Report of the Attorney General's Committee on Administrative Procedure, which accepted the role of administrative agencies in the structure of American government but recommended reforms in administrative procedure that eventually became the basis of the Administrative Procedure Act.[11]

Presidents Truman and Eisenhower enlisted the experience of former President Hoover in creating the Commission on Organization of the Executive Branch of Government, which proposed that the adjudicatory functions of the Federal Trade Commission and the National Labor Relations Board be taken away and given to a newly created Administrative Court of the United States.[12] John F. Kennedy, while still the President-elect, asked James M. Landis, formerly dean of the Harvard Law School and a member of several agencies, to prepare a report on the state of the administrative process. The Landis Report was scathing in its criticisms of the agencies for their inefficiency and their failure to formulate policy effectively.[13] President Nixon appointed the President's Advisory Council on Executive Organization, also known as the Ash Council, which recommended that the major regulatory agencies be replaced in their collegiate form by single administrators whose decisions would be reviewable by a new administrative court.[14]

That so many Presidents have felt compelled to seek comprehensive assessments of the administrative process and that the resulting studies have so consistently proposed changes of such a fundamental, even radical, character is suggestive of a persisting sense of uneasiness and concern about the problematic place of administrative agencies in the machinery of modern government. To these presidentially inspired studies must be added a series of searching critiques of the administrative process, published within approximately a decade of each other, by three of the most thoughtful of recent administrative agency members, Philip Elman of the Federal Trade Commission, Louis J. Hector of the Civil Aeronautics Board, and Newton N. Minow of the Federal Communications Commission.[15]

The history of the modern administrative process can be seen, then, as having been marked by an extended sense of crisis. At each stage of this history, the sense of crisis has been phrased in terms of a dominant concern. Eventually, each dominant concern has subsided in intensity as a satisfactory theoretical explanation has been fashioned or responsive legislation enacted, only to be succeeded by a differently formulated concern that has become dominant in its place.

The emergence of each new concern has not, of course, caused the earlier ones to disappear completely. They have remained and continued to trouble new generations of lawyers and scholars. But they have come to be regarded as part of the inevitable, even intractable, imperfections that attend all human endeavors, requiring periodic attention and adjustment, rather than as glaring anomalies that call into question the central justifications for the administrative process itself.

The enduring sense of crisis historically associated with the administrative agencies seems to suggest that something more serious than merely routine criticism is at work. As one examines this history, one begins to believe that the dominant concern of any given period is in fact only the manifestation of a deeper uneasiness over the place and function of the administrative process in American government, and that each generation—however earnestly and plausibly it has formulated its uneasiness—has in fact been speaking to this same underlying problem. This may explain why, despite the fact that each generation has fashioned solutions responsive to the problems it has perceived, the nation's sense of uneasiness with the administrative process has persisted.

The criticism that historically has been directed toward the administrative agencies is significantly different in tone and quality from the criticism, robust though it often has been, that regularly has attended the manner in which Congress and the courts carry out their respective responsibilities. Those institutions have been challenged primarily with questions concerning the proper limits of their undoubted powers, the wisdom of particular decisions as a matter of policy or the national good, and the efficiency of the processes by which they reach their decisions. Most of these criticisms have been directed at actions and defects existing at the margins of institutional power, at temporary aberrations and malfunctions rather than at the legitimacy of the institutional power. On those few occasions when the criticism has been directed at the legitimacy of the institutional power itself, the power has survived wholly intact, its legitimacy undiminished.[16]

By contrast, the criticism of the administrative agencies has been animated by a strong and persisting challenge to the basic legitimacy of the administrative process itself. Criticisms of this character are stated in the reports commissioned by Presidents Roosevelt, Truman, Kennedy, and Nixon, as well as in an extensive body of literature analyzing the federal administrative process.[17] That such criticism has so often been phrased in terms of crisis suggests that it is too serious, too fundamental, perhaps too deeply implicated in principle, to be met by theoretical constructs or by incremental adjustments of the kind that governments routinely rely upon when anomalies or inefficiencies of recent appearance or temporary duration seem to require a response.

The subject of legitimacy is concerned with popular attitudes toward the exercise of governmental power. Such attitudes focus upon whether governmental power is being held and exercised in accordance with a nation's laws, values, traditions, and customs. That the legitimacy of the federal administrative process should still be in question at this late date may be surprising. But institutions of which so much is demanded, no matter how deep their historical roots, can hardly be expected to gain and sustain public acceptance when the very basis of their existence and their legitimacy is so consistently and forcefully challenged. Institutional legitimacy is an indispensable condition for institutional effectiveness. By endowing institutional decisions with an inherent capacity to attract obedience and respect, legitimacy permits an institution to achieve its goals without the regular necessity of threatening the use of force and creating renewed episodes of public resentment. Since the authority of any institution, as Max Weber so effectively argued, rests ultimately upon a popular belief in its legitimacy,[18] substantial, persisting challenges to the legitimacy of governmental institutions must be regarded with concern, for such challenges threaten to impair the capacity of government to meet its administrative responsibilities effectively.

But how do governmental institutions achieve a status of legitimacy in the American political setting? Why have the federal administrative agencies failed to achieve a status of legitimacy as complete as that of other governmental institutions? And what steps can Congress or the administrative agencies take to enhance the legitimacy of the administrative process?

The recurrent sense of crisis attending the federal administrative process results from the failure of many Americans to appreciate the relevance of four principal sources of legitimacy to the role that administrative agencies play in American government. The legitimacy of the administrative process may be supported by public recognition that administrative agencies occupy an indispensable position in the constitutional scheme of government. The policies and performance of administrative agencies may further be accepted as legitimate to the extent that the public perceives the administrative process as embodying significant elements of political accountability. In addition, the effectiveness of administrative agencies in meeting their statutory responsibilities may enhance their legitimacy by strengthening public support in a nation that always has been impressed by effective performance. Finally, the legitimacy of the administrative process may be enhanced by the public's perception that its decision-making procedures are fair.

The sources of crisis in the administrative process include the failure of administrative agencies to conform to the constitutional scheme of separation of powers, the departures that the administrative process makes from judicial norms, public ambivalence toward economic regulation, public concern with bureaucratization, public skepticism of administrative expertise, the fact that administrative agencies lack a direct political accountability, and the problems created for administrative policy making by broad delegations of legislative power. These sources of crisis impair the legitimacy of the administrative process, often unfairly because many of the judgments underlying these sources of crisis are misconceived as conclusions of historical fact, misinformed as judgments of administrative practice, or indiscriminately general as assessments of agency performance.

The quality of administrative justice—the fairness of an agency's procedures, its interest in the protection of individual rights, its commitment to the attainment of just results—is an essential source of administrative legitimacy. Formal and informal administrative processes may be evaluated in order to demonstrate the integrity of the procedures by which the federal administrative agencies discharge their important decision-making responsibilities and to expose areas where improvement is desirable.

Questions of legitimacy give rise to an intricate and perplexing inquiry, filled with theoretical and practical subtleties. Government has little choice but to confront these subtleties if, as Charles L. Black, Jr., has written, it is to command 'among its citizens an adequately strong feeling of the legitimacy of its measures, of their authentic governmental character as distinguished from their debatable policy and wisdom.'[19] The failure of the federal administrative agencies to still the recurrent sense of crisis with respect to their legitimacy—to persuade the American people 'of their authentic governmental character'—thus presents questions worthy of a serious quest for understanding, even if because of the difficulty of such questions, the quest should finally lead, in Erikson's phrase, 'only to perpetual failure.'

Notes

1. See L. White, The Republican Era, 1869–1901, at 211–14 (1958).
2. Report of the President's Comm. on Administrative Management 41 (1937).
3. 11 U.S. (7 Cranch) 382 (1813).
4. Frankfurter, The Supreme Court in the Mirror of Justices, 105 U. Pa. L. Rev. 781, 793 (1957).
5. E. Erikson, Childhood and Society 23 (2d ed. 1963).
6. See L. Jaffe, Judicial Control of Administrative Action 28–86 (1965).
7. J. Dickinson, Administrative Justice and the Supremacy of Law in the United States (1927).
8. 5 U.S.C. § 551 et seq. (1970).
9. H. Friendly, The Federal Administrative Agencies: The Need for Better Definition of Standards 5–6 (1962).
10. FTC v. Ruberoid Co., 343 U.S. 470 (1952) (Jackson, J., dissenting).
11. Report of the President's Committee on Administrative Management (1937); Final Report of the Attorney General's Committee on Administrative Procedure, S. Doc. No. 8, 77th Cong., 1st Sess. (1941).
12. Commission on Organization of the Executive Branch of the Government, Report on Legal Services and Procedure 61–62 (1955).
13. Report on Regulatory Agencies to the President-Elect, Submitted by the Chairman of the Subcomm. on Administrative Practice and Procedure of the Senate Comm. on the Judiciary, 86th Cong., 2d Sess. (Comm. Print 1960).
14. A New Regulatory Framework: Report on Selected Independent Regulatory Agencies (1971).
15. Elman, Administrative Reform of the Federal Trade Commission, 59 Geo. L. J. 77 (1971); Elman, A Modest Proposal for Radical Reform, 56 A.B.A.J. 1045 (1970); Elman, The Regulatory Process: A Personal View, BNA Antitrust & Trade Reg. No. 475 at D-1-D-5 (1970); Hector, Problems of the CAB and the Independent Regulatory Commissions, 69 Yale L.J. 931 (1960); Minow, Suggestions for Improvement of the Administrative Process: Letter to President

Kennedy from Newton N. Minow, Chairman, Federal Communications Commission, 15 Ad. L. Rev. #146 (1963).

16. Perhaps the most notable recent example was the failure of several Southern states, after the decision in Brown v. Board of Education, 347 U.S. 483 (1954), to establish a theory of interposition of state sovereignty as a qualification upon the authority of the Supreme Court. See Cooper v. Aaron, 358 U.S. 1 (1958); Bush v. Orleans Parish School Board, 188 F. Supp. 916 (E.D. La. 1960).

17. See, e.g., J. Beck, Our Wonderland of Bureaucracy (1932); M. Bernstein, Regulating Business by Independent Commission (1955); J. Sax, Defending the Environment (1971); H. Vreeland, Jr., Twilight of Individual Liberty (1944); The Politics of Regulation (S. Krislov & L. Muslof eds. 1964); The Crisis of the Regulatory Commissions (P. MacAvoy ed. 1970).

18. M. Weber, The Theory of Social and Economic Organization 130–32 (T. Parsons ed. 1947). See R. Bendix, Max Weber: An Intellectual Portrait 412–17 (1960).

19. C. Black, Jr., The People and the Court 42 (1960).

Is There A Crisis In Regulatory Accountability?

C. GRAHAM

The regulatory framework is in crisis and in urgent need of reform.

Dieter Helm 'Rewrite the rules for regulation' *Financial Times*
7 April 1993.

...the present system has worked relatively well and a very great deal
better than that which preceded it.

Sir Bryan Carsberg 'Reflections on the Regulation of
Privatised Companies' speech given on 26 April 1994
to the University of Manchester.

...the fundamental problem lies not so much with the regulatory
bodies themselves but with the peculiar secrecy associated with
British government

Tony Prosser 'Regulation of Privatised Enterprises:
Institutions and Procedures' in L. Hancher and M. Moran (eds.)
Capitalism, Culture, and Economic Regulation,
Clarendon Press (1989), p. 158.

Introduction

There has been, since about 1993, a rapidly growing public debate about
the accountability of the regulators of privatised companies, or public
utilities as they shall be called throughout this paper.[1] Interesting and
important as this debate has been, it has mainly been conducted with
the aim of advancing particular policy positions in the hope they might be
adopted by government. The aim of this paper is to try and set these
arguments within a wider context of debates about the control of discretion and the allocation of authority which, in their turn, reflect underlying arguments about the constitutional law and practice of Britain.
The underlying thesis of this paper is that the difficulties with accountability of the regulators can only be solved, or put on a sounder footing,

in the context of wider changes to our constitutional structures and practices.

In order to accomplish this objective, the first part of the paper will summarise the current debate. The second part of the paper will then examine current regulatory structures in the light of this debate in order to try and identify to what extent the various views are supported by the evidence. The third part of the paper will examine the proposed solutions for the problems of the accountability of the regulators. The final part of the paper will tackle the linkages to wider debates about discretion and the constitution of Great Britain and make some suggestions, both incremental and radical, for improving the accountability of the regulators.

Before going any further, it is worth reflecting on what we mean by accountability. In a very general sense, a person is accountable if they have to give reasoned justifications for their decisions to some other person or body who has a reasonable right to require such justifications. This definition stresses accountability after the decision is taken but, for accountability to be meaningful, there has to be some awareness of the basis on which the decision was taken or the process by which it was taken. In the current context, our interest is in accountability to the public, in other words, not simply the internal accountability of civil servants to line managers. Accountability can take many forms and the legislation which sets up the current regulatory system provides a number of mechanisms, such as Annual Reports, references to the Monopolies and Mergers Commission (MMC) and duties to give reasons in certain circumstances. In addition, there are generic devices such as judicial review, investigation by the National Audit Office (NAO) and Parliamentary select committees. The regulators have also taken the initiative by publishing consultative documents, holding workshops and seminars and making public statements about their decisions. Given that there are a variety of accountability mechanisms, why has there been such fierce criticism?

The Debate Over Accountability

The critics' argument is that these accountability devices have failed to prevent the regulators from making serious mistakes in their substantive decisions. These criticisms come from very different perspectives and are by no means consistent. One common criticism is that there was, at the time of privatisation, a regulatory bargain expressed in the shape of the prospectus. This bargain seems to be seen as relating to both the structure of the industry on privatisation and the regulatory philosophy that would underpin its operation in a privatised form. It has been argued that both sets of guarantees have been broken. Thus, to use the most widely cited example, British Gas has been subject to increased competition and fundamental restructuring. As regards regulatory philosophy what started as light touch, temporary regulation has become creeping over-regulation.[2] A different view is that the regulators have failed to use their powers adequately to protect strategic areas of the economy. This argument surfaced most clearly in the debate over the future of coal in this country and its relationship to energy policy. The Trade and Industry Select Committee commented that they did '...not regard the way the Director General [of Electricity Supply] had discharged his duties as satisfactory. Our concerns...relate to the Director General's over-reliance on competition and apparent lack of urgency in solving problems'.[3] At their extremes, these criticisms point in different directions. One line argues for the retreat of the regulators, the other argues for them taking a strategic view of industrial policy objectives.

Another area where the regulators have been subject to criticism has been over consumer protection. Thus, for example, it has been argued that the business customers of utilities have benefited more from price controls than the domestic customers.[4] It has also been argued that shareholders have benefited at the expense of consumers, that the workforces have lost out, directors have been over-paid and that the social obligations of the utility companies have taken second place to profit seeking.[5] As with the other arguments, this is hotly disputed, not least by the regulators, but their response will be dealt with later.

Before going any further, it is worth commenting that underpinning some of these criticisms are substantive disagreements over the objectives of regulation. This comes across clearly in Peter Hain's work where he argues for the regulators to take a strategic role in relation to industrial policy matters. Although this might arguably be within the legal remit of their powers, it was hardly the role envisaged for them at the outset, as I shall explain later. The same point could be made in relation to those commentators who argue that the regulator should, if possible, concentrate solely on matters of economic efficiency, leaving social obligations to government.[6] Thus the arguments about accountability may simply be ways of disguising disagreements over substance, a common phenomenon in the United States. From arguments about what procedures agencies should follow, resulting initially in the Administrative Procedure Act 1946, to the regulatory reform movement of the 1980s, disagreements about the legitimacy of agency action and the substance of decisions have frequently been fought out on procedural and constitutional terrain. The British solution is not to concentrate on procedures but to seek to either replace the regulator, or diminish the regulator's powers, in favour of a person or body whom you trust to make the right decisions, such as a Minister or a commission. Aside from being disingenuous, there is a more serious problem since it is not clear that changing accountability arrangements in this way will necessarily improve the decision making process.

What then are the defects identified in the existing mechanisms of accountability by the critics? The critics have three main inter related lines of attack. The first and most important criticism relates to the width of discretion vested in the regulators personally. As Veljanovski puts it: 'The flaws in the present system arise from the wide discretion given to the regulators to make determinations and negotiate compliance with the utilities within a system which has little regard for due process and accountability.'[7] Because of this discretion a system of personalised regulation has arisen where the personality of the regulator is alleged to be crucial to the decisions taken and the relationships between the regulators and other parties, notably industry. The example always given here is the antagonistic relationship between Sir James McKinnon and British Gas.[8] Related to this are various process concerns, as the quote indicates. Regulators are under no general duty to give reasons, they are said not to be transparent in their dealings with other parties and to operate on the basis of vague criteria and standards of proof when making decisions. The third criticism is that there is a confusing division of responsibilities between the regulators and other government agencies. An example might be the current debate over who should regulate subscription television: Oftel or the Independent Television Commission?

The regulators are not without their defenders, most notably Sir Bryan Carsberg and Sir Christopher Foster.[9] The gist of their defence is that, although the regulatory structures may not be perfect, they are a good deal better than their critics allow and that the proposed cures may be worse than the disease which has been diagnosed. This is a different view of the regulatory experience and, in order to assess the validity of the competing claims, we need to examine the legal structures in place and how they have coped with regulatory developments in the light of these criticisms.

Regulatory Structures and Accountability

In this section I want to examine the allocation of authority between the regulators and other agencies; the relationship between the regulators and government and the legislative mandate given to the regulators before going on to look at accountability devices. In doing so, I hope to cast some light on the issue of why bringing the regulators to account is problematic and begin to suggest that the issue is wider than that of the regulators alone. One of the problems in assessing what were the objectives set for the regulatory bodies after privatisation has been the absence of any clear public statement by the Government of the rationale of regulation. There are, of course the two Littlechild reports.[10] These only dealt with matters of economic regulation, in a narrow sense, and some of the assumptions contained within them, most notably that regulation was only a way of holding the fort until competition arrived and a preference for non-discretionary regulation, now look somewhat naive. When it came to presenting the proposals to Parliament, discussion of regulation was minimal. In the electricity White Paper, the matter was discussed in only five paragraphs. The White Paper on water privatisation, although containing a longer discussion, is similarly vague on the principles behind regulation. It does not, for example, contain any discussion of the relationship between environmental quality matters and charging for water, something which has become a matter of acute controversy. Foster's account[11] suggests that, initially, civil servants had not had the opportunity to think deeply about regulatory policy and had to improvise a set of arrangements for British Telecom which were then used as a model for subsequent privatisations.

Government Powers over Regulators

Let us look at the allocation of authority, specifically the relationship between government and the regulators. For whatever reasons, one of the objectives of creating regulatory bodies was to have the major decisions taken by the regulators, rather than by government Ministers. They were expected to operate, in some sense, independently of government. This is indicated in the statutes by the general powers and duties of the respective Director Generals (DGs) which they can exercise without government interference. Unlike nationalised industries, government can only issue formal directions to regulators in specific circumstances. Thus the Secretary of State may give specific directions to the Director General of Telecommunications (DGT) and the Director General of Water Services (DGWS) in the interests of national security, to the Director General of Electricity Supply (DGES) to preserve the security of buildings used for electricity supply and in cases of civil emergency and to the Rail Regulator in times of hostilities, severe international tension or great national emergencies.[12] Aside from such limited circumstances the Secretary of State can only give a Director General directions on what matters he or she ought to have regard to in deciding whether or not to exercise any of their functions under the legislation or in deciding the priority of matters which ought to be reviewed. With the exception of telecommunications, any such directions have to be published in the Annual Report of the regulator.[13] No such formal directions have ever been given outside rail.

This simple picture is, inevitably, misleading. Aside from creating the initial competitive environment within which regulators had to work, government has always retained substantial reserve powers. Perhaps the clearest example of this is in telecommunications where, between 1984 and 1991, government retained the power to license new telecommunications operators and operated a duopoly policy in order to protect Mercury. Although the duopoly policy has ended, the power to issue licences to new operators is still in the hands of the Secretary of State. It is instructive to look at the area of references to the MMC because the threat of such a reference is often perceived as the regulator's greatest weapon and one which they have allegedly used to bully companies.[14] Leaving aside the Gas Act, these provisions fall into two categories. In telecommunications and water the Secretary of State has limited or no powers to prevent references to the MMC. In electricity and rail, the Secretary of State has a wide discretion to direct the MMC not to proceed with such a reference.[15] There is similar variation in the Secretary of State's powers to intervene when the regulator and the licence holder have agreed a variation. This goes from the one extreme of rail in not having a power to intervene at all to electricity where the Secretary of State has a broad power to prevent any modifications. In telecommunications, gas and water the power is limited to specific circumstances, notably if the Secretary of State feels that a reference to the MMC is more appropriate.[16]

Gas is an interesting case because of the limitations on the powers of the DGGS. Under the 1986 Act the DGGS has no jurisdiction in the commercial and industrial areas. Hence the original reference to the MMC in 1988 came from the Director General of Fair Trading after complaints from industrial users channelled through the Gas Consumers Council. Gas experience has also involved parties other than the regulator in implementing the remedies proposed by the MMC.

This is a hotch potch of provisions and it is not clear why they should be so different for each industry. Although no formal direction has ever been given under any of these sections, and although the Secretary of State can only prevent a reference being made, not initiate one, these legal provisions suggest that it would be foolish of a regulator not to consult the

Secretary of State on any proposed reference to the MMC. If this is indeed the case, and if it has happened in the past[17] or may happen in the future, it suggests that we need to be concerned not only with the accountability of the regulator's decision-making processes but also the accountability of the processes of inter-agency consultation. This point will be made in other contexts.

Aside from powers over the modification of licences, government retains an array of other important powers in each of the industries. The electricity industry is notable for the extent of these reserve powers. The Secretary of State may require public electricity suppliers to have available generating capacity from non-fossil fuel sources, the Secretary of State sets the fossil fuel levy, may give directions about the maintenance of fuel stocks at generating stations and gives consent for the construction of generating stations and overhead power lines. In addition the Secretary of State has the power to make regulations relating to the supply and safety of electricity and may grant exemptions from the need for an electricity licence.[18] In the water industry Guaranteed Service Standards are set by the Secretary of State as are the quality standards which have to comply with EC obligations. These obligations are enforceable by the Secretary of State[19] and they have been the subject of much controversy and debate, especially between the DGWS and the quality regulators. In rail, the Secretary of State can grant exemptions from the licensing requirement, exempt railway facilities in respect of access contracts, exempt passenger services in respect of franchise agreements and decide appeals on closure decisions made by the RR. Most importantly, the Secretary of State can pay grants and subsidies to operators to cover their public service obligations, in relation to railway goods services and for the provision of facilities for freight haulage.[20] These are all substantial powers and it should be observed in passing that there are not even the minimal process require-ments which have been imposed on the various Director Generals here. This also applies to the setting of the initial price formulae for the period immediately after privatisation by the Ministers. The over generous nature of these formulae have created major problems for the regulators' sub-sequent activities.[21]

Inter-Agency Relationships

These are the direct powers which government retains over the regulators. An additional problem is the confused and confusing relationship that the regulators may have with other agencies. This has occurred in two different contexts. The first relates to social obligations while the second concerns what might be called 'functional' divisions. When the regulatory agencies first started their operations social obligations were not perceived as a major part of their agenda. Arguably, there is a social agenda within the legislation but, in any event, the regulators have had to become involved in social issues as a response to mounting public concern. There are two good examples of the problems regarding social obligations; energy efficiency and water poverty.[22] Taking the latter first, the central question is to what extent water is an essential public service or simply a commodity like any other? The problem is that a significant number of people do not have a sufficient level of income to allow them to purchase sufficient quantities of water at current rates. This results in, among other outcomes, disconnections. The problems over the division of responsibility become most apparent when charging policy is considered. To what extent should the DGWS take into account people's ability to pay and insist or encourage some form of special tariff for low income users?[23] Or, is this a matter for the Department of Social Security when considering benefit rates? The problem, in terms of accountability, is that both have a responsibility but because the procedures for acting jointly are unstructured it becomes difficult to ascertain responsibility.

Another highly problematic area is that of energy efficiency. The first moves here were made by Ofgas who created an 'E' factor in the price control for British Gas which, roughly, allowed them to approve energy savings schemes. After the Rio summit in 1992, the government, in partnership with a number of energy companies, set up the Energy Savings Trust (EST) whose aim was, in part, to help the government meet the Rio targets. The intention was that the EST's work would be funded mainly through 'E' factor projects and a similar device to be introduced in electricity. This policy has been thrown into utter confusion by the decision of the new Director General of Ofgas, Clare Spottiswoode, that funding such projects was equivalent to tax-raising by Ofgas and was either illegal or undesirable, a position she first made clear in public in evidence to the Environment Select Committee in March and May 1994. Subsequently, a more detailed paper was produced which argued that energy efficiency measures could be more effectively encouraged through market mechanisms rather than regulatory action. In particular, it argued that it was not Ofgas' role to take into account the environmental or redistributive effects of such schemes. Relying on the criteria set out in the paper, albeit after some delay, the Director General did not approve the five projects submitted by British Gas. Regardless of whether or not you agree with the Director General's views, this does make energy efficiency policy look a mess, especially as the Director General of Electricity Supply appears to have addressed these concerns in a more measured way.[24]

The problem of functional divisions is a pervasive problem. The division between economic and quality regulation in the water industry has led to some highly publicised and controversial debates between the NRA and Ofwat and the division of functions between the RR and the Franchising Authority looks equally problematic. The most high profile example has been over the issue of pit closures and the future of the coal industry. The difficulty here was that many of the energy policy issues fell outside of the remit of the DGES. Although he was criticised by the Trade and Industry Select Committee to some extent this criticism misses the point that his remit was limited to the electricity industry. A similar problem is occurring in telecommunications with the breaking down of the barriers between the telecommunications and the broadcasting industries. The problem in all these areas is similar. Decision making is not the preserve of one body, it must inevitably be the outcome of negotiations between agencies. Such negotiations will be conducted without the benefit of any legislative framework which seeks to ensure openness and accountability to a wider public. This is a problem that cannot entirely be solved by the amalgamation of agencies, a point that I shall return to.

Legislative Mandate

Although in their public statements the regulators stress that their main aim is consumer protection, this does not follow in a straightforward way from the legislation. The regulators' primary legal duties are: first, to ensure that all reasonable demands for the product of their industry are satisfied or, in the case of water, that water companies carry out their activities properly and, secondly, that the companies are able to finance the carrying out of their activities.[25] *Subject* to these duties, they have an array of secondary duties which include, among others, promoting competition, protecting consumers, promoting efficiency and economy of the industry and taking into account the interests of pensioners and the disabled. There are a variety of other duties, which vary from industry to industry but could not be categorised as, in any sense, economic duties. Thus, for example, the DGT has to ensure that sufficient telecommunications services are provided in rural areas and to enable persons providing telecommunications services to compete effectively in the provision of those services outside the United Kingdom. The DGWS has a specific responsibility to protect the interests of customers in rural areas and the DGES is required to protect certain Scottish rural consumers.[26] There are two points about these duties. First, they may pull in different directions and will require the regulator to balance conflicting interests. Secondly, they combine both economic and social injunctions; the duties cannot be read simply as imposing economic injunctions. Thus inevitably the regulator must have discretion when making decisions because the outcome is not simply an arithmetical result of known and agreed data with known and agreed weights.[27]

The granting of a wide discretion to Ministers is quite commonplace in British public law. It is a relatively recent development to grant such wide powers to a named individual. Previous practice has tended to give such powers to a group of people, such as the Civil Aviation Authority or the Independent Broadcasting Authority,[28] although the historical precedent apparently used was that of the Director General of Fair Trading. The DGFT's position is different in that, at least under competition legislation he works, in effect, with the approval of the Secretary of State. The regulators enjoy a more independent position than the DGFT.

Taking all these factors into account, we can see that the regulators have a wide discretion. There are at least two ways of ensuring that this discretion is not abused, or too many mistakes are not made. One is the traditional approach of British government's which might be called the 'good chaps' approach whereby a trustworthy person is appointed to the appropriate job. This was nicely put by David Walker:[29]

Club membership is a better guarantor of the *safeness* of the new regulatory bodies than formal controls. In other words, the *sound chap* instincts of both ministers and Whitehall advisers are a much better guide to the way the new regulatory regimes have been put in place than administrative theory

The other is through imposing certain checks and balances and requirements of accountability and it is to those devices that I now turn.

Accountability Devices

Procedures   What is remarkable about the legislation is that it by and large leaves procedural matters up to the discretion of the regulators. The formal duties imposed on a regulator are in respect of licence modifications and enforcement proceedings. Before making a modification to a licence, a regulator must give notice that he or she intends to make the modifications, setting out their effect. He or she must give reasons why they propose to make the modifications, they must give an opportunity to make representations about the proposals and consider any such

representations.[30] This might be considered almost a symbolic consultation period. For example, the recent changes to the electricity price
formulae were announced before the end of this period, even though it
had been assumed that the relevant decisions had already been taken.
Similar procedures exist when a regulator wishes to issue a formal enforcement order to stop a breach of licence conditions. In this case, the
company concerned has a right of appeal to the High Court essentially
on the grounds that the regulator was not acting within their powers.[31]
These provisions cover only a limited range of the regulators' powers.
There are also extensive decision making powers contained within the
legislation and the licences where there are no formal procedural requirements. This can be illustrated, and the implications for accountability
examined, by looking at three separate areas: the policy making function
of regulators, their power to determine disputes about access to a network
and their power to determine individual disputes. If we assume that
decision making runs in a spectrum from policy making to determining
individual cases, then these areas cover the spectrum, with access disputes
representing an interesting hybrid: a dispute between individual companies but one which is likely to have general implications.

Individual consumer disputes   I shall start with disputes between individual
customers and the companies. There are many areas where, if the company and the customer cannot reach agreement, the regulator has the
ultimate decision. Thus, for example, the DGES is empowered to decide
disputes over the duty to supply, powers to recover charges and expenditure, power to require security, additional terms of supply and special
agreements.[32] Similar provisions exist in relation to gas and water.[33]
Telecommunications was treated differently, perhaps because the relationship between the utility and the customer is a contractual one, as opposed
to the statutory scheme in the other utilities, but this has now been
modified by the Competition and Service (Utilities) Act 1992. This Act
now gives the DGT power to resolve disputes over individual standards,
discrimination in fixing charges, billing disputes and deposits.[34]

What is notable about these statutory powers is that they do not
attempt to set down any common procedure. Section 23 of the Electricity
Act set the pattern followed in other statutes by stating that the practice
and procedure to be followed in connection with any determination under
that section shall be such as the Director shall consider appropriate. This
gave rise to some controversy when the Competition and Service (Utilities) Act was before Parliament. In particular the lack of any general

requirement placed on the regulators to give reasons was heavily criticised, especially in the House of Lords. The Government, after initial reluctance, tabled amendments placing an obligation on the regulators to give reasons for their decision in certain circumstances, notably disputes about guaranteed service standards, the new powers given to the DGT and Section 23 of the Electricity Act and the new Section 30A of the Water Industry Act.[35] Despite some pressure to require oral hearings for such disputes, or to place these functions under the supervision of the Council on Tribunals,[36] the Government made no further concessions. The regulators have agreed to a measure of 'informal' supervision by the Council over their procedures for determining disputes.[37]

It would be wrong to imply that the regulators carry out their decision making functions under these powers in an arbitrary and unstructured way. Both Offer and Ofwat have issued detailed guidelines explaining the procedures that they will use for handling disputes. Indeed Offer goes further and publishes many of its decisions which give detailed reasons for decisions, as well as building up a useful body of case-law. By contrast, determinations made by Ofgas and Oftel are not published and do not enter into the public domain.[38] The problem, as ever, is one of consistency in practice, compounded by the failure to implement certain provisions. Thus, for example, Ofgas has decided not to use its statutory powers to make regulations prescribing individual standards of performance, relying instead on the voluntary scheme produced by British Gas. This has the effect of putting any dispute resolution procedures outside the statutory framework. Whether the solution is to give supervision of these functions to the Council on Tribunals is an open question. It may be the best available alternative but perhaps such procedures need to be considered in a wider context.

Interconnection disputes   The next area that I want to examine is interconnection disputes. Perhaps the defining characteristic of a natural monopoly is the existence of a network which it is uneconomic to duplicate due to economies of scale. One of the critical questions for the development of competition in any industry with such a network will be the terms and conditions for access to that network. Although there were attempts in the early 1980s to open up access to the gas and electricity networks they were miserable failures, in part because the ultimate decision on access rested with the industry which had most to lose from competition. The privatisation statutes and licences changed this position, obliging the network operators to allow use of their networks and leaving the final say in cases of dispute with the regulator.[39] Again, what is striking is the lack of any procedural obligations being placed on the regulator.

Ofgas took full advantage of this when it issued its first direction on common carriage. The Direction itself was not published, but details of the approach that Ofgas would take to the issues were published as a means of guidance to British Gas and potential competitors.[40] From the terms of the notice it appears that Ofgas developed its approach initially through meetings solely with British Gas and not with its potential competitors. Events in this area have been overtaken by other developments but it is interesting that Ofgas has taken apparently a loose informal approach to issuing such directions. In telecommunications, the DGT has involved a wider range of parties and undertaken a greater consultation process through an industry workshop on interconnection. The Rail Regulator has consulted extensively inside and outside the industry and, more than any other industry, rail will depend on access to facilities run by others.[41] What ought to be evident from this area is that we are dealing with a decision which has individual affects on the companies directly involved as well as important policy implications for the rest of the industry. The problem is to develop a procedure which can recognise this and separate out matters of general concern, which should be open to all interested parties to comment on, and matters of individual concern which will involve elements of commercial confidentiality and can only be discussed between the parties and the regulator. The final decision needs to be open to scrutiny so that the individual decision can be seen to fit into the general policy framework. On this basis, the first direction issued by Ofgas was unsatisfactory as there did not appear to be a clear separation of general issues from particular ones. In defence of Ofgas, this may have been due to the difficulty of obtaining information from British Gas and, given the rapidly changing gas market, it may not be a pointer to future behaviour.

By comparison, Oftel's recent procedures for dealing with interconnection issues would seem to be a model of their kind. After detailed consultation, including industry workshops on the specific issue of interconnection, they issued a detailed consultation document on the future regulation of the telecommunications industry; *A Framework for Effective Competition*. In addition, a series of public meetings have been held around the country and Oftel made provision for telephone comments, as well as providing Freepost for written comments. In line with the usual practice, written comments were made publicly available on receipt in Oftel's library. Oftel have now published a statement which sets out their conclusions on certain issues, such as moving to incremental costs for the basis of interconnection charges, which will be the subject of further consultation.[42]

General policy making   This brings us finally to matters of general policy making. In all the legislation there are a number of matters that the legislation either did not resolve or did not address. The regulators have, however, felt impelled to take action under their general powers and duties. Good examples are the development of quality standards in telecommunications and gas and the debate over future methods for water charging. It was recognised early on by Oftel that the price cap system provided companies with an incentive to downgrade the quality of service. A similar problem existed in gas, and I want to focus on that. Aside from the general wrangling with British Gas, Ofgas attempted to open up this debate through seminars with interested parties, consultation documents and a summary of replies to the consultation document. Again, there was no statutory framework and what was substituted was a loose framework of meetings and discussions with interested parties supplemented by intensive negotiation with British Gas, including participation by the Gas Consumers' Council. A similar procedure has been followed in development of policy on debt and disconnection.

The position in water is different. Water companies have power to charge but, after the year 2000 the Water Industry Act provided that such charges could not be fixed by reference to rateable values.[43] The government has now decided to allow the use of rateable values after that period although not to allow the use of council tax bands. The problem has been to determine what system should replace charging by rateable value and this debate has taken place in the context of a general increase in water charges so that it is politically highly charged. Water companies must have a charges scheme in place which adheres to the provisions of their licence and in particular does not breach the clauses on undue discrimination. The DGWS appears to have no power to reject a charges scheme as long as it complies with the obligations in the legislation and licence. Ofwat has approached this issue in an open but procedurally unstructured way. There have been many consultation documents, surveys of customers and trials of different charging methods.[44] There does not appear to have been much dialogue between the proponents of various different charging methods and the issue of whether it is possible to construct an acceptable metered tariff has not been raised very often. Reasons for this might include: the way metering is associated with price increases, the lack of powers of the DGWS, an expressed governmental preference for a particular solution and the lack, until recently, of convincing alternatives to metering. The criticism of Ofwat is not that they are operating a closed, secretive process. They have done the opposite and produced a great deal of information. The criticism is that they have not listened to alternative views which, for our purposes, is better seen as a criticism that the status of the proceedings is unclear.[45]

It needs to be mentioned here that the legislation also makes provision for institutional representation of the consumer interest, both domestic and industrial, as well as certain other interests. The arrangements differ from industry to industry, not only in terms of their legal basis but also as regards their effectiveness.[46] The regulators also attend meetings of the Public Utilities Access Forum (PUAF) which serves as a venue to interchange ideas.[47] Interest associations, such as the Major Energy Users Council which have attempted to lobby the regulators have also developed. The first DGT attempted to regularise contacts through instituting the Telecommunications Forum but this has now been wound up under the second DG who has produced a number of initiatives aimed at making Oftel's activities more transparent, for example, a second round in licence modification proceedings which will allow parties to comment on each other's submissions.[48]

The lesson that we ought to take from this discussion is that the procedural arrangements across the utilities are less than adequate. The problem is not a lack of good will on the part of the regulators, but the lack of any framework within which to work. This is a commonplace problem in British public administration but it does not mean that it is therefore not worth tackling. I will return to what might be done later but just add that this observation does not imply that the only alternative is American style legalism.

Information   Another aspect of accountability is the publication of information so that the public can have some idea of what activities the regulators are carrying out. Again, as is the British practice, the matter of publishing information is left up to the discretion of the regulators. They are given the power to publish information but no general duty to publish information with the exception of information with respect to levels of performance and an annual report.[49] All the regulators have published substantial amounts of additional information and have undertaken some quite innovative practices, in a British context. Thus, for example, it appears to be general practice that all responses to consultation documents will be made available to the public, unless the author stipulates otherwise. The DGWS has demonstrated the greatest commitment to openness of the regulators through publishing his general letters to finance and regulatory Directors of the water companies. In addition, when he asks for reports from Customer Service Committees a common format is imposed to enable the results from each region to be compared. This may be a management tool but it is also very useful for outside observers. In terms of producing information, Ofgas seems to have done less than the other regulators which may be more of a reflection on a small body regulating a relatively small group of companies, unlike the water industry, rather than a conscious decision.

The problem in information may lie less at the level of the regulator than at the company level. Here again, Ofwat has been in the lead in publishing information about company performance in a variety of contexts, not simply the standard overall performance measures. The other regulators have been able to accomplish less, hindered by a combination of lack of powers and the more competitive nature of the industries in question which has meant that claims for commercial confidentiality have to be taken quite seriously. Nevertheless, they have still succeeded in putting more information about the industries into the public domain than was the case under nationalisation.

Checking mechanisms   There are two major checking devices contained within the legislation. The first is a right of appeal to the courts against the decision of a Director General to make an enforcement order and the second stems from the Director General's inability to impose a licence amendment upon a regulated company without consent. The first provision has only been used once,[50] but it does exist, and it is over-simplified for commentators to assert that there is no right of appeal against decisions of the Director General. It is limited to, broadly, whether the Director General acted within his or her statutory powers. Although not an appeal on the merits of a decision, it does serve as some constraint. As regards references to the MMC two points have been made. The first is that, because of the costs to a company of a reference to the MMC, the regulator is often able to force through modifications without basic procedural safeguards.[51] The second is that the arrangement is one sided because, although the regulator may make a reference, the company may not. The second point is really a disguised plea for an appeal procedure, something that I will deal with later. As for the first point, just as an MMC reference takes up the resources of a company, so will it take up the resources of a regulatory agency. It will probably take up more of the agency's resources, on a percentage basis, than that of the company's. In the context of telecommunications and judicial review this point was recently made by the Director General of Telecommunications and this is so regardless of whether the reference is widely or narrowly drawn.[52] So far, outside the gas industry, there have been relatively few references to the MMC but there are signs that this may be about to change. Thus after the electricity and water price control reviews there were three references to the MMC and BT has recently refused to accept the DGT's proposals on number portability which has lead to another MMC reference.[53] Thus there seems to be some evidence that companies are now more willing to let the MMC report on an issue. Whether the MMC is any better than the regulators is another question. The MMC has been heavily criticised on both procedural and substantive grounds in the competition law area and their recommendations on the gas industry were not accepted by the Government.[54] In the context of the bus industry the MMC has had serious problems acting as a general regulator. It has called for a general review and suggested a specialist regulator instead of the current arrangements.[55] This suggests that you cannot simply displace the problem to the MMC.

Aside from the limited appeal rights in that statute there is always the possibility of judicial review of a decision of a regulator or some other form of challenge in a court. In a judicial review case the court examines three aspects: whether the regulator acted within his or her powers, whether they followed fair procedures and whether they acted rationally or not. It is important to realise that the courts take a very limited view of their functions under any of these tests. The question of the ambit of powers is a question of statutory interpretation, that is, the courts' view of what Parliament intended in the statute. The courts apply very flexible tests for the fairness of procedures as they recognise that the fairness of a procedure will depend on the circumstances of the case. Finally, when the courts apply a test of rationality, this is a very limited test. In its traditional formulation they are simply seeking to ensure that the public body has not behaved so unreasonably that no reasonable public body could have taken that decision.[56] To put it another way, the courts will tend to defer to the decisions of the agency unless there is something exceptional in the case. Perhaps in part because of these limitations, very few judicial review cases have been brought against the regulators. Indeed, I know of only five, not counting the Mercury litigation, which will be discussed below, of which only two actually reached a decision in court.[57] By comparison, judicial review is much more common against the competition authorities, although no decisions of the MMC have ever been overturned.

The Mercury case, however, indicates that the courts may be more receptive to such cases in the future.[58] This case involved a challenge by Mercury to the DGT's interpretation of condition 13 of BT's licence, which provided the framework for deciding disputes over interconnection agreements. The dispute between Mercury and BT would have been referred to the DGT pursuant to an agreement between Mercury and BT for dealing with questions of interconnection which incorporated the terms of condition 13. In other words, the DGT to some extent looked like an arbitrator deciding a matter of interpretation of the contract and Mercury duly sued in the Commercial Court starting the action by writ, as opposed to judicial review. This meant that they avoided the procedural protections provided for public bodies under the judicial review procedure, notably the requirement of leave and the short time limit, and that they were utilising a procedure which was able to deal with a large amount of evidence, submissions of expert witnesses and cross-examination. The DGT, supported by BT, claimed, among other points, that judicial review was the only suitable procedure for this type of challenge. This argument was rejected in all three courts which heard the case. The point about this case is not that the courts made substantive decisions, this is in essence a procedural decision, but that they were willing, at least in theory, to listen to arguments that the DGT had, on a critically important issue, misinterpreted the extent of his powers and the available approaches. This issue is also a highly controversial economic one and it can be doubted whether courts are an appropriate for dealing with such issues. Nevertheless, they were prepared to take it on and this suggests that the courts may be willing to entertain a wide variety of challenges in the future. As the industries become more competitive, there is the likelihood of more challenges as competitor companies will have the resources and the incentive to mount such challenges.

I cannot leave this issue of the courts without brief mention of the question of damages and compensation. The issue here is not so much obtaining damages against the regulator but whether it is possible to obtain damages against a company for breach of a regulatory requirement. Under the legislation, where the regulator has made a final enforcement order there is a duty placed on the relevant company to comply with that order. That duty is owed to any person affected by contravention of the order who may enforce that duty by an action for damages.[59] Given the Director Generals' role in enforcing the licence conditions, it seems highly doubtful that there is any private right of action for breach of a licence condition if the DG has decided not to act, although there has been some discussion of this possibility.[60]

The other checking device is the possibility of intervention by the Ombudsman (Parliamentary Commissioner for Administration) on the grounds of injustice caused by maladministration. All the regulators are within his jurisdiction but no complaints were brought before 1991 and only a handful since then. None of the complaints have been accepted for a full investigation but it has recently been reported that a complaint against the DGGS has been referred to the Ombudsman over her behaviour regarding energy efficiency and this might have a different outcome.[61]

Outside the courts and the Ombudsman there are the Parliamentary checking devices of which the most important are the National Audit Office (NAO) and the select committees. The NAO is responsible for, among other things, carrying out checks on the economy, efficiency and effectiveness of the operation of public bodies and all the regulatory offices fall within its remit. It has so far only investigated Oftel which resulted in a detailed report and oral hearings before the Public Accounts Committee at which the Director General was given a fairly tough time.[62] Valuable though this scrutiny may be, it is subject to a number of well known limitations, for example, the merits of policy objectives cannot be queried and it is only *ex post facto* scrutiny, plus the additional factor that scrutinising the work of the regulatory agencies can only ever be a small part of the programme of the NAO and PAC. The PAC has asked the NAO to undertake a general survey of the regulatory framework within which the electricity, gas, telecommunications and water industries work and the NAO has agreed to do this.[63] The NAO will have to tread a very fine line here to avoid trespassing on matters relating to the merits of policy objectives.

As regards select committees, prior to 1992, the Energy Select Committee had a good record of issuing informative and critical reports on a number of energy matters.[64] After the 1992 election the Department of Energy became part of the Department of Trade and Industry and in consequence the select committee was abolished, although not without protests. The current situation is that three of the industries fall within the jurisdiction of the Select Committee on Trade and Industry, water falls within the jurisdiction of the Select Committee on the Environment and rail falls within the jurisdiction of the Select Committee on Transport. All of these bodies have conducted investigations and issued reports in areas relating to the regulation of utilities. In terms of putting information into the public domain and encouraging debate on the issues this has been extremely valuable. The Committees have not, however, been able to succeed in obtaining major changes in government policy as, for example, is illustrated by the Government responses to the committee reports on the coal industry and the privatisation of British Rail. This is an inherent weakness in the Select Committee system because there is no legal duty on the Government, or indeed the regulators, to respond to Select Committee reports, let alone explain why they are or are not accepting their recommendations. The committees are also limited in that they are not well resourced.

What is lacking in this system is any select committee which specialises in the regulated industries, such as the old Select Committee on Nationalised Industries, which is able to conduct investigations of issues across the industry, for example, differing approaches to cross-subsidy. Given that Select Committees are charged with scrutinising Departmental policy, rather than the regulators, again regulation will only be a part of their concerns and it is less likely that they will be able to develop a fruitful dialogue with the regulators or to pursue issues on a long term basis, as has arguably been the case with the Treasury and Civil Service Select Committee.

Conclusions To what extent are the critics right? There is much force in the general criticisms: the legislative mandate is unclear, the division of powers between the regulatory agencies, government and other agencies is opaque, the procedures followed by the regulators are inconsistent across the field, although arguably better than much public administration in Britain, and the existing checking mechanisms are limited and weak. What therefore is the way forward?

The Critics' Solutions to the Regulatory Crisis

Rules

One obvious solution to the problem of discretion is to structure that discretion by the use of rules. Cento Veljanovski, for example, has proposed a Regulatory Charter where the government would provide a clear statement of the principles governing regulation. This would be buttressed by agency policy statements outlining priorities, procedures and a workplan and there would also be a policy document produced by a working party consisting of: all the regulators, the OFT and the MMC, which would cover: entry assistance, the relationship between competition and social obligations, the identification of areas of permanent regulation and those in which competition will replace regulation and principles for determining the reasonable rate of return for utility assets. Finally, any significant modification to a utility's licence terms would only take place in formal regulatory proceedings by the MMC, at pre-determined intervals. The burden of proof for increased regulation would be on the MMC and all proposed regulation and licence terms should be required to pass a cost-benefit analysis.[65]

It is not clear how these various documents relate to one another. To take an example used by Veljanovski, to what extent is it the government's charter which sets the rules on entry assistance as opposed to the working party's policy document? To what extent could an individual regulator operate a different approach? There are more fundamental objections. First, these proposals advocate taking decision power away from regulators and giving it to the MMC and government. I will deal with the problems that this would entail later. Secondly, these proposals assume a great deal more foresight on the part of the regulators and associated agencies than seems possible in practice. There is an assumption here that the relevant public bodies have all the information, can predict the future reasonably accurately and are able to come to some sort of binding agreement. This simply is not a realistic picture of any regulatory system, let alone any policy-making process.[66] If relevant agencies tried to carry out this approach it would clearly slow down the decision-making process substantially and allow the companies to tie up the proceedings in court if they so wished. Thirdly, insofar as these procedures are considered important, Veljanovski devotes no thought to the process implications that they raise. The policy document produced by the joint working party is not simply something with no implications for people outside government, it affects numerous interests who will wish to have a say. In the absence of procedural rights, this is simply shifting the problem somewhere else. Finally, one problem that might arise is that, because of the difficulties of amending the framework documents, agencies might seek other ways of changing policy, for example, through adjudication, or by placing little weight on the formal documents. This has happened in the planning field through, for example, the increasing use of appeals to the Minister and through imposing restrictions on the content of development plans.[67] Again, the effect is simply to shift the procedural problems from one arena to another.

A more subtle proposal emanates from Sir Christopher Foster.[68] He proposes that the regulators should concentrate primarily on the enforcement of what he calls the 'economic regulatory offences' as opposed to considering issues of social regulation. The point here is not that economic regulation is a matter of precise science, but that there is a framework within which such evaluation may take place, as opposed to social regulation where there is no such agreed framework. His proposal is that social objectives, such as quality or environmental objectives, are primarily a matter for the political process and that these decisions should be made explicitly and transparently within that process, not through the regulatory process as a substitute. The virtue of this approach is that it seeks to provide a clear distinction between governmental and regulatory roles and, within the latter, provides a framework for structuring the discretion of the regulator. This approach depends upon a particular interpretation of the purposes of regulation and the relationship between economic and social objectives and it is not one that commands widespread agreement.[69] There are also reasons for thinking that use of the regulatory process may be a more effective way of implementing social goals than use of the political channels. Consider the problems with the take-up of benefits as opposed to certain types of low user tariff schemes.

Government intervention

A general theme of many of the commentators is that governments should have more power or influence over regulatory decisions.[70] Veljanovski's Regulatory Charter is one variant of this but it comes across more clearly in Hain's contribution. He suggests that the Secretary of State would draw up guidelines for Parliamentary approval and that the regulators should be required to submit rolling plans of action which Ministers would approve. This would allow the regulatory regime to be assessed against various performance targets.[71] Similarly Corry et al argue that:

> Regulators are civil servants whose responsibility it is to implement government policy, and whose frame of reference should change with any change of government or relevant legislation.[72]

This means that Ministers should set the framework for policy in any particular area and be able to intervene if decisions are perverse or contrary to government objectives. The idea is that Ministers are responsible for policy, regulators for its implementation. 'Policy is for Government, regulation for regulators'.[73]

There are two, related, difficulties here. First, these suggestions assume that there is some relatively clear cut distinction between policy and implementation. There is much political science literature that warns us against this assumption and the history of the nationalised industries and recent events surrounding Next Steps agencies, such as the confusion over whether the Home Secretary or the Chief Executive of the Prisons Service was responsible for disciplining the Governor of Parkhurst Prison after the escape of three life sentence prisoners,[74] should warn us that there is no easy distinction between policy and implementation.[75] Without some more procedural protections, or open government requirements, relying on a self-policing division of functions is likely to obscure accountability, particularly where the agencies concerned do not have competing interests, as is the case with the purchaser/provider split in the health service. Secondly, the whole point of the structure was to have independent regulators. Although government never articulated publicly what they wanted the regulatory structure to achieve, from the context of privatisation and the structure of the statutes it seems clear that they wanted to leave most of the decision making outside the hands of the Minister. Whether this was for good reasons, expertise, or bad ones, avoiding accountability, matters not for the moment. As Sir Christopher Foster points out either regulators are independent or they are not.[76] Compare, for example, the position of the Rail Regulator, who is under a temporary duty until the end of 1996, to take into account guidance given by the Secretary of State, with the position of the Franchising Director who is required to fulfil the objectives laid down by the Secretary of State.[77] It seems implicit in most contributions, and is clearest in Corry et al, that government would be given greater powers to intervene than is the case at present. Presumably this would mean some sort of general power of direction, unlike present arrangements. Lying behind this idea seems to be some sort of assumption about the accountability of Ministers to Parliament for the exercise of their powers. The history of the use of such directions in the context of nationalised industries suggests that this would do very little to increase accountability; indeed, it is likely to have the opposite effect. Nor is it clear from the same history that greater political intervention would lead to better results, as is again evident from the history of nationalised industries.

Regulatory Rationalisation

To deal with the problems of the overlap of responsibilities, the critics have proposed that there ought to be some measure of rationalisation of regulatory agencies. These proposals have varied from Peter Hain's suggestion of one utilities commission to a variety of other suggestions.[78] For example, Veljanovski would merge OFTEL, the ITC and the Radio Authority to form an Office of Communications, gas and electricity would merge to form an Office of Energy Regulation and there would be a new Office of Transport Regulation.[79] From the other end of the political spectrum this is supported by Corry et al who argue that there should be sectoral regulators dealing with the main multi-utility markets: energy, communications, transport and water.[80] There is a great deal of intuitive attraction in these arguments which bring with them the idea of sectoral policies. Clearly the various industries inter-relate and one of the increasing problems will be that of overlap between the industries. This is perhaps most noticeable in the relationship between telecommunications and broadcasting but is also likely to occur when electricity companies enter the market for gas supply, to use just another example. The case against, insofar as this has been discussed publicly, was put neatly by Tim Eggar:

A specialist regulator can develop the depth of understanding of each industry. The changes which are coming in the gas and electricity industries are sufficiently complex to require the undivided attention of a specialist before the case for a single energy regulator could be properly considered.[81]

This largely avoids the issue by assertion, although it suggests that sectoral regulators might not have as deep an understanding of the individual industries within their remit. Three points can be made on this debate. First, it is not obvious that merging two or more organisations under one title would automatically lead to better coordination of decisions in the respective areas. To what extent in the pre privatisation days did the Departments of Energy and Transport have coherent and coordinated policies? Secondly, by making preliminary discussions about coordination a matter of internal debate for a regulatory body it is possible to reduce accountability because important debates will take place within the regulatory body and the conclusions presented to the outside world. One advantage in the water industry of separating economic and quality regulation has been that it encouraged Ofwat to initiate a public debate on what the costs of water quality were. Thirdly, this proposal does not deal with the primary problem, which is the division of powers between government and the regulator, most clearly seen in the dispute over the closure of parts of the coal industry. All this is simply to say that there may be arguments both ways; that there may be costs as well as benefits to regulatory rationalisation and that the arguments in any one sector need to be looked at carefully.

Regulatory Commissions

One of the popular suggestions for the reform of the regulatory offices is to replace a named individual as head with a regulatory commission. Corry et al is a representative example of this approach, linking it with the idea of sectoral regulators, but this is not a necessary connection.[82] The proposal is that the Commission should be made up of 'individuals with independent expertise in the individual industries making up the sector... chaired by an independent commissioner perhaps having expertise in the sector as a whole'.[83] They add that it might also be possible to include individuals with other relevant policy expertise, for example representing the consumer.

To what extent would these proposals improve accountability? The first question is what type of commission is envisaged? One alternative would be a commission of 3–5 individuals, on the US model, in order to keep discussion manageable. Given the criticisms levelled at the individual regulators presumably some form of balance on the Commission would be required. This could be done on party lines, as is not uncommon in the US, or on the basis of interest. What are the relevant interests? Corry et al identify six: customers, shareholders, managers, suppliers, market entrants and employees. Of this group customers divides into domestic and commercial, so there are in effect seven different interests. If you took five as the maximum number then probably suppliers, shareholders and employees would have to be omitted, on the grounds that there are other mechanisms to make their views known. The point is that the selection of the interests to be represented would be a difficult process, let alone the selection of individuals. Of course, the individuals concerned would not be representatives of their interests, in the sense of delegates. However, in a small panel of people personal idiosyncrasies will still intrude, although there may be a greater element of checking by the collective. Lawyers will remember the contribution of Lord Denning to jurisprudence while a member of the Court of Appeal, a three person body. If, on the other hand, a large regulatory commission, say of 15–16 people, is envisaged, this seems to create other problems. It would inevitably slow down the decision making. Assuming that the commissioner were not full time, expertise would reside in the staff and this would be, in effect, an internal check on the discretion of the staff.

How is the commission going to operate? The US model depends largely on reactive quasi-judicial hearings, where the bulk of staff present a case and the Commission, aided by a small number of their own staff, decide. At least three British commissions follow this pattern: the Civil Aviation Authority (CAA), the ITC and the MMC. However, only the CAA attempts 'to combine a massive technical knowledge with a system of trial type public adjudication'.[84] By contrast, neither the ITC nor the MMC hearing process is public. Judicial hearings might do for some issues, such as the review of price controls, but it is less suitable for others, for example, policy development. Presumably commissioners could each be responsible for specific areas of development, for example the various directorates of OFTEL, the approach of the European Commission, but again the issue of the openness of regulatory procedures needs addressing.

What about decision taking? A key question here is to what extent the process of discussion amongst the commissioners would be open. In the US, it is quite common for there to be requirements for meetings of all the commissioners to be open to the public and to be obliged to create a record. Commissioners are required to give reasons for their decisions and this may lead to minority opinions being given. If it takes place in closed session, then all the old problems of accountability recur with an additional one—the written reasons may not reflect the discussions within the group of commissioners—a complaint found in the US. If in the US with its more searching judicial review it is possible to protect commission decisions from scrutiny it will be much easier in the UK with its weaker judicial controls. This suggests that open decision taking ought to be the norm, which would be unprecedented in the UK context.

Commission decision taking will inevitably tend towards a greater degree of compromise and consensus than decisions by a single individual.[85] If this is the case it may not lead to better decision making. Although there are virtues in consensus decision making there are also dangers. It is unclear that the idea of regulatory commissions would lead to better decision making. The EOC has been criticised quite severely over the years for the lack of a strategy, IBA and ITC decision making has also been castigated and it is a common complaint amongst competition lawyers that the decisions of the MMC are inconsistent.[86] None of these examples suggest that the commission approach automatically produces better decisions, or indeed more accountable ones, although there are other variables in play here. Certainly it would not, on its own, be a substitute for improvement of the other procedures and mechanisms of accountability. There would still be a need for reasoned decision, for access to information and scrutiny by other bodies, as well as rights of appeal.

Procedural Matters

Perhaps rather oddly, the critics have not focused that much on the procedures operated by the regulators. There has been plenty of criticism of the closed nature of the procedures and the lack of openness,[87] but rather less in the way of prescriptions for reform. Broadly the critics' prescriptions have centred around two: the duty to give reasons and the need for some open, public hearings. The lack of a general duty to give reasons is one of the great gaps in British public law and Sir Bryan Carsberg admitted that he used this gap as a means of making a challenge to his first price control review more difficult, on the advice of counsel.[88] The point has now been conceded as regards resolution of individual disputes, it is accepted as a general principle in the Code of Practice on Access to Information and the recent decisions of the courts suggest that they are more likely these days to find situations when a duty to give reasons will be implied.[89] As for public hearings, the regulators are experimenting with this device, although it is not always given this name. Most recently Oftel has held a series of public meetings around the country in order to discuss the issues raised by its consultation document; *A Framework for Effective Competition*. Oftel has also held workshops, seminars and other meetings where policy issues are discussed amongst interested parties, as have Ofgas and Ofwat. These are not, of course, public meetings, but meetings with interested parties, some of whom represent sections of the public.

The critics have been somewhat slow to recognise the extent to which the regulators have adopted an innovative approach to their procedures. For example, Oftel very early on adopted the practice of putting all responses to its consultation documents on the public record, unless otherwise specified[90] and this practice has been followed by the other regulators and adopted now by government departments. The regulators have also genuinely sought to consult the consumer interests, not solely through whatever statutory procedures are in place, but also through a variety of less formal mechanisms, such as the Public Utilities Access Forum and various regional groupings which fulfill a similar purpose. This is all largely a matter for the discretion of the regulators and what is lacking is any consistent practice across the sectors and any benchmark against which to assess the performance of an individual regulator. There is no equivalent of the American Administrative Procedure Act, nor does the Council on Tribunals have any jurisdiction to look at the procedures in general terms, although they have sought to have some influence on procedures relating to the resolution of disputes.

Appeal Rights

One of the frequent points made is that there should be more appeal rights, in particular from decisions made under the licence, such as the Mercury/BT interconnection decision, or interpretation of the licence by the regulator.[91] As a lawyer, I might well ask—what sort of appeal? If a *de novo* appeal on the merits of the case is envisaged this would seem to turn the appeal body into the regulator and the regulator into the prosecutor. Such a division of functions is a recipe for disaster, as the example of the Air Transport Licensing Board shows.[92] If it is not a *de novo* appeal on the merits then it begins to look suspiciously like appeal on a point of law or judicial review.

A second point which is often made is that the system should distinguish between major and minor appeals in advance of the case having to be decided. Only 'major' appeals would go to a full hearing. There is clearly no problem with ruling out frivolous and vexatious appeals but this is a different idea. Someone will have to decide whether or not the case is suitable for an appeal and this could only be the appeal body or, perhaps, another government agency, say the OFT or the DTI. It would be most peculiar for an appeal body to decide not to hear appeals because they feel, in advance, that the case is not important enough. Where would the appeal against this decision lie? There is precedent for a governmental filter in the competition legislation but then this looks less like an appeal mechanism and more like a means for government to start an investigation in a particular area. This whole argument looks peculiar from a lawyer's point of view. If there are appeal *rights*, then people should be allowed to exercise them, subject to time limits and having an arguable case. It is no part of the appeal body's function, in advance of the case, to decide whether the case is sufficiently important to hear.

Oversight Mechanisms

One suggestion which seems to have a strong level of agreement among all the commentators is that there should be a Select Committee on Regulated Industries, even though there are a number of warnings as to the limits of its effectiveness.[93] There would seem to be no good case against this idea, although the practicalities of reform of the rules of the House of Commons might be technically tricky.

What about other oversight mechanisms? Sir Christopher Foster has suggested that, insofar as economic matters are concerned, the MMC should conduct retrospective reviews of classes of economic offences, such as discrimination, predatory pricing, preferably across all the natural monopolies.[94] These reviews would have no effect on past decisions made nor have any other binding force but it would act as guidance to the regulators on how the MMC might be expected to consider similar cases that come to it later, as well as an audit of the handling of those offences. He adds that the Director General of Fair Trading could make similar references to the MMC that would be helpful for clarifying issues of importance to natural monopoly regulation. As a way of getting an overview of certain regulatory problems this does seem to be a helpful suggestion and it may be that this need not be limited to economic matters in the way that Sir Christopher suggests. For example, why could not issues relating to universal service across natural monopolies not be referred to the MMC?

Conclusions

Is there a crisis in regulatory accountability and, if so, what is the way forward? The critics can be characterised as having two strategies: the imposition of rules and giving more powers to different people, that is, Ministers. At best, there is an implicit assumption here that Ministers are more accountable than regulators. The defenders are rather more sanguine and suggest that, although there are some problems, these can be solved by incremental change. I want to suggest that the critics are right in suggesting that something more than incremental change is needed; however, the defenders are right in suggesting that the proposed solutions are likely to be no solution at all and may even make the situation worse.

There is an immense literature on the rules versus discretion debate which raises two important points.[95] First, rules and discretion are not alternatives. Any regulatory system, or system of administration, is a combination of rules and discretion and there are advantages and disadvantages to the use of rules as opposed to discretion and vice versa. In addition, there is the question of what type of rules should be implemented. To move toward a formal, rule based system will neither necessarily increase accountability nor will it improve the effectiveness of the system as is illustrated by the attempt to run much of the social security system between 1980 and 1986 on the basis of rules contained in delegated legislation and the first attempts at rule making by the Securities and

Investment Board under the Financial Services Act.[96] The second point is that by creating rules you may simply be moving the point of discretion, rather than removing discretion. As for the accountability of Ministers, this is simply a convenient myth, which should not be retailed amongst adults and is dangerous to tell to children. Are then the defenders right and the only prospect is incremental change, dealing with the most severe problems?

I think not, but this answer needs to be given in context. One way of viewing developments in public administration since the mid 1970s is to see it as a search for new institutional forms to replace the old idea of services delivered centrally by large Departments under the control of elected representatives. Instead there has been an attempt to separate out functions and to introduce some of the aspects of competition and markets in public services. Two obvious examples are the purchaser/provider split in the health service and the creation of Next Steps agencies in the civil service, the latter being aimed at, among other things, separating out management and delivery of services from policy matters. The privatisation of public utilities and their subsequent regulation is an example of this development. There is, implicitly, a separation of functions between the government Department, the regulator and the company. In theory, government looks after strategic policy matters, the regulator deals with regulatory issues and the company acts as a commercial entity. This arrangement is akin to a new separation of powers and it has the potential advantage that, because the various players have different interests, it will be self-policing. Thus, for example, the company's duties to its shareholders are not akin to the regulator's duties as contained in the legislation. The purchaser/provider split in the health service is a clearer example because there the bodies do have, in theory, very different interests. The purchaser wishes to obtain the maximum amount of services for the minimum cost, while the provider wants to get the best price for their services. The provider is limited in doing this by, in part, the existence of market mechanisms.

The point is that privatisation and the creation of regulatory agencies is part of a wider process of institutional reform in the United Kingdom which has raised major questions about the effectiveness of our constitutional structures for providing accountability for the activities of public agencies.[97] Thus it must be remembered that any proposals for change as regards regulators must take account of these developments and that any general developments may also have an impact on regulatory agencies. In an ideal world, or even a better organised polity, there would be some sort of institution responsible for a systematic look at all these issues, such as the Administrative Conference of the United States or the Conseil d'Etat in France, but in Britain there is no such body.[98] The following remarks are, therefore, indicative, and would need fleshing out. They are, however, a set of lines of inquiry which should lead to some useful conclusions.

The relationship between government and the regulators

There are three issues: the relationship between government and the regulators, the question of procedures and the issue of what are regarded as fundamental rights. The first, and most difficult problem, is that of the relationship between government and the regulators over which looms the convention of ministerial responsibility. The difficulty here is to find a settlement which is able to withstand changes in government and changes in political aims because all governments have a strategic interest in these industries. How should the powers be divided? First, it would seem to be accepted by everyone that the government should have specific powers of direction in cases of national emergency. Secondly, the idea that Ministers should give some interpretative guidance to the regulators in how to carry out his or her functions is a good one.[99] What is flawed in the present system is that, with the exception of the Rail Regulator,[100] no such guidance has been given publicly and that, if there has been any suggestion about how powers should be exercised, this has been done informally. This suggests that government should be obliged to give policy guidance to regulators about how they should interpret their conflicting duties and that this advice should be published. Guidance should be general and not directed at specific cases, otherwise it becomes directions rather than guidance.[101] It would help to provide a way to prioritise statutory duties and to balance conflicting ones. It would need to be formally issued as guidance. In addition, there also needs to be some mechanism for ensuring that this guidance is not subverted by informal discussions and this suggests that contacts between regulators, Ministers and representatives of Ministers, i.e., civil servants, should be placed on the public record. In other words, a publicly available minute of such meetings should be kept. There is a precedent for this in the publication of minutes of meetings between the Chancellor of the Exchequer and the Governor of the Bank of England. Careful thought would need to go into how this obligation was structured. The point of such detailed procedures is not to politicise the regulatory process but as an attempt to force government to clarify its thinking on general regulatory policy matters and to put that thinking into the public domain. In theory, such a proposal should increase accountability by making it clear what were the Government's views on particular matters. It does not represent an increase in governmental power but an attempt to structure that discretion and bring its exercise out into the open.

What about the specific powers of intervention held by the Government? My personal predilection is to abolish these and make references to the MMC solely a matter for the regulator. There are also numerous other powers of intervention that the Government retains. The general approach should be that these powers are given to the regulator although there will be exceptions to this general rule. For example, why not give the power to make Guaranteed Service Standards to Ofwat or licensing in telecommunications to Oftel, rather than those powers remaining with the Minister? There will be other examples, but the general presumption should be that the regulator makes the decisions within a policy framework which is clearly laid down by government.

The *quid pro quo* for this increase in power of the regulators should be an increase in their accountability. This may lead to the idea of a board or commission of regulators. As mentioned above, this is perfectly feasible, but does not solve the main problems. Let me begin with one, relatively uncontroversial, proposal. There needs to be a Select Committee on Regulated Industries covering at least the four existing industries and rail.[102] It will, of course, need adequate resourcing. The regulators and the industries will also appear before other Select Committees on specific issues, such as the environment, but the main focus of the Select Committee on Regulated Industries should be on questions of regulation, both industry specific and across industries. In addition, it should have a role to play in the appointments process. Potential regulators, or commissioners, would need to have their appointment endorsed by the Select Committee. Before coming to a decision, the Select Committee would be required to hold public confirmation hearings. Given the make-up of Select Committees, I would anticipate that the government's nominee would be endorsed in the majority of cases, although a safeguard could be built in the form of a *de facto* appeal to the House of Commons. In addition to these Parliamentary checks, the NAO and PAC would retain their current roles of scrutinising the economy, efficiency and effectiveness of the regulators.

The relationship between this new committee, the existing Departmental Select Committees and government needs careful thought. To take government first, the five areas mentioned are covered by three departments: Trade and Industry, Environment and Transport. Simply having a Select Committee asking generic questions about regulatory policy would no doubt stimulate an effort at coordinating responses between the departments and might lead to some part of the government machine, such as the Cabinet Office, being given responsibility for generic regulatory issues. As for the relationship with other Departmental Select Committees, the current standing orders of the House of Commons allow for a sub-committee to be set up to examine any matter affecting two or more nationalised industries and this could be adapted for regulated industries which would provide the Select Committee with part of its jurisdiction. It would also need powers to examine issues arising in relation to one industry. Finally, there would need to be some way of sorting out overlaps between this new committee and existing committees, such as a provision for joint sub-committees.

Procedural issues

Oversight alone would not be enough, some thought needs to be given to regulatory procedures. There needs to be a structurally independent voice for the domestic consumers in each industry, modeled on the Gas Consumers Council. This would be controversial as the existing consumer committees in electricity and water, and their regulators, would argue that the current arrangements do provide such a voice. Without going into this issue in detail, two points can be made. First, under current arrangements, consumer committees must represent the interests of domestic and industrial consumers. Large industrial consumers do not need such help, witness the work of the Major Energy Users' Council, and the interests of these two classes may pull in different directions, especially in a competitive market. Secondly, there is a tension between representing the consumer, an advocacy role, and being part of the regulator, a role requiring the arbitration of competing interests. I am not convinced that current arrangements properly resolve this tension.[103]

There needs to be detailed work done on a common set of procedures for regulatory decision making. This does not imply a move towards American style legalism but instead is aimed at providing some consistency among regulators and some minimum standards that should be adopted. The type of procedure will vary depending on the decision under consideration. Decisions on individual disputes should take a different form from, for example, interconnection decisions or from policy making decisions. There needs to be variety of procedural forms tailored to the issue in question. These procedures cannot be developed *ex cathedra* but should be developed on the basis of a survey of current regulatory practice and a view on what constitutes best practice; the same way, historically, that the American Administrative Procedure Act was developed. It should be clear, however, that I do not think that the American Administrative Procedure Act's division between rule making and adjudication is likely to be suitable in British circumstances. A *sine qua non* of any such procedures must be a duty to give reasons and to respond to arguments raised in the proceedings. Finally, comes the question of openness. With a structurally more open procedure there will need to be more formal rules about what information is publicly available, in particular what information the regulated industries will have to make available in public hearings. An implication of such procedural changes is that the courts would be able to play a greater role in the review of regulatory decisions if they so wished. Such procedures and rules on openness should not be voluntary but this does not necessarily mean that legislation is required. It may be that a Code of Practice, such as the Code of Practice on Access to Government Information, could be created.

If sectoral regulators are not created, and even if they are, thought needs to be given to opening up the relationships between the various agencies concerned with decision taking. Thus, for example, the DSS will still be responsible for deciding on the standard rate of benefit and the amount included within that for utility bills. The process by which that is decided and the decision whether or not to subsidise the poor through direct payments or tariff schemes needs to be brought into the open.

Fundamental rights

Finally, some thought needs to be given to the general duties placed on the regulator. At present they are rather a hotch potch of duties which are, in general, biased towards an economic approach to regulation. The task of the regulator is to balance conflicting interests within the context of an overall approach set by the government of the day. In other words, the general duties of the regulator should reflect the need to balance interests and leave open the question of whether economic or social approaches should predominate. The mix to be struck between an economic and a social approach should be a matter for government decision and reflected in its guidance to the regulator. What also has to be made clear is to what extent we think people's fundamental human rights are affected by regulatory decisions. Although a 'right to a cheaper telephone service or to choose your electricity supplier' may not be a fundamental human right,[104] the provision of basic services like heating and water may well be regarded as a fundamental right. There needs to be further debate on what exactly are the core social obligations provided by utilities.

These suggestions have the merit of falling in line with general developments in thinking about the re-constitutionalisation of government in this country. The idea is not to provide a once and for all solution but to devise a framework that can accommodate differing political views of the regulatory process and that is self-correcting, that can detect problems and suggest solutions.

Notes

I received very helpful comments on this paper from Rob Baldwin, Aileen McHarg, Colin Scott, Tony Prosser and Peter Vass. My thanks to them all. Any opinions or factual errors are solely my responsibility.

1. For the purposes of this paper I shall concentrate mainly on electricity, gas, telecommunications and water. Examples from broadcasting and rail will be used occasionally but not airports nor the Post Office.
2. A good example of both these criticisms is C. Veljanovski, *The Future of Industry Regulation in the UK* (1993), London, European Policy Forum; pp. 22–4 and 50–60. For 'creeping interventionism' from another perspective see Dan Corry, David Souter and Michael Waterson, *Regulating Our Utilities* (1994) London, Institute of Public Policy Research.
3. See Trade and Industry Select Committee *Energy Policy* HC 237 1992–3, para 291 although note that this criticism is prefaced by: 'He has no powers in respect of some of the more serious problems in the electricity supply industry, such as generators' charges and the size of the fossil fuel levy.' Similar criticisms are voiced by P. Hain, *Regulating for the Common Good* (1994), London, GMB; p. 15 and D. Helm HC 326 (1992–3), Vol. 1, pp. 65–70.
4. National Consumer Council, *Paying the Price*, (1993) London, NCC.
5. See J. Ernst, *Whose Utility? The Social Impact of Public Utility Privatization and Regulation in Britain*, (1994), Open University Press, Buckingham.
6. C. Foster, *Privatization, Public Ownership and the Regulation of Natural Monopoly* (1992), Oxford, Blackwell, Ch. 9.
7. C. Veljanovski, 'The power of the regulator' in *But Who will Regulate the Regulators?*, (1993), London, Adam Smith Institute, p. 25.
8. See Veljanovski, *The Future of Industry Regulation in the UK*, pp. 60–1.
9. See Sir Bryan Carsberg 'Reflections on the Regulation of Privatised Companies' speech given on 26 April 1994 to the University of Manchester; Sir Christopher Foster, *Privatization, Public Ownership and the Regulation of Natural Monopoly* (1992), 'Natural Monopoly Regulation: Is Change Required?' paper given at Centre for the study of Regulated Industries Academic Forum 14 September 1993 in P. Vass (ed.) *Regulating the Utilities—Accountability and Processes*, CRI Proceedings No. 7 (1993); 'Who or what regulates the Regulators?', paper given to conference at University of Hull on 19 April 1994.

10. *The Regulation of British Telecom's Prices* (1983); *The Economic Regulation of Privatised Water Companies* (1986).

11. Op cit. pp. 124–5.

12. Telecommunications Act 1984 (TA) Sec. 94; Electricity Act 1989 (EA) Sec. 96; Water Industry Act 1991 (WIA) Sec. 208; Railways Act 1993 (RA) See 118. But there is apparently no such power under the Gas Act!

13. TA Sec. 47 (3); Gas Act 1986 (GA) Sec. 39 (2); EA Sec. 47 (2) and 50 (20 (c); WIA Sec. 27 (3) and 193 (2) (b); RA Sec. 69 (2) and 74 (2) (c).

14. C. Veljanovski 'The Need for a Regulatory Charter' in P. Vass (ed.) *Regulating the Utilities—Accountability and Processes* CRI Proceedings No. 7 (1993) at 4.

15. TA Sec 13 (5) and (6) (directions only in the interests of national security); WIA Sec 14; EA Sec. 12 (5); RA Sec. 13 (5). In gas there was originally no power for the Secretary of State to intervene but this will be changed in the Gas Bill so that gas is identical to electricity. See Gas Bill Sched. 3, para. 22 (4), new section 24 (4A).

16. TA Sec. 12 (5) and (6); EA Sec. 11 (4); WIA Sec. 13 (4) and (5); RA Sec. 12; Gas Act Sec. 23 (4) and (5).

17. It was reported that, just before the 1992 General Election, the Energy Secretary, John Wakeham, had given British Gas assurances that Ofgas would review the pricing formula in the light of changes to British Gas's industrial business in order to prevent a reference to the MMC by the Office of Fair Trading. See *The Financial Times* 16 January 1992.

18. EA Sec. 5, 29, 32–7.

19. WIA Sec. 39 and 67.

20. RA Sec. 7, 20, 24, 44, 136–7 and 139. Compare the very different duties of the Franchising Director who is required to fulfil the objectives given to him by the Secretary of State: RA Sec. 5.

21. Note Sir James McKinnon's comment that the initial value of X in the gas industry had been set 'To get the company off to a good start.' In (1993) *Utilities Law Review* 119 at 120.

22. Similar problems exist in relation to fuel and telecommunications.

23. Assuming for the sake of argument that this could be done without breaching the licence conditions on undue discrimination.

24. For background see Environment Committee *Energy Efficiency in Buildings*, HC 648 1992–3: paras 36–46 and HC 648 II pp. 71–6. On the change of position and problems created see Environment Committee HC 328 i–iii 1993–4. For the Ofgas decisions see Ofgas *The Efficient use of Gas: The role of Ofgas* (1994) and Ofgas decision of February 1992. For Offer's position see *Energy Efficiency* (1992), *Energy Efficiency: The Way Forward* (1992), *The Supply Price Control: Proposals* (1993) paras. 4.41–4.52, *The Distribution Price Control: Proposals* (1994) paras 4.1–4.18. My thanks to Ken Bailey for this information.

25. These primary duties do not apply to the RR: see RA Sec. 4. Promoting competition is a primary duty for the electricity regulator and will be a primary

duty for the gas regulator under the new Gas Act; see EA Sec 3 (1) (c) and Gas Bill clause 1.

26. Generally see TA Sec. 3; EA Sec. 3; WIA Sec. 2 and RA Sec. 4. There is no such duty owed to rural consumers in the Gas Act. Note that promoting competition in generation and supply of electricity is a primary duty of the DGES and will become one for the DGGS by virtue of the new section 4 to be inserted by the Gas Bill.

27. For more detail on these arguments see T. Prosser 'Privatisation, Regulation and Public Services' (1994) *Juridical Review* 3 and A. McHarg 'Accountability in the Electricity Supply Industry—The Role of the Regulator' (1995) *Utilities-Law Review*, 34–42. My thanks to Peter Vass for the last point in this sentence.

28. Now the Independent Television Commission.

29. D. Walker 'Enter the Regulators' (1990) *Parliamentary Affairs* 149–58 at 155.

30. TA Secs. 12 and 15; GA Secs. 24 and 28; EA Secs. 11 and 14; WIA Secs. 13 and 16; RA Secs. 12 and 15.

31. TA Sec. 18, GA Sec. 30, EA Sec. 26, WIA Sec. 21.

32. EA Secs. 16–23.

33. See GA 14A, to be replaced by a new sec 27A which will cover connections, undue discrimination, security deposits and disputes over meters; WIA Sec. 30A (general power to determine disputes), 45 (6A) (reasonableness of expenses for connection to the mains), 49 (metering conditions for connection to the main), 53 (2A) (dispute over compliance with certain conditions), 56 (determination of requests for non-domestic supplies), 64 (2A) (disputes over the supply of water by separate service pipes) 105–107, 112, 113 and 116 (disputes over sewerage systems) 150A (billing disputes).

34. See now TA Secs. 27A, 27F, 27G, 27I. However, the provisions regarding billing disputes in telecommunications and other industries have never been implemented. See K. Bailey and G. Carney 'The Strange Case of Billing Disputes' (1995) *Utilities Law Review*, 60–1.

35. See, for example, HL Debs Vol. 536, cols. 1032–7 5 March 1992. The duty to give reasons was added at HL Debs Vol. 536 cols. 1504–5 13 March 1992.

36. The Council is a permanent statutory body with the general duty of supervising tribunal organisation and procedure: see Tribunals and Inquiries Act 1992.

37. See Council on Tribunals *Annual Report* HC 78 1993–4 para 2.10. The Council describes this as an interim measure, as yet no formal steps have been taken.

38. For Offer procedures see (1994) *Utilities Law Review* 51–2; for Ofwat procedures see MD83 of 24 August 1992.

39. TA Sec. 8 (1) (b) and BT licence Conds. 13A and B; GA Secs. 19–22 to be amended by the Gas Bill Sched 2, paras 16–20; EA Sec. 7 (2); RA Sec. 17–22.

40. Ofgas *Paying the way for gas competition* (1989).

41. See Rail Regulator *Railtrack's Access Charges for Franchised Passenger Services* (1995), *Ticket Retailing* (1995).

42. Generally see Oftel *A Framework for effective Competition* (1994) and 'Effective Competition: A Framework for Action', Oftel Press Release 25 July 1995.
43. WIA Sec. 145.
44. Ofwat *Paying for Water* (1990); Ofwat *Paying for Growth* (1993); Ofwat *Future Charges for Water and Sewerage Services* (1994) are the main publications.
45. For the government's decision to allow the use of rateable values after the year 2000 but not a system based on council tax bandings, see 257 HC Debs cols. 1056–9 Written Answer, 4 April 1995 and the Secretary of State's letter to the Chairs of the water companies and the service associations quoted in Public Utility Access Forum Information Bulletin, April 1995.
46. See C. Graham, unpublished report to the National Consumer Council.
47. PUAF was formed in 1989 by a group of concerned individuals from organisations representing low income consumers. It received the endorsement of the regulators who have supported it indirectly in various ways through the provision of meeting space and some facilities. It is funded through membership subscription, membership is not open to the industry, and by contributions from some regulators. It produces a regular information bulletin as well as holding regular meetings. These meetings are the prime function of PUAF and are attended on a regular basis by representatives of the regulators as well as representatives of the non-statutory organisations. PUAF members see the meetings as an important opportunity to quiz the regulators about policy matters, to pick up hints about how to present arguments and to understand the regulatory timetable. PUAF has also expanded outward by creating telecommunications and water issues sub-groups which meets regularly with the regulators to discuss policy issues. PUAF will also organise seminars and conferences but it will not take any position on current issues itself. It is a procedural facility for its member organisations.
48. See Oftel *Consultation Procedures and Transparency* 21 March 1995 and in general Oftel *Doing Business with OFTEL* (1994).
49. TA Secs. 27C, 48 and 55; GA Secs. 33C and 39; EA Secs. 42, 48 and 50; WIA Secs. 193, 201; RA Secs. 71, 74.
50. By British Gas in relation to Ofgas orders regarding price rises for projects by Thames Power and Coryton in 1991. British gas eventually dropped the action. My thanks to Peter Spring for this reference.
51. Veljanovski, op. cit., note 14 at p. 4.
52. As the DGT put it at a workshop on Interconnection and Accounting Separation: '... eager though OFTEL is to seek practical solutions, its resources are ... severely constrained. The same people who would be in the vanguard of examining practical solutions on incremental costs and capacity charging will also inevitably be involved in dealing with the court case.' See (1994) *Utilities Law Review* 103.
53. See Oftel Press Release 27 April 1995.

54. On the MMC see R. Whish *Competition Law* (1993; 3rd ed.) 92, 692, Trade and Industry Select Committee *Takeovers and Mergers* HC 90 (1991–2), *Financial Times* 10 April 1995.

55. See Cm 2309 paras 6.85–7. My thanks to Tony Prosser for this reference.

56. *Associated Provincial Picture Houses v Wednesbury Corporation* [1948] 1 QB 223.

57. *R v Director General of Gas Supply ex parte Smith* (1986); fair procedure in meter tampering cases; an action by National Power against Ofgas over the supply of long term interruptible gas in 1991 which was dropped; a case against the DGT by information service providers which was settled by the DGT accepting that he had acted beyond his powers, an action by the Coalition for Fair Electricity Regulation (COFFER) against the DGES over his interpretation of the economic purchasing requirement for regional electricity companies which was denied leave and, most recently *R v Director General for Electricity Supply ex parte Redrow Homes* 22 February 1995, *The Times*. There has been some consideration of taking judicial review proceedings against the DGWS on various aspects of metering but this has so far come to nothing. My thanks to Aileen McHarg for the COFFER reference.

58. *Mercury Communications v Director General of Telecommunications* 9 February 1995 (House of Lords), 22 July 1994 (Court of Appeal); both unreported. See also *Telecom Corporation of New Zealand v Clear Communications* (Privy Council) unreported but discussed at (1995) *Utilities Law Review* 17–20.

59. See EA s 27(4) and (5); TA s 18 (5) and (6), WIA s 22, RA s 57 (4) and (5).

60. See N. Green 'Recent Trends in Regulatory Law' paper given to conference at the University of Hull, 21 April 1994.

61. Personal communication from the Association for the Conservation of Energy.

62. National Audit Office *The Office of Telecommunications: Licence Compliance and Consumer Protection* HC 529 1992–3; Public Accounts Committee HC 123 1993–4.

63. Committee of Public Accounts Press Notice 19 July 1995.

64. See for example HC 15 1985–6 Regulation of the Gas Industry, HC 307 1987–88 The Structure, Regulation and Economic Consequences of Electricity Supply in the Private Sector; HC 64 1989–90 Industrial and Commercial Gas Prices; HC 205–1 The Cost of Nuclear Power; HC 91–1 1990–1 Energy Efficiency; HC 113 1991–2 The Consequences of Electricity Privatisation.

65. Veljanovski op cit., note 2, pp. 82–5. A more thoughtful piece on the same lines in D. Helm 'British Utility Regulation: Theory, Practice and Reform' (1994) *Oxford Review of Economic Policy*, 10, 17–39. Corry et al, op cit. note 2 at p. 81 seem to have some similar ideas.

66. As John Kay puts it 'However much one might like to define the rules precisely and leave them unchanged for a period of years or decades, it is fantasy to believe that this is a realistic approach to regulation,' from 'The Regulation of Monopolies' in Adam Smith Institute *But Who will Regulate the Regulators?* (1993) at p. 15.

67. See Patsy Healey 'The Role of Development Plans in the British Planning System: An empirical assessment' (1986) *Urban Law and Policy* 1–32.

68. Op cit., note 6 at ch 9.

69. Compare John Ernst, op cit., note 5, Tony Prosser, op cit., note 27 and Aileen McHarg, op cit., note 27.

70. The proposal of Clare Spottiswoode, the gas regulator, that the government should be able to call for an independent investigation into important regulatory decisions is another example of this theme. See *The Financial Times* 18 April 1995.

71. Op cit., note 3 at p. 22.

72. Op cit., note 2 at p. 80.

73. Tim Eggar, Institute of Economic Affairs Conference speech 21 November 1994, p. 9 of transcript.

74. See HC 1444 1994–5, Questions 34–72.

75. See M. Hill 'The policy-implementation distinction: a quest for rational control' in S. Barrett and C. Fudge (eds.) *Policy and Action* (1981) London, Methuen: P. Greer *Transforming Central Government* (1994), Buckingham, Open University Press especially at 78 and Home Affairs Select Committee *The operation of the Prison Service* HC 144–I 1994–5.

76. Op cit., note 9 at p. 103.

77. RA Secs 4–5.

78. See Hain op cit., note 3 at p. 23.

79. Formed from the CAA and the rail regulators but not, oddly, anything to do with buses or apparently roads.

80. Op cit., note 2 at pp. 76–8, 93 and 95.

81. Institute of Economic Affairs Conference speech 21 November 1994, p. 8 of transcript. See also Sir Bryan Carsberg 'Regulation: Special versus General', Institute of Economic Affairs Conference Speech 22 November 1994.

82. D. Corry et al, op cit., note 2. Other advocates include Peter Hain, op cit., note 3 p. 23.

83. D. Corry et al, op cit., note 2 at p. 85.

84. R. Baldwin *Regulating the Airlines* (1985), Clarendon Press at 153.

85. A point made by Sir Bryan Carsberg, op cit., note 81 at p. 6.

86. On the EOC see G. Applebey and E. Ellis 'Formal Investigations: The Commission for Racial Equality and the Equal Opportunities Commission as Law Enforcement Agencies' (1984) *Public Law* 236–76; V. Sachs 'The Equal Opportunities Commission—Ten Years On' (1986) *Modern Law Review,* 49, 560–92. Recent publicity over the Chairwoman of the EOC, Kamlesh Bahl, suggests that even a Commission approach does not necessarily get away from personalisation. On the ITC see, generally, T. Gibbons *Regulating the Media* (1991), London, Sweet and Maxwell at 80–8 and *R v ITC ex parte Television South West* 30 March 1992, *The Times*.

87. See Veljanovski, op cit., note 2 and National Consumer Council, op cit., note 4 at pp. 101–11.

88. Op cit., note 9 at p. 15 of transcript.

89. Most importantly *R v Secretary of State for the Home Department ex parte Doody* [1994] I AC 531.

90. For recent developments see the Oftel documents mentioned in note 48.

91. For example, Veljanovski op cit., note 2 at p. 84; John Baker *Financial Times* 6 April 1994; Sir Bryan Carsberg, op cit., note 9 at p. 19 of transcript.

92. See Rob Baldwin op cit. at 41–8 and the comment on p. 41: 'If there was a single reason why the ATLB system of licensing was eventually perceived to have failed it was the manner in which appeals were decided. This power allowed Ministers to review not only politically significant decisions but also issues of Board judgement.'

93. See Veljanovski op cit., note 2 at p. 85; Hain op cit., note 3 at p. 22; Corry et al op cit., note 2 at p. 93; Foster op cit., note 9 at p. 103, C. Graham 'Regulatory Crisis: A Myth?' *Energy Utilities* (1994), June, 20–23 and Spottiswoode as reported in *The Financial Times* 18 April 1995.

94. Foster op cit., note 9 in the 1994 conference piece.

95. For a selection see J. Jowell *Law and Bureaucracy* (1975) Port Washington, (NY), Dunellen; Denis Galligan *Discretionary Powers* (1986) Clarendon Press and D. Feldman, 'Review Article' (1994) *Public Law* 279–93.

96. On financial services see J. Black 'Which Arrow? Rule Type and Regulatory Policy' (1995) *Public Law* 94–117. On social security see M. Hill *Social Security Policy in Britain* (1990), Chs. 5–7.

97. For example, M. Freedland 'Government by Contract and Private Law' (1994) *Public Law* 86–104 and N. Lewis 'Reviewing Change in Government New Public Management and Next Steps' (1994) *Public Law* 105–113.

98. The academic community and independent policy analysts do provide valuable information and analysis but they do not, on their own, have the institutional weight within government that such a body would have.

99. See McHarg, op. cit., note 27 for this idea which is a development of the current arrangements; see note 13 and accompanying text.

100. RA Sec 4 (5). For the guidance see HC 662 1993–4.

101. On the distinction between guidance and directions see *R v Secretary of State for the Environment ex parte Lancashire County Council* [1994] 4 All ER 165. The distinction is not without difficulties: see *Laker Airways v Department of Trade* [1977] QB 643 discussed in R. Baldwin 'A British Independent Regulatory Agency and the Skytrain Decision' (1978) *Public Law* 57.

102. Arguably it should also cover airports, airlines, broadcasting, the Post Office and related transport industries.

103. For more discussion of this issue see C. Graham op cit., note 46.

104. Corry et al op cit., note 2 at p. 82.

ANNEX

Summary of Recommendations

The following table gives a brief summary of recommendations on various issues. The commentators singled out have been chosen as representatives of particular positions who have developed their own views most fully. My apologies to those who were omitted. My apologies also for the necessarily schematic summaries of each commentator's views.

Issue	Cento Veljanovski	Dieter Helm	Sir Christopher Foster	Dan Corry et al	Cosmo Graham
Rules	Government to provide Regulatory Charter—a clear statement of principles governing regulation; joint working party of regulators, OFT and MMC to produce policy document on various issues.	Common set of financial rules through a White Paper, guidelines or initiative of regulators. Also common basis for efficiency comparisons.	As clear a distinction as possible to be drawn between social and economic matters—regulators to concentrate on economic matters.	Central framework set by Ministers, common division of powers for regulators, accompanied by guidelines governing relationship between regulators, regulatees and consumer bodies and clear statement of how regulators intend to pursue their objectives.	Government to give policy guidelines to regulators regarding statutory duties. Guidance to be published.
Relations with government	Rationalisation of powers of Secretary of State—reduction of powers in electricity.	See Rules and Role of MMC.	No greater government influence than already exists.	Ministers to set the framework for regulatory decisions. Right of intervention if decisions perverse or contrary to government policy.	Specific government powers of intervention to be reduced.

Regulatory rationalisation	Office of Communication, Office of Energy Regulation, Office of Transport Regulation.	Office of Communication. Office of Energy Regulation. Office of Transport Regulation.	No.	Single regulatory departments dealing with each of the main multi-utility sectors—energy, transport and communications—and with water.	Worth considering.
Regulatory Commission Procedures	No.	No.	No.	Yes.	Possible.
	Adversarial, open hearings before the MMC. Reasons for decisions to be given.	Reasons for decisions to be given.	General procedural guidance to be given, as well as reasons for decisions.	Major regulatory decisions to be preceded by public consultation, including public hearings. Full reasons to be given.	Common set of procedures for regulatory decision making either through Code of Practice or legislation. Open up relationship between agencies.
Appeal rights	Regulatory decisions to be appealable.	Not considered.	Wider scope for appeals, possibly to MMC.	Proper appeal procedures to be established.	No change.
Role of MMC	Major licence modifications to be determined by MMC and MMC to adjudicate on regulatory disputes.	Automatic referral of major licence changes at MMC, MMC to report to Secretary of State.	Conduct retrospective reviews of economic offences across all natural monopolies.	As now—power to restrict scope of references to MMC.	Retrospective review of economic and social matters cutting across utilities could be helpful.
Parliamentary oversight	Create Regulated Industries Select Committee.	Further steps needed.	Would not quarrel with new Regulated Industries Select Committee.	Establishment of new Parliamentary Select Committee.	Establishment of Regulated Industries Select Committee, perhaps supported by NAO.
Other	Private rights of action for breach of licences and Regulatory Charter.	None.	In time will be a need for damages and compensation.	New independent consumer representative bodies.	New independent consumer representative bodies.